TED MORGAN

SIMON & SCHUSTER
New York · Toronto · London
Tokyo · Singapore · Sydney

WILDERNESS AT DAWN

*The Settling of
the North American Continent*

SIMON & SCHUSTER
Simon & Schuster Building
Rockefeller Center
1230 Avenue of the Americas
New York, New York 10020

10 9 8 7 6 5 4 3 2 1

Library of Congress Cataloging-in-Publication Data

Morgan, Ted
    Wilderness at dawn : the settling of the North
American continent / Ted Morgan.
        p.   cm.
    Includes bibliographical references and index.
    1. North America—History.   2. United States
—History—Colonial period, ca. 1600–1775.
3. Canada—History—To 1763 (New France)
I. Title.
E45.M67   1993
970—dc20   93-2628
                                               CIP
ISBN: 0-671-69088-4

Overleaf: "View of St. Anthony's Nose" by John
William Edy after George Bultelel Fisher. New York
Public Library Print Collection

*This book is for Eileen Bresnahan, born in Washington, D.C.,
of a Virginia mother and a Massachusetts father,
and raised in Kansas City, Missouri.*

CONTENTS

Part Four:

AMERICA
FOR THE AMERICANS

INTRODUCTION

People who find themselves at the juncture of worlds passing and worlds coming tend to be crushed like insects.

When William Faulkner traveled to Stockholm in November 1950 to collect his Nobel Prize for literature, he stopped off in Paris on the way home to Mississippi and was prevailed upon to speak at the Sorbonne, where I was then a student. A friend of mine was part of the welcoming committee that went to the Hotel Lutétia on or about December 12 to escort the Nobel laureate to the university. They found him so drunk he could barely walk. The fatigue of the journey, a touch of the flu, the Stockholm ceremony, which he said was "as long as a Mississippi funeral," had all conspired to make him turn to his anesthetic of choice, bourbon.

Backstage in the Sorbonne's packed auditorium, they plied Faulkner with black coffee as they debated whether to call the whole thing off. In the auditorium, where I was sitting, the crowd was getting fidgety and began to clap. A desk and a chair were brought out on stage, and Faulkner soon followed under escort. After a tremendous ovation, he said, in English: "The big difference between Europe and America is that we are still adding stars to the flag." Then his head slumped on his crossed arms and he spoke no more.

It was the shortest speech I ever listened to, and one that I never forgot. The idea of "adding stars to the flag" brings to mind a continent filling with people, with each star representing territory won from previous occupants through diplomacy or conquest. Implied is a quest that can never end. In this sense, the American flag is unlike any other, because it's an add-on flag, with room to grow.

What I would like to do in this book is tell the story of an empty continent filling with people, from the time of the first arrivals before recorded history. This will not be the "Great Man" version of events, but the story of the men and women, red, black, and white, who were in North America ahead of the great men.

I'm looking for what Hawthorne called "a sort of home-feeling with the past."

No race of men originated in the "New World." The residents of our continent came over water or crossed a temporary land bridge from Asia. Each wave of people had a different reason for making the trip. The Asians who crossed the Bering Land Bridge and were misnamed Indians came as refugees from the Ice Age. The Spanish came as conquerors, the French as traders, and the English as settlers and religious seceders. The Africans came in chains.

The idea of a great expanse of land waiting to be filled is central to the spirit of this country. At the start there was an empty continent, not *terra incognita* but *terra in vacuo*. After crossing the Bering Land Bridge about seventeen thousand years ago, transplanted Asians had the Western Hemisphere to themselves until the time of white occupation. Thus, the very idea of "the Age of Discovery" is false. When the white man arrived, the continents of North and South America had already been discovered by a people who had settled them from the Seward Peninsula to the Tierra del Fuego. That discovery was never recorded or mapped, because these first settlers had no written language.

American history is essentially different from the history of other nations in that the people were ahead of the government. That is, they arrived in places where there was no government, whether the place was Plymouth, or Ohio, or Utah. America is a much more grass-roots-created continent than Europe; it was made by the many and not by the few, by Native Americans and slaves and squatters as much as by statesmen.

In this sense, I am writing a collective biography of ordinary Americans. Those who are usually in the background of history will be in the foreground. Instead of presidents and generals, the characters are people like the shipwrecked Spaniard Cabeza de Vaca, the itinerant North Carolina preacher Charles Woodmason, and the freed slave Jeremiah. This is the story of mail carriers, sodbusters, circuit-riding judges, and Indian agents, of the people who were too busy occupying the land to make a claim on history.

It was Frederick Jackson Turner who first taught us not to look toward Europe to understand America, in *The Significance of the Frontier in American History*. Look at our land policies and the apportionment of our states, he said. Look at our trading posts becoming railroad stations, at our trails widening into turnpikes.

Follow the arteries made by geology, follow the tongues of settlement along the rivers, follow the frontier as it expands and contracts like a human skin covering the continent.

Follow the salt springs that enabled the settlers' cattle to cross the mountains . . . follow the army posts opening the way into Indian territory. In Europe, the frontier was a boundary between two densely populated nations. In America it meant the edge of settlement, as the Massachusetts General Court defined it in 1704, when it ordered five hundred pairs of snowshoes to be provided to counties "lying frontier next to the wilderness."

There wasn't one frontier, there were three, English, French, and Spanish, and eventually they collided. Florida belonged to Spain for three hundred years, and the French were exploring the American heartland via the Mississippi River when the English settlers were still hugging their narrow Atlantic strip. And just over the hill, there was always the Indian, making the frontier a battle line and also a porous line of red-white exchange.

On the other side of the line was the settler, who might or might not be English. The frontier was multinational, and even the English colonial frontier was remarkably diverse; it included the Puritan frontier, with its doctrine of the voluntary covenant; the Virginia frontier, class-conscious and silver-buckled; the Quaker frontier of Pennsylvania, refusing to vote funds for a militia; and the South Carolina frontier, with more slaves than white settlers.

The fabled individualism of the frontier, where passive obedience to government did not apply since there wasn't any, was mitigated by the settlers' need to act in unison, to build houses, to plant crops, to defend themselves. Transportation depended on crossing rivers, which meant that the ferryman had to be on duty. As soon as the settlers had irrigation, they had to regulate the distribution of water. In the mining camps of California, they wrote their own laws covering claims. Herding cattle and building railroads were other forms of collective labor. The West, which fostered the ideal of individual escape, also became the seedbed of voluntary associations, from the early colonial compacts to the river pilots' union and cattlemen's groups—as well as vigilante associations.

As the frontier kept moving, it left behind an ever-growing area that was no longer frontier, which I will call the hinterland. This hinterland had law and government, institutions and stability, in contrast to the anarchy and insecurity of the frontier. What made America was not just the hinterland, and not just the frontier, but the tension and interaction between the two.

Much of our national life can be defined according to frontier and hinterland attitudes. Take our two national pastimes, football and baseball. Football is a frontier game, because it has to do with the conquest of territory. The aim of the game is to invade the other team's land and settle there until you've crossed the goal line. As on the frontier, time of possession is everything.

Football is a metaphor for land hunger, a ritualized reenactment of the westward movement, going back to colonial times. Look at the names of some of the teams in the NFL, the Patriots, the Redskins, the Cowboys, the Broncos, the Forty-Niners, the Chiefs, the Raiders, the Buffalo Bills, and the Oilers, all names connected with different stages of the frontier epic. Look at the way a first down is measured. Officials bring out the chains, which are a vestigial replica of the surveyors' chains and a reminder of the men who marked off the wilderness, dividing it into ranges and townships and sections.

On their hundred-yard-long turf-covered universe, football players act out the conquest of the frontier. And just as they fought the taking of their land on the real frontier, Native Americans today protest the appropriation of their past on the football field, in the use of team names like Redskins and Chiefs, and in the hoopla of fans painting their faces, wearing chicken-feather headdresses, and waving foam-rubber tomahawks. In the game itself there are emulations of Indian customs, such as the huddle, which is a stylized Indian powwow, and the gauntlet that each player must run upon entering the stadium.

Football breeds a defiant frontier attitude, because someone is out to get you and you're not going to let him. As the late linebacker Lyle Alzado once said: "I don't think there is anyone on this earth who can kick my ass." Another great linebacker, Lawrence Taylor, once said that his purest joy was to hit someone so hard he could see the "snot bubble out of his nose." And here's the Chicago Bears coach Mike Ditka defining the frontier ethic as well as the game of football: "It's people hittin' each other, that's what it's all about. I'm tired of the skill." Skill gets taken for granted, while there's a degree of physical punishment reminiscent of life in the wilderness. The limits to that punishment are suggested by some of the penalties, such as "piling on," "unnecessary roughness," and my personal favorite, which has a colonial ring in its phrasing, "coming unabated at the quarterback when offsides."

There's no unnecessary roughness penalty in baseball, a game with a refined hinterland sensibility, which was gentrified from the start, when A. G. Spalding organized the Knickerbocker Base Ball Club in 1845 in Manhattan, for "men of high taste." Baseball teams seem to be named by bird-watchers (the Orioles, the Blue Jays, the Cardinals), zookeepers (the Cubs, the Tigers), and believers in the Supernatural (the Angels). In baseball, there's no fighting over territory, since the convention has been established that the teams will take turns occupying the same field. In baseball, you play out the inning no matter how long it takes, and there's no time anxiety, but in football you're running against the clock, it's a game of seconds, just as life and death on the frontier were determined in seconds. In baseball, there's always a team sitting in the dugout, but in football, there are always two full teams on the field, man on man, and until the fifties, the same players played both offense and defense. Unlike baseball, in which games are called on account of rain, football is still mostly played in frontier weather conditions of rain, snow, and ice. Baseball players might work up a sweat running bases, but that's pretty much the extent of their discomfort, because there's comparatively little physical contact. Baseball is a game of the civilized hinterland, while football harks back to the epic qualities of the frontier, which continue to live in the American psyche.

The settling of the North American continent is an epic written in the blood and sweat of ordinary men and women, and like all epics it originates with the oral tradition, with tales told round the campfire, with the language of scouts and squatters, of trappers and land agents, of Iroquois braves and plantation hands speaking their Gullah patois, of all the tongues that were wagging in an American way.

They spoke of the scale of nature, the distances traveled, of God's punishment and His blessings; of the state of permanent warfare with the native people; of the human cost of redeeming the wilderness and a life without precedents; of democracy and slavery, deeds and misdeeds, laws and outlaws.

But instead of being an epic of great warriors and high deeds, it was an epic of the multitudes, of mundane events and minor characters, of incremental advance and retreat, of clearings in the forest and compasses and chains, a quilted patchwork pieced together from strips of settled land, an aggregate that kept expanding over the centuries until it assumed its present shape.

Beringia
Land
Bridge

Asian
Migration
from Siberia
to North
America
c. 15,000 B.C.

ALGONKIAN

UTO-AZTECS   PUEBLO

SIOUANS

QUIVIRA
INDIAN

Arkansas R.

Colorado R.
GRAND
CANYON

INDIANS

CIBOLA
INDIANS

Tiguex

Pacific Ocean

YUMA

Acoma   Cicuye
(Pecos)

PALO DURO
CANYON

Red R.

APACHE

El Paso

Ures

NEW

SPAIN

1528
VELASCO
1532
MATAGORDA PEN.
1534
Alice

Rio Grande

Kms.
0 ———— 300
0 ———— 300
Miles

Culiacán

Routes
of Coronado
1540-42

NEW
GALICIA

French
claims
by 1600

Spanish
claims
by 1600

Compostela

© A. Karl / J. Kemp, 1993

Mexico City

Vera Cru

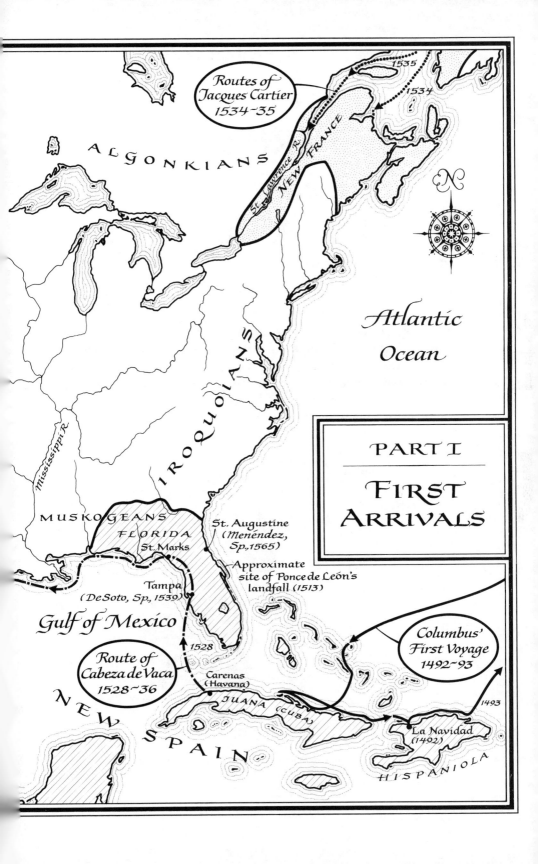

Routes of
Jacques Cartier
1534~35

1535

1534

ALGONKIANS

St. Lawrence R.

NEW FRANCE

N

Atlantic

Ocean

IROQUOIANS

Mississippi R.

PART I

FIRST
ARRIVALS

MUSKOGEANS

FLORIDA

St. Marks

St. Augustine
(Menéndez,
Sp., 1565)

Approximate
site of Ponce de León's
landfall (1513)

Tampa
(DeSoto, Sp., 1539)

Gulf of Mexico

Columbus'
First Voyage
1492~93

1528

Route of
Cabeza de Vaca
1528~36

Carenas
(Havana)

1493

NEW SPAIN

JUANA (CUBA)

La Navidad
(1492)

HISPANIOLA

CHAPTER ONE

THE FIRST
FIFTEEN
THOUSAND
YEARS

Fleeing the hazards of the Ice Age, Early Man crossed over
the Bering Land Bridge onto the uninhabited continent of
North America, circa 15,000 B.C. Until the arrival of the
white man in the sixteenth century, these people of Asiatic
origin had the continent to themselves, and developed a
number of highly evolved native American societies.

Douglas W. Schwartz, School of American Research

This willow-twig effigy found in a cave on the Colorado River was
carbon-dated 4000 B.P. Made by the first Americans, and sometimes
pierced by miniature spears, it probably figured in ceremonies conducted to ensure success in the hunt.

We speak of Christopher Columbus being the discoverer of America, although millions of human beings had occupied the continent for untold ages.

T. W. DAVENPORT, *Indian agent in Oregon in 1850*

S t. Lawrence Island, an inhabited but treeless gravel pit, sits more or less halfway between Siberia and Alaska, on the U.S. side of the International Date Line. Once a six-hundred-foot-high hill in the middle of the Bering Land Bridge between Asia and North America, it was the crossroads of two continents. Today it is covered by the Bering Sea. The change stems from the fact that for the last fifteen thousand years the planet has been in one of its warm "interglacial" periods.

During most of the last million and a half years, however, much of the earth has been in a deep freeze. This Ice Age period is known as the Pleistocene. It arrived in a rush of wind and a curtain of blue-white light, in the rumbling and crackling of ice mountains moving like slow prehistoric beasts, gouging out basins, pulverizing rock into sand, scouring valleys with the stones caught in its basal ice, leaving a trail of eroded "whale-back" hills, abrading and grinding and rearranging the land, obliterating all living things.

We are no more than the creatures of glacial cycles, of mile-high slabs of ice doing their drowsy two-step, advancing and retreating over North America, Europe, and Asia. Glaciologists tell us that these catastrophic cycles are determined by little wobbles of the earth as it rotates around the sun. A tilt in the axis of our home planet changes the angle at which the sun's rays strike. It doesn't take much. A little tilt, a little wobble, a little drop in the average temperature, and soon dry winds are lifting evaporated moisture off oceans, moisture that will later fall as snow at high latitudes, feeding and expanding existing glaciers.

Instead of thawing in spring, the winter ice accumulates until it forms continent-sized ice cubes. At some point, these glaciers locked up so much water that the global sea level fell 350 feet. This meant that, in areas where the sea floor was shallow, the continental shelf was exposed. One area where this occurred was the Bering Sea, which was drained like water in a bathtub, and where the sea floor became a plain.

Some unglaciated enclaves remained between the ice sheets, in areas where there wasn't enough rainfall to nourish their spread. One was Beringia, which included eastern Siberia, much of western Alaska, and of course the dried-up sea floor in between. This anomalous piece of real estate, where the sea had retreated and the glacier hadn't moved in, covered 1.3 million square miles. It was composed of Siberian mountains to the west, Alaskan mountains to the east, and a grassy plain in between.

"Land bridge" is a misnomer: Beringia was a subcontinent, a refuge for the frantic animals and men out of northern China and Mongolia, who were fleeing the Big Ice. They found a land teeming with game, but it was too good to last. With each interglacial, the ice melted and the tub filled up again, sending two- and four-legged occupants running for the high ground.

St. Lawrence Island and a few others like it are the only unsubmerged remnants of the land bridge visible today. This dreary mass of black lava and gravel, ninety miles long and thirty-five miles wide, flat except for an elongated ridge maybe three hundred feet high, is one of the former highlands of central Beringia. It has the raw, exposed look of land above the tree line, with patches of waterlogged, grassy tundra, a few wild flowers, and edible plants such as duckweed and Labrador tea, growing close to the ground. There is a sixty-day growing season here, so it takes a plant years to flower.

On St. Lawrence, you're never far from the uninviting gray sea, with its short choppy waves. Eight months of the year, the island is surrounded by ice pack, and in the summer months it's often fogged in. Bering Air, scheduled to fly in daily from Nome, cancels about half its flights because of weather conditions.

Winters are long, dark, and icebound. Summers are foggy. But there's a population of about fifteen hundred, gathered in the two towns of Savoonga and Gambell. The island has been continuously inhabited since pre-Christian times. Dog skulls found here were carbon-dated to 100 B.C. The skulls were broken, brains having been extracted to tan hides.

Residents today have the standard Eskimo physique, a high-trunked body with short arms and legs, compact and flat-faced. They still stretch walrus hides on racks to make skin boats for hunting whales. They also have aluminum boats with outboards, but when the whale hears the motor it dives out of range. There isn't a single road on the island, so transportation is by dune buggy.

Eskimo kids race through the gravel on Honda Big Reds, playing dune-buggy tag.

The beach is a whale boneyard, littered with jaws and carcasses. The bowhead whale, a slow swimmer beloved of hunters, arrives in the spring and stays three months. In the winter, residents fish through the ice and hunt deer. They can't plant trees, or vegetable gardens, or any kind of crop, for under the thin soggy layer of tundra lies permafrost, frozen solid thousands of feet down. You won't find any burrowing animals here, no moles or gophers.

On St. Lawrence Island, as in the rest of Alaska, there is a curious mix of prehistoric conditions and modern appliances, a confusion of epochs, as if Ice Age people had somehow been provided with outboard motors and television sets. Alaskan license plates say THE LAST FRONTIER, but this is a frontier with more tourists than homesteaders—five hundred thousand Alaskans and 750,000 tourists a year. Polar bears scavenge in the dumpsters of fast-food outlets, and the Malaspina glacier, a thousand feet high and bigger than Rhode Island, provides the backdrop for overcute gift shops with names like The Gold Dust and Pecos Pete's.

From Nome, a gold-rush town on the Seward Peninsula, 150 miles south of the Arctic Circle, it's an easy drive into the estuary of the Nome River, which is still littered with abandoned gold dredges. Walking in the tundra is like walking in rice paddies; the surface ice that thaws in the summer doesn't drain off, because of the permafrost a couple of feet below ground. There is about the same amount of rainfall here as in the Sahara, which is why it was never glaciated. Plant life survives, because the permafrost keeps the water on the surface, like a form of irrigation. The tundra is in fact an irrigated desert.

On the Seward Peninsula and St. Lawrence Island, it is possible to get a feel for that lost land of Beringia, the route of the first men to step onto the continent of North America. There had of course been animals in North America for many millions of years, going back to the dinosaurs. One who originated in the "New World" twenty-five million years ago was the three-toed horse, a skeleton of which was found in Crawford, Nebraska. It took the eohippus millions of years to convert its tender toes into hardhorned hooves. The two side toes regressed, while the center toe grew into a hoof, an adaptation to dry ground. The horse also developed high-crowned teeth for chewing grass. Then, at some point when the land bridge was exposed, the horse skipped to Asia and became extinct in North America, until the conquistadors brought it back in the sixteenth century.

Fifteen million years ago, there were camels in North America the size of greyhounds. A hundred of their skeletons were found in Sioux County, Nebraska. Camels small and large are American in origin. Like the horse, they crossed into Asia over the land bridge, where the traffic was obviously two-way. In the other direction came the Asian repertoire of big beasts: mastodons with mandibles the size of forklifts, woolly mammoths with their long shaggy coats, and two-ton ancient bison, hairy and matted. All lumbered over the land bridge into the New World, leaving behind the species that couldn't make it across, such as the woolly rhinoceros.

One day, in mid-Pleistocene, around 35,000 B.C., a speck appeared on the Siberian tundra. It moved upright on two legs, but it wasn't an ape, for it had no fur. This seemingly helpless mammal, lacking tusks or claws or other apparent means of defense, had been slouching along for a few hundred thousand years, working his stance to the vertical, exercising his fingers to bend so they could hold tools, growing a chin, putting some space between his hairline and his eyebrows, and enlarging his brainpan from its original pea size. This dullard had been around for many millennia but still didn't know enough to tame animals, grow crops, or build a boat. He did know enough, however, to leave Central Asia when it started turning to desert, and to follow his dinner into Siberia and onto the land bridge.

Then, between ten and twenty thousand years ago, came the interglacial that flooded the Beringian refuge. Scampering to dry ground, man moved inland and southward from the edge of Alaska. Maybe he came over in previous interglacials, but it's unlikely, since all the evidence we have now points to his arrival during the third and final interglacial—the one, incidentally, that we are still in today.

There is plenty of evidence, however, of animal migration long before man. In 1979, near the inland city of Fairbanks, Alaska, a mining company stripping the gravel-laden ice from a hillside thought to contain gold dislodged Blue Babe, a two-ton prehistoric bison carbon-dated 34,000 B.C. Growing up in the Fairbanks area, Blue Babe was attacked at the age of eight by a lion, who took a couple of bites out of her flank and then left her for

dead. Clawmarks on the nearly intact carcass identified her at-
tacker.

Blue Babe is a rather famous bison, the only large prehistoric
mammal ever recovered from permafrost in the United States. She
is on exhibit at the University of Alaska Museum in Fairbanks and
is indeed bright blue, owing to a chemical reaction that took place
when the iron and phosphorus in the carcass were exposed to air.
Her ancestors must have crossed over from Asia during the second
interglacial, circa 40,000 B.C.

And what about man? He was happily living in Beringia,
around 15,000 B.C., when the warming trend became a threat. The
glaciers were melting, and the sea level began rising, and soon the
dry sea floor of the Beringia plain was inundated again. It was like
the Biblical flood, only more gradual. The western plain flooded
first, barring the route back to Siberia. Man had no choice but to
go east, into the empty quarter of eastern Beringia, which lacked
the lush grasslands of the central plain. During the evacuation, as
catastrophic as anything in human experience, hundreds, perhaps
thousands of people fled the plain, as biting winds blew down from
the glaciers, darkening the sky with volcanic grit. Imagine families
separated and children lost, a scene of confused alarm and desperate flight as the tide broke through the straits, linking the Arctic
Ocean with the Bering Sea for the first time in thousands of
years, drowning the plant life, and disrupting the great animal
herds.

These men were not explorers seeking a new world, but panic-
stricken refugees escaping a natural cataclysm. They moved in
small increments, finding animals who were not frightened of
them, never having seen hunters before. They moved from bison
watering holes to migratory flyways teeming with seabirds. If a
place got too crowded and the food scarce, they moved on.

Some moved eastward into Alaska and Canada by way of a
deglaciated corridor along the Yukon and Mackenzie rivers. Some
moved farther south, along the eastern foothills of the Rockies,
down through Montana, Wyoming, and Colorado, where there
were no more glaciers and they could breathe a little easier. Some
kept trudging south, into Mexico and Central America, crossing
the Isthmus of Panama into Colombia, down along the coast of
Chile, where, at Monte Verde, in a dried-up creek channel near
the Pacific, mastodon bones were found alongside wood fragments
carbon-dated 11,000 B.C. Others traveled on down to the very tip

of South America, the Land of Fire, a distance of about twelve thousand miles.

The trip took roughly 1,250 years. Averaging about ten miles a year, the marchers moved along corridors with walls of ice on both sides. As the cold wind blew off the glaciers, they crossed frozen lakes and rivers, working their way south, not knowing where they were going or what they would face. It was the Great Pilgrimage of Early Man. The first American families aren't those who came over on the *Mayflower* but those who came out of Central Asia, Mongolia, northern China. They would become the ancestors of the North American Indians, as well as of the Mayans, Aztecs, Incas, and all other south-of-the-border inhabitants.

These people occupied two continents, and the amazing thing was that when they arrived nobody was there. Nobody onshore throwing spears at them. Nobody sniping at them from behind a tree. Nobody saying, "Get off my land." Here were two entire continents, absolutely uninhabited by man, and they would have it to themselves for, let's say, fifteen thousand years.

Beringian man made an explosive entrance as the new and dominant predator on the American continents. He had the stone-point technology to kill the grazing mammoth and browsing mastodon, the ground sloth and long-nosed peccary, huge bisons and prehistoric beavers the size of bears. Without precedents to guide them, these early men were absolutely, perilously on their own. It took them centuries to develop survival strategies.

Each geographical zone required a different approach. The men who stayed in Alaska invented ivory goggles as protection against snow blindness; semiburied houses made of sod-covered driftwood; ivory bolas (long cords with weights on the end) to hunt low-flying water fowl; rainproof coats made of strips of sea-lion intestine sewn together; parkas with bibs so that the fur near the throat wouldn't freeze from the moisture on the breath.

Whatever their destination, as they occupied hundreds of different habitats and climates, the various groups had one thing in common: the quest for food was their organizing principle. Throughout the year, they moved around to follow the game. Fisher-hunters on Alaska's Kotzebue Sound, right on the Arctic Circle, stayed in their winter quarters until April, hunting hares and caribou. Then they moved into snow houses on the ocean ice, where men hunted seals and women processed the meat. When the ice melted, they went back on land.

Hundreds of such small-scale societies sprang up in all sorts of places, some of them downright inhospitable. At a site on Tukuto Lake, in the arctic foothills of northern Alaska's Brooks Range, archaeologists found half-burned willow twigs, birch-bark basket fragments, and flakes from stone blades. Caribou herds migrated to the lake year after year, and the hunters were ready for them. Wood pegs standing upright in the ground may have been used to stretch the hides. If the size of the herd decreased, the group controlled its own birthrate through the spacing of children and population dispersion.

Remnants of spear handles and wooden swivels used to keep harness lines from tangling show that these people had made two important advances: point hafting and the domestication of dogs. Attaching stone points to a long stick with a haft was the essential advance; it gave man power over animals many times his size. Dogs gave man mobility. Instead of drying the caribou meat where they killed it, men who had dogs pulling sleds could carry it back to their camps. But every advance has a price tag; in this case, it was the need to produce a surplus of salmon to feed the dogs. In another example, the archaeologist Jean Aigner, while excavating a site on the Aleutian island of Unalaska, found the mummified body of a woman in a cave. The dissected cadaver had the blackened lungs of a three-pack-a-day smoker. Evidently she had been tending the seal-oil lamp in unventilated quarters—a prehistoric health hazard.

How, you may ask, do we know so much about Early Man in North America? There are no journals or diaries to work with, not a single piece of paper. What does remain is an unintentional, nonverbal archive. History begins with written records, but prehistory is revealed by buried clues—skeletons, potsherds, flintpoints, bits of charcoal, burial goods, textile fibers. This is the great subterranean library of Early Man, and archaeologists are its librarians.

Archaeology is a form of time travel. In a cave in Colorado, thirty-two figurines were found, each the size of a hand and made from a single twisted willow twig. They were effigies of mountain sheep. Several were pierced with miniature spears. These artifacts gave archaeologists a glimpse into the soul of Early Man, who believed that he could improve his chances in the hunt by creating a magic image of his prey.

American archaeology flowered during the depression. The good people at the WPA provided the funding for the first large-scale excavations because they were labor-intensive and took a lot of unemployed men off the relief rolls. With diggers shoveling, and clerks labeling and filing, thousands of Indian sites around the country were located, and rough chronologies of occupation were established based on ceramic sequences (the most recent were closest to ground surface).

Chronologies remained approximate until the astronomer Andrew Ellicott Douglass, who was studying the impact of sunspots on climate, went to Arizona in the 1920s to look at tree rings. Examining the rings on yellow pines near Prescott and Flagstaff, Douglass noticed that in dry years the rings were narrow and bunched together, whereas in wet years they were wider apart, forming a distinctive pattern. Some of these Arizona pines were five hundred years old, going back to pre-Columbian times. Douglass realized that, if he could match the patterns on the trees with the patterns on the beams in prehistoric ruins, he would be able to date the ruins, since he knew the age of the trees.

But there was a gap between the sequences he found in the beams of the ruins and the live-tree patterns, which didn't go back far enough. To bridge the tree-ring gap, Douglass went into Hopi villages and obtained permission to cut into their ancient beams, promising to cap each beam with a turquoise to keep the spirits away. On June 22, 1929, in the Arizona village of Show Low, a team of his gap hunters found a fire-scarred roof beam that overlapped with both his living-tree sequence and one of the prehistoric beams in the ruins. "The history within that carbonized bit of beam held us spellbound," Douglass wrote. He was able to date it to A.D. 1237. The astronomer had found the first reliable method of dating the construction of prehistoric sites.

Tree-ring dating was limited in its uses, for it could only go so far back, and certain types of trees, such as the giant sequoia in California, did not prove useful; also, the technique wasn't much good in places like northern Alaska, above the tree line.

Still, dendrochronology, as tree-ring dating became known, was a breakthrough, helping to point archaeology in the right direction, for in the first quarter of the twentieth century, American archaeologists were barking up the wrong tree. The reigning scholars denied the existence of the Bering Land Bridge and Ice Age man. They mocked the theory that Early Man had crossed the land bridge in pursuit of Ice Age mammals and gone on foot across North and South America. They believed man had come later, by boat, and were looking for prehistoric craniums to measure, the way it was done in Europe. But no Early Man skulls had ever been found in North America. The only other way to prove the Bering Land Bridge theory was to find a projectile point in close proximity with the bones of an extinct Ice Age mammal; this would place man the hunter at the site of the kill.

The scene shifts to a summer day in 1925, in the northeastern corner of New Mexico, close to the Texas border. A black cow-hand named George McJunkin, who works for the Crowfoot ranch, is riding along the Cimarron River, near the town of Folsom, following the tracks of a stray cow. He nudges his horse into the narrow valley of a dry creek with high embankments of yellowish-red clay, looking intently at the ground. A flash of white catches his eye. He stops his horse, notices something sticking out of the embankment, and dismounts to take a closer look. He finds a bone, bigger than any he's ever seen. When he pulls at it, it breaks off in his hand, and he takes the fragment back to the ranch.

J. D. Figgins, director of Denver's Museum of Natural History, heard of McJunkin's find and sent a party to the site in 1926. They started chipping away at the top of the embankment with chisels. One day, when they were about ten feet down, a chisel struck what Figgins later described as "a wedge-shaped fragment of flint, an inch in width by three quarters of an inch in length, lying in a fixed position, adjacent to a bison rib." This tiny flint projectile, this Folsom point, in perfect contact with a bison rib, was proof that Early Man had coexisted with a species of Ice Age bison known to have become extinct by 6000 B.C.

If there was a Folsom point, there had to be a Folsom man, although his remains were not found in the arroyo embankment— or anywhere else, for that matter. Eventually, however, the team did find the skeletons of thirty bisons, and nineteen of the beautifully made Folsom points, fluted on each side for nearly their entire length. Considering that Folsom man had only stone and deer-antler tools, this was an achievement on the order of the Sidewinder missile.

It would take another quarter-century to produce an accurate method of dating that could probe back as far as the Pleistocene. This time, the discovery was a by-product of World War II atom-bomb research.

Its inventor was Willard F. Libby, a University of Chicago scientist whose work in separating uranium isotopes was essential to the success of the first atom bomb. While studying radioactivity, he found that, although the carbon in the air was mainly nonradioactive carbon 12, there was also a small quantity of radioactive carbon 14.

When plants absorb sunlight and water during photosynthesis, they retain the carbon and exhale the oxygen, which is exactly the opposite of what human beings do when they breathe. The plants absorb the carbon dioxide, with its component of radioactive carbon 14. Animals absorb the plants, and man absorbs animals and plants. So, all living organisms contain a small amount of carbon 14.

Libby, who won the Nobel Prize in chemistry in 1960, found that, when the living organism dies, the carbon 14 in the tissues is released, or lost, at a fixed rate. He further determined that 50 percent of the carbon 14 in a dead plant or a bison bone or a piece of wood or a prehistoric skeleton was lost after 5,730 years, and half of the remaining carbon 14 was lost in another 5,730 years, and so on.

To test his theory, Libby prevailed on a curator at the Chicago Museum of Natural History to let him have a board from the funerary boat of an Egyptian pharaoh—in the interest of science. He chopped the board into kindling and threw the kindling into an electric furnace, burning it down to charcoal. He ground up the charcoal and applied a Geiger counter to it, which gave him a reading that the board was 3,621 years old—only a little more than a hundred years off the known age of the wooden boat, 3,750 years. Libby had found the long-sought chronometric tool that could date practically anything except stone and metal. Any object or fragment made of wood, soot, grass, dung, antler, or tusk, bone, clam or mussel shell, basket fragment, or textile fiber could now be accurately dated.

This was to archaeology as the rudder was to navigation. Soon samples began arriving in Libby's laboratory from museums all over the world. Prehistoric craniums of international repute, pondered over by the great Leakey himself, or given shelf space at the Musée de l'Homme in Paris, were sent to laboratories to be carbon-dated. A juvenile skull found in Borneo in the 1960s out-performed all others, yielding an age of forty thousand years.

Dates obtained by the Libby system are not B.C. but B.P. (Before Present), with 1950 as year zero. Isolating the carbon 14 sounds like purest wizardry to the layman. The sample must be cleaned, then burned, to convert it to carbon dioxide. In the case of skeletal remains, the bone has to be melted away with hydrochloric acid to get at the soft and combustible collagen, which is burned and converted into gas that is piped into a machine called a "proportional counter." But, as arcane as the process sounds, carbon-dating entered popular culture during Ronald Reagan's second term, when he said: "When I go in for a physical nowadays, they don't ask me my age, they just carbon-date me."

Thanks to carbon-dating, which is accurate to about 40,000 years, the story of Early Man was brought within a time frame. Once Libby provided the tool for reconstructing prehistory, archaeologists went digging. At the Old Crow site in the Yukon territory, which was once the easternmost part of Beringia, a serrated caribou skin scraper was carbon-dated 5000 B.P. Cut and butchered bones were carbon-dated 30,000 B.P. All indications are that man was on the North American continent thirty thousand years ago, on that unglaciated strip known as Beringia, and started moving south when the glaciers melted.

We can follow Early Man's southward march along a trail of carbon dates. By 19,000 B.P., he was in Pennsylvania, not far from Pittsburgh, on Cross Creek, a small tributary of the Ohio River. Fifty feet above the creek, archaeologists found a natural recess in a sandstone cliff with one of the longest occupational sequences in the Western Hemisphere. Discovered in the seventies and dubbed Meadowcroft, the site revealed more than a dozen layers of occupation. At the deepest level, the diggers found a bit of basketry dated 19,999 B.P.; on the surface, beer cans and a junkie's hypodermic.

At the Kimmswick site, twenty miles south of St. Louis, a three-inch point was found in 1979 on top of some mastodon bones carbon-dated 11,000 B.P. This is the only mastodon kill in the United States that has been linked to Early Man. A second point was found at the same site a year later, in direct contact with a mastodon bone. This proves that man and mastodon coexisted in Missouri eleven thousand years ago. The Kimmswick point (called a "Clovis point," after the place in New Mexico where it was first discovered) showed a lot of flake scars and some crude fluting. It was an earlier model than the Folsom point, but effective enough to kill the forest browser with the huge molars.

Refugees from the interglacial were in Alabama by 15,000 B.P. We learned this from the dig at Russell Cave, in the northeast corner of the state, less than a mile away from the Tennessee line.

One can imagine the first extended family to arrive at this big sheltered cave congratulating themselves on their good fortune. The cave had a dry floor to sleep on. It faced east and was warmed by the morning sun. It was protected from the winds, and there was plenty of water at their front door from a pool fed by an underground stream. It was high enough so that, when the pool flooded in the spring, the water didn't reach the cave level.

It wasn't a bad life for 10,500 B.P., which was the carbon date for the earliest skeleton found there, that of a two-year-old child. These people, whose skeletons tell us they were short, and suffered from bad teeth and arthritis, had evidently arrived over the ice-free corridor in the Missouri Valley and settled in this spacious, well-situated Alabama cave. They kept a fire going during the cold winter months, made their chert points, dug pits for food storage, and prepared hides for clothes. They were comparatively well off.

From Wilson Butte, Idaho, where archaeologists found bone tools carbon-dated to 14,500 B.P., to Florida's Charlotte Harbor, where the shell of a giant prehistoric tortoise was found penetrated by a wooden spear, the evidence was abundant and widespread: Early Man, or Paleo-Indian man, was everywhere, in every corner of the United States, living in small groups, often at some distance from one another. Thinly settling the vast surface of available land, the Indian in North America developed 160 language families that survived long enough to be studied, with twelve hundred or more dialects. Scientists estimate that the time needed to spread across the land, adapt to different climates, and evolve so many languages must have been twenty-five thousand years, which more or less jibes with the carbon-dating.

As for learning about the survival techniques of Early Man, the so-called Chubbuck site was another breakthrough, demonstrating that nine thousand years ago large bands of well-organized hunters on the Great Plains were able to hunt buffalo herds successfully on foot.

In 1957, an amateur archaeologist named Jerry Chubbuck was driving along Big Sandy Creek in eastern Colorado, north of the Arkansas River, between the towns of Kit Carson and Cheyenne Wells. He came upon a dry gulch where wind erosion had exposed a sight so remarkable that he stopped his car—not one skeleton, not ten, not a hundred, but a continuous bed of bones lying in the gulch, a weaving, serpentine line of bones 170 feet long, in neat, separated piles. A pile of limb bones, a pile of skulls, a pile of pelvic girdles, and so on.

After obtaining permission from the owner of the land and notifying the University of Colorado, Chubbuck began to dig test pits with his friend Sigurd Olsen. The "river of bones" (all belonging to an extinct form of straight-horned bison weighing more than a ton) was dubbed the Chubbuck-Olsen site. At the deepest level of excavation, thirteen complete skeletons were found that the hunters had not touched. At the next level were partly butchered skeletons. And on top, lined up along the arroyo, were the piles of single bones, which were carbon-dated 8500 B.P.

The wealth of remains—not just bones, but projectile points and scraping tools—provided enough clues to reconstruct a prehistoric bison hunt. Early Man compensated for the handicap of being on foot by maneuvering the bisons into stampeding off the high embankment.

Try to visualize a companionable herd of bison, grazing in the valley. Suddenly they are spotted by a party of hunters approaching from the north, keeping the breeze in their faces so the more than two hundred bison won't pick up their scent. The hunters position themselves in groups on three sides to funnel the herd toward the arroyo to the south. Once in place, the hunters rise, hallooing and yelling and throwing their spears, counting on the herd to flee en masse. The terrified animals close ranks and stampede, plunging off the embankment and into the gulch. The first ones off are crushed by the others. In a matter of minutes, the hunters kill or wound ninety-three bulls, 101 cows, and sixteen calves. The calf skeletons at the site were only a few days old. Knowing that bison calves are born in May or June gives us the season of the kill. After the attack, the hunter's first task was to move the carcasses to flat ground for butchering. Next, the bison were rolled over on their stomachs, and the hide was cut down the back and pulled down on both sides to form a kind of mat to put the meat on. Then the hunters cut the front legs and shoulder blades to expose the choice hump meat, and threw the bones back into the gulch, where they were stacked in piles.

They liked the tongue best. Tongue bones were not found in a pile, but scattered throughout the deposit, suggesting that they were eaten sushi-style as the hunters worked. If the hunters had women with them, some of the meat might be stewed in skin containers, the water kept boiling with heated rocks. A lot of the meat had to be dried and carried out. Maybe they had dogs to carry the load; these would eat part of the meat. Of the 210 buffalo killed, about 150 were completely butchered. To stalk, butcher, and prepare that much bison meat, the group of hunters must have been fairly large.

It is safe to say that about nine thousand years ago large bands of well-organized hunters on the Great Plains were getting the protein in their diet from buffalo.

Other clues to the life-style of Early Americans were found on the farm of Teed and Mary Koster, near Eldred, Illinois. Drawn to the area when farmers plowing their fields started turning up potsherds, archaeologists found a site with fourteen levels of occupation, going back to 8500 B.P. At the deepest level were four dog skeletons the size of fox terriers, some of the oldest domesticated dogs found in the United States. Each dog was buried in a separate pit, showing the esteem in which they were held. These people were hunter-gatherers, traveling perhaps several hundred miles in their search for deer. They needed dogs to flush the deer out and run them to ground.

At the Koster site, archaeologists could see the technology improving from layer to layer. Fishhooks made from deer toes appeared around 8000 B.P., at about the time stone net-weights arrived on the scene. But these changes occurred at a snail's pace. Early Man was on slow time, absorbed in the search for food. The conditions were not auspicious for creative thinking. For instance, in 8000 B.P., men used stone axes that were grooved in the middle so they could tie on the handles with wet rawhide. It took them three thousand years to figure out that, if the ax was grooved at three quarters, it had better balance and more striking power.

From 8500 to 4000 B.P., the changes were minor. Man had settled into an adequate and sustainable way of life, hunting white-tailed deer, catching the plentiful river fish, and eating wild plants such as marsh elder and goosefoot. There was no crowding or competition with other groups, and population increase was slow. The society was seemingly immune to change, perhaps because the life span was so short. Death came from disease more often than from old age. The skeletons found at Koster revealed tuberculosis of the spine, arthritis, and birth deformities. There were also a number of fractures (bones broken perhaps in the hunt) that did not mend properly.

Even more resistant to change was Cochise man, down in the

southeast corner of Arizona. By 9000 B.P., he was grinding wild seeds with milling stones. He didn't acquire projectile points until three thousand years later, and it took him another three thousand to come up with the mortar and pestle. All that time, he lived in caves at high altitudes, building up rubbish heaps for archaeologists to study. Finally, he settled in the valleys. It's all too easy to reproach Cochise man for his many millennia of inglorious stagnation, but archaeologists aren't judgmental. They know there's no steady advance from grain-grinding lowbrow to doctoral candidate, no smooth progress from Stone Age to nuclear family. They know that, when a society works reasonably well, there is little incentive to change it.

A pretty good case can be made for the hunter-gatherer way of life, an existence based on the four seasons of food supply. In the fall, Early Man in America pitched his camp in the plains to harvest hickory nuts. In the winter, he moved to the river bottoms to hunt deer and migratory fowl. In the spring, he fished in the swamps and ponds, and in the summer he collected mussels and snails and harvested sunflower seeds, marsh elder, and wild strawberries.

They didn't deplete their resources, because they weren't equipped to take more than they could use. Storage facilities were nonexistent. They seemed to have an instinct for keeping their population in balance with their food supply. The Eskimos, for instance, practiced infanticide and gerontocide—leaving the old people on the ice to die. The idea wasn't to accumulate in excess, just enough to get by. For thousands of years, they lived a healthy outdoor life. They didn't settle in villages that grew into towns, and they didn't have the epidemics that decimated the crowded and unsanitary cities of Europe. They never developed the successful Old World combination of plant raising and animal husbandry, because they didn't have any livestock—no oxen to pull plows, no pigs or sheep.

What makes agriculture the "next step" in human progress? Perhaps hunter-gatherers gradually switched to farming because the game fled or the population drastically increased. They probably didn't see it as a change for the better. They had developed strategies to get the most food with the least effort, and they loved the hunt, the satisfaction of bringing back the game. As Margaret Mead said, a man is never happier than when he's going hunting. But the shift to agriculture gradually occurred, first showing up south of what is now the Mexican border, where there were no endless plains stocked with buffalo, no river systems for transportation and fish, and no bottom lands.

South of the border, man learned to domesticate wild grasses and plants, and to make pottery in which to store food. By 4000 B.C. or so, they were planting squash, peppers, avocados, and corn. And by 1600 B.C., they had settled communities and were on their way to a number of mini-civilizations, such as the Olmecs and the Mayans, whose achievements included bar-and-dot calendars, a written script, and a knowledge of mathematics and astronomy. The Mayans not only had a calendar but prophesied that the world will end on December 24, 2011.

Among the accomplishments of these societies can be counted the single most important contribution to North American Indian civilization—namely, corn. All known civilizations have been based on one of just six plant species: wheat, barley, millet, rice, corn, and potatoes. The magic plant for the Americas was corn, or maize, developed from a wild, seed-bearing tall grass that was repeatedly hybridized until small, inch-long cobs began appearing in central Mexico. Seeds fell in ground manured by humans, and the plant was domesticated, and turned out to be amazingly adaptable. In theory, you could grow it anyplace where there was a 120-day growing season. It was the perfect crop for people who didn't have plows, because it grew without tending, it husbanded itself. American civilization as we know it would never have existed without the gift of corn.

The hard evidence that the corn route went from South to North America is fairly recent. In 1959, the archaeologist Richard "Scotty" MacNeish narrowed the search down to central Mexico's Tehuacán Valley, northeast of Puebla, where there were a large number of dry caves.

He visited thirty-one caves before frustration made him turn to a pile of forms that local schoolteachers had filled out for the Puebla museum director, describing the location of caves they had spotted on outings with their students. The first two turned out to be duds, but he agreed to go look at a third with Bertha Martinez, the teacher who had identified it. It was a hot six-mile uphill trudge through thick stands of cactus and mesquite, but MacNeish saw at once, from the amount of vegetal material under the goat dung that covered the cave floor, that it looked promising.

With two helpers, and using only trowels, he dug a six-foot

square to a depth of six feet, taking the dirt out with buckets to sift it through a mesh screen, and getting down to preceramic layers of occupation. On January 27, 1959, one of the assistants came up to MacNeish with something in his hand—a dirt-encrusted corncob less than an inch long. Although prosaic in the extreme—no trumpets, no roll of the drum—it was a stirring moment, for he was holding the ancestor of North American corn. This corncob and two others that MacNeish found were later carbon-dated to 5600 B.P.

MacNeish could now trace the corn route from the Tehuacán Valley to Bat Cave in New Mexico, where corncobs dated between 4000 and 5000 B.P. had been found. From 4000 B.C., corn crept northward. There was an intermediate period during which Early Man started to plant while still hunting and foraging. The very act of planting, however, changed his habits, his schedule, and his mind-set.

Foraging for wild plants required going where the plant was, whereas farmers plant the crop where they are. Foraging is nomadic and episodic, farming sustained and sedentary. Your sense of time changes with farming, because you can't just take life as it comes, knowing that if you go to a certain clearing in April you'll find goosefoot: you have to plan ahead, pick a suitable field, manure the ground with fish bones, build a storage facility for seeds and food surpluses.

Farmers are in a different relationship with nature, because they are working the land instead of taking what it naturally offers. They are affecting the outcome with their farming skills, and altering the landscape by chopping trees and digging canals. The forager's attitude toward nature is deferential; he is grateful for its bounty and leaves the landscape alone. But the farmer's attitude is territorial; the piece of land he works becomes *his* field, the crop *his* crop, grown with the sweat of *his* brow. Instead of hunting, he must learn to assume a defense role, as land disputes arise and marauders raid planted fields.

With farming comes a change in the type of dwelling. Some foragers lived in holes in the ground called pit-houses, which were simple to dig wherever they went. But the farmers needed permanent dwellings close to the planted fields, and a different kind of living space, including storage and milling rooms. So, with farming came a change to multiroom surface housing, constructed of wood and mud, and later of stone.

And if corn comes, can pottery be far behind? Pottery wasn't convenient for the foragers—it broke too easily. The hunters preferred to use the stomachs of the animals they killed to cook their food. But in farming villages, pottery was essential for storage and food preparation. It didn't unravel like baskets, and it could be sealed, protecting what was inside from insects and rodents. Used for cooking, it could be placed directly over the fire or left on a bed of coals to simmer unattended, freeing the prehistoric housewife for other tasks. And, given thorough boiling in pots, more plants were edible.

With farming and a settled village life, you need an organized labor force, a storage system with a food surplus, and a trade network, all of which require some kind of authority and a chain of command. When the tribe turned to farming, it became hierarchical and lost the egalitarianism of the hunter-gatherer. There's still a strain of nostalgia in the American psyche for the anarchic individualism of the forager; consider Thoreau or Kerouac, or the twentieth-century subculture of the drifter—people who would rather not have a fixed address. Even the aluminum-can retrieving of the homeless is reminiscent of the hunter-gatherer instinct.

Farming entails a more efficient organization of time. When you don't have to spend all your time in the food chase, you can think of other things, such as fixing the roof, making prettier pots, choosing a chief, and musing on the possibility of an afterlife. People suddenly have time for organized religion, and a priestly class is born. A theory of the hereafter is formed, in which it is held that the dead will go to another land to rejoin their ancestors. According to their position in the farming society, which has gradually divided into social classes, the dead are buried with more or less pomp. At the Koster site in Illinois, corn makes its appearance in 200 B.C.—having taken more than two thousand years to get there from New Mexico. A hundred years later, you start seeing the dead sprinkled with red-ocher pigment and buried with ceremonial grave goods, such as rattles and flutes.

A rudimentary mercantile economy developed to satisfy the need for grave goods. Say there was a flint quarry nearby; people could trade it for copper from Lake Superior. The copper was beaten into large ax-blades intended only as decorative objects, to be buried with an Important Personage as he ventured into the Great Beyond. And since people had some spare time, they started building burial mounds.

But land ownership also creates a scenario for conflict. Somebody else wants the same land, and you have to defend it. The random skirmishes of hunter-gatherers become regular cycles of war and peace over boundaries. That's why a number of skeletons found at various sites had multiple arrow points in their bones (the bow and arrow having come in circa 2000 B.C.). Others had butchering marks in the neck bones, indicating decapitation. Still others showed signs of ritual sacrifice, perhaps borrowed from the Aztecs, for whom sadism and high aesthetics went hand in hand. At the Spiro, Oklahoma, site, a jar full of amputated human hands was found, indicating some Aztec-like mutilation. Engraved shell designs and stone statuettes unearthed among grave goods sometimes show costumed men holding detached heads.

With the spread of corn and the shift to farming in some parts of North America, mini-civilizations flourished as they had south of the border. Though perhaps not quite as brilliant as the Mayans, in that they never developed a handwriting or built stone pyramids, these *norteamericano* efforts could qualify as an Indian Renaissance that flowered and died long before the arrival of the white man in the sixteenth century. These people had a history, but not in the sense of documents that can be read by historians; rather, it was the buried history of a mortuary cult, which had to be dug up and dated by archaeologists.

During the twenty-three hundred years between 1000 B.C. and A.D. 1300, a number of agricultural societies in various locations took the lead and produced indigenous civilizations as startling in their way as the better-known Mayans and Incas, and completely removed from the post-contact stereotype of the primitive Indian.

Ohio, where people were living in caves, as early as 2000 B.P. was the crucible. The site on the Scioto River—outside Chillicothe, in south-central Ohio—is one of the earliest mound-building communities, occupied by 3000 B.P. and abandoned by 1500 B.P. This farming society preceded the arrival of corn. At first they planted pumpkins and squash. The earliest corn found there was carbon-dated 2300 B.P. It was a completely indigenous society, not a copycat influenced by South America. Who knows why it was abandoned? Maybe, with the introduction of the bow and arrow, the trade caravans were ambushed by bandits, and the flow of grave goods was interrupted. Or maybe the practice of taking wealth out of circulation by leaving it with the dead left those people impoverished. But while it lasted, for fifteen hundred years, there was here, for the times, an affluent society based on a wide-ranging trading system.

In one grave, four leading citizens were found covered with hundreds of sheets of mica, then a layer of earth, then a second layer of mica. Mica was expensive, and there was the additional cost of packaging and shipping the fragile sheets, which came from the Blue Ridge Mountains of North Carolina. Also in the graves were large copper ornaments, beaten flat and carved in the shape of two-headed eagles, falcons, and hands; copper was another expensive and distant item, from Lake Superior. Further grave goods included engraved conch shells from the Gulf of Mexico, large ceremonial points made from North Dakota chalcedony (a kind of quartz), and a great many beautifully carved ceramic pipes, works of art that match the carved jade of the Incas in finesse.

One in particular has a bowl representing a roseate spoonbill (habitat Florida) astride a fish; another shows a curious female figure, the pipe bowl between her shoulders, the hole for the removable stem in the small of her back. The woman has swollen breasts and a distended abdomen. Her legs are up. She is evidently in the early stages of labor. Perhaps the pipe was meant to be smoked by midwives before attending a birth. In any case, for the honored dead, nothing was too good. The finest work of the best artisans was placed in their graves without stinting, as if today's Japanese billionaires were buried with their recently acquired Van Goghs and Monets.

These Chillicothe people are called Adena, the name of the estate where some of their mounds were discovered. They moved millions of cubic feet of earth to make pyramid-shaped mounds, exclusively for burials. They lived in outlying residential communities, where they tended their fields; the mounds were their ceremonial and social centers. It was a society of the leaders and the led, the latter not being granted the same splendid burials as the former. The common folk were cremated in a gruesome manner—their heads, arms, and legs were cut off, their bodies then drained of blood and set on fire over open pits until they were reduced to ash and bone. The shaman dismembered the bodies with his fine obsidian blade. The shaman's grave contained obsidian "blanks" (large unfinished pieces), his squirrel-skin medicine bag, and the jawbone of a wolf. Obsidian, incidentally, is a volcanic glass that came from the Rocky Mountains; it must have been carried on someone's back halfway across the continent.

Adena blended into Hopewell, a similar society, also named after a nineteenth-century estate. It flourished more briefly, from 200 B.C. to A.D. 400. Hopewell mounds were uncovered during the construction of locks for the Ohio Canal, and the laying of tracks for the Central Ohio Railroad. The principal mounds, however, are in Newark, Ohio, outside Columbus.

From Ohio, the Adena-Hopewell burial-mound culture spread in different directions. Hundreds of years after the abandonment of the Ohio sites, sites appeared in Alabama and Georgia. Near present-day Tuscaloosa, in western Alabama, on the Black Warrior River, there is a large Adena-Hopewell-style burial complex known as Moundville, which prospered from A.D. 900 to 1400, with a population of three thousand and satellite communities totaling perhaps ten thousand. This was the Indian Renaissance of the Southeast. Small triangular stone points show they had the bow and arrow, and the pottery tempered with crushed shells show that they had an early form of Tupperware. They had floodplain agriculture based on corn, beans, and squash, long-distance trade, the emergence of highly organized chiefdoms, an increased territorial instinct leading to warfare, and enough discretionary time to build their great burial mounds.

As in Ohio, these people used cradleboards to flatten babies' skulls, and sweet-gum twigs to clean their teeth. The red liquid found in bloodroot was used as body paint, and animal-hair brushes were used to paint pottery. Finely carved stone palettes were used to mix the paint, which was made of red iron ore, ground kaolin (a fine white clay), and yellow ocher. A trade network that went from the Great Lakes to the Gulf of Mexico provided them with lavish grave goods. The long-nosed masks cut from copper sheets started appearing in burial sites alongside skeletons carbon-dated 1000 B.P. But by the time De Soto ventured into Alabama in the 1540s, Moundville had been abandoned. While it lasted, it was a ceremonial center, like a cathedral town in France, with a public building for religious worship, a crafts center, game courts, a sweathouse, and of course, the culture's signature structures, the burial mounds.

The high point of this riparian heartland mound culture was the Cahokia federation, which flourished from 1000 to 1250 A.D., overlapping the time of the signing of the Magna Carta in England (1215). It was located right across the river from present-day St. Louis, at the confluence of the Illinois, Mississippi, and Missouri rivers. Situated on a creek where today there is a highway, it has been called the first real American city north of Mexico. In its prime it had a population of thirty thousand. Location, then as now, was everything: the people here had water for irrigation, navigation for trade, and plenty of flatlands.

Standing on the flat top of Monk's Mound, the largest man-made prehistoric structure in the United States, one can see, ten miles away, the Gateway Arch and the skyscrapers of downtown St. Louis. Traffic flows down Interstate 55-70, where a navigable creek once brought the grave goods. A housing subdivision covers other mounds. About a hundred mounds have been preserved, some ridged and some flat-topped, but many more have vanished.

Monk's Mound is a hundred feet high, with a base as long as three football fields, graded sides, several large terraces, and a log stairway to the top, upon which once stood wooden structures. It covers fourteen acres, and in the ranks of construction projects it's right up there with the pyramids of Thebes and the Zuggurats of Uruk. It's the centerpiece of a city that existed five centuries before Columbus.

It was obviously an "incipient empire" of trade, with a network of stations along the waterways, one of them in Wisconsin, halfway between Cahokia and the Lake Superior copper mines. The Cahokians had salt from briny springs fifty miles away, and flint from a quarry a hundred miles away, from which they made stone hoes that became an export item with brand-name recognition. Apparently, they had a favorable trade balance. Up the creeks and rivers went the hoes and other goods, and back came shells from the Gulf of Mexico, thirteen hundred miles away, copper from Lake Superior, mica from the Carolinas, and chert from Oklahoma. They had a corn surplus, plenty of timber in the surrounding forests, abundant game, and many picturesque-sounding wild plants, such as prairie dock, compass plant, tickseed, and spiderwort. Of course, they had thirty thousand mouths to feed, and we can only imagine the logistics of such an endeavor when everything had to be carried by hand. But they had docks and warehouses, and labor was recruited from outlying areas.

The inventiveness of this farming society was revealed with the discovery of the remains of forty-eight cedar posts the size of telephone poles, planted in a circle. This was a horizon-sighting calendar. When the Cahokians lined up the posts with the rising sun, they could figure out the summer and winter solstices.

A less desirable aspect of the society was revealed with the excavation of Mound 72, a ridge-topped mound only seven feet high that contained three hundred graves. The tale those graves told was one of wretched excess, in terms of both grave goods and human sacrifices. There was every indication that a Great Leader —six feet two inches tall, according to his skeleton, which was carbon-dated 1050 B.P.—had been accompanied by some of his people into eternal continuance. The Great Leader was found lying on a bed of twenty thousand shells covered with mica, and surrounded by 750 arrow points. Four skeletons nearby were without hands or heads, but their arms were interlocked, suggesting that they had been his *consiglieri*. The chief was also buried with a sizable number of lesser folk, including 118 females between the ages of fifteen and twenty-five; their youth suggests that they did not die a natural death.

Around A.D. 1100, at the peak of their power, the leaders of Cahokia ordered another public-works project, the building of a stockade around the inner city. They cut down an estimated eighty thousand trees for their fence of twelve-foot-high upright poles, with protected entrances and guards on raised platforms at seventy-foot intervals.

The first stockade was double-walled, as the archaeologists could tell from the postholes. But when the stockade was rebuilt, in A.D. 1200, it had only one wall. It seems that the Cahokians were running out of wood—a thirteenth-century example of re-source depletion. There was no Sierra Club to tell them they were overlogging, so they cut down their forests and didn't replant. Losing its cover, the game fled at a time when the human popula-tion was increasing. The Cahokians became victims of their own success, with too many mouths to feed, and developed a negative trade balance. The labor force grew discontented, and they went right into a recession. By A.D. 1300, Cahokia was abandoned, and its splendid mounds were covered with weeds and underbrush, monuments to man's overreaching.

In their prime, however, the mound-building societies ex-tended from the Great Lakes to Florida, and from the Atlantic Coast to Oklahoma. They shared an adaptation to floodplain habi-tats, a ranked society, a religion based on the differentiated treat-ment of the dead, a trade network, and a love of majestic public buildings. Unearthed skeletons dating from A.D. 1000 show signs of violent death, disclosing what anthropologists call "increasing inter-group conflict," meaning that the tribes were at war with one another.

•   •

In the winter of 1888, Richard Wetherill and his brother-in-law Charlie Mason were riding across a seven-thousand-foot-high plateau in southwestern Colorado called Mesa Verde, tracking strays that had wandered off with a bunch of wild cattle. It was December 18, and they were following tracks through the snow; underbrush scratched the legs of their horses as they rode. They dismounted and walked out on a point of bare rock. Half a mile away, on the opposite side of the canyon, they saw an opening in the cliff face. Through the white haze they could make out the ghostly outline of dwellings, of ruined walls and broken terraces, of a round tower rising in the fading afternoon light. Forgetting the strays, they clambered down to the bottom of the canyon and up the other side, to the once-inhabited gap in the rock face. They had discovered a lost civilization.

Richard Wetherill gave up ranching to devote himself to the excavation of the city in the cliff. Colorado had only been a state since 1876, and there weren't any laws, state or federal, protecting prehistoric ruins. Later he would be blamed for not using methods devised a generation after his death. He just went at it with pick and shovel. When a shovel blade scraped pottery, he scooped it up with his bare hands. Some said he was no more than a pothunter, and Wetherill himself boasted when drunk that he was known as "the vandal of the Southwest." He was certainly no archaeologist, in method or intent, the profit motive being uppermost in his mind.

In 1898, he moved to Chaco Canyon, another amazing prehistoric site of stone ruins and great ceremonial buildings. His aim was to apply for a homestead on the site of the ruins so he could excavate them, which was a little like going to Egypt and laying claim to the pyramids.

Around the ruins, there was a Navajo reservation the size of Massachusetts, with a population of twenty-five thousand. Wetherill opened a trading post, buying Navajo blankets and selling illegal liquor, among other things. He bargained with the shy, brown-skinned women who had woven the blankets. When they were ailing, his wife doctored them. He slipped their husbands pints of white lightning and settled their disputes, all the while waiting for title to the ruins.

But times were changing, and in 1906 Congress passed an act to preserve Indian ruins from vandalism. In 1907, the Chaco Canyon site was made a part of the Navajo reservation, under federal supervision. Wetherill was out of luck and settled for a 113-acre homestead on the reservation fringe. His ire focused on the super-intendent of the Navajo Agency, William T. Shelton. "I've forgotten more about the Navajos than Shelton'll ever know," he said.

Be that as it may, Shelton's reports to the Indian Service charged that Wetherill was cheating the Navajos and selling them liquor, that he was stealing their burros and cattle, that he was acting as if they were his serfs, abusing them and beating them and keeping them in his private jail.

Nineteen ten was a dry year, and the grazing was poor. Navajos dug water holes to keep their cattle alive. At 6:00 P.M. on June 22, Wetherill and one of his cowboys, Bill Finn, were driving a small bunch of cattle down a bend in the Chaco Canyon, at a point where a wagon trail winds through the rock to the mesa. The cattle were raising dust, and the men hiding behind the rocks seemed like part of the landscape. Shots were fired as the two riders passed, and Wetherill slipped from his saddle and sprawled in the sand. Finn galloped off, followed by Wetherill's big sorrel horse, stirrups swinging.

A Navajo rose from behind the rock and crouched over the fallen body. "Are you sick, Anasazi?" he asked. Wetherill had been killed by a shot through the heart. The Navajo pointed the muzzle of his rifle at the dead man, fired again, and blew away the right side of his head.

At the trial in Denver, it came out that the Navajo owed Wetherill money, and had turned his debt into a grievance. As a boy, he had seen his father killed by a band of cowboys. The Navajo was sentenced to five to ten, which reflected on Wetherill's reputation as an abusive exploiter of the Indians. He was not an admirable figure, but there was one thing that could never be taken from him—the exquisite moment when, through the snow sprinkling the piñon, he came upon the city in the cavern, the remnants of a lost society.

The ruins that he discovered, Mesa Verde and Chaco Canyon, were linked, the one being practically a continuation of the other. The earlier one was Chaco, the center of a unified and far-ranging culture from A.D. 900 to 1150.

Between 1038 and 1054, according to the carbon-dating of the logs, the Anasazi people of the Chaco Canyon built veritable San Simeons, five-story stone houses with five hundred rooms each. They preferred communal housing, and built houses a city block long, right up against the ocher cliff, with intricately designed ceremonial centers called "kivas." These houses didn't have foundations, stairs, or hallways. One room led into the next, and the upper stories were reached by ladder. The corners, not being dovetailed, eventually pulled apart. The ceilings were made of split juniper shakes plastered with mud.

But in their scale, in the strength and beauty of their construction, and in their unprecedented use of stone, the Chaco structures were the highest architectural achievement of the Native American. The Anasazi people built a city of stone, with thirteen major housing complexes and several hundred smaller ones, covering more than ten thousand acres. The construction required an enormous community effort. With stone axes, they felled and trimmed thousands of ponderosa pines from forests thirty miles away, and quarried millions of pounds of stone that had to be carried, dressed, and fitted. Then the brickwork had to be finished and chinked.

Chaco became the capital of a southwestern civilization, and a regional trade center, a sort of early shopping mall. The trouble its inhabitants took to acquire a desired item is illustrated by one of the more interesting skeletons found there—and also one of the smallest—that of a macaw. How did these gaudy parrots, originating in southern Mexico or Central America, arrive alive in Chaco Canyon? Someone had to bring them on foot over a distance of more than two thousand miles. It must have been a costly trading item. The Chaco people kept live macaws as pets, and used bird feathers for their ceremonial costumes. "O Mother Earth, weave for us a garment of brightness," say their Navajo descendants even today. They also had copper bells, shell trumpets, ceramic incense-burners, and painted wood tablets.

The kind of resource pooling they had to do required good management and the rise of a leadership class. For a while, they prospered, but the boom gave way to a bust. All it took was a drought, which, according to tree-ring evidence, took place in the Chaco area from 1130 to 1180. During those fifty years, with rainfall scarce and unpredictable, the system collapsed. They gradually abandoned their laboriously built stone dwellings and places of worship and moved south to more fertile land, perhaps to Texas. The whole remarkable system of roads, irrigation canals, granaries, and multistory houses, with awnings made of bark and willow twigs to provide shade in the work areas, fell into ruin.

Chaco Canyon is empty now. Willows rustle in the blue wind.

Mesa Verde lies eighty miles north of Chaco, in the southwestern corner of Colorado, a landscape that is humbling to man. You climb seven thousand feet to a flat-topped plateau covered with juniper and pine, more lush than Chaco. The sides of these high plateaus are steep sandstone cliffs, forming ravines with the sides of other mesas. Out on the bare rock, where Wetherill once stood, you look down about a hundred feet to a big overhang like the beak of a cap, and under the overhang there is a long cave with the ruins of stone houses.

A total of six hundred separate cliff dwellings have been found at Mesa Verde. The biggest one, Cliff Palace, is like a resort condominium, with more than two hundred rooms. Some of the smaller caves have only three or four rooms apiece. The beams they used were carbon-dated from A.D. 1209 to 1270, just after Chaco. These people, also Anasazi, had long been living on top of the mesa, where they grew corn and beans in small plots and hunted deer and rabbits. At the beginning of the thirteenth century, for some reason—perhaps for warmth at a time when the climate was cooling, or to protect themselves from enemies—they moved into the alcoves in the porous sandstone cliff-side.

They made their houses out of breadloaf-sized sandstone blocks, which they worked with harder cobbles from the stream at the bottom of the ravine. Limited in height by the cave roof, the miniature castles they designed had round towers and fine stone walls of shaped blocks aligned in straight courses. They flattened the uneven floors of the caves and had front yards in which they threw their garbage and buried their dead rolled up in yucca mats.

They continued to farm their plots on the mesa top, moving up and down the cliff face with the help of hand- and toe-holds they had cut into it. These cliff ladders were coded—that is, you had to know which foot to start out on, or halfway up you'd be in big trouble. We can try to imagine these Anasazi men and women clambering up and down the almost vertical sides of the cliffs with baskets on their backs, using shallow finger-holds. It was a risky commute, as we can surmise from a pair of child-sized crutches found among the graves.

But, as in Chaco Canyon, water was the problem. By 1300, the cliff dwellings were abandoned. The population, which had grown to several thousand, left the mesa in search of arable land. Climate changes forced them to regress to the hunter-gatherer stage. Thus, from 1000 B.C., with the rise of the Adena culture in Ohio, to A.D. 1300, with the collapse of the Mesa Verde cliff culture, Indian civilizations flourished and became extinct. The cliff dwellings remained hidden for nearly six hundred years, until Wetherill happened by. When the white men arrived in North America in the sixteenth century, they knew nothing of what the Indians had achieved, for they saw not the great cities that once had been, but tribal societies with a subsistence economy, living in wigwams and mud huts, and deserving, it seemed to them, the designation of savages. They knew nothing of the legacy that is still kept alive in the Navajo "Nightway Chant":

> *With Harmony may I walk,*
> *With Harmony behind me, may I walk,*
> *With Harmony above me, may I walk,*
> *With Harmony below me, may I walk,*
> *With Harmony all around me, may I walk. . . .*
> *It is finished in Harmony,*
> *It is finished in Harmony.*

CHAPTER TWO

THE EXPLORATION FEVER

Between 1492 and 1540, exploration fever raged in Europe. Among the many expeditions, two landed in North America: Ponce de León arrived in Florida in 1513, and Jacques Cartier reached Canada in 1534.

Elizabeth Waldo-Dentzel Collection, Northridge, CA.

In Joshua Shaw's *Coming of the White Man,* a ship appears on the horizon line, with the sun rising behind it, while in the foreground four Indians on a bluff are seen in various attitudes of terror. One is sitting bent over with his arms over his head, one is shielding his face with his arm, and one is carrying a hatchet as if already knowing he is going to have to defend himself against an invader. Below, on the shore, an Indian skiff has landed and one of the Indians is already out of it, running like hell. They know that nothing good is going to come of this.

*One hundred and fifty years elapsed between Columbus'
first voyage in 1492 and the settlement of Jamestown in
1607. What happened in that interval was the Spanish
entrada.*

J. H. PARRY

Before the marriage of Ferdinand and Isabella in 1469, there
was no Spain. She was ruler of the western half, Castile,
while he ruled in Aragon, in the east. Various provinces
had been fighting the Moors for seven hundred years, in what was
called the *reconquista*, a combined patriotic war and religious crusade. During this long struggle, Spain developed a particularly
combative form of Catholicism and a low tolerance for other faiths.
A warrior class sprang up, men who were good with the horse and
the sword, and considered ordinary work beneath them. Commerce was for the Jews, crafts for the Moors, farming for the
peasants, and fighting for the *hidalgos*.

With its large population of Jews and Moors, Spain was the
only multinational and multiracial country in Western Europe. But
after the two halves of the nation were united, the Catholic majesties proceeded to expel non-Spaniards. The Inquisition hit its
stride in 1483 under the Dominican monk Torquemada, who per-
suaded Ferdinand and Isabella to expel any Jews who refused to be
baptized. The deadline was 1492. It was in January 1492 that the
last Moorish stronghold, Granada, was captured. The Moorish
King Boabdil surrendered the Alhambra and saw a large silver
cross raised over the city, and Christian banners unfurled. One of
those who witnessed his submission was a Genovese navigator
named Columbus.

The year 1492 was a hinge between eras, in which royal un-
dertakings expressed both the religious persecution of the Dark
Ages and the adventurous expansionism of the "Age of Discovery."
Less than four months after Ferdinand and Isabella paraded
through Granada, Columbus' voyage was approved, and the *reconquista* was exported to the other side of the Atlantic. He sailed for
the "New World" on August 3, the deadline for the exile of all
unbaptized Jews.

The son of an Italian wool weaver, Columbus had tried for
years to find financing for his voyage. A bit of a scholar, a bit of an

intellectual, he had read and annotated a volume of Marco Polo's travels, with its account of visiting the Great Khan's court in Peking. This started his imagination working overtime. What if, instead of taking the long overland route eastward, you sailed westward and came at Asia from the other side? What a coup—never before attempted, and eliminating the middlemen who had a lock on the lucrative spice trade.

Today this seems absurd, because anyone looking at a globe can see that sailing west from Spain would lead straight to North and South America. But at that time North and South America did not exist in the European mind, or on European maps. The first globe, produced by Martin Behaim of Nuremberg in 1492, showed Zipangu (Japan) on the other side of a narrow Atlantic, an ocean decorated with mermaids and sea serpents. Columbus' misguided scheme was based on hopelessly inaccurate data about the size of the planet, the width of the Atlantic, and the proximity of Asia by sea. His detractors predicted he'd wind up in the drink, food for the monsters on the map, but he went anyway; in this he was very much in the American grain, very much a part of the "Sometimes a Great Notion" tradition.

After unsuccessfully approaching the kings of England, France, and Portugal, Columbus went to Spain in 1484. He lobbied, he made friends, he followed the itinerant court from city to city. It took him two years just to obtain an audience with the royal couple, and another six to win their approval. Originally, it was a mercantile undertaking, intended to fill the royal coffers, not a religious quest. Columbus was appointed admiral of the sea and governor general of all the lands he might discover. According to the articles of agreement, he would receive one-tenth of all the resources obtained from those lands.

Columbus set out on August 3, 1492, from the port of Palos in southern Spain, in three light ships called "caravels," with about ninety men and a letter of introduction to the Great Khan of Asia. With good weather, fair winds, and a stopover in the Canary Islands, he landed on October 12 on a small island in the central Bahamas, which he named San Salvador. This was the start of the Spanish Empire in the Americas.

Columbus thought he was off the coast of mainland China, for he wrote in his log: "It is certain that this is tierra firma and that I am off Zayto and Qyinsay" (two cities in China) "a hundred leagues more or less" (there were three leagues to a mile). In fact, he was on a speck in the Caribbean that the Indians called Guana-hani—perhaps the same island the English later called Watling.

On San Salvador, archaeologists have recently uncovered a number of objects that Columbus specified he had given to the natives—green and yellow glass beads, broken crockery, a coin, a belt buckle—objects found nowhere else in the central Bahamas. These trinkets are the earliest memorabilia of the Spanish *entrada*.

Columbus, as historian J. H. Parry put it, "did not discover a New World; he established contact between two worlds, both already 'old.' " The Indians, after all, had already been in the "New World" for fifteen thousand years. Some tribes had lived since 6000 B.P. on the islands that Columbus "discovered," according to recent digs.

Columbus' landing marked the beginning of the relationship between the late-fifteenth-century Spaniards, with their ocean-going vessels and expansionist ambitions, and the American Indians, with their Stone Age technology and isolated society. The Indian civilizations had already flowered and declined by A.D. 1200. At that time, Spain didn't exist, France was a collection of dukedoms, and England did not yet have the Magna Carta.

Columbus' first contacts set the pattern for all the others, the Spanish, French, and English. Thinking he was in Asia, or, as it was called, the Indies, Columbus called these people Los Indios and labeled them uncivilized and deficient. Therefore, it was all right to exploit them, to kidnap them and bring them back to Spain by force as slaves, and to make them work in the mines. During their wars with the Moors, the Spanish had formed the habit of capturing and mistreating prisoners, and the Indians suffered the same fate.

Like Columbus, the settlers of all of North America—of Quebec, Jamestown, and Plymouth—would believe that the white men didn't have to treat the Indians the way they treated one another. Columbus wrote in his second letter: "As soon as I had landed on the first island . . . I had several Indians taken prisoner." He had a job to do, and needed guides. From San Salvador, Columbus sailed southwest to the northern coast of Cuba, where he found Indians smoking roll-your-own cigars, which they lit with firebrands. Then he headed east to the next big island, which he called Hispaniola, and which is now divided between Haiti and the Dominican Republic. There he found what he'd been looking for, Indians wearing pendants made from gold dust panned in riverbeds.

On December 24, his flagship, the *Santa Maria*, went aground. The men were probably sleeping off a drunk, having been up all night carousing with the Indians. The Arawak chief gave him men to help unload the smashed ship, and this too was typical—the initial Indian response to the white man was friendly and helpful, until he got to know better. The chief also loaned Columbus two houses in which to store his supplies.

At this point, Columbus had a problem: now that he had only his two smaller ships, he lacked the room to take all his men back. The solution was to leave some men behind and build them houses from the planks of the dismantled *Santa Maria*. This little settlement on the northern coast of Haiti was called La Navidad. Thirty-nine men volunteered to stay on for a year, hoping for first crack at the gold.

La Navidad, today a Haitian farming village called En Bas Saline, was excavated from 1984 to 1987. The carbon-dating of pottery shows that the site was occupied from 1300 to 1500. Tiny bits of glass, as well as the charred post of a European dwelling, confirm Columbus' presence. Also discovered were a bone from a rat that must have left the sinking *Santa Maria*, and the fragment of a pig jaw. These animals were unknown in the Americas before Columbus. Pigs were bred so successfully on Hispaniola that they became a nuisance, and licenses to hunt them down were issued in 1508.

After settling his volunteers right next door to the Arawak king's large Indian village, Columbus sailed back to Spain on January 16, 1493. It was only three months since his arrival, but he apparently wanted further instructions before trying to find the Great Khan.

He took with him the seven prisoners captured on San Salvador, to show Their Spanish Majesties. They were taken to Barcelona, a garrison town full of soldiers and whores. Some of these Indians, it is believed, were carriers of syphilis, and passed it on to the Spanish whores, who passed it on to Spanish volunteers in the army of Charles VIII of France, who was starting out on an Italian campaign. This explains the raging outbreak of syphilis, a disease previously unknown in Europe, in Naples in 1495, during its occupation by the French army. Hundreds of pre-Columbian skeletons have been found in the Americas with syphilitic bone lesions, whereas there were no verifiable signs of syphilis in Europe before Columbus.

Columbus' second trip was altogether different, lasting two

and a half years, from September 1493 to March 1496, and leading to the founding of the first planned settlement in the Americas. He left with a fleet of seventeen ships and twelve hundred colonists hungry for gold. Priests were brought along for the conversion of the natives; they would henceforth be a fixture on Spanish expeditions.

Columbus landed at Dominica on November 3, 1493, and coasted along a number of other islands, known today as Guadeloupe, Antigua, St. Croix, the Virgin Islands, and Puerto Rico. At St. Croix, some Indians fired arrows at his ship; they had heard of the men with shiny helmets and sticks that spat fire. On returning to La Navidad, Columbus had an unpleasant surprise. The settlement was in ruins, and none of the thirty-nine men he'd left behind had survived. Fed up with the Spaniards' lust for gold and girls, the Indians had stopped being helpful.

Sailing seventy-five miles east, Columbus founded the town of La Isabela on the northern shore of the Dominican Republic, on a limestone bluff far from fresh water. This was a poor site to select, overlooking a reef that made for difficult anchorage, but here began the ongoing relationship between Old World and New. In 1990, on the site of La Isabela, archaeologists dug up the stone foundations of Columbus' principal settlement, which included a storehouse, a powder house, a hospital, a church, and a cemetery with skeletons whose arms were folded across their chests in the Christian manner. The archaeologists found jars of mercury that the settlers, who were less interested in working the land than in trading for gold, used to separate the yellow stuff from the ore. They found roof tiles and a kiln for firing pottery. One archaeologist, who unearthed the ceramic rim of what looked like a chamber pot, commented, "We'll never get closer to Columbus than this."

On La Isabela, Columbus the successful navigator became Columbus the inept island governor. Giving in to public pressure, he began asking the natives for a gold tribute, and initiated a system of forced Indian labor to help the settlers work their lands, just as the Spanish had done in the Canaries.

Columbus still believed, or forced himself to believe, that he was in Asia; his career, his title, his coat of arms, and his cash rewards all depended on it. In April 1494, he sailed with three ships to explore Cuba. To maintain his credit with the king, he made the crew swear, on penalty of having their tongues torn out if they recanted, that the island was part of the Asiatic mainland.

He returned to La Isabela in March 1495, just in time for an Indian rebellion. In an attempt to "pacify" the island, he took five hundred Taino Indian prisoners, sending them to Spain to be sold as slaves. Other Indians were put to work in the gold mines, and other islands were raided to make up labor shortages. As the Indians boarded the ships, they were told they were going to see their departed ancestors in heaven. Instead, upon arrival in La Isabela, they were sent underground, to the mines. Those who fought back had their arms cut off and were sent back to their villages as warnings. Within fifty years of Columbus' first voyage, the Tainos of Hispaniola had been exterminated.

In the meantime, Spain's rivals were playing catch-up. Henry VII, the first Tudor, had turned down Columbus, but granted his support to Giovanni Caboto, a onetime Venetian real-estate salesman who had caught the Asia bug by reading Marco Polo. Trying to outdo his Genovese colleague, he proposed a shorter and cheaper northern route to neutralize the Spanish advance. But Henry VII was chintzy, he didn't want to lay out large sums; Caboto sailed with only one ship, the *Matthew*, and eighteen men, around May 20, 1497.

By June 24, he had reached the coast of Newfoundland, the first man to land in North America since Leif Eriksson in the year 1000. He sensed the land as he approached, in the smell of fir trees and the flight of coastal birds. Like Columbus, he thought he had found Asia. Caboto stayed less than a month, departing on July 20 and reaching Bristol on August 6. The round trip had taken two and a half months. He went ashore only once, to fill the water casks.

Pleased, the king gave Caboto ten pounds and a twenty-pound annuity, as well as a second patent, this time for a larger, five-ship expedition. Soon after they left in 1498, one of the ships put into an Irish port in distress. That was the lucky one; the other four were never heard from again.

Meanwhile, in Hispaniola, the downward spiral had begun. The turning point came when Columbus sent five hundred slaves to Spain, which displeased Queen Isabella, who launched an inquiry into how they could be freed. Columbus was ordered home; he sailed on March 10, 1496, and reached Cádiz on June 11, leaving Hispaniola in the care of his brothers, Bartolomé and Diego.

Court squabbles and financial problems kept him in Spain for two years, but finally Ferdinand and Isabella agreed to a third voyage, with two hundred settlers (including ten convicted murderers, two of them gypsy women) and six ships. A register of the cargo, or *libro de armadas*, was recently found in the Spanish archives by the historian Eugene Lyon. From this document we know that Columbus' third voyage was stalled by sailors refusing to sail unless they collected their back pay, but something seems to have been worked out, and he set sail on May 30, 1498.

On returning to Hispaniola, Columbus found that his own men had rebelled against his brothers. Word of the uprising soon reached Spain, causing Ferdinand and Isabella to lose faith completely. They sent out another emissary, Francisco de Bobadilla, to replace Columbus as governor and chief magistrate. He arrived on August 23, 1500, in Santo Domingo, a harbor town on the southern coast of the Dominican Republic founded by Bartolomé Columbus in 1496. The situation had deteriorated badly. Diego Columbus was in Santo Domingo hanging rebellious Spaniards.

When Columbus refused to hand over his powers, Bobadilla had to arrest him, and he was brought back to Spain in chains. By the time he landed at Cádiz in November 1500, there was a little discovery boomlet. As he wrote, "They all made fun of my plan then; now even tailors wish to discover."

Though not a tailor, Amerigo Vespucci, the continent namer, was in trade. The Florentine-born son of a notary, he worked for the Medicis, and was sent to Seville in 1492, to help out in a Medici-owned ships'-chandler business. In 1496, he became manager of the agency, and was one of the chandlers who fitted out ships for Columbus' second and third voyages. The two Italians became acquainted.

While Columbus was on his third voyage, Vespucci started on his first, in 1499, as navigator on a Spanish expedition under Alonso de Ojeda. Having sailed with Columbus, with whom he had quarreled, Ojeda knew the route. When they reached the coast of what is now Guyana, next door to Venezuela, Vespucci apparently left Ojeda and sailed south along the coast of Brazil, which he believed to be the shore of Asia. Back in Spain, he was eager to mount a second expedition, but the Spanish monarchs, who already had their hands full with Columbus, turned him down; he offered his services to Portugal.

After setting out from Lisbon on May 13, 1501, he again sailed down the coast of Brazil, and returned in July 1502. But this time he became convinced that the strange unmapped landmass was not

Asia but some other place. "These regions," he wrote in 1504, "we may rightly call *Mundus Novus*, a New World, because our ancestors had no knowledge of them. . . . I have found a continent more densely peopled and abounding in animals than our Europe or Asia or Africa." He also made quaint remarks about the Indians—how barbarous they were, not using napkins when they ate.

Vespucci's letter spoke of four voyages, though the evidence seems to show that he went on only two, or possibly three. His first alleged voyage, in 1497, appears to have been an attempt to upstage Columbus as the first to discover the Mundus Novus. It appears that he simply made up a voyage that never took place. As Emerson put it, "Strange that broad America must wear the name of a thief." In 1508, the Spanish hired Vespucci as chief navigator for the Casa de Contratación, or House of the Indies, founded in 1503 by Queen Isabella to handle trade with the colonies. In addition to administering trade, the Casa scheduled the ships, laid out the shipping routes, and funded mapmaking and navigation schools. Although he may have been a liar, Vespucci was clearly a master navigator.

Columbus, in the meantime, was struggling to regain the confidence of his royal backers. In early 1502, however, Ferdinand and Isabella appointed a new governor to Hispaniola, Nicolás de Ovando, the prototypical *hidalgo*, commander of the military-religious Order of Alcántara. He sailed in February, with the largest fleet ever to leave for the "New World"—thirty-two ships, twenty-five hundred men, and twelve Franciscan friars.

As a consolation prize, Columbus was allowed to go sailing one more time, on the condition that he stay away from Hispaniola. In June 1502, he was back in the Caribbean, along the coast of Honduras, with four caravels. He still believed he was headed for Asia, writing his royal patrons that "from there to the river Ganges there are ten days." Then he landed in Panama, which he said is "in Mango province, which is next to that of Cathay." He wandered around for two years, suffering many vicissitudes, such as running aground in Jamaica, before returning to Spain in September 1504.

Columbus led four expeditions to the Caribbean over a period of twelve years, years of heartache and mismanagement, of repression in Hispaniola and disgrace in Spain, but also, in terms of his later reputation, of triumph. He returned from his last voyage a broken man, and died two years later, in May 1506. It was not

North America that Columbus discovered, but a bunch of Caribbean islands, and bits of shoreline in Central and South America. He also helped spread the myth of the westward route to the Indies, which lived on for a century after his death, even when it was known that a Mundus Novus lay between Europe and Asia.

By the time Ovando arrived in Hispaniola in 1502, the Spanish had been there for ten years. They had not extended settlement to any other island, but the population of Hispaniola had increased to about ten thousand. Ovando founded fifteen towns, including Puerto Real in 1504, on the northern coast of Haiti, near Columbus' original settlement of La Navidad. According to recent digs, which uncovered a cathedral with stone-gargoyle drain spouts, Puerto Real in its prime had about a hundred households, and was built on the model of the Castilian town, with Indians serving as slaves.

This use of forced labor was regulated and legalized under Ovando into a system called the *encomienda*. Indians provided labor in return for wages, protection, and Christian instruction. The Indians seem to have been cruelly used. The *hidalgos* chased them with greyhounds, which led them to coin the word *aperrear*—to cast to the dogs. To make them better man-hunters, the dogs were raised on human flesh; one Spaniard would say to the other, "Give me a quarter of an Indian for my dog, and I'll pay you back when I have one."

When the Indians died off in Hispaniola, thousands more were recruited from neighboring islands and unloaded at Puerto Real. Madrid, however, was repeatedly told that the Indians were free men. Only in 1510 did the settlers' cruelty become public knowledge in Spain, when visiting Dominicans who complained to the king.

The debate on Indian treatment would go on for the rest of the Spanish colonial period, with the crown coming down much of the time against brutality, thanks to the lobbying of the Catholic clergy. In 1512, the Laws of Burgos were drafted, inspired by King Ferdinand. They stipulated that pregnant women were not required to work in the mines after their fourth month. Any Spaniard found beating an Indian would be fined five gold pesos. Any Spaniard calling an Indian a *perro* (dog) would be fined one gold peso. By 1519, when a smallpox epidemic nearly wiped out the Taino population, the Spaniards had leapfrogged to other locations. In 1508, they sent an expedition to the Isthmus of Panama.

In 1509, they occupied Puerto Rico, where from thirty to fifty thousand Tainos lived. In 1511, they occupied Cuba, from which Cortez launched the conquest of Mexico in 1519. But they still didn't know where they were.

The Spaniards conquered the Aztecs in Mexico and the Incas in Peru, and dug up so much gold and silver that the sudden influx of precious metals started an inflationary spiral in the Spanish economy. In North America, however, they were less fortunate, and their attempts, in the next half-century, to settle the mainland are a chronicle of hardship and death.

The first attempt by Juan Ponce de León in Florida came to nothing, but illustrates some of the difficulties of exploration, from hostile Indians to interference by the mother country. Ponce, a courtier and soldier, had fought at the siege of Granada, and sailed with Columbus on his second trip, in 1493, at the age of thirty-three. Nine years later, he sailed again, as Ovando's deputy. In 1508, he was sent to explore Puerto Rico, which was next door to Hispaniola. According to the Spanish historian Antonio de Herrera, in his *General History of the West Indies*, first published in 1601, Ponce had been told by some Indian servants that there was plenty of gold on the island, which they called Borrinquen. Ponce and other Spaniards never doubted the misinformation they picked up from the Indians. The word "gold" made them suspend their disbelief.

Once again we see a friendly reception from the Indians, whose chief, Agueybana, wanted to exchange names with Ponce so that they could be sworn brothers. Agueybana obligingly showed the Spaniards the streams where gold was panned. Ponce decided to stay, brought settlers in, and was named governor of the island in 1509. Some villages were built, and the Indians were put to work digging for gold. They were forcibly distributed among the settlers, according to the *encomienda* system. A young nobleman, Christopher Sotomayor, founded a town that he named after himself, and took the local chief's sister as his mistress.

In 1511, the Indians rebelled, attacking the Spaniards all over the island and killing eighty. Three thousand Indians destroyed the town of Sotomayor and killed its founder, who had ignored a warning from his mistress. Ponce had only about a hundred men left, and fought back with ambushes and dawn attacks. He also had a fierce attack dog, Bezerillo, "who made wonderful havoc among those people," wrote Herrera, "so that the Indians were more afraid of ten Spaniards with the dog than of 100 without him." Bezerillo was such an asset that he received a crossbowman's pay on the expedition's books. He died a hero's death, shot by a poisoned arrow while swimming after an escaping Indian.

Ponce pacified the island, but was replaced as governor as the result of a court intrigue. Wanting to do something for him, King Ferdinand gave him a patent to discover the island of Bimini. Ponce had heard, writes Herrera, about "a spring or river, where old people bathing themselves became young again." Here began the search for the Fountain of Youth. The Spaniards were predisposed to believe in such places, which the medieval tradition said existed.

Ponce fitted out three ships at his own expense and sailed from Puerto Rico on March 3, 1513. He landed on the coast of Florida, somewhere between Daytona Beach and Cape Canaveral, on March 28. Since Sunday, March 27, was Easter Day, *Pascua florida* in Spanish, he called the place Florida. He believed it to be an island.

When he went ashore to take possession, Indians tried to seize his boat. Ponce didn't want to provoke them, but after one of his sailors was hit on the head with a cudgel he had to fight back. Two of his men were wounded with arrows. This seems to have been one of the rare occasions on which the Indians opened hostilities.

In April and May, Ponce sailed south, hugging the shore, "on that place which enters the sea like a sleeve," writes Herrera, "and yet did not perceive that it was a continent." He rounded the keys, then sailed up the Gulf of Mexico side of Florida 150 miles or so, as far as Sanibel Island, where there was another battle, on June 11. Ponce was attacked by eighty canoes full of archers with shields, whom he kept at bay with crossbows and harquebuses. At this point, he turned back. He and his men had sampled every brook and puddle they had seen, but instead of the Fountain of Youth had found nothing but hostile Indians.

That same year, Ponce went to Spain to report to the king. Favorably impressed, Ferdinand knighted him and gave him a coat of arms with three islands on waves. When Ponce boasted that he was skilled at subduing the savages, Ferdinand asked him to raid the Caribs of Guadeloupe on his way back to Puerto Rico. Spaniards believed the Caribs were the most savage of savages, cannibal-pirates surviving on plunder, who lived in Guadeloupe and some of the other islands, and sometimes raided Spanish settlements.

The idea was to capture some Caribs and sell them as slaves in Puerto Rico and Cuba. The king did not realize that no one in his right mind would buy a Carib, since they refused to work and were so fierce they had to be kept in chains. Even in chains, they worked at their fetters with sharp stones until they could run away.

So Ponce's little armada sailed from Cádiz in the fall of 1514, and when they made their landing at Guadeloupe, laundresses were sent under guard to wash the men's clothes in a stream. For the Caribs, this was an opportunity not to be missed to improve their diets. They surrounded the laundresses and their guards, and carried them off. Wary of following them into the jungle interior without guides or trained dogs, Ponce made no attempt at rescue, but sailed on to Puerto Rico.

The next seven years, until 1521, constituted a fallow period for Ponce. King Ferdinand died and was succeeded by Charles V, and during the change of reigns colonial ventures were held in abeyance. In addition, Ponce was being investigated in Spain for gubernatorial malpractice, which further delayed his voyages.

While Ponce was rusticating in Puerto Rico, the discovery sweepstakes continued. The teen-aged Spanish king was more interested in exploration than his more senior royal colleagues, Henry VIII of England and Francis I of France. And in 1517 he had an interesting offer from a Portuguese captain, Ferdinand Magellan. A great wanderer in the Portuguese service, Magellan went to Spain when he was refused promotion, just as Vespucci had gone to Portugal when refused a mission by Spain.

Magellan proposed, once again, to go westward to reach Asia. He sailed five ships on September 20, 1519, and went down the coast of South America. In October 1520, he entered the three-hundred-mile-long maze that bears his name, with its narrows, bays, islands, and dead-end branches. And, God knows how, he picked his way, operating on instinct by seat-of-the-pants navigation, and emerged on November 28 into the shimmering Pacific, spread out like a huge semicircular gray-green welcome mat.

Then it was ninety-nine days to Guam, without fresh food. They would go on, Magellan told his men, even "if they had to eat the leather chafing-gear on the ships' yards," which is exactly what they did. After Guam, he headed west until he hit the Philippines, in March 1521. A month later, having made the mistake of taking sides in a tribal conflict, he got a poisoned arrow through the leg, and it killed him. Thus did a great voyage end in foolish bravado.

The return to Spain was under the command of the Basque navigator Sebastián de Cano, who was awarded a globe with the inscription *Primus Circumdedisti Me* ("you were the first to encircle me"). The circumnavigation disproved the theory that Asia was next door to the "New World."

By the time Magellan was in the Pacific, Ponce de León had cleared his name and sailed on his second trip to Florida, with five ships and two hundred men. According to Gonzalo de Oviedo in his *History of the Indies*, Ponce now realized that he had been deceived on the fountain, but, being imbued with the spirit of the fountain, he was returning "to youthful and thoughtless deeds" by going to settle Florida, even though he was white-haired and sixty-one.

He took along a number of friars to help with conversions. By this time, the Inquisition had stuck its nose in the "New World" in a particularly absurd manner—by introducing the *Requerimiento*, a document designed to be read in Spanish to uncomprehending Indians, asking them if they agreed to accept the teachings of the Catholic Church. "If you do not do this," the *Requerimiento* said, "or if you maliciously delay in doing it, I certify to you that with the help of God we shall forcefully enter into your country and shall make war against you in all ways and manners that we can, and shall subject you to the yoke and obedience of the church." Since the Indians could not understand a word of what was being said, the *Requerimiento* amounted to a license for conquest.

A skirmish followed Ponce's landing in Florida, and the captain found himself in the front line. He was hit by an arrow, and died after being taken to Havana, in July 1521. This first attempt at settling U.S. territory came to nothing, thanks to a spirited Indian defense on the beach.

Giovanni da Verrazano, who had moved to France in 1506 from his native Florence, became the next explorer. A syndicate of Italian merchant bankers in Lyons, already an important banking center, was interested in finding new sources of silk, and agreed on a joint venture with King Francis I. Verrazano agreed to look for a westward passage to Asia, and was given a ship of the Royal French Navy. He reported directly to the king, but the Italians in Lyons supplied most of his funds, as well as a second ship.

He sailed on January 17, 1524, and made landfall on March 1 at what is today Cape Fear, North Carolina. In his letter to the king, written when he returned, he said that on that coast they found an old woman with a young maid, two infants, and a child of about eight. So what did they do? "We took a child from the old woman to bring into France, and were about to take the young woman, who was very beautiful and of tall stature, but we could not for the great outcries that she made. . . . Being far from the ship we purposed to leave her behind, bearing away the child only."

Verrazano sailed up the East Coast past New Jersey and into New York Harbor, but only stayed a day. Moving fast, he had missed the Chesapeake Bay and the mouth of the Hudson. He continued up the Maine coast to Newfoundland, covering a lot of ground but exploring nothing, and then returned to France, where he was anchored at Dieppe on July 8, 1524, the date of his letter to the king. But by that time, Francis I was away on his Italian campaign. Verrazano found private backing and was off again, in 1527, this time to Brazil. On a third voyage, in 1528, he stopped at a Caribbean island, where some Caribs killed him as he waded ashore and he ended up as dinner.

In the meantime, the Spanish continued to send out expeditions to American shores, for failure was not a deterrent. On June 17, 1527, another fleet left, under the command of Pánfilo de Narváez, a one-eyed veteran of the Mexican campaign. Narváez had a royal charter to explore Florida, which meant everything north of Mexico.

He sailed with five ships and six hundred settlers and soldiers, stopping forty-five days in Santo Domingo to buy horses and re-supply. During the layover, 140 men deserted, having sized up their leader, described in chronicles as "the most incompetent" of the conquistadors. When he left Santo Domingo, it was the hurricane season. He lost two ships off the southern coast of Cuba, along with sixty men and half his eighty horses. He wintered in Cuba's Cienfuegos Bay, and it was not until April 15, 1528, that Narváez landed on the western coast of Florida, somewhere near Tampa. This was the great moment of disembarkation, which included raising the flag, having a monk read the *Requerimiento* on a beach empty of Indians, and then setting up the portable altar and celebrating mass with Spanish wine and communion wafers. His was the first group that would explore the interior of the United States, eighty years before Jamestown. Despite their blunders and *hidalgo* brutality, it was a plucky effort.

Narváez took forty horsemen and 260 men on foot into the

interior, leaving a hundred men on the beachhead with his three remaining ships. They soon came upon an Indian village, where he saw something that shocked his Catholic sensibility. The Indians had recovered some wooden cargo cases from a Spanish wreck, and were using them as coffins. In each box lay a corpse covered with painted skins. To put a stop to this idolatrous use of Spanish property, Narváez ordered his men to burn the packing cases and the bodies—in a first display of arrogance.

Things went badly thereafter. On June 17, Panfilo forded the Suwannee River, about 150 miles north of Tampa, and one of the mounted men drowned with his horse in its swift current. That night, they ate the horse for dinner. On June 24, they reached the chief town of the Apalachee people, near Tallahassee, where they stayed for nearly a month.

The Indians harassed them, firing arrows from behind trees or under logs when they went out singly or in small groups to water their horses. The Apalachees were expert bowmen, able to hit the joints in the Spanish armor. Their bows were so strong that no Spaniard could bend them. And they used the swamps' natural cover so well that they were hard to hit with a crossbow bolt or a harquebus bullet. As Cabeza de Vaca, the treasurer of this doomed expedition and one of its four survivors, would later write in his *Relación:* "There were those who swore they had seen two red oaks as thick as the upper part of the leg, pierced through from side to side by arrows. . . . The bows they use are as thick as an arm and twelve palms in length, which they discharge at 200 paces with great precision."

Under constant attack, Narváez took a lot of casualties in men and horses. He didn't have enough horses to carry his wounded, and those men who weren't wounded were sick. They had reached a spot on the coast south of Tallahassee, near the town of St. Mark's, and Narváez decided that the only way out of this mess would be to build some boats and try to get to Mexico. He would rather face the sea than the Indians.

Of course, there was no one in the company who knew how to build a boat, and they had no forge, no iron, no tow, no resin, no rigging, and no tools. But they had an ingenious fellow who made bellows from deerskin, and nails and saws and axes from crossbows, stirrups, and spurs. They managed so well that, by September 20, 1528, they had finished five longboats, each caulked with palmetto fiber and pitched with resin from pine trees; the ropes and rigging were made from the manes and tails of the horses they had butchered, the sails from their own shirts, and the oars from trees that grew there.

And all the time that they were at work, the Indian danger was constant. When they sent a party of men out for shellfish, ten of them were killed, even though they were wearing steel armor. Not to mention the misery of marching around in armor in the Florida summer, with chiggers and ticks burrowing under.

When they finally embarked, there were 242 men left out of the three hundred who had gone into the interior. Hoping to reach the northernmost Spanish settlement in Mexico, they headed west, following the coastline, and found some friendly Indians, who gave them water and fish. But these same friendly Indians attacked them during the night and killed three men. Narváez was struck in the face with a rock, and had to be moved to the boat reserved for the sick and wounded.

They reached Pensacola Bay, and Mobile Bay, where once again they were attacked, and crossed the mouth of the Mississippi on the last day of October 1528. As they continued westward, along the Louisiana coast, the sea got rough, and the boats capsized, and Narváez and most of his men were drowned. About eighty survivors were thrown on shore, among them Cabeza de Vaca, who found himself, half drowned and naked, on a small island south of Galveston, Texas, probably Velasco Island. He was soon joined by Andrés Dorantes and Alonzo de Castillo, whose barge had also capsized, and by Esteban, a slave. The Indians lit fires to warm them and gave them fish and roots to eat.

And so began, with a shipwreck, the enforced visit of Cabeza de Vaca among an Indian tribe in Texas. In a bewildering role reversal, the conquering Spaniard now became an indentured servant of the native people. It was the *encomienda* in reverse. Cabeza de Vaca and his three friends remained eight years among the Indians, gaining an understanding of them that no other Spaniard had. Cabeza de Vaca lost his Spanish-colonial identity and became a different man.

Although he was often mistreated by the Cahoques Indians on the island, he began to see them as no other Spanish soldier had— as human beings. He admired their ingenuity. In fishing with the bow and arrow, for instance, they could feel on their legs the undulations the fish made below the water's surface. They were also generous and affectionate. When a child died, the whole village wept for a year.

They were not, as the Spanish explorers tended to believe, all alike. Different tribes had different customs. Cabeza de Vaca heard from Indians that another group of Spanish survivors up the coast had resorted to eating the dead washed up onshore. They were cutting their fellow Spaniards into strips and turning them into jerky. This "produced great commotion among the Indians." It was another role reversal; the Spaniards routinely dubbed all Indians cannibals, but in this case the Spaniards were the cannibals and the Indians were shocked, since this particular tribe considered cannibalism as seriously taboo.

Cabeza de Vaca was put to work as a medicine man, but there wasn't much he could do, considering the state of European medicine in 1528. His method was to bless the sick, breathe on them, and recite prayers for their health. He also prayed that none of his patients would succumb, for he was worried that the Indians might burn him alive for malpractice. His reputation rose when he treated an Indian who had an arrow point next to his heart. By probing, he found that the point had passed through the chest cartilage. When he cut the chest open, he saw the point, aslant, and managed with great difficulty to draw it out, then sewed the Indian's chest up with a deer-bone needle.

Cabeza de Vaca also had to perform demeaning tasks that left no doubt about his status in the tribe. He fetched water and wood, and dragged canoes on portages. He was given the womanish job of pulling sharp submerged roots from the saltwater marshes, and his hands were so raw they bled. These Indians were hunter-gatherers, who moved from the island to the mainland on their food rounds. When they dug for shellfish in brackish waters, Cabeza de Vaca was put to work setting up their houses, made of mats and branches, with a floor of crushed shells.

He had previously been so finicky about food that he had refused to touch horsemeat, but was now purged of all pride, and found himself eating what the Indians ate—that is, ant eggs, worms, lizards, snakes, and deer dung. If he was thrown a scrap of meat, he had to eat it raw, for if he put it on the fire another Indian would grab it.

As time passed and the Indians got used to having him around, he was given more freedom, and managed to set himself up as a sort of itinerant peddler between coastal and inland tribes. He brought conch shells and sea snails from the coast and traded them inland for deerskins and flints. Like a friendly traveling salesman, he was always ready with a joke or a bit of news. By now, he knew some of the lingo. He drank the evergreen-bush brew and played with the kids.

On his peddling routes, Cabeza de Vaca was surprised by two things. First, the number of languages they spoke—"We passed through many and dissimilar tongues," he wrote. Second, the difficulty of travel, for the tribes were always fighting among themselves. It was not just the intrusion of the white man that made them belligerent; "all these nations, when they have personal enmities, and are not of one family, assassinate at night, waylay, and inflict gross barbarities on each other." In almost every case, neighboring tribes were enemies.

In 1532, he was taken off the island and down the coast about a hundred miles to the Matagorda Peninsula, which a tribe inhabited during the wild-pecan season. He and his fellow captives were given as slaves to the chief. In midsummer, the tribe migrated inland for the prickly pears. This was the best time of the year, when they had plenty to eat. But even when there were food shortages, Cabeza was surprised by their optimism. They would tell him not to be sad, for soon there would be prickly pears— when he knew that the pear season was five months away.

This went on for two more years, until, in 1534, the four men were able to escape. They proceeded down to southern Texas and crossed the Rio Grande into northern Mexico, over a route that can only be surmised. Eventually, they began to see villages, adobe houses, women doing their laundry with the soaplike yucca root, and people who worked the land. The Indians there regarded Cabeza and his companions as itinerant holy men. He picked up a large following, "and as we had to breathe upon and sanctify the food and drink for each and grant them everything they would come to ask, it may be seen how great was the annoyance."

Then they moved into the Sonora Valley, to the present-day town of Ures, about 150 miles away from the Gulf of California. They began to hear tales of the cruelty of the Christians, who burned and destroyed the Indians' towns and left them in dread. And as they proceeded southward, to the Yaqui River, they saw signs of their presence—burned-out villages, skeletons hanging from trees on Spanish ropes, and clusters of buzzards by dirt roads. After his years with the tribes, Cabeza could no longer identify with the Spanish-imperial ideology. In sympathy with the Indian victims, he was horrified to see that the first Spaniards he met were on a slave-catching expedition.

After six years of going native, when he got back to so-called civilization, in Vera Cruz, it took him a while to adjust. When he was given clothes, "I could not wear any for some time, nor could I sleep anywhere else but on the ground." Back in Spain, he wrote the *Relación* of his trans-Texas trek, which was published in 1542 and remains one of the most remarkable early narratives of discovery, because his experience broke down his system of beliefs.

While Cabeza was stranded in Texas, France got back into the exploration game. In 1532, King Francis I gave the master navigator Jacques Cartier six hundred *livres* to mount an expedition "to discover New Lands in a New World." Cartier made three voyages of discovery that established the French in Canada, in 1534, 1535, and 1541.

On his first trip, taking two ships and sixty men, he reached the eastern coast of Newfoundland on May 10, 1534, and waited for the ice to melt in the straits leading into the Gulf of St. Lawrence. To the explorer, entering an unmapped landscape that was his to decipher, the gulf must have seemed a watery labyrinth, with its innumerable islands, bays, and capes. Cartier felt his way as though playing blindman's buff, as he sought the "great abbreviation" to Marco Polo's Cathay.

On July 6, while exploring Chaleur Bay in a longboat, he saw two fleets of canoes coming toward him. These were Micmacs, who had been in the area for thousands of years, hunting caribou and moose in the winter, and fishing in the summer. They seemed overjoyed to see the white men, Cartier reported, but when they surrounded his longboat he fired over their heads to scatter them. The next day, they were back, brandishing pelts on sticks, and when Cartier offered the chief a red cap, the Micmacs expressed their pleasure by throwing salt water over their heads.

Ten days later, in Gaspé Bay, he ran into a band of two hundred Iroquois on a mackerel-fishing trip with their chief, Donnaconna. At once, there was a climate of mutual suspicion. When the French rowed ashore to mingle with the Indians, the latter sent most of their young girls into the woods, having perhaps already suffered sexual harassment from European fishermen. Cartier's first contacts led him to remark that the Indians were "wonderful thieves, who steal everything they can carry."

On July 24, when Cartier raised a thirty-three-foot-high cross on a little island in Gaspé Harbor, taking possession for his king,

Chief Donnaconna immediately saw the cross for what it was, a token of conquest. Clad in a black bearskin, he went out to Cartier's ship and harangued the navigator from his canoe, pointing to the cross and then to the ground, to make it very clear that the ground belonged to him and that Cartier was a trespasser.

Not having found gold or spices, Cartier needed something tangible to bring back to his king, and in Donnaconna's visit he saw an opportunity. Offering the chief an ax, he leaned over the gunwale so that Donnaconna would approach and take it. But when his canoe came alongside, it was held fast by Cartier's sailors, and Donnaconna and the four other occupants were hoisted aboard, "which surprised them greatly."

After seizing the Indians, Cartier was quick to reassure them, telling them that "he would not hurt them, and showed great signs of love." He gave them food and drink, explaining that the cross was merely a signpost, so that he could find his way back with more presents. Wine improved Donnaconna's frame of mind, and he agreed to let Cartier take two of his sons back to France. "We dressed his two sons in shirts and livery, and red bonnets, and to each gave a brass chain to put around their necks, of which they were greatly pleased." The Indians were transformed into imitation Europeans and robbed of their native identities.

The significance of Cartier's first voyage wasn't the passage to Cathay, which didn't exist, but the meeting with the Indians. Although he showed a little more finesse than the Spaniards, there was inevitably a gradual deterioration from friendliness to hostility; in Cartier's case, the turning point came with the ax deception.

Cartier went home in August, his first trip having turned out to be a reconnaissance of the gulf. He had not found the St. Lawrence River, but was on the right track. After staying in the French port of Saint-Malo no longer than it took to outfit his ships and recruit his crew, he sailed back to Canada in May 1535, and headed up the now familiar coast in July. Thanks to the guidance of Donnaconna's two sons, Taiogagny and Agaya, who were anxious to get home, he went right into the St. Lawrence River.

On September 8, they saw the great rock where Quebec would one day stand; Donnaconna came to meet their ships with twelve canoes, and the French and the Indians broke bread and drank wine. Now that they were no longer captives of the French, however, the two sons had a change of attitude. Cartier was counting on them to pilot his ships upriver, but they sulked and stalled, saying the river wasn't worth exploring, and avoiding Cartier when he came looking for them.

Cartier did not realize that Donnaconna had a political strategy. Since he wanted most-favored-tribe treatment, his policy was to prevent Cartier from going upriver and making friends with other tribes. He intended to maintain his position as middleman between the French and the Indians in the interior. The next day, Donnaconna staged a morality play to deter the French. Three Indians costumed as devils, their faces painted black, with horns "as long as arms," their bodies covered by dogskins, sailed past Cartier's boats in a canoe, while the rest of the tribe wailed onshore. When Cartier asked them what was going on, they said their God had made an announcement, which was that there would be so much snow and ice upriver that all the French would perish. The French laughed and told the devil-faces that their God was a fool and that Jesus had told them they would have blue skies and sunshine.

Upriver Cartier went, on September 19, and reached the site of present-day Montreal on October 2; more than a thousand Indians came to greet them, throwing so much cornbread into their longboats "that it seemed to be raining bread." "One of the most attractive features of Indian society," wrote Cartier, "was the spirit of hospitality by which it was pervaded. Perhaps no people ever carried this principle to the same degree as the Iroquois." This turned out to be a minority view of the "savage Iroquois."

Cartier climbed to the top of Mount Royal, where he had a magnificent panorama, with the Laurentians to the north, the Adirondacks to the south, and the great river flowing out of sight. But a few miles upstream, he saw a series of boiling rapids that were obviously unnavigable, and he knew that for the moment he could go no farther.

On October 11, Cartier was back at the site of Quebec; here, in his absence, the sailors had built a log fort mounted with ships' guns, which indicated a further deterioration in friendly relations. Sensing the change, Cartier set up night watches and strengthened the fort with deep ditches and a drawbridge.

He and his men now had to spend the winter in the fort and on their boats, for it would be imprudent to risk a stormy crossing of the Atlantic. The ships lay frozen up in ice twelve feet thick, and onshore the snow was four feet deep. It was so cold that the wine froze in its casks. In December, scurvy broke out among the

Indians, and fifty died; even though Cartier banned Indians from the fort, the French got sick too. By February 1536, of the 110 men in the company, eight were dead, fifty were dying, and fewer than ten were in good health. Too weak to dig graves in the frozen ground, the survivors buried the dead in the snow.

And the men kept dying. One day, when there were twenty-five French dead, Cartier left the fort to go walking on the ice and caught sight of Agaya, whom he had seen twelve days before gravely ill, with a knee swollen "to the size of a two-year-old baby," and rotten gums and teeth. To what did he owe his miraculous recovery? asked Cartier. Agaya said it was the juice from the leaves of a certain tree called "Hanneda" (perhaps hemlock or white cedar), and obligingly had nine or ten branches brought to him by two squaws, who showed Cartier how to grind the bark and the leaves and boil them in water.

His men at first refused to sample the evil-smelling potion, but finally one or two agreed to taste it, and felt better at once, recovering their strength; then they all took it, and were much improved. "If all the doctors of Louvain and Montpellier had been there," wrote Cartier, "they would not have done so well as this tree did in eight days." With their herbal medicine, the Indians were more advanced than the Europeans.

When spring came, Cartier prepared to return to France. To ensure the king's backing for a third voyage, he needed to bring some Indians with him; this time, he kidnaped ten, including Donnaconna, not one of whom ever saw his home again. That night, the Indians came to the shore, howling like wolves, but made no attempt to free their chief; Cartier sailed on May 6, 1536.

It was not until five years later, in August 1541, that Cartier returned to Canada. At the site of Quebec, on August 23, there was an embarrassing moment when he had to explain to the new tribal leader that none of the Indians he had taken with him in 1536 had returned. It was of course fatal to deposit Indians in French society, for they had no immunity to germs. A cold could kill them, and did, and all ten died. Cartier covered up by saying that Donnaconna was dead but the others "had stayed in France as great lords."

This last voyage, on the Spanish model, complete with cattle, goats, and pigs and two hundred settlers, including fifty convicts released from French jails, was the most ambitious and least successful of the three. Cartier built a fortified settlement eight miles upstream from Quebec, which to the Indians was an invasion of their land. In the winter, they began attacking the French who ventured outside the fort to cut wood, and by the spring of 1542 had killed thirty-five. In June, Cartier admitted defeat and went home with the survivors. By this time, France was mired in religious wars, giving the Indians of Canada a fifty-year respite from further colonial ventures.

CHAPTER THREE

THE
SPANISH
PRESENCE

In terms of the occupation of North America, the sixteenth century was the Spanish century. From 1540 to 1600, Spanish captains went from California to Kansas and established bases in Florida and New Mexico.

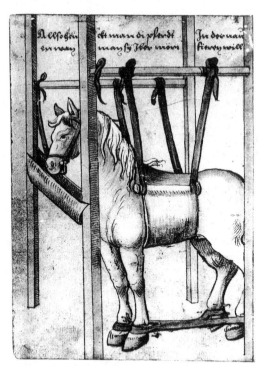

Das Trachtenbuch des Cristoph Weiditz
(von seinen resisen nach Spanien, 1529, und den Niederlanden, 1531–32).

In order to protect his horses during the rough sea voyage, De Soto hung them up in harnesses so that their feet did not touch the ground and brought them ashore with a pulley system.

Over there I have placed under their Highness'
sovereignty more land than there is in Africa and
Europe.

CHRISTOPHER COLUMBUS

I n March 1987, a Florida developer started bulldozing a real-
estate parcel in downtown Tallahassee, less than a mile from
the state capitol, in order to put up an office complex. When
Calvin Jones, an archaeologist with the Florida Bureau of Archaeological Research, saw the excavation, an alarm bell went off in his
mind, a feeling he recognized as "site sense," an instinct he's developed in twenty years of digging in Florida.

He asked the construction foreman if he could take a look, and
unearthed pieces of Spanish olive-jars, the all-purpose containers
of the sixteenth century. The developer then agreed to a two-week
delay, and Calvin Jones rounded up some volunteers for a quick
dig. They found five Spanish and Portuguese coins of the sixteenth
century, some iron nails, some faceted beads, and a crossbow tip,
known as a "quarrel." They found small S-shaped pieces of rusted
iron, which didn't look like much until they realized that the pieces
fit together.

And then they knew what they had uncovered: the camp of
Hernando De Soto, the most brutal of the Spanish conquistadors
to venture into the United States in the sixteenth century; in the
winter of 1539–40, he commandeered an Apalachee Indian village.
The half-inch-long pieces of iron were links in a coat of chain mail.
Spanish soldiers threw away these ten-pound iron shirts, which
were not only misery in the summer but ineffective against Indian
archers. For Calvin Jones, the rusty little links, roughly 450 years
old, were solid evidence of the hardships of the De Soto expedition,
as for three years it roamed through eight southern states.

When De Soto's fleet of nine ships left Havana and landed in
Tampa Bay on May 25, 1539, with a force of 570 men and 243
horses, they brought all of Spanish civilization with them, from
visored helmets right down to the molds for making communion
wafers. They also brought attack dogs and the ancestor of the
South's long-snouted razorback hog, a mobile and self-reproducing
source of food.

72

It took De Soto five days just to land, because he didn't want to scrape bottom, which would have displeased the royal auditor who had come along for the ride. The very first incident set the tone of the entire *entrada:* some horsemen taking a look around came upon ten Indians, and, whoever fired first, the result was two dead Indians.

Then De Soto had an incredible stroke of luck, finding in an Indian village a survivor of the Pánfilo de Narváez expedition by the name of Juan Ortiz, who in his twelve years with the tribe had picked up the language. Ortiz had been put to work keeping carrion-foraging wolves away from the burial mound. De Soto had arrived at the tail end of the mound societies, to the destruction of which he would make a major contribution.

De Soto took Juan Ortiz with him as interpreter and began his inland march. In every village, he asked the Indians where the gold and silver were. Wanting to be rid of these unwelcome visitors, they invariably pointed to the nearest trail out of town. According to De Soto's secretary, Rodrigo Ranjel, the Spaniards abducted women, whom "they desired both as servants and for their foul use and lewdness," but the Indian women fought back. "They are of such stuff," Ranjel wrote, "that one woman took a young fellow named Herrera, who stayed alone with her and behind his companions, and seized him by his private parts and had him worn out and at her mercy."

Although De Soto found no gold, his expedition was productive in that it gives us a picture of the southern United States sixty-seven years before Jamestown. The area he went through consisted of large villages called chiefdoms, with sparsely populated areas in between. In each village he visited, De Soto repaid the hospitality of the chief by taking him hostage, along with other captives who were used as porters, and women who were kept as camp followers.

The Indians had to interrupt their planting to defend themselves against this troop of marauding Spaniards. But his passage was disruptive in another way as well. Just as De Soto's beads and brass bells entered the Indian trading system, the germs of his men entered the Indian bloodstream. The Spanish presence was followed by epidemics, population loss, and the collapse of the village system.

It's a myth to think that the Indians lived an illness-free existence before the arrival of the white man. There were, however, plenty of European diseases that they didn't have, among them smallpox, bubonic plague, scarlet fever, typhus, cholera, measles, and diphtheria.

With his system of abducting porters and stealing village grain reserves, De Soto made himself rather unpopular. After wintering in Tallahassee, he crossed into Georgia in the spring of 1540 and fought his first major battle. Attacked by a force of four hundred warriors, he beat them back, killing between thirty and forty, while the rest dived into two big ponds as night was falling.

De Soto placed guards around the ponds and waited for the Indians to come out. The Indians covered their heads with water lilies and moved soundlessly through the water, looking for unguarded spots on shore. At the sound of any ruffle on the pond's surface, the mounted Spaniards took their horses in to catch the waterlogged Indians. Eventually, all but twelve surrendered, and these diehards were pulled out by the hair, put in chains, and kept as porters.

Ranjel was appalled by De Soto's cruelty, "which was a grievous thing to see," and admired the courage of the Indians. Five of those captured would not tell where their village was, "although they burned one alive in front of the others, who suffered the same fate for not talking . . . and to martyrs such as these the Romans built a statue in the Forum."

By October 1540, De Soto was in Alabama, and on October 18 there was another big battle at a town called Mabila, near today's Selma. In this fracas, De Soto was wounded and eighteen of his men were killed. To extricate himself from a tight spot, he set fire to the town, burning his own supplies, including the ornaments for saying mass, and the pearls he planned to take back to Cuba. By this time, 102 of his men had died, some by arrow and some by fever, but, instead of becoming discouraged, he was more determined than ever to find riches. From Alabama he headed west into northern Mississippi, and wintered in the area around today's Tupelo. Christmas came, and there was a snowstorm, and it was just like the city of Burgos in northern Spain, thought Ranjel, only colder.

In March 1541, their winter camp was attacked; twelve more Spaniards died, and they were short of food besides. It was amazing what they endured, wrote Ranjel. He had never thought the day would come when he would see a Spanish knight, the brother of a marquis, who had two thousand ducats of income, crawling on his hands and knees and digging his fingers into the ground to pull out some edible plants.

By now, about 225 of his 547 men and 150 of his 247 horses were dead, and yet De Soto continued his march, heading west into Arkansas, propelled by his vision of gold. In Arkansas, where they spent the winter of 1541–42, the Indians taught them how to snare rabbits. Juan Ortiz died, leaving De Soto without an interpreter, so that when they started out, in March 1542, they were unable to ask for directions and often lost their way.

By the time De Soto reached eastern Arkansas, not far from the Mississippi, he was ill with a fever and had lost his manic optimism. Now he wanted to reach the sea and get off this bad-luck continent. In May, they came to the Mississippi, somewhere south of Memphis, and started building barges. But on the other side of the river, De Soto was confronted with the largest war party that he had yet encountered—seven thousand warriors, according to Ranjel, with two hundred canoes. Every day, the canoes went out and showered the Spaniards with arrows.

On May 21, 1542, De Soto died of his fever, after three years of aimless and frantic movement, having accomplished exactly nothing except the devastation of the lands he had passed through. His men were relieved, and his body was thrown into the Big River. It took them another year to escape through Texas and across the Gulf of Mexico to Vera Cruz, which 312 survivors reached in the summer of 1543.

The enslavement of men and women, the many pitched battles, the destruction of villages, the psychological shock of defeat, the looting, and the epidemics destroyed a social system that had been thriving when De Soto landed in Tampa in 1539. Fifty years later, the world of the chiefdoms—Apalachee, Ocute, Coosa, Pacacha, and others—had vanished.

In 1886, near Dodge City, Kansas, a corroded sword blade was found inscribed with the name Juan Gallego and this message in Spanish: "Do not draw me without reason, do not sheathe me without honor." If genuine, how did this sixteenth-century Spanish sword find its way to the Great Plains? Juan Gallego was a soldier in another prodigal Spanish expedition, which was roaming around the Southwest at the same time De Soto was moving through the Southeast. But, unlike the previous Spanish *entradas*, which sailed from Hispaniola and Cuba, this one started in

Mexico and went overland into the United States, as far as central Kansas.

Mexico, or New Spain, now under the government of a Spanish viceroy, was divided into provinces named after those of Spain. Two years after his arrival in 1535, the first viceroy, Antonio de Mendoza, heard from a Franciscan friar much given to exaggeration that there were fabulous cities to the north, rich with gold. Mendoza believed him and ordered a full-scale *entrada* under the command of his protégé, twenty-seven-year-old Francisco Vasquez de Coronado.

Having to outfit the expedition at his own expense, in the hope of recouping his investment by finding gold, Coronado mortgaged his estate to raise fifty thousand ducats, and got a matching sum from Mendoza. By February 1540, at the very time De Soto was wintering in Tallahassee, Coronado had recruited 250 horsemen and seventy men on foot, plus a large number of Indian auxiliaries. This small army gathered at Compostela, about seventy-five miles northwest of today's Guadalajara, where the viceroy passed it in review.

It was a long way up the Pacific Coast of Mexico, seven hundred miles of mountain and jungle from Compostela to Culiacán, and another thousand miles to what is today the Arizona border. At this point, Coronado took a small detachment of horsemen east into New Mexico, leaving the pack train to follow at its own pace. In July, they reached the so-called fabulous cities, which turned out to be a half-dozen mudball hamlets on the Arizona–New Mexico border, about fifteen miles west of the present town of Zuni.

The Franciscan braggart Friar Marcos, who had come along, was now completely discredited, and in August Coronado wrote the viceroy: "We have all become very distrustful of the father provincial, and were dismayed to see that everything was the reverse of what he said."

Deciding to winter in New Mexico, Coronado headed east about two hundred miles to a group of villages near today's Albuquerque. Resenting the intruders, who wanted to occupy their dwellings and eat their corn reserves, the Indians fought back. Coronado laid siege to the principal village for forty days, using scaling ladders to invest their multistory houses. In the interest of "pacification," he had thirty Indians burned at the stake.

A scouting party continued eastward and found the largest village yet, called Cicuye (today's Pecos, twenty miles east of Santa

Fe), with five hundred warriors and four-story houses. The scenery was spectacular, with huge wind-sculpted rocks, nature's cathedrals, taller than the Giralda bell tower at Seville, which is 275 feet high. In Cicuye they found a captive Indian from Florida whom they nicknamed "the Turk" because of his swarthy coloring. The Turk, a bit of a con man, saw a chance to escape Cicuye. In the sign-language conversation that ensued, with much tapping of jewel-inlaid sword hilts and clinking of coins, he told the Spaniards what they were all too willing to hear, that in Quivira there was plenty of *oro*—why, his king took siestas under a tree festooned with gold bells.

Off galloped the gullible Coronado on another great trek, leaving on May 5, 1541, and continuing eastward into the Texas Panhandle, near today's Amarillo. Then he pressed forward with a detachment of thirty riders, including the Turk, across the westernmost strip of Oklahoma, which he claimed for Spain as he crossed it, and into western Kansas. There Coronado and his party saw the vast and overwhelming expanse of the Great Plains buffalo country, which the Spaniards called the Staked Plains—because to them the bluffs looked like log stockades. They marveled at the huge herds of "humpbacked cows," and the tribes of seminomadic Apaches they called Querechos, with their dog travois, "troops of dogs loaded with poles."

Coronado and his party were the first to hunt buffalo on horseback, using the musket and the pike. The horseless Indians had to ambush them at water holes or employ stampeding strategies. He wrote the king of Spain that for forty-two days he and his men had lived only on buffalo, "which are very fierce and brave animals." They got as far as today's Great Bend, Kansas, right smack in the middle of the state. But there was no tree with gold bells. There was instead a wigwam village of Wichita Indians.

Having spent every peso he had without finding anything, Coronado was annoyed at the Turk for luring him into a desert, and had him strangled in his sleep. Then he headed for home, in the spring of 1542, leaving behind three friars in New Mexico to teach the gospel; they soon attained martyrdom. Unknowingly, he determined the limits of the Spanish Empire in North America, for his countrymen would never cross the Great Plains.

Whereas the Spaniards kept trying to secure a foothold north of Mexico and failing, the French succeeded, by sending the Huguenot navigator René de Laudonnière to Florida in 1564. He sailed into the estuary of the St. Johns River on June 22 and settled on a bluff near today's Jacksonville, a site so pleasing, he said, that "melancholics would be constrained to change their nature." His men measured out a piece of ground to clear and build their fort, which they called Caroline. Friendly Indians helped, gathering palmetto leaves for the roof. Indians had lived on the St. Johns since at least 4000 B.P., which is the carbon date for pottery found at the Tick site—some of the earliest pottery in North America.

But the situation at Fort Caroline soon deteriorated, for the usual reason—food shortages. Things were so bad, wrote Laudonnière, "that some of my soldiers ate privately the bodies of newborn puppies." Some malcontents mutinied, stole a ship, and sailed to Cuba. Then the Indians killed two of his carpenters for stealing corn, and he retaliated by burning their village.

"Hard times can change good will among men," commented Laudonnière. The French traded the shirts off their backs for a little fish. When they complained about high prices, the Indians said, "If you value your merchandise so highly, eat it, and we will eat our fish." In their starving, mendicant state, the French had lost their prestige. Their misery was so great that they crushed roots in mortars brought for making cannon powder, and ground fish bones into meal. The persistent irony of the settling of the United States is that the land of plenty was in fact a land of hunger for all these expeditions. Why didn't they do more hunting and fishing? Perhaps insecurity outside the fort prevented it. The soldiers were so thin, said Laudonnière, that the bones pierced their skin. When he finally got some corn, the men ate it husks and all.

Then the French began to find arrows stuck in the ground with scalps hanging from the ends, a sign of coming war. Laudonnière resolved to abandon the fort and sail back to France, but on August 3, 1565, just as he was getting under way, men and supplies arrived from France in seven ships.

Meanwhile, at the court of Philip II in Madrid, in early 1565, the Spanish ambassador to France arrived with alarming news: France had planted a colony in Florida. The thirty-eight-year-old monarch pondered the situation. His strategy was to establish an extension of Spain's Mexican empire on Florida's Atlantic shore, a forward operational base supplied from Havana that could control the sea lanes.

It was humiliating that the French had succeeded on their first try where Spain had so often failed. And now the French were positioned right on the plate fleet's Gulf Stream route. Soon French ships out of Fort Caroline would be attacking Spanish ships loaded with gold and silver. And to make matters worse, these Frenchmen were Huguenots—heretics who had settled on the lands granted to Spain by the pope, which gave Spanish retaliation the fervor of a crusade.

So now, in 1565, because of a failing French outpost on the Florida coast, came the first outbreak of hostilities between two colonial rivals in the "New World." The curtain was rising on a never-ending war, sometimes broken by truces. For more than two centuries, the three principal colonial powers, France, Spain, and England, would be embattled, with the Indians caught in the middle. The Franco-Spanish hostilities in Florida turned the "New World" into an annex of the European warfare in the Old.

To go after the French, Philip II needed someone tough, experienced, and perhaps a little unscrupulous. He chose Pedro Menéndez de Avilés, a veteran of many voyages to Mexico as captain of the treasure fleets. He had recently been sentenced by the Casa de Contratación to twenty months in jail, for smuggling. Now, however, the convicted smuggler was given a three-year contract to settle Florida and drive out the French.

This would be no haphazard expedition. The phase of prospecting by semi-autonomous adventurers was over. The phase of great-power rivalry in the "New World" had begun. Financed by the king, Menéndez would take with him a ready-made urban population, with all the required crafts and professions, such as stonecutters, blacksmiths, carpenters, smelters, weavers, tanners, sword-makers, crossbow repairmen, coopers, bakers, brewers, and barbers who doubled as surgeons. Every possible need had been anticipated. Half the 250 soldiers were also *labradores*, ready to farm the land. Twenty-six were bringing their families. He even had a notary, with twenty-four reams of paper and a pot of ink. He was prepared, upon landing in Florida, to reproduce down to the last detail a Spanish municipality, complete with church bells.

Menéndez left Spain on June 27, 1565, and reached the Florida coast on August 28, with five ships and six hundred men. On this very day, the French reinforcements, under another Huguenot navigator, Jean Ribault, arrived in Fort Caroline.

Forty miles south of the French settlement, Menéndez found a pleasant harbor, its shore fringed with live oaks and swamp cabbage, and unloaded his soldiers and settlers, his olive jars and munitions cases. Curious Timucua Indians watched, chewing on hardtack and biscuits that the Spaniards had handed out, as one of the four friars said mass on shore. This was the founding of St. Augustine, the oldest continuously settled city in the United States.

The French and the Spanish were now about forty miles apart, the distance between St. Augustine and Jacksonville. At Fort Caroline, the French soon learned through Indian word of mouth that the Spanish were down the coast. As a Spanish historian put it, "In those provinces news travels from *cacique* to *cacique* faster than it does through the mails of Europe."

Ribault and Menéndez were impetuous men, the sort who want to get the job done right away, and they both attacked at once, one by land and the other by sea. Ribault sailed for St. Augustine on September 10, with his seven ships and two hundred men, but hurricanes tossed his little fleet on shore near Cape Canaveral.

In the meantime, Menéndez took five hundred men overland, in a comedy of errors that turned to his advantage. They started out around September 15, led by burly Basque axmen to hack through the brush. Those who couldn't swim were carried across the streams on pikes. It was raining hard, and their clothes were drenched, and their powder was wet.

On the evening of September 19, Menéndez arrived on the outskirts of Fort Caroline, camped in a grove a mile away, and prepared to attack at dawn on the 20th. In the French fort that night, Count de la Vigne was captain of the guard. The downpour was so bad that he took pity on the sentinels and sent them to bed. Who would be crazy enough to attack in such foul weather?

At dawn, Menéndez found the fort unguarded and caught the French in their nightshirts. About 135 Frenchmen were killed; a fortunate forty-five escaped by jumping over the stockade into the woods. They found a boat and sailed back to France. The Spanish flag now flew over the ramparts of Fort Caroline, which was renamed San Mateo. Menéndez found some impious Huguenot books and some blasphemous playing cards decorated with chalices and hosts, and had them burned.

When Menéndez and his men got back to St. Augustine, he heard that there were some shipwrecked Frenchmen in the vicinity. These were the hurricane survivors, who had marched a hundred miles north from Cape Canaveral and were recuperating on Anastasia Island, just across the inlet from St. Augustine.

When Menéndez found them, they were too weak to resist; according to an eyewitness, the priest Solis las Meras, "When all were tied, the *adelantado* asked if they were Catholics or Lutherans. . . . Jean Ribault answered that all were of the New Religion; and then he began to repeat the psalm *Domine, Memento Mei*, having finished which, he said that from dust they came and to dust they must return." But when Menéndez asked again if any among them were Catholic, eight sailors raised their hands.

The ones who refused to abjure were marched off behind the dunes and stabbed to death. To this day, the inlet is called Matanzas (slaughter) Bay. Menéndez buried them and, in lieu of gravestones, placed this sign: "I do not do this as unto Frenchmen but as unto Lutherans."

Thus was the religious intolerance of Europe carried to the New World on the point of a sword. In no more than a month, Menéndez had purged Florida of Frenchmen and heretics. The Spanish would have the area to themselves until the founding of Charleston by the English a century later.

Lacking the silver of Mexico and the gold of Peru, Florida remained an impoverished backwater of the Spanish Empire. The king was willing to subsidize St. Augustine with an annual contribution called the *situado*, because he wanted his window on the Atlantic. But there were always shortages, and the Indians had to be impressed into service with their food and their labor. Consequently, instead of kneeling and kissing hands, they were soon picking off isolated settlers.

And now, seventy years after Ponce de León's landing in Florida, and fifty years after Cartier's first trip to Newfoundland, the English began taking an interest in the New World, making it a three-cornered game of grab. This was the result of Protestant England's being more or less constantly at war with Catholic Spain, and of Queen Elizabeth's coming to the throne in 1558. Eager to challenge the Spanish monopoly in the New World, she sent out expeditions of her own. The soldier-navigator Humphrey Gilbert sailed to Newfoundland in 1583, and found an international fishing fleet of thirty-six vessels already there. Gilbert and his crew toasted "the Pope and ten shillings" (the price of a hundred pounds of dried codfish for Catholics to eat on Friday). He stayed there only a month, and drowned on the return voyage when his ship sank in a storm.

Two years later, Gilbert's half-brother, Sir Walter Raleigh, sent out an expedition that landed in April 1585 on Roanoke Island, off the coast of North Carolina. These 108 colonists stayed a year and then came home. Raleigh recruited a second group of 117, which arrived on Roanoke Island in July 1587. This was the famous "Lost Colony," which completely vanished.

When the supply ship anchored at Roanoke in August 1590, the only clues to the fate of the settlers were the word CROATOAN carved in capital letters on the gatepost of a log palisade, and a few belongings, such as books torn from their covers, maps and pictures spotted by rain, and a rusted suit of armor.

Croatoan was what the English called present-day Hatteras, sixty miles south of Roanoke. Although they were never found, the settlers were believed to have moved to another location, perhaps settling in an Indian village in Hatteras. Many years later, in 1650, the Croatoan Indians migrated from Hatteras to mainland North Carolina, where they were known as the Lumbees. Some of them were fair-haired and blue-eyed. Among their family names were the names of Roanoke settlers such as Dial, and there was a curious singsong in their speech, reminiscent, it is said, of Elizabethan English.

With the failure of the first English expeditions, it was left to Spain to make the last important *entrada* of the sixteenth century, when Juan de Oñate went into New Mexico. This was an overland trip, in the tradition of Coronado. Oñate's mission was to pacify New Mexico and convert the Indians. His underlying motive, in the *hidalgo* tradition, was the search for gold and silver. In exchange for outfitting the expedition at his own expense, he was given the rank of captain and the title of *adelantado*.

On December 19, 1597, Oñate started the long march northward with a column of four hundred soldiers and settlers, reaching the Rio Grande at the site of El Paso on April 20, 1598, and continuing along that great river into New Mexico. Oñate crossed the desert later called the Jornada del Muerto, where one member of the advance party died of thirst, past the sites of Albuquerque and Santa Fe, and in August 1598 he reached the Chama River, a tributary of the Rio Grande in northern New Mexico; here he decided to build his capital, which he called San Gabriel. It remained the capital until Oñate's successor, Don Pedro de Peralta, founded Santa Fe in 1610.

In San Gabriel, the first order of the day, as per instructions, was building the church, which was dedicated on September 8, 1598. "In the afternoon," reported Oñate, "the whole camp celebrated with a good sham battle between Moors and Christians, the latter on foot with harquebuses, the former on horseback with lances and shields." On September 9, the Franciscans divided New Mexico among themselves into parishes.

The second order of business was exploration, and Oñate, also in September, sent his sergeant major, Vicente de Zaldívar, eastward into buffalo country with some men. Zaldívar's report provides an early account of life among the sixteenth-century buffalo-hunting Indians, fifty years after Coronado had first seen them in central Kansas. Zaldívar came upon a *ranchería* of *vaquero* Indians, five hundred tents strong. "The dressing is so excellent," he observed, "that water will not go through even in a downpour, nor will the leather harden." The sergeant major bought a complete tent to take back to Oñate. He was quite amazed at the pliancy and lightness of the leather. Despite its size, it weighed only two *arrobas* (an *arroba* was twenty-five pounds). To carry their tents, the Indians had medium-sized dogs. "It is very amusing to see them travel," wrote Zaldívar, "dragging the poles in single file, most of them blistered by the harness. To load them the Indians hold the dogs' heads between their legs. . . . They run with a gait as if they had been trained with fetters."

Thinking that the buffalo were like ordinary cattle, Zaldívar attempted to corral a herd that he might bring back to San Gabriel, but failed completely. "We tried a thousand ways to catch them and round them up," he wrote, "but in no way was this possible. They killed three of our horses and badly wounded 40 others. . . . They attack sideways lowering the head gently, and in this manner they easily tear asunder whatever they happen to hook." Zaldívar admired the ease with which the Indians, lacking guns or horses, were able to hunt them, "concealed in ambush at their watering places." The Spaniards, with their superior technology, were unable to bring back a single live buffalo.

While Vicente de Zaldívar was exploring buffalo country, his brother Juan, who was Oñate's *maese de campo*, had taken some men southwest into the land of high, windswept rocks. On December 3, Juan de Zaldívar reached the fortified Indian town of Acoma, built on the flat top of a steep, high rock, about thirty miles west of today's Albuquerque. This "sky pueblo," perched on the mesa of red sandstone 357 feet above the gray sage of the valley, had been occupied since the days of Coronado, and is still occupied today. Upon approaching it, one sees something akin to a grounded aircraft carrier in a remote and treeless landscape of huge rocks with fantastic shapes.

Juan de Zaldívar asked the Acoma Indians for food and water; these they gave grudgingly, for they had barely enough to feed their own people. When he asked for flour, they said they had none but would grind some corn and the Spanish could come back for it. He returned for the flour on December 4, 1598, with eighteen men. According to Oñate's treasurer, Alonso Sanchez, one of the men, "a soldier named Vivero, took two turkeys from the Indians, and they killed him from one of the terraces." Then the entire pueblo rose up in arms, with Indians grabbing Spaniards and beating their heads against the rocks, and women throwing stones from terraces. The braves put on the dead Spaniards' helmets and waved their swords and threw their bodies off the cliff.

Bernabé de las Casas, the soldier who was holding the horses at the bottom of the rock, saw some Indians running toward him brandishing swords and shouting that he was a bastard murderer. A half-dozen Spaniards had jumped off the cliff and were still able to ride, and Bernabé helped them onto their horses and galloped off. But thirteen of the party of nineteen were killed, including Juan de Zaldívar. It was a blow to Spanish soldiery, and there had to be a reprisal or the Indians would lose respect for the Christian conquerors.

When Vicente de Zaldívar got back from the buffalo country, Oñate sent him to Acoma with seventy men to avenge his brother. Upon arriving on January 21, 1599, they found the Indians well fortified on the mesa, armed with the weapons they had taken from the Spanish dead, and wearing their coats of mail. They shouted and boasted and called the Spaniards scoundrels and Castilian whoremongers, and stayed up all night dancing and carousing, in a high state of excitement. At dawn, the Spaniards attacked, with a feint on one side of the rock while the main body scaled it on the other side. The fighting lasted for two days, and so many Indians were killed that they asked for peace. "The weather was favorable," said the report, "being so cold that our harquebuses never overheated, even though they were fired all day."

Five hundred Indians were taken prisoner, and about seventy males were sent to stand trial in Santo Domingo, the mission headquarters that Oñate had founded, farther south on the Rio Grande, just before it forks with the Jemez. This was one of the first trials to be held in the United States, eight years before the founding of Jamestown. A Spanish defense attorney appointed for the Indians took an oath to plead their case as best he could.

Various Indians took the stand and testified about the battle. One had an alibi—he was out tilling his fields on that day. Another said the whole thing had started when a soldier stole some turkeys. A third one said it had started when the Spaniards demanded food and blankets. Several soldiers gave their side of the story. The trial was conducted in strict keeping with Spanish jurisprudence, and all the Indians were found guilty. On February 12, 1599, Oñate pronounced the sentence: All the men over the age of twenty-five would have one foot cut off and would have to serve twenty years of serfdom. Those between twelve and twenty-five would simply have one foot cut off. The scene can be imagined—Indians waiting their turn in line, approaching the block, and then being held down as the man with the ax chopped off one of their feet. A lot of mutilated Indians were sent back to Acoma. Oñate's brutality had a deterrent effect; after another punitive campaign, in 1601, east of the Rio Grande, there was no more Indian trouble in New Mexico for nearly a century.

Life went on in San Gabriel, which by 1601 had a population of five hundred, for the viceroy had sent reinforcements in December 1600. Oñate, resenting that the viceroy had appointed several captains, said: "The viceroy can wipe his ass with his commissions." By this time, it was clear that New Mexico was no El Dorado. In fact, it was a white elephant for the Spanish crown. Instead of bringing in revenue, it cost money. The men were cranky, and it was hard to keep them in rein. Because they couldn't feed themselves, they sent parties out each month to steal from the Indians. It was that or starve. The Indians didn't have a surplus; they were so careful with their corn that when the men carried their baskets they had women follow behind to pick up the spilled kernels. As for the land, it was limitless prairie, with extreme climate changes, and it bred innumerable mice, bedbugs, and other vermin.

And yet Oñate had to send the viceroy glowing reports. You had to tell the boss what he wanted to hear if you wanted more funds and more men, and if you wanted to remain in charge. If you said there was no hope of gold and silver, you might be recalled in a hurry. Of course, if you went too far, you might be in for a *residencia*—a complete audit of your administration by the Council of the Indies. So Oñate reported that fifty thousand Indians had been pacified. The friars were learning the Indian vernacular. The wheat was sown and harvested, and a flour mill was under construction. In some villages, the Indians wore crosses and worshiped as Catholics.

Oñate was not the viceroy's only source of information. Under the Spanish system, anyone with a gripe could write him in Mexico City. In March 1601, one of Oñate's captains, by name Velasco, made a number of damaging charges, accusing Oñate of murdering two of his captains. One, Pablo de Aguilar, was decapitated, he said. Another, Alonso de Sosa Albornoz, had begged to go back to New Spain. Oñate had allowed him to leave, but sent some men to bushwhack him in a ravine, and they stabbed him to death and covered his body with stones. "The fact is," wrote Velasco, "that we are all depressed, cowed, and frightened, expecting death at any moment."

Oñate had developed a case of galloping megalomania, Captain Velasco went on, and several witnesses had heard Vicente de Zaldívar address him as "majesty." His treatment of the Indians left much to be desired. "Your lordship may well imagine how this treatment, entering their houses, taking their women, and causing them a thousand such annoyances and vexations, will incline them toward us to accept baptism and our Holy Catholic faith." It was really a shame, Captain Velasco said, since "the Pueblo Indians are the most meek, humble, and timid people ever seen. . . . They are so simple that they tried to protect themselves against firearms by making shields from mats and from the little willow shutters of their windows."

On the basis of Captain Velasco's complaints, the viceroy sent an inspector, Francisco de Valverde, to New Mexico, at a time when Oñate was off exploring. Valverde concluded that there was general dissatisfaction among the settlers, who had expected great riches and felt cheated. The winters were harsh, and they were always shivering by the fire. The main firewood, cottonwood, was very smoky. Moreover, the summers were as hot as the winters were cold. People slept in their vegetable gardens to escape the plague of bedbugs. Oñate levied a tribute of one blanket a year from each Indian. When the soldiers came through, they took the blankets right off the women's backs, leaving them naked. Valverde did not meet a single person who wanted to stay in New Mexico.

The dossier against Oñate was piling up in the viceroy's office. In 1601, the friars turned against him, for their conversion efforts were frustrated by the soldiers' brutality. "If you who are Christians cause so much harm," the Indians told the friars, "why should we become Christians?" One of the priests, Juan de Escalona, wrote the viceroy on October 1, 1601, that Oñate was to blame, in that he refused to plant a community plot. This was a year of drought, Escalona went on, and the Indians had so little for themselves that they were eating charcoal and dirt ground up with seeds, and "any Spaniard who gets his fill of tortillas here feels as if he had obtained a grant of nobility." It was pointless to preach the gospel, which was despised as the message of their tormentors.

But, between complaints from the field and action in Spain, years passed. In 1603, another viceroy was named, the marquis of Montesclaros. He decided that New Mexico was a failure and wrote the king as much. By now, there was another king, Philip III, who turned against Oñate and wrote Montesclaros in 1607 to stop subsidizing the expedition. In 1608, Oñate resigned, completely demoralized, leaving New Mexico with a small party of loyal friends, and with his twenty-two-year-old son, whom he had brought along in 1597 as a twelve-year-old boy. In pursuing fame and fortune in New Mexico, Oñate had lost a fortune of perhaps four million dollars in today's terms, and ten years of his life.

Upon his return to Mexico City, Oñate found that an ungrateful crown had indicted him on thirty criminal charges, among which were that:

• He had reported New Mexico to be rich and fertile when it was poor and sterile.

• He had belittled the clergy.

• He had insulted the royal inspector.

• He had insisted on being addressed in public as "majesty."

• He had lived scandalously with women of the camp, both married and unmarried.

• He had sent a party of soldiers from the camp at the risk of their lives to pick wild fruit for his enjoyment.

• He had murdered two captains.

Oñate was sentenced to pay a sixty-two-hundred-ducat fine and to perpetual exile from New Mexico. In 1609, Philip III decided to make New Mexico a royal colony after all, now that the British had a foothold in Virginia. Peralta was appointed governor and founded Santa Fe, setting the course for Spanish New Mexico for the next 250 years.

At the end of the sixteenth century, Spain was the only European power with colonies in the United States. There was one in Florida and one in New Mexico, plus assorted missions; France and England as yet had nothing. Spain had earned its colonies with many fruitless ventures, the blood of its captains, and the creation of a vast bureaucracy at home. The paper trail and the blood trail kept the system together. The more possessions you had, the more *letrados* (law-school graduates) you needed. And the more *letrados* you had, the more regulations they drafted. The investigation of a term of office, or *residencia*, could take ten years. "If death came from Madrid," said one viceroy, "we should all live to a very old age." The system was slow, corrupt, and cumbersome, but it managed to creak along.

The history of America's settlement has been written and taught from an Anglocentric point of view, partly because England ousted Spain and France, partly because many of the early *entradas* concentrated on plunder rather than settlement, slaughtering Indians as they went. It's not a particularly uplifting tale.

And yet it should be remembered that the first white men to settle in the United States were not religious dissidents, as in Plymouth, or mercantile companies, as in Jamestown, but the emissaries of the Catholic empire of Spain, orthodox and loyal, bearers of the sword and the cross. These subjects of the king wanted to win the honors that the Spanish monarchy conferred and to gain a heavenly reward by saving heathen souls.

Sometimes, as in Mexico, and sometimes not, as in Florida and New Mexico, there was a windfall of precious metals, which in the sixteenth century kept Spain afloat as the leading world power. Sometimes, when it was worth their while, the Spaniards tried to establish settlements, but they did not succeed until 1565, with St. Augustine. And with the soldiers came friars, some of whom were humane men appalled by cruelty. It's probably pointless to judge them by contemporary moral standards, or to compare them with the French and English colonizers, whose conduct was sometimes no less cruel. Suffice it to say that the Spaniards covered a lot of ground in the United States, from California to Kansas, and what they saw, no other white man had seen.

CHAPTER FOUR

THE
FRENCH
FRONTIER

Between 1603 and 1633, Samuel de Champlain established the French in Canada, eventually founding the city of Quebec. With his discovery of the water route from the St. Lawrence River to the Great Lakes, he gave the French access to the Mississippi River and the North American interior.

What's all this fuss about a few acres of snow?

VOLTAIRE

In August 1867, a Canadian farmer by the name of John Lee, who lived in the town of Cobden, about seventy miles west of Ottawa, took a job clearing land for the Ottawa Forwarding Company, the steamboat company on Muskrat Lake. Lee enlisted as helper his fourteen-year-old son, Edward George, who was on summer vacation from school, and they cleared mixed hardwood and pine at the edge of the lake, chopping the trees down, cutting them into logs, then pulling them up and burning them. "We burned timber that would make a man's fortune nowadays," Edward George Lee later recalled.

One hot day, father and son were working on neighboring Green Lake. A big old fallen red pine lying downhill, with its top in the little creek that wound out from the southern end of the lake, caught the boy's attention. John Lee chopped the trunk into three logs, two of which Edward George drew away with their team of oxen. But the third log wasn't chopped clean off, and when he

New York Historical Society

This is the astrolabe that Samuel de Champlain dropped in 1613 near Green Lake while on the expedition that discovered Lake Huron. It was found in 1867 by a Canadian farmer's son.

hitched the oxen to it he had to pull it around sideways to break it away. As the log swung away, it pulled back the moss like a blanket. There on the ground, where the moss had been, a round yellow object glinted, nine or ten inches across. Edward George picked it up and saw that it had an arm across it, and figures engraved on it, as well as the date 1603. It was an astrolabe, a navigational instrument to observe the positions of the stars.

The French explorer Samuel de Champlain had first come to Canada in 1603, and Green Lake had been on the route of one of his expeditions, in 1613. He had set out with four men and two canoes from the site of today's Montreal, where the St. Lawrence splits in two. He started up the St. Lawrence, but almost drowned in rapids south of today's Cornwall. He headed north to the other branch, the Ottawa, but that was also rough going, so he advanced instead along a line of three connected lakes, Olmstead, Green, and Muskrat, portaging from one to the other.

The portages were difficult, wrote Champlain, "on account of the wind having blown down pine-trees one on top of the other, which is no small inconvenience, for one must go now over and now under these trees." Champlain was carrying three harque-buses, three canoe paddles, and his cloak, and in pushing through the tangle of trees he dropped his astrolabe, which remained cov-ered by moss and the fallen pine for 254 years, until Edward George Lee found it on that summer day in 1867.

Captain Overman, the Ottawa Forwarding manager, claimed the astrolabe for the company, promising to give Edward George ten dollars for it. "Poor Pa let them have it," Edward George Lee later recalled, "but if I had gotten it up to the house, Ma would not have let them have it that day. . . . I never saw a farthing, nor hide or hair of the compass since."

Captain Overman turned the astrolabe over to the Cassels, owners of Ottawa Forwarding, who sold it for five hundred dollars to a New York collector, Samuel V. Hoffman, who left it to the New York Historical Society, which has recently returned it to the Canadian government.

France in 1600 was a powerful and united nation, ancient nurse of arts and letters, eldest daughter of the church. Her popu-lation was sixteen million, compared with eight million in Spain and 5.5 million in England. Her king was Henry IV, a Protestant who converted to Catholicism in order to wear the crown.

Henry saw the advantage of establishing colonies in North America ahead of the English, and offered the fur monopoly to anyone willing to underwrite an expedition. For a couple of hundred years, Newfoundland fishermen had been trading for bea-ver pelts, which milliners in Paris and Amsterdam shaped into fashionable hats. Chaucer's merchant in *The Canterbury Tales* (circa 1390) had "upon his head a Flanders beaver hat."

The Company of New France was founded; its investors would finance the expedition, keep 90 percent of their profit, and give 10 percent to the crown. In 1603, Samuel de Champlain, an experienced navigator, was sent on a reconnaissance trip. This born explorer would spend the next thirty-two years, until his death in 1635, commuting between Canada and France on an al-most annual basis. He crossed the Atlantic twenty-nine times, log-ging over a hundred thousand miles.

On this first trip in 1603, Champlain stayed less than three months, following Cartier's route into the gulf and up the St. Lawrence. It was sixty years since the Indians had seen a Frenchman; old offenses were forgotten, and they offered Champlain a feast with ten kettles of meat. He was appalled at their manners, for "they feed very filthily, and when their hands are greasy they rub them on their hair, or else on the hair of their dogs." He was, however, impressed by their birch-bark canoes, "so light that a man can carry one of them easily." Like Cartier before him, he believed that the St. Lawrence would lead him to the South Sea and Cathay.

In August 1603, he went back to France, then set out the following April with Pierre de Monts, director of the Company of New France. They took two ships, seventy-nine settlers, and forty crewmen, but, instead of sailing into the St. Lawrence, they decided to look for a spot in a milder climate, and sailed along the southern coast of Nova Scotia into the Bay of Fundy. Bypassing Campobello, they entered Passamaquoddy Bay and sailed up the St. Croix River, the present boundary between Maine and Canada's New Brunswick Province. Ten miles up the St. Croix, they landed on a small island, a tree-covered slab of rock known today as Dochet Island.

They called it St. Croix, and at the time it was the only American settlement north of the Spanish towns of New Mexico. They finished their houses just in time for winter: the first snow fell on October 2. Having learned nothing from Cartier's experience, they relied on a diet of salt meat, and many came down with scurvy. Their mouths, Champlain reported, "had large pieces of superfluous fungus flesh . . . and their teeth barely held in place and could be pulled out with the fingers without causing pain." The ones who stayed healthy were those who hunted rabbit, skated on the ponds, and threw snowballs. Thirty-five died, nearly half the company.

Another bad winter would wipe them out, so Champlain and de Monts spent the summer of 1605 sailing down the Maine coast, to the Kennebec and Saco rivers, looking for a better site. They visited the harbors of Boston, Plymouth, and Cape Cod, but were put off by hostile Indians. The coast was then heavily populated with Indian villages. Several years before the Pilgrims arrived on the same coast in 1620, many of these Indians had died in an epidemic, making it possible for the Pilgrims to settle there. Champlain was also handicapped by not having an interpreter. At one village, he used sign language to ask about snowfall, pointing to his white collar with one hand while wiggling his fingers with the other.

So, instead of moving the French settlement to Massachusetts, de Monts decided to take his people across the Bay of Fundy to a snug harbor on the northern shore of Nova Scotia, today's Annapolis Basin. The St. Croix buildings were dismantled, and in the fall the men were ferried across the bay to the new location, Port Royal. There they built a fortified village, with a well, a big kitchen, and a pigeon loft near the gate.

In their second winter, they lost twelve of the remaining forty-five men to scurvy. You have to feel sorry for the nameless clods who went out with one-year contracts as salaried workers, without a clue as to what they were getting into, and who died far from home without even making a footnote to history.

In 1606, fifty more men arrived from France to make up for the losses, and Champlain once again ventured down the New England coast. In October, sailing down the Atlantic shore of Cape Cod, the French put in at Chatham, site of a good-sized wigwam village of Almouchiquois. They passed out rings and bracelets to the Indian women, but the men sent the wives into the woods and started taking down their wigwams. The French were ordered back on board ship, but five stayed behind and got drunk. The next morning, October 15, as they were sleeping it off, a large group of Indians came quietly over the hill and fired a salvo of arrows. The French ran toward the shore, crying, "Help, help, they are killing us." As they screamed, four of the five fell dead in the water. It was the first skirmish of the Indian wars in Massachusetts.

The French landed an armed party to bury the dead near a cross they had planted. They rescued a survivor, who had an arrow in his chest. The Indians fled inland, but when the French had gone and the tide was low, Champlain wrote, "this rascally crew came back to the place of their murderous deed, uprooted the cross, dug up one of the dead, took off his shirt and put it on . . . and besides all this, turning their backs toward the barque, they made mock of us by taking sand in their two hands and casting it between their buttocks, yelping the while like wolves." Verrazano had already noted that the Indians of the New England coast "exhibit their bare behinds."

It was clear to Champlain that New England was not for him

and his men. The Indians were murderers, and such thieves that "if they cannot lay hold of a thing with their hands they try to do so with their feet." So they went back to Port Royal and endured a third winter (1606–7). This time, only seven died of scurvy, for it was a relatively mild winter, and they improved their diet with fish and game. But in May 1607, a ship arrived from France to announce the cancellation of the fur-trading monopoly. The venture was a bust: poachers were trading for beaver up and down the St. Lawrence, and there was nothing the company could do about it.

The Port Royal colony was abandoned, and Champlain took everyone back to France, where de Monts managed to wangle a one-year extension for his monopoly. Champlain left with a new group in 1608, but this time he was determined to settle on the St. Lawrence, where he could control the river traffic and the poaching. On July 3, he reached the site of Quebec. There, at the forested base of the 165-foot-high sheer rock wall, a hundred feet from the water's edge, he made his third attempt at settlement. Two-story row houses with balconies were built in a circle, as well as a warehouse. Land was cleared for gardens, and later a palisade was added, along with some more houses and storage sheds, and a small convent. This bare-bones fortified log village remained Champlain's Quebec for twenty-seven years.

His real ambition, the reason he kept coming back and taking risks, wasn't the beaver trade but a desire to find the passage to Cathay. He still thought that North America was an island leading to another sea and Asia. But if he wanted to find Cathay, he had to make friends with the tribes, in order to obtain guides. As part of his good-neighbor policy, he agreed in 1603 to help the Hurons make war against their Iroquois enemies. This decision was devastating to the French in the long run, ushering in a century of warfare with the Iroquois, who were supported by the Dutch and the English. And all for the lure of a nonexistent Cathay.

In July 1609, Champlain was asked to join a war party of Hurons and Algonquins who were marching on the Iroquois. He and a few of his men joined the warriors at Trois-Rivières on the St. Lawrence. There was a long portage to the Richelieu River, and they headed south in a shallop to the 125-mile-long, island-filled lake that would eventually be named after him, straddling the border of New York and Vermont. When the shallop stalled in some rapids, Champlain continued by canoe to the Quebec–New

York border at Rouses Point and entered the lake with sixty Indians and twenty-four canoes (and, by the same token, "discovered" New York State).

The two hundred Iroquois had never seen a firearm, and Champlain advanced with his cord lit, his powder primed, and his harquebus ready. The obvious targets were the chiefs, wearing the three big plumes.

When the Indians drew their bows, he took aim and fired, and from that single shot two chiefs fell to the ground, for he had loaded his musket with four balls. Then his companions fired from the woods, and the Iroquois took flight. This was Champlain's finest hour, but he showed some mercy, forcing his Indian allies to stop torturing a prisoner. They had lit a fire, and each had taken a brand and burned the poor wretch a little at a time. Then they tore out his nails and burned the tips of his fingers and his *membrum virile*. Finally, they scalped him, pierced his arms near the wrists, and tore out his sinews with sticks. "I felt pity at seeing him treated this way," Champlain reported. The Indians agreed to let him give the captive the coup de grâce, "and with one shot I allowed him to escape all his tortures." But once the man was dead, they opened his body and threw his bowels in the lake, chopped off his head, arms, and legs, cut his heart into several pieces, and ate it.

By this time, the industrious Netherlands, land of commercial capitalism, home of the work ethic, had entered the exploration game, having, after years of struggle, negotiated a truce with Spain in 1609. That same year, the Dutch East India Company hired the English navigator Henry Hudson, who specialized in looking for a short route to Asia over the Arctic Ocean. He was propelled by the delusion that he would find an ice-free sea around the North Pole.

So he sailed out of Amsterdam in the *Half Moon* in April 1609 and headed up the coast of Norway to the Arctic Ocean. But he hit some ice packs, and the crew mutinied. Rather than go home empty-handed, he decided to look for the Northwest Passage, turned around, went back down the Norwegian coast, caught the Labrador current to Newfoundland, and was off Nova Scotia by July, heading down the New England coast to New York Bay. Then up the 350-mile-long river he went, getting about halfway, as far as Albany; here he found the water only seven feet deep, and turned back.

At about the same time Hudson was in Albany, Champlain was at Ticonderoga. Converging in the vast expanse of North America, the man who had a river named after him came within 120 miles of the man who had a lake named after him.

Hudson's trip was memorable for several reasons. For one thing, Hudson realized that this mighty river was not the road to Asia. For another, the journal kept by one of his crew members, Robert Juet, offers the first recorded example of white men's deliberately getting an Indian drunk. On one occasion, wrote Juet, "our master [Hudson] and his mate determined to try some of the chief men of the country, whether they had any treachery in them. So they took them down into the cabin and gave them so much wine and aqua vita that they were all merry. . . . In the end one of them was drunk . . . for they could not tell how to take it."

The river trip was a curious mixture of friendliness and hostility, of Indians offering them furs and tobacco one day, and attacking them in war canoes the next. On October 1, an Indian climbed up on the *Half Moon*'s rudder to the cabin window and stole a pillow, two shirts, and two bandoliers. The mate shot and killed him. The men put down a longboat to retrieve their things, and a lone Indian swam toward it and tried to capsize it, "but our cook took a sword and cut off one of his hands, and he was drowned." The following day, there was another battle, arrows against muskets, and so it went, until they were out of New York Harbor and headed for home.

Hudson entered New York Harbor on September 3; on September 5, Champlain sailed out of the St. Lawrence, bound for the Fontainebleau court of Henry IV, to whom he brought a belt made of porcupine quills, two scarlet tanagers, and an account of his muskets-against-arrows victory. The following year, 1610, good King Henry was assassinated, and his nine-year-old son succeeded him as Louis XIII.

Champlain continued to shuttle between Quebec and France. In keeping with his plan to remain on good terms with the Indians on the St. Lawrence, and to pick up information about routes to Cathay, he instituted a sort of "visiting-fellow" exchange program, under which young Frenchmen went to live with a tribe for a year or so, and young Indians came to live with the French. It was, in the words of the Champlain historian J. C. W. Armstrong, "the first step of a French feasibility study for western expansion." One of the first of these young Frenchmen was Nicolas de Vignau, who went to stay with some Hurons on Allumette Island, with Chief Tessouat as his mentor.

De Vignau was the sort who likes to ingratiate himself by telling people what they want to hear; upon returning to Quebec in 1612, after his year with the Hurons, he told Champlain that he had reached the sea that led to Cathay, via the Ottawa River, and had seen the wreck of an English ship on shore. The Indians with him, he said, had taken the scalps of the crew of eighty, sparing only one English lad, whom they were holding for the French.

By this time, Champlain had heard of Hudson's discovery, in 1610–11, of the huge bay named after him a thousand miles to the north of Quebec. His curiosity was aroused. He took de Vignau back to France and made him swear to the truth of his tale in two affidavits signed before two La Rochelle notaries. On May 27, 1613, he and de Vignau and some guides set out in two canoes from the site of Montreal; it was on this trip that he lost his astrolabe.

Champlain reached Allumette, a large island twelve miles across, heavily forested with pine, opposite today's Pembroke, Ontario. There the moment of truth came. Chief Tessouat was waiting for them. The chief, a self-appointed toll-keeper, used his strategic position on the island to regulate river traffic. Champlain told him that de Vignau claimed to have reached Lake Nipissing, the large lake to the west that was one of the routes into Lake Huron.

"Nicolas," said Chief Tessouat, "is it true that you say you were among the Nebicerenes?"

After a long pause, de Vignau said, "Yes, I was there." "You are a downright liar," Chief Tessouat said, "you know very well that you slept at my side every night with my children. If you were among the Nebicerenes, it was in your sleep."

De Vignau tried to brazen it out, but Champlain told him that, if they proceeded on the trip and it turned out he was lying, he would have him hanged. At this point, de Vignau fell to his knees, weeping and begging for pardon. "Give him to us," the Indians said; "we promise that he will not cry any more." But Champlain needed him alive, to explain to his people in Quebec the failure of the trip. And so they backtracked, reaching the Lachine Rapids on June 17, 1613.

But even though de Vignau was lying, his stories made Champlain want to explore the places where he claimed to have been. Champlain made the crucial trip in July 1615, and it gave him the brass ring, the Great Lakes, which might be seen as a gigantic combination lock with five tumblers, each of which had to be picked separately. This time, he set out with two big canoes, ten Indian paddlers, a white servant, and another graduate of the exchange program, Etienne Brulé. The route up the Ottawa was familiar as far as Allumette Island. Then the Indian guides unlocked the first tumbler, which was perhaps the most important geographical secret that the continent had to divulge—the route to Lake Huron via the Mattawa River, Lake Nipissing, and the French River.

The deep-channeled French River, lined with high banks of red and gray granite, was the travel route of the Ojibwa Indians. On August 1, 1615, Champlain paddled along the outcroppings of colored granite into Lake Huron's Georgian Bay, not yet suspecting that this huge body of water, this freshwater ocean, was connected to four others, and led to the great river that split the continent from north to south. One can imagine the sense of awe upon entering a lake so large that only its circumference was visible on the horizon line. It must have been like some primal vision of the planet, like that of the character in Jules Verne's *Journey to the Center of the Earth:* "I had not yet looked down into the unfathomable depths in which I was about to be engulfed."

Champlain landed near the present Lake Huron harbor town of Midland, and portaged to Lake Simcoe, in the middle of the strip of land between Georgian Bay and Lake Ontario. At a large village where the town of Orillia now stands, he picked up five hundred Indians, for once again he had agreed to join the Hurons on a military expedition against the Iroquois. His guides, drawing maps on bark with bits of charcoal, showed him the way. He could never have found it without them, for they had to lake-hop and portage along the northern shore of Lake Ontario, across Cranberry, Balsam, Cameron, Sturgeon, Pigeon, Buckhorn, and Rice lakes, and down the Trent River to the Bay of Quinte at Trenton, on Lake Ontario's northern shore.

The Bay of Quinte was a twenty-mile-long inlet that threaded its way past islands and peninsulas into Lake Ontario, another watery vastness. Two- and three-foot breakers rammed its pebbly shore. Champlain missed Lake Erie, and if he'd explored the northern shore of Lake Huron he might have found the entrance to Lakes Superior and Michigan, but two out of five wasn't bad.

Continuing along the northern shore of Lake Ontario in September 1615, he crossed the eastern tip at today's Kingston into what would one day be New York State, paddling into Sackets Harbor, near Watertown.

In the harbor, Champlain and his men hid their canoes and headed overland for a fortified village of about seventeen hundred Onondaga Indians, who had settled in longhouses north of today's Syracuse. On October 10, he arrived before the Indian fort on the edge of a small lake. In the ensuing battle, Champlain was hit twice, in the leg and in the knee, and was forced to retreat. He was unable to take a fort of Indians armed only with bows and arrows, when he had muskets. He had to be strapped inside a wickerwork basket and carried back to the lakeshore, where, luckily, his party's canoes were still waiting. After spending four long and dreary months recuperating with the Indians near Lake Simcoe, he got back to Quebec in the spring of 1616, like one risen from the grave. Indeed, the Indians had reported that he was dead. This was his last expedition outside Quebec: two arrow wounds were enough. He now spent more time in France, and made his final voyage to Quebec in 1633, two years before his death at sixty-eight years of age. He had logged thirty-two years in New France, off and on, but the settlement did not grow beyond its modest level of about a hundred persons.

Champlain succeeded in finding the most remarkable feature of the interior of North America: that is, the network of five connected lakes. Their combined area added up to the largest surface of fresh water in the world. Lake Huron was the hub, with two lakes to the left of it and two to the right. Lake Superior, like a headwater, discharged into Lake Huron through the St. Marys River at Sault Sainte Marie. The sausage-shaped Lake Michigan, directly south of Lake Superior, also flowed into Lake Huron through the Straits of Mackinac. Lake Huron was connected to Lake Erie via the St. Clair at Detroit, and Lake Erie was connected to Lake Ontario, the smallest but second-deepest lake, at Niagara. Lake Ontario discharged into the St. Lawrence, which emptied into the Gulf of St. Lawrence, the French navigators' point of entrance in Canada. Thanks to Champlain, these great interlocking lobes of water left by the Ice Age were now available to the French as a system of transportation that provided access to the heartland.

In 1634, a year before his death, Champlain sent out Jean

Nicolet, one of the young men who had lived with the Indians. Nicolet followed Champlain's route into Lake Huron, canoeing along its northern shore, past Manitoulin and Drummond islands, and reaching Sault Sainte Marie, where Lake Superior poured into the lower lakes. Changing course, he entered Mackinac Inlet, a lovely inland waterway, and reached the northern shore of Lake Michigan, which he discovered. Heading into Green Bay, he took the Fox River to Lake Winnebago. There the Indians told him a great river was three days' journey away.

He could have taken the Fox and portaged over to the Wisconsin, where the town of Portage stands today. This would have led him right into the Mississippi, but Nicolet wanted to get back to Quebec before the autumn storms. You can't blame him: Lake Michigan without a map is a daunting prospect.

But the various pieces of the puzzle were beginning to fit together, and while the English were patiently settling their New England and Virginia towns, the French were charting straits and portage paths. They eventually learned how to travel from Quebec to New Orleans. Portages became campsites, cleared for easy landings, where you might find company, or a letter hanging from a branch, or a cross left by a missionary.

The water route, however, was both a trump and a trap, encouraging travel rather than settlement. You could cover a great distance over a ready-made route, but the land was yours in name only, because you hadn't cleared it or built on it. The English settlers advanced more slowly, clearing and building as they went, each group sinking roots, the next group going a little farther, while the French were taking their swift canoe trips. When the final struggle came in the eighteenth century, the English had a compact area of dense settlement with a population of two million, whereas the French had Quebec on the St. Lawrence and New Orleans on the Mississippi, like the handles on a two-thousand-mile-long jump rope, with the wilderness in between and a population of less than one hundred thousand.

Quebec under Champlain stagnated, because no one wanted to go there. The French were stay-at-homes; they didn't have the strong imperial impulse of the Spanish or the mercantile tradition of the English. France was still in many ways feudal, lacking a vigorous middle class. The wealthy liked to spend their money on titles of nobility or army commissions. Quebec wasn't attractive to farmers, because the growing season was a brief 150 days, and fruit trees would die when temperatures dropped below zero. In addition, the St. Lawrence was frozen solid for three and a half months, and there was dangerous pack ice in the gulf another three months, so that the colony was cut off from France at least six months a year. At home, there were company disputes, and the shareholders didn't give a damn about anything except making 40 percent on their money; most of the time France was at war, so there was only a trickle of royal support.

Given these circumstances, it's understandable that enthusiasm for New France in the mother country was lukewarm. People didn't go to Quebec voluntarily, they were sent, as landless laborers impressed into the army, or refugees from the poorhouse. In 1627, there were fifty-five settlers, and only one and a half acres of land had been cleared, by Louis Hébert, who died that year. Until 1628, not one plowshare was drawn by oxen. By comparison, the English in Jamestown numbered two thousand in 1627, and there were two hundred Dutch on the Hudson.

Missionaries were the exception to this lack of enthusiasm. In 1615, they started living among the Hurons of Georgian Bay. These seventeenth-century French monks were less dogmatic than the Spanish and less moralizing than the English. Through prolonged immersion in the tribal society, they learned as much as, if not more than, they taught, gaining a depth of understanding of the Indian that was unique in the colonial experience. The thinly settled French had come upon populated lands requiring a policy of accommodation with the native people. The missionaries became the agents of that accommodation—France's ambassadors to the wilderness.

Gabriel Sagard, for instance, was a Recollet lay brother who accompanied a friar to a Huron village on Georgian Bay and stayed there from June 1623 to the autumn of 1624. His experience, recounted in *Long Journey to the Country of the Hurons*, taught him to take into account the Indian point of view.

The question was, who were the real savages? Sagard was appalled when the Indian women ate the lice they picked off their children. He was horrified when on canoe trips the men urinated in the same bowls they ate their cornmeal in. But the Indians were equally disgusted at his use of a handkerchief. "They say we place what is unclean in a fine white piece of linen," he wrote, "and put it away in our pockets as something very precious, while they throw it on the ground. . . . When a savage one day saw a Frenchman fold up his handkerchief after wiping his nose, he said to him laughingly, 'if thou likest the filth, give me thy handkerchief and I will soon fill it.' "

As Sagard got to know the Hurons, he came to admire their patience. They started fires by turning a twig in a wooden groove, and took the time to hide corn along their route in little birch-bark bags. He was also impressed by their generosity, so much in contrast to French greed and competitiveness. They always shared what food they had, and when Sagard told them that France had many beggars wandering the countryside, "they found it very bad . . . and thought it was due to a lack of charity, and blamed us greatly, saying that if we had some intelligence we would set some order in the matter, the remedies being so simple."

As for religion, Sagard saw that they had one of their own, which was integrated into the daily life of the tribe. They believed in a God who was in harmony with nature, and who could bring the sunshine and the rain. They threw grease in the fire and said "*Papeouekou*, make us find something to eat." They asked Sagard to pray when heavy rains were ruining their corn crop; he did, and the rains stopped. They asked him to kill the thunder, which they thought was a bird. They believed the earth had a hole in it, and the sun went into the hole when it set.

Sagard saw that the Hurons set great store by dreams, which they took as omens or instructions. The sick were encouraged to act them out. One sick woman, Sagard wrote, "asked one of the young men to make water in her mouth, and she had to swallow it, which she did with great courage, hoping to be cured by it." Then a number of girls were assembled at the sick woman's couch and asked which young man they wanted to sleep with. Those they named were brought in and consummated the act in the presence of the sick woman.

Many of the missionaries, however, particularly the Jesuits, did not acquire Gabriel Sagard's spirit of tolerance. Bent on conversion, they disparaged the Indians' system of beliefs. Outwardly benevolent, the missionary movement was extremely disruptive. To have the blackrobes coming around and telling you that your religion was no good, and that you should change gods, must have been disheartening, to say the least.

As they spread the gospel, the missionaries also spread disease. Half the Hurons in the Georgia Bay area died between 1634 and 1640, and the survivors began to blame the blackrobes. The

Indian shamans, who were trying to preserve tribal ways, told their flock that the missionaries were poisoning them.

Another disruption of the Indian way of life was the beaver trade. Hunting among the Hurons was a regulated activity. You had to stay on good terms with the spiritual powers who helped you find game. You had to respect the game you hunted. The Chippewa on Lake Huron and Lake Superior believed that each animal species had its "keeper of the game."

To appease the keeper, certain rules had to be observed. In fishing, the jaws of an otter were tied to the fishnet. When hunting beaver, the Indians moved from place to place, before the hunter's shadow became known to the beaver's shadow. A flat porcupine bone was placed on the fire to indicate the direction of the hunt. The hunter and the hunted both belonged to the same spiritual kingdom. The beaver had the power to change himself into other animals' forms, and could only be caught with the consent of the keeper of the game.

When the French fur traders arrived in the Huron region, there were beavers in the millions. Using them only for their own needs, the Indians hunted them sparingly. But now, offered European goods like kettles and knives, they abandoned their conservationist principles and hunting rituals, moving from a subsistence economy of balance with their resources to a trade economy of supply and demand. Beaver pelts were the ticket to gracious living and to the power of the iron muzzle. The "natural ecologist" became a consumer. To improve their standard of living, the Indians overhunted.

The traders encouraged them to get out on the ponds in the winter, when the beavers' coats were thickest, and trap the animals in the air pockets under the ice. The whole set of rituals and taboos, the belief in the keeper of the game—all was forgotten in the rush for pelts so the Indians could buy brandy and glass beads.

Some of the beaver dams (little animal-built water systems that regulated the flow of streams and creeks in the dry season) had been in use for centuries; now, in their indiscriminate hunting, the Indians broke those dams, and the water in the beaver ponds spilled out, resulting in lowered water tables and the loss of tons of stored-up topsoil. In response to the French fur traders, the Indians overkilled the beaver and wrecked their environment.

The French wanted to change the Indians and they did, but not in the way they expected. The Indians were changed because the fabric of their society unraveled. Overhunting made them give up the ritual of the hunt. The blackrobes told them to dump their gods and adopt Christianity. Strange illnesses, about which their shamans could do nothing, carried them away. The combined presence of the fur trader and the missionary was extremely destructive. The Indians knew it, knew that they had lost a vital part of their being, and knew that overkilling beaver was a form of spiritual decay. An Algonquin chief told Father Paul Le Jeune: "I have seen the time when my dreams were true; when I saw moose or beaver in my sleep I would take some. . . . Now our dreams and prophecies are no longer true. . . ." The compact with the spirit world was broken.

The introduction of alcohol amounted to an additional epidemic. North American Indians did not make fermented or distilled beverages, as some Indians south of the border did. The French fur traders brought it to them, and it was a catastrophic introduction. According to the Abbé Belmont, who wrote a *Treatise on the Brandy Trade*, the Indians had no sense of their own tolerance level, no cultural conditioning as to the social uses of strong drink, and no social or moral inhibitions concerning drunkenness. Nor was there any concept of personal sin, or of shame. They believed that liquor produced a welcome transformation of the personality, and that they were not responsible for what they did while in an altered state. They were binge drinkers, wrote the Abbé Belmont. "We were not long in seeing drunken men killing each other, husbands burning wives, wives dishonoring husbands, and fathers putting their children in cauldrons."

Francis Parkman wrote: "The Spanish slaughtered the Indians, the English pushed them away, and the French embraced them." But the French embrace was fatal, not only in spreading disease, but in engendering among them a sense of hopelessness. In May 1633, an Indian chief came to Quebec with eighteen canoes and told Champlain: "I am but a tiny animal that crawls on the earth. You French are the great of this world, you make everything tremble. . . . But if I say something it's only something I've picked up, accidentally. . . . You will build a house that is a fortress, then you will build another house . . . and then we will be nothing but dogs that sleep outdoors. . . . You will grow wheat, and we will no longer look for our sustenance in the woods, we will be no better than vagabonds. . . . You pinch our arms, and we will tremble." To reassure him, Champlain replied, "When our great house is built, our sons will marry your daughters, and we will be one people." But his vision of a Franco-Indian merger never came to pass. When one set of aspirations collides with another, there's bound to be a loser.

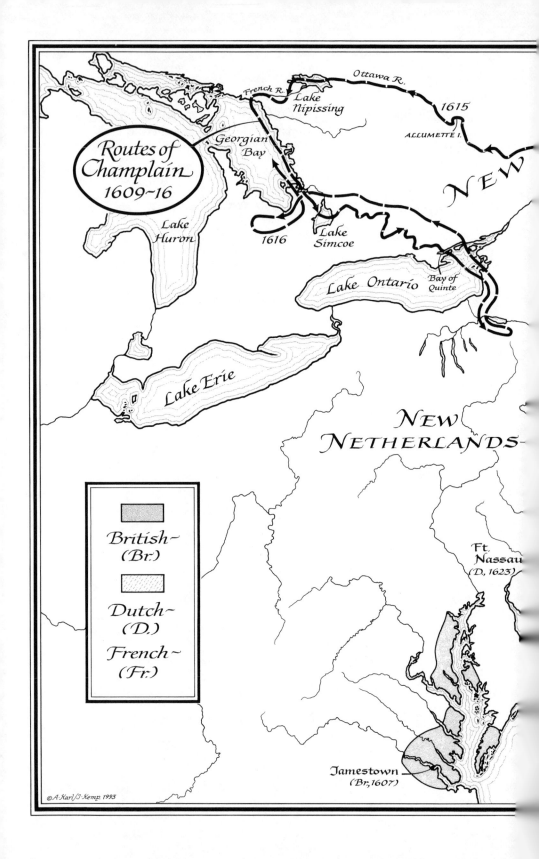

Ottawa R.

French R.

Lake
Nipissing

1615

ALLUMETTE I.

Georgian
Bay

N E W

Routes of
Champlain
1609~16

Lake
Huron

1616

Lake
Simcoe

Lake Ontario

Bay of
Quinte

Lake Erie

N E W
NETHERLANDS

British~
(Br.)

Dutch~
(D.)

French~
(Fr.)

Ft.
Nassau
(D, 1623)

Jamestown
(Br, 1607)

© A·Karl/J·Kemp. 1993

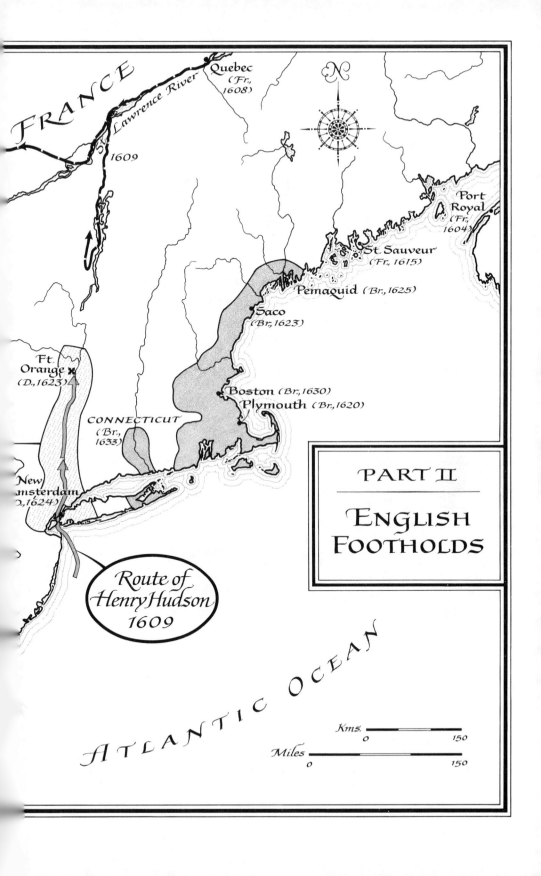

FRANCE

Quebec
(Fr.,
1608)

St. Lawrence River

1609

N

Port
Royal
(Fr.,
1604)

St. Sauveur
(Fr., 1615)

Pemaquid (Br., 1625)

Saco
(Br., 1623)

Ft.
Orange
(D., 1623)

CONNECTICUT
(Br.,
1633)

Boston (Br., 1630)
Plymouth (Br., 1620)

New
Amsterdam
(D., 1624)

Route of
Henry Hudson
1609

PART II

ENGLISH
FOOTHOLDS

ATLANTIC OCEAN

Kms.
0   150

Miles
0   150

CHAPTER FIVE

THE JAMESTOWN FRONTIER

Latecomers to the settlement of North America, the English established a foothold at Jamestown in 1607. A mercantile company ran Jamestown until 1624, when it was taken over by the crown.

This watercolor of the ruins of Jamestown, painted in 1860 by William C. Hopler, evokes the romance of early settlement rather than its misery.

For a transitory enchanted moment, man must have held his breath in the presence of this continent, compelled into an esthetic contemplation he neither understood nor desired, face to face for the last time in history with something commensurate to his capacity for wonder.

F. SCOTT FITZGERALD

Finally, in 1607, with the Spanish well ensconced in Florida and the French hanging on in Canada, the English landed between them, in Virginia. The settling of Jamestown has all the elements of a horror story—that is, of expecting a land of milk and honey and finding instead suffering and death. The monsters on the map were real, although not exactly as drawn.

The impetus for English settlement of the New World was private and mercantile, fueled chiefly by the profit motive. Merchants were still looking for a shortcut to the spices of the East. Nutmeg, cinnamon, cloves, ginger—all these were in such demand that an importer could lose five out of six ships and still make money. Also, the idea of a Greater England, breaking out from its island limits, was in the air. With the decline in farming and the flight to the cities, colonization was seen as a solution to the unemployment problem, and a way of getting rid of such unwanted elements as "rogues, vagabonds, and sturdy beggars."

The rising English merchant class had begun to organize joint-stock companies, pooling their capital and selling stock shares to investors. Sir Ferdinando Gorges, an armchair explorer who never spent a day in North America, had the idea of starting a company to colonize the New World. This pompous and blustering fellow, Plymouth's fort commander, got some local merchants interested. Together with some London merchants, they asked the king for a charter. It was fashionable to invest in this early form of venture capitalism. The backers, including the earls of Pembroke, Montgomery, and Southampton (Shakespeare's patron), formed an Elizabethan *Who's Who*.

The timing was right. James I, who had succeeded Queen Elizabeth in 1603, had ended the long war with Spain, which had drained funds from colonization efforts. James, who ruled until 1625, was the son of Mary, Queen of Scots. When his mother was sentenced to death for plotting against Queen Elizabeth, the twenty-one-year-old James acquiesced in her execution. By the time he assumed the English crown, he had already proved himself an able king of Scotland.

In April 1606, a royal charter created two companies, which were empowered "to make habitation . . . into that part of America, commonly called Virginia." One was the North Virginia Company of Plymouth, which, under the direction of Sir Ferdinando Gorges, came to nothing. He sent two ships and 120 men to Maine's Kennebec River, but they soon returned, for the earthly paradise was a howling wilderness.

The other was the South Virginia Company of London, formed by a group of rich speculators looking for a passage to Cathay, as indicated by the company's 1606 instruction to choose the river "which bendeth most towards the Northwest, for that way you shall soonest find the other sea." One-armed Captain Newport, "a mariner well-practiced in the Western parts of America," was in charge of the three ships that left England on December 19, 1606, with 105 settlers and a crew of thirty-nine.

The London Company, which operated the Virginia colony from 1607 to 1624 as a private venture, bore a striking resemblance to the savings-and-loan companies of the 1980s. In each case, "junk bonds" were sold to finance highly speculative real-estate ventures, and there was a mishandling of funds that crossed the line into swindling.

For instance, in 1615 and 1617, the English crown, which supported the company but did not wish to pay for it with public money, ordered all the parishes of the Church of England to contribute to the funding of a school for Indian children in Virginia, to be called Henrico College. The college was never built, and the company used the funds to help pay for its annual supply ship to Jamestown.

In 1612, the failing company extracted from King James the permission to conduct lotteries, which amounted to an invitation to print money. In their eight years of operation, the lotteries brought in twenty-nine thousand pounds, and kept the company afloat. But irregularities were eventually brought to the attention of Parliament. The lottery manager, Gabriel Barbor, was charged with embezzling seven thousand pounds, and one of his receivers with pocketing the receipts. In 1620, the king banned the lottery, and four years later, torn by dissension and under attack, the London Company was bailed out by the government and turned into a crown colony.

It took Captain Newport more than four months to sail his three ships—the *Susan Constant*, the *Godspeed*, and the *Discovery*— to the shores of Virginia with their 105 passengers. The *Discovery*, a two-masted pinnace, was hardly more than a thirty-foot-long rowboat with sails. Yet it carried twenty-one men plus enough food and water for the trip. In today's terms, imagine a four-month ride in an oceangoing subway car at rush hour.

For six weeks, troublesome winds kept the three ships within sight of England. Then they stopped in the West Indies for three weeks, visiting various islands, and one colonist died from heat exhaustion while on a hunting trip. Captain Newport had trouble finding the Virginia shoreline, but on April 26, 1607, he finally entered Chesapeake Bay, flanked by Cape Charles and Cape Henry, where he made his first landing.

The colonists did not realize that they had arrived in one of the most heavily populated Indian communities on the Eastern Seaboard. There were perhaps fourteen thousand Indians between the bay and the falls of the James River. The region was in fact so crowded that the Indians themselves called it "the densely inhabited land." Thirty-two of the tribes were of the Powhatan people, ruled by a chief whose name was Wahunsonacock (whom the English called Powhatan), who ruled from a village on the York River, the next river north of the James, above today's Gloucester Point. Indian villages dotted the waterways, and houses resembling bark Quonset huts gave off a pleasant smoky smell from the fires that were kept going.

Everywhere the white men went, there were Indians. When Captain Newport sent a scouting party in a small boat to the Cape Henry shore, Indians carrying their bows in their mouths sneaked up on the English and fired arrows, wounding Captain Gabriel Archer and one of the sailors, Matthew Morton. Undaunted, they entered the James River between today's Newport News and Norfolk, heading into Hampton Roads and upriver. For two weeks, they looked for a site, sailing up as far as today's Hopewell, where the Appomattox runs into the James. They proceeded cautiously —without maps, over unfamiliar terrain—searching for a spot that would meet the criteria of their instructions: a healthy and defensible place with a good harbor, where the river bent to the northwest.

On May 13, they decided on what seemed to be a large, snout-shaped island on the northern shore of the James (south of today's Williamsburg). They made this choice even though the land was linked to the mainland by a sandy neck or isthmus, which was submerged at high tide (it was completely washed away in the 1700s). The island was flat and low and half covered with tall marsh grass. The other half was forested with pine, with swamps to the north, and a marshy inlet emptying into the James. Something should have made them wonder why no Indians were living at such a choice spot. They would soon discover the reason. The brackish water of the river estuary produced typhoid and dysentery, and the mosquitoes that bred in the summer carried malaria. The place was a death trap, but, not knowing what the summer would bring, they picked the semi-island because it was easy to defend and had deep waters close to shore. One of the colonists, George Percy, reported: "The 13th of May we came to our seating place . . . where our ships do lie so near the shore that they are moored to the trees in six fathoms water."

Although an eventual disaster for the settlers, Jamestown was a brilliant choice from the crown's perspective, for it delivered the Chesapeake Bay to the English. Hub of the Atlantic Seaboard, the intricate Chesapeake, 193 miles long and twenty-five miles wide, was an inland sea with long tidal reaches and deep-water inlets. It was a unique display of geographical lacework, of 150 rivers and creeks, of a bay with an indented shoreline four thousand miles long, rivaling the French water route via the Great Lakes. For, though it was a contained system, blocked by the Appalachians, it opened a multitude of water routes to the green-wooded, rich-topsoiled land of Virginia, and offered a path to the sea over which colonists could ship their commodities from their own back doors. All in all, the Chesapeake was a providential find.

But not for the first settlers, who had set out on this long and dangerous voyage with as much preparation as for a weekend jaunt to the Channel Islands. They continued to wear linen and wool in the Virginia summer. They knew nothing about Indian tactics, which included driving the settlers inside their enclosures to keep them from planting. Fifty-four of the colonists were listed as "gentlemen," a euphemism for layabouts. They came with their footmen, and were "ten times more fit to spoil a commonwealth than either to begin one or help to maintain one," according to John Smith. Luckily, there were also a number of artisans, such as carpenters and bricklayers.

John Smith was a twenty-seven-year-old veteran of "that university of warre" in Europe. He had survived a number of escapades so improbable that the Victorian clergyman and novelist Charles Kingsley commented: "Fellow, either thou art the cunningest liar that ever earned a halter or else thou hast done a deed the like of which man never ventured." Smith did provide leadership at Jamestown, and deserves credit for his strength of character, excellent maps, and genuine affection for the New World.

There was certainly a dire need for leadership among the Jamestown novices whose mission was to hang on to their shoreline frontier for England, three thousand miles away. One of their instructions said, "In all your passages you must have great care not to offend the naturals," but it was hard to follow. Violence broke out four days after their May 14 disembarkation, when an Indian tried to steal a hatchet and was struck by a settler. Then Captain Newport, who had remained with his three ships while the settlers finished their fort, went exploring up river. On May 22, he found some Indians who were "our kind comrades." On May 23, he visited Powhatan, who offered roasted deer and guides. But on May 24, there was more theft. Two bullet bags containing shot and trading toys were missing. All was eventually restored, and Captain Newport gave the Indians the toys they had stolen, while "making it known to them the custom of England to be put to death for such offenses." On May 25, hung over from too much sack and aquavit, Powhatan was described as "very sick." On May 26, the Indians attacked the unfinished fort, in retaliation for the May 18 incident. The Indians were repulsed, thanks to the nearby ships' guns. There were seventeen wounded, one dead.

The settlers soon realized the necessity of an organized defense. During the day, they had to guard their workmen; at night, they had to stand watch, an added burden for the already discouraged and overwrought Englishmen. The Indians targeted stragglers. On May 29, Eustace Clovell came running into the fort with six arrows in him, crying "Arm! Arm!" He died six days later. On June 4, Indians hiding in the long grass "spied a man of ours going out to do his natural necessity, and shot him in the head and through the clothes."

By June 15, they had finished their triangular fort, made of a high palisade of pointed logs planted in the ground, with a base 420 feet long and two sides three hundred feet long. At each corner, a half-moon-shaped earthen platform was raised, upon which cannon were mounted, firing out through openings in the palisade.

This was a model that had been pioneered in Ireland, which the English were colonizing, and where they built fortified towns for protection against rebels.

On June 22, Captain Newport sailed back to England, promising to return with supplies within twenty weeks. Now the settlers' diet was reduced to small quantities of wheat and barley boiled with water. The grain had already lain twenty-six weeks in ships' holds and was filled with worms. Their drink was brackish water, consumed after hard labor in extreme heat.

To strengthen and restore their souls, they had religion—common prayer morning and evening, two sermons every Sunday, and holy communion every three months. Yet God was not in strict attendance, for, as John Smith later recalled, "the continual inundations of mistaking directions, factions, and numbers of unprovided libertines near consumed us all. . . ."

In his *Discovery of the Plantations of the Southern Colony in Virginia by the English*, George Percy gave a chilling recital of the almost daily deaths that began to diminish the small colony in August: "The sixth of August there died John Asbie of the bloody flux" (dysentery). "The ninth died George Flower of the swelling. The tenth died William Bruster, Gentleman, of a wound given by the savages. . . . The 14th, Jerome Alicock . . . died of a wound. The same day Francis Midwinter and Edward Morris (Corporal) died suddenly. The 15th there died Edward Browne and Stephen Galthorpe. The 16th there died Thomas Gower, Gentleman. The 17th, Thomas Mounslie, the 18th, Robert Pennington and John Martin, Gentlemen, the 19th Drue Piggase, Gentleman, the 22d there died Captain Bartholomew Gosnold, of our council. . . . They shot off all the ordnance in the fort in his honor. . . ." (Gosnold had captained a 1602 expedition to Newfoundland, where he discovered and named Martha's Vineyard). "The 24th died Edward Harington and George Walker. . . . The 28th died Thomas Stoodie" (Thomas Studley, keeper of the stores). In that one month of August 1607, there were nineteen deaths.

It was not what the colonists had been led to expect. Virginia had been described in the London Company's promotional literature as an earthly paradise, where gold mines and the spice route awaited. One such pamphlet was entitled *Joyful News Out of the New-Found World*. Morale at Jamestown in September 1607 was understandably low, and resentment focused on the nominal leader, who had in May been elected president of the seven-member Council described in the instructions. He was Edward Maria Wingfield, one of the original London investors to whom the 1606 charter had been granted, and the only one of that group to sail with the settlers.

He seems to have been a little too conscious of his own importance, and there was considerable grumbling, mainly concerning his role as distributor of the food stores. Council members drafted written charges against Wingfield, who was accused of having plenty while others starved, and of playing favorites.

To Wingfield, it was a mutiny. He accused his accusers of stealing from the common store. "It is said I did much banquet, and riot," he said, "I never had but one squirrel roasted." The Wingfield case raised the issue of equality for the first time among white men in America. In England, class distinctions were deeply ingrained, spelled out in such texts as this 1562 *Book of Homilies:* "Every class of people . . . hath appointed to them their duty and order. Some are in high degree, some are in low. Some kings and princes, some inferiors and subjects. . . ."

As a gentleman and a founding member of the London Company, Wingfield was hoping to maintain class distinctions in the New World. His defense was that lower-class citizens had no authority to make accusations about stores. John Smith, Wingfield argued, was little better than a servant, being the son of a yeoman (small farmer).

But at Jamestown class distinctions evaporated in the face of hardship; Wingfield was found guilty of stealing stores, imprisoned, and deported. Another member of the Council, George Kendall, was put to death for attempted mutiny in December 1607. These were early examples of frontier justice, far from the social stratification of London and Hampton Court.

Captain John Ratcliffe, the new president of the Council, ruled during a period of anarchy and disease. By September, wrote George Percy, the settlers were still living in tents "and in holes in the ground." They were "in miserable distress," Percy went on, "groaning in every corner of the fort, most pitiful to hear . . . some departing out of the world, many times three or four in a night. In the morning their bodies trailed out of their cabins like dogs to be buried."

When Captain Newport returned in January 1608, about a month later than his promised twenty weeks, there were thirty-eight settlers left alive of the original 104. Newport brought 120 new settlers, more than making up for the losses. Whatever its faults, the Virginia Company of London was efficient in the recruitment of settlers. In a classic case of misleading advertisement, Jamestown was billed as "Earth's Only Paradise"; when you got there, you found out that it was a hellhole under siege.

Under instructions to bring back gold, Captain Newport had returned to Jamestown with two gold refiners and two goldsmiths. "The worst mischief," wrote John Smith, "was our gilded refiners, with their golden promises. . . . There was no talk, no hope, no work, but dig gold, wash gold, refine gold, load gold." Captain Newport marched his refiners forty miles inland in his hunt for nonexistent mines. They dug and dug, found a little fool's gold, and ended up filling the ships' holds with cedar.

In April 1608, another ship arrived, with twenty-eight gentlemen and twenty-three laborers. By that time, twenty-eight more settlers had died. In October, Captain Newport was back, with two ships and seventy new recruits, including eight German and Polish glassmakers, and the first two women, Mrs. Forrest and her maid, Anne Burras, who soon married the carpenter John Laydon. At this point, the Jamestown population stood somewhere around two hundred, though the figure changed from day to day.

In London, the investors wanted to start seeing some profits, and now placed their hopes in glass, pitch, and tar. When Newport left Jamestown in the late fall of 1608, he took with him "trials, pitch, tar, glass, frankincense and soap ash, with that clapboard and wainscot which could be provided."

John Smith had been named president of the Council in replacement of the lackluster Ratcliffe, but the settlers' situation had not improved. Disease and Indian harassment continued to restrict mobility, cutting down on planting, hunting, and fishing. There was plenty of food out there, but it wasn't worth an arrow through the neck to go looking for it. Smith instituted a policy of "if you don't work you don't eat," while complaining of greenhorn settlers. "All the trash they could get in London was sent to us in Virginia," he wrote.

Under Smith, there was some progress, and by the spring of 1609 they had planted thirty acres of corn, their three sows had increased to sixty pigs, and they had five hundred chickens. Jamestown was becoming a viable concern, though Indian relations did not improve. In the winter of 1608–9, during a corn shortage, Captain Ratcliffe took twenty-six men to trade with Powhatan.

When he accused the Indians of trying to cheat him in the way they bagged the corn, they hid in the fields, attacked his men while they were carrying the corn to their ship, and killed all but two. According to George Percy, Ratcliffe was "bound under a tree naked, with fire before [him]. And by Powhatan's women his flesh was scraped from his bones with mussel shells, and before his face thrown into the fire. And so for want of circumspection, he miserably perished."

On the other side of the ledger, Smith wrote that, when they were on short rations that winter, "it pleased God (in our extremity) to move the Indians to bring us corn, ere it was half ripe, to refresh us, when we rather expected they would destroy us."

In May 1609, they discovered that their corn reserves had rotted in the casks. Because there were too many mouths to feed, Smith sent two hundred of his flock out to the shore to live on fish and oysters. They did better than the settlers inside the fort.

In London, armed with a new charter, the Virginia Company increased its powers. Company leaders believed that the council system was not working, and that some sort of one-man rule was needed if Jamestown were ever to run profitably or help expand English influence. Reflecting this dual purpose, the new charter made the company officers governors of a province, empowered to deal with questions of government and land management. New shares were issued, at twelve and a half pounds apiece. But since there was no dividend, stockholders were offered profits in land, at a hundred acres per share. This was the first appearance of individual land ownership at Jamestown. In addition, the company pledged to improve the quality of its recruits, so that "the lascivious sons, masters of bad servants, and wives of ill husbands" would now be excluded. A governor was appointed to enforce company policies. So began the second phase of Jamestown colony—after the do-it-yourself period, a time of garrison-style military rule.

Since the designated governor, Lord De la Warr, was not feeling well, he sent his lieutenant governor, Sir Thomas Gates, a seasoned veteran of the Netherlands campaigns. Gates left England with the largest contingent so far—nine ships and five hundred settlers. But one ship sank in a storm, and the ship that Gates was on ran aground in the Bermudas.

In August 1609, the seven remaining ships arrived, with three hundred new settlers, among whom, Smith wrote, were "many unruly gallants packed thither by their friends to escape their destinies." This was no longer his problem: in September, he was seriously wounded in a gunpowder explosion and had to go back to England. When he left, on or about October 4, there were 490 settlers in Jamestown, armed with three hundred muskets. George Percy was left in charge until the arrival of Gates.

That winter of 1609–10, with a crowd of new settlers and inadequate food reserves, became known as "the starving time." It was the absolute nadir for Jamestown, with many more deaths than the first year. Percy had to string men up for robbing the stores. Soon they were down to eating their horses, their dogs and cats, rats and mice. They cursed the company's treasurer in London, Sir Thomas Smythe, for failing to send supplies. "So miserable was our estate," wrote Percy, "that the happiest day that some of them hoped to see was when the Indians had killed a mare—they wished whilst she was boiling that Sir Thomas Smythe was upon her back in the kettle."

Having eaten all the animals, the colonists fell to eating humans. An Indian they had killed and buried was disinterred, and they ate him "boiled and stewed with roots and herbs." "Some have licked the blood which hath fallen from their weak fellows," Percy noted.

One man murdered his pregnant wife, threw the unborn child into the James River, chopped up the mother, salted her, and ate her. The man had to be hanged by the thumbs with weights on his feet to extract a confession, Percy said. John Smith, writing about events that took place after his departure, made this spousal cannibalism sound humorous by saying that the man had powdered his wife before eating her. "Now, whether she was better roasted, boiled, or carbonated, I know not, but of such a dish as powdered wife I never heard."

Nor had the settlers been able to negotiate a peace with the Indians, who were "as fast killing them without the fort as the famine and pestilence within." Oblivious to actual conditions, the London directors were instructing the settlers to deal with the Indians "by all lawful means." So began the credo that the only good Indian is a dead Indian. George Percy wrote his brother that he had attacked an Indian village ruled by a queen, and had taken her and her children to his boat. He had wanted to keep the children captive, but, "a council being called, it was agreed to put the children to death, the which was effected by throwing them overboard and shooting out their brains in the water. . . ."

On May 24, 1610, Sir Thomas Gates, the lieutenant governor long shipwrecked in the Bermudas, arrived at Jamestown and was appalled by what he saw. Only sixty settlers had survived the starving time, whereas there had been about three hundred when John Smith had left the previous October. Of those sixty, scarcely ten could be called able-bodied, according to a young man named Ralph Hamor, who arrived with Gates. After listening to the survivors, all "accusing or excusing each other," Gates decided to abandon the colony.

All embarked on June 7 in four small boats down the river. But as they sailed down the James, they spotted a skiff coming upriver. It was Lord De la Warr, finally arrived to assume his duties as governor, with 150 men. The hand of God! They now had supplies, men to make up some of the losses, and the will to start anew. But, practically upon landing, Lord De la Warr came down with both of the maladies of the place, scurvy and dysentery, and remained on his sickbed for the rest of his stay, while Gates governed.

De la Warr left Jamestown in March 1611 at the age of thirty-three with his health permanently damaged. Acting Governor Sir Thomas Dale arrived in May with three hundred more men. At this point, the turnaround at Jamestown began. In Dale's five years of governing Jamestown, he showed himself to be both tough and astute. It was said that he ruled by the gospel, the knout, and the firing squad. Stealing an ear of corn, or committing blasphemy, was punishable by death. Swearing was punished with a bodkin—a large needle for punching holes in leather—through the tongue.

Deserters were hanged, or broken on the wheel, or shot to death. Work was regulated at so many hours per day, and idlers were given the lash. It was a regimented and authoritarian garrison life. Twice daily, the bell tolled for church services.

Dale also introduced a policy of giving three acres of land to settlers who had satisfied their obligation to the company (those who hadn't paid their way over were on seven-year indentures). This marked the start of the capitalist system in English America. Land transfers to settlers, begun in 1614, were described by Ralph Hamor: "When our people were fed out of the common store and labored jointly in the manuring of the ground and the planting of corn, glad was that man who could slip from his labor: nay the most honest of them in a general business would not take so much faithful and true pains in a week as now he will do in a day; neither cared they for the increase, presuming that howsoever their harvest prospered, the general store must maintain them, by which we reaped not so much corn from the labors of 20 men as three men have done for themselves."

All these reforms worked together. Powhatan's daughter Pocahontas had been taken hostage in 1613, because Powhatan was holding eight English soldiers. A hostage exchange was proposed, but John Rolfe, a settler who had arrived in Virginia in 1610, had developed a strong attraction to the young princess. Having lost a baby daughter on the voyage and buried his wife soon after arriving, Rolfe was understandably lonely.

Disturbed by his growing affection for a "heathen," he wrote to Governor Dale with a baffled Anglican sincerity that "my hearty and best thoughts are and have a long time been so entangled and enthralled in so intricate a labyrinth that I was even wearied to unwind myself thereout." It was love in the New World, but it was also détente, not unlike the European marriages of teen-age infantas with mature kings in order to cement alliances. Rolfe rationalized his lust, by accepting the match as a "godly tax" in the interest of improved Indian relations. If only the policy of mixed marriages had spread, the sole quarrels between Indians and colonists might have been marital.

The peace with Powhatan lasted eight years. During this period, farmers were safe to plant tobacco, which gave to the expanding Virginia colony the special character that Puritanism gave to New England. The experimenter in tobacco as well as in marriage was John Rolfe, who seems to have collected some West Indian seed during the time he was shipwrecked in Bermuda. After a few years of trial and error, to improve "the byting tast" of the native weed, he found the right combination of soil and seed, and in March 1614 shipped four barrels of the leaf to London. This was the most momentous fact in the history of Virginia, and one of the most momentous for all America.

For the cultivation of tobacco saved Virginia, the first English colony, despite some early naysayers, including King James, who believed that smoking was harmful. But already there was a tobacco lobby claiming that, the more you smoked, the better you felt; promoters made up jingles such as "Earth ne'er did breed / Such a jovial weed." This colonial propaganda is in direct line to Marlboro Country, or to the old Lucille Ball program, with Lucille saying, "Give your husband a carton of Philip Morris," and Desi Arnaz chiming in with "Smart move!"

Whatever the royal reservations, the reason for planting tobacco was simple: in England it sold for three shillings a pound. Virginia became a one-crop colony, exporting twenty-five hundred pounds in 1616 and more than one million pounds in 1628. The tobacco leaf should have been on the Virginia flag as the maple leaf is on Canada's. Tobacco depleted the soil, and was labor-intensive, and slavery was waiting in the wings, but in the 1600s it was the road to riches, the substitute for undiscovered gold.

It took a lot of skill and year-round hard work to grow tobacco. In January and February, tiny seeds were arranged in seedbeds in parallel rows, and covered with brush to protect them from frost. In May, the young slips were transplanted to open fields; after a certain number of leaves appeared, the slips were topped to hasten the growth of the broad lower leaves. The topping was done with the thumb, and it was said that you could always tell a tobacco planter by the thickness of his thumb. The plants had to be "suckered"—removing small shoots that spring from the junction of each leaf with the stalk. They had to be inspected for flea beetles, cutworms, and hornworms, and watched for diseases such as hollow stalk. They had to be weeded until they reached their full growth, five to seven feet, in six weeks.

When the leaves began to spot and discolor, the plants were cut off at the base with a tobacco knife and left in the fields to wilt. Then they were brought in for "sweating," as it was then called. It took the planters a few years to figure out that the best way to cure tobacco was not to keep it in piles on the ground under a cover of hay, but to suspend it on lines in a barn where the air circulated. After three to six weeks of curing and thorough drying, the brittle leaves were bound together in small bundles called "hands," and packed into wooden casks or hogsheads four feet high and two feet in diameter. Workers placed the "hands" in smooth layers and packed the hogsheads tight, but not too tight (which was called "squeezing it to death"), secured the head, placed the hoops, and weighed and marked each hogshead with the planter's trademark. Then the hogsheads of Sweet-Scented or Oronocco (the two kinds of leaf) were hauled to the wharf in two-wheeled ox carts, loaded onto small sloops, called "flats," which were anchored in the nearest creek, and floated downriver to the warehouse. If hogsheads arrived at the warehouse with broken staves, there was likely to be pilfering. In his 1782 *Essay on Tobacco*, William Tatham wrote: "I believe it would not be hard to prove that Negro attendants at the Richmond warehouses [have enjoyed] the choicest chewing tobacco."

All this planting, transplanting, topping, suckering, weeding and worming, cutting and curing, binding and packing required a large work force. At first, indentured servants were used, but as they won their freedom and became landowners themselves, slavery was slowly introduced. The first slaves were brought to Jamestown in a Dutch ship in 1619, and in a 1625 census, ten were listed in Jamestown proper.

There was a period in which black slaves and white servants overlapped on the plantations, working and living together, though Robert Beverley, the early historian of Virginia, observed that "some distinction is made between them in their clothes and food." As late as 1669, there was a Virginia court case in which a white woman servant complained of having to take orders from a Negro overseer.

But, over time, the planters tended to acquire an all-slave labor force. For one thing, the white workers disliked working alongside the slaves. For another, the planters preferred slaves, finding them more docile and cheaper to keep. Also, they reproduced themselves, and it was difficult for them to run away. And, as Robert Beverley observed, whereas white servants worked for their freedom, blacks "are called slaves, in respect of the time of their servitude, because it is for life."

When the weed became the staple of the Old Dominion, much of the colony's social and political life was affected by it. There was a growing body of tobacco legislation—crop limitations, for instance, and inspections for quality and weight. The affairs of the colony became interwoven with the staple when tobacco became legal tender, as in: "I will give you ten hogsheads of tobacco for your horse." This form of barter became law in 1640. Public servants and soldiers, as well as taxes and court fines, were paid in tobacco. Tavern bills were settled in tobacco. Reluctant tithe-payers saved their trashiest weed for the guardians of their souls. When ninety young ladies arrived at Jamestown in 1619 as prospective brides, each was redeemed with 120 pounds of Virginia leaf.

There were drawbacks. Using tobacco as a currency meant that debts were paid seasonally, and the weed itself was perishable and of uneven quality. King James, who detested tobacco, was forever curtailing and taxing production. He could not ban it, for he needed the revenue, and had no wish to ruin the colony. After 1614, "all Rustica was cleared to plant Tabacum," in the words of Sir Thomas Dale.

Sir Thomas left Jamestown in 1616, aboard the same ship that took John Rolfe and Pocahontas back to England (where she died of smallpox). By this time, the colony had spread up and down the James River. Four hundred settlers were dispersed in six new settlements: Henrico lay upriver, at the falls of the James, five miles south of today's Richmond; Kecoughtan was about forty miles downriver, right on the Chesapeake, at today's Newport News; Dale's Gift lay at today's Cape Charles, on that spit of land that drops down from eastern Maryland to close off the Chesapeake, and was employed in salt production. Three collective farms were named after an ancient English land unit, the Bermuda, West, and Shirley hundreds. At Bermuda Hundred, downriver from Henrico, on a looping section of river known as "the curls," they were making pitch and tar and potash; at West and Shirley hundreds they planted tobacco. There was less disease, thanks to the application of sanitation laws, and no starvation, thanks to the cash crop of tobacco and their own farms. At Kecoughtan they planted twenty-five hundred acres of corn. Jamestown was becoming Virginia. The Indians kept thinking, "Now they have all the land they could possibly want." But they were wrong. The "coat-wearing people," as the Algonquins called them, always wanted more.

Sir Thomas Dale entrusted the colony to one of his Netherlands captains, a tough and disciplined soldier named George Yeardley. He used his position to acquire land and became known as "the right worthy statesman for his own profit." With prosperity, the planter mentality became self-seeking and greedy. Wanting to organize a militia, William Capps was put off with excuses by his fellow planters, who told him: "Now, sir, here's another devil. You know amongst most men the old proverb is, charity begins at home. Take away one of my men, there's 200 plants gone, that's 500 weight of tobacco. Yea, and what shall this man do but run after the Indians?"

The Indians at that time were friendly, lulling the settlers into a false sense of security. Yeardley taught some to fire muskets so they could bring him game. When Captain Samuel Argall arrived early in 1617 to replace Yeardley, he found Jamestown a neglected town, with "but five or six houses, the church down, the palisades broken, the bridge [to the mainland] in pieces, the well of fresh water spilled, the storehouses used for the church. . . . The savages as frequent in their [the settlers'] houses as themselves, whereby they were become expert in our arms, and had a great many in their custody and possession . . ."

Argall went back to a policy of firmness, and announced a series of new laws in May 1618. Foremost among them was one "against teaching Indians to shoot with guns on pain of death to learner and teacher." Others included the injunction that every man must plant two acres of corn, and the stipulation that every person had to go to church on Sundays and holidays or be put in irons.

That year, a drought was followed by hailstorms, spoiling both the corn and tobacco crops. Supplies that had taken five months to cross arrived in poor condition. On the bright side, Thomas Lambert discovered air-curing, and Argall wrote the company that "Mr. Lambert has found out that tobacco cures better on lines than in heaps and desires lines to be sent. . . ." But shortages bred dissatisfaction, and complaints began reaching London that Argall was embezzling stores.

The still-unwell Lord De la Warr was sent back out to Virginia to reassume his governorship, but died en route. So the company sent Yeardley for a second term. By the time he arrived in April 1619, Samuel Argall had already left.

Yeardley's second term as governor was the start of Jamestown's third period—after anarchy and military rule, the boom years. In 1619, 1620, and 1621, the company sent over forty-two ships and 3,570 men and women. That the colony could absorb such numbers was a sign of its vigor and prosperity. The numbers were due in part to the new management in London, under the energetic leadership of Sir Edwin Sandys, son of the archbishop of York and treasurer of the company, who pushed through big budgets and stepped up the recruiting.

The company's vision had changed. The goal was no longer simply commercial. Jamestown was seen as a permanent outpost of England in the New World, with a sort of embryonic social and political life. Thus the company sent out women, writing in its report that "the plantation can never flourish till families be planted, and the respect of their wives and children fix the people on the soil." But with every improvement came problems. There were so few women for so many men that breach-of-promise incidents arose, with women pledging to marry several prospective husbands. A law had to be passed that, if a woman promised herself to more than one, "she shall for such offense undergo either corporal punishment [such as whippings] or other punishment by fine." Thus, in 1624, Eleanor Sprague, who was promised to Richard Pierce, was put on trial because she had been overheard in conversation with Robert Marshall; when he asked her, "Art thou mine?," she replied, "Yes, with all my heart, and thou art mine art thou not?" And they began discussing what they would wear at their wedding.

In some matters, the London Company had a different agenda from that of the Virginia settlers. London frowned on basing the colony's prosperity on the vice of smoking. Tobacco led to the dispersal of the colony. Settlers were increasingly far-flung, and could not attend divine service unless each plantation had a minister, which was impractical.

In its efforts to diversify the economy, the company sent out Frenchmen with vines and silkworms, but these halfhearted attempts to bring silk and wine to Virginia came to nothing. Six Italians were also sent out to build a glass furnace to make trading beads, but soon after their arrival one of them murdered his wife. George Sandys, Sir Edwin Sandys' brother, who was treasurer in Jamestown, said of the Italians in 1623: "A more damned crew never vomited." There was also a shipbuilding project. But all attempts at diversification failed: tobacco was king.

There were several methods of acquiring land. Investors in London could take their profits in land and send over settlers who formed "hundreds." By company decree, they had to be at least ten miles apart, and tended to become autonomous mini-colonies, with their own backers, recruiters, and transporters. Indentured servants who had worked out their terms were given thirty acres. There were special deals—an apothecary was allowed to bring over his two children free if he promised to continue to exercise his profession in the colony. Boys over fifteen who were a burden to the London parishes were taken off their hands by the company.

But the biggest inducement to settle was the head-rights system launched in 1618. This awarded fifty acres for every person whose passage over was paid. If you brought over ten servants, you were entitled to five hundred acres, on condition that the land be farmed within three years. The head right was not for a particular piece of land, but the right to stake out acreage wherever you could find it; this fostered chaotic and piecemeal expansion with minimum oversight. There were plenty of loopholes to exploit: A Virginia gentleman returning from a vacation in England could claim a head right. So could a sailor touching at a Virginia port. A head right might require no more than taking an oath in a county court before a friendly judge. Captains on tobacco ships entered head-right claims each time they landed at Jamestown. No one checked for duplicate entries. Fraud became an integral part of land acquisition. A study of head rights in local Virginia records showed that, between 1635 and 1639, eighty-two thousand claims were made, adding up to a nice parcel of land—4.1 million acres.

Many of these head rights were for indentured servants. Indenture was a modified form of the apprenticeship system that had existed in England for centuries. It was widely accepted that apprentices should be bound out to masters to learn various trades, and it was only natural to extend the system to the colonies. In 1619, John Pory, a member of Parliament who had come out with Yeardley, wrote: "Our principal wealth consists of servants."

Recruiting servants became a cottage industry. Agents, or "crimps," brought the men in, got them registered, and turned them over to a merchant or captain, who sold the indenture to a planter on arrival. They roamed as far as Ireland, where a disgruntled recruiter reported in 1669 that men were "loath to leave the smoke of their own cabin if they can but beg near it." At a time when prison sentences were harsh (death was the punishment for stealing anything worth more than a shilling), a journey to the New World attracted some of the more downwardly mobile sectors of society: petty thieves, runaway apprentices, husbands who'd deserted their wives. A number of convicts were given the choice between jail and indenture. It was said that America was a haven for the godly and the convicted, and Virginia got the convicted.

As the ship neared the Virginia shore, convicts were handed wigs, fictitious trades were invented, and arrangements were made. After it landed, the planters came aboard and walked the prospects up and down, chatting them up and feeling their biceps. It was like a cattle market or a horse fair, except that these were talking horses. Of course there were servant problems—the convicts poxing the daughters of the colonists, disobedience, runaways. Once legislative assemblies were formed, much of their time was spent in drafting laws governing servant behavior.

Indications are, however, that the arrival in Virginia was a big letdown after what the recruits had been led to expect. Richard Frethorne, a young servant from Manchester who arrived in December 1621, thought he was coming to "Earth's Only Paradise." Instead, his cloak was stolen aboard ship, and all he was given to eat during the voyage was peas and loblolly (a thick gruel). Upon arriving, he was sent to Martin's Hundred, five miles downriver from Jamestown. Rather than paradise, he found a land of sickness, "as the scurvy and the bloody flux and divers other diseases." He had been promised venison but never saw any, "and people cry out all day and night, 'Oh that they were in England without their limbs,' and would not care if they lost any limb to be in England again, yea though they begged from door to door."

Frethorne was sent to load and unload ships in Jamestown, where a gunsmith named Jackson befriended him, lending him a cabin and giving him some codfish. But he desperately wanted to go home, and wrote his parents to see if they could arrange it, adding that he did not have one penny to buy spice or sugar or strong waters, "without which one cannot live here. . . ." At Martin's Hundred, he was underfed. "I have eaten more in a day at home than I have allowed me here for a week." He asked his parents to send him some cheese, and pack it so that "there are coopers' chips between every cheese or the heat of the old hold will rot them."

The shift from martial law to a more representative type of rule, whereby the colonists had a say in the matters that affected them, came about through the leadership of Edwin Sandys, who believed that cooperation was helped by participation. When a group became large and complex enough, there came a point where all sorts of problems arose that had to be legislated and adjudicated, and in Virginia that point had been reached.

Thus, on July 30, 1619, in the choir of the Jamestown church, Governor Yeardley presided over the first legislative assembly ever convened on the North American continent. It was called the House of Burgesses, and it was unicameral, consisting of the governor, six counselors, and two burgesses from each of the ten settlements. According to the proceedings of the first assembly, laws were passed against idleness, gaming, drunkenness, and excess in apparel. Two other matters involved forest diplomacy. There was a complaint against John Martin for sending a shallop into the bay to trade with the Indians, and taking their corn by force when they refused to trade. Another complaint was against the interpreter

Henry Spelman, for conferring with Chief Opechancanough. He was accused of having "spoken unreverently and maliciously against the present Governor." Running down the governor to an Indian chief was seen as close to treason, and Spelman was sentenced to a seven-year term of indenture.

The early court records of Virginia—that is, the few records that survived the burning of the Richmond State Court Building during the Civil War—provide a kind of archaeology of private behavior that doesn't usually get into history books. Ordinary people's lives are revealed as they were centuries ago. Through their misdemeanors and felonies, we can see how they spoke and how their minds worked.

For instance, in 1625, Edward Sharples, clerk of the Virginia Council, was sentenced to have his ears cut off for leaking Council proceedings to the Privy Council in London. This problem goes back a long way, as does marital discord. In August 1625, at the Bermuda Hundred, there was such a racket coming from the house of the Johnstons that the plantation commander, Mr. Bransby, sent over two of his servants, who found Mr. and Mrs. Johnston fighting on the bed. Bransby went over and told Johnston that "if he did beat and abuse his wife any more he would beat him tightly." At which Johnston got his musket and pointed it at Bransby, saying: "What have you to do here, you had best keep back or I will make you stand back." When the case came to trial, Bransby's comment to the court, reflecting the origins of some of the settlers, was: "This trouble I have for parting Newgate birds and Bridewell whores" (referring to two famous London prisons). Charged with "continual squabbling and misuse of his wife," and contempt against the plantation commander, Johnston was fined forty pounds.

And here is the first case of sodomy to be brought to trial in America: In August 1624, the good ship *Ambrose* was riding on the James River, and a crew member, Richard Williams, "being then in drink," asked the cabin boy, Couse, to lay a clean pair of sheets on his bed. Then Williams "would have Couse come into ye bed to him," which Couse refused, so Williams cut Couse's codpiece (a pouch then worn at the crotch of men's breeches) "and made him go into the bed and then lay upon him . . . and so by force he turned him upon his belly, and so did he put him to pain in the fundament and did wet him and after did call for a napkin." In an early example of capital punishment, Williams was put to death for buggery, while the cabin boy was indentured to a colonist. Some months later, in February 1625, a colonist named Thomas Hatch said that in his view Williams had been put to death wrongfully. For expressing this opinion, Hatch was sentenced to be whipped from the fort to the gallows and back, and to be set in the pillory and lose one of his ears.

Generally, however, in those years of Yeardley's second term, from 1619 to 1621, things seemed to be going well, and a 1620 report to the London Company said: "Every man planteth himself where he pleaseth and followeth his business securely." New plantations were spreading out along choice veins of fertile soil. The colony was now divided into four boroughs: Jamestown, Charles City, Henrico, and Kecoughtan (renamed Elizabeth City). The company's single complaint was that the planters liked only "their darling tobacco, to the overthrow of all other staple commodities."

When Sir Francis Wyatt arrived at Jamestown in October 1621 to relieve Yeardley as governor, he "found the country in very great amity and confidence with the natives," from whom he received a welcoming message. He replied that he held the peace so firm the sky would fall before he dissolved it. Seldom was a gun or a sword worn, and the bad old days of guard duty were long gone.

But the Indians had begun to see the Jamestown colony for what it was—an invasion. To their consternation, fresh settlers were arriving by the thousands and spreading inland from the banks of the James. They were taking lands that didn't belong to them and had to be stopped. It was now or never. In the fall of 1621, Chief Opechancanough, Powhatan's brother and successor, assembled some of the other chiefs. At a ceremony during which Powhatan's bones were disinterred, they all pledged a concerted attack upon the plantations. Their aim was to rid themselves of the settlers.

But even as they planned the attack, they befriended their enemy. Opechancanough was friends with George Thorpe, who was in charge of building a school at Henrico for the "children of infidels" (he was also the first settler to distill corn whiskey). Thorpe built a house with a lock and a key for Opechancanough. The Indian chief admired it so much that he locked and unlocked his door a hundred times a day. And when the Indians said they were afraid of the English mastiffs, Thorpe had some killed in their presence, to the great displeasure of their owners.

Set for March 1622, the attack was well thought out. The Indians had the advantage of surprise, and benefited from the company's system of placing the "hundreds" ten miles apart: they could be separately attacked without giving the alarm. Word was sent out to all Indian villages to meet on the hour and day appointed. The pretense of friendliness was maintained to the end, so that two days before the attack, the Indians guided some lost settlers through the woods with much kindness.

On the morning of March 22, the Indians came as usual with provisions to sell: turkey, deer, fish, fruit. They sat down at breakfast with the planters, and then, according to the governor's report, "the Indians attacked the settlers, whom immediately with their own tools they slew most barbarously, not sparing either age or sex, man, woman or child." They also killed the men they found at work in their fields, "well knowing in what places and quarters each of our men were."

The surprise was not complete, however: a converted Indian warned his master, Richard Pace, "who had used him like a son." Pace at once rowed across the river to give the alarm. In this way, Jamestown was spared.

The attack was nonetheless devastating. Out of a population of twelve hundred, 347 settlers were killed at thirty-one different sites. Three members of the Council were among the victims— Nathaniel Powell, who had been in Jamestown since 1607 and owned a six-hundred-acre plantation; the kindly George Thorpe; and the man who, through his marriage to Pocahontas, had been the architect of détente—John Rolfe, who had returned to Virginia in 1618 after the death of his wife. In many cases, the bodies of the settlers were mutilated, and the Indians "carried some parts away in derision, with base and brutish triumph."

At Martin's Hundred, where there had been 140, only sixty-two remained, including the by-now frantic Richard Frethorne, who had noticed the Indians "of late growing very bold." He had seen a marksmanship contest between an Indian and one of the planters, Mr. Charles. When they fired at a bit of white paper, "the Indian hit it at the first, but Mr. Charles could not hit it." Now Martin's Hundred was destroyed, with but two houses left standing, and a piece of church. The survivors were told that they must go out and live off the land, eating the bark of trees and the mold upon the ground. "I thought no head had been able to hold so much water as that which doth daily flow from mine eyes,"

Richard Frethorne wrote his sponsor in Manchester, Mr. Bateman, "and my humble request is that I may be freed out of this Egypt."

George Sandys, the Jamestown treasurer, was a broken man. Dispersal, he felt, was the cause of the tragedy. Their instructions to keep the "hundreds" ten miles apart had come from men in London "who know nothing of Virginia. . . ." Each family was too far from its neighbor, and the only reason was land greed. And now "the living were hardly able to bury the dead. . . ."

From the Indians' viewpoint, the attack had been an attempt to rid themselves of the English occupier. It had, however, two unintended consequences. First, it created a loss of court support for the London Company, which was taken over in 1624 by the crown. Second, it gave the settlers a good reason to go after the Indians.

Now the English planters embarked upon a policy of extermination and enslavement borrowed from the conquistadors, under instruction from the company, which had once advised them to treat the Indians with kindness. In a letter from London on August 1, 1622, the settlers were told to wage total war, "surprising the Indians in their habitations, intercepting them in their hunting, burning their towns, demolishing their temples, plucking their wares, carrying away their corn, and depriving them of succor or relief."

The settlers were only too glad to oblige, although it took them a while to get back on their feet. Adding to their woes, a supply ship landed some poisoned beer, which killed two hundred. The total number of deaths from disease in 1622 was six hundred, but the company made up for the losses by sending sixteen ships with eight hundred more settlers. Since they seemed to have no trouble finding recruits, news of the massacre must have been hushed up.

In the countermassacre, armed bands of settlers went out hunting Indians. The Virginia Council reported to the London Company on January 20, 1623: "In all places we have slain diverse [Indians], burned their towns, destroyed their wares and corn. . . . We have slain more of them this year than hath been slain before since the beginning of the colony." Another progress report was sent to London on January 30, 1624: "We have to our uttermost abilities revenged ourselves upon the savages on this river, cut down their corn in all places. . . . Burning down the houses they have reedified, and with the slaughters of many have enforced them to abandon their plantations. . . ." Thus were the Indians cleared from the James River area. From this initial Tidewater base, settlers would soon spread, and the seventeenth-century plantation society would blossom.

But the London Company's days were numbered. Edwin Sandys was under investigation, charged with taking kickbacks from a baker and loading ships with goods for the private gain of investors. He was also charged with printing books and ballads describing the "happy state of the plantation, which was most unreasonably put in practice this last Lent [of 1622], when the colony was in most extreme misery."

These rosy books and ballads had kept the colony going. Without reinforcements, Jamestown would have failed. It is estimated that, in its eighteen-year existence (1606–24), the company sent out a total of 7,289 settlers, of whom 6,040 either died or went back to England. That's about six out of seven.

In 1627, there were about fifteen hundred settlers, divided into fifty plantations, with few Indians left on the James River. The colonists were reaching out along the water routes, the York and the Potomac, breaking the brown-green forest cover with tilled clearings, frame houses, tobacco sheds, and wharves poking into the tidal waters. There was a rising class of wealthy planters, like George Yeardley, who had twenty-four servants. No family of planters was so poor that it did not have hogs and poultry, and malt and barley to make good ale; few had to drink water, and the better sort were well furnished with sack and aquavit. They were all applied to their labor, growing enough corn and tobacco so that they didn't have to get food from the Indians. Indentured servants who had served their terms could obtain land at favorable rates and join the plantation society. In the Virginia Assembly of 1629, seven burgesses were ex-servants. With the easy acquisition of land, Virginians became upwardly mobile, except for the slaves.

CHAPTER SIX

THE PILGRIM FRONTIER

In 1620, the English gained a second foothold on the Atlantic coast of North America when a group of religious dissidents landed at Plymouth. Like Jamestown, this was a private venture, not backed by the crown.

Leiden Pilgrim Document Center of the Municipal Archives, Boisotkade 2A, 2311 PZ Leiden.

The "Old Hundredth," in Ainsworth's Psalter, was sung by the Pilgrims in their services.

But here I cannot but stay and make a pause, and stand half amazed at this poor people's present condition; and so I think will the reader, too, when he well considers the same. Being thus passed the vast ocean, and a sea of troubles before in their preparation . . . they had now no friends to welcome them nor inns to entertain or refresh their weatherbeaten bodies; no houses or much less towns to repair to, to seek for succour. It is recorded in Scripture as a mercy to the Apostle and his shipwrecked company, that the barbarians showed them no small kindness in refreshing them, but these savage barbarians, when they met with them (as after will appear) were readier to fill their sides full of arrows than otherwise. . . . What could they see but a hideous and desolate wilderness, full of wild beasts and wild men.

WILLIAM BRADFORD

In December 1620, while Jamestown was still in its difficult years, another group of settlers landed in Plymouth Bay, six hundred miles to the north. This singular group had not come for any of the reasons that had motivated its predecessors—not for gold or spices, not for conquest or conversion, not to take advantage of a head-rights offer. Not for any of these reasons had the pilgrims come, but out of their dire and inescapable need to sustain themselves as outcasts.

The Pilgrims are our first example of that restless American mobility that was supposed to have originated on the frontier. They left Scrooby in England for Amsterdam in Holland, and Amsterdam for Leiden, and then decided they must leave Leiden. There was nowhere left to go but the New World, and this was the Pilgrim paradox: in order to maintain their spiritual life intact, they chose the one place where the forces of change would create the very fragmentation they were so desperate to avoid. In seeking to salvage their community, they destroyed it. And yet in the process they made a brave attempt.

Puritanism rose in the 1560s in England among those who wanted to purify the Anglican Church of all vestiges of Catholicism. They didn't want the ring in marriages, or the sign of the cross in baptisms, or bowing and kneeling, or brocaded vestments.

At first, the Puritan clergy was punished with fines and exactions. But then the group split into sects. The breakaway branch, known as Separatists, or Brownists (after one of their leaders, Robert Browne), was more extreme; its members refused to attend the state church and wanted no ecclesiastical hierarchy (from bishops to pope to king). They wanted nothing more than a pastor proclaiming the Word. Their religion was a rule of life, a hunt for God's intention. These men, who argued all day about the nature of salvation, were considered dangerous, and many were jailed under Queen Elizabeth, who had made Anglicanism the state religion.

One of their congregations formed in the unlikely hamlet of Scrooby, a post station in central England, on the Great Northern Road between London and the North Country, near today's Sheffield. John Robinson, a Cambridge graduate, thirty years old in 1606, was the pastor, and burned with the true Separatist fire. The whole thrust of his beliefs was the submergence of the individual to the common good, and the perfectibility of man through "walking with God." "Never honor a gay coat more than a virtuous mind," he said. Two prominent members of the congregation were William Brewster, the postmaster's son, who had also gone to Cambridge, then known as "a vile cess-pool of sedition," and William Bradford, the seventeen-year-old son of a small landholder. Bradford writes that they were "hunted and persecuted on every side, so as their former afflictions were but as flea-bitings in comparison of these which now came upon them. For some were taken and clapped up in prison, and others had their houses beset and watched night and day, and hardly escaped their hands."

So, in 1607, they decided to leave the land of their birth for Holland, where they did not know the language or have any assurance of employment. They were willing to pull up stakes in order to live according to their own dictates, without any thought police.

The Scrooby Pilgrims were betrayed by the captain they had hired to take them to Holland. On their departure, the authorities searched them for money—"Yea, even the women, further than became modesty," wrote Bradford. After a series of false starts, they finally reached Amsterdam in 1608, and sang their hymns on the banks of the Zuyder Zee.

It was the Golden Age of the Dutch Republic, but they stayed in Amsterdam less than a year, not wanting to get caught up in the quarrels of the two English Separatist congregations already there.

On February 2, 1609, the Pilgrims, now numbering about a hundred, moved to Leiden, a walled city on the Rhine, only twenty-two miles southwest of Amsterdam. Holland's second city had a population of forty thousand (a third of them refugees) and a famous university. By now, the pattern was set—the Pilgrims moved somewhere, found something amiss, and moved on to a supposedly better place.

In Holland, Bradford wrote, "they heard a strange and un-couth language" and "they saw the grim and grisly face of poverty coming upon them like an armed man," but at least they now had religious freedom. The Dutch left them alone. Leiden was in fact a haven for members of almost every religious group known to man: Roman Catholics, Eastern Orthodox, Jews, gypsies, Lutherans, Dutch Mennonites, Dutch Reformed, German Reformed, Walloon Reformed, English and Scottish Reformed, English Separatists (our brave band), Libertines, Remonstrants, Rijnsburger Collegiants, Moslems, Moravians, Quakers, Huguenots, Russian Mennonites, Czech Reformed, and Polish Socinians (Unitarians).

They settled in, and bought houses with stepped gables, and William Brewster operated his Pilgrim Press. In 1619, the English government complained to the Dutch that one of his books, an attack on the king, was "vented underhand" in London. The Dutch were pressured to seize the type and arrest Brewster, who went underground upon his release. But after that the threat of extradition hung in the air.

The Pilgrims thought of leaving. Besides extradition, they feared that if they remained in Holland their community would unravel. The danger was that the young people would vanish into the Dutch melting pot. This had already happened to other religious dissidents, such as the Huguenots. It was natural for young people to grow into local ways, learn the language, marry local girls. All this would eventually lead to the complete destruction of the congregation.

America beckoned. The trip was expensive, dangerous, and full of hardships. But negotiations were begun with the Virginia Company of London, and the Pilgrims presented their case in a petition to the company in December 1617: "We are all weaned from the delicate milk of our mother country; and are inured to the difficulties of a strange and hard land. . . . We are knit together as a body, in a most strict and sacred bond and covenant. . . . It is not with us as with other men whom small things can discourage,

or small discontentments cause to wish themselves at home again."
This was a declaration of singularity. They were saying: We are
not like others, we are toughened by exile, and up to any challenge.
They knew that self-reliance was their only hope.

They also had to lobby James I, who in January 1618 was told
that a group of Separatists wanted a grant in northern Virginia.
"What profits might arise in the parts they intend," he asked, and
was told, "Fishing," to which he replied: "So God have my soul!
'Tis an honest trade! It was the Apostles' own calling." James I was
a good deal more farsighted than Louis XIV of France, who
banned the Huguenots from Canada. He would, however, give the
Pilgrims nothing in writing, because that might seem like condon-
ing Separatism. But he did let it be known that he would "connive
at them and not molest them, provided they carried themselves
peacefully."

As always with the Pilgrims, things did not go smoothly. The
Virginia Company was riddled with dissension and on the verge of
bankruptcy. Then Thomas Weston stepped in, the moving spirit
of a company that called itself the Merchant Adventurers of London. Weston steered the Pilgrim project through (for his own
less-than-philanthropic reasons), and conditions were drawn up.
Finally, he chartered the 180-ton *Mayflower* and the sixty-ton
Speedwell for the voyage.

About fifty-three members of the congregation left Leiden for
Southampton on the last day of July 1620. Bradford and Brewster
were in this first contingent, but not John Robinson, "by strong
necessity held back." In his written farewell to the others, Robinson called for a truly communal vision: "Let every man repress in
himself, and the whole body in each person, as so many rebels
against the common good, all private respects of men's selves, not
sorting with the general conveniency. And as men are careful not
to have a new house shaken with any violence before it be well
settled and the parts firmly knit, so be you, I beseech you, brethren, much more careful that the house of God, which you are and
are to be, be not shaken with unnecessary novelties or other opposition at the first settling thereof."

And so they took the fourteen-mile canal trip from Leiden to
Delfthaven, past tidy farms and country houses with tulip gardens,
a sharp contrast with the landscape of their destination. Then, at
Delfthaven, they boarded the *Speedwell* to Southampton, where for
a week the *Mayflower* crew had been loading her stores and prepar-

ing for a long voyage. They had packed hardtack, salted down beef, and filled casks with beer and water.

Weston had rounded out the passenger list with a group recruited in England, some Separatists and some not. A total of 120 passengers were divided between the two ships, eighty-four going in the *Mayflower* and thirty-six in the *Speedwell*. And then the *Speedwell* sprang a leak, which was seen as a cheap trick on the part of her captain, Mr. Reynolds, to avoid the voyage and weasel out of his contract to remain a year in America. She remained in England; of her passengers, eighteen were crowded onto the *Mayflower*, and the other eighteen waved them farewell. "Those that went back," wrote Bradford, "were for the most part such as were willing to do so, either out of some discontent, or fear they conceived of the ill success of the voyage."

When the *Mayflower* sailed out of Plymouth on September 16, 1620, the project was already compromised: of the 102 passengers, only forty-one were from Leiden, and only two, Brewster and Bradford, were from the original Scrooby congregation. Forty had been recruited in England, without regard to religious origin, and there were eighteen servants and three hired men. It was a mixture of Saints and Strangers, essentially middle-class, coming from all over England. The Pilgrims were in a minority, and considered the others to be "ill-conditioned people, who will never do good, but corrupt and base others."

The striking thing about the *Mayflower* was its smallness— ninety-six feet long at the waterline by twenty-five feet wide. It was sturdy and squat, with three strong masts, oak timbers, linen sails, and miles of tarred hemp rigging, but the dark, low-ceilinged, "tween-decks" section for the passengers was badly cramped for a hundred–odd people on a two-month voyage.

"Think of it as a cottage where a hundred people are always home," said one of the crew aboard the replica that now sits in Plymouth Harbor. I tried to imagine life down there for fifty men, twenty women, and thirty-two children: the absence of privacy, the noise of small children, the smoke of cooking with coal, the stench of chamber pots, the seasick passengers throwing up, the stormy nights on straw mattresses, the travails of the pregnant women, and people always in one another's way. This claustrophobic prelude of detention before the endless spaciousness to come was a mighty test of the passengers' patience.

The trip took sixty-seven days, and there were the usual bad moments. Both the sailors and the weather were hostile. John

Howland was licked up by a wave and swept overboard, then fished up and saved. The only death among the passengers was William Button, servant to Dr. Fuller, the Pilgrims' surgeon. He expired on November 16, but Elizabeth Hopkins gave birth to a son around the same time, balancing the ledger. Always on the lookout for omens that God was with them, Bradford received one en route: an arrogant sailor told the seasick Pilgrims that he hoped to throw them overboard and take their property, but before the trip was half over he took sick, died, and was himself thrown overboard.

At dawn on November 19, they saw Cape Cod, "wooded to the brink of the sea." On November 21, they anchored in what is today Provincetown Harbor, "wherein 100 sails of ship may safely ride." They saw so many whales that Captain Jones and other experienced fishermen said there was surely three or four thousand pounds' worth of whale oil out there. They found beds of fat mussels, but all those who ate them were "caused to cast and scour" (vomit and diarrhea). Another problem was the shallowness of the water; the *Mayflower* had to stay a mile offshore, and the men had to wade "a bow shot or two" to reach land in freezing weather, the start of many colds and coughs.

Their patent was for Virginia, but they were well beyond its limits, outside all established authority. Already mutinous speeches were heard from some of the Strangers, whom no one had the power to command. The adult males were quickly summoned to the ship's cabin to sign a compact, which called for a "civil body politic," able to enact laws. They invented their own government, without royal parchment or seal, because of the unreliable non-Pilgrim elements among them.

Then came a month of reconnoitering, of sending out parties to find a suitable site, of trudging up and down the beach and across sand dunes "much like the downs of Holland" in their half-armor, southward, by the Great Pond, to the Nanset Trail leading to the Cape. The Pilgrims landed their shallop, a sort of big rowboat with a mast and sails, and oars for eight men. Packed below decks, it had taken the carpenter more than two weeks to reassemble. Upon landing, the shallop crew saw few if any Indians. A plague in 1616 and 1617, doubtless brought by European fishing parties, had struck down thousands. This was seen as God's judgment—divine providence had made forest clearing for immediate occupation possible.

When the Pilgrims sent out a party for firewood, they found

no persons or habitations. "The savages had died like rotten sheep," according to Edward Winslow. It had happened so fast they were not "able to bury one another; their skulls and bones we found in many places lying still above ground, where their houses and dwellings had been." It was quite unlike Jamestown, which was teeming with Indians.

On November 25, they saw some Indians with a dog, who ran into the woods. The next day, they found what looked like graves with grave goods such as bows and arrows, which they left mainly untouched. "We thought it would be odious unto them to ransack their sepulchers." Because of their own religious beliefs, the Pilgrims respected the Indians' rites, an altogether startling departure from earlier settler practice. The attitude paid off. The Pilgrims were the first of the early groups (with the possible exception of Champlain) to develop a successful forest diplomacy.

Soon, however, necessity prevailed. When the Pilgrims found some baskets of corn, and an old ship's kettle, they faced a difficult choice. "We were in suspense what to do with the corn and kettles," wrote Bradford, "and at length, after much consultation, we concluded to take the kettle and as much of the corn as we could carry away with us." They intended to pay the Indians back, but there was no way for the Indians to know this. On November 30, the Pilgrims found some bowls and trays, and "we brought sundry of the prettiest things away with us. . . ." Then, in a deserted wigwam village, they saw wooden bowls, earthen pots, and baskets made of crab shells, "and some of the best things we took away with us." Three times in the first month, they stole from the Indians, though they intended to pay them back with trade goods.

In December, the shallop started down the coast. The ocean spray froze as it splashed the crew's clothes, covering them "many times like coats of iron." At Eastham, they fired their muskets in the morning to see if the damp had spoiled the powder, then continued along the shore to what today is Barnstable. The blinding snow and rain concealed the entrance to the inlet. On December 21, they sounded Plymouth Harbor in the shallop, and on that day, aboard the *Mayflower*, William Bradford's twenty-three-year-old wife, Dorothy, fell overboard. He never mentions her in his otherwise undissembling account, which suggests she may have committed suicide.

On December 26, 1620, the *Mayflower* finally came into Plymouth Harbor, though there is no mention in any of the Pilgrims' accounts of the famous rock. Their first order of business was to build houses; they decided that single men would bunk with families, "so we might build fewer houses," Bradford wrote. This was where the Pilgrims were different from the settlers at Jamestown and Quebec. They had arrived as families. They had also arrived with a primarily not-for-profit ideology, being essentially a conservative affinity-group bent on self-improvement.

As they built their houses, they continued to live aboard the *Mayflower*, which remained in the notch of the Cape Cod hook until April 5, 1621. But since the ship had to be berthed in deep water, a mile off shore, it was quite a commute. In the bitter Plymouth winter, many settlers died, and so did many crew members.

Comparing the solidarity of the Pilgrims with the selfishness of the crew, Bradford saw the latter as emblematic of the doomed and unenlightened Old World they had left behind, whereas the Pilgrims represented a spiritual rebirth in the New. For the crew, who "had been boon companions in drinking and jollity in the time of their health and welfare, began now to desert one another . . . saying they should be infected by coming to them in their cabins." One sailor complained that a friend whom he was helping was not dying fast enough. The boatswain, an arrogant young man who had often cursed the passengers, now grew weak and told Bradford: "You, I now see, show your love like Christians to one another, but we let one another lie and die like dogs."

The six or seven healthy Pilgrims took care of their sick, fetched wood, cooked, "washed their loathsome clothes," and did all those things "which dainty and queasy stomachs cannot endure to have named," willingly and without grudging. It was a test, to see if they could live up to their principles, which they did, although they lost fifty people, nearly half the company, and their graves were "leveled and sown, lest the Indians should take advantage of their weak and wretched state."

Such a high level of compassion and self-sacrifice would prove impossible to sustain. There is in the Pilgrim enterprise a built-in dilution of noble purpose. Their ideology was the right one for the hard early years—submersion of the individual, teamwork, the greater good. But when things improved, the Pilgrims became pragmatists, making a virtue of necessity.

You could see it in small things, such as widows and widowers remarrying soon after the deaths of their spouses. Although this would have been unthinkable in former times, Edward Winslow had been a widower for only seven weeks, and Susanna White a widow for twelve, when they married; in Plymouth, the family was the most desirable unit. You could see it in behavior induced by hunger, when men took green ears of corn from the common plot, for which they were whipped.

In February, when Miles Standish and Francis Cook had their tools stolen in the woods, they became more conscious of defense, and brought different sorts of cannons in from the ship. They realized that the community must be organized along military lines, which was a long way from pacifistic Pilgrim doctrine.

They also began to formulate a foreign policy, as the result of an event that seemed almost miraculous—the appearance in their midst on March 16, 1621, out of the blue, of an English-speaking Indian. He was Samoset, an Algonquin from Maine, where he had shipped out with English fishermen. Samoset gave the Pilgrims crucial intelligence on Indian strength in the area. He also introduced them to Squanto, who spoke better English than he did, having spent two years in London after being captured on the Cape Cod coast in 1615.

At first, Squanto gave them practical help, showing them how to manure the ground with alewives (a sort of herring), without which, in this depleted soil, nothing grew. He also taught them how to fish, showed them the lobsters in Plymouth Bay, and gave them shad roe, for which Bradford was grateful, recalling Seneca's epistle, "that a great part of liberty is a well-governed belly."

Samoset and Squanto showed the Pilgrims that they could not remain isolated, but must take part in regional politics. Thus, on March 22, 1621, they signed a mutual defense treaty with Chief Massasoit of the Wampanoags against the marauding Narragansetts, cementing the friendship with "a pot of strong water." The pact featured the main element of forest diplomacy, the alliance with one tribe against another, for it stated, "If any did unjustly war against him, we would aid him, and if any did war against us, he would aid us."

Squanto became a double agent, taking kickbacks from the tribes on promises that he would prevent the English from attacking them. He played to Indian superstition, spreading the word that the English had the plague buried in their storehouse, which they could send forth at will. But, despite evidence of his misdeeds, he was clearly too useful to dispense with.

With a few interruptions, Bradford, who became governor in

1621, stayed in office until his death in 1657. At first, he was pestered with complaints from his London backer, Thomas Weston. When the *Fortune* arrived in November 1621, with thirty-five new recruits (not quite replacing the fifty lost during the winter), and some cheap suits from Birching Lane (London's Canal Street), there was also a letter of remonstrance from Weston, furious that the *Mayflower* had been sent back empty. "That you sent no lading in the ship is wonderful, and worthily distasted," he wrote. "I know your weakness was the cause of it, and believe more weakness of judgment than weakness of hands."

It was a bit much to have gone through so much suffering and death and then be reprimanded for it by a mere investor. When the *Fortune* left for England, however, she was "laden with good clapboard as full as she could stow, and two hogsheads of beaver and other skins." In less than a year, the Pilgrims had mastered the fur trade, having sent up a shallop to a point near today's Medford on Massachusetts Bay, where the Indian women sold them the beaver coats off their backs. Beaver became the Pilgrims' cash crop.

In June 1622, Weston wrote to say that he had sold his shares in the company, "so I am quit of you." This news came aboard the ships *Charity* and *Swan*, which bore sixty of Weston's men to start a second colony. The Pilgrims were alarmed, for New England was becoming a haven, not only for religious dissenters, but also for roving bands of fortune-hunters and speculators in embryonic principalities. Equally alarming was the news that arrived from Captain John Huddleston, master of the *Bona Nova*, who told them about the March massacre at Jamestown: ". . . I will so far inform you that myself with many good friends in the south colony of Virginia have received such a blow that 400 persons large will not make good our losses. . . . Happy is he whom other men's harms do make to beware. . . ." That summer, the Pilgrims built a good fort with sound timber, mounting the ordnance on its flat roof. They hoped it would be finished before the Indians in their area heard about the Jamestown massacre, which might give them ideas.

Weston's people sponged off them all summer, until they moved to a place they called Wessagusset, in the Boston area, near where Weymouth is today. These new settlers had no religious background, and turned out to be nothing but trouble. The Pilgrims notified the Indians that the new recruits were a distinct group, hoping to forestall guilt by association. Weston's settlers were disorderly and wasteful, kept Indian women, and planted little or no food. In the winter, they sold their clothes and bed coverings for corn, and became servants of the Indians, cutting their wood and fetching water for a capful of kernels. When the Wessagusset men left in 1623 to join the English fishing fleet in Maine, the Pilgrims were rid of an unwanted neighbor.

In 1623, there was a major change of direction in the Plymouth colony, which could be seen as another compromise of Pilgrim principles. At first, all labor was shared, and all products were placed in the public store. The less productive received as much as the hard workers. Bradford saw that collectivism didn't work, and went over to a free-market economy, assigning a lot to each household, with an acre per head. This system, he wrote, had "a very good success, for it made all hands very industrious. . . . The women now went willingly into the field, and took their little ones with them . . . to set corn, which before would allege weakness and inability." Gone was the system where "the strong man had no more in division of victuals and clothes than he that was weak and not able to do a quarter the other could."

But then more settlers arrived who were not up to the "Old Standers." In July, the *Ann* brought some whom Bradford considered so unfit that he sent them back on the next ship. The remaining newcomers complained that instead of beef and mutton they had to make do with a mess of boiled clams and a jar of water.

Once they experienced the reality of Plymouth life, they "were much daunted and dismayed, and according to their diverse humors were diversely affected; some wished themselves in England again; others fell a-weeping, fancying their own misery in what they saw now in others. . . . In a word, all were full of sadness."

By 1624, Plymouth had a population of 180; the first cattle had arrived, one bull and three heifers, which proved a morale booster. But with growth came new difficulties, such as a rising crime rate. The first law enacted in the record book, on December 27, 1623, read: "All criminal facts, and also all matters of trespass and debts between man and man, should be tried by the verdict of twelve honest men, to be empaneled by authority, in form of a jury upon their oath." And so the trial by jury was established on the North American continent.

In March 1624, there arrived aboard the *Charity* a so-called minister, John Lyford, with his wife and four children, perhaps sent by the London backers to spy. Bradford had him pegged for a dissembler and a hypocrite, for "he bowed and cringed and would have kissed their hands if they would had suffered him." He allied himself with a chronic malcontent, John Oldham, in various efforts to subvert the colony.

Bradford learned that Lyford was sending letters aboard the returning *Charity*. Fearing their contents would hurt the Pilgrims' cause in England, Bradford went out in a shallop to retrieve and read them; the future of the colony was at stake, and he was its chief magistrate. As he suspected, Lyford's letters were full of slanders and false accusations. He wrote that the Pilgrims were intolerant of outsiders, that he had seen much waste of tools and vessels, and so on. Bradford made copies and kept some of the originals, in order to produce Lyford's own handwriting as evidence.

Both Lyford and Oldham became habitually insubordinate. When Miles Standish ordered Oldham to take guard duty, he refused, calling Standish "a beggarly rascal," and pulling a knife on him. Finally, a town meeting was called, in which both men were charged with conspiracy to destroy the government. When Lyford's letters were produced, he was at first struck dumb, and then collapsed, calling himself a reprobate and an "unsavory salt."

Oldham and Lyford were banished from the colony, and went to Nantasket, in Massachusetts Bay (today's Hull). Lyford then went to Salem, and was later hired as minister for Martin's Hundred in Virginia, where he died.

Sixteen twenty-five was the turning point for Plymouth, when, as Bradford wrote, the Pilgrims first felt the sweetness of the country. That year in London, the plague struck, killing 41,313, an amazing number. That year also, John Robinson died in Leiden, his hope of joining the Plymouth congregation unrealized. Bradford maintained Pilgrim discipline, keeping strict watch over sinners, and making sure that everyone attended divine service. The colony was spreading on both sides of the original town, and it was decided that each colonist should have twenty acres besides the single acre they already had, with five acres on the water.

But just when things were going well came a serious threat, in the form of a rival, incompatible colony about twenty miles away, where Quincy is today. A certain Captain Wollaston started a plantation there in 1625, on a hundred-foot-high hill overlooking

Boston Harbor, with some partners and about thirty indentured servants. The first year was discouraging, and Wollaston decided to take some of the servants to Virginia and sell their indentures, leaving nine or ten behind. One of Wollaston's partners, who also stayed behind, was a former lawyer by the name of Thomas Morton, who according to Bradford was "a pettifogger" who had "left his country for his country's good."

Morton, in turn, wrote an amusingly anti-Pilgrim account of his adventures in the New World called *New England Canaan* (published in Amsterdam in 1637). He claimed to have arrived in 1622, "where I found two sorts of people, the one Christians, the other infidels; these I found most full of humanity and more friendly than the others. . . ." The Indians, he said, were "much like the wild Irish." Their senses were keener than the Europeans', and there were Indians who could tell a Spaniard from a Frenchman by the smell of his hand. Their greatest failing was their fondness for strong drink, "for they will pawn their wits to purchase the acquaintance of it . . . and it happened that a savage killed himself when he was drunk, a gun being charged and the cock up, he set the mouth to his breast, and putting back the trigger with his foot, shot himself dead."

With Wollaston gone, Morton told those servants who had stayed behind: "You see that many of your fellows are carried to Virginia, and if you stay you will also be carried away and sold for slaves." He proposed that they set up a free republic, to trade and plant and live as equals. He would cancel their indentures and make them partners, and they would support and protect one another.

Merrymount, as this seventeenth-century commune became known (its site is marked on Route 3 in Quincy), represented everything the Pilgrims detested. Morton and his men were fun-loving and hard-drinking; they laughed at religion, did not keep the Sabbath, swore and scoffed, and slept with Indian women. They offered an alternative to the holier-than-thou Pilgrims. Bradford was horrified, calling Morton "Lord of Misrule," and saying that he maintained "a school of atheism," and that what he and his group earned in trade they spent in drunken revels.

For his part, Morton saw the Pilgrims as bigots and hypocrites. "They differ from us," he wrote, "in the manner of praying; for they wink when they pray because they think themselves so perfect in the high way to heaven that they can find it blindfolded."

He accused them of making defamation a principle, by acting in the manner of the verse: "Stick candles 'gainst a virgin wall's white back, If they'll not burn at least they'll black."

In Morton, we have the first appearance in America of a counterculture, challenging the conservative orthodoxy of the Plymouth colony. In contrast to the priggish and judgmental Pilgrims, Morton didn't moralize. He lived by his own libertine convictions and antiestablishment, laissez-faire permissiveness. He was completely open about his raunchy republic, telling how "the lasses in beaver coats" had been "welcome night and day."

In the spring of 1627, to celebrate the season and the naming of Merrymount, Morton put up a Maypole with the help of his Indian friends. An eighty-foot-long pine was raised, wreathed in garlands and ribbons, and topped with the spreading antlers of a stag. The celebrants broke open the wine and beer, and danced hand in hand with Indian squaws around the pole, to the firing of muskets and the music of fife and drum, as they sang a poem that began: "Drink and be merry, merry, merry, boys."

To Bradford, the pagan ritual of the Maypole was the crowning insult. From that day on, Morton wrote, "the precise Separatists . . . sought occasion . . . to overthrow our undertaking and destroy our plantation quit and clean." But there was another reason why the Pilgrims wanted to shut down Morton's operation. He was undercutting them in the beaver trade, by offering incentives to the Indians that Plymouth could not match—not only parties and booze, but, more important, guns. Since the Indians could not obtain guns from the Pilgrims, they sold their beaver pelts to Morton.

According to Bradford, Morton "taught the Indians how to use the guns to charge and discharge . . . and what shot to use for fowl and what for deer." He sent them out hunting, and they grew fond of guns, "accounting their bows and arrows but baubles in comparison." Now they were better fitted than the English themselves, with muskets and pistols, and molds to make shot, and screw plates to make screw pins. And if they had known how to make saltpeter, they would have made their own gunpowder.

In Bradford's view, Morton was selling the blood of his brethren for gain, because armed Indians were a terror "unto them who lived strugglingly." When the Plymouth people told Morton that he was in violation of the king's 1622 proclamation banning the sale of guns to Indians, he replied that the king was dead (James I had died in 1625). They saw that they would have to use force, and put the Pilgrim enforcer, Miles Standish, on the case. William Hubbard in his *History of New England* described Miles as "a little chimney soon fired . . . a man of very little stature, yet of a very hot and angry temper." In 1628, he took eight men to Merrymount, where they found Morton and his men too drunk to fight. One man was so drunk he ran his nose onto the point of a sword.

In Morton's account, Miles Standish, whom he called "Captain Shrimp the quondam drummer," arrived with his men "as if they had been tailed one to another, as colts to be sold at a fair." Morton agreed to lay down his arms "to save the effusion of so much worthy blood." They roughed him up a little and deported him to England. He returned a year and a half later, but times had changed. The Puritans were in Boston, and their stern governor, John Endecott (whom Morton called Captain Littleworth), had in his absence chopped down the Maypole. In December 1630, after being charged with wounding an Indian, Morton was arrested and shipped back to England, this time for good. In the Pilgrim mindset, any dissent was subversive, and Morton had to go.

By 1630, Plymouth was a fortified village of three hundred, all of whom belonged to one Separatist congregation and were independent of all English control. But with prosperity came dispersal. When farmers increased the number of their cattle, they wanted more land for grazing, as well as for tilling, and so they moved away from Plymouth. Bradford saw them scattering all over the bay, going "to their great lots . . . and the town in which they [had] lived compactly till now was left very thin and almost desolate." Miles Standish and John Alden went to Duxbury, across the bay, which meant that they were too far to bring their families to church at Plymouth, and "sued to be dismissed and became a body of themselves—and so they were dismissed, though very unwillingly." Bradford's worst fear—the splintering of the congregation —was now accomplished. Duxbury had its own church.

To prevent further scattering, good farms were offered to "special persons, who would promise to live at Plymouth, and be helpful to the church, and the Commonwealth." The land for this expansion was bought from Chief Massasoit by the General Court. But these farms, like Duxbury, were across the bay, which was not a solution, for the settlers didn't want to commute from Plymouth every day. Eventually, they too broke away, incorporating as Marshfield in 1640. They thought only of their own conceived necessity, wrote a disappointed Bradford, "and this I fear will be the ruin of New England, at least of the churches of God there, and will provoke the Lord's displeasure against them." It was a curious frontier dynamic: Bradford, as governor, trying to prevent expansion in order to keep the original congregation together, while the settlers took off with their unstoppable momentum.

Bradford was further disheartened by the growing incidence of crime among the Pilgrims. How could the community maintain itself with such disorders? The whole idea of Plymouth was that they would "walk with God" and improve their private conduct through religious observance, but it wasn't working out that way. John Billington, one of the original *Mayflower* group, was not a Pilgrim, "and I know not through what friends shuffled into our company," wrote Bradford. In 1621, he had been "laid neck and heels" for insubordination. And now, in 1630, he killed a man in a hunting dispute and was sentenced to death in the colony's first capital case. It was a matter of great sadness to Bradford that a man who had gone through the terrors of the first winter with them had to die by the executioner's hand. But, just as the containment of the colony was impossible, so was the maintenance of Pilgrim purity.

Bradford was confronted with two of the quandaries of the American experience: One, as long as there was land to move to, you could not get people to stay put. Two, it was impossible to maintain ethnic or religious purity in a country where all sorts of new people kept arriving.

And so the court at Plymouth was kept busy with a wide range of offenses—slander, drunkenness, theft, burglary (for which the letter "B" was burned into the hand), receiving stolen goods, hanging laundry on the Lord's day, keeping three swine unringed, smoking tobacco on the highway. Some crimes were peculiar to the New World. A Duxbury woman, charged with "dalliance with an Indian," was sentenced to be whipped through the town streets, and to wear a badge on her left sleeve. The Indian, who was judged to have been allured and enticed, got off with a whipping.

Indentured servants committed many sexual offenses, in part because they were not allowed to marry until their term was up. This was daunting for young men, and there were many cases of fornication and illegitimate births. This lack of normal sexual outlets led Bradford in 1642 to lament "a very sad accident of foul nature." He was shocked by the grossness of the crime, but his honesty as a chronicler would not let him omit it: "Horrible it is to mention, but ye truth of ye history requires it."

A teen-aged servant, Thomas Granger, "was detected of buggery (and indicted for ye same) with a mare, a cow, two goats, five sheep, two calves, and a turkey. . . . He was first discovered by one who accidentally saw his lewd practices towards the mare. . . ." The Pilgrims followed Old Testament law, and in this case Leviticus had written that "the man who lies with an animal: He must die and the animal must be killed." The problem at Granger's trial was identifying which turkey and which goat and which sheep were involved. Since no one could identify the five sheep from his description, all the sheep he tended were brought before him in a kind of police lineup so that he could point out the guilty ones. Granger watched as the animals were cast into a pit and killed, and then he was put to death, in September 1642.

Appalled at all the wickedness, Bradford searched his soul for an explanation. He concluded that the devil was more powerful "in these heathen lands," and was trying to shame the godly colony. Also, that wickedness, when dammed up by strict laws, broke through more violently.

In 1644—faced with more departures, which would further weaken the congregation—the Pilgrims considered undertaking yet another removal as a body, this time to Nauset, a tract on the outer cape (today's Eastham, south of Wellfleet). But they soon saw that Nauset would be worse than Plymouth, for it was fifty miles away, removed from all other settlements, with a worse harbor, worse soil, and too many Indians. And so they remained in Plymouth, even though its population was dwindling. The betrayal of the departed young, already a danger in Holland, had finally come to pass.

Bradford's acute sense of failure was poignantly expressed: "And thus was this poor church left like an ancient mother grown old and forsaken of her children . . . her ancient members being most of them worn away by death, and those of later time being like children translated into other families, and she like a widow left only to trust in God. Thus, she that had made many rich, became herself poor."

As Bradford grew old, his thoughts returned to the early years, when scurvy had thinned the ranks and they had pulled together for the common good. He had been there from the first, when a handful of convalescents had fired their matchlocks over the graves of the fallen. And so he wrote his history of the colony year by year, "that their children may see with what difficulties their fathers wrestled." He got as far as the years 1647 and 1648, for which he wrote the headings but left the pages blank. He could not go on. It was too disheartening.

Now his time was taken up by such matters as the boundary dispute with the Massachusetts colony, which involved some highly prized marshland. Bradford returned to the study of Hebrew, which contained no disappointments, and tied him in closely with tenets of his faith. He died in 1657, at the age of sixty-seven, beset by an overwhelming sense of loss. He had tried to keep the congregation exactly as it was, but that had been impossible in the New World, whose essence was change.

CHAPTER SEVEN

THE
DUTCH
FRONTIER

The Dutch were a colonial power in North America for a brief forty years. They landed in New York Harbor in 1624 and were ousted by the British in 1664, though many Dutch settlers remained.

New York Public Library

This Dutch view of New Amsterdam in 1673 shows the town in the background and native Americans in the foreground. Attention is given to their style of dress, their weapons, their wigwam, and to animals indigenous to the New World. The towering squaw on the right blots out the Wall Street stockade and the soldiers on the quay.

New Amsterdam . . . never became more than a small commercial center during the Dutch regime because its hinterland was only thinly colonized and because the whole province was but a minor holding in the worldwide operations of Dutch mercantile enterprise.

D. W. MEINIG

T hough their country was small, the Dutch were all over the place, picking up bits and pieces of real estate—in the Orient, where they held Ceylon and Formosa, and in Brazil, Africa, and North America. It was the Dutch East India Company, founded in 1602, that had hired Henry Hudson to look for a Northeast Passage. By July 1610, he was back in Holland, reporting that he had found a fine harbor with limitless farmland on the river that bears his name. Wasting no time, the Amsterdam merchants sent a ship out that same year, and five more in 1611. In 1614, they built a little fort on an island in the Delaware River, called Fort Nassau, which was flooded in 1617 and abandoned.

In 1621, the West India Company was founded to handle the Atlantic trade; three years later, thirty families were landed in Manhattan, with the Virginians to the south and the Separatists to the north. In 1624, Fort Orange was built on the site of Albany, between the Mohawk and Hudson rivers, at the portage that circles the Cohoes Falls. Peter Minuit arrived in 1626 for a six-year term as governor and bought Manhattan for sixty guilders' worth of trading goods, which must have seemed like a good deal to the Indians, who owned all of New Jersey and Long Island, with its wampum-producing quahogs. New Netherlands was established on its American Rhine, a minor cog in the great worldwide Dutch mercantile conglomerate.

The period of Dutch settlement lasted for only about forty years, which wasn't long enough to compile much of a colonial record. The Dutch were traders, bottom-line-oriented, indifferent to imperial strategies. They didn't develop strong Indian alliances. Nor were they particularly interested in religious conversion. They built a few haphazard settlements, but basically did only what they had to do to get the fur trade going. They built Fort Orange upriver to receive the goods, and headquarters in Manhattan, that great natural pier, to berth the Dutch merchantmen who carried

153

the goods. When Peter Minuit arrived, there were already a few houses, and a tower with a bell, obtained when a Dutch fleet sacked Puerto Rico in October 1625.

It was a business operation like Jamestown, a joint-stock company operated out of Amsterdam and financed by investors, who wanted a return on their money. The company sent out governors with detailed instructions that clothed the profit motive in religious rhetoric. They were told, for instance, to deal honestly with the Indians in buying land, and not to obtain it "by craft or fraud, lest we call down the wrath of God upon our unrighteous beings."

Be that as it may, the Dutch were not averse to shortcuts. In Manhattan, the company's chief commercial agent, Isaac de Rasieres, made an interesting discovery, which he communicated to the Amsterdam merchant Samuel Bommaert. The Indians on Long Island had "an oblong bead that they make from cockle-shells, which they find on the seashore, and they consider it as valuable as we do money here, since one can buy with it everything they have." De Rasieres had discovered wampum, which the Dutch began to buy from the Long Island Indians to use as currency in Fort Orange, to buy beaver. Having access to wampum was like owning a bank.

In 1627, de Rasieres visited Plymouth to learn the extent of the Pilgrims' trading efforts. Though remembering the welcome they had received in Holland, the Pilgrims now considered the Dutch as commercial rivals. Bradford had already told them not to trade around Buzzards Bay or Narragansett. The Dutch replied that they had the right to trade where they liked. Bradford said he would expel by force anyone entering his territory to disturb his trade.

Such was the situation when de Rasieres landed at Plymouth in October in a boat carrying sugar, linen, and a stock of wampum. He was the son of Huguenots, who, like the Pilgrims, had been sheltered by the Dutch. In his amicable talk with Bradford, he mentioned the circular pieces of shell, polished, drilled, and ground, which the Indians used as money. Intrigued, Bradford bought fifty pounds' worth, which allowed the Pilgrims to extend their fur trade up and down the coast of Maine. Between 1631 and 1636, they sent to England more than twelve thousand pounds of beaver, which greatly contributed to the reduction of their debt. They had the Dutch to thank for this.

Reporting on his visit, de Rasieres noted that the Indians in the Pilgrim area of influence "are better behaved than ours, because the English give them the example of better ordinances and a better life." That was quite a compliment, showing that the Pilgrims were an example to other colonists.

Generally, however, the Dutch disliked the Puritans, whom they called Janikers (Johnnies). The easygoing Dutch thought of them as a race apart, with their punitive laws and their unhealthy preoccupation with the sins of the flesh. Their government seemed more despotic than any monarchy. They banned cooking on Sunday, eating beans that they had baked the day before.

Perhaps on the advice of de Rasieres, the West India Company sent out a clergyman in 1628 to raise the moral standards of the settlers. But the Reverend Jonas Michaelius was not destined to be happy in the New World. After seven weeks, his wife or "yoke-fellow" died, leaving him a widower with two small daughters and a servant problem. He also developed an aversion for the Indians, whom he described as strangers to all decency and "stupid as posts."

Michaelius kept a diary, so we know what he thought of the Indians, but rarely are we privy to what the Indians thought of the whites. The Moravian missionary John Heckewelder, however, recorded the story handed down by the Delaware Indians of their moment of contact with the Dutch:

A long time ago, when there was no such thing known to the Indians as a people with white skin, they saw a boat come in, and were hailed in a language they did not understand. . . . A large barrel was brought forth by the white men, and something was poured into a glass, which the assembled chiefs passed along, smelling but not tasting. A warrior jumped up and harangued them on the impropriety of returning the glass full, and said he would drink it himself, and soon he was staggering about, and they bemoaned him, thinking he had expired, but he woke up and said he wanted more.

Then the man with the red clothes gave them beads, axes, and hoes, and said they were going home but would come back next year with more presents, but at that time they would want a little land to sow some seeds in order to raise herbs to put in their broth. When the whites returned they laughed at the Indians, who had the hoes and axes hanging from their necks as ornaments. . . . Familiarity daily increasing between them and the whites, the latter now proposed to stay with them, asking only for as much land as the hide of a bullock would cover, which hide was brought forward and spread on the ground. This request they readily granted, whereupon the whites took a knife, and began to cut the hide into a rope not thicker than the finger of a child, so that by the time the hide was cut there was a great heap. Then this rope was drawn to a great distance and brought around so that both ends met, and it encompassed a large piece of ground. The Indians were surprised at the superior wit of the whites, but did not want to argue about a little land, for they had enough. The whites asked them from time to time for more land, proceeding higher up the Hudson, so that they believed they would soon want all their country, which at this time was already the case.

There is no rancor in this account, but a kind of fatalism, as if the Indians had accepted the idea of being cheated out of their land. In fact, the Dutch were fairly scrupulous in their land deals, and after 1630 insisted on written deeds, because of the Indian habit of wanting to sell the same piece of real estate more than once.

The Dutch had a system of patroonships, under which a man who brought over fifty settlers could buy a large piece of land. In July 1640, to give one example, an Amsterdam tanner by the name of Cornelius Melyn became patroon of Staten Island, which was named in honor of the States General, the Netherlands form of government. Like Manhattan, Staten Island had been bought by Peter Minuit, and Melyn was shown the original deed, marked by a number of Indians, and listing what they had received: duffles, kettles, axes, hoes, wampum, drilling awls, Jew's harps, and various other wares.

Melyn arrived with forty-one settlers, some cattle, and farm implements. They began to build houses and plow land. He had a little trouble with the Indians over hunting rights, which he argued they had forfeited as a result of the original sale. But they said they could not be without the liberty of hunting, and promised to give him ten or twelve deer a year, and some turkeys, which they did. There was peace temporarily, but in 1643 the Indians attacked, burned his farms, and killed some of his people. Melyn had to run for his life.

He returned to Holland in 1647 aboard the *Princess*, which hit a reef off England. Eighty-one of about one hundred passengers aboard were drowned. Melyn survived after eighteen hours on a makeshift raft in the Atlantic, but lost his six-year-old son.

By 1650, Melyn was back on his Staten Island property with twenty settlers. The Indians said there must be a new sale, which he protested, saying that once a thing was sold it must remain sold. The Dutch didn't pay for anything twice, he said, though he would give them a little something to maintain the friendship— and he passed around some duffles, kettles, wampum, awls, and needles. They cried, *"Kenne, Kenne, Oritnietap,"* which he was told meant "Thank you, good friend."

In the next five years, Melyn's little colony grew to about seventy settlers and sixteen farms, each with its oxen and milk cows, and calves for increase. Soon he began to recover his losses. But, in 1655, hundreds of Indians attacked Manhattan and Staten Island, killing sixteen of his people, including his twenty-two-year-old son. Melyn, his wife, and forty-nine others were taken captive and held for thirty-one days, until a ransom of fourteen hundred guilders (more than twenty times the cost of Manhattan) could be raised. It was a Job-like tale—one son killed by Indians, another drowned, his houses and barns burned, his cattle and farms destroyed, his goods stolen. Melyn went back to Holland; he had had enough.

In the matter of Indian relations, the Dutch were less adroit than the Pilgrims, and about on a par with the Jamestown settlers. One minister, Johannes Megapolensis, who spent six years among the Mohawks, found that in his conversion efforts he was rowing against the current. "When we pray, they laugh at us," he reported.

Megapolensis had one promising recruit whom he took in and taught for two years until the Indian could read and write Dutch. He presented this lone convert with a Bible, but the fellow took to drink, pawned it, "and became a real beast, who is doing more harm than good."

Aside from conversion, which was not one of their priorities, the Dutch had the usual problems with the Indians (land disputes, trespass and property damage, and attacks on settlers). The authoritarian and brutal governor, Willem Kieft, launched an Indian war that lasted from 1642 to 1647. He told the settler David De Vries: "I want to make these savages wipe their chops." De Vries was shocked when, in February 1643, Kieft sent his men across the Narrows to Staten Island and they massacred eighty Indians. "Some came to our people in the country with their hands or legs cut off," he wrote, "and some holding their entrails in their arms.

. . . Did the Duke of Alba in the Netherlands ever do anything more cruel?" The Dutch were as bad as the Spanish. Among the governor's innovations was setting a bounty on Indian scalps—the going rate was ten fathoms of wampum. But Kieft's policy failed to wipe out the Indians or make them submit, and war discouraged settlement. It actually caused departures to outnumber arrivals.

When De Vries met with sixteen Long Island chiefs on March 4, 1643, one of them said: "When you first arrived on our shores, you were sometimes in want of food. We gave you our beans and corn, and let you eat oysters and fish. And now for our reward you murder our people." The chief had a bundle of sticks in his hand and laid one down—marking the first count in the indictment.

"The men you left here to barter our goods were treated by us as we have treated our own eyeballs," he went on. "We gave them our daughters for wives, by whom they had children. And now their blood is murdered in a villainous manner." And he laid down a second stick, the second count in the indictment. Two sticks meant war, which was bad for settlement and bad for trade.

The Dutch were good traders but lacked empathy, and understood the Indians less well than the French or the English. They didn't catch on that Indians never forgot a grudge. In 1642, when Claes Rademaker was murdered in Albany, the Indian who did it said that as a small boy, he had come with his uncle to trade beaver, but that some of the Swannekins (Dutch traders) had robbed his uncle and killed him. The boy swore revenge, which he nursed until he was grown.

Peter Stuyvesant, the peg-legged soldier who debarked in May 1647, was a far abler man than Kieft. Upon arriving, he found the settlers wild and loose in their morals. They were given to cheating, smuggling, fraud, and the sale of beer and brandy to the Indians. His was a reform administration, which enacted stricter fire-control laws and an excise tax on imported wine and liquors. He made peace with the Indians and tried to put a stop to the selling of guns, which was routine at Fort Orange. In 1648, he arrested the New Amsterdam armorer, Geritt Barendt, who was selling the West India Company's guns to private dealers—who then sold them to the Mohawks at a huge markup. But, once begun, the sale of guns couldn't be stopped, because the Indians would hold back their pelts until they got some. So Albany became the Mohawk arsenal.

There were always squabbles between the Fort Orange traders and the Indians. The Dutch grumbled that the Indians killed their cattle. The Indians griped that they had to pay wampum to get their guns fixed. When the Dutch explained that the gunsmiths had to be paid for their work, the Mohawks snapped back that "the French are doing more for their Indians than you are for yours," which was a way of upping the ante. Enterprising traders called "bushlopers" went into the woods to intercept the Indians before they reached Fort Orange, and their sales pitch was usually laced with rum. Concerned about drunkenness in the tribes, the sachems asked the traders to "put the bung on your casks."

Because the emphasis was on beaver pelts to the detriment of everything else, New Netherlands didn't grow the way New England did. In the early 1650s, it had a population of about two thousand, most of whom were in Manhattan to enjoy the proximity of Fort Amsterdam, which was a joke, with its ten soldiers, its cows and goats grazing on the ramparts, its streets like cow paths, and one house in four a grogshop. Even when it was called New Amsterdam, New York was a mongrel, where people of many backgrounds, religions, and languages coexisted.

The first Jews to cause a stir in North America landed in New Amsterdam in September 1654 as refugees from Pernambuco, the major port city on the hump of Brazil, today called Recife. Pernambuco kept changing hands, having been taken by the Dutch from the Portuguese in 1630 and retaken by the Portuguese in 1654. These twenty-three Sephardic refugees arrived stone broke. There was at that time one important Jewish merchant in New Amsterdam, Jacob Barsimon, who had a certain amount of capital. But Johannes Megapolensis, back from his mission to the Mohawks, reported to his superior in Amsterdam in 1655 that Barsimon would not lend the Jewish refugees a single stiver (one-twentieth of a guilder).

Peter Stuyvesant, the son of a Calvinist minister, thought of Jews as "Christ-killers" and was not particularly desirous of having them on his turf. He recommended to the directors in New Amsterdam that they be deported as indigent. But the Jewish investors in the West India Company lobbied for their admittance, and the company replied on April 25, 1655, that the refugees could remain there and trade provided that the poor among them did not become a burden to the company.

By this time, in the spring of 1655, more Jews had arrived from Holland, and Megapolensis wrote his superior a letter that stands as the first anti-Semitic document originating in the New World. He reported that the Jews planned to build a synagogue in New Amsterdam, which "causes a great deal of complaint and murmuring. These people have no other God than the Mammon of unrighteousness, and no other aim than to get possession of Christian property, and to overcome all other merchants by drawing all trade towards themselves." Megapolensis asked his superior to urge the directors of the company to deport "these godless rascals, who are of no benefit to the country, but look at everything for their own profit."

The company, however, allowed the Jews to remain, and to worship quietly in their homes, suggesting that they build their houses close together—an intimation of the ghetto or "Jewish-quarter" policy. The issue turned into one of those conflicts bound to arise between company policy and the men in the field. Although unable to get rid of the Jews, Stuyvesant thought up various kinds of harassment. When five affluent Jewish merchants from Amsterdam joined the colony in 1655, they were barred from owning houses, employing Christian servants, or taking part in the retail trade. When Jacob Barsimon petitioned in November 1655 to be allowed to do guard duty instead of paying the exemption tax, he was turned down and told he could leave the colony if he wanted to, which he did. And so did most of the other New Amsterdam Jews, either to the commercial hub of Barbados, where there was a thriving Jewish community, or back to Europe.

If they had stayed, they would soon have been under English rule, for the Dutch venture on the Hudson ended without a bang and with scarcely a whimper on August 26, 1664, when four British men-of-war arrived near Staten Island to take possession, and met no resistance. Stuyvesant had to go home and explain himself: The fort was indefensible. He didn't have the manpower. Provisions were low, the burghers were terrified of looting, and the chief gunner had come to him and said: "What can my lord do? He knows that there is no powder, and that most of it is good for nothing. . . . Were I to commence firing in the morning, I should have used all of it up by noon."

And so New Amsterdam, like Pernambuco, changed hands, and the cards were reshuffled in the international game of whist the colonial powers played. New Amsterdam became the property of the king of England's brother, the duke of York. New Netherlands by then had a population of close to ten thousand, of whom fifteen hundred were in New Amsterdam. The Dutch were treated with benign neglect and pursued their commercial activities. New York retained its cosmopolitan flavor, and Albany long remained Dutch. Women wore close-fitting dresses, the insides of houses were lined with Delft tile, and the floors were scrubbed till the boards looked planed. The Puritans said the Dutch kept their houses cleaner than their bodies, and their bodies cleaner than their souls.

The transition was almost painless, as can be seen by following the progress of William Beekman, who had arrived with Stuyvesant in 1647 at the age of twenty-three, a young man seeking his fortune. Two years later, he married, and when one of his neighbors said that his wife had been observed "in the bush with another man," he sued for slander. He bought a farm in Harlem, but had to abandon the Harlem frontier when Indians threatened to burn it—they had already killed three farmers near the Hellgate.

With his shrewd business sense and acquisitive nature, he was by 1658 a member of the upwardly mobile Dutch establishment— he owned land, a brewery, a flour mill, and slaves, and was a leader of the militia. By the time the English took over in 1664, he was one of New Amsterdam's most affluent citizens, with an estate of three thousand florins. When he balked at signing a loyalty oath to the king of England, he was threatened with the confiscation of his property and changed his mind. The important thing was to maintain one's estate, whatever flag flew. By 1678, he was an alderman, and by 1683 he was one of the eighteen members of the newly created Assembly.

William Beekman made the transition from Dutch burgher to founder of a New York dynasty, and the way this was done is a case study of how old money got that way. The first principle was to hold public office. William's son Henry, born in 1652, was a member of the Assembly from Kingston, a justice of the peace, and a captain in the militia. The Assembly had its moments of rebelliousness; in 1692, Henry Beekman was one of those who asked for an accounting of the troops employed on the Albany frontier, to make sure there was no payroll padding.

The point of being well connected politically was to obtain favorable land patents at a time of widespread corruption under Governor Benjamin Fletcher, who made New York City a haven for pirates in exchange for a share in their profits. William Nicoll, the Speaker of the Assembly, was legal adviser to the pirates. The payoffs were in Spanish dollars. Fletcher's land grants were equally notorious. There was one on the Mohawk River, given to the merchant William Pinhorne for an annual quitrent of one beaver skin, that had fifty miles of river frontage.

In 1697, elbowing in on this bounty, Henry Beekman obtained a tract of land the size of an English shire with twenty miles of river frontage in Dutchess County, embracing the present town of Rhinebeck. When the earl of Bellomont arrived in New York in May 1698 to replace Fletcher, he was so shocked by the giveaways that he sent him back to England under arrest for malfeasance. Bellomont asked London for "a good judge or two and a smart active attorney general and I will God willing . . . break all these extravagant grants."

Henry Beekman was fortunate that similar land grants had recently been made to well-connected English landowners in Ireland. You couldn't break the New York grants without creating a precedent for breaking the Irish grants. The issue was held in abeyance until the death of Bellomont in 1701. He was replaced by Lord Cornbury, who was more flexible. And Beekman, as leader of the new Assembly, was a member of the committee charged with voiding some of Bellomont's projected acts, such as "an act for vacating, breaking, and annulling several extravagant grants made by Col. Fletcher."

Besides political connections, it was important to be active in church affairs. The equation was, religion plus money equals status and power. Henry Beekman, who became the political boss of Ulster County, was a generous presence in the Dutch Reformed Church, to which he gave forty-four acres in Rhinebeck to build a church. One measure of his influence was the passing of the Bolting Act in 1694. Traditionally, the city of New York had the privilege of "bolting," or sifting, all the flour that the colony exported, according to strict regulations as to the quality, weight, and packing of flour. This was quite a cottage industry. The city had bolting supervisors, bread viewers, and bread supervisors to prevent the various sorts of fraud, such as selling bran flour.

This lucrative bolting monopoly of Manhattan dwellers so irked Henry Beekman and some of the other Ulster notables that they bribed the governor and his council into passing the Bolting Act, which rescinded the privilege; henceforward, each county could do its own bolting. Beekman helped collect the four hundred pounds in bribes, including a hundred pounds for the governor. Almost everything he did in the Assembly had some bearing on his business and land interests.

Another dynastic principle was to marry well. Henry's son, Henry, Jr., married a Livingston and then a Van Cortlandt, and became, through the dowries of his wives, the largest landholder in Dutchess County. Following in the family tradition, he was a member of the Assembly and a colonel in the militia. He was also sheriff of the colony for five years, and eventually a census taker. He found that, in 1730, of the colony's fifty thousand inhabitants, the city and county of New York contained more than eight thousand.

As these big landholders intermarried, they pulled the strings in upstate New York. Henry, Jr., ran Ulster, designating its two assemblymen and controlling perhaps five of that body's twenty-six votes. Beekman, Livingston, Pawling—these were the recurring names in the Assembly, as though by birthright. In his capacity as sheriff, one of Henry, Jr.'s duties was to find jurors for grand and petit juries in every county of the colony. There were times when he was able to stack the jury to help a friend, as in the case of Governor William Cosby, who decided that he wanted a thousand acres that the city of Albany had an option to buy from the Mohawks.

Cosby arranged for the Mohawks to come and complain to him that Albany's option had been fraudulently obtained. Then he summoned the mayor of Albany, asking him to bring the deed so that it might be read before the complaining Indians. After the deed was read, the governor handed it to one of the Indians—who tore it to pieces and threw it into the fire, once Governor Cosby, with a motion of his hands, had made him understand what he was expected to do. There was such a stink over this that a grand jury was convened in Albany, and would have indicted Cosby had not the sheriff, Henry Beekman, Jr., "taken care to put some upon the jury who did all they could to intimidate the others," according to grand jury testimony.

Henry, Jr., retired from the Assembly in 1758, at the age of seventy, and lived to be eighty-eight. He had no surviving children, but there were by then many other Beekmans, for his sons and nephews had tended to have large families, extending their influence through sheer numbers. Two of his grandsons were Chancellor Robert R. Livingston, the negotiator of the Louisiana

Purchase, and Edward Livingston, who was secretary of state under Jackson.

For the Indians, it didn't matter that much who the colonial power was, since they invariably found themselves divested of their lands and their rights while the settlers prospered. For instance, there was a growing whale industry on Long Island, and the Indians were good at going out in small boats and harpooning them. It was accepted practice for the English whalers to pay part of the Indians' wages in liquor and gunpowder. There was also money in "drift whales" that washed up onshore. But, whereas Christians finding drift whales were entitled to a quarter of the proceeds, sharing with the proprietor, the duke of York, Indians finding drift whales were awarded "such reasonable satisfaction as has been usual," according to a council ruling in 1675. There were two sets of laws, one for colonists and one for Indians.

Nor did it matter who the colonial power was, in terms of the decline of the Indian population of the New York and Long Island area. Whether under the Dutch or the English, the tribes were decimated, not by a conscious policy of extermination, but simply as a result of contact with the white man. An English settler in Long Island, Daniel Denton, wrote in 1670: "There is now but few upon the island, and those few no ways hurtful but rather serviceable to the English, and it is to be admired how strangely they have decreased by the hand of God since the first settling of those parts; for since my time [1644], when there were six towns, they are reduced to two small villages, and it hath been generally observed that when the English come to settle, a Divine Hand makes way for them by removing or cutting off the Indians either by wars one with the other, or by some raging mortal disease."

CHAPTER EIGHT

THE
PURITAN
FRONTIER

In 1630, another group of religious dissidents, the Puritans, founded Boston and spread into Massachusetts and Connecticut. Expansion was fueled by thousands of newcomers who left England in the so-called Great Migration. By 1640, there were 35,000 English settlers in North America.

The Puritan hated bear-baiting, not because it gave pain to the bear, but because it gave pleasure to the spectators.

MACAULAY

The difference between a failed colony like New Netherlands and a successful colony like New England was not financial backing from home, the volume of Indian trade, the form of government adopted, or the imposition of a religious orthodoxy; it was numbers. New Netherlands and New France failed because they were thinly settled; Virginia and New England succeeded because colonists came by the thousands during periods of crisis in England.

Charles I succeeded James I in 1625, when his older brother, Henry, died. Charles was small and shy and stammered a bit. Even Van Dyck, in his triple portrait, does not quite manage to make him look regal. Because his wife was the sister of the French King Louis XIII, he was thought of as soft on Catholicism. Trouble was not long in coming. There was a strong Puritan party in the House of Commons, and when Parliament started impeaching bishops, the king arrested some of its members. Finally, Charles dismissed Parliament and locked up the Puritan leaders. In a return to personal rule, he reigned without an elected legislature for eleven years.

This period, from 1629 to 1640, coincided with the Great Migration, which sent twenty thousand Englishmen to the shores of New England. What was a trickle in 1607, and a stream in 1620, became a flood after 1629. A large number of Englishmen, made miserable by economic depression, unemployment, poor harvests, and religious persecution, did not want to live in their own country.

In 1633, William Laud, a longtime advocate of religious uniformity and authoritarian royal government, was named archbishop of Canterbury. He was in favor of the wearing of surplices, the railing off of the communion table from the congregation, and other "popish" practices. With Laud at the helm, the Tower of London was soon crowded with pamphlet-writing Puritan lawyers. William Prynne had his ears cut off, was branded on both cheeks with the letters "SL" (for "Seditious Libeler"), and was sentenced to life imprisonment. His crime was calling actresses "notorious whores"—acting was one of the queen's hobbies.

In this constrained political climate, the sentiments of thousands of dissidents were summed up in a couplet that appeared in *The London Magazine:*

> *We are on tiptoe in this land,*
> *Waiting to pass to the American Strand.*

After the Pilgrims had led the way, Charles began to grant more patents to other groups, such as the New England Company. John Endecott, a Puritan veteran of the wars in Holland, sailed with about fifty settlers in June 1628 and landed in September at Naumkeag, renamed Salem. There he found Roger Conant, who had left Plymouth and with a few others built some huts in 1626.

Five more ships brought three hundred colonists, including two ministers, Samuel Skelton and Francis Higginson, who founded the first Puritan church in North America. Though dogged by bad luck, Higginson held fast to his Puritan conviction that everything was "God's pleasure." When his four-year-old daughter, Mary, died of smallpox at sea and was "buried in the bowels of the great Atlantic," he saw her passing as God's will.

She had been freed from a world of misery, for she was a cripple, with a twisted spine and crooked knees. Higginson was ordained in Salem on August 6, 1629, but died after only a year in the colony, leaving a wife and eight children. His last sermon was titled: "What Went Ye Out into the Wilderness to See?"

That was a particularly appropriate question for "persons of competent estates," such as John Winthrop, a Cambridge graduate with a five-hundred-acre property. Why would he abandon his green English acres? In 1629, like other Puritans, he went through a crisis of pessimism concerning the state of England. He could no longer hide his dislike of the Catholic queen, and of the king's behavior. He saw a sick society, a countryside full of beggars, horse thieves, "lewd bailiffs," and orphans, a land of "wandering ghosts in the shape of men." He wrote his wife of "evil and declining times." Feeling a need to start over, and wanting to take part in a worthy enterprise, he joined the Massachusetts Bay Company (the reorganized New England Company), which had a grant in the area where Endecott had already landed.

In May 1629, Winthrop wrote his wife that the Lord would provide "a shelter and a hiding place for us and ours." On August 26, 1629, he signed the so-called Cambridge agreement with the eleven other leaders of the company. They pledged to arrive in New England by September 1, 1630, and each put up a bond as a guarantee that they would sell their estates in England. But their stroke of genius was to arrange for the management of the company to remain in their hands rather than under the control of directors in England, as had been the case with previous voyages. In this way, they freed themselves from all controls in the mother country. There would be no board of investors thousands of miles away to hound them, no distant government by whim. Thanks to the device of the movable charter, the Massachusetts Bay Colony was self-governing from the start, as well as self-financing.

They sailed in April 1630, with five ships and about six hundred settlers. Discipline was strict. On Winthrop's ship, the *Arbella*, two men "who pierced a rundlet of strong water, and stole some of it," were laid in bolts. Two men "falling at odds and fighting," contrary to the orders posted on board ship, had to walk the deck all day with their hands tied behind them. A man who "used contemptuous speeches in our presence" was laid in bolts. A servant who had given a child a trinket in exchange for the child's biscuit ration, which he sold to other servants, was suspended from a bar by the hands, with a basket of stones around his neck, for two hours. This was definitely a law-and-order outfit.

The arrival, on June 12, 1630, was less than joyous. Endecott's people, who had been there nearly two years, were in a shabby state, most of them living in wigwams, with not enough crops planted to feed themselves. One of *Arbella*'s passengers, Thomas Dudley, who had been the earl of Lincoln's steward, described the scene in a letter to the countess of Lincoln. The settlement was "in a sad and unexpected condition, above 80 being dead the winter before; and many of those alive weak and sick; all the corn and bread amongst them . . . hardly sufficient to feed them a fortnight."

Immediately there was a religious squabble. The Salem minister, Samuel Skelton, refused Winthrop and Dudley communion because they could not show to which Congregational church they belonged in England. "Salem, where we landed, pleased us not," Dudley wrote.

Dudley's eighteen-year-old daughter, Anne, was on board with her husband, Simon Bradstreet. Like the others, she had heard Winthrop's shipboard sermon, "Model of Christian Charity," in which he reminded the group of the great work ahead and warned against lapsing into chaotic individualism. He asked them to "knit together in their work as one man." But they found that they could not knit with the people of Salem, who treated them poorly and failed to extend the hand of friendship.

America was an escape hatch, where you could start over, but it also fostered dispersal rather than a spirit of community. The Winthrop people could not remain with the Salem people, but had to move on in a secondary exile, shunned in their newfound land as in their homeland. What were they but new Adams, as in the following lines by Anne Bradstreet, the first real poet America produced?

> *Who like a miscreant's driven from that place*
> *To get his bread with pain, and sweat of face:*
> *A penalty impos'd on his backsliding race.*

The wilderness was not a deliverance, but "a penalty impos'd."

The new arrivals headed south, first trying Charlestown, between the Charles and Mystic rivers. They set up their tents there, but left when some of their people started coming down with dysentery. Next they crossed the Charles to the Shawmut Peninsula, two miles long, a mile wide, and almost an island, joined to the mainland by a low-lying neck of land. This peninsula, renamed Boston, was an odd choice for settlement; there was little room for growth, and more settlers were arriving. From the start, there was dispersal. One group, led by Sir Richard Saltonstall, went to Watertown, and another, led by William Pynchon, went to Roxbury. But the towns were close together, a contrast to the more far-flung dispersal at Jamestown, which had led to the massacre in 1622.

The new settlers soon began creating the way of life that they wanted without any interference from England. As Winthrop's son John, Jr., later wrote, they had "all things to do, as in the beginning of the world." Two hundred died in the winter of 1630–31, including Winthrop's son Henry, who drowned in a creek, and Lady Arabella Johnson (of the house of Lincoln, which went back to William the Conqueror) and her husband, Isaac, who had come "from a paradise of plenty and pleasure into a wilderness of want." They died, as usual, of scurvy, but in February 1631 a ship carrying lemons brought relief. About eighty of the faint-hearted—"cowards and degenerates," Dudley said—gave up and went back to England in that ship. But there were plenty more arrivals, and by 1632 the Bay Colony had two thousand settlers. The number doubled by 1634, and doubled again by 1637.

For thirty years, from 1630 to 1660, they pursued their "errand in the wilderness" without interference. According to the New England model, each town was built around a church and a congregation. The simple, practical government structure consisted of a governor, a lieutenant governor, and a number of assistants. To vote or to hold elective office, you had to be a member of the church. To join the church, you had to describe your past life and your conversion.

Land was distributed, each lot representing enough space for a house, a garden, and an orchard. The farmland was divided in strips so that everyone would have some plowland, woodland, pastureland, and meadowland. Some land was held in common, for the village green, or for the future.

It was a community of small landholders on a brine-washed coast of ledge and sandy beach, with a strong and fully realized social order—a frontier of medieval English villages, still using the common-field system, inhabited by people who had come to America not because they wanted change, but to preserve their way of life from a meddling king.

It was a cattle frontier along the Charles, a prim and proper colony of long-winded pulpit rhetoric and cold feet in the meeting-house, where merchants in lace collars mingled with farmers in homespun breeches; where the governor wore a ruff, lace waist-bands, and white gloves, and was escorted by halberdiers. It was a class-conscious frontier, discriminatory and undemocratic. The seating plan of the church was based on the age, estate, and dignity of the townspeople, with everyone jockeying for better pew posi-tion. It was a frontier where not the tiniest green sprout of individ-ualism could grow, and where the formerly oppressed rather quickly adopted the methods of their oppressors. In Boston, the Puritans were soon cutting off dissidents' ears and branding them, as had been done to the Puritans themselves in England. In June 1631, Philip Ratcliff, a servant who was clearly out of his mind, convicted of "most foul, scandalous invectives" against the church and the government, had his ears chopped off. This led Edward Howes, a relative of Winthrop's, to write from London: "I had heard divers complaints against the severity of your govern-ment."

Winthrop might have replied that when the wilderness is on your doorstep you have to govern with a firm hand. It was impor-tant to maintain order, by keeping Sabbath, ringing the hogs, and girdling the trees. Idleness was a criminal offense, called "mis-spence of time." Winthrop was fighting a process of disruption, a falling away of Puritan ideals into chaotic individualism. "I think there are some persons who never showed so much wickedness in England as they have done here," he wrote.

Among those guilty of un-Puritan-like conduct was Win-throp's own deputy governor, Thomas Dudley. As the earl of Lincoln's steward, he had made loans to tenants on the earl's es-tates, a practice he carried to Massachusetts, advancing seven and a half bushels of seed corn to farmers and demanding ten back at harvest time. He was charged with "oppressing usury" and forced to resign.

The original Puritan concept called for a settlement that stayed put, a "city on a hill," but the Massachusetts frontier con-tained the germ of continuous expansion. Thousands of new arriv-als had to be settled, and a buffer had to be created against the French in Maine, who were bound "to prove ill neighbors (being papists)," wrote Winthrop. In 1633, John Winthrop, Jr., was sent with twelve men to Agawam (now Ipswich) to start a plantation there, "lest an enemy, finding it void, should possess it and take it from us."

But the central dilemma of the frontier was, as always, Indian relations. William Wood, who spent four years in the Bay Colony, between 1629 and 1633, wrote in *New England's Prospect* that the Indians were courteous and hospitable, helping "wandering, benighted coasters" who were lost on their paths, which were seldom broader than "a cart's rut." They could find their way in the wilderness as well as any Londoner could find Charing Cross, and were of "a kind and affable disposition." Wood conceded that Indians could do things that the Europeans could not, such as catch beaver, animals "too cunning for the English, who seldom or never catch any of them." They could also scrape, trim, sew, and soften the beaver skins. In fact, there seemed to be no end to their skills: They could make bark canoes, collecting bark in the summer when it peeled off easily. They could make wampum, boring and drilling the shells and polishing and stringing them with much skill and patience. For Wood, however, the idleness of the Indians was a problem. To the Puritans, working meant regular hours, but for the Indians, it meant periods of inactivity alternating with months of hard labor on a hunting trip.

The Puritans were careful to buy the land they occupied, and they were pretty pleased with themselves for their virtuous acquisitions. Cotton Mather observed that "the good people of New England have carried it with so much tenderness towards the tawny creatures among whom we live, that they would not own so much as one foot of land in the country without a fair purchase."

That meant nothing to the Indians, whose concept of land wasn't based on ownership but on use; the land belonged to those who hunted and farmed on it. What did signing a deed mean to people who had no written language? How could they appreciate the concept of an absentee landlord? The Indians sold the land but delayed their departure with clauses giving them the right to fish, hunt, and gather nuts, which led to further complications. It is a mistake to think that because there was unlimited land the Indians treated land cessions lightly. Edward Winslow noted that every sachem in New England knew "how far the bounds and limits of his own country extend; and that is his own proper inheritance."

Since the Indians were on their Boston doorstep, the Puritans deemed it necessary to place them under the English court system. They were charged with violating laws they didn't know existed. In Plymouth they were expected to keep the Sabbath. Fornication was not a crime within their own culture, but in Puritan New England they were punished for it. Indians were arrested by English constables, dragged off to English jails, examined by English judges, tried by English juries, convicted and sentenced under English law, and whipped in an English town square in front of jeering English townspeople.

Despite all this, the Indians took every opportunity to ask for redress if the offense was against them. In September 1632, an Indian complained that his wife had been "solicited to incontinency" by a young settler, who was whipped in front of the Indian couple. They were "very well satisfied," having evidently understood the Puritan concept of adultery as a crime. That same September, Josiah Plaistowe and two servants were convicted of stealing corn from the Indians. He was degraded from the title of "gentleman" and fined five pounds. His men were whipped. The Indians learned that they would be treated fairly in court, despite some laws that seemed discriminatory (one law banned Indians from "hankering about" English homes).

To the Puritans, Indian relations, like everything else, were ordained by God. It was God who had caused the Indians to abandon the coast, so that they could move in. "If God were not pleased with our inheriting these parts," Winthrop wondered, "why did he drive out the natives before us? And why doth he still make room for us, by diminishing them as we increase?"

In 1633, another epidemic carried away a good many Indians on the Connecticut River. This was the signal for further expansion, for the Bay Colony towns were "like a hive overstocked with bees," in the words of Cotton Mather. The Connecticut Valley beckoned, with its great four-hundred-mile-long river, the only river flowing down the entire length of New England. Originating on the Quebec side of the Vermont border, it forms the border between Vermont and New Hampshire. It then crosses Massachusetts and Connecticut and empties into Long Island Sound. The Dutch had been the first to explore it, when Adrien Block sailed up it in 1614 in the *Onrust* (Restless), and had an island named after him.

The gradual foray into Connecticut was the beginning of the

westward movement. It engendered a four-cornered struggle that involved the Bay Colonists, the Plymouth Pilgrims, the Dutch, and the Indians. The main actors included three soldiers—Captain John Underhill, and Lieutenants Lion Gardiner and John Mason —and one Puritan entrepreneur, William Pynchon.

In 1631, a Connecticut sachem visited Boston and Plymouth to ask the English to settle on his river, for the river tribes were being terrorized by ferocious newcomers called Pequots, whose name meant "killers of men." In 1632, the Dutch bought land at Saybrook, at the mouth of the river, but didn't settle it. Early in 1633, Edward Winslow, then governor of Plymouth, came to Boston with William Bradford to confer with John Winthrop about setting up a joint trading post on the river to trade for beaver and hemp. Despite their desire to jump in ahead of the Dutch, they decided against it, because of the three or four thousand warlike Pequots in the area. Navigation was also difficult, because of the ice and the violent current. "We thought not fit to meddle with it," Winthrop wrote. These drawbacks did not deter the Dutch, who in June 1633 bought a mile of river frontage at today's Hartford. They built a fort with two cannons and set up a trading post they called the House of Good Hope.

In September 1633, the English trader John Oldham reconnoitered the river and came back singing its praises. So the Pilgrims decided to go ahead and brave the Dutch, and sent Lieutenant William Holmes up the river with a prefab house all ready to go up. Some compliant sachems were willing to sell him land, whether it belonged to them or not. One can imagine the scene when the Pilgrim barque reached the Dutch fort. The cannoneers standing by with lighted match, the New Netherlands banner floating above them, the sound of the drumbeat echoing on the river, the order to stop.

"What are your intentions?"

"To go upriver and trade."

The Dutch threatened at first to fire, but, when the Pilgrims insisted that they would proceed, the Dutch refrained from opening fire on the people to whom they had granted asylum in Leiden. The Pilgrims went upriver a few miles, to the site of today's Windsor, and built their post, feeling that they had done the Dutch no wrong. There was plenty of room for everybody.

The situation was ripe for strife, needing only an incident to trigger it. That arrived in the person of a confirmed troublemaker by the name of John Stone, a sea captain and trader from the West Indies, who had taken some cattle from Virginia to Boston and was now on his way back to Virginia. While in Boston, he was caught in bed with a married woman, Mrs. Bancroft. When he was brought in irons before the governor and charged with drunkenness and adultery, he "spoke contemptuously of the magistrates," calling one of his judges, Roger Ludlow, a "just ass." The Boston Puritans, failing to appreciate the pun on "justice," fined him one hundred pounds and banished him.

Sailing down the Atlantic Coast in January 1634 with a crew of eight, Captain Stone decided to take a look at the Connecticut River. He kidnaped a couple of Pequots to guide him. When three of his men went ashore with the Indians on January 21, the Pequots killed them and then boarded Stone's ship and shot him and the rest of his crew with the loaded guns they found on board.

Even though Stone was a disreputable fellow, who had just been banished from Boston, the Puritan authorities had to think of the larger issue of forest diplomacy. To let the murder of an English trader go unpunished (particularly when he was reported to have been roasted and eaten) would be to invite further attacks on the trading posts already established there. Happily for the settlers, the Pequots were then warring with their neighbors, the Narragansetts, as well as with the Dutch. They did not want to make enemies of the English.

In November 1634, a Pequot delegation arrived in Boston with gifts and wampum. They explained that Captain Stone had taken two of their men captive, and so they had retaliated. "This was related with such confidence and gravity," said Winthrop, "as having no means to contradict it, we inclined to believe it."

Nonetheless, the Puritans insisted that the Pequots must deliver the guilty men to English justice. They replied that, of the nine Indians who had taken part in the attack, seven were either dead of the pox or slain by the Dutch. But they agreed to deliver the remaining two and to pay a tribute of four hundred fathoms of wampum, as well as forty beaver and thirty otter pelts. In return, they asked for the friendship of the English, and invited them to settle on their river.

The invitation was timely, for at the September 1634 meeting of the General Court there had been a heated debate when a group from Newtown (Cambridge) had asked for permission to remove to Connecticut. They had already sent a boat up the river that June. This group was led by Thomas Hooker, a dissenter fleeing arrest in England, who had arrived in Cambridge in 1633. Hooker argued that Cambridge was cramped, their fields were too rocky, and they didn't have room for their cattle.

Winthrop told Hooker and his people that they ought not to bolt, since they were all knit in one body. He added that in Connecticut they would encounter the Dutch and Pequot threats. But Hooker insisted on "the strong bent of their spirits to move thither." The court was divided—fifteen for and ten against. There was so much dissension that they broke up, and later met again, deciding that it was better to enlarge Cambridge than to allow the move to Connecticut.

This could only be a temporary solution. The westward movement was under way, encouraged by the pox that continued to rage on the Connecticut River. In 1634, the Indians died "like rotten sheep," Bradford wrote. They were too sick to fetch wood for fire and burned their wooden dishes, and even their bows and arrows, for fuel. The Pilgrim traders at Windsor got them wood and water, made them fires, cooked their food, and buried their dead. Not one of them got sick. If you walk with God, you will stay healthy.

The Indians were in terrible shape, with the pox boils breaking and running into one another, and "their skin cleaving by reason thereof to the mats they lie on. When they turn them, a whole side will flay off at once, and they will be all of a gore blood, most fearful to behold." What was horrible for the Indians was good news for the Bay Colonists, for, as Bradford wrote, "Some of our neighbors in the Bay, hearing of the fame of the Connecticut river . . . began now to prosecute their settlement with great eagerness."

In 1635, the General Court reversed itself, giving four different groups "leave to remove whither they pleased, so as they continue under this government." The conquest of Connecticut was under way. A group from Watertown settled Wethersfield, south of Hartford; a group from Dorchester settled right next to the Pilgrims, already at Windsor; a group from Roxbury went farther north on the river, to the site of Springfield, Massachusetts; and Hooker's people settled Hartford. By April 1636, Hartford had its own court, the first case being that of Henry Stiles, for "trading a piece with the Indians for corn."

By then, the Connecticut River was dotted with small settlements of newcomers infringing on one another in the wilderness. The Dorchester people squatted on land that belonged to the Pilgrims. From Plymouth, William Bradford fumed that it was "an attempt not only to intrude themselves into the rights and possessions of others, but in effect to thrust them all out."

The Pilgrims, however, not wanting to fight with their brethren, or to live in continual contention with them, "fell to treaty." Under the agreement signed in May 1637, they sold most of their land to the Dorchester intruders, keeping only the river frontage at Windsor. "Thus was the controversy ended," wrote Bradford, "but the unkindness not so soon forgotten."

In spite of their grudge, the Pilgrims gave their neighbors a helping hand, storing their goods and canoes, finding them guides, and lending them food, particularly during the first winter, when they lost much of their cattle and were reduced to eating acorns. Thirteen of them were so distressed they went back to Massachusetts, minus one who fell through the ice and drowned.

The leader of the Roxbury group was the wily William Pynchon, who combined religious piety with the profit motive. A member of the inner circle of the Bay Colony, he was one of the select few to sign the Cambridge agreement, by which they had agreed to emigrate in person with their families. Like the others, he was a devout Puritan; he had sold his land in England for sixty pounds and paid a subscription fee of twenty-five. Soon after reaching Salem, he moved to Roxbury, serving as one of the eighteen assistants of the new government. He was also treasurer of the company, collecting funds from town rates and fines to settle bills for materials, labor, and salaries.

Pynchon spent his capital on a boat to enter the beaver trade on the coast of Maine. He did very well, and, with the colony taxing his beaver at the rate of twelve pence per pound, he was soon its biggest taxpayer. His wife died during the first year at Roxbury, leaving him with five children, and he soon remarried a widow, Mrs. Frances Samford.

But the beaver trade in Maine declined, and he found Roxbury overcrowded and too close to Boston; he decided to move into the wilderness to the west and start a trading post. His plan was to go far enough upriver to intercept the beaver that the Indians were bringing down to the Dutch. He had met John Oldham, who had been deported from Plymouth and had been up and down the

Connecticut, describing "the many desirable places . . . fit to receive many hundred inhabitants."

Once Pynchon got permission from the General Court in 1635, he wrote Jonathan Brewster, the Pilgrim agent at Windsor, asking him to give "house room" for the goods of a party arriving from Boston. In the initial party were only Pynchon and seven others, including his son-in-law, Henry Smith, and a minister, George Moxon. That first march westward, from the cluster of settlements fringing the bay to the Connecticut Valley, was a mere hundred miles. To Pynchon, however, it was a journey into the unknown. He wondered what kind of neighbors the Indians would be, and how his people would feed themselves.

Pynchon went fifteen miles above Windsor and chose a spot where the Indian overland trail from Boston intersected with the Connecticut River. Anyone traveling downriver would have to break at the falls there; it was a perfect spot for his warehouse. The only problem, he wrote, was that the best ground was "encumbered with Indians." Finally, he bargained with them for four or five miles of land on both sides of the river. The deed was signed by eighteen Indians with their marks, and the price was eighteen fathoms of wampum (a fathom being six feet), eighteen coats, eighteen hatchets, eighteen hoes, and eighteen knives, plus particular presents to the chiefs.

By the end of the summer of 1635, Pynchon's house and warehouse were built, and he had started receiving trade goods from Boston. He eventually wound up his other business there and removed himself permanently to this loose circuit of river towns. The advantage he enjoyed of being the northernmost trader on the river gave him a virtual monopoly. He also had strong bay connections and could move the goods efficiently. He hired an Indian interpreter and started making his own wampum, buying loose shells and hiring Indian women to string them, until he had an inventory of twenty thousand fathoms.

This seemed more like the triumph of individualism than the Puritan compact. One man, with a small group of friends, had broken away from the main colony. He built a town, which he called Springfield, after his birthplace outside London. You could see it go up—houses with thatched roofs, the wooden frames of the chimneys covered with mortar. The birth of government was contained in the first commonsense rule: every house had to have a ladder in case of fire.

The first houses had river frontage, and narrow paths led to the training ground and the burial ground. At the foot of a lane was a wharf. In the 1636 agreement to found a town, the second article limited its size to "fifty families rich and poor." As new problems arose, bylaws were added: A man could fell a tree to make a canoe for his own use but not to sell it. No person could wash or water hemp or flax in the brook (an early antipollution law). No inhabitant could sell his house lot to a stranger without advising the select townsmen (the concept of zoning). Eventually, there were two public buildings, the meetinghouse and the jail. The emphasis on corporal punishment in the first towns can be partly explained by the fact that jails were too expensive to maintain. It was cheaper and easier to whip and brand offenders.

While Pynchon was building his town on the river, something else was afoot in England. The earl of Warwick, who held a modest patent "from the Narragansett to the Pacific," turned it over in 1631 to fifteen Puritan lords and gentlemen. In 1635, John Winthrop, Jr., was named "first governor of the river Connecticut" by this group, and set off for the New World to claim his territory. But when he got to Boston in October, he learned that the Dutch had been on the river since 1623. He sent twenty men to build a fort at the mouth of the Connecticut, which they called Fort Saybrook, after two of the patentees, Viscount Say and Lord Brooke.

They took possession of a point of land just above the mouth on the left-hand or western side, between two coves, and began to fell trees. But a military engineer was needed to design and command the fort. Experienced officers were in short supply in New England, and had to be imported from the mother country.

This was how Lieutenant Lion Gardiner, lately in the prince of Orange's service in Holland, was recruited by the patentees to serve four years as commander of Fort Saybrook, at one hundred pounds a year. When he arrived in March 1636 with his wife, he was disappointed to see a mere clearing. There were no houses or fields for planting. He designed a square palisaded fort with an earthen embankment, a moat, a drawbridge, and at each corner a cannon with a range of one mile, which could reach Poverty Point, across the river. Soon the fort was home to twenty-four men, women, and children. They planted some corn two miles away.

There were new complications on the Pequot front. The Pequots had failed to turn over the two surviving murderers of Captain Stone to the Boston authorities. The Bostonians were now planning to return their presents, which the Pequots would interpret as a declaration of war. Gardiner pleaded for leniency, at least until his fort was completed. War might start any day, and he would be a prime target. When John Oldham came by in April 1636, on his way to Block Island to trade with the Narragansetts, Gardiner complained that he was being left "at the stake to be roasted." His contract did not mention scalping, and he was in no mood to play the sacrificial lamb.

On May 20, 1636, the trader John Gallop, sailing near Block Island with his sons and a servant, spotted Oldham's pinnace, its deck swarming with Indians. He rammed the pinnace and boarded as the Indians jumped overboard. He tied up four who were too slow to escape, but, knowing their skill at untying themselves, he threw them bound into the sea.

Gallop found Oldham's warm body under an old fishing net, his head cleft to the brains. His hands and legs were gashed as if the Indians had been in the process of cutting them off. It was an odd murder, written off to Indian unpredictability, for Oldham had traded regularly with the Narragansetts and was on good terms with them. The question was, what should be done about it, and should it be linked to the difficulties with the Pequots?

On June 18, Jonathan Brewster sent a warning letter to Fort Saybrook, saying, "The Pequots have some mistrust that the English will shortly come against them." He feared a pre-emptive strike.

On July 4, 1636, in Boston, the newly created Standing Council (responsible for military matters) instructed John Winthrop, Jr., to give the Pequots an ultimatum. Either they would comply with the terms of the 1634 treaty and turn over the two Indians who had killed Captain Stone, or the treaty would be null, which would mean war. That July, there was a conference at Fort Saybrook attended by some Pequot chiefs plus Sassous, the sachem of the Western Niantics. They were told that, if they would "clear themselves of these matters," the English would "not refuse to hearken to any reasonable proposition from them for confirmation of the peace." Captain Stone's killers had to be handed over with more tribute. If the treaty was void, the English would "revenge the blood of our countrymen as occasion shall serve." The Pequots offered tribute, but the English delegates "said they would have their lives and not their presents." And that was where things stood in July 1636.

On August 25, 1636, the Standing Council sent a punitive expedition under the command of John Endecott to Block Island, with orders "to put to death the men, but to spare the women and children, and to bring them away, and to take possession of the island." From there, they were to go to the Pequots to demand the murderers of Captain Stone and the other English, one thousand fathoms of wampum for damages, and some of their children as hostages. If the Indians refused, they were to "obtain the reparations by force."

Second in command was Captain John Underhill, another of those colorful officers whose services were available for hire. A nominal Puritan, Underhill had lost his position as captain of the Boston militia for being a follower of the heretical Anne Hutchinson. He was also a colonial Don Juan, always in trouble with the Boston authorities. For staring at Miriam Wilborne during a lecture, he was charged with adultery. Mistress Wilborne was something of a scarlet woman, having been accused of going to meeting with "wanton open-work gloves slit at the thumbs and fingers for the purpose of taking snuff."

Captain Underhill insisted that he had not looked at her "with lust." The judge, Hugh Peter, asked why he had not looked at other ladies present as well, and he replied, "Verily they are not desirable women." This frank response was seen as proof of guilt, and Underhill was suspended from the church.

The raid on the Narragansetts on Block Island with ninety volunteers was a fiasco. When the Indians saw the armored Englishmen tramping on the beach, they slipped into the forest. "They observed the old rule," wrote Captain Underhill, "tis good sleeping in a whole skin." The English killed a few stray Indians and looted the Narragansett village. "Many well-wrought mats our soldiers brought from thence, and several delightful baskets."

They then sailed from Block Island Sound past Fishers Island to Long Island Sound and Fort Saybrook, where they stayed for four days with Lieutenant Gardiner, who was not overjoyed to see them. Realizing that a raid on the Pequots could only mean trouble, he told Underhill: "You come here to raise these wasps around my ears, and then you will take wing and flee away."

When the raiding party entered Pequot country, the Indians at first came running, crying, "What cheer, Englishmen, what cheer, what do you come for?" But when the English did not reply, the Pequots realized they were not there to trade, and began to cry, according to Underhill, "Are you hoggery, will you cram us?" That is, Are you angry, will you kill us, and do you come to fight? Once again the Indians slipped off into the high grass and wooded interior, though the raiders managed to kill one, burn some wigwams, and take as much corn as they could carry.

Now the wasps were raised, and Gardiner was repeatedly harassed. The Pequots shot three men he had sent to stand guard in the cornfield. In October, he sent five men to gather hay at Calve's Island, four miles north, near the Lyme shore. The Pequots caught one named Butterfield, killed him, and ate him. The place became known as Butterfield's Meadow.

On February 22, 1637, Gardiner took ten men and three dogs a half-mile from the fort to burn weeds and reeds where the Indians might hide. Each man carried his matchlock with a length of match. Four Indians rose up out of the flaming reeds and ran off. When more Indians were sighted, two men threw down their guns and ran back to the fort. The Indians attacked and "kept us in a half-moon," Gardiner wrote. "Thomas Hurlbut was shot almost through the thigh, John Spencer in the back into his kidneys, myself into the thigh, and two more were shot dead. . . ." The Indians were so close they had to be fought hand to hand with swords. The knowledge of what would happen to them if they were taken alive gave them added strength. Gardiner was shot so full of arrows that his buffcoat looked like a pincushion, but it saved him.

When they got back to the fort, Gardiner faced the two cowards who had fled, and decided to draw lots to see which of them would hang. But the two were spared at the intercession of the other men, who argued that they needed every able body. Having bandaged his wounds, Gardiner went out with eight men to retrieve the abandoned muskets, and found a body with an arrow through it, "which I took out and cleansed it, and presumed to send to the Bay, because they had said that the arrows of the Indians were of no force."

It was a time of great stress for the Connecticut settlements, which were isolated from one another and easy to pick off. Pynchon in Springfield asked Roger Ludlow in Windsor for help, and Ludlow replied: "If the case be never so dangerous, we can neither help you, nor you us. . . . What we plant is before our doors, little anywhere else. . . . Our people are scarce able to stand on their legs"—because of watch and ward duties.

In April 1637, the Pequots attacked Wethersfield, below Hartford, where the settlers had dispossessed Sachem Sowheag, contrary to their agreement to let him live on his own lands. On April 23, the Pequots raided workers in the fields, killing six men and three women and taking two girls captive. They butchered the livestock and burned the storehouses and haystacks. A day or two later, Gardiner saw a flotilla of Indian canoes coming down the creek beyond the marsh. Billowing from them, sail-like, were the shirts and smocks of their victims. They sailed right past the fort, mocking the garrison. Gardiner fired his cannon, and one shot broke the bow off the canoe carrying the two girls, but the Pequots pulled up to a narrow beach and got away. The girls were later rescued by the Dutch. The oldest was about sixteen, and when she was asked how she'd been treated, she said, according to Underhill, "they did solicit her to uncleanness," but she had refused to "sin against my God."

The Wethersfield massacre spurred the English to action. On May 1, 1637, the General Court in Hartford mobilized a force of ninety men, forty-two from Hartford, thirty from Windsor, and eighteen from Wethersfield. An initial detachment left Hartford on May 10 commanded by John Mason, a lieutenant in the English army who had arrived in Boston in 1632 to serve as a militia leader. He was described as "tall and portly, but nevertheless full of martial valor."

Mason moved to Windsor in 1635 and became a freeman, but not a member of the church, which meant that he could not vote. Initially, he was disappointed by the "vacant wilderness" and the discrimination against bachelors, who were fined as an inducement to wed. Although Mason wasn't a Puritan, he had to go to Sunday service to avoid a five-shilling fine, and sat through the tedium of a three-hour service in a meetinghouse that was so cold in winter that the water froze in the baptismal fonts. Churchgoers dropped broken pieces of old bullets into the collection box: everything was for appearance's sake, and it was important to be seen putting something in the box. After the meeting, he had to eat cold food for dinner, because cooking was banned on Sunday. For this he had left London and its pleasures—for this village of shacks thatched with grass, and dirt paths where cattle strayed.

In the spring of 1637, when Lieutenant Mason marched on the Pequots with Captain Underhill and ninety English soldiers, about two hundred Indians from other tribes were also with them. This small army sailed from Saybrook on May 19, entering the Pawcatuck River, which today forms part of the border between Connecticut and Rhode Island. They marched three miles and came to a field near today's Mystic, where some Indians told them that the Pequots had two "almost impregnable forts."

Mason's plan was to attack the smaller of the two forts first. Massacre was the objective. "We had formerly concluded to destroy them by the sword and save the plunder," he wrote. That night, "the rocks were our pillows," and they heard the enemy singing in the fort, "with great insulting and rejoicing." Before dawn on May 26, they stormed the fort, killed some Indians in a wigwam, and went looking for more. Then they got a firebrand and set some wigwams on fire. "The Indians ran as men most dreadfully amazed."

"Many were burned in the fort," wrote Captain Underhill, "both men, women, and children. Others, forced out, came in troops . . . twenty and thirty at a time, which our soldiers received and entertained with the point of a sword. Down fell men, women, and children; those that escaped us fell into the hands of the Indians that were in the rear of us." Mason estimated that between six and seven hundred Pequots were killed, whereas the English had two killed and twenty wounded. Underhill wrote: "Our Indians came to us, and much rejoiced at our victories, and greatly admired the manner of the Englishmen's fight, but cried, mach it mach it: that is, it is naught, because it is too furious, and slays too many men." ("Admire" then meant "be surprised at," and "naught" meant "naughty," or "wicked." The Indians were shocked at the ruthlessness of the English.)

Those Pequots who escaped were hunted down in a swamp. The river Indians, whom the Pequots had often terrorized, were paid a bounty to go after survivors. "Happy were they who could bring in their heads to the English," Mason said. Only about two hundred Pequots escaped, and went to live with other tribes. They had in effect ceased to exist as a people, although today their descendants have made a comeback by operating the Foxwoods Casino on their two-thousand-acre reservation in southeastern

Connecticut. The extermination of the Pequots delivered the Connecticut River to the English settlements. The victorious river towns emerged with a heightened sense of their own sovereignty, and in 1639 formed a separate government from Massachusetts.

Another result of the war was the formation—in 1643, in Boston—of the New England Confederation, uniting Massachusetts, Plymouth, Connecticut, and New Haven (Rhode Island and Maine were excluded because of their political and religious uncongeniality). The articles of agreement included a limited mutual-defense treaty.

The war also provided an early example of profiteering. In March 1638, when the Connecticut settlements were suffering war-induced food shortages, the commissioners at Hartford asked William Pynchon to buy five hundred bushels of corn from the Indians at five shillings apiece. When Pynchon began to waffle over the terms of the contract, the Hartford court sent Lieutenant Mason to Springfield to stiffen his resolve.

On March 21, 1638, Mason called on Pynchon. They were standing outside Pynchon's house, and Mason was explaining why he was there, in his loud, blustering way. Pynchon suggested they go inside and speak in private: it was not a good idea to let the Indians know they were short of corn. "I care not who knows it," said Mason. "I have brought some cloth and wampum, to trade some corn with the Indians, and I desire you to deal with them for us and to bind them to a bargain and bring it down."

Pynchon said it was pointless to bind the Indians to a bargain or to pay them in advance, since they never kept their promises. Wanting no part of Mason's dealings, he said, "I will neither make nor meddle to bind you to a bargain."

Seeing Pynchon as a shirker in an important colonial matter, Mason asked, "What hurt can it be to you? I pray, sir, let me know, for it is a dark riddle to me."

To calm Mason down, Pynchon brought in Parson George Moxon, who said, "An Indian promise is no more than to have a pig by the tail." As soon as the Indians sensed there was an English shortage, they would raise the price, saying that their corn had been ruined by the snow, or that the river was too high for them to bring it down.

When Pynchon finally agreed to buy some corn for six fathoms of wampum a peck with delivery to Springfield, or eight fathoms a peck with delivery to Hartford, Mason became convinced that he was manipulating the price to make a bigger profit. It looked to Mason as though Pynchon, having cornered the grain market, was just chasing the almighty shilling, in violation of every Puritan principle.

At the next session of the General Court in Hartford, Pynchon was charged with deliberately raising the price of corn for his private gain, and was summoned to stand trial for "unfaithful dealing in the trade of corn." Pynchon denied being a speculator, but was found guilty and fined forty bushels of corn. He felt that the whole trial was a Hartford conspiracy to rob him of his trade, "a plain turning me out of the saddle." Thomas Hooker, now pastor of the Hartford church, saw Pynchon as a grasping profiteer and said, "I do assure you, we know him from the bottom to the brim, and follow him in all his privy footsteps."

Pynchon went back to England in 1652, and died there ten years later. His son John remained in charge in Springfield, where he ran the trading company and the town.

As for the officers in the Pequot War, Captain Underhill returned to Boston and continued chasing skirts. Lieutenant Mason was eventually elected deputy governor of Connecticut, and settled the town of Norwich, on the Yantic River. Lion Gardiner bought an island on Long Island Sound, which was named after him, and which his family still owns.

Once the Pequots were gone, there was nothing to stop the white advance. The Connecticut settlements mushroomed along the river bottoms, the towns advancing in close formation. The frontier was not a line or boundary, but a fluid, shifting zone, expanding and contracting, where Indian and settler traded and mingled and fought.

As the frontier was pushed farther out, the hinterland, once frontier itself, was modified. Its land was cleared, its towns were founded, and its Indians were gone. It could now develop as a normal English colonial community. On the one hand, there was an endless repetition of the frontier phenomenon; on the other, an ever-larger area that was no longer frontier. As the hinterland looked back to England, both emulating and resenting the mother country, the frontier looked back to the hinterland with the same mixture of emulation and resentment.

The frontier was in a permanent state of emergency, with its own laws and particular crimes such as neglect in keeping the watch, and its own sort of people, some of whom were the victims of Puritan banishment—"the offscourings of civilized society," as Timothy Dwight described them. The frontier was brutal, as when a captive Indian woman in Deerfield during King Philip's War "was ordered to be torn to pieces by dogs." The hinterland was utopian, as when four Indian boys were sent to Harvard College.

In the hinterland, there was a strict class system in which everyone had an assigned status, whereas the frontier was egalitarian. Servants became landowners, and women ran schoolhouses and became, through repeated marriages, considerable landowners. The involvement of townspeople in government was greater on the frontier, because the population was thin and the offices were numerous. There were fence viewers, haywards, constables, cask inspectors, hog ringers, gravediggers, tithing men, and on and on.

When the frontier became hinterland, people no longer wanted to serve in these minor municipal offices. They couldn't be bothered, being engrossed in their own self-advancement. They became more selfish and litigious. Once there was no common enemy, they started taking one another to court over trifles.

The Puritan ideal of being "knit as one" began to unravel in the hinterland; such an ideology needs a visible threat to be sustained. The Puritan principle that extravagance destroys the state competed with the desire of prosperous colonists to show off. This conflict led to legislation against "ornamented or wanton clothing . . . whereby the nakedness of the arm may be discovered in the wearing," and other proscribed articles, such as lace, gold thread, and ruffs. There were also forms of hidden ornamentation, such as the wider use of decorated chamber pots, on the bottom of which might be found the king's portrait or a humorous jingle such as:

> *Treat me nice and keep me clean*
> *And I'll not tell you what I've seen.*

The frontier, which was in a more or less constant state of siege, continued to enforce the Puritan ways strictly. In Springfield, where John Pynchon had taken over from his father, there was the case of the virtuous wife. Sarah Smith testified that in October 1655, when her husband was away, she had occasion to go to the meadow for two lost calves. There she ran into Robert

Bartlett, who "upon a sudden turned full butt upon me and laid hold on me . . . and impudently and immodestly he kissed me with his mouth upon mine . . . and did shamefully handle my nakedness. . . . I, considering his filthy unclean purpose, was very earnest with him to let me go. . . . He did again desire to fulfill his filthy lust, but I refused . . . and he did at length let me go." Bartlett was remanded to the court at Cambridge.

In the hinterland, there was a loosening of morals as people gave in to their lust. Elizabeth Bennett was sent back to England for "unchaste miscarriage" (abortion). There was also the witch-craft hysteria, a hinterland phenomenon imported from the Puritan counties of England, and centered in Salem. Initially, the Puritan view was that evil came from the wilderness. But in the hinterland, the equation of Satan and the wilderness gave way to the idea of Satan as your neighbor. Instead of seeing the devil in swarms of mosquitoes, poisonous snakes, and inimical Indians, you had the woman next door giving birth to a monster. Witchcraft was an irrational response to the dilution of Puritan orthodoxy.

Transmitting values from one generation to the next was a tricky business. True religious ardor gave way to ersatz obser-vance. Church attendance was eventually drained of all fervor. The generation that had fought for its religious freedom could pass on the freedom but not the fight.

By 1640, when the Great Migration was over, there were about thirty-five thousand Englishmen in America: sixty-five hundred in Virginia, a thousand in Maryland, fifteen thousand in Massachusetts, three thousand in Plymouth, fifty-seven hundred in Connecticut, and two thousand farther north. The worst was over, the starving time and the plagues. In thirty-three years, be-tween 1607 and 1640, half the original states were founded. These were the seed years, when the hard lesson of self-reliance was learned.

Conditions in England did not allow much monitoring of life in the colonies. Charles I, having ruled without Parliament since 1629, summoned it back into session in 1640 on the advice of the peers. All the pent-up resentment of the legislators vented itself in a Grand Remonstrance with two hundred clauses, one of which censured "the corrupt part of the clergy, who cherish formality and superstition." There was open revolt, and in 1642 Charles left London for the north, to govern from York. The rise of Oliver

Cromwell encouraged the Puritans, who no longer felt they had to flee to America. If the Grand Remonstrance had not passed, Cromwell might have fled to Massachusetts. Instead, there was civil war, and the defeated king was handed over to Parliament and tried for treason in 1649. When Charles was beheaded on January 30, Cromwell said he had "cut off the king's head with the crown on it."

Cromwell ruled as lord protector from 1653 until his death in 1658, and had exactly the same problems as the king. He dissolved Parliament, because he could not control it. But under his rule there was greater religious tolerance in England than in New England. Cromwell had a live-and-let-live attitude toward other Christians, and even the Catholics were better off under his protectorate.

In 1660 came the restoration of the Stuarts under Charles II, for most Englishmen favored a return to a stable and legitimate monarchy. Once again the Puritans were hounded—they could assemble no more than five, and must stay at least five miles away from places where they had formerly preached. The Puritan Revolution collapsed, and the crown began once again to interfere in colonial affairs, threatening to impose the Anglican Church.

The king sent four royal commissioners on an inspection tour of New England in 1665. One of them, Colonel Cartwright, reported that the Puritans continued to banish Quakers and to punish them for returning. "They have beaten some to jelly," he said. The Puritans were less democratic than Charles II, who wanted freemen admitted even though they were not church members. "Those whom they will not admit to the communion they compel to come to their sermons, by forcing five shillings from them for every neglect," Cartwright continued. "Yet these men thought their own paying of twelve pence for not coming to prayers in England was an insupportable tyranny." They were also imposing a five-pound fine for observing Christmas.

Along with the bad news of the Restoration came a smallpox epidemic in Boston, a drought in 1662, and a war with the Indians in 1675. In King Philip's War, attacks began on the ring of frontier towns that screened the older hinterland settlements, and more than six hundred settlers were killed. But in the reprisals, the power of the New England Indians was broken, and Philip was killed in August 1676.

In the settlers' view, the Indians were obstacles to progress. Before anything constructive could be done, they had to be driven back. Their savage cruelty, their bloodletting, their "revengeful, devouring jaws" (in the words of John Bartram, the "father of American botany") made their removal necessary. Anyone who doubted that the Indians must be removed had only to read the captivity tales then circulating: accounts of the ghastly treatment of white captives by Indians were a popular literary genre.

In Maine, the English and the French were neighbors. English settlers were at Pemaquid Point, a peninsula in today's Lincoln County, and the French were a few miles north, on Penobscot Bay. A small number of farmers had settled at Pemaquid, which was protected by the Fort Charles garrison. Among them was Thomas Gyles, a strict Puritan, who had brought his wife and five children and purchased several tracts of land.

In 1689, the French incited their Indian allies to attack the Pemaquid settlement. On August 21, Thomas Gyles took some workers and three of his sons to one of his farms on the river, three miles above Fort Charles, to harvest his wheat. While they were eating during their midday break, they heard guns from the fort.

Then, from behind a rise near the barn, about thirty Indians discharged a volley of shot. Thomas Gyles' ten-year-old son, John, heard the shot whistling, and heard his father call out, "What now! What now!" The boy ran off, a cutlass-waving Indian in pursuit. He fell down, and when the Indian picked him up, he saw his father on the ground, with blood boiling out of his shoes, and a half-dozen holes in his waistcoat. The Indians covered his father's body with boughs.

John Gyles would end up spending six years with the Indians. The captives were taken by canoe to Penobscot, where the French had a fort, and where a Jesuit priest gave John a biscuit. The little Puritan refused to eat it, "fearing that he had put something in it to make me love him, for I had heard tell of the Papists torturing the Protestants, so that I hated the sight of a Jesuit."

His Indian master took him up the Penobscot River to a village where a number of squaws were dancing in a circle. One of them pushed him into the ring, and the others grabbed him by the hair, but his master put down a pledge for his release; a bag of corn, or a blanket, could redeem a captive from the squaws' cruelties.

The next day, they portaged from lake to lake until they got to a village on the Eel River in Canada, where there were other captives, from Dover, New Hampshire. From time to time, a shriveled squaw would pick up a shovelful of hot embers from the fire and throw them at a captive's chest; if he cried out, the Indians would laugh and say, "What a brave action our grandmother has done."

When it was John's turn to be burned, a little girl set down a bag of corn in the ring and took him by the hand, making signs for him to leave the circle. It was a sort of lottery, in which some captives were tortured and others were adopted.

Winter came, and the river froze over, and the Indians laid up their canoes until spring. John Gyles went out and carried the gear for a hunting party of ten with only two guns. For days, there was no game, and nothing to eat, though the Indians told him "bye-bye, great deal moose." They finally chased one down in a swamp, where it had caught a hind leg in the exposed roots of a large tree knocked over by the wind.

When the ice broke up in the spring, they canoed down the St. John River, to a place where they planted corn and fished for salmon, which they ate until the corn was ripe. They dried the corn and put it into "Indian barns"—that is, holes in the ground, lined and covered with bark and fir.

In his second year of captivity, John Gyles was turned over to another group of Indians, in a village where some braves were dancing. One Indian grabbed him by the hair while another beat him across the back and shoulders. Then a tomahawk was placed in his hand and he was ordered to get up and dance, and sing in Indian. But a fierce Cape Sable brave said, "Shall we who have lost relatives by the English suffer an English voice to be heard among us?" They beat him with an ax handle, and not one showed the slightest compassion. It was the worst day of his captivity.

John managed to crawl away on his hands and knees, and when the Indians came after him, he hid in a swamp. He heard hallooing and whooping, and the Indians came so close he could hear some of them calling, "Chon! Chon!," but he didn't come out.

He found his way back to the first village, and in the third winter of his captivity, he was sent with a young Indian to fetch a killed moose on a cold and cloudy day. When they found the carcass, it was evening, and a snowstorm was coming up; they built a small fire with rubbish. In the morning, they butchered the moose, and John put on the skin as a coat, but it soon froze stiff as a hoop around his knees. His snowshoes also froze, and they marched the whole day without fire or food, and his toes and fingers grew numb, and he didn't think he could go another foot, and then he got drowsy and felt an urge to sit down, though he knew this would be his final sleep.

When they got to the village, the Indians cried out, "The captive is froze to death." They cut the shoes off his feet, and soon, before the fire, his blood began to circulate. But his feet up to his ankles were black and bloated with blood blisters, and the Indians said, "His feet will rot, and he'll die."

Then the skin on his feet came off in one piece, like shoes, leaving his toes without nails; the tips of his toes turned black, so that he had to cut them off with a knife. The Indians advised him to apply fir balsam, but wondered aloud if it was worth it, for he would surely die. He dragged himself on his elbows over the snow from tree to tree until he found some, which he cooked in a clam-shell until it was like a salve, then applied it to his feet and ankles. Within a week, he could hobble about on his heels with a cane, and thanked God they had enough provisions so that they didn't have to break camp for fifteen days.

When they did, the Indians made two little hoops in the form of snowshoes and tied them to his feet, and he followed on his heels, sometimes waist-deep in snow, but it was walk or die.

One day at the village, John was chopping wood and binding it with hemp when an ill-natured young fellow threw him back-ward, sat on his chest, and pulled out his knife, saying he had never killed an English person. John, who was by now fifteen and spoke their language, said, "It would be more manly to go to war than to kill a poor captive doing chores." But the young Indian began to stab him, so John grabbed him by the hair and tumbled him off, then followed up with fist and knee until the Indian said he'd had enough. The other Indians saw the blood running down his chest from the stab wounds; when he told them what had happened, they commended him.

After six years, his Indian master died, and there was a dis-pute over who owned him. He was now sixteen, and looked like an Indian, tanned and long-haired. He was sold to a French trader, who was of the Papist persuasion his parents had so detested. The trader and his Indian wife were good to John, though, and released him after three years, in 1698.

He got back to Boston on June 28 of that year, having been absent eight years, ten months, and twenty-six days, and having seen, as he thought, much of the goodness of God at an early age. His tale of captivity was published and went into several editions. Such was life on the frontier, where violent death and captivity were commonplace regardless of age or gender, while in the hinterland the sleep of men was undisturbed and they died of natural causes.

CHAPTER NINE

FRONTIERS
IN COLLISION

With the three European powers in North America
spreading out from their original settlements, collision was
inevitable. By 1681, the French had gone down the
Mississippi as far as the Gulf of Mexico. To counter their
efforts, the Spanish established bases in Texas and at
Pensacola. In 1680, the Pueblo Indians of New Mexico rose
up against the Spanish in the only successful Indian revolt
against a colonial power.

New York Public Library

This view shows Quebec, the capital of New France, in 1718. At
that time, Boston was the principal town of the English colonies,
and the Spanish had St. Augustine.

193

*We do think that America was built on the idea that
people went to dangerous places and they went to
frontiers and they did the things that should be done.*

JOAN SUTHERLAND
(wife of former hostage
Thomas Sutherland)

Missionary accounts were the French version of captivity tales. Alone among the Indians, the missionary was forced to adopt their ways while trying to teach them his. The French Jesuits went out looking for martyrdom to earn their place in heaven and found instead nature's purgatory. Each year, they sent back their field notes, which were published in France and enjoyed a wide readership.

The Jesuits thought they were bringing the word of God to a heathen people. But the Indians had their own religion, which made more sense to them than Christianity. One of the first Jesuits to come to the Great Lakes was Claude-Jean Allouez, who established a mission at Sault Sainte Marie, among the Hurons, in 1665. Father Allouez found the Indian beliefs "false and abominable," and yet Indian sacrifices to idols had a cross-cultural resemblance to offering the body and blood of Christ at mass. When Father Allouez was stranded, he prayed. When the Indians approached a rapids, they offered presents to the river divinity. On the eve of battle, the Indians fasted and waited for a dream of victory, much as Father Allouez sometimes fasted while waiting for God's message. The Indian medical rituals, like preparing a feast for the sun, were not so different from the priest's rituals of holy water and last sacraments.

But Father Allouez didn't see it that way, and wrote disapprovingly about the Hurons' "libertinism, debauches, indecent dances and shameful acts of concubinage." The suspicion was mutual. The Indians didn't think much of either Allouez's religion or his wilderness skills. They teased him mercilessly about his canoeing. At portages, they said they would call a child to carry him. Sometimes they took pity on him and carried his sacred vessels.

"The slight esteem in which they held me," he wrote, "caused them to steal every article of my wardrobe that they could, and I had trouble keeping my hat, the wide rim of which seemed to them well suited against the heat of the sun." At the end of the day, they gave him neither food nor blanket, and he fasted, slept under the stars, and prayed.

Father Allouez's mission was a bust. He got nowhere with his Christian morals. When he tried to instruct the Hurons about bad thoughts, one replied: "I do not know what it is to have bad thoughts." When he built a chapel out of bark, no one came. Since they didn't respect him, they paid no attention to his sermons, and he was compelled to abandon his post.

His predicament was typical of the stagnation of New France. As the English advanced in wedge formation on their cramped Atlantic Coast, the French were skipping like stones on their limitless water routes. The contrast was partly due to an accident of geography, for the rivers along the Atlantic Coast gave no access to the interior beyond the Appalachian chain. This great highland system, the eastern counterpart to the Rockies, extended from the Gaspé Peninsula in Quebec to Alabama, and formed a natural obstacle between the Atlantic Coast and the lowlands of the continental interior. To gain access to the interior, one had to go all the way north to the St. Lawrence and follow the intricate water system of the Great Lakes and the Mississippi River.

The French had the access, but not the population or the right approach. They didn't emigrate as families, and they weren't bonded by a commonly held religious dissent. They had none of the regimentation and personal austerity of the Puritans. The English, on the other hand, had the population and the right approach, but not the access. By 1640, when there were thousands of English settlers in New England, Virginia, and Maryland, there were only about three hundred in New France. The great men of the English settlements were leaders of communities, such as William Bradford and John Winthrop, whereas the foremost men of New France were adventurers, such as Cartier, Champlain, and La Salle. In England, the king was preoccupied with civil war, and the emigrants were left on their own. France did not have a pool of dissatisfied subjects wanting to leave home. It had missionaries, and it had soldiers and adventurers, but the average Frenchman didn't want to emigrate.

New France changed when Louis XIV and his finance minister, Jean-Baptiste Colbert, took it over in 1663, replacing the joint-stock companies that had been founded in the 1620s. Now the

French king began to take a personal interest in Canada. He read reports, and wrote notes in the margin. In 1663, he sent an emissary to consolidate the few French settlers around Quebec. Their farms were spread out along the St. Lawrence, because they all wanted river frontage. "Not only are they unable to learn the land," the royal instructions noted, "but they give the Iroquois a great facility to slit their throats."

The king's first priority was the Iroquois, who murdered the priests and then mocked them by wearing their robes. Louis sent the Carignan regiment of thirteen hundred to New France with flatboats to carry the troops upriver, twenty men to a boat. This show of force brought an uneasy peace.

Soon New France had a governor. Then, in 1665, the energetic Jean Talon arrived to fill the role of *intendant* (a combination accountant and quartermaster). He brought a program for a genuine colonial economy, an economy that wasn't based only on beaver. Talon encouraged immigration and cleared land for settlement. He built a brewery and a tannery, imported horses, and subsidized the raising of sheep. Since there was a shortage of women, he encouraged marriage to Indian women by offering each a dowry of 150 livres. The same year Talon arrived, however, the first shipment of "daughters of the king," from orphanages in France, also docked.

Louis de la Hontan, an officer with the Carignan regiment, wrote home that a cargo of women had been sent out "under the direction of some stale old nuns." Upon arrival in Quebec, the nuns "divided them into groups, some fair and some brown, some fat and some thin, some big and some little."

In fifteen days, all had been disposed of. "I am told that the fattest went off best," wrote de la Hontan, "upon the apprehension . . . that they would hold out better against the nipping cold of winter. . . . [Marriages were] concluded on the spot in the presence of a priest and a public notary, and the next day the Governor General bestowed upon the married couple a bull, a cow, a hog, a sow, a cock, a hen, two barrels of salt meat, and 11 crowns; together with a coat of arms."

These efforts led to growth, and when Talon took his first census, in 1666, New France had a population of 3,215, of whom 2,034 were men. (New England had ten times as many by then.) This small but growing population was kept under careful surveillance through detailed correspondence between the *intendant* and

Paris. Even the death of a donkey was reported. When a replacement was sent, a note around its neck stated the use that was to be made of it.

Talon left in 1672 to become valet of the king's wardrobe. He was replaced by Frontenac, one of many destitute provincial noblemen who came to the New World to make a new life. He took advantage of the truce with the Iroquois to pursue further exploration efforts. Under his orders, Louis Joliet, the Canadian-born son of a wagon-maker, set out. He arrived in December 1672 at the mission of Father Jacques Marquette. This Jesuit missionary's first mission had been on the Michigan side of Sault Sainte Marie, but he later moved to St. Ignace, on the northern side of the Straits of Mackinac, between Lake Michigan and Lake Huron.

On May 17, 1673, Marquette and Joliet set out along the northern shore of Lake Michigan, with two canoes and five other men, "firmly resolved to do all and suffer all." They did. One of the first landmarks they encountered was Green Bay, which they called Stinking Bay, because of its putrid salt-sea smell. Indian guides took them over the portages and through the marshes where the wild rice grew, onto the Fox River, and into Lake Winnebago. They followed the Fox again to the site of today's Portage, Wisconsin, near the divide where the Fox heads east and the Wisconsin heads west. A mile-long portage, its route obstructed by marshes and lakes, took them to the Wisconsin, and they floated westward into the American heartland. As the river's stream broadened, they saw roebuck and buffalo, and trees of unknown nomenclature.

On June 17, at today's Prairie du Chien, Wisconsin, their canoe shot out into the parent current of the Mississippi, which seemed to carry a volume of water greater than the united rivers of all Europe. As night fell, and the sun dropped behind green meadows, its light glowing red in the sky, a range of hills cast shadows on the Father of Rivers, and on the tiny figures in their canoes, Marquette a speck of black in his cassock. Could he and Joliet have any idea of the vastness of the area they had acquired for France? Could they have even begun to imagine the watershed, with thirty-five thousand miles of navigable waters converging into one?

The journey grew easier. They followed the flow of the river down the Indian Interstate with no concerns but the daily spectacle of river life: a huge catfish, a herd of elk, a flock of wild turkeys. They saw Indians who had never encountered a white man, a tribe whose chief taught the French explorers the use of the calumet, a pipe of polished red stone with a two-foot-long stem. Smoking it made everyone friendlier, and they decided to adopt it as a sort of passport through Indian country. Their curiosity was piqued by women with their noses or ears cut off—adulterous wives—and by transvestites, "who assume the female dress, and keep it all their lives. . . . They never marry, and glory in debasing themselves to do all that is done by women. . . . "

June turned into July as they rode the current, and only once did they encounter hostile Indians. After the rapids at today's Cairo, Illinois, where the Ohio joins the Mississippi, they were attacked by mosquitoes, and used their sailcloths as netting. Indians told Marquette that he was ten days from the sea, but on July 17, when they reached the confluence of the Arkansas and the Mississippi, they decided to turn back. With the Gulf of Mexico only three hundred miles away, the French were worried about falling into Spanish hands and began the laborious trek upriver.

Marquette returned to his mission. Joliet went on to Quebec, but on the rapids above Montreal his canoe capsized. Two of his men were drowned, and he lost his journals and nearly his life. During a second trip, in 1674, to establish a mission among the Illinois Indians, Marquette contracted dysentery and died on the way home, at the mouth of the river that bears his name. He had hoped to give his life for the glory of God, and he finally got his wish.

It would take another nine years for Marquette's exploration of the Mississippi to be completed, by Robert Cavelier de La Salle, who went the rest of the way, to the gulf. La Salle arrived in Canada in 1666, at the age of twenty-three, and for a while he kept a farm eight miles above Montreal. The Seneca Indians who camped on his grounds told him about a river of a size beyond calculation, with warm waters of a reddish color. With his imagination fired up, La Salle convinced himself that this great river went to the Pacific and was the route to Cathay. Of this he was so sure that his property was nicknamed "Little China."

In July 1669, he took nine canoes and twenty-seven men to Lake Ontario, where he ran into Louis Joliet, who was returning from an unsuccessful mission to Lake Superior to look for copper mines. La Salle claimed to have gone as far as the Ohio River at today's Louisville on this occasion, but no one knows for sure. He appears to have been a fabulator as well as a great explorer. In 1672, Frontenac sent La Salle to build a fort where the St. Lawrence empties into Lake Ontario, at today's Kingston. Besides its military use, it would serve as a warehouse to receive furs.

Two years later, La Salle went to France and saw the king, who gave him a royal patent for the fort. He came back to Quebec saying, "The king told me this," and "The king told me that." His name-dropping was the start of his difficulties, turning the two most powerful lobbies in Canada against him—the licensed fur traders and the Jesuits. The first saw him as an interloper cutting into their trade, while the second were concerned about his selling liquor to the Indians.

In 1677, when someone tried to poison his food, he blamed the Jesuits, and returned to France to counter their campaign against him. On this trip, he met his one true friend and cohort, Henri de Tonty, soldier son of a Neapolitan banker. Tonty's left hand had been shot off in Sicily, and he replaced it with an artificial metal hand covered with a glove, which he sometimes used as a club. La Salle presented the king, who liked big ideas, with a plan to build a ship on the Great Lakes, and in 1678 he brought a ship's carpenter back with him to Canada.

In Quebec on October 10, 1678, La Salle attended Governor Frontenac's "Brandy Parliament," where leading merchants and clergymen debated the merits of selling liquor to the Indians. The arguments against were that liquor jeopardized religion and family values: wives prostituted themselves for a glass of brandy, drunken parents killed their children. It also ruined trade, because the Indians bought goods on credit, sold them for booze, and fell into debt.

The chief advocate for maintaining the liquor traffic was La Salle. If the French didn't sell it to them, he argued, someone else would. The profits would go to the English and the Dutch. There would always be someone to "introduce by moonlight some bottle into their cabins." La Salle said that drunken Indians committed fewer excesses than would take place at a town fair in Brittany. He favored educating them to use alcohol in moderation.

Joliet, also in attendance, supported strict prohibition; he had seen what happened to the Indians when they drank. But the pragmatists won the debate, and the liquor traffic continued.

In December 1678, La Salle set out with Tonty and his carpenters to the western end of Lake Ontario, portaging around Niagara Falls into Lake Erie, where he proposed to build his ship. He had begun to develop symptoms of what seems to have been a kind of paranoia. He suspected that the Jesuits planned to form "a new Paraguay," setting up independent communities of Christianized Indians under their control. He believed that they hoped to stop his exploration efforts by informing the Spanish of his plan to find the great river. La Salle accused the Jesuits of stirring up the Indians against him by saying he wanted to take over their fur-trading routes. He allowed his hatred of the Jesuits to become obsessive, attributing everything that went wrong to them.

In fact, his shipbuilding activities on the eastern end of Lake Erie, near today's Buffalo, angered the Senecas, who planned to burn the ship. Nor were they pleased when he erected two blockhouses at the mouth of the Niagara. In the spring of 1679, his ship was finished and named the *Griffin*, after the mythological beast, half eagle, half lion.

"I will make the *Griffin* fly above the crows," La Salle said. In August, he took the *Griffin* into Lake Huron via today's Detroit and learned something about the weather on the Great Lakes "graveyard of ships" (he had already dubbed the western end of Lake Ontario Cap Enragé—"the enraged Cape").

By September, in Lake Michigan's Green Bay, he decided to send the *Griffin* back to Niagara with a load of furs, but stayed behind with four canoes and fourteen men. Because of autumn storms on the southern half of the lake, it took him forty-three days to paddle down along the western shore over to the St. Joseph River, on the eastern shore.

Up the St. Joseph he went, building a fort near today's Niles, Michigan, at the portage between the St. Joseph and Kankakee rivers. Then he set forth down the Kankakee, crossing Indiana and Illinois, and hooking into the Illinois River south of today's Joliet. The Illinois, he found, was as deep and broad as the Seine in Paris. Moving down the Illinois Valley, he paddled past the sites of such present-day river towns as Morris, Marseilles, and Ottawa, and came to an Indian village at the site of today's Utica, where he took about twenty bushels of corn from an Indian storage pit, because it was winter and food was scarce.

In January 1681, having been joined by Tonty with ten men and four canoes, his eight-canoe flotilla reached the string of small lakes above today's Peoria, where he came to an Indian village whose chief told him the sea was twenty days distant.

Above Peoria, La Salle built another fort, called Crèvecoeur —"Heartbreak." Concerned about the *Griffin*, he went back to his

Lake Ontario fort in February. While Tonty, whom La Salle had left in charge, was reconnoitering, his men burned Crèvecoeur and deserted it, leaving this message etched on a plank: "We are all savages." (Or, in another version, "We have withdrawn.") This was only the first of La Salle's woes. In May, he learned that the *Griffin* had vanished with all hands. It had probably sunk in a storm.

Early in December 1681, La Salle set out again with Tonty and six canoes, using the Kankakee-Illinois route to reach the Mississippi. The dunes on the shore of Lake Michigan were under deep snow, and at Utica the Illinois River was frozen.

By February 6, 1682, he was at the confluence of the Illinois and the Mississippi, upon which floated great chunks of ice. He had to wait a week before embarking. Down the river he went, to reclaim the land for France, passing the mouths of the Missouri and the Ohio, stopping at the Chickasaw Bluffs, near the site of today's Memphis, to build a small stockade, Fort Prud'homme. Then he traveled down to the Arkansas, past the point where Marquette had turned back.

Soon they began to see alligators sunning themselves on the banks, and were astonished to learn that these scaly monsters were hatched from eggs. They saw the bright flash of feathers in tall rushes, and Indians sleeping on scaffolds over smoke fires to drive away the mosquitoes. Farther on, they came to a village of Taensa Indians with an elaborate temple. It had an altar and a great shell on the door plaited all around with hair. The temple was a remnant of one of the ancient burial-mound cultures that were rapidly disappearing.

Next they went down the stretch of the Mississippi that today forms the border between Louisiana and Mississippi, past what would one day be Vicksburg and Natchez, into Louisiana, and past Baton Rouge. On April 6, they came to a place where the river branched into three channels, running with a strong current along low marshy banks. La Salle tasted the water and pronounced it brackish. According to the engineer Minet, whose memoir of the trip was discovered in 1985, the oarsmen, who had drunk quite a bit of the water, said: "You will pardon us, monsieur, but we find it not salty." La Salle lost his temper and insisted that it was.

The river was lined with cypress trees hung with moss, and broken up into swamps and bayous. When they shot birds, the alligators caught them in their jaws, and the travelers managed to retrieve only one out of seven. Then they crossed Lake Pontchartrain and went into the Gulf of Mexico, on April 9, 1682. They landed on a small palm-and-cypress-covered island, where they buried a lead plate indicating possession. La Salle signed a parchment, which was countersigned by a notary he had brought along. Then they shouted "*Vive le roi*," sang the "Te Deum," and fired three volleys.

As La Salle gazed out at the huge expanse of gulf shimmering under a clear spring sky and heard the roar of the combers, he could reflect that he'd done it, he'd gone the whole route. The French had now navigated the Mississippi through most of its 2,348-mile course, beginning at Lake Itasca in northwestern Minnesota and ending in the Gulf of Mexico; the Mississippi, with its lattice of tributaries covering a labyrinthine expanse, its great lateral branches of the Ohio to the east, and the Missouri to the west; the Mississippi, winding and looping chameleonlike through its swampy floodplain, as the shapes of its banks and shoals were continuously modified by tides and currents.

Thanks to the water route, Louisiana became the unlikely extension of Canada. With an area that now extended from the Appalachians to the Rockies, and from the Gulf of St. Lawrence to the Gulf of Mexico, La Salle had made France the colonial power that owned the most real estate in North America—on paper.

On his return trip up the Illinois, La Salle traveled only half as fast against the current. Along the way, at today's Utica, Illinois, he built a fort at the top of a great slab of rock (sheer cliff on three sides) now known as Starved Rock. He must have picked up a touch of malaria from a Mississippi mosquito, for in May he was seriously ill, delirious and rambling.

When he returned to his fort on Lake Ontario, La Salle learned that his backer, Governor Frontenac, had been replaced by a naval officer. This meant another trip to France, for he felt surrounded by enemies. His state of mind can best be seen in a letter he wrote, before leaving for France, to one of his supporters, the Abbé Bernou, who had asked him who his friends in Canada were. "I know of no friends in this country," La Salle replied; "to all appearances they are enemies, more subtle and secret than the rest. . . . I open my mind to nobody, I distrust everybody. . . . If I am wanting in expansiveness and show of feeling towards those with whom I associate, it is only through a timidity which is natural to me, and which has made me leave various employments where I could otherwise have succeeded."

At Versailles, he still held a strong hand, and managed to convince the king to back a mission to the mouth of the Mississippi. His plan was to build a chain of forts along the river, harass the Spanish, who were in Florida and New Mexico, and organize an anti-Iroquois Indian federation.

The king agreed to supply a ship and a hundred men if La Salle raised another hundred men and three smaller ships. The summer of 1684 found La Salle in the port of La Rochelle with the captain of the king's ship, Tanguy Le Gallois de Beaujeu. La Salle and the captain did not hit it off. When La Salle learned that Madame de Beaujeu was the head of a women's organization that supported the Jesuits, he found the captain guilty by association, and refused to share information with him. He wouldn't even tell Beaujeu that their destination was the Gulf of Mexico. "There are very few people who do not think that his brain is touched," Beaujeu wrote.

The four ships and two hundred men left La Rochelle on August 1, 1684. During the crossing, Minet, the engineer, became convinced of La Salle's dementia. "Monsieur de La Salle," he wrote, "always had five or six spies on the bridge. One could not say a word that was not wrongly interpreted. . . . I tried to calm his mind, which would become sour over nothing. But I was no more exempt than the others. He said that I was spying on his activities."

On September 28, they reached the island of Hispaniola, and landed at Petit Goâve, on the southern shore of Haiti, which had recently been taken over by the French. Suffering perhaps from another bout with malaria, La Salle was taken ashore delirious. His illness, which Captain Beaujeu said was "as dangerous to the mind as to the body," lasted nearly two months. His ravings, according to Minet, were invariably about the plots against him.

On November 25, they set sail again, but La Salle refused to board the flagship, the *Joly*. Instead, he went aboard the smaller supply ship, the *Aimable*. Thereafter, he and Captain Beaujeu communicated by letters that were rowed back and forth between the two ships. Minet thought the captain was a highly experienced sailor and a reasonable man, whereas La Salle's behavior grew increasingly erratic.

They sailed along the southern coast of Cuba and then took

the Yucatán channel between Mexico and Cuba into the gulf, aiming at a point on the American coast where they hoped the Mississippi Delta would be, instead of hugging the shore from Florida. This turned out to be a serious mistake.

La Salle had not taken the longitude of the Mississippi in 1682, and now, two years later, the ships hit the coast on December 20 near the border of Louisiana and Texas and headed west instead of east, past Galveston Bay, as far as Texas' Matagorda Bay, four hundred miles west of their destination. La Salle convinced himself that this was the Mississippi Delta, because Matagorda Bay looked like a river delta, with its long outer peninsulas, lagoons, and inlets.

Upon landing and exploring a bit, he could not find a river, only lakes and marshes. Minet and some of the others were sure he was wrong, and had second thoughts about staying on an unknown shore with a demented leader. When La Salle ordered Minet to land, he refused. La Salle was in the bay with the pilots, taking soundings, waiting for high tide, and arguing over the depth. When the pilots told him the bay was only nine feet deep, he said, "So much the better, only merchant ships will be able to come in."

On February 20, 1685, the *Aimable* was brought into the bay along a marked channel, but its captain, Aigron, managed to wreck it. La Salle was convinced he had done it deliberately, and blamed Beaujeu. In the meantime, his soldiers and settlers onshore were dying, two and three a day, from drinking the brackish water and eating bad food.

On March 12, Captain Beaujeu left, along with Minet and about twenty others. La Salle accused Beaujeu of having been bribed by the Jesuits to scuttle the entire expedition. On the trip back to France, knowing he would have some explaining to do, Minet prepared a list of charges against La Salle, among which were financial irresponsibility and homosexuality: "Why did he borrow money at 100% interest? . . . Why did he have young and handsome valets and make them sleep with him? . . . Why did he find fault with everything and quarrel with everybody?" As it turned out, Minet spent a few months in prison on charges of desertion; Aigron was given a long prison term for intentionally wrecking his ship; and Captain Beaujeu's naval career was cut short.

In Texas, La Salle entered Lavaca Bay and moved up the Garcitas Creek, where he built a fort. His men, meanwhile, died of dysentery, food poisoning, and rattlesnake bites. Twenty lay under a sailcloth suffering from the venereal diseases they had contracted in Haiti. He had alienated the local Indians, the Karankawas, by taking some of their canoes, and they started picking off stray workers.

Despite La Salle's erratic conduct, the fort was completed, a plot of ground was tilled, and the meat from their hunts was cured. La Salle mustered his strength for a trip through southeastern Texas, to search for the Mississippi. In 1685 and 1686, he went west and north. Finally, in 1687, he went east, with about thirty men. By this time, he had lost their confidence, and they were conspiring against him. Why, they said, must we always be slaves to his whims and victims of his foolish expectations? What can we do but kill him to put a stop to our miseries? One of his men had sworn to kill him because his brother had been left behind and found by the Indians.

On March 19, on the Brazos River, west of today's Houston, two of the men hid in the tall grass and ambushed La Salle. Addressing his corpse, one of them said: "There you lie, great Pasha, there you lie." And so, in death and madness, ended the career of a great explorer.

The French now had a vast domain they couldn't possibly manage, stretching from Quebec to Louisiana. They built forts at key points, which doubled as trading posts, and the missionaries kept the Indians in line. There was a fort at the eastern end of Lake Ontario, and a fort at Niagara, and a fort at Pittsburgh, and a fort guarding the portage from the Kankakee to the St. Joseph. There were forts at either end of Lake Champlain. From the St. Lawrence, above Montreal, there was a thirteen-mile portage to the Richelieu River, which took them right into Lake Champlain. At the southern end of the lake there was a portage to Lake George, and from Lake George they could reach the Hudson.

They added forts as the need arose and the English threat increased. There was one on Lake Winnebago, guarding the Fox-Wisconsin portage; one at Erie, Pennsylvania, guarding the portage to French Creek; one at the Straits of Mackinac; and one at Sault Sainte Marie.

The settlement efforts in Quebec did not match the great feats of exploration. Quebec was a city of blasted hopes, a fortress with a few guns on the cliffs of Cape Diamond. The small population inhabited rows of scruffy cabins, and stray Indians begged for food. In New France, as on the New England frontier, there was a reprobate factor, and the *intendant* (administrator) Demeulles lamented in 1683 that the country was full of people who had come to "escape their crimes" and indulge their "vicious habits." It seemed that the population was made up of convicts and "daughters of the king," among whom whores outnumbered orphans. The Sun King himself was losing patience with Canada, where nothing ever seemed to go right. If the government distributed seed, it was left to rot. Some of the farmhouses outside Montreal were nothing but speakeasies. Eight hundred men were running around in the forest drinking brandy with Indians instead of tilling the land.

Probably the biggest mistake the French monarchy made, under the influence of the Catholic clergy, was to ban Protestants from Canada and Louisiana. The English monarchy allowed its dissidents to emigrate, and it was the Puritan migration that made New England. In 1685, Louis XIV revoked the Edict of Nantes, which had granted the Protestants religious tolerance. In the next few years, some two hundred thousand persecuted Huguenots left France. Some went to the English colonies; in Canada, the door was closed. The Sun King managed to ban the one and only group of Frenchmen who wanted to emigrate and were hardworking and clean-living. Canada was Catholic, and the church called the tune, and this eventually cost the French their presence in the New World.

With the French spreading out all over the map, it was only a matter of time before they bumped into the English and the Spanish. The wars of Europe were eventually exported to North America. When England declared war on France in May 1689, this was the first European war to have a North American front. Frontenac, who was back in Canada for a second term as governor, sent three raiding parties into English territory: one to Schenectady, one to Salmon Falls on the New Hampshire border, and one to Fort Loyal, where Portland, Maine, is today. The New England frontier was subjected to plunder and destruction.

The Treaty of Ryswick in 1697 ended the fighting, temporarily. The three-cornered war among the French, English, and Spanish, each with its Indian allies, would continue for another half-century. It was in fact a war for the mastery of the continent.

The initial collision between France and Spain was an aftermath of the La Salle expedition. The Spanish, who were in Florida and New Mexico, had no idea that La Salle had landed between them on the Texas coast in 1684. It wasn't until a year later, in

July 1685, that they captured a pirate ship in the Bay of Campeche, off the Yucatán Peninsula, and took 120 prisoners. One was a deserter from the La Salle expedition in Petit Goâve. By name Denis Thomas, he gave a deposition in Vera Cruz stating that the French, under the leadership of Monsieur de La Salle, had planned to land on the gulf and build a fortress there, and that the king had appointed him "Viceroy of the Micicipy." His willingness to talk did not help the twenty-two-year-old sailor-pirate, who was hanged in September 1686 with the other 119 captured men.

The Spanish now knew that La Salle had landed a force on the gulf on territory they claimed. But they didn't know where he had landed, or why. In the spring of 1686, the War Council of the Indies met in Madrid and advised the king that "His Majesty's prompt action is necessary to pluck out the thorn which has been thrust into the heart of America."

The Spanish spent the next four years prowling the fifteen-hundred-mile-long northern shore of the Gulf of Mexico, sending out a total of five expeditions by sea and four by land. In April 1687, a naval expedition actually sailed into Matagorda Bay and found the wreck of La Salle's supply ship, but they did not explore inland, where, a few miles away, they would have found the fort with a few people still alive. That August, other Spanish ships found the mouth of the Mississippi, but no La Salle.

The man who found the fort was Alonso De León, the governor of Coahuila Province in northeastern Mexico. In May 1688, he heard that there was a Frenchman living among the Indians north of the Rio Grande and set out to find him. He turned out to be another deserter, Jean Géry, who was sent to Mexico City to give his deposition. Géry had gained some eminence in a Texas tribe of Coahuiltecan Indians. He had learned the lingo and married into the tribe, and had a half-breed daughter.

Alonso De León set out on March 24, 1689, from today's Monclova in Coahuila Province, 150 miles from the Rio Grande, with a total of 113 men, including soldiers, priests, and servants, 720 horses, and eighty-five mule-loads of supplies. He crossed the Rio Grande on April 2, a little to the south of today's border town of Guerrero, then headed due east across Texas, through mesquite thickets and prickly pear, crossing the Nueces and Frio rivers, and, on April 14, the Guadalupe, which took him right down to Matagorda Bay. On April 22, he reached Garcitas Creek and saw the ruins of the French fort on a rise.

On the frame of the main gate these dates were inscribed:

1684–168 . . . The final numeral of the second date had not been entered. The gabled fort and its outbuildings had been set on fire, and the floors were covered with debris—broken furniture, bits of glass, pottery shards, torn and mildewed books. Three skeletons were found, including one wearing a dress with an arrow in its back. The Spaniards figured that the others had been thrown to the alligators in the creek. If there had been any doubt as to the nationality of the occupants, a cultivated field enclosed by a picket fence would have given them away, for they had been growing endives and asparagus.

Two survivors were found in an Indian village sixty-five miles away. They told how La Salle had overworked his men and made them spend long hours in the water trying to salvage the supplies on the sunken *Aimable*. They said that many died of diseases and the rest were killed by Indians.

Finding the fort motivated the Spaniards to settle the area where the French threat had arisen, and Alonso De León soon established a Franciscan mission in the piney woods of East Texas, on the Neches River. This worked to the advantage of the French: it was better for them to have the Spanish in Texas than at the mouth of the Mississippi. La Salle's mistake had turned out to be a red herring, which threw the Spanish off the scent. By 1718, they were firmly ensconced in Texas, having founded San Antonio with a presidio and a chapel called the Alamo, and brought in some settlers from the Canary Islands. They also had three more missions, two on the Rio Grande and one at today's Goliad, about sixty miles north of Corpus Christi. In 1722, a fort was built on the site of La Salle's on Garcitas Creek.

The general agitation over La Salle had led the Spanish to explore the gulf coast more thoroughly than before, and to take further measures against French encroachment, such as establishing a fort in Pensacola Bay in 1698. The French were not far behind, sending the sieur d'Iberville in 1699 with five ships and one thousand men to finish what La Salle had begun. That January, five fleur-de-lys flags appeared in Pensacola Bay. The French said they were looking for deserters and asked if they could drop anchor in the harbor. The answer was an emphatic no. Iberville was in fact looking for the mouth of the Mississippi, which he found in March. Then he sailed eastward into Biloxi Bay, landing two hundred settlers in a cove at the site of today's Ocean Springs, Mississippi.

Now the French had finally driven a wedge between the Spanish settlements in Pensacola and East Texas. The Spaniards wanted to oust them, but were overextended. When Iberville's brother, the sieur de Bienville, built a fort twenty-seven miles from the mouth of the Mobile River, about forty miles east of Biloxi, they did nothing to stop him.

To understand this uncoordinated strategy, we must view Spain's holdings north of the Rio Grande as the unwanted or least favorite children in a large imperial family that included sterling-silver Mexico and twenty-four-carat-gold Peru. Having no mineral wealth, Florida and New Mexico cost the Spanish monarchy money instead of filling its coffers, and their strategic importance was arguable. Florida had some strategic value in protecting the sea lanes for the Spanish treasure-fleets. In New Mexico, however, the harvest of souls was the only reward.

In Florida, which then included portions of Georgia and Alabama and was divided into four provinces, the Franciscan missionaries were the shock troops. As Friar Pareja put it, "We are the ones who are conquering and subduing the land." Of the first three lasting settlements on the territory of the United States—St. Augustine in 1567, Jamestown in 1607, and Santa Fe in 1610—two were Spanish. St. Augustine and Santa Fe were the northern spurs of Spain's empire, the one supplied by sea from Havana, the other by land from Mexico over the Chihuahua Trail.

This "Spanish tier" of the future United States has been neglected in accounts of settlement. One reason is that Spanish Florida didn't last, whereas Plymouth did. Another is that Plymouth was Protestant and self-governing, whereas the Spanish colonies were extensions of a Catholic monarchy.

In what would become an English-speaking country, the experience of the English colonies elbowed aside the French and Spanish experiences, just as France and Spain were elbowed out of North America. But, from the point of view of the frontier, the Spanish colonies have a definite fascination. In New Mexico took place the one and only example of an Indian rebellion that succeeded in expelling the colonizing power: the Pueblo revolt of 1680.

Spanish colonization was a gargantuan but arthritic piece of work directed from Madrid. The legal tradition and the bureaucracy were transmitted to the New World intact, creating a system that was overregulated and undermanned. In Spain, there were no religious dissidents, as there were in England, but a lot of ambitious men who wanted to make a quick fortune in America, as well as plenty of missionaries who wanted to save souls. All these men, whether soldiers, civil servants, or friars, were in theory but not in practice under the absolute authority of the crown, which could in theory hire and fire them at will. Spanish society in the American colonies resembled Spanish society at home, saturated with clericalism and rigid bureaucratic thinking.

In the thinly settled Spanish colonies, Indian labor was the key to survival. A bewildering set of regulations governed labor relations, but, whatever name they went by, they boiled down in practice to the exploitation of a ready-made nation of peons. When the crown said that the Indians were freemen, the translation from the Don Quixote–style Spanish double-talk was that they were free to work for nothing, just as the *hidalgo* was free to bear arms and the friars were free to convert.

However, aside from the common denominator of Indian peonage, New Mexico and Florida developed in different ways. Florida was poor, floated on brackish waters, and was held together by mandrake roots. It was at the bottom of the list for royal subsidies. Sacked by Drake in 1585, St. Augustine, on the northern frontier, was turning into a slum, known as a place of exile for troublesome friars, governors with a stain on their blotters, and soldiers with a drinking problem.

Life seemed to proceed as a series of disasters. In the spring of 1649, the supply fleet that left Vera Cruz for Cuba had yellow-fever-carrying mosquito larvae in its water casks. The epidemic killed one-third of the Havana population before moving north to St. Augustine, where many Spaniards died of the "black vomit," including the governor, Benito Ruiz. Ten years later, a measles epidemic killed ten thousand Florida Indians, almost wiping out the Timucua in the south. Instead of becoming settled, Florida was becoming depopulated.

The turning point for St. Augustine came in 1670, when the Council of the Indies approved funds for a masonry fort. This created a construction boomlet that lasted for a quarter of a century. The fort was a response to the English settlement of Charleston. English traders offering guns and Venetian beads lured the Indians away from the friars and their communion wafers. It was no contest. The abandoned Spanish missions were soon overgrown with loblolly pine and live oak.

Fifteen hundred miles to the west, in Spain's other northern spur, New Mexico, there was a stagnation worse than that in Florida. Pedro de Peralta, who replaced Juan de Oñate as governor in 1610, reported to the viceroy: "No one comes to America to plant and sow, but only to eat and loaf." And how else could they eat and loaf except by exploiting the Indians?

Peralta had arrived with nine Franciscans, and by 1616 there were twice that number, fanning out among the Pueblo villages. They used Indian labor to build their churches and houses, and then used them again as sacristans, bell ringers, organists, cooks, and gardeners. The mission influence was twofold. The Spanish took from the Indians their labor and their corn, but they also gave by introducing wheat, cattle, plows, irrigation, lime mortar, roof beams, masonry, and other practical improvements. They taught the Indians trades like carpentry and smithing, and used surplus grain to feed poor Indians outside the missions, which helped them meet their conversion quotas.

Interfering in the Pueblo way of life, they tried to ban polygamy and ceremonial dances. They treated the Pueblos like irresponsible children, as can be seen from the instructions that Friar Ruiz left for his successor in Jemez, thirty miles west of Santa Fe: Don't let the Indian women work in the fields, because all they want to do is "join the older youths in wanton and wicked dalliance." Don't let them sit together in church, because all they do is gossip. Don't let the children at catechism cover the lower parts of their faces with their serapes, "for then they eat grains of toasted maize and chew nasty stuff they are addicted to."

In 1622, Alonso de Benavides arrived in Santa Fe as chief prelate for the New Mexico missions, and also as the representative of the Inquisition, which made him the equal of the governor. After eight years of driving his missionaries to break their conversion records, he wrote a self-promoting *Memorial* for the king in which he claimed that there were now twenty-five missions, each with its own church; over ninety villages; and more than sixty thousand Pueblo Indian converts. According to Benavides, there were more converts than there were Indians in New Mexico.

Under Benavides, the missions spread to Hopi villages in northeastern Arizona. Isolated by the natural buffers of their mesas, the Hopis were astonished to see, in August 1629, three enterprising Franciscans arrive in the village of Awatovi, atop Antelope Mesa, about sixty miles north of today's Flagstaff, Arizona.

The leader of the three, Francisco Porras, was a remarkably

able man, who introduced Spanish plants and animals to promote economic self-sufficiency, organized work details, taught Hopi children to read and write, and built a fine adobe church with a steeple, a copper bell, a choir loft, and an altar stone. He was so capable, in fact, that in 1633 the local shamans, whose authority he was undermining, had him killed by poisoning his food.

The mission continued to prosper under his successors, although in the 1650s it was tainted with scandal. Alonso de Posada, one of the Franciscans at Awatovi in 1654, took an Indian mistress and ordered two of the soldiers at the mission to kill her Indian lover. The scandal fueled the quarrel between the friars and the governors, who were constantly trading charges and investigating one another. The crux of the matter was labor management: the governors needed Indians for their private projects, such as tanning hides, weaving, and gathering piñon nuts; but the missionaries wanted the Indians for their own work projects.

One of the friars' weapons against the crown-appointed officials was the Inquisition, which Benavides had brought to New Mexico in 1622. The friars would bring Inquisition charges against a corrupt governor for some religious lapse, as in the case of the governor who came to Sunday mass in Santa Fe and made soldiers who were kneeling in prayer stand up and salute him.

The governors retaliated by investigating the missionaries for brutal treatment of the Indians, charging that the friars made them wear hair shirts and carry heavy crosses in penance. Government policy toward the Indians and the friars changed with the personality of each governor. Governor Lopez, for instance, undermined the friars by giving the village of Tesuque permission to go ahead with their kachina dances. He said they were only "Indian foolishness" and there was no harm in them.

The Franciscans responded by prohibiting the dances throughout New Mexico, and in 1661 they raided a number of villages and destroyed sixteen hundred masks, covering over the kivas (ceremonial rooms).

In 1675, Governor Juan de Treviño decided to cooperate with the friars in stamping out native religious practices, which were now seen as subversive. Forty-seven shamans were arrested. Three were hanged, one hanged himself, and the other forty-three were whipped. At this point, seventy Tewa warriors stormed into Santa Fe to demand the release of the prisoners. The governor complied, contributing to the making of a native leader.

One of the shamans who had been whipped and released was a Tewa Indian named Popé. He fled north to Taos, known for its rebellious spirit, his head filled with plans of vengeance.

For the next five years, he shaped those plans. It was said that a god from the underworld had appeared to him and given him a mission. It was said that three devils had appeared, shooting flames of fire from their extremities, and told him to rid the land of all Spaniards.

Popé developed a network of emissaries in the villages, who spread the word that the Spanish god had brought drought and hard winters. The Spanish had so burdened them with tasks that they had no time to till their own fields. Not only could they no longer produce the surpluses they needed for trade, they could not even feed themselves. They must bring back their own gods, who would give them more corn than the Spanish god, by wiping out the mission system. They must regain control of their villages by driving the Spaniards out of New Mexico.

Popé's plan required the united action of all the pueblos. On a given day, there would be a simultaneous attack of the thirty-three missions left in the declining system. Santa Fe would be surrounded and cut off, its trails being guarded against messengers. The attack would be timed to begin just before the arrival of the annual provision train from Mexico in September. They would catch the Spaniards at a vulnerable moment.

In 1680, there were about twenty-five thousand Indians left in New Mexico, including six thousand warriors. They outnumbered the 2,350 Spaniards almost three to one. (The Spanish had the same problem as the French: they were undermanned for the area they held. Santa Fe, with a population of one thousand, had the biggest garrison—250 men.)

Popé was a charismatic leader with popular support and a remarkable strategic sense. His emissaries in the pueblos offered various incentives, saying that every Indian who killed a Spaniard would be rewarded with an Indian woman. If he killed four, he would get four; if he killed ten or more, he would have a like number of women. This wasn't a rebellion in the name of freedom. It was a conservative uprising to restore traditional ways, and religious practices that predated the Spaniards.

The revolt was set for August 13, 1680. To alert the pueblos, Popé tied as many knots as there were days until the revolt into ropes of maguey fiber, and sent riders carrying the ropes among the tribes. If the villages agreed, they were to send out smoke signals.

In Santa Fe, Christian Indians leaked word of the attack to Governor Antonio de Otermín. In response, Popé advanced the date of the ambush to August 11. That day, a Sunday, Otermín was about to go to mass when Pedro Hidalgo, one of the soldiers from the nearby Tesuque mission, arrived with terrible news. A party of painted warriors had been seen in a ravine outside Tesuque. Father Pio, one of the best-liked missionaries, had gone out to meet them, and saw that they were on the warpath. "What is this, my children, are you mad?" he asked. Those were his last words. After killing Father Pio, the Indians had taken all the mission's cattle and horses and gone into the sierra.

At once Otermín tried to notify his *estancias* (ranches). But the trails were guarded, and his messengers couldn't get through. Those few places that got wind of the rebellion didn't believe the news. The trouble with the territory, Otermín reflected, was that the *estancias* were too far apart.

The scene at Tesuque was repeated at all the missions, and twenty-one out of thirty-three Franciscans were killed. The astonishing thing, a Spanish report noted, was "that all of them rebelled on one day and at one hour." This was unprecedented in New Mexico, where the Indians had been obedient vassals for so many years.

The Indians, it could be said, were only repaying the Spanish, who had hanged their shamans and destroyed the kivas and kachina masks. At Jemez, the friar in charge was taken to the cemetery, stripped naked, and told to get down on his hands and knees. The Indians took turns riding him and whipping him, and finally killed him with war clubs.

At the pueblo of Sandia, south of Santa Fe, the floor of the church and the foot of the communion rail were covered with human excrement. Two chalices and a crucifix were found in a basket of manure, and a full-length statue of St. Francis had its arms hacked off.

In every mission and village, Spanish bodies were piled up in front of altars or in the street. In Santa Fe, Governor Otermín, realizing that the Indians were armed with the weapons of slain soldiers, collected about a thousand Spaniards in the governor's palace and its outbuildings and waited for the attack. The siege began on August 15. Five hundred Indians surrounded the city.

Among them was Popé, who wore around his waist a sash of red taffeta taken from the convent at Galisteo.

Otermín fought off the first attack, but a couple of days later the Indian reserves arrived, twenty-five hundred strong. They cut off the water, and by nightfall had set fire to half the city. The whole town, Otermín wrote, "was a torch and everywhere were war chants. . . . What grieved us the most were the dreadful flames from the church and the scoffing and ridicule which the wretched Indians made of the sacred things . . . intoning the *alabado* [a hymn to the sacraments] and other prayers with jeers."

Otermín was trapped. Outside were three thousand frenzied Indians, bent on massacre. Inside were one thousand Spaniards who had nothing to drink except what they had collected in jars and pitchers. Outside the cries of the warriors, inside the weeping of the women and children. Otermín either had to engage the enemy or die. His men heard mass at dawn on August 20, and the horsemen galloped out, followed by men on foot. Certain of victory, the Indians had spent the night in celebration, singing that the Spanish god was dead. Otermín and his desperate men surprised them, and within a few hours the Indians were in flight, leaving behind three hundred dead. Otermín suffered an arrow wound in the face and a gunshot wound in the chest.

He quickly decided to abandon Santa Fe and headed south with his people toward the Rio Grande. As they marched, they passed the debris of war, burned-out houses, and the rotting carcasses of horses lying in the road. South of Isleta, they joined up with another troop of refugees, led by Lieutenant Governor Alonso García. In mid-September, they reached the Rio Grande, and Otermín took a muster. There were 1,946 persons. The Spanish death toll was 380 soldiers and civilians and twenty-one priests.

It was a triumph for Popé. His two major objectives, to eliminate the mission system and to drive out the Spaniards, had been achieved. For the first and last time in North America, the native people had defeated and thrown out the colonizer, and the land was returned to its original settlers.

Popé at once emphasized the true nature of his rebellion. Every vestige of the conquest had to be expunged. The Indians were told to bathe in the rivers and scrub themselves with soapweed to wash away all traces of baptism. They were told to drop their Christian names and void their Christian marriages. They were told, "Don't speak Spanish, and plant only the crops of your ancestors, maize and beans."

Wearing a bull's-horn headdress, Popé toured the villages, proclaiming the new order. "We are quit with the Spaniards now," he said, "and shall live as we like and settle wherever we see fit." At Santa Ana, south of what would one day be Albuquerque, he presided over a feast at which he cursed the Spaniards and Christianity while drinking from a chalice, and addressed the other Indian leaders as "holy father."

Once again the Pueblo Indians prayed at their kivas. They donned masks and danced the kachina. But soon it became apparent that they could not go back to the old ways, having been Hispanicized beyond return. The invaders had been there since 1600, under fourteen different governors. Only octogenarians remembered pre-Spanish times. Were they supposed to stop planting wheat, uproot their orchards, throw their horses and cattle into the Rio Grande, destroy their guns? Many villagers did not. Some continued to speak Spanish. Some kept their Christian wives. Some hid church vessels. New Mexico's tribal societies had become irretrievably hybrid.

Otermín, in the meantime, had settled in El Paso del Norte, today's Ciudad Juárez. He and his people were told to stay put until the reconquest of New Mexico could be achieved. But it was twelve years before Diego de Vargas undertook the campaign at his own expense. By that time, Pueblo unity had broken down. Popé turned out to be as repressive as the Spaniards, exacting tribute from the villages. The tribes once again were split into warring factions.

In 1692, de Vargas reconnoitered in New Mexico for four months, meeting no resistance, and decided that the time was ripe for reconquest. On October 4, 1693, he headed north again, with one hundred soldiers, eighteen Franciscans, some Indian auxiliaries, and seventy-three families of settlers. In Santa Fe, some Tanos Indians had turned the governor's palace into a housing complex, and weren't about to give it up. De Vargas stormed the place, killing between seventy and eighty of the defenders.

The Spaniards were back in New Mexico, but they couldn't repeat their old methods. De Vargas went on a good-will tour of the villages, taking the olive branch to the mesa top. He stood as godfather at the baptism of Indian children. Spanish officials no longer came around every May and October to collect tribute.

Indian forms of worship were tolerated, and the beat of drums was heard in the land.

The Pueblos were given a measure of autonomy, while the more distant Hopis were now outside the Spanish sphere of influence. In any case, the eighteenth-century strategic context was different, for New Mexico was now more of a defensive bastion than a mission outpost. An example of the change was that in 1791 a petition arrived in Santa Fe from the Pueblos in Isleta, asking for the removal of a priest because he wouldn't let them perform their corn dance or go out on their traditional rabbit hunt. The priest was removed.

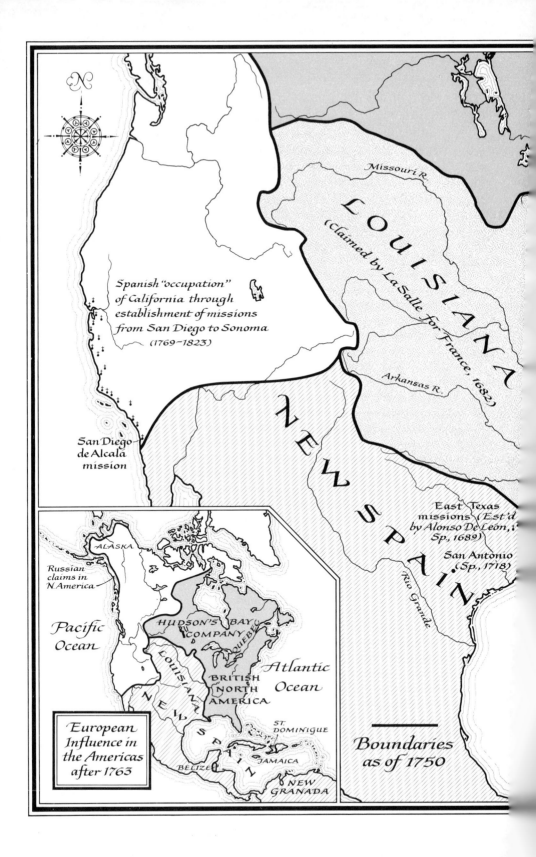

N

Spanish "occupation"
of California through
establishment of missions
from San Diego to Sonoma
(1769–1823)

San Diego
de Alcala
mission

L O U I S I A N A
(Claimed by La Salle for France, 1682)

Missouri R.

Arkansas R.

N E W   S P A I N

East Texas
missions (Est'd
by Alonso De León,
Sp, 1689)

San Antonio
(Sp., 1718)

Rio Grande

European
Influence in
the Americas
after 1763

ALASKA

Russian
claims in
N. America

Pacific
Ocean

HUDSON'S BAY
COMPANY

QUEBEC

LOUISIANA

BRITISH
NORTH
AMERICA

Atlantic
Ocean

NEW SPAIN

BELIZE

ST.
DOMINIGUE

JAMAICA

NEW
GRANADA

Boundaries
as of 1750

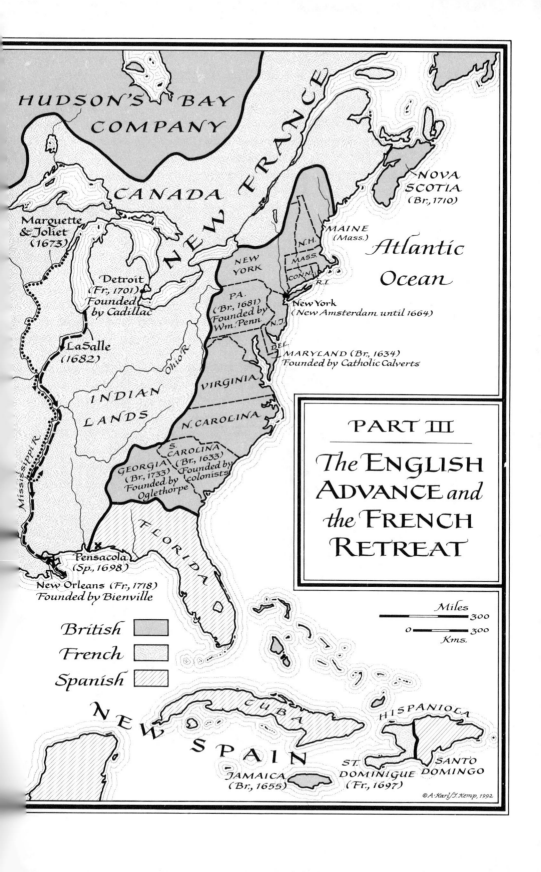

HUDSON'S BAY COMPANY

CANADA

NEW FRANCE

NOVA SCOTIA
(Br., 1710)

Marquette & Joliet (1673)

Detroit (Fr., 1701) Founded by Cadillac

LaSalle (1682)

Ohio R.

INDIAN LANDS

Mississippi R.

NEW YORK

N.H.

MAINE (Mass.)

MASS.

CONN.

R.I.

Atlantic Ocean

PA. (Br., 1681) Founded by Wm. Penn

N.J.

New York
(New Amsterdam until 1664)

DEL.

MARYLAND (Br., 1634)
Founded by Catholic Calverts

VIRGINIA

N. CAROLINA

S. CAROLINA (Br., 1633) Founded by colonists

GEORGIA (Br., 1733) Founded by Oglethorpe

FLORIDA

Pensacola (Sp., 1698)

New Orleans (Fr., 1718) Founded by Bienville

British
French
Spanish

NEW SPAIN

CUBA

HISPANIOLA

JAMAICA (Br., 1655)

ST. DOMINIGUE (Fr., 1697)

SANTO DOMINGO

PART III

The ENGLISH ADVANCE and the FRENCH RETREAT

Miles
0 — 300
0 — 300
Kms.

© A. Karl/J. Kemp, 1992

CHAPTER TEN

THE
MANORIAL
FRONTIER

Between 1680 and 1730, the Virginia tobacco planters,
while living on the edge of the wilderness and still subject
to Indian raids, emulated the architecture and manners of
the English gentry.

Colonial Williamsburg Foundation

In Georgian houses on the manorial frontier, there were architectural details such as this handsome staircase.

A Southern gentleman is someone who can shoot like a South Carolinian, ride like a Virginian, drink like a Kentuckian, make love like a Georgian, and be proud of it as an Episcopalian.

CLARE BOOTHE LUCE

On the frontier, a gentleman is any adult white male who is not in jail at the moment being alluded to.

BERGEN EVANS

William Fitzhugh, the twenty-year-old younger son of a dealer in woolens in the English town of Bedford, about fifty miles north of London and twenty-five miles west of Cambridge, arrived in Virginia in 1671. He seems to have broken with his family, with whom he did not communicate. His assets were an enterprising nature, a little capital, and some knowledge of English common law, which was then so scarce in the colonies that he lost no time in launching a law practice.

One of his clients was a wealthy widow named Rose Gerard, who had inherited property from her late husbands, John Tucker and Thomas Gerard. She saw in Fitzhugh a young man of some distinction, with a maturity beyond his years, and proposed that he marry her eleven-year-old daughter, Sarah Tucker. He seemed more refined than the rough-hewn native Virginians. The marriage took place in 1674, and Sarah was sent to England for two years to round out her education.

As her dowry, she brought Fitzhugh everything he needed to start a plantation except the land itself: a pair of slaves, three cows, six ewes and a ram, some hogs, a bay gelding, furniture, china and glassware, and kitchen equipment. In addition, she had inherited five thousand pounds of tobacco from her late father; in Virginia, this was ready cash.

Settlement had by then spread several hundred miles from the original landing at Jamestown. The population had moved north and west along the rivers that ran more or less parallel to the James. The riverfront land along the James and the York had been claimed by earlier arrivals, so Fitzhugh had to go farther north, to the Northern Neck, between the Rappahannock River and the Potomac's estuary. At the western end of the Northern Neck, he and his bride bought a thousand-acre plantation on the Potomac, near today's Stafford.

This was then Virginia's northern frontier, still vulnerable to Indian raids and heavily forested, with undefined borders. At the same time, however, it was a gentrified frontier, where the threat of attack existed side by side with Restoration manners and amenities. The men wore wigs and ordered expensive books from London. The women wore the latest fashions and had servants to polish the family silver. English manorial life had been transplanted to the New World on this late-seventeenth-century Virginia frontier.

Fitzhugh built a fine house of thirteen rooms, including four reception rooms hung with tapestries. There were expensive brick chimneys, four good cellars, Turkish carpets, diamond-shaped and leaded windowpanes, brass andirons for the fireplaces, looking glasses, gilt-framed family portraits, and a marquetry writing table for Fitzhugh's voluminous business and legal correspondence.

Besides the main house, there were slave quarters, a dairy, a stable, a hundred-foot-square garden, and an orchard of twenty-five hundred apple trees, enclosed by a locust fence "as durable as a brick wall." The seven white indentured servants included a carpenter, a glazier, and an accountant. From his wharf on the Potomac, Fitzhugh sent his tobacco downriver by flatboat to ports with oceangoing ships. The small inland growers with no river frontage also sold their tobacco to him.

Almost effortlessly, Fitzhugh settled into the Virginia ruling class, the landed tobacco gentry. In 1677, a year after moving to his plantation, he was elected to the House of Burgesses, the oldest legislative body in English-speaking America. As a lawyer, he came to represent some of the leading colonists of his time. As a justice of the peace in Stafford County, he sometimes ruled on cases in which he had a personal interest. As a colonel in the militia (not having had to climb the rungs of promotion), he collected the tobacco tax levied to support the Potomac garrison. In fact, he was accused of cheating the county by misrepresenting the amount of tobacco that was due and keeping some for himself. But this charge turned out to have been fabricated by his political enemies.

Fitzhugh held the natives in contempt and transmitted his English superiority with every gesture and locution. He was an Anglican and a Tory, a churchgoer and a good husband, a man who "never courted unlawful pleasures with women." By 1686, when his wife was twenty-three, he had given her five "pledges of our conjugal affection." He boasted that he never suffered from gout because he always avoided hard drinking and overeating.

His religious piety and protestations of virtue concealed a flinty materialism. What mattered most to him were luxuries from England. He had a passion for silver. With each ship from London came candlesticks, snuffers, saltcellars, porringers, chafing dishes, sugar bowls, and plates by the dozen. Each piece was engraved with his initials and coat of arms, it being part of the Virginia planter tradition to make claims of kinship with English nobility.

Around this secure bastion of Englishness was a society based on slave labor, and a community terrified by Indian alarms. To Fitzhugh, the Indians were a nuisance. He rarely mentions them in his letters, although he lived through a period of Indian raids from the north, and had friends who fought and were killed by them.

The slaves were the answer to his labor problems, just as the river was the answer to his transportation problems. His pioneering reliance on slave labor guaranteed the success of his plantation, but there is no evidence that he ever considered the slaves as anything more than merchandise.

Because he lived too far away from the ports of Gloucester and York, where the slaves were auctioned, Fitzhugh often got the dregs. He had to write his friend Ralph Wormeley to do his buying for him, complaining: "I understand there are some Negro ships expected in York now every day. I am so remote, that before I can have notice they'll all be disposed of, or at least none left but the refuse."

On one occasion, he felt he'd been skinned because he was sold a female slave who was mute. In June 1681, he wrote John Buckner, a fellow lawyer-planter, asking that "you make some abatement for your dumb Negro that you sold me. Had she been a new Negro, I must have blamed my fate not you, but one that you had two years I must conclude you knew her qualities, which is bad at work worse at talking, and took the opportunity of the softness of my messenger to quit your hand of her." This was in the same category of annoyance as ordering glassware from London, having it arrive broken, and demanding a refund.

Buckner was the man who brought the first printing press to Virginia in 1682, the year following the imbroglio over the mute slave. He was ordered not to print anything without royal permission, in keeping with the policy announced some years before by Governor William Berkeley that education and printing were a menace to sound colonial government. "I thank God there are no free schools nor printing," Berkeley said, "and I hope we shall not have them these hundred years; for learning has brought disobedience, and heresy, and sects, and printing has divulged them, and brought libels against the best government. God keep us from both!"

The colonial governors did not act in the tobacco growers' best interest. They wanted to increase tax revenues by sending as much tobacco to England as possible, which made prices drop. When they hit bottom in 1682, the Assembly was prevented by the governor from passing a crop-curtailing law. Organized bands in the Gloucester area started destroying the crop, and the militia had to be sent out after the plant cutters. Fitzhugh sympathized with "the pluckers and the cutters," writing in June that "the lowness of tobacco has utterly discouraged me, and if the market this year rises not, I have small encouragement to run so great a risk."

On balance, however, the planters prospered, and Fitzhugh reported four years later that he now had twenty-nine slaves, "a choice crew of Negros," as he termed them. He put a stop to his purchasing, figuring they would increase naturally. "The Negros being a considerable parcel of breeders," he wrote, "will keep the stock good forever." He was also able to increase his landholdings, to such an extent that, when he died, he left fifty-seven thousand acres.

He was not, however, a happy man, feeling condemned to remain in Virginia while longing to return to England. "I have a long time in a strange land struggled hard with fortune's adverse hand," reads a letter of May 1685. "Society that is good and ingenious is very scarce," he wrote in 1686, "and seldom to be come upon except in books. Good education of children is almost impossible, and better be never born than ill bred, but that which bears the greatest weight with me, for I now look upon myself to be in my declining age, is the want of spiritual helps and comforts, of which this fertile country in everything else is barren and unfruitful."

In 1690, he put the plantation up for sale in London, or in exchange against a comparable English property, but there were no takers. He would even have settled for Scotland or Ireland, but he was trapped in Virginia. Unable to go home himself, he sent his eleven-year-old son to school there in 1698. In spite of his sober habits, he was carried off by dysentery in 1703, at the age of fifty-two. He left a large estate to his two surviving children, and founded a Virginia dynasty.

If there was anything "American" about planters like Fitzhugh, it was their immersion in the tobacco economy, the Oronocco way of life, which had nothing comparable in England. An aerial view of late-seventeenth-century Virginia would show breaks in the brown-green forest cover, like bald spots along the rivers. On closer inspection, one would see fields with tidy rows of big-leafed plants, hunched slaves moving slowly between the rows, curing sheds, and planked wharves poking into the brackish tidal waters. All around the Chesapeake was the murmur and hum of a world based on tobacco.

From the small farmer, known as "the man of one hogshead," to the big planters, the men of so many thousand "hills" (running to about four thousand hills an acre), all were fixated on tobacco. The seed plants were transplanted to the field when "they be grown to the breadth of a shilling." Then came the hilling, planting, topping, suckering, weeding, worming, and cutting. Some planters used turkeys to go after tobacco worms. The curing could take six weeks before the tobacco was "in case."

Sometimes smoke fires had to be lit under the hanging leaf, as the planter Robert Carter explained: "In funky, foggy weather, when tobacco is just upon turning, we are forced to make smothers in our house to dry it. . . ."

The cured leaf was stripped and stemmed and prized (packed into hogsheads), and the hogsheads were loaded aboard ship. There was a little ritual with the captain—a round of drinks, and toasts to a prosperous voyage, a lucky market, and a happy return.

The planters' dealings with the London merchants were antagonistic. From the Virginia end, the relationship was seen as a tug-of-war between hardworking planters and grasping merchants. From the London end, it was a battle that pitted the punctual merchant against the quick-to-borrow-and-slow-to-pay planter. The merchant might write that the tobacco had lost weight during the passage, to which the planter replied that it had not lost weight but had been "pillaged." Since each letter took an average of four months, these discussions were prolonged.

In spite of all the difficulties, the mutual recrimination between merchants and planters, the drops in prices, the taxes in England, the droughts, and the hailstorms, the tobacco economy was entrenched in Virginia. After 1680, there was a decline in the stream of indentured servants, which led to a switch to slaves, who became available in greater numbers just at the time when planters could afford them.

Far from being inferior, slaves from West Africa carried a unique advantage over the white man, which was the sickle-cell gene. This genetic trait produced abnormal sickle-shaped red blood cells that conferred partial but inherited immunity to malaria and yellow fever. The slaves could work in the mosquito-infested tidewater areas of Virginia and remain healthy.

The replacement of servants by slaves became a system for keeping laborers in perpetual bondage. Perhaps the tradition of indentured servants conditioned Virginians to accept slavery without qualms, but there were crucial differences. Unlike the indentured servants, the slaves could not work off their term of service and become freemen and landowners. They could never be accepted into the Chesapeake society. They formed a permanently disenfranchised and excluded group, without outlets for expression.

A 1705 Virginia act declared "the Negro, mulatto and Indian slaves within the dominion to be real estate." Later it was decided that a Negro convicted of murder or arson could be sentenced "to have the right hand cut off, the head severed from the body, the body divided into four quarters, and head and quarters set up in the most public place of the country." The European lawmakers who had thought up drawing and quartering for regicides could not have done better.

Religious instruction was initially withheld from slaves, because of the belief that Christians automatically become freemen. Conversion, in other words, would discharge a slave from bondage. In Maryland, in 1671, however, they passed an act that slaves who became Christians remained slaves.

Slavery introduced racial tension into southern frontier society. Racial cases began turning up in court dockets. In 1681, in Henrico County, a group of freemen and servants gathered with a half-dozen Negro and mulatto slaves on a hot August afternoon to drink some cider after cutting weeds in an orchard. One of the white women, the wife of a Quaker, made giddy by the combination of heat and hard cider, began to focus her amorous attentions on a handsome mulatto lad. There was an accusation of rape.

The judge who questioned the woman wanted to know whether she had seduced the lad and trumped up the rape charge as an excuse for an angry husband. Witnesses testified that the tipsy coquette had brought it on herself with her sexual teasing, and that the slave had at first shunned her in order to stay out of trouble. The slave was acquitted. This story, perhaps the first example of a black man charged with raping a white woman in America, would repeat itself over the years in every slave state.

The black man in Virginia had little hope of advancement. But for the white man, the tobacco economy remained an arena of rapid social ascent, where the son of a grocer or a cooper could become landed gentry. In 1670, William Byrd I, the son of a London goldsmith, inherited a plantation on the James River from an uncle, Thomas Stegge, a sea captain who had struck it rich as an Indian trader.

William Byrd I applied himself to increasing his inheritance, following in his uncle's footsteps in the Indian trade. He added to his regular income the profitable sideline of importing slaves. By the time he died, in 1704, he was one of the richest men in Virginia, having succeeded in expanding his uncle's estate at the falls of the James River to forty-seven hundred acres.

In his son and namesake, William Byrd II, we have, not an unreconstructed Englishman like William Fitzhugh, but a divided being, a weld of the Old World and the New. His inbred Englishness was leavened by an instinctive though unarticulated "Americanness." Byrd was an eighteenth-century Englishman with the values of his class and a highly organized code of conduct, but he was also a product of the frontier experience. He was a sort of frontier fop, a combination of Restoration dandy and tidewater plantation owner, not at all straitlaced like Fitzhugh, with strong allegiances to both his Virginia home and his English roots.

Born in Virginia in 1674, he was sent to school in England when he was seven. In 1690, when he was sixteen, he spent a year in Holland "to imbibe some of the fine business sense of the Dutch." Then it was back to England for law studies. After passing his bar exam in 1695, when he was twenty-one, he returned briefly to Virginia, but was soon in England again, employed as an agent for the colony.

Only when his father died in 1704 did he return to manage the family plantation, Westover, near today's Charles City. In 1706, at the age of thirty-two, he married Lucy Parke, the daughter of a prominent English officer. Lucy had four children, with two daughters surviving infancy, and Byrd recorded their life together at Westover in a secret journal. He kept it in shorthand learned from a how-to book of the period called *A Pen Plucked from an Eagle's Wing*. This journal provides one of the rare glimpses into the marriage and private life of a colonial planter in Virginia in the early eighteenth century.

Lucy and William Byrd are presented in the diary as a constantly squabbling but reconciling couple. It was a tempestuous marriage. Lucy Parke Byrd was a high-strung woman, given to tantrums. For reasons that baffled her husband, she was customarily indisposed, out of humor, melancholy, or in poor health. In her sudden storms and unpredictability, she was like the wilderness at the edge of the plantation that had to be tamed. She required the same kind of management as Byrd's lands, based on patience, alertness, and a system of rewards and punishments. "She was in the wrong," Byrd observed in a typical entry. "For my part I kept my temper very well."

Many things about Lucy angered Byrd, including her treatment of slaves. When, in March 1712, he found her beating her maid, Jenny, with tongs, he lunged toward her to take the tongs away, and "she lifted up her hands to strike me but forbore to do it." She then gave him "abundance of bad words" and put her hands around her neck as though to strangle herself, "but I believe in jest only," Byrd noted. "After acting a madwoman for a long time, she was passive again." It should be said that Byrd's own methods for punishing slaves were less than exemplary, as shown in this entry concerning a slave boy: "Eugene pissed abed again for which I made him drink a pint of piss."

When the slaves were good, however, there were distributions of the delicious mead that Lucy Byrd prepared. And when Lucy herself was good—or, more precisely, when Byrd wanted to get back in her good graces after a quarrel—he "rogered" or "flourished" her. A fight in the morning was followed by a "flourish" in the afternoon, and he observed on one occasion that "the flourish was performed on the billiard table." Afterward, she read to him from a sermon by the noted preacher Archbishop John Tillotson, and Byrd was moved "to tears of repentance."

Byrd was normally up early, but when Lucy was out of sorts he stayed in bed to do a little wife-wooing. "I rogered her," he writes, "by way of reconciliation." Sex was seen as the cure for her recurring indispositions and bad humors, as when he reported that she had "a hysteric fit pretty violently which lasted about an hour." After the medication, she usually improved; as he observed, "I gave my wife a powerful flourish and gave her great ecstasy and refreshment."

Though it helped them to make up, the "rogering" did not stop the quarrels. On one occasion, they fought when he accused her of eavesdropping on him from the top of the stairs. Another time, the issue was her insistence on plucking her eyebrows before the governor's ball, which Byrd feared would make them late.

Byrd was intriguing, an early-American anti-Puritan libertine with healthy appetites and the sexual candor of a Boswell. He liked to get "merry but not drunk," and "rogered" his way through life. Unlike the pious Fitzhugh, who mourned the absence of a church, Byrd had one nearby but kept the Sabbath casually, playing billiards with his cousin on a Sunday morning "because there seemed to be no more harm in it than in talk." He considered church to be "a gentleman's club with a faint interest in religion," where the right sort of people could meet and gossip. Still, he was proud of having the best pew.

Byrd remained intensely class-conscious. When a planter's daughter married her uncle's overseer, he noted: "To stoop to a dirty plebeian without any kind of merit is the lowest prostitution." At the same time, he was a learned man who had a library of 3,625 books, and who read Dutch, French, Italian, Latin, Greek, and Hebrew.

Although a hedonist—he carefully listed every sexual encounter and every dish he ate at meals—Byrd was hardworking. He spent long days on the many-faceted plantation business, and bragged about his self-sufficiency: "I have no bills to pay and half a crown will rest undisturbed in my pockets for many moons. . . . I have my flocks and my herds. . . . We sit securely under our vines and our fig trees without any danger to our property."

On rising, at six, he would read a hundred verses of Homer before shaving, and then take a light breakfast of hot chocolate before seizing the day and its immediate crises—a dog had killed a lamb, a neighbor's horse had broken his fence, and a neighbor's hogs were rooting in his pasture. A bear cub had been shot as it sat in the vines eating grapes. A woodsman wanted permission to shoot birds in the marsh.

On a large plantation, there were always personnel problems, such as a drunken overseer, or shiftless slaves pretending to be sick. Byrd saw them all as backsliders, liars, and thieves. It never changed: When one needed paint, another had the key to the store-room. The herdsman let the cattle stray, and the gardeners cut trees down without permission. The house servants stole rum and watered what was left. Moll the cook missed the sauce and spoiled the plum pudding.

In his tobacco business, Byrd felt hounded by regulations. The planters weren't allowed to export a finished product; they could only ship the leaf. He tried trimming the center stem to cut freight costs, but that was banned by an Act of Parliament. It seemed absurd that, after growing the stuff, he had to import his own smoking tobacco from London.

But Byrd remained a staunch booster of tobacco as a panacea. He wrote: "We should hang bundles of it round our beds and in the apartments where we most converse. . . . The pass to our stomachs should be also safely defended by chewing this great antipoison very frequently."

Although the frontier was receding, there was still a general aura of insecurity; as late as the 1730s, Byrd built an underground passage from the plantation house to the river in case he was sur-prised by Indians. His anxiety led to recurring dreams of mutila-tion and death. He dreamed that lightning had almost put out one of his eyes; that a funeral coach had stopped at his front door; that a coffin had been brought into his house and thrown into the hall.

Like his father before him, Byrd was elected to the House of Burgesses and named to the Council of State, which served as a kind of supreme court. Most of the twelve seats were controlled by the intermarried clique of big planters.

Byrd was also receiver general of the revenues, and in this role he came into direct conflict with Alexander Spotswood, who in 1710 became governor of Virginia. Byrd had gubernatorial ambi-tions of his own, which were dashed with Spotswood's arrival. Spotswood was a war hero, wounded at Blenheim. The duke of Marlborough put Byrd in his place by writing him, "No one but soldiers should have the government of a plantation."

Byrd did his utmost to subvert Spotswood's efforts to reform the revenues, the tobacco economy, and the judiciary, until Spots-wood complained about him to the Board of Trade in London. In danger of losing his office of receiver, which was worth four hundred pounds a year, Byrd went to England in 1714 to argue his case, arriving in London in July. When he remained in England, Spotswood pointed out that Byrd could not continue being receiver general while living in London. Byrd had to sell the office for five hundred pounds.

In 1716, tragedy touched his life when Lucy came to London to see him and died there of smallpox. "Gracious God," he wrote in a letter, "what pains did she take to make a voyage hither to seek a grave." In less than two months, however, he was courting an heiress and resuming his restless sexual prowling. He ended up spending twelve years in England.

By the time the fifty-two-year-old Byrd returned to Westover in 1726, he had a new wife, Maria Taylor, who would give him four more children. Before long, he had become involved in Virginia's long-festering dispute with North Carolina over a strip of land thirty miles wide, north of Albermarle Sound. The second Carolina charter claimed the land for Carolina, but a number of settlers who held Virginia land grants lived in the area. Were they Virginians or North Carolinians? To whom should they pay taxes? Since both provinces claimed them, they paid neither.

In 1728, under the impetus of Governor William Gooch of Virginia, the two provinces got together and appointed a joint commission, with four commissioners from North Carolina, three from Virginia, and two surveyors on each side. One of the Virginia commissioners was William Byrd II, who thus took part in a great colonial ceremony, the running of a boundary line.

The line was run in two expeditions, one in the spring and one in the fall of 1728. Aside from the seven commissioners and four surveyors, the crew included forty men and a chaplain. The men were needed to carry the packs, provisions, and bedding, clear the underbrush, carry the chains, and mark the trees.

From the start, the Virginians cultivated a superior attitude, patronizing the Carolinians and treating them like poor relations. They informed the Carolina commissioners that they planned to travel in style, with tents for themselves and their servants, and "as much wine and rum as will enable us and our men to drink every night to the success of the following day, and because we understand there are many gentiles on your frontier who never had an opportunity of being baptized we shall have a chaplain to make them Christians. . . . And whoever of your province shall be desirous of novelty may report on Sundays to our tent and hear a sermon."

The Carolinians jocularly replied that they couldn't possibly meet such high standards, but that "what we may want in necessaries we hope will be made up in spiritual comfort from your chaplain, of whom we shall give notice as you desire to all lovers of novelty and doubt not of a great many boundary Christians."

On March 5, 1728, the seven commissioners, bewigged gentlemen in London suits, stood on a beach covered with blue-and-white conch shells at Currituck Inlet, off the Atlantic shore. Byrd, who deemed the Carolina commissioners to be comical bumpkins, made fun of one of them because his coat, waistcoat, and breeches were "of different parishes." As breakers flew over the inlet with a great smacking sound, the commissioners argued about the point where the line should start—should it be the spit of sand on the northern shore of the inlet, or the high ground two hundred yards beyond? They agreed on the high ground, since the sand spit was ever shifting and often submerged, whereas they wanted a fixed and certain landmark. They planted a cedar post there, engraved with "NC" on one side and "V" on the other.

Then they rested for a day, tasting oysters as savory as Colchesters from Wellfleet, and coming upon a hermit who lived with a woman in a bark-covered hut like Indians. They did not sow or plant, Byrd observed, but lived on oysters and milk from the neighbor's cows. For Byrd, this was a glimpse of a future America, where crude democracy had worn down civilization.

On March 7, they began running the line westward from the first cedar post, with the surveyors setting up their tripods and sighting through their levels, and reading the gradations on the measuring rods, while the men with the chains marked out short, straight sections. The line split a plantation belonging to William Harding, which was a major annoyance: now that his land was half in Virginia and half in North Carolina, he would have to take out two patents and pay for a new survey of each.

They had to cut through thickets of briars and brambles, and were glad when they advanced three miles in a day. The pace gave Byrd a chance to observe the borderers, a rough and ready lot who had a reputation for sheltering runaway slaves and criminals. The men were loafers, and the women did all the work.

North Carolina in general he thought of as "lubberland," where people were "intolerably lazy." He made no allowance for the fact that, whereas Virginia had been settled for more than a century, these people were recent arrivals, at an earlier stage of development.

And yet, all along the line, they were invited to stay, and wined and dined. If there was a pretty girl around, the commissioners made the most of the opportunity. On March 12, they invited "a tallow-faced wench" with a sprained wrist to drink with them, lifted her up, "examined all her hidden charms, and played a great many gay pranks . . . the poor damsel being disabled from making any resistance by the lameness of her hand. All she could do was to sit still and make the fashionable exclamation of the country, 'flesh alive and tear it.' "

The greatest obstacle of the expedition, they knew, was a huge swamp, thirty miles north to south and ten miles across, which had never been traversed by a white man, and which Byrd named the Dismal Swamp. On March 14, they reached it, having advanced about twenty miles from Currituck Inlet in a week. A team of twelve men was sent through to mark the line, while the commissioners traveled around it.

The commissioners stayed at Timothy Ivy's plantation, eighteen miles away; the men in the swamp caught fevers from sleeping on wet ground and drinking bad water. At night, they covered the ground with strips of cypress bark and spread their bedding on the bark, but water seeped up between the strips and soaked them. They couldn't keep a fire going, because the moisture in the soil put it out, so they had to keep a sentry on duty to rekindle it every fifteen minutes.

On March 28, Byrd got word that the "Dismalites" had run the line. "What a mass of mud and dirt is measured up in this filthy circumference," he wrote. Moving quite quickly westward, the party covered about thirty miles in six days, and reached the banks of the Meherrin River, near today's town of Severn, on April 3. There they decided to stop the expedition until the autumn, for the rattlesnakes were crawling out of their winter quarters and the men were tired and wanted to see their families. In six weeks, they had gone about seventy-three miles.

On April 6, the Virginians took leave of the Carolinians and decided to visit the Indian village of Nottaway Town, where the population of two hundred entertained them with war dances to the beat of a drum. Byrd's fellow commissioner William Dandridge said he wanted to see whether Indian women were different from white women. The following day, Byrd saw that Dandridge's ruffles were smudged with ponchoon, the purple-red dye that the Indian maids used for body paint. As for Byrd, "a grave matron," the chief's wife, whispered in his ear that, "if her daughter had been but one year older, she would have been at his devotion." "They are a little mercenary in their amours," he added, "and seldom bestow their favors out of stark love and kindness." But the price was reasonable, "a princess for a pair of red stockings." On April 9, he left Nottaway and headed home to Westover.

When the boundary commission reconvened in September, Byrd met up on the 19th with the Carolinians, who had so many provisions he asked them if they intended to carry the line to the South Seas: they had five hundred pounds each of bacon and brisket, whereas the Virginians were relying on game for their meat. The next day, on the Meherrin again, their landlord sold them his homemade brandy, which made them so rowdy that a damsel helping in the kitchen "would have been ravished if her timely consent had not prevented violence." The commission's revels sometimes took on the exuberance of a party at Animal House, and in this case their landlady, thinking herself unsafe "in the hands of such furious lovers, fortified her bed-chamber and defended it with a chamber-pot charged to the brim with female ammunition."

Now that they were in wilderness country, with not a white settler to be seen, Byrd hired a Saponi Indian hunter-guide, Ned Bearskin, who "seldom discharged his piece in vain." They had some difficult days of broken stony ground with impenetrable thickets, but still managed eight or nine miles a day.

On October 5, 1728, the Carolina commissioners dropped a bombshell: they said they were going home, having been ordered to run the line thirty or forty miles west of the Roanoke and no farther. Byrd asked them why they hadn't said so before. The Virginians would push on, he said, since they had only been on the job seventeen days and their governor expected them to run the line to the mountains.

But one of the Virginia commissioners, Richard Fitz-William, was a troublemaker; he sided with the Carolinians and demanded to see the Virginia governor's written orders. The third Virginia commissioner, William Dandridge, took out his pencil and said in a comical tone that, since Fitz-William insisted on minutes, by gad, he would take a minute of that. "Without preface or ceremony," the infuriated Fitz-William grabbed a club "big enough to knock down an ox" and brandished it at Dandridge, who was scratching with his pen. As Byrd stopped Fitz-William's arm in mid-swing, deflecting the blow, Dandridge "saluted him with the title he had a good right to, namely of son of a whore." Fitz-William called for help to his servant, who said, "That's none of my business, if the gentleman will run himself into a broil, he may get out of it as well as he can."

On October 7, Fitz-William left with the Carolina commissioners, who had "stuck by us as long as our good liquor lasted," Byrd wrote, "and were so kind as to drink our good journey to the mountains in the last bottle we had left." The Virginians trudged on for another eighteen days, and on October 25 they saw the peaks of the Blue Ridge Mountains ten miles away. One was so high it hid its head in the clouds, and another was like a stack of chimneys, with a precipice they dubbed the Despairing Lover's Leap. By this time, they were running short of bread, and the horses were so thin their ribs showed, so they decided to go home, back along the line, the way they had come.

On November 22, they dispersed to their respective homes, having been out close to ten weeks. In their quest for a boundary, they had crossed marshes, swamps, steep hills, and craggy rocks, going as far as today's Stokes County, North Carolina, where the Hanging Rock State Park is. They had run about two-thirds of today's Virginia–North Carolina boundary, which is a straight line running right across landscape features rather than following them.

William Byrd lived on until 1744, but running the boundary line was the high point of his life. In the wilderness, he lost his class-conscious Virginia-gentleman outlook and joined in the camaraderie of the venison kettle and the rum jug. In this sense he was American, and also in his changing view of slavery: on July 12, 1736, he wrote to the earl of Egmont, Georgia's first president of the trustees, congratulating him on the ban on slaves there, which was surely a departure from the interests of his class.

"I wish my lord we could be blessed with the same prohibition," he wrote. "I am sensible of many bad consequences of multiplying these Ethiopians amongst us. They blow up the pride and ruin the industry of our white people, who seeing a rank of poor creatures below them, detest work for fear it should make them look like slaves. . . . It were therefordh worth the consideration of a British Parliament, my lord, to put an end to this unchristian traffic of making merchandise of our fellow creatures."

This was easy for Byrd to say at the age of sixty-two, after building up an impressive fortune with the help of slave labor. Even so, he defined America as a place where a man can change his mind, where people aren't frozen into their positions because of vested interests. Already, Byrd discerned what Emerson would express: "If you put a chain around the neck of a slave, the other end fastens itself around your own."

CHAPTER ELEVEN

THE CHESAPEAKE FRONTIER

After the mercantile companies and the religious dissidents came a new form of English colony, the proprietary province, in which the royal grant was bestowed upon a single person, a family, or a small group of investors. The first of these was Maryland. Founded in 1633 as a colony for Catholic gentlemen, it became a land of opportunity for indentured servants.

> *. . . things are changed now,*
> *At the Hoe I daily work,*
> *And Bare-foot go,*
> *In weeding Corn or feeding Swine,*
> *I spend my melancholy Time.*

> *EBENEZER COOK*

The founding of Maryland in the 1630s was directly related to the position of Catholics in England. Since England had a Protestant monarch, excommunicated by the pope, and since Catholics were loyal to the pope, they were seen as the Vatican's fifth column. They weren't massacred and expelled, as the Huguenots were in France, but a sweeping body of anti-Catholic legislation had been passed—Catholics could not bear arms, travel freely, or practice their faith openly. Those who attended a university or who held public office were required to take a loyalty oath.

If you were a Catholic in seventeenth-century England and you wanted to make something of yourself, you had to play the game of pretending to be an Anglican. This was what George

Calvert did. A closet Catholic who outwardly conformed to the Anglican faith in his marriage and in the baptism of his four children, he began his political rise in 1604 with his appointment as secretary to King James I's chief minister, Robert Cecil, the earl of Salisbury.

Calvert's rise was steady. He became clerk of the signet, and clerk of the council, and, in 1619, one of two secretaries of state. This made him one of the king's men, sent out on delicate missions, at the heart of diplomatic negotiations.

Then, in 1625, at the height of his career, he abruptly resigned and announced his Catholicism. His policy of bringing about a rapprochement with Catholic Spain through a royal marriage had failed, and after his resignation, since he no longer held public office, he decided to profess his faith openly. As a personal favorite of James I, he remained in the good graces of James' son, Charles I, who had married a French queen and was thought to be sympathetic to Catholics.

King Charles made Calvert Lord Baltimore, the name coming from one of his properties in County Longford, Ireland. Calvert then turned his attention to the New World, which had long been a sideline of his. In 1609, he had been one of 812 subscribers to the Virginia Company, paying twenty-five pounds for two shares, and in 1622 he had joined Sir Ferdinando Gorges' Council for New England. Now, in 1625, he obtained a grant for Newfoundland and sent some people out to start a cod-fishing station.

As it turned out, there were two things wrong with Newfoundland. One was that the French were on the St. Lawrence and did not appreciate his horning in. The other was that it was much colder than anyone had told him. After his move there in 1628, he wrote King Charles that, "from the midst of October to the midst of May, there is a sad face of winter upon all this land, both sea and land so frozen as they are not penetrable, no plant or vegetable thing appearing out of the earth until it be about the beginning of May. . . ."

Calvert's Newfoundland mission came at a time when the king was experimenting with alternatives to the joint-stock company as a vehicle of colonization. One alternative was the proprietary province, patterned on the ancient palatinate of Durham, an English province on the Scottish border that had been turned over to a feudal lord to guard it against Scottish raids. The same thing could be done in the New World. Individuals could be given royal grants to protect and settle specific places. The proprietor could declare war, raise troops, pass laws, punish or pardon, appoint officials, and distribute land as he saw fit. He could even take out mortgages on the land.

In 1632, George Calvert was granted about seven million acres north of the Potomac. He wanted to call it "Crescentia." The king suggested "Terra Maria"—after his wife, Henrietta Maria, daughter of one French king, Henry IV, and sister of another, Louis XIII. Calvert died in the same year that he received the grant, his health impaired by his stay in Newfoundland.

His two sons, Cecil and Leonard, inherited the property, the former staying in London to do the necessary lobbying, the latter leading the first group of settlers. They planned to follow their father's vision and make the new colony a refuge for the Catholic gentry of England. There would be large landed estates, veritable baronies, with the conferring of titles and a courtly manorial life. The advantage to the monarchy was that Maryland would be a buffer against the Dutch and the Swedes on the Delaware in the ongoing New World checkers game.

In mid-October 1633, the *Ark* and the *Dove* sailed down the Thames under the command of Leonard Calvert. It carried seventeen gentlemen investors, mostly Catholic, and a hundred–odd servants, mostly Protestant. After swearing allegiance to the crown, they sailed westward through the Strait of Dover, stopping at Cowes on the Isle of Wight to pick up three Jesuit priests. They started across the Atlantic on November 22. On March 3, 1634, they had their first glimpse of the magnificent Chesapeake, an Indian word for "Great Shellfish Bay."

It was only twenty-six years after the first landing at Jamestown, but what a difference. Stopping off in Virginia, they picked up a fur trader, Henry Fleet, to interpret and negotiate with the Indians. Fleet, who knew the area, also helped with site selection, taking them into the estuary of the Potomac, which one of the Jesuits, Father Andrew White, described as "the sweetest and greatest river I have ever seen. . . . The Thames is but a little finger of it."

Fearful of an Indian attack, they first stopped at St. Clement's Island, part of the Heron Island chain, then four hundred acres, now eroded down to forty. Here, at last, they breathed the air of religious freedom, and Henry Fleet got a good real-estate tip: some Yaocomico Indians down the Potomac were abandoning their village and were willing to sell their attractive waterfront property.

Up the St. Marys River they went, to land at the site on

March 27 and negotiate a deal with the Indians, who were friendly. The Indians stayed among them for a while to teach them the ropes. They taught them how to plant corn on land that wasn't cleared of stumps and root systems, using the hill method.

When the Indians moved out in 1635, the Maryland settlers built a square palisaded fort with 360-foot sides, mounted with cannons. They placed their cabins inside. Since there were no Indian raids, however, they found they didn't need the fort, and tore it down.

Aside from occasional Susquehannock alarm from the north, this was the Peaceable Kingdom. The settlers could go fishing and hunting without falling into an ambush. Much of their good luck had to do with timing, or the virtue of being second. Jamestown, being first, had borne the brunt of hardship.

For the first time in the history of English settlements, a colony came close to religious tolerance. The Calverts knew that they could not impose Catholicism as the Puritans had imposed their creed in Boston. Catholicism would never be the religion of state in England, and therefore had to be practiced discreetly. The Calverts adopted tolerance in Maryland because they hoped for tolerance in England. Their policy was to let every man practice the religion he wanted.

Cecil Calvert's instructions to his brother were quite explicit. He must be "very careful to preserve unity and peace amongst all . . . and that they suffer no scandal nor offense to be given to any of the Protestants . . . and that for that end, they cause all Acts of Roman Catholic religion to be done as privately as may be, and that they instruct all the Roman Catholics to be silent upon all occasions of discourse concerning matters of religion." When the Jesuits built a chapel at St. Marys in 1641, the second Lord Baltimore demanded that they surrender the building.

In the 1649 Act Concerning Religion, religious tolerance became the law of the colony, and remained so, with a Cromwellian interruption, until the Glorious Revolution of 1688, when the Protestants took over. Maryland in its early years was the only colony where Quakers were tolerated, although they were resented, because in court they would "presumptuously stand covered," and because they refused to testify under oath, serve as jurors, hold office, or perform military service. There was a bit of everything in Maryland, including Puritans and Dutch and Swedish Reformed, and by 1660 the population had grown to seventy-five hundred.

The irony was that a colony intended as a neo-Catholic feudal refuge ended up as a godsend for impoverished Protestants. Once again, the original vision was trampled underfoot by all those racing for available land. Cecil Calvert underestimated the man-land ratio in his "Conditions of Plantation," which set out the terms of acquisition. At first, any gentleman bringing over five servants was entitled to purchase a thousand acres. Then it was changed to twenty servants and two thousand acres, and it kept going through changes until it became a modified head-rights system, where, the more servants you brought in, the more acreage you got.

There were basically three kinds of servants: indentured, who signed a contract in England and were bound to serve terms that varied depending on their age and skills; convicts, who turned Maryland into a colony of jailbirds; and free-willers, who were given a number of days to find an employer who would advance the price of their passage. The free-willers were told by the crimps in England to expect a life of ease, but more often than not their hopes of a job were blasted and they found themselves obliged to accept unprofitable servitude.

When Maryland opened its first courts, in 1638, legislation concerning servants was one of the priorities. At that time, because of the number of runaways, "unlawful departure" was punished by hanging. Later a law was enacted that no one could travel outside his own county without a pass, which was a nuisance to the freemen, who were suspected of being runaways if they forgot their pass.

Servants were protected from ill treatment, such as being forced to work on the Sabbath. In one case, Captain Thomas Bradnox, a justice of the peace in Kent County—across the bay, in eastern Maryland—was accused of beating a servant named Sara Taylor. According to the testimony, he beat her with a rope while his wife held her down, leaving twenty-one marks on her back and arms, saying, "Now spoil me a batch of bread again."

Sara Taylor bared her back in court to show the three commissioners the marks. An eyewitness said he had seen Bradnox hit her on the head with a three-footed stool because she had picked up a book. "You dissembling jade," he shouted, "what do you do with a book in your hand?" Sara Taylor was released from her indenture because of the "inveterate malice" of her master. But as a justice of the peace, Bradnox was well connected in the courts, and Sara was restored to him on appeal.

Bradnox, however, got a sort of out-of-court settlement when his wife cuckolded him. Some time later, she was charged with adultery with John Salter. When Salter told her that he would force her to go to bed with him, she had replied that it was not necessary to use force, for "by fair means you can do much."

Salter's breeches were soon "down in his hand," while she lay on the bed "with her coats up as high as her breast." Bradnox appeared and grabbed his wife "by the birth," dragging her across the floor "in an inhumane manner." Salter came to her rescue. The men scuffled. As Salter left, Bradnox threatened to shoot him. "Old Tom, do thy worst," Salter said, "I fear thee not." Then Bradnox brought some drinks to his wife's bedside and asked her "to pledge him a dram, and forget all malice or cause of discord that was betwixt them." He was so drunk he fell down and suffered a nosebleed.

In another servant-master case, Jacob Lumbrozo, the first Jew to settle in Maryland, was charged with aborting Elizabeth Wild, a maid in his employ. According to the testimony, he had intercourse with her against her will, throwing her on the bed and covering her mouth with a handkerchief when she tried to cry out. On learning she was pregnant, he gave her a purge made of juniper berries, and soon she passed "a clod of blood as big as a fist." When Lumbrozo saw it in the chamber pot, he told her, "Your body is clear. . . ."

Lumbrozo was jailed, but this was not the only time he was in trouble with the law. A native of Lisbon, naturalized in 1663, he was an educated man and a jack-of-all-trades, who practiced medicine and the law, quoting from Scripture and poetry in his summations. He also acted as "commissionated appraiser" of estates, and kept an inn in his house on Nenjemoy Creek in Charles County, at the southwestern tip of Maryland. There he hunted wolves for bounty and traded with the Indians for furs, always wearing a beaver hat and a black cloak.

Lumbrozo was a sort of New World Shylock, maligned by the community, and dragged into court on a number of charges. Once he was sued for defamation for saying that one Mary Empson had "a pocky whore's back" (the pox being syphilis). Another time, he was charged with receiving stolen goods. Perhaps the most unusual charge against him was one that strained the limits of religious tolerance in the colony. In 1658, at the court of St. Marys, he was charged with blasphemy against "Our Blessed Savior, Jesus Christ."

His accuser, John Fossett, testified that, when he had said to Lumbrozo that Christ was "more than man, as did appear by his Resurrection," Lumbrozo replied that "his disciples stole him away." What about miracles? asked John Fossett. To this Lumbrozo replied, "Such works might be done by necromancy, or sorcery." "Then you do take Christ to be a necromancer?" Fossett asked. Lumbrozo laughed, but did not reply. Though he argued in his defense that he had not intended to say anything derogatory, this theological discussion landed Lumbrozo in jail. He was released in a general amnesty on the occasion of Oliver Cromwell's death in the same year, 1658.

This case demonstrates Maryland's complete lack of freedom of expression. People were constantly being arrested for "sundry and contemptuous and scandalous words." You could drag your neighbor into court for calling you "a factious fellow." This was only feasible when the population was small, or the courts would have been swamped, so most of the slander cases turn up in the early years. One man was fined for calling another "a hog-stealing fellow from his cradle," and Henry Clay sued Dr. Thomas Ward for calling his wife "a burnt-assed whore." Under Charles Calvert, the third Lord Baltimore, Edward Erbery got twenty lashes in 1665 for calling the members of the lower house "pitiful rogues and puppies," and the Assembly itself "the turdy, shitten Assembly."

Since there were no jails until the 1650s, each justice of the peace kept an assortment of irons for branding malefactors, one with an "H" for "hog stealers," another with an "R" for "runaways," and still others with an "M" and a "T" for "murderer" and "thief." Every sheriff was equipped with ducking stools and whipping posts. When they finally did build county jails, prisoners had to pay for the cost of their imprisonment; anything else would have been "an encouragement of offenders."

With the increased presence of slaves came a whole new body of legislation. In 1664, a law was passed prohibiting the marriage of white women servants and Negro slaves. Any woman servant marrying a slave had to serve her master during the life of her husband, and all their children were slaves. Instead of preventing miscegenation, this law allowed unprincipled masters to encourage such marriages, in order to turn their women servants into slaves. It was repealed in 1681, on the grounds that the marriages were often due to "the instigation, procurement, or connivance of the masters."

The slaves would remain slaves, but the ascent of the indentured servants was nothing short of prodigious. Wherever tobacco was planted, labor was needed, and there was a steady influx of young unmarried males, who swiftly rose to landowning status. Once they were "out of their time," their master had to give them their "freedom dues": fifty acres of land, a year's supply of corn, a suit of clothes, an ax, and a hoe. Of course, the fifty acres were usually in the form of a head-rights warrant, which meant that the servant had to find the land himself and pay for the survey and the patent, so there was a transition period when he had to work for wages to raise the money.

Still, by 1642, eight years after the first landing, twenty-five servants had become freeholders. Alongside the manorial estates were the small farms of servants, now freemen on the rise.

Some became members of the Assembly and pushed through the passage of proservant legislation. John Hatch was sheriff of St. Marys in 1647. Robert Vaughan was justice of the peace on Kent Island for twenty-six years. Vaughan's length of service was the exception: malaria and dysentery were still killers, and a short life span created a high turnover in public office. There were always opportunities opening up for young men, some of whom served as justices even though they were illiterate.

After 1680, more servants arrived from Ireland. Some of them, hardworking and shrewd, did extremely well, but others fell victim to the flaws in their character. A study in contrasts were two young Irishmen who arrived in Port Tobacco, on one of the Potomac's many inlets, in 1703.

Having had some legal training, Thomas Macnemara bound himself as clerk to the lawyer Charles Carroll. He courted his employer's niece, and married her once his term was up. Starting his own practice in a Maryland that by then was under Protestant rule, he had to sign an oath abjuring the Catholic Church. "A dose of squills" (a diuretic), he told his friends, "will clear my stomach of those oaths."

Specializing in defending habitual criminals, Macnemara was popular with his fellow lawyers. He was the sort who would always stand a drink and crack a joke. In 1710, however, he killed a Quaker boatman in a quarrel. Indicted for murder, he entered a plea of "homicide by chance medley," meaning in the heat of battle. As punishment, he was branded on the right hand with the letter "M." Incredibly, he was reinstated as a lawyer, which attests to the serious shortage in the colony. In 1712, he was charged with "attempted buggery," which he plea-bargained down to simple assault. He got off with a fine of fifteen hundred pounds of tobacco. In 1720, he died of natural causes. On a copy of his will, which was found in the probate record, someone had written in the margin: "A most troublesome and seditious person."

In 1703, eighteen-year-old Daniel Dulany also arrived at Port Tobacco, from Dublin, where he had studied law for a term at the university. He was a free-willer, looking for an employer to pay his passage. One can imagine him on the deck of the ship, gazing at the immense blue Potomac and finally at the dock, where prospective employers waited.

Among them was an important citizen, Colonel Plater, a leading Maryland lawyer, attorney general of the province, and receiver of revenues for the Patuxent River District. He needed a clerk. Spotting Dulany, and liking the look of him, Plater was pleased to hear that he had studied the law. When he asked Dulany to write a few lines, he saw that the young man had a neat hand and a sober, deferential manner.

Saved from indenture, Daniel Dulany served six years of apprenticeship, learning the laws—which wasn't that hard, because there weren't that many. In 1709, he was admitted to practice, serving the four counties on the western shore, between the Potomac and the bay—St. Marys, Charles, Prince Georges, and Calvert. The courts were in session in March, June, August, and November, on successive Tuesdays. On the first Tuesday of those months, the circuit-riding lawyers arrived with their clients at Seymour Town (today's Leonardtown, in St. Marys County), by ferry or on horseback. The second Tuesday, they were in Port Tobacco for the Charles County court; the third, in Prince Georges; and the fourth in Calvert. These latter two county seats were little more than a courthouse and a tavern.

In 1710, only a year after he'd launched his practice, Dulany came to the attention of the new attorney general, William Bladen, doubtless through the recommendation of Colonel Plater. He was named clerk of the indictments and prosecutor of Her Majesty's pleas for Charles and St. Marys counties. He handled crown cases, as a federal prosecutor does today, and for each case he was paid one hundred pounds of tobacco.

A lot of cases involved indentured female servants charged with bastardy. The usual penalty was a fine or a whipping. Jane

Addison, for instance, was presented to the grand jury for "incontinent living" with a Negro known as Saucy Jack. Convicted of "bastardy," she was given twenty-five lashes. Then she was charged with murdering her newborn child, but Dulany could not find enough evidence to indict her.

In 1711, by then twenty-six, Dulany married nineteen-year-old Charity Courts, who had already been married, at sixteen, to a neighborhood tobacco planter. Her husband had died a few months later, making her a teen-age dowried widow. Her father had also left her two plantations in the best tobacco country—Martin's Freehold, 150 acres on the Potomac, and Hargage's Hope, one hundred acres just off the Potomac. Because of the short life span, there were always plenty of widows and widowers. It made for an upwardly mobile society.

Charity died in the year of their marriage, and her inheritance reverted to her family's estate. Nonetheless, by 1712, having been in Maryland less than ten years, the penniless Dublin free-willer Daniel Dulany had become a part of the planter oligarchy. In 1713, he moved to Prince Georges County, where there was still a lot of cheap land, and built a home on the Patuxent River, at Nottingham Town, halfway between Port Tobacco and Annapolis. It was twenty-two miles each way, an easy day's ride.

He began to buy land, a tract here, a tract there, and started appearing in court records as Daniel Dulany of Prince Georges County, Gentleman. To work the tobacco fields, he bought his own indentured servants. He married into one of Maryland's ruling families, that of Colonel Walter Smith, who was blessed with six daughters. From Nottingham he concentrated his practice on the Annapolis courts, such as the provincial court, the will-probate court, the chancery court, and the vice-admiralty court.

Dulany continued to invest his legal fees in land bargains, and by 1720 had increased his holdings to twenty-seven thousand acres, not counting his wife, Rebecca's dowry. He had become one of the largest landowners in the colony. This was the year his friend and fellow Irishman Macnemara died, leaving little more than the clothes on his back—good old Mac, whose bond he had once paid to keep him out of jail, and whose salty stories had made his sides split.

That same year, Dulany moved to the colonial capital of Annapolis, which had taverns, an inn, a September fair, and horse races. He entered politics and was named attorney general. In

1723, he came full circle when he prosecuted an indentured servant who had stolen a nightgown and six quarts of brandy. Dulany showed no mercy to this member of the caste to which he had almost belonged, and the thief was sentenced to hang. In another case he tried, that of a female slave who had committed an ax murder, the sentence was hanging on a ridge above the public highway, where everyone could see her.

His second wife, Rebecca, like his first wife, Charity, died young—two of those faceless women of the early English colonies who briefly reared children and ran households before becoming forgotten names on their family trees. Dulany married another widow with a good estate, Henrietta Chew. In 1742, he was sworn into the Governor's Council, and lived out his last years as a leading citizen of Annapolis, with a fine house and a good set of family silver. When he died in 1753, he had been in the New World almost exactly half a century—fifty years of patient accumulation, which made him the hero of an authentic rags-to-riches story.

CHAPTER TWELVE

THE
BLACK
FRONTIER

The second proprietary province was South Carolina, founded in 1663 by eight investors. The settlers took up the cultivation of rice, which required considerable manual labor. By 1729, there were twice as many slaves as colonists in South Carolina.

R U N   A W A Y,

From the Subscriber's Plantation in Prince William's *Parish,*

T W O   N E G R O   F E L L O W S,

Named MINOS, and CUDJOE;—they are both ſtrong-made Fellows. Minos appears to be near 40 Years old, Cudjoe about 26 :—They are marked a little above the right Breaſt with the Letters PB.——Whoever apprehends the ſaid Negroes, and lodges them in the Work-Houſe, or delivers them to my Overſeer, at Cooſaw, ſhall receive FIVE POUNDS Currency for each, on applying to Mr. JOSEPH ATKINSON, Merchant, in Charles-Town, or at Cooſaw, to

P I E R C E   B U T L E R.

South Carolina Historical Society, Charleston

In colonial South Carolina, where for a time there were more slaves than whites, runaways could find sanctuary in Spanish St. Augustine, and many did.

Eyeless in Gaza, at the mill with slaves.

JOHN MILTON

On January 22, 1737, the *South Carolina Gazette* reported a "Very Melancholy Accident." A Negro boatman was taking his master's son by canoe down the Ashley River to Charleston, where the boy was attending school. The canoe capsized, and they both drowned. Their bodies were found "sticking in the mud in the said river, their arms clasping one another." It would be hard to find a better image to illustrate the nature of slavery: two bodies, one black, one white, arms entwined in a fatal embrace. And nowhere did slaves become such a large percentage of the population as in South Carolina.

The impulse for the settlement of Carolina came from the congested little Caribbean island of Barbados, off the coast of Venezuela. Barbados was a gold mine, the gold being sugar, and the miners, or cane cutters, being black slaves. The annual export was worth more than that of all the North American English colonies combined. But Barbados grew so crowded (there were several hundred big planters) that many wealthy investors, aspiring planters, and servants who had finished their terms wanted to move on.

In 1663, Charles II issued a charter to eight proprietors under the same sort of arrangement that had been made with Calvert in Maryland. All were rich and titled, and some were Barbados planters. That August, one of the proprietors, Lord Albemarle, recommended to the governor of Barbados that the island overflow might settle in the new colony and plant commodities including "wine, oil, raisins, currants, rice, silk, etc. . . . ."

In April 1670, 150 colonists from England and Barbados disembarked at the mouth of the Ashley River and were led by a friendly Indian to a sheltered site which they called Charles Town. A hundred more arrived in 1671. From the start, there were two unusual features about Carolina. The first was its slave system, a replica of the Barbados structure, which was transplanted to North America. The second was location. The Carolinians had settled on the fringes of territory claimed by Spain. St. Augustine was 250 miles away. "We are here settled in the very chaps of the Spaniards," one of the settlers wrote a proprietor, Lord Ashley, in London.

So here was a colony based on slavery and profit, in search of a cash crop, a colony with a foreign neighbor and Indians nearby to trade with. The climate, subtropical and unhealthy, could "break even the strongest constitution."

The first site of Charles Town, sixty miles up the Ashley River, was so filled with malaria that the English used it as a reference in describing a place they did not want to go: "I'd rather live and die in Carolina," the saying went. Tales were told of ships landing 150 settlers of whom a hundred died the first day. No one knew, of course, that malaria and Carolina's other chief malady, yellow fever, which caused hemorrhaging and vomiting blood, were spread by the mosquito.

In 1699, by which time Charles Town had been moved to a peninsula where the Ashley and Cooper rivers joined, there was a yellow-fever epidemic. "The dead were carried in carts," wrote Hugh Adams, one of the survivors, "being heaped up one upon another worse by far than the Great Plague of London, considering the smallness of the town. Shops shut up for five weeks; nothing but carrying medicines, digging graves, carting the dead."

On the bright side, there was a two-hundred-day growing season and plenty of rainfall, and the forests were full of deer. "There is such infinite herds," wrote the settler Thomas Ashe in 1682, "that the whole country seems but one continued park." Indian porters by the hundreds came into town to deposit deerskins at the warehouses on the wharves. The skins were loaded onto London-bound packets to be made into buckskin breeches.

Another readily available resource came as a by-product of clearing pine-covered land. Burning the wood cooked out the tar, which was in demand by the Royal Navy, to waterproof cordage and caulk ships. One could also make pitch, a clear liquid used to caulk seams, by boiling tar in round clay holes in the ground. As long as ships were made of wood, there was a market for tar and pitch. By 1717, Carolina was exporting forty-four thousand barrels a year. In 1705, to lessen the Royal Navy's dependence on foreign sources such as Sweden, Parliament authorized a bounty of four pounds per ton on Carolina tar and pitch. In 1701, a Carolina planter estimated that the timber on his land would yield ten thousand pounds sterling's worth of tar, "but I can make little advantage of it till I can compass a good gang of negroes."

That was the hitch—the system would collapse without slaves. In the early frontier days, when they were clearing land

and surviving on deerskins, cattle-raising, and naval stores, settlers, slaves, and Indians all worked together, sharing the hard life on this exposed fringe of the English-speaking coastal settlements. Common hardships diminished social barriers. Elias Horry, a French Huguenot on the Santee River, north of Charles Town, reported in 1697 that he "worked many days with a negro man at the whipsaw." Carolina had the same climate as Brazil, and, for a while, the same racial mixing, with its mulatto quotient. The products of unions between blacks and Indians were known as Mustees.

All this came to an end with the introduction of a crop ideally suited to the Carolina climate and geography. The crop was rice. It became the same sort of gold mine that sugar was in Barbados. In fact, the seed that accidentally found its way to Charles Town from Madagascar was called "Gold Rice" because of the color of its hull. (In this case, both the product and the labor came from Africa.) John Thurber, a captain in distress, put into Charles Town for repairs in 1685 or thereabouts, and gave some of his Madagascar seed rice to one of the early settlers, Dr. Henry Woodward, who planted it. In 1715, a grateful South Carolina Assembly voted to give Captain Thurber one hundred pounds "for bringing the first Madagascar rice into this province."

A different strain of rice was already being grown by the time Thurber arrived, for on April 23, 1672, only two years after the first settlers landed, at a little ceremony on the Ashley River, the lord proprietors were given a barrel of it. Yet it was the successful planting of the Madagascar seed that made rice a staple. By 1690, some planters were petitioning to pay their quitrents with it, just as the Virginia planters were paying theirs with tobacco.

Ten years later, Edward Randolph, collector of customs for the Southern Department of North America, reported: "They have now found out the true way of raising and husking rice. There have been above 300 tons shipped this year to England, besides about 30 tons to the Islands." Three hundred and thirty tons, or 660,000 pounds, seemed phenomenal, but soon the exports would be in the millions.

They had "found out the true way." At first settlers planted rice in inland freshwater swamps. This meant reclamation of the swamp, digging up the cypress trees and underbrush, a job no white man wanted to do. To avoid sinking in the swamp muck, you had to hop from one exposed root system to the next, while avoiding the water moccasins and the alligators.

Then they built a reservoir on higher ground at one end of the swamp, so that they could flood it, and a strong earthen dam at the other end, so that they could drain it. The reservoir and the dam had locks in the form of long wooden boxes called "trunks," with hinged doors at each end to let the water out. The trouble with this inland-swamp method was controlling the amount of water needed. A freshet (overflow) could flood the swamp when the rice was "in blossom" and destroy it. In a drought year, the reservoir wasn't full enough to cover the planted rice when the time came, and the blackbirds devoured the crop.

The genius of the rice-planter society, like the genius of the French in using portages, or the genius of the Virginians in air-curing tobacco, was to discover a system suited to its own environment. In the coastal area north and south of Charles Town, there were a number of more or less parallel tidal rivers with picturesque names—the Waccamaw, the Pee Dee, the Santee, the Cooper, the Edisto, and the Combahee. Down where these rivers emptied into the Atlantic—on the wrinkled Carolina coastline, with its multitude of inlets and islands—the water was salty, and salt kills rice. But up those rivers, the water was fresh, and when the ocean tides rose and fell, the fresh water was backed up and drawn down, which afforded a natural cycle of irrigation for the growing of rice.

The planters used the tidal ebb and flow of these freshwater sections of the rivers to flood and drain their rice, figuring it out by trial and error over a period of time. On January 19, 1738, an advertisement in the *South Carolina Gazette* announced that William Swinton was offering two fields "overflow'd with fresh water every high tide. . . ." It was a tricky business; the reclaimed swampland along the riverbanks had to be low enough so it could be flooded at high tide, and high enough so it could drain at low tide. The land in each field had to be fairly level, so that it could be flooded evenly. Embankments had to be built around fields to protect them from freshets. The same system of trunks applied, to keep the water in or let it out.

It was an ingenious way of using nature, thanks to tides and gravity, but it also required an enormous amount of manual labor. The planters were lucky that some of the slaves had cultivated rice in their African homelands. Once the thickly timbered swamps were cleared, the embankments had to be built. In the fields, canals and ditches had to be dug, and trunks had to be made and fitted. After that was done, wagons arrived with sacks of seed rice, and the job of planting began. The seeds were planted in the greasy black soil of the reclaimed cypress swamps by labor gangs—a hoe gang to cut the seed trenches, followed by a sowing gang, with one slave to drill the hole, the second to place the seed, and then a third to cover the hole.

After planting, the fields were flooded from two to four days. When you could feel the grain under water begin to "pip," the field was drained to allow the rice to throw a root. The "trunk-minding" gang was in charge of water control. When the rice sprouted, the field was hoed, then flooded again for two or three weeks, then drained for a final hoeing and weeding, then flooded a third time and drained for the harvest.

The rice crop was harvested with sickles in September or October. By that time, the soil was boggy, having been underwater for a month or more. Once the rice was harvested and gathered in bundles, it was taken to a barn to be threshed by hand. The bundles were arranged in rows on the ground, and the slaves walked between the rows with sticks, flailing away to separate the grains from the straw. The threshed grain was taken to a winnowing house, a structure on posts twenty feet off the ground with a grate in the middle, through which the grain was dropped, in the hope that a breeze would blow away the remaining straw and the empty hulls. Then came the hand milling, with a wooden mortar and pestle, to remove the hull, which took even longer than threshing and winnowing. In winter, the stubble of last year's crop had to be burned. The fields were then kept submerged until February.

It was a triumph of muscle over machinery. Who but a slave would have worked in mud and stagnant water, bare-headed in the malarial August heat, when the planters had fled to Newport and Saratoga? Who but a slave would have rolled a wheelbarrow filled with mud up a slippery gangplank to plug leaks in the embankment caused by water-rat nests, or gone into a trunk to pull out a trapped alligator? The land of the laughing darky this was not, and an overseer on one of the Pee Dee River plantations reported: "I can see a goodeal of obstanetry in some of the people." Even the malaria-resistant slaves had health problems, although the overseer wrote, "The people here keeps healthy, all but Lidia who I think is playing Posom."

With the growing use of tidal rivers for irrigation, the Carolina lowlands became an area of rice plantations and slave concentration. Like tobacco, rice was one of those crops that created a specific life-style. It was as rewarding for the planter as it was demanding for the slave. It brought great fortunes, and it brought great pain. It also caused planters much annual anxiety, for so many acts of nature had to go just right to ensure a successful crop.

Like the Indians, rice planters who lacked tidal frontage sometimes prayed for rain. The minister of Sheldon Church in Beaufort County, home of the Combahee River plantations, was once asked by his congregation to deliver such a prayer. Following his prayer book, he asked the Lord to send "such moderate rains and showers that we may receive the fruits of the earth." Upon which an old river planter got up from his pew and stomped out, exclaiming: "What in hell do I want with moderate rains and showers? It will take a regular trash-moving, gulley-washing downpour to do my crop any good."

Most years, however, they harvested the rice, and the demand was so great that in 1702 Queen Anne's government listed it as "an enumerated commodity." This meant, according to the Navigation Act of 1660, that it could only be exported to England, on English-built ships. A heavy duty of one pound, six shillings was charged when the rice entered England, and eight pence per hundredweight. The planters got rich in spite of duties, mainly because they did not have to pay for labor. The slaves were a capital investment whose only cost beyond their initial purchase price was their upkeep, and who, thanks to their sickle-cell resistance to malaria, sometimes outlived their masters. Not only that, slaves were an investment that doubled and tripled by breeding new generations of slaves.

Year by year, as the production of rice increased, so did the number of slaves. By 1708, the slave population had caught up to the whites; there were about four thousand of each. After 1708, the blacks outnumbered the whites. By 1720, there were twelve thousand slaves and seven thousand whites. In 1729, when the colony produced ten million pounds of rice, there were twenty thousand slaves, twice the number of colonists. By 1740, when forty-three million pounds of rice left Charles Town and Georgetown, there were twenty-five thousand whites, as opposed to forty thousand blacks.

Henry Melchior Muhlenberg, a German-born Lutheran who landed in Charles Town in September 1742, wrote in his journal: "The heathen slaves are so numerous here that it is estimated that there are 15 for every white man. . . . One also finds here many

slaves who are only half black, the offspring of those white Sodom-
ites who commit fornication with their black slave women. This is
a horrible state of affairs."

There were other problems. The planters complained that
slavery wasn't as profitable as people thought. Slaves had to be fed,
dressed, and housed whether they worked hard or not. And what
about the shirkers and all the old men and women who couldn't
work any more, and the little children? What about their sullenness
and trickery? Why did they pretend to misunderstand what was
said to them when it suited their purpose to do so? They were
constantly undermining the system. Why, they even bragged
about it in their gullah patois, or "salt-water brogue," one of them
saying: "De buckruh [master] habe scheme, and de nigger habe
tricks, en ebery time de buckruh scheme once de nigger trick
twice." All told, the planters told one another, they were doing the
slaves a favor.

Also, the planters worried that the slaves might eventually rise
up. As Benjamin Martyn, who served as secretary to the Georgia
trustees in London, observed in 1741: "The greater [the] number
of blacks which a frontier has, and the greater the disproportion is
between them and her white people, the more danger she is liable
to; for those are all secret enemies, and ready to join with her open
ones on the first occasion." By that reasoning, the white population
of Carolina had forty thousand secret enemies in 1740. The more
the population ratio tilted toward the blacks, the more tightly the
slaves were bound in ropes of regulations.

The planters looked for signs of unrest, imagining them
whether they existed or not. Their fears expressed themselves
in all sorts of ways, including the fear of slaves raping white
women, whereas in reality, black women slaves were raped by
white planters.

Not all the fears were imaginary. When Benjamin Martyn said
that the secret enemies were ready to join with the obvious ones,
he was describing an actual situation. Just as a kind of forest diplomacy had developed with the Indians, a slave diplomacy was now
emerging. Spain had begun to use the slave issue to harass the
Carolina English. The idea was to offer St. Augustine as a haven
for runaway slaves. If a slave could make it to St. Augustine—250
miles away from Charles Town, but quite a bit closer for the ones
on the Combahee and Savannah rivers—he was free. This lure was
used to good effect. As early as 1687, ten Carolina slaves escaped

to St. Augustine and asked for sanctuary, which was given on condition that they take religious instruction and convert to Catholicism. In this way, Spain was able to combine conversion of the heathen with harassment of the English. Of course, for slaves, the risks were high. They had to get past Indians who would turn them in for the bounty. If they were captured, the punishment was severe. Three slaves heading south in 1697 were caught and emasculated. But that didn't stop others in whom the hope of freedom was stronger than the fear of mutilation or death.

In 1733, the Spanish king, Philip V, published a proclamation outlining the proper policy toward escaped slaves: if they converted and spent four years as public servants, they would be freed. The harboring of runaways now had royal authority.

The Spanish policy succeeded beyond all expectations, leading to the development of what amounted to the first underground railroad—between South Carolina and Florida. When Manuel de Montiano arrived in St. Augustine in 1737 as governor, there were so many runaways that he settled them in a fort two miles north of town, called Fort Mose, and organized them into a militia company. By 1738, the settlement housed as many as seventy-nine freed slaves. A priest was assigned to catechize them, and Spanish officers taught them military drill. Some married Indian women and started families. Each arriving runaway was formally welcomed in a little ceremony in which he was told that he was an equal in the eyes of God and instructed on the conditions of his freedom.

When the news got out that in St. Augustine there was a colony of freed slaves who had been given land to till and guns to fire against their former masters, it was like a beacon sending out a powerful signal to the slaves of Carolina. In the spring of 1739, Lieutenant Governor William Bull expressed his concern to the Assembly at Charles Town. Perhaps they should send some scout boats to patrol Southern coastal passages. Or offer bounties to the all-white colony of Georgia—twenty pounds for each adult scalp with both ears.

In the midst of the meeting, word arrived that four slaves had stolen some horses, killed one white man, and wounded another. The runaways were heading south. "Four or five who were cattle-hunters and knew the woods," the official account went, "some of whom belonged to Captain MacPherson, ran away with his horses, wounded his son, and killed another man. . . . They reached Augustine, one only being killed and another wounded in their flight. They were received there with great honors. One of them had a commission given to him, and a coat faced with velvet."

On May 9, 1739, William Bull wrote the duke of Newcastle, who was secretary of state in England, about the incident. The people of the province were concerned, he said, "to find their property now become so very precarious and uncertain." There was a growing awareness "that their negroes, which were their chief support, may in little time become their enemies, if not their masters, and that this government is unable to withstand or prevent it."

The colony was in a state of high alert. A Security Act was passed requiring all white men to carry firearms to church on Sunday. All this led to the largest slave revolt of the colonial period, the Stono Rebellion. On September 9, 1739, about twenty Angolan slaves gathered near the western branch of the Stono River, twenty miles west of Charles Town. They broke into a store that sold small arms and powder, killing two storekeepers and leaving their heads on the front steps. They then killed a local planter and his son and daughter, and turned south on the road to Georgia and St. Augustine, pillaging and killing as they went. More slaves joined up, and they marched to the beat of drums and shouts of "Liberty." When they got to the Edisto River, thirty miles south of Charles Town, they halted, with the militia in pursuit. That afternoon, the slaves were easily defeated. Forty-four were killed or executed, whereas the death toll for the whites was twenty-one.

Although quickly extinguished, the Stono Rebellion was a warning, which led to a prohibitive duty on new slaves in order to limit imports. That December, the Charles Town merchant Robert Pringle wrote his brother: "We shall live very uneasy with our negroes while the Spaniards continue to keep possession of St. Augustine, and it is a pity our government at home did not encourage the dislodging of them from thence."

Determined to lance the boil of St. Augustine and its colony of freed slaves, Governor James Edward Oglethorpe of Georgia laid siege to the city in the spring of 1740. The population of twenty-four hundred was herded inside the fort, and the forty freed slaves in Fort Mose fought against the English militia alongside Montiano's five hundred men. The English took Fort Mose and brought artillery to Anastasia Island. Oglethorpe also had seven frigates, with a total of thirty cannons firing from the river.

Thanks to the fort's *coquina* (shell-fragment limestone) walls, the Spanish withstood a thirty-eight-day siege, from June 13 to July 20. There were daily bombardments, but only two Spanish fatalities. Governor Montiano had allies behind Oglethorpe's lines: mosquitoes, gnats, and sand flies. In the summer heat, these insects wrought havoc, bringing malaria and yellow fever, and were far more destructive than cannons. Oglethorpe lifted the siege and went back to Georgia, his military reputation ruined.

There aren't many women mentioned in these accounts of early settlement. Women then didn't become explorers, or sail ships, or bear arms. They came to the New World as the wives of settlers or as indentured servants, to share the frontier life of the men, but escaping the attention of historians. Every so often, a woman emerged from anonymity—Hannah Dustin, the scalper of Indians; Margaret Brent, who strode into the Maryland Assembly in 1648 and pleaded in vain for "vote and voice."

In South Carolina, in the 1740s, a teen-age girl made a substantial contribution to the economic life of the colony by introducing the cultivation of indigo, an essential dye for English textiles. Eliza Lucas is an early model of those self-reliant frontier women whose strength of character and managerial abilities made them the equals of men. Though born in the Caribbean, she was English through and through, homesick for London and loving "the English taste." But she was shaped and molded by the circumstances of her life in America, where she became a plantation manager at an early age.

In 1738, her father, Lieutenant Colonel George Lucas, had brought his wife and two daughters to Carolina (two sons were at school in England). He had previously been stationed in Antigua, where Eliza was born in 1722, and then in England, where she was educated. Colonel Lucas came to Carolina to work three plantations he had inherited from his father, one on the Combahee, one on the Waccamaw, and the third, where they lived, on the Wappoo, a salt creek that connected the Ashley and Stono rivers. The plantation was sixteen miles by land and six by water from Charles Town. Within months of their arrival, Colonel Lucas was called back to Antigua, where he had been named lieutenant governor. He left behind his daughters and his ailing wife, and entrusted the plantation to Eliza. Later he was taken prisoner during a war with France. He died in prison in Brest in 1747.

Miss Lucas had an interest in botany; as she wrote in one of

her numerous letters, "I own I love the vegetable world extremely." From Antigua, her father sent her batches of seeds, including ginger, lucerne (alfalfa), and *Indigofera tinctoria*. The idea
was that she would experiment and try to come up with a cash
crop to pay for the mortgage on the property and the upkeep of its
twenty slaves.

On July 1, 1739, she wrote her father: "I have greater hopes
for the indigo than any of the rest of the things I have tried." And
yet it took her three seasons before she managed to grow a successful crop. Something always went wrong—the grasshoppers ate the
plants, or a late frost limited the harvest.

By 1742, however, she had a crop, and her father dispatched
a highly paid indigo expert named Cromwell from the island of
Montserrat to oversee the complicated process of extracting the dye
from the leaves. This required the construction of three connecting
brick vats. The first one, called the "steeper," was filled with water.
Then the cut plants, thick and full of juice, were thrown in and
allowed to ferment from twelve to thirty hours, depending on how
hot a day it was. Care had to be taken not to rub the bluish powder
off the leaves.

The liquid was then drained off into the second vat, or "bat-
tery," and whipped with paddles to coagulate the solids. The
paddling had to stop at exactly the right moment. At this point,
the liquid was drained off into the third and smallest vat, called the
"Young Devil," where the solids were allowed to settle with
the help of lime to assist the congealing of the indigo particles. The
water at the top was then drawn off. Workers scooped up the goo
at the bottom and poured it into small cloth bags, which were hung
up to drain.

When the bags were taken down, the contents, almost black
in color, were spread on a flat surface to dry for several days in the
shade. Once dried, the indigo was cut into squares like fudge, and
the result was the "blue gold" of Carolina, which came in three
grades: Fine Copper (for wool), Fine Purple (for linen), and Fine
Flora, which had an iridescent sheen like burnished metal, for silk.

Cromwell built the vats and processed the harvest, but his
indigo lumps were of poor quality. Although he blamed the climate, he was actually sabotaging the process himself by adding too
much lime. He did not want Carolina indigo competing with the
Montserrat production. Perhaps he thought he could trick Eliza
because she was a woman. If so, he was wrong. She found him out

and fired him, writing her father that he was "a mere bungler." Through trial and error, she learned to make superior indigo. She discovered that the time of harvest was important for color, and that the indigo had to be watched night and day when it was in the vats. She also learned to protect the plants from grasshoppers and locusts. As generous as she was innovative, Eliza devoted her entire 1741 crop to making seed, which she distributed among her neighbors, several of whom were Huguenots familiar with indigo cultivation.

By 1745, the monopoly of Spain and France was broken, and indigo soon became the highland staple in Carolina, with the lowlands on tidal rivers reserved for rice. The indigo sold in England for between three and twenty shillings a pound. By 1748, demand was so great that it was made an enumerated commodity and subsidized by a government bounty of an additional sixpence a pound. In 1750, sixty-three thousand pounds were exported to England. Five years later, the annual export total had grown to more than a million pounds, and the indigo planters were described as being "full of money." In 1767, a ship leaving Charles Town with 141,000 pounds of indigo was recorded in the *South Carolina Gazette* as "the richest ship that has sailed from this port," except for one in 1759 that had sailed with more than two hundred thousand pounds.

It was mainly due to Eliza Lucas, who had turned her love of botany into a cash crop more lucrative than tobacco or rice. "I have the business of three plantations to transact," she wrote a friend in England, "which requires much writing and more business and fatigues of other sorts than you can imagine." She kept the books, and sent the accounts to her father. She made handwritten copies of her voluminous correspondence in a parchment-bound book and looked after the other crops. She saw to the curing of bacon, the boiling of soap, the molding of candles, the shearing of sheep, and the carding of wool, among other things. Continuing her experiments, she started a fig orchard and planted oaks for future navies.

To get it all done, she "took time by the forelock," rising at five. When a neighbor told her this would make her look old before her time, she replied that sleeping was basically a waste of time, "the emblem of death," more "breathing than living." Her schedule was to read till seven, see that the servants were on the job, and have breakfast; then came an hour of playing music, followed by an hour of French or shorthand. After this interval of self-improvement, the rest of the day was devoted to plantation management, with time out for such occasional activities as drawing up wills for her neighbors.

Steeped in the work ethic, she believed that to be poor in a country as plentiful as Carolina was proof of laziness. In the management of her slaves, she noted, "Nobody eats the bread of idleness when I am here, nor are any overworked." To overwork slaves, she believed, was not good business. It was like galloping a horse until he dropped. In 1741, she took the time to teach "a parcel of little negroes" to read, and planned to hire a schoolmistress for the others.

Her work was stressful, and she suffered headaches. The medicine she needed took six months to arrive from England. Sometimes it seemed that her youth was vanishing while she tended to business. As she observed, "I shall begin to think myself an old woman before I am a young one, having such weighty affairs upon my hands." And sometimes she felt so fragmented, so pulled in different directions, that she was "forced to consult Mr. Locke over and over, to see wherein personal identity consisted and if I was the very same self."

Though Eliza lived in a world of considerable refinement, it was still the frontier. She wrote in April 1746: "We have been in great confusion about the Indians, the negroes were in such dread of them I could not make them mind their work." Tribes still raided plantations near Charles Town, interfering with the slaves' productivity. Eliza worried about Spanish incursions and Cherokee attacks, writing on one occasion that the Cherokees "have been insolent and 'tis high time they were chastised."

In the meantime, her father, concerned that she would become a spinster, suggested two suitors, whom Eliza rejected out of hand. "Not for all the riches in Chile," she said. Eliza would make her own selection, although a childhood friend in England said she would die an old maid because she was so hard to please. It was true that she didn't have much time to socialize, and her visits to Charles Town were few and far between.

Her dearest friends were Charles Pinckney and his wife, an older couple with whom she sometimes stayed. He was a leading citizen, Carolina's first native-born lawyer, who would one day be chief justice of the colony. She was devastated when Mrs. Pinckney died in 1743, but a year later, at twenty-two, she married the widower, who was twice her age, which had tongues wagging. But her practical mind told her that she already knew him to be the best of husbands.

Once married, she spent most of her time at Belmont, the Pinckney plantation on the Cooper River. The Lucas plantation at Wappoo Creek was lost to her father's creditors; his debts were greater than the profits from indigo. She continued her experiments at Belmont, this time with flax and hemp. She also wove her own silk, from which she made her own dresses, two of which can be seen today—one in the Powder Magazine in Charleston, the other at the Smithsonian. With Charles Pinckney she had fourteen happy years, giving birth to two sons and a daughter, who were sent to school in England. When Charles died in 1758, she was a young widow of thirty-six—"well left," as the saying went, with family properties, and some two to three hundred slaves. She lived into her early seventies, until 1793, a small, purposeful woman who under frontier conditions drove herself to give the very best, making strict resolutions which she reviewed daily. George Washington served as one of the pallbearers at her funeral.

Perhaps the most curious passage in her correspondence is one dated 1741, concerning Hugh Bryan, a revivalist disciple of George Whitefield, who "had been very much deluded by his own fancies, and imagined he was assisted by the divine spirit to prophesy Charles Town and the country as far as Ponpon Bridge should be destroyed by fire and sword to be executed by the negroes before the first day of next month. He to town—60 miles—twice besides sending twice to acquaint the governor with it. People in general were very uneasy tho convinced he was no prophet, but [feared] the dreaded consequence of such a thing being put into the heads of the slaves and the advantage they might take of us."

To announce a forthcoming slave rebellion in a colony with a black majority was like shouting "Fire!" in a crowded theater. Hugh Bryan, in his nutty way, was articulating their deepest fear, and, as Eliza Lucas pointed out, just saying it might give the slaves ideas, particularly one year after the Stono Rebellion. In Charles Town, the official reaction to his prophecy was the threat of a grand-jury indictment.

Hugh Bryan was another type peculiar to the American frontier, the revivalist who has broken away from mainstream Anglicanism. On the frontier, where there weren't any churches, unorthodox forms of religious worship flourished, whereas the hinterland remained under strict clerical control, whether Puritan,

Quaker, or Anglican. Hugh Bryan sometimes preached to slaves, predicting they would revolt and gain their freedom, which did not increase his popularity among the Charleston planters.

His mentor, the Methodist George Whitefield, had made his reputation preaching in frontier communities. Whitefield didn't go by the book, because people on the frontier didn't have prayer books. He got up on a stump in a forest clearing, or on a cart by the side of a road, and gave them a hell-raising sermon of his own devising, which departed considerably from the religious texts. He worked the congregation up to such an emotional pitch that they started clapping their hands and shouting "Amen!" in a kind of blatant American improvisation. Whitefield's comment on Anglicanism was that the bishop of London knew no more about Christianity than did Mahomet.

Carolina seems to have attracted more than its share of bizarre evangelists. There were also eighteenth-century cults, like the Weberites, who practiced a hundred miles from Charles Town between 1759 and 1761.

Jacob Weber was a Swiss who arrived in Carolina at the age of fourteen, and who "experienced grace" in 1756, after indulging his corrupt nature, as he put it, in his youth. He felt the urge to preach, and started in a casual way by having his neighbors come around to sing a few hymns on Sundays, after which he would read them a sermon from a prayer book. The more people admired Weber, the more he admired himself. He began to think he didn't need a book—he would just make it up out of his head. He began to attract followers. A sect was hatched under Jacob Weber's leadership, with two principal disciples, Schmidt and Dauber. As Weber explained it, he was God the Father, Schmidt was the Son, and Dauber was the Holy Spirit. One feature of the services, according to the Lutheran theologian Henry Melchior Muhlenberg, who was told about the sect when he revisited Charleston in 1774, was that followers of both sexes went about naked "and practiced the most abominable wantonness."

One day, a Lutheran preacher, Christian Theus, attended a Weberite meeting, at which the three leaders were on a raised platform while the faithful sat at their feet. Schmidt addressed him: "Little parson, do you believe that I am the redeemer and savior of the world and that no man can be saved without me?" Certainly not, Theus replied, at which the three leaders said he had committed a grave offense and must be sentenced to death. They asked the congregation whether Theus should be hanged from the nearest tree. No, replied the faithful, he has blasphemed God and offended the holy assembly and must be drowned in the deepest depths. Seeing that they were working themselves up into a state of collective hysteria, Theus ran down to the bank of a nearby river, where he was lucky enough to find a Negro boatman about to push off. The man took him aboard, with the Weberites in hot pursuit.

The three leaders soon fell to quarreling, and Weber and Schmidt decided that Dauber was not doing a good job as Holy Spirit: he was too lukewarm and uncharismatic. So they assembled the faithful and dug a pit in the forest. They placed a mattress at the bottom of the pit, threw Dauber on the mattress, filled up the pit with more mattresses, and trampled on the mattresses until Dauber suffocated. The Holy Spirit went out of him for good. Then Weber quarreled with Schmidt and said he was the devil. He had the faithful chain Schmidt to a tree, surround him, beat him with sticks, throw him on the ground, and trample him until he was dead.

This was the sort of thing one could get away with on the frontier, where law enforcement was nonexistent. But reports of strange doings eventually reached Charles Town, and Weber was arrested, tried, and hanged. He left a memoir for his children in which he said that he had been corrupted by Satan.

CHAPTER THIRTEEN

THE SALZBURGER FRONTIER

Georgia, the last colony founded by the English in North America, in 1733, was conceived as a refuge for "poor persons of London." But among the early settlers were some religious dissidents expelled from Austria, who did their utmost to maintain their separateness, refusing to melt into the pot.

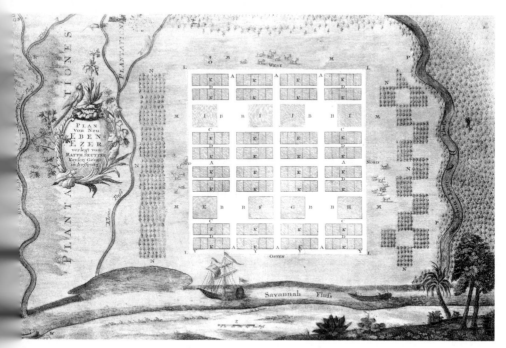

New York Public Library

This view of the Salzburger colony of New Ebenezer in 1747 shows a neat grid plan of settlement on the Savannah River, with one square for marketplaces and another for church and school.

In the far South the sun of autumn is passing
Like Walt Whitman walking along a ruddy shore.
He is singing and chanting the things that are part of him,
The worlds that were and will be, death and day.

WALLACE STEVENS

In the eighteenth century, social reform replaced religious dissidence as a motivating factor for colonization. Citizens of England still went to jail for debt, and could not get out until the debt was paid. But behind bars there was no way to pay. Why not help poor debtors emigrate to America?

The man behind the impulse was James Edward Oglethorpe, soldier and politician. In 1729, he chaired a House of Commons committee investigating prisons, and helped push through an act to send unemployed debtors to America. His plan was to "procure a quantity of acres . . . and to plant thereon a hundred miserable wretches who being let out of gaol by the last year's act, are now starving about the town for want of employment."

Oglethorpe mobilized the forces of piety, including the celebrated reformer Dr. Thomas Bray, known as "the great little man." Bray's lobbying efforts had resulted in legislation to free several thousand debtors. In July 1730, Oglethorpe asked the king for a grant of land south of Carolina to settle "poor persons of London." This request was favorably received, since the crown saw an advantage in having a buffer colony between Carolina and Spain.

Oglethorpe and his nineteen associates, mainly rich and titled men, were granted a twenty-one-year charter in 1732 for the land between the Savannah and Altamaha rivers. In the fall of 1732, he left England with the first group, 125 "sober, industrious and moral persons." They landed at Charles Town in January 1733 and proceeded south to the site of the trader Muskrove's old post at the Yamacraw Bluffs, above the Savannah River. There they founded the city of Savannah. A year later, the first non-English contingent arrived—a group of persecuted Lutherans from Salzburg, Austria.

Georgia became a multipurpose colony: part reform experiment, part buffer state, part Protestant refuge, and part would-be silk producer. It was the last colony founded by the English in North America, and the only one founded in the eighteenth cen-

266

tury. Alone among the colonies, it tried for fifteen years to enforce the prohibition of rum and slaves.

In drafting their statutes for the approval of the Privy Council and the king, the London trustees did not ban slaves on moral grounds, but on the practical grounds that they created more problems than they solved.

"Experience has shown," the trustees wrote King George II, "that the manner of settling colonies and plantations with black slaves or negroes has obstructed the increase of English and Christian inhabitants, who alone can in case of a war be relied on for the defense and security of the same . . . and has exposed the colony to the insurrection, tumults, and rebellions of such slaves. . . ."

The trustees asked for a fifty-pound penalty on every slave imported into Georgia. In August 1735, an act to that effect was reported by the Privy Council to be "proper to receive," and was confirmed, enacted, and ratified.

At once the planters complained that "Georgia can never be a place of any great consequence without negroes." The trustees replied that slaves, who cost at least twenty pounds per head, were more expensive than white settlers, for whom five pounds paid the passage. Besides, they added, Georgia had been incorporated specifically to help poor Englishmen and Protestants persecuted in other countries—preference should be given to them.

The planters countered that they could never grow rice without slaves: the work was too hard and the heat too intense. The whites couldn't work "half-submerged in water the way the negroes did" without getting sick. The trustees in London were adamant, however. On March 17, 1747, their secretary, Benjamin Martyn, wrote: "If any persist in declaring they cannot succeed without negroes it would be of service to the colony as well as themselves for them to retire into any other province where they will be freely allowed the use of negroes." In fact, the opposite happened. As residents from South Carolina bought lands in Georgia, they brought their slaves in, despite their initial promises to abide by the laws of the colony.

Intending to enforce the ban, the trustees told the authorities in Savannah to issue warrants for constables to seize the slaves. But this created considerable discontent, and in 1748 the proslave planters sent an emissary, Major Alex Horton, to Savannah to plead their case. Horton said that the presence of slaves was well known all over Georgia and that everyone winked at it. He went on to report that the most common toast in taverns was "to the one thing needful," by which were meant Negroes.

The president of the colony, William Stephens, wrote the trustees on July 21, 1748, that the presence of slaves had created a real dilemma: enforcing the ban would exasperate the settlers and cause some of them to move to Carolina.

Under pressure, the authorities in Savannah gradually sided with the colonists against the absentee trustees. In January 1749, the five Savannah magistrates wrote Benjamin Martyn in London that, after consulting with "the best inhabitants," they had come to the conclusion that the introduction of Negroes would make Georgia a flourishing province.

Discussion shifted to the conditions under which slaves should be admitted. In order to prevent immoral behavior, the trustees now said, the slaves must be instructed in the Christian religion by a Protestant minister. There must be no carnal mixing or marriage between blacks and whites. Reasons now were found why slaves should be admitted, such as the number of hands needed for the culture of silk.

On August 8, 1750, a new act from the trustees repealed the ban on slaves. By 1760, Georgia had a population of six thousand whites and thirty-six hundred blacks.

The only settlers in Georgia who sincerely did not want slaves were the Salzburgers, a group that, in terms of frontier experience, provides a curious example. Conventionally, the frontier is seen as an agent of assimilation, furthering the breakdown of Old World values and the birth of American identity. But the Salzburgers, who staked out their site on the Georgia frontier in 1734, wanted to remain exactly as they were. Like the Pilgrims, they had left their homeland because they had been hounded out of it (by Leopold von Firmin, the zealous Catholic bishop of Salzburg, who in 1731 expelled twenty thousand Protestants). They came to Georgia to practice their faith without interference and wanted as little as possible to do with the rest of the colony. The Salzburgers didn't like outsiders of any kind, whether white, Indian, or black. They were determined to keep speaking German, and to do things their way. Their greatest fear was that the land around them would be sold to non-Salzburgers, giving them unwanted neighbors.

They had to balance their standoffishness with civic obligations: jury duty in Savannah, military service, etc. They also contributed to the economic life of the colony by building the first flour mill. Basically, however, they were on their own, and wanted to keep it that way.

The first group of seventy-eight Salzburgers arrived on March 5, 1734, impoverished by confiscation and exile, with their thirty-two-year-old pastor, Johann Martin Boltzius. The young Boltzius (who had run an orphanage in what is today the German city of Halle) served as both spiritual and temporal leader. From the very beginning, Boltzius kept his settlers separate. Rarely did they take their differences to the English authorities. Aiming at self-sufficiency, they had their own doctor, constable, school, and orphanage.

Oglethorpe gave them some land twenty-five miles northwest of Savannah, on a bluff six miles from the river. He had chosen the site for its strategic advantage, but it turned out to be a poor selection. The soil was too sandy for agriculture, and the nearby creek was so choked with dead trees that boats couldn't navigate. In spite of the drawbacks, the Salzburgers settled there, calling their settlement Ebenezer, which means "Stone of Help."

Much time in the first year was spent nursing the sick and burying the dead, who succumbed from dysentery after drinking bad water. Wolves and bears devoured their cattle and hogs. Boltzius did not complain. When members of his flock came down with dysentery, he told them that sickness was salutary, reminding man of his frailty and dependence on God. Their physician, Andreas Zwiffler, who wasn't really a doctor but an apothecary, was killing more people than he cured with his bloodletting and self-concocted medications.

In 1735, eleven children were born and baptized but only four survived, and twenty-one adults died, passing into what Boltzius called "happy eternity." These losses were eased by a second transport, of fifty-four, which arrived in Ebenezer in January 1735, and a third transport, of about fifty, which arrived in February 1736. In the first four years, however, half the original settlers died.

Oglethorpe initially resisted the Salzburgers' pleas for relocation, not wanting them to leave defensible high ground. But when they found a strip of oak forest on the river a few miles away, he came to visit. On February 10, 1736, he gave the Salzburgers all sorts of reasons why the move was inadvisable. Settlement on the Savannah River was reserved for Englishmen, he said, and the Salzburgers would have trouble there because they didn't speak

English. As for crossing the river, that wasn't possible, because of promises made to the Indians. Nevertheless, after a dramatic confrontation with Boltzius, he agreed to the move. He needed the Salzburgers; they were his only evidence that white men could prosper in Georgia without slaves.

After an initial epidemic of malaria, illness and deaths decreased dramatically in the Salzburgers' new location, and settlers applied themselves to building and planting. The work was hard. Yet, in spite of all the difficulties, they had built sixty houses and an orphanage by 1737. Indian corn was planted, and there was a herdsman for the cattle. Although the forests were stocked with deer and the rivers with sturgeon, these settlers did not hunt and fish at first, because in the old country fish and game were reserved by law for the gentry. Shooting a turkey now became a way of affirming their newfound freedom.

By June 1738, there were 146 settlers, but no court of justice was needed in the crime-free settlement. Red Bluffs, or New Ebenezer, had the reputation of being an amazing place, where all the inhabitants lived in harmony with their minister, and there were no idle, drunken, or profligate people.

Boltzius described the reality rather differently in exhaustively detailed reports to his superiors in Germany. He had to expel bad apples like the Bavarian distiller George Roth, who from the start had been the most vexatious man in the entire first transport, arguing over trifles, gruff with everyone, cursing and beating his wife.

Josef Ernst and his wife were two other malcontents, as bad as the Roths, with no sense of the upright. When Ernst injured a woman by grabbing a saw out of her hands, Boltzius had him sent to Savannah for trial, against his usual practice. Ernst was convicted but got off with a suspended sentence and came back to New Ebenezer.

As for Zwiffler, he was so useless as a doctor that Boltzius made him constable, in charge of night patrols, to prowl about with a lantern and sword. Zwiffler protested to Boltzius, "You do not value my art, but wish to make me into a peasant," and returned to Austria, miffed.

Christopher Ortmann, the schoolmaster, was another who complained that his talents were being ignored. Boltzius felt that at the age of fifty-five he was too old for the job. When Ortmann's wife accused three honest and conscientious Salzburgers of stealing melons and beans from her garden, Boltzius told her that she must recant this ugly rumor before the entire congregation, speaking on the theme: "Oh, if only I could put a lock on my mouth." He was not surprised to see her develop a huge boil on the neck, which was God's punishment.

Then there was Maria Haberfehner, who shocked the congregation by getting an Indian woman drunk on rum in order to steal her honey. He saw God's justice done when she died in October 1736, for she had been a greedy and wicked woman.

When, on July 16, 1738, Andreas Grimminger stole three pounds from Johann Pletter, Boltzius asked Grimminger whether he would rather be punished by the community or sent to Savannah for trial. Grimminger opted for the former, and his sentence was to guard the cattle until Christmas without pay.

With a mixture of discipline and fairness, Boltzius managed to keep his congregation in line. His method was to keep them busy, for he believed that, when they weren't working, they were thinking about sin. One of his favorite words was *asotisch*, meaning "sinful." As a strict Lutheran pietist, obsessed with the conditions of salvation, he preached against such esoteric sins as "work righteousness," "self-made piety," and "bourgeois honesty."

At the same time, he was a practical man, serving the congregation as mayor, magistrate, quartermaster, town planner, law enforcer, and therapist. Besides being intimately involved in the lives of his parishioners, he had the authorities in Savannah and the Indians in the forest to contend with, and tried to stay on amicable terms with both.

Boltzius arrived with preconceptions of the noble savage based on the literature of the period, but was quickly disillusioned. The Indians, whose notions of private property were vague at best, helped themselves to whatever was handy, shooting a stray cow for the bell around its neck, or killing one of their steers for a single haunch, just as they did with deer.

Boltzius wanted as little as possible to do with the Indians, which was also the way he felt about blacks. He wrote Oglethorpe in March 1739: "We humbly request that the Lord Trustees never allow negroes to be brought to the vicinity of our town to be used as slaves for the white people here, as we know from experience that neither houses nor gardens will be safe from theft, and that our very lives will not be safe from these savage people."

Despite the lack of slaves, New Ebenezer became a success.

By 1739, there were 250 head of cattle and four miles of fields, and the colony was at last self-sustaining. There were still cases of malaria, but the death rate was down. Boltzius could see the fate of the three transports he had welcomed in this German proverb: "Death for the first, hardship for the second, bread for the third."

Unlike the Salzburger frontier, Savannah was rife with divisiveness. William Stephens, a planter commissioned by the trustees to report on the colony, arrived in Savannah on November 1, 1737. Entering a pub, he was instantly regaled by a regular with a litany of complaints—the want of Negroes, the conditions of land sale, and more.

Stephens, who had arrived with servants and workmen to build his house, found Savannah in a state of near anarchy. The ban on rum was openly defied. Constables neglected the execution of warrants. In the rare cases where rum sellers actually came to trial, the jury almost always acquitted them. Stephens had two of his own servants brought before a magistrate for visiting rum shops, which had become as common as gin shops in London.

Strolling around town on December 30, Stephens was struck by the number of uncleared lots, as well as others once cleared and now going to ruin. The land was overrun with rubbish and seemingly abandoned. One reason was that people were leaving Georgia for Carolina, because of the slavery situation. He had met a man named Mercer, just back from Carolina, and had said to him in a jocular way, "I understand you intend to butter your bread on both sides"—i.e., take land in both provinces. But Mercer had replied that he had suffered so much in Georgia that the trustees were welcome to his land. Stephens made light of it, saying, "Some go, and others arrive."

To implement his reports, Stephens mixed with the malcontents in the taverns. There, in the spring of 1738, he heard rumors of Oglethorpe's troubles with Parliament. Prospects were gloomy, people said, and the colony was little removed from bankruptcy.

In Savannah, Stephens found outlaw behavior of every conceivable sort. A man named Etherington developed a reputation as the first white cattle-rustler, slaughtering stray cows in the woods, salting the meat, and selling it to ships' captains. He was jailed, and when he escaped, many said it was perhaps better to have him lost than found.

In the first months of 1739, it seemed to Stephens that Savannah's population was dwindling, and that those who remained "were one size above the lowest rank." And there were other changes—in July, a gallows was built on a bluff for the execution of three sailors who had killed a man aboard a ship docked in the harbor.

At the gallows on August 3, one of the sailors was so eager to be hanged that he climbed up the ladder more nimbly than the hangman, fastened the rope to the beam himself, and, turning to the spectators, told them he was ready to die. The second went to his fate quietly, but the third made a great lamentation, claiming he had slept through the whole thing, and went on so that he was given a reprieve. When General Oglethorpe returned that October, he revoked the reprieve, asking how it was possible for a man to sleep through a noisy murder taking place a few feet away. The sentence was about to be carried out when Oglethorpe changed his mind and reprieved him once more.

As time passed, it became clear that more people were leaving Savannah. Planters were getting around the no-slave rule by moving their slaves back and forth between South Carolina and Georgia. But, in spite of these desertions, Georgia was growing in other directions. Augusta, 130 miles north of Savannah, had become an important fur-trading post. South of Savannah, the Scotch highlanders were settled in Darien and below, on the Altamaha.

Meanwhile, in New Ebenezer, the Salzburgers had finished their mill on Abercorn Creek in 1740; this was a boon to the entire colony, for many of the sloops coming from New York with flour were being captured by the Spaniards. Some Salzburgers now had horses, which in their homeland had been a luxury reserved for the rich, and mounted herdsmen rounded up their cattle.

In their spare time, they came to Boltzius with their quarrels and secret fears. There were husbands who beat their wives, and wives who beat their husbands. One woman worried that she was more attached to her husband than to Jesus. Several backsliders wanted to leave, and there was nothing Boltzius could do to keep people against their will. He wrote home, "Here in America it is almost the fashion to move from one place to the other and run to a place where people can live as they please according to their carnal ends."

With his medieval mind-set and self-righteous nature, Boltzius saw the country outside Ebenezer as evil incarnate. Savannah was a sink of iniquity where "abominable horrors are being practiced quite with impunity . . . through adultery and fornication."

The blacks and the Indians were just as evil, if not worse.

"Much harm is caused here and there by the negroes," he reported, "and the most atrocious things are done by and among them. . . ." He was referring to allegations that in Augusta two slaves had raped a little Dutch girl.

In August 1740, Boltzius heard that a Negro had set fire to Charles Town. And these were the people that the Georgia colonists were yearning for! He prayed that "our dear God will protect us at our place from the importation of those more harmful than useful negroes."

The Negroes, however, were not an immediate threat, whereas the Indians were. Boltzius' early efforts at friendship had backfired, and that August he went to Savannah to complain to the authorities about the Uchee Indians. They had become so brazen that they rode through the Salzburgers' fields stealing corn and stamping the beans. They shot pigs and chased cattle with their dogs. They rode into town and stole shirts from clotheslines, and anything else they could get their hands on. On his return, Boltzius gathered the congregation and told them they had to be firm: "The more friendly we are and the more we give in and trade with them . . . the more we will have them around our necks and suffer trouble."

Eventually, it was the language problem, and not the immorality in Savannah or the Negroes or the Indians, that wrecked the Salzburg colony. For a while, Ebenezer continued to prosper. The residents introduced sheep, and grew mulberry trees that produced 464 pounds of silk in 1748. They won the contract to supply the lumber for the first church in Savannah, and started selling wood to the West Indies. Their forests were well stocked with longleaf pine. In order to keep slaves out, Boltzius applied himself to recruiting white German servants whose terms were up.

But the colony never had more than three hundred souls, and malaria continued its ravages, particularly among children. Two of Boltzius' four children died of fever within a week. Health conditions didn't really improve until malaria could be controlled in the twentieth century. It wasn't so long ago that blacks in Georgia called a newborn baby a "come-see," deciding whether it wanted to remain in this life or not.

Boltzius himself had a twenty-year bout with malaria, which weakened him as he got older. He suffered another kind of blow in 1750, when, after resisting slavery for fifteen years, he had to resign himself to it because the antislavery law was repealed. Members of his own congregation bought slaves. But when he died in 1765, at the age of sixty-three, having served the Lutherans of Ebenezer for more than thirty years, the colony was thriving. The importance of a strong leader on this kind of ethnic frontier settlement was underscored by his incompetent successor, Christian Triebner, who arrived in 1769. He got off on the wrong foot by starting a quarrel over the management of the mill. A married man with three children, he was accused of improprieties with a young girl. Triebner was dismissed but not replaced, and Ebenezer was for some time left without a pastor. And now the Salzburgers began to lose their spiritual focus. Their distinctive society began to unravel as they became more worldly, indulging in such amusements as horse races.

They had always been apolitical, and as the revolution approached, they had little reason to take sides. When the British captured Savannah in 1778, the redcoat commander, Colonel Archibald Campbell, went to Ebenezer, where the settlers reaffirmed their loyalty to the king. After the revolution, the colony limped along. As long as it was on the frontier, it was able to maintain its German identity, for isolation kept it from melting into the pot. But in the early nineteenth century, when it was surrounded by English-speaking settlements, young people began to rebel against speaking German. Finally, the congregation requested that the sermon be given in English. When the pastor stubbornly retained German, his flock dwindled away. As Boltzius had warned, slavery also helped wreck the colony, for, with slaves doing the work, the whole idea of the value of labor was lost by the others, and the settlement dwindled away. It became a ghost town.

When I visited the site on the Savannah River in the summer of 1991, there was nothing left but the cemetery where Boltzius is buried, a little museum that was once the orphanage, and the Jerusalem Church, the oldest house of worship in Georgia. Some of its bricks, handmade by the congregation, are indented with Salzburger fingerprints. Outside the one remaining cabin, connected to a separate kitchen by a walkway called a "dog's trot," were two mulberry trees, attesting to the Salzburgers' success in silk spinning. When I walked over a fragrant pine-needle floor down to the river, six wild turkeys rose out of the underbrush on the bank, surprisingly swift in flight.

CHAPTER FOURTEEN

THE QUAKER FRONTIER

The last proprietary province was Pennsylvania, founded by William Penn in 1682. Although his finances and his health suffered in its maintenance, Penn established the Quaker principles of pacifism and religious tolerance.

National Gallery of Art, Washington, D.C.

In a Quaker cemetery in rural England, William Penn was laid to rest in 1718.

A philosophical Quaker, full of mean and thrifty
maxims . . .

JOHN KEATS

U nlike most of the early colonial leaders, William Penn believed in treating the Indians with fairness. He saw no
point in fighting them if he could possibly get along with
them. As he wrote the Delaware chiefs on August 8, 1681, before
his first visit to America: "I am very sensible of the unkindness and
injustice that hath been too much exercised towards you by the
people of these parts of the world. . . . But I am not such a man.
. . . I have great love and regard towards you. . . ."

That regard was reciprocated. The Delawares gave Penn a
wampum belt depicting a white man and a red man with hands
clasped in friendship. When Penn died in 1718, the Delawares sent
his widow a cloak sewn from the skins of wild animals "to protect
her whilst passing through the thorny wilderness without her
guide."

William Penn and Plymouth's William Bradford appear to
have been the two most complex figures in the first century of
English settlement in North America. These two men stand out
from the others as the Great Dissenters, whose vision and purpose
helped found colonies despite seemingly insurmountable difficulties. What ennobles Penn is not that he stumbled, but that he
aimed high.

Was his conversion to Quakerism an act of youthful rebelliousness against his father the admiral? It was to all appearances a
genuine conversion, costly to Penn in many ways, placing him at
odds with his father and his country. In contemporary terms, it
was as if one of the Joint Chiefs of Staff had a college-age son who
came home one weekend with his head shaved, wearing a saffron
robe, to announce that he had become a Hare Krishna.

In seventeenth-century England, the Quakers were as much
of an eccentric fringe group as the Hare Krishnas are today. The
well-known practice of addressing everyone as "thee" may seem
quaint to us now, but then was considered seditious. Pronouns
were part of the regulated class system; to call one's father or the
king "thee" was an act of egalitarian defiance.

Equally radical were Quaker refusals to remove their hats before a judge, take oaths, or swear allegiance to the king (which was seen as civil disobedience). The Quakers quoted Matthew: "Thou shalt not forswear thyself, but shalt perform unto the Lord thine oaths." They dealt only with God. To top it off, they were pacifists and refused to go to war, which was treasonable.

Admiral William Penn was a pillar of the English military establishment, the outstanding sailor of his time, a captain of the fleet that captured Jamaica in the second Dutch war. In 1661, his seventeen-year-old son came home from Oxford, but it was not the between-terms break. He had been expelled for objecting to the prayer book and refusing to wear a surplice. Upset over his Quakerish leanings, the elder Penn gave the boy a good whipping. To the admiral, the Quakers were a bunch of lunatics. He had spent his entire life doing battle in the king's service, but the Quakers refused to fight. He was a good Anglican, and they disrupted church services. Or perhaps he thought of Solomon Eccles, the fashionable Quaker music-master, who had walked naked through Westminster Hall with a chafing dish full of fire on his head, crying out, "Repent! Repent!"

The admiral sent his son to Ireland, where in 1667, at the age of twenty-three, he heard the Quaker preacher Thomas Lowe speak on "there is a faith which overcometh the world, and there is a faith which is overcome by the world." Penn came home addressing his father as "thou" and "thee," and refused to take part in Christmas festivities or attend the christening of his sister's child. He became such a nuisance that his father threw him out of the house.

At this particular time, Quakers were often fined and jailed for holding their meetings. The young Penn was first arrested in Cork, Ireland, and sent to the Tower in close confinement (no exercise or fresh air). Released in July 1669, he was arrested again in August 1670 on London's Gracechurch Street and charged with "preaching to an unlawful, seditious, and riotous assembly"—he had been addressing a group of Quakers in the street after they were locked out of their meetinghouse. He was acquitted by the jury, but fined for refusing to remove his hat in court. When he couldn't pay the fine, he was sent to jail. In Newgate Prison, he learned that his father was dying, and wrote him on September 5, 1670: "I am more concerned at thy distemper and the pains that attend it than at my own mere imprisonment which works for the best."

The admiral died, leaving his son 120,000 acres in County Cork. Although he was jailed again in 1671 for speaking at a Quaker meeting, Penn settled down after his marriage in 1672. But he did not give up his beliefs, and remained active in Quaker affairs. It was as an arbitrator in a Quaker dispute that he became involved in the New World.

Unwilling to take their legal quarrels to government courts, the Quakers had developed their own machinery of arbitration, called "Gospel Order," which involved using other Quakers as judges. In 1674, Penn was asked to settle a dispute between two Quakers who had bought a large tract of land in what is today New Jersey. One of the men, John Fenwick, had leased his share of the land to two investors as the collateral for a loan.

The experience of arbitration gave Penn the settlement bug. He felt that he could do better than these two bumblers, and launch a Quaker colony in America. The answer was single ownership. In 1680, Penn petitioned the king for a grant. He was thirty-five at the time, living with his wife, Gulielma, and their two children at Warminghurst, his Sussex estate. A prominent Quaker and author of tracts like *The Sandy Foundation Shaken*, he was always on the edge of legal trouble. But he had the wit and grace to make himself popular at the court of Charles II, and counted the king's brother, the duke of York, among his friends.

Penn's ability to operate with one foot in the Quaker camp and the other at court helped him to fulfill his ambition of bringing persecuted Quakers to America. It was an easily transplantable religion, having no priests, no tithes, no sacraments, and no cathedrals. Along with his religious mission, there was the profit motive. He could make money by selling land, as Fenwick and the others in New Jersey had attempted.

Penn's request was based on a debt owed by the crown to his father for feeding his sailors out of his own pocket. Penn said in his May 1680 petition that he felt he "had a debt upon the Crown of about 16,000 pounds of money lent by my father for the victualing of the Navy in 1667. . . ."

The grant sailed past the bureaucratic shoals and whirlpools in less than a year. In February 1681, Penn was accorded "a certain tract of land in America, to be erected into a province and to be called by the name of Pennsylvania." The king may have welcomed a petition ridding England of a passel of troublemaking Quakers. Penn later wrote his friend Lord Romney: "The government at home was glad to be rid of us at so cheap a rate as a little parchment to be practiced in a desert 3000 miles off. . . ." In fact, this "desert" was a province the size of England, forty-five thousand square miles of prime American real estate nicely tucked in between New York and Maryland.

Penn turned out to be a great promoter. He wrote appealing pamphlets and sold maps of Pennsylvania with charming drawings of trees, inviting streams, and smiling Indians. Between July and October 1681, he sold 320,000 acres to 259 buyers. By the time he sailed in August 1682, he had sold another three hundred thousand acres to 250 buyers. But, instead of making money, Penn was mired in debt, because of the massive initial expenses of colonization. His own business manager, Philip Ford, however, served as a friendly banker, who paid his bills but charged him compound interest and a commission on every transaction. Ford skimmed enough money to open a drygoods shop in London's Bow Lane. Before his departure, Penn gave him the mortgage to three hundred thousand acres of land in Pennsylvania to pay off a 2,851-pound debt.

Although the conventional image of Penn suggests "the Quaker Oats costume of shadbelly coat and cocked hat, eternally dispensing peace and yard goods to the Indians" (in the words of F. B. Tolles), he was in fact an absentee landlord. From 1681, when he acquired Pennsylvania, to the time of his death in 1718, he spent less than four years on site.

On his first trip, he came as a visitor, without his family, arriving in October 1682 and remaining through 1683 and much of 1684. In less than two years, he accomplished something remarkable, creating a colony that could remain unfortified and undefended because of its friendly relations with the Indians.

Next he turned to the business of laying out Philadelphia, the site he had bought from five Swedes. There were Assembly elections, boundary negotiations, and additional land purchases from the Indians. By August 1683, he was already complaining about the rise in the price, "which now is dear, that which would have bought 20 miles not buying now two."

Whatever the price, new land was necessary, for in 1683 there was an impressive movement of population into the colony. More than thirty ships brought several thousand settlers. One of the first was the Bristol pewterer Thomas Paschall, who cleared six acres five miles from Philadelphia and built himself a house with a chimney. He wrote a friend in Bristol that Swedes, Finns, and Dutch were his neighbors on the river, "and this I can say, I never wished myself at Bristol again since my departure." The Indians were starting to speak English, and Paschall heard one of them say: "Swede no good, Dutch man no good, but Englishman good."

Pennsylvania was the first colony to attract a large number of German settlers. The chief figure among the early arrivals was a Frankfurt lawyer, Francis Daniel Pastorius, whom Penn had met on his travels to Germany. Pastorius became the agent for a group of Frankfurt Quakers and Mennonites who bought fifteen thousand acres from Penn's agent in Rotterdam. Pastorius feared an impending end-of-the-world disaster in Europe. He came to America to find a place of refuge "for upright people, while God poured out his cup of wrath over sinful Europe."

He sailed in June 1683 with forty-two settlers, and arrived in Philadelphia on August 20 after a rough crossing, only to find that Penn, in spite of his protestations of friendship and his promises, had reneged on the land deal. The Germans had bought fifteen thousand acres in one piece, on a navigable stream, plus three hundred acres outside Philadelphia, and three city lots. Penn didn't want to give them such a large amount of contiguous acreage, but Pastorius refused to be wedged in among the English. They compromised on an initial grant of six thousand acres. It was not on a navigable river as promised, but east of the Schuylkill.

The Frankfurt partners felt defrauded, and the merchant Jacob Vandewalle wrote Penn on August 24, 1684, "We cannot imagine why you have made so many difficulties . . . and have presented us impossible conditions." Their enthusiasm for emigration dimmed, and they did not follow Pastorius to Germantown, as the colony was called.

Pastorius set about making Germantown a community unto itself, a state within a state. He supervised the clearing of the land, which was all overgrown with forest, wishing for a dozen stout Tyrolese to fell the thick ash trees. He recalled God's penance to Adam, that he should eat his bread in the sweat of his brow. Pastorius often walked the six miles to Philadelphia, finding the people there honest. There were even posters in the street saying that so-and-so had found this or that and the loser should call for it.

He first encountered those "who are erroneously called savages" at Upland (today's Chester), a Swedish settlement where he had gone to buy supplies. (The Swedes had been there since the 1640s, having bought land for a piece of baize.) When he offered the Indians a dram of brandy, they wanted to give him sixpence, but he wouldn't take it. Soon they started visiting Germantown, and Pastorius hired them as day laborers.

Pastorius felt that they had learned dishonesty from the settlers. One crafty fellow pledged his carrying strap as security that he would bring them a turkey, but instead brought a buzzard that he tried to pass off as a turkey. Another, having previously been cheated with watered-down liquor, tested the brandy by sticking his finger into the jug and then poking it into the fire to see whether it lit up.

Pastorius found his unadorned life in the Pennsylvania wilderness a satisfying antidote to the "Sodom" of Europe. The contrast was uppermost in his mind when, in June 1692, he learned of an earthquake in Jamaica that had destroyed most of its capital, Port Royal, and killed twenty-five hundred of its inhabitants. He labeled the disaster God's punishment, for Jamaica was an outpost of European immorality. Fashionable women wearing high head-dresses had been buried up to the waist, and could not be dug up or removed, remaining vertically planted in the ground, stiff in death, "and obliged to play the role as it were of the devil's pillory posts."

In contrast, the citizens of Germantown were law-abiding and orderly, and their sins were venial. The court records covering fifteen years do not show a single violent crime. Reynier Peters was fined twenty shillings for calling the sheriff "a rascal and a liar" on the open street. George Muller was fined for betting that he could "smoke above one hundred pipes in one day." Peter Keurlis was fined five pounds for selling more than the prescribed limit of a gill (quarter-pint) of rum or a quart of beer to his tavern customers.

The days of Germantown's independence were numbered. In 1701, when Pastorius asked that the community be allowed to keep its separate government and exemption from county taxes, his request was turned down. Germantown became a township of Philadelphia County, subject to county courts and taxes. Pastorius resigned as agent for the Frankfurt company and became a school-teacher in Philadelphia. He died in 1719, at the age of sixty-eight, having spent thirty-six years in Pennsylvania, a great deal longer than Penn himself.

•   •

After a little less than two years in Pennsylvania, Penn sailed for England in August 1684. His mission was to defend the interests of his colony in its boundary dispute with Maryland, which pitted the Calverts against the Penns. Instead of appointing a deputy governor to serve in his absence, he distributed the power among a council of eleven, including ten Quakers, seven of whom were First Purchasers (500 acres or more).

At this time, thousands of new arrivals were creating all sorts of pressures on the colony, and factions were forming among the Quakers. Penn himself said at a Quaker meeting on New Year's Day 1684, "Brother love is not to be met with as freely in this our Philadelphia, as I on my part desire." But go he must, leaving Pennsylvania rudderless and staying away for fifteen years, beset by a series of financial crises.

In 1688, the fourth year of Penn's absence, John Blackwell, a Puritan, was appointed deputy governor. But Blackwell only lasted a year, finding the Quakers ungovernable. His parting shot upon being dismissed in 1689 was: "Each prays for his neighbor on First Days [Sundays] and then preys on him the other six."

By the time Penn came back to Pennsylvania, in September 1699, his finances were in such a mess that he had deeded the entire colony to his business agent, Philip Ford, as collateral for loans. Ford rented it back to him for 630 pounds a year. Penn's wife and elder son had died, and he was remarried to a merchant's daughter, Hannah Callow-Hill, a woman half his age. They had a second family of three sons and a daughter, and a lot of problems.

Philadelphia was now a city of five thousand, but Penn spent most of his time on his eighty-four-hundred-acre estate, Pennsbury, twenty-six miles northeast of the city. There he had built a three-story house with a brick façade overlooking the Delaware River. The estate had the Quaker mix of simplicity and comfort, with brickwork in the austere "English Bond" pattern. The only decoration was a plank bearing the initials "WP" and the year "1683" embedded above the door. Stone steps led down from the front door to a privet-lined garden with odd plants like Love Lies Bleeding, which sprouts filamentlike red fronds. More steps led down a gravel path lined with tulip poplars and white wood benches to the river's edge, where Penn's twenty-seven-foot-long barge waited to take him to Philadelphia by oar and sail, a five-hour trip. The pace of life was leisurely, in a time when clocks did not yet have minute hands.

Some may be surprised to learn that William Penn the virtuous Quaker kept slaves. The fact is not mentioned in his biographies and is only revealed in the exhaustive seven-volume edition of his papers published in the 1980s by the University of Pennsylvania. Despite his lectures about God and brotherly love, it seems that Penn failed to question the propriety of owning a human being. Slavery was commonplace among the Pennsylvania Quakers, the only opposition coming from Germantown. In February 1688, Pastorius helped draft an antislavery protest to be read at one of the monthly Quaker meetings in Philadelphia. "Ye Quakers do here handle men like they handle there the cattle. . . . Have these Negroes not as much right to fight for their freedom as you have to keep them slaves?"

A few years earlier, in 1685, William Penn had written his Pennsbury steward, James Harrison, from London, instructing him to train a man and a boy as gardeners. "It were better they were blacks," he wrote, "for then a man has them while they live." Penn wrote Harrison again on July 11, 1685, about a fisherman slave that he wanted sold: "If the black, that is the fisher, be there still, let Jos. Cart have him at full price."

Some slave-owners felt it was morally wrong to separate married slaves by selling one and keeping the other. Penn had no such compunctions. In 1700, while living in Pennsbury, he and his wife, Hannah, had two married house servants, Jack and Rarthenia. When Hannah Penn suspected Rarthenia of stealing some linen (although she had no proof), arrangements were made to send her back to Barbados and sell her there. Jack was desperate to go back with her, but, as Hannah Penn wrote the secretary of the province, James Logan, on July 23, 1700, "I am loath to let him go because our washing approaches." Perhaps there would be time, she added, for Rarthenia to come up from Philadelphia by boat to see her husband one last time before she was taken away. The correspondence ends there.

When William and Hannah Penn returned to England in 1701, they left behind James Logan to collect rents and taxes, sell land, and settle accounts. Logan accumulated far more power than his title of clerk of the Council and secretary of the province would indicate, but was frustrated by the Quakers' pacifism, including their refusal to contribute to the cost of defense in the war with France.

In London, Penn had other concerns. He was sinking in a bog of debt. In 1702, when his daughter Laetitia married the Quaker merchant William Aubrey, he was forced to borrow three thousand pounds from his son-in-law. It was a sort of reverse dowry. When Aubrey dunned Penn, the normally mild Hannah Penn called her son-in-law "that muck worm."

In Pennsylvania, there was quarreling among the Quaker factions, and the dream of a Quaker state was evaporating with the huge influx of non-Quakers, such as the Welsh, who left place names like Bala-Cynwyd. Penn was so broke and so fed up with wrangling that he put the entire colony up for sale for thirty thousand pounds, saying privately that he'd take twenty thousand. When word got out that Pennsylvania was for sale, the settlers were less willing than ever to pay their rents and taxes.

In fact, Penn had no right to sell, for in 1702 Philip Ford died, and his estate had a strong legal claim to the colony. The matter ended up in the courts, where it dragged on for years. Ford's widow, Bridget, claimed that Pennsylvania was hers, whereas Penn argued that he had been defrauded with bloated accounts and an "unreasonable and voracious computation of compound interest." He had been bilked, he claimed, by his number-crunching, money-grubbing steward.

Penn was despondent at the end of 1703, describing himself as an "old, kind, and abused landlord," hounded by his surrogate children, including the disputatious ones in Pennsylvania, the greedy family of his steward in London, his dunning son-in-law, and now, as was about to happen, his own son.

William Penn, Jr., was as much of an embarrassment to Penn as he himself had been to his father the admiral. Arriving in Pennsylvania in February 1704, the young Penn went to live at Pennsbury, where he kept his horses and hounds. At first, he seemed to like the country squire's life. Frustrated by his lack of income, he began coming into the city, and got involved in the training of the militia—quite an affront to his father's Quaker pacifism.

In the militia, according to the reports William Penn received from James Logan, young Penn met a gang of "loose fellows" who indulged in "revels and disorders." Logan had already warned Penn about his son's "youthful sallies." It all ended in court, after young Penn and his friends got into a street brawl with a night watchman. Penn, Jr., prudently decided to leave the colony, and sailed for England only nine months after his arrival.

In 1705, William Penn had a slight stroke, "a troublesome swimming in the head," which prevented him from writing letters. He never regained his health or financial footing, and in 1707 was obliged to sell Warminghurst. As one of his friends put it, his lot was always "to have wormwood mingled with his drink."

For Penn, the cause of his travails was his colony. "O Pennsylvania, what hast thou cost me?" he lamented. "Above thirty thousand pounds more than I ever got by it, two hazardous and most fatiguing voyages, my straits and slavery here, and my child's soul almost . . ."

The Ford suit moved slowly through the courts, and in 1708 the estate was awarded 2,908 pounds for back rent that Penn owed Philip Ford. Penn either would not or could not pay. In January 1709, at the age of sixty-three, he was sent to Fleet Prison, where he stayed until October, when he was able to borrow more money and settled out of court with the Fords for seventy-six hundred pounds. In return, they gave up all claims to the ownership of Pennsylvania. To make good his new loans, Penn once again tried to sell the colony. He was on the verge of succeeding, in 1712, when he suffered a crippling stroke. He lingered on in a vegetable state until his death in 1718. Pennsylvania had cost him his life as well as every penny he had.

After Penn's death, a powerful Quaker merchant class came into existence, and Philadelphia, with its straight streets paved and curbed, its flagstone sidewalks, and its spacious harbor, soon outdistanced Boston as the number-one commercial center in America. The city's success came from urban planning and the Quaker businessman's reputation for honesty: "Their yea was yea and their nay was nay." They formed a kind of international tribe, with colleagues in all the big port cities, from Halifax to London, from Hamburg to Lisbon. But this sense of being a "peculiar people" vanished as they grew prosperous. It's hard for a group to maintain qualities rooted in dissent once the group is no longer persecuted. To some extent, the virtues of simplicity and egalitarianism went out the window. As the Quakers got rich, they began buying silver watches and expensive furniture. They started wearing curled periwigs and ribbons in their hats. Some secretly had their portraits done.

Philadelphia changed too. By 1702, James Logan estimated that only one-third of the population was Quaker. Churches of other denominations were built alongside the meetinghouses with their rows of hard benches. The Friends were so engulfed by hordes of Scotch and Irish that in 1730 one of the monthly meetings noted the disturbances taking place, "under the pretense of keeping a day to a saint called Patrick."

The Scotch-Irish started coming in after 1717 and moved west of Philadelphia into the valleys between the Delaware and the Susquehanna. They adapted easily on the frontier, having already learned the lesson that you have to fight for what's yours. They had left behind a quasi-feudal society of high rents and tithes paid to churches they didn't belong to. In America, they heard, poverty was unknown; every man was his own landlord, and no tithes were collected. Pennsylvania was known as "the best poor man's country," the most productive mixed-farming region in America. As the Scotch-Irish pushed westward, they strained the policy of good relations with the Indians, squatting on their lands and defending illegal occupation by force of arms. James Logan wrote to Hannah Penn in 1726, "There are at this time near 100,000 acres possessed by persons who resolutely sit down and improve without any manner of right or pretense to it." They landed and headed west—overlooking the visit to the land office. If someone threw them off the land, they came right back, with their log cabins, their pegs in the wall, their three-legged stools, and their pot-valiant prowess. "A settlement of five families from the North of Ireland," wrote Logan, "gives me more trouble than 50 of any other people." He wondered who the real savages were.

The frontier began thirty miles north or west of Philadelphia. These people, who had left behind the intolerable institutions and restraints of their homeland, wanted also to move beyond the reach of the bailiff and the judge in the New World. The frontier was the answer, where they had the freedom to go where they wanted and do what they pleased. It was impossible to reproduce the strictures of the Old World, because the physical scale was so different. The frontier represented a way of moving out of reach. If you couldn't marry an heiress, or live in a brick house, or attend a famous university, or inherit your father's legal practice, you could at least move on. If there were class differences, they were based on how well you ran your farm and kept your garden. There was no concept of "minority group," no "period of adjustment," no "Immigrant Aid Society." Nor was there instant assimilation.

People hung on to their language and ethnic identity as a form of armor against the wilderness. When did a man start saying that he was a Pennsylvanian rather than a Scotch-Irishman or a German? The first generation was tied to the Old World, and the second was caught between the two, but the third generation, American-born, looked resolutely westward.

One of those Pennsylvania borderers was Edward Marshall, a Bucks County hunter and frontiersman, sometimes employed as a chain carrier by surveyors. In 1735, the twenty-five-year-old Marshall was approached by Timothy Smith, sheriff of Bucks County, with a job offer. Marshall, a strong and sturdy young man, was an experienced forester who knew the area. All Smith wanted him to do was go for a walk, for which he'd be paid five pounds. Marshall agreed, wondering what it was all about.

Marshall was one of three men recruited by Smith on orders from Thomas Penn, who with his two brothers, Richard and John, had inherited Pennsylvania from their father. The sons, like their father, were always borrowing money and embroiled in lawsuits. They owned acres by the millions but remained in England, living on loans and expectations and sinking deeper into debt.

In 1732, Thomas Penn went to Pennsylvania to clear the family debt; he remained there nine years. His brother John wrote from London, estimating their debt at seven thousand pounds and saying that he faced debtor's prison. "To be continually dunned for debts is certainly the most uneasy life a person can live under," John said, "nor indeed is it to be supported."

To raise cash, the brothers thought of a land lottery. They would sell forty-shilling tickets and distribute one thousand acres of Pennsylvania land among the winners. But the Quakers would say that a lottery was immoral, Thomas cautioned. John Penn responded that, "as there is no fraud in it . . . no person even the most godly can gainsay it." The real obstacle was that some of the land selected for prizes still belonged to the Indians. There could be no lottery until the title was cleared. They couldn't just seize Indian land, which went against all the principles established by their father. However, they didn't have the money to pay a fair price, and they were under pressure. In the summer of 1734, Thomas Penn met with the Delaware chiefs at Durham, a place on the Delaware, southeast of today's Bethlehem, where there was an iron foundry. At this meeting, as the Delaware Chief Nutimus later testified, Penn "kept begging us and plaguing us to give him the land," but would not meet their terms. The Indians replied, in effect: No more token payments!

At this point, the wily agent James Logan, employed by the sons as he had been by the father, found an old scrap of paper going back to 1686, two years after Penn had first left Pennsylvania. It was a deed, dated August 28, and signed by three Delaware chiefs, who agreed to the sale of a tract of land north of Philadelphia, in the fork of the Delaware and Lehigh rivers. The description of the boundary of the tract was extremely vague. It began at a certain white oak opposite the falls of the Delaware, then continued up the Delaware as far as a spruce tree at the foot of a mountain, and then along the mountain to another white oak, "from which said line the said tract or tracts hereby granted doth extend itself back into the woods as far as a man can go in a day and a half."

It was not unusual for early deeds to include walking or riding clauses, a method of measuring distances that the Indians understood. But according to the 1686 deed, the tract, although paid for, had never been walked. And now, half a century later, Thomas Penn claimed that the land was his, that Nutimus and his fellow chiefs owed it to him, and that they must organize a walk to measure the extent of the tract. A meeting was arranged at Pennsbury in May 1735 to discuss the matter with the Delaware chiefs.

Before that meeting, Thomas Penn decided to prepare for the boundary walk by secretly hiring a party of three walkers to find the best route and blaze the trail. Thus, when the line was walked, they would not waste any time finding their way; they could cover more ground and encompass more acres.

The subterfuge of the trial walk came to light more than a century later, when this note was found in Thomas Penn's private papers: "April 2, 1735. Timo. Smith expenses on traveling ye Indian purchase, 5 pounds." Sheriff Smith was the subcontractor who hired the three walkers, among them Edward Marshall. Smith was paid a total of fifteen pounds, plus fifteen for "ye three men who traveled ye purchase." They were slow getting under way, and orders arrived from Penn on April 29 that the walkers "should immediately be sent on foot on the day and a half journey." Penn wanted to know the results of the walk before his meeting with the Delaware chiefs on May 9.

On that day, the chiefs arrived at Pennsbury for their meeting with Thomas Penn and James Logan, who was experienced in Indian negotiations. According to the deposition given by one of the chiefs, Tedyuscung, at an inquiry into the Walking Purchase conducted in 1762, Logan told Chief Nutimus: "It would not be worth your while to trouble yourself about these lands; if you do, you'll make the big trees and logs and great rocks and stones tumble down into our road." In Indian talk, according to Tedyuscung, such words were a threat of hostilities.

When Nutimus protested, Logan belittled him, saying: "I look upon you as the little finger of my left hand." Despite Logan's bullying, the results of the meeting were inconclusive, because some of the Indian chiefs were missing.

Two months later, in July 1735, the lottery tickets went on sale, even though the Penns were still short of land. They were counting on collecting fifteen thousand pounds, more than enough to pay their debts. A prospectus was issued, but the lottery didn't catch on. The Quakers boycotted it, and the drawing had to be postponed until August 1736. Even then, so few tickets were sold that Thomas Penn was faced with the unpleasant prospect of returning the money that had been collected. He devised a new scheme, according to which ticket holders could convert their tickets into a right to buy land at fifteen pounds per hundred acres. This netted eighteen hundred pounds, but the land in question was the land at the fork of the Delaware, which still had an Indian encumbrance on it.

By the summer of 1737, the walking of the 1686 tract had taken on some urgency, for those who had converted their lottery tickets would soon want to claim their land. Another meeting with the chiefs was arranged in Philadelphia on August 24. This time, a copy of the 1686 deed and a map of the area were shown to the chiefs. The deposition of an Indian who had been present at the original signing was read as further evidence. The chiefs said they were satisfied that the land had indeed been sold and agreed that it should be walked. They insisted, however, that Indian observers accompany the walkers. Four chiefs signed the agreement on August 25: Nutimus, Teeshacomin, Lappawinzoe, and Manawkyhickon.

What they did not know was that the map they had been shown was doctored. The area covered was the stretch of the Delaware that today forms the border of New Jersey and Pennsylvania, between Trenton and Easton. At Easton, the Lehigh River, then called the West Branch of the Delaware, flowed into the main north-south branch. About twenty-five miles south of the Lehigh, there was another waterway, Tohickon Creek, which also flowed from the west into the Delaware. On the doctored map, Tohickon Creek was called the West Branch of the Delaware, making the area seem much smaller than it was. The Indians were under the impression that the walk would run parallel from the Delaware to a point that was presented to them as the West Branch of the Delaware, but that was in fact Tohickon Creek. It would be about sixteen miles from the point of departure in Wrightstown Township to the point where the walkers would reach Tohickon Creek, a bit north of today's Pipersville; whereas it was fifteen miles farther to the crossing of the Lehigh.

Once the Indians had signed, it didn't take long to get the walk started. Timothy Smith was instructed to round up three strong walkers, including Edward Marshall, "that man of the three which traveled and held out best" in the trial walk. The others were James Yeates of Newtown and Solomon Jennings, who had a spread on the Lehigh. All three were young, strong, and athletic, used to the wilderness. Each man was to be paid five pounds, but, as an incentive bonus, the man who walked the farthest would be given five hundred acres, which made the walk a race. Edward Marshall said he was determined to win the prize or lose his life in the attempt.

On September 19, 1737, just before sunrise, there was quite a gathering to be seen around the big chestnut tree on John Chapman's farm, near the Wrightstown meetinghouse, the spot where the walk would start. Timothy Smith was there, and so was Benjamin Eastburn, the surveyor general for Pennsylvania. The Indians watched gravely, but the white spectators and officials were in a festive mood.

Everyone looked eastward as the sun started rising over the horizon. When it was fully visible, at about six, the signal was given, and the walkers, who were touching the tree, started out over Great Durham Road. Yeates went off at such a clip that Marshall jogged to catch up, but one of the Indian observers pointed out that running was not allowed. They headed north, parallel to the Delaware on the Durham road into Buckingham Township, then into Plumstead Township through Gardenville, and Bedminster Township through Pipersville. North of Pipersville, they came to Tohickon Creek, where the Indians thought they were going to stop, according to the map they had been shown. But the white men waded across the creek, which was low in September, continuing across Tinicum Township and into

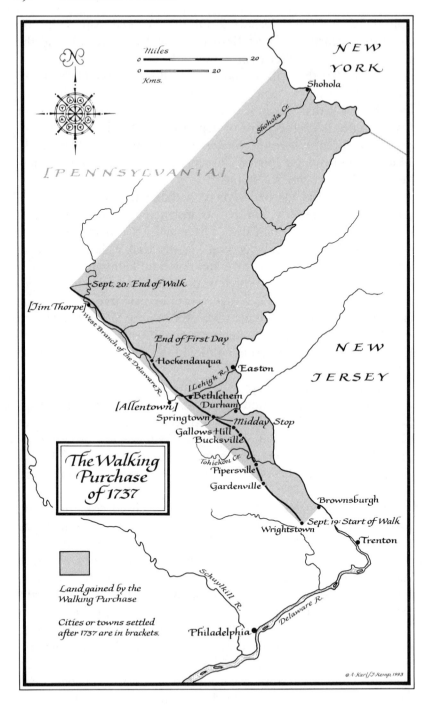

Miles
0 _____ 20
0 _____ 20
Kms.

NEW YORK

Shohola

Shohola Cr.

[PENNSYLVANIA]

Sept. 20: End of Walk

[Jim Thorpe]

West Branch of the Delaware R.

End of First Day

Hockendauqua

Easton

[Lehigh R.]

NEW JERSEY

Bethlehem
Durham

[Allentown]

Springtown

Midday Stop

Gallows Hill
Bucksville

Tohickon Cr.

Pipersville

Gardenville

Brownsburgh

Sept. 19: Start of Walk

Wrightstown

Trenton

The Walking
Purchase
of 1737

Land gained by the
Walking Purchase

Cities or towns settled
after 1737 are in brackets.

Schuylkill R.

Delaware R.

Philadelphia

© A. Karl / J. Kemp, 1993

Nockamixon Township. At this point, after nineteen miles, Solomon Jennings gave out.

Marshall and Yeates continued across Nockamixon Township and into the southeastern corner of Springfield Township, where they came to a rise known as Gallows Hill. Here the Durham road went east to the Durham iron foundry, four miles away, and would have taken them back to the Delaware, but they veered away from it and took an Indian path north-northwest, in the direction of today's Bethlehem and the Lehigh River. They went on another three miles until they reached Cook's Creek, where they stopped for a spartan fifteen-minute lunch break, having covered twenty-eight miles in seven hours. That was four miles an hour, a brisk pace to maintain.

They started out again at 1:15 P.M. and walked another five hours, still heading north-northwest over Indian trails. According to Alexander Brown, one of the mounted attendants, "Marshall and Yeates, who were tall light thin men, well formed for walking, walked as fast as they could to avoid running and kept a horse in a middling journey's pace." They crossed the Saucon River and the Lehigh, or West Branch of the Delaware, where Bethlehem is today.

At this point, the Indian observers realized that something was seriously wrong. The walkers were no longer following the Delaware, but had marched off into the interior. To the Indians, the language of the deed, "as far as a man can go in a day and a half," meant an average day's walk by an average man. But these fellows were racing like demons, as though their lives depended on it.

The Indian observers objected that the walkers weren't following the river, and were going too fast. "You run," said one. "That's not fair. You was to walk." One of the Indians complained that he was having a hard time keeping up because his shoes were no good, and said he should be given a new pair; some of the mounted attendants began to let the Indians ride. As for Marshall and Yeates, they kept going until six-fifteen, following the Lehigh to a spot near the Indian village of Hockendauqua, today a suburb of Allentown, where they saw Timothy Smith waiting for them on horseback with a watch in his hand, shouting at them to "pull up," because time was up. Marshall grabbed a sapling and called out, "I'm almost gone. A few poles further and I would have fallen." They had covered about forty miles in one day.

Rest that night was sweet, although the white men were disturbed by the chanting in the nearby Indian village, which was the home of Chief Lappawinzoe, one of the signatories of the agreement. There was plenty of food and drink to restore the valiant marchers, and Yeates in particular drank his fill. When the walkers rose, at dawn on September 20, they discovered that the Indian observers were gone, as well as some of their horses. An emissary was sent to the village. The observers had informed Chief Lappawinzoe that something shady was going on. When the emissary arrived, asking for the observers, the chief told him to go to the devil.

It took time to round up the horses, so they didn't get going until eight. This meant that the six-hour half-day would end at two in the afternoon. Marshall was off at the same hell-for-leather pace, with compass in hand to hold his course in the wilderness, while the hung-over Yeates tried to keep up. At 1:30 P.M., half an hour before the finish, when they had to climb a steep hill north of a bend in the Lehigh, Yeates collapsed, and Edward Marshall knew that he had won the prize. When he stopped, at two o'clock, four miles north of today's Jim Thorpe, between two mountain ranges, he had covered about sixty miles. This was no mean feat, considering the absence of bridges and roads. To mark the spot, Timothy Smith and the others placed stones in the forks of five chestnut oaks.

Then it was up to Benjamin Eastburn and his team of surveyors to run the line at a right angle to the line that had been walked, northeast until they hit the Delaware, at Shohola Creek, which took them four days. As a result of Marshall's marathon, the Penns collected a large triangular piece of land, with the Delaware forming the base, about a hundred miles long, winding and twisting north from the outskirts of today's Trenton, through the Musconetcong, Scotts, and Kittatinny mountains, and making a sharp turn west at today's Port Jervis, New York, where it forms the boundary with Pennsylvania, up to Shohola Creek. The two sides of the triangle were the line that was walked between Wrightstown and Jim Thorpe, of about sixty miles, and the line the surveyors ran from Jim Thorpe to Shohola, about fifty miles.

On his way back to Bucks County, Timothy Smith rode by an Indian village and saw an Indian grab a gun and hide behind a log. Clearly, the Indians were not happy about the outcome of the walk. Later one of the old chiefs Smith saw said, "No sit down to smoke, no shoot a squirrel, but run all day long." The walk had not been done in the intended spirit of the deed.

As for Edward Marshall, a couple of months after the walk, he happened to be in the Indian town where Chief Lappawinzoe lived, and heard the chief proclaim his dissatisfaction. The walk had not been fairly done, nor the course honestly run. Next spring, they were coming down to Philadelphia, each man with his buckskin, to take back their land. But they were powerless to respond, and there was no redress; the fraud simply festered until a chance for revenge came with the outbreak of the French and Indian War in 1754, when some of the Delaware tribes sided with the French. The chiefs told the missionary John Heckewelder that "they never would have joined the French . . . had they not been so shamefully dealt with" in the matter of the Walking Purchase.

As if it wasn't enough to cheat the Indians, Thomas Penn also cheated Edward Marshall, who never got his five hundred acres. Marshall and his family found some land to farm in Mount Bethel, in the uppermost corner of Northampton County. When hostilities broke out, Northampton and its outskirts were particularly hard hit. In November 1755, there was an attack on a Moravian village on the eastern side of the Lehigh, about two miles northwest of Bethlehem. By September 1757, 115 settlers had been killed in Northampton County alone.

The Indians were simply trying to get back the land they had been cheated out of. When they got to within twenty miles of Easton, settlers took their threshed corn, cattle, and household goods and fled to New Jersey. Marshall's farm was about fifteen miles north of Easton, on Jacoby Creek, in Upper Mount Bethel. Although he was right on the New Jersey border, he stayed put, with his wife and nine children. In May 1757, he went on a day's logging expedition with a neighbor, above the stream. While he was gone, a war party of sixteen Indians attacked his house. One of them threw a coat over a beehive, causing swarms of bees to riot.

Five of his children ran for the woods to escape the Indians and the bees, and his fourteen-year-old daughter, Catherine, was shot as she ran. She hid in a stream and stopped the bleeding with the hem of her dress. Mrs. Marshall, eight months pregnant, was taken prisoner and dragged off. As they approached the Poconos on uphill paths, she was unable to keep up, and so they killed her and scalped her. Her body was found some time later, along with the remains of unborn twins. The Indians, probably without knowing it, took their revenge on the man whose feat of athletic prowess had paced the land that was taken from them. During a second attack, in August, Marshall's oldest son, Peter, was killed.

Edward Marshall survived the hostilities and remarried. His second wife was a German woman whose father had been killed by Indians. One of the things they had in common was the grief of losing members of their family in Indian raids. The devastation of the colony was also a form of revenge against the Penns for Marshall, making rents and taxes impossible to collect.

Marshall lived on into his seventies, regaling his grandchildren with tales of the frontier days.

"What did you do when you came across an Injun, grandpa?"

"Why, I just shut one eye, and we never met again."

And here's the one we've all seen in a hundred westerns, although it may have first happened on the Pennsylvania frontier in the 1750s: "Once I saw an armed Injun 150 feet away, moving in and out of the trees. I got behind a tree and took my hat off and stuck it on the tip of my ramrod and moved it from one side of the tree to the other. A shot rang out, knocking the hat off, and the Indian rushed forth with a yell, tomahawk in hand. I dropped him at 30 feet."

Edward Marshall knew the two faces of the wilderness, its menace and its beauty. Once, while walking in the forest, he came upon a panther cub that was so like a kitten that he let it be.

CHAPTER FIFTEEN

THE HINTERLAND IN 1750

As the frontier kept moving westward, it left in its wake an ever-growing area of settlement that was no longer frontier. In this hinterland, Indians were no longer a threat. The wilderness was cleared to make room for an Anglo-American landscape of tidy towns and tilled fields.

New York Public Library

In the civilized hinterland in 1750, there were cities like New York with hose-and-ladder fire companies. Beneath the elaborate cartouche with swirling scrollwork and foliage, there is an invitation signed by clerk Isaac Roosevelt: "You are hereby notified of a meeting of the Hand-in-Hand Fire Company . . ."

I despair not of preferment before I die.

A PHILADELPHIA BARBER
IN *1744*

In 1750, North America was a three-cornered continent, as it had been for a century and a half. The English remained in their compact area of settlement, which stretched down the Atlantic Seaboard from Maine to Georgia. There were no inland provinces, though land-hungry settlers were moving into western Pennsylvania, and frontiersmen were already in Ohio. The colonial population was about 1.3 million. Writing in 1751, Benjamin Franklin opined, "Our people must at least be doubled over 20 years."

The term "our people" covered quite a religious and ethnic mix of Presbyterian Scotch-Irish, German Lutherans, French Huguenots, and Dutch and Swedish Reformed, in addition to the core group of early English settlers—Anglicans in Virginia, Dissidents in Massachusetts, Catholics in Maryland, and Quakers in Pennsylvania, who were now being swamped by the others.

Georgia's southern frontier, on the Altamaha River, was one hundred miles from St. Augustine, Spain's principal Florida outpost, but things had been fairly quiet on the frontier since Oglethorpe's siege of 1740. In New Mexico, the other zone of Spanish occupation, the subjection of the pueblos had been achieved, though settlements were now subject to Apache and Comanche hit-and-run raids. In Texas, the Spanish presence was represented by a string of missions on the Pecos and the Rio Grande. The Spanish population of North America was negligible compared with the English colonies—about five thousand in New Mexico and three thousand in Florida.

As for the French, they covered a vast surface, from Quebec to New Orleans, through their control of the waterways, from the St. Lawrence to the Great Lakes to the Mississippi to the Gulf of Mexico. They were at Niagara and on Lake Huron and Lake Ontario. They were at Crown Point, at the southern end of Lake Champlain, and at the headwaters of the Mississippi, on Lake Itasca, in northwestern Minnesota. They had forts on the principal rivers, such as Fort Miami at today's St. Joseph Michigan, Fort Pontchartain at Detroit, and Fort Crèvecoeur on the Illinois. On the Gulf of Mexico, they were at Biloxi and Mobile. Soon they would build four forts in Pennsylvania, between Pittsburgh and Erie.

The interior was known to the French as "the Illinois country," and a few small settlements had sprouted there. One was Sainte Geneviève, founded about 1750, on the western bank of the Mississippi, forty miles below St. Louis. This, the first permanent European settlement in Missouri, consisted of nine farmers, their families, their *volontaires* (hired hands), and their slaves. Nearby was Fort de Chartres, built in 1719 to protect the lead mines.

The French population in North America was about seventy thousand, or roughly one-twentieth of the population in the English colonies. The French strategy was to guard the water routes and the trade routes, and to use Indian allies to harass their imperial rivals.

These three great European powers, with their conflicting North American claims, were on a collision course. Spain, England, and France each held pieces of the continent with borders that were imprecise and elastic, always expanding and contracting. There was bound to be conflict; it was only a matter of where and when. The English and the Spanish had already fought in Florida. In 1750, the French and the English were staking out the same territory, south of Lake Erie, where the Allegheny and Monongahela rivers joined to form the Ohio. Did this land belong to Virginia, Pennsylvania, or France? The question of ownership might at any moment lead to a frontier incident that could drag the hinterland into a war.

Life in the hinterland was one of growing refinement, because of the decrease in the number of Indians and the increase in wealth. With the rolling back of the wilderness came the slow growth of culture. You could see the change in sash windows with small square panes, and in three-story brick houses with twin chimneys. You could see it at Boston book auctions, and at college commencements at Harvard and Princeton. An American elite was forming, with American architects like Peter Harrison in Newport and American inventors like Benjamin Franklin. In Quaker Philadelphia, there was a theater. In Virginia, there was a planter society free to pursue outside interests on estates that seemed to run themselves. A code of honor developed alongside slavery; there was a new etiquette, a sense of noblesse oblige, a refinement of personal behavior. It was important to know how and when to remove one's hat.

Boston was a city of merchants and artisans, like Apollon de Rivoire, a Huguenot who arrived from France in 1715 at the age of thirteen as apprentice to a silversmith. His exiled family had gone first to Holland and then to Guernsey. De Rivoire eventually set up his own shop on Ann Street and changed his name to Revere, "merely," as he put it, "on account that the bumpkins should pronounce it easier." In 1729, he married; in 1735, he had a son named Paul.

By 1750, those who wished to emigrate to America had a wide variety of colonies to choose from, each with its proven attractions. They could practice their trades in Boston or New York. They could grow tobacco in Virginia or Maryland, or rice in South Carolina. If they were bargain-hunting for land, they could take the wagon trails to western Pennsylvania and North Carolina. If they found Philadelphia or Annapolis a little cramped, it wasn't that far to the Carolina Piedmont. By 1760, North Carolina had a greater population than New York, ranking fourth behind Virginia, Massachusetts, and Pennsylvania (thanks to William Penn's German connections).

Growth was slow in New York. Large estates gobbled up all the land in the Hudson Valley, and the settlers could only come in as tenants. The Iroquois checked northern expansion in the Mohawk Valley. The patroons dodged taxes through their influence in the Assembly, although, to hear them tell it, they were sorely put upon.

One man who knew the real story of land grants in New York was Cadwallader Colden, surveyor general of the colony since 1722. The Edinburgh-educated son of a Scottish clergyman, he had arrived in America in 1710, at the age of twenty-two, and moved to New York in 1715. The whole colony, he knew from experience, was built on fraud—land fraud in the patents, and the defrauding of the Indians in trade. To give but one example, a Mr. Faulconnier, who had a part in a patent containing two million acres, "boldly put Indian names on certain places which were never heard of by Christians who have lived near these places nigh 30 years."

Colden was a bit of a whistle-blower: constantly writing the governors that the security of the colony depended on honest dealing with the Indians. New York had a fort and trading post at Oswego, on the southern shore of Lake Ontario, only sixty miles from the French fort at Kingston. In one typical case, Colden reported, some Indians had come to Oswego to trade. The Albany trader Nicholas Schuyler had sold them some small rum casks filled with water. The linen rags with which the bungs were tightened had been soaked in rum. Schuyler knew that the Indians never opened a cask on the road, and that this particular group had four hundred miles to go. But on the way home, they met some men of another nation and opened a cask in friendship. When they realized they had been tricked, they returned to Oswego, feeling sorely vexed. The fort's commanding officer informed the governor, who had Schuyler prosecuted, but since he was a member of the Assembly, the prosecution was dropped and the whole thing was winked at. Later the scurrilous Schuyler was appointed to build the fort at Saratoga.

Colden warned that cheating the Indians was incredibly shortsighted, for the friendship of the Six Nations was paramount. They were keeping the other tribes from going with the French. In April 1748, Colden went to Onondaga, south of today's Syracuse, to confer with the Indians and try to keep their friendship. When he arrived, they hoisted the Union Jack and beat the drums. Colden told the sachems of the Six Nations that they were bound in friendship by a strong silver chain. If the chain ever turned rusty, it should be brightened up again.

For the time being, the Six Nations remained loyal, Colden believed. It worried him, however, that the cheating at Oswego continued. The Mohawks complained about high prices, and said they could get cheaper goods from the French, who were probably selling at a loss. Two and a half years later, in October 1750, Benjamin Franklin wrote Colden that the Pennsylvania frontiersman Conrad Weiser "is just returned from Onondaga and gives a melancholy account of the declining state of the English and the increase of French interest among the Six Nations."

The situation was deteriorating on the frontier, while the hinterland was secure and prosperous. Skilled artisans and professional men were now arriving at the ports of entry along with the usual consignment of indentured servants. Gottlieb Mittelberg, hailing from Württemberg in Germany, who landed in October 1750 in Philadelphia, was an organist. He brought with him the first church organ to arrive in Pennsylvania and took it to St. Michael's Lutheran Church, where people came from far and wide to hear him play.

Mittelberg had taken his organ down the Neckar and the

Rhine to Rotterdam, and across the Channel to Cowes. The Rhine boat passed through thirty-six customs houses—such was the nit-picking red tape of Europe. On the long, transatlantic voyage, the men were packed like herring, the drinking water was polluted, and the biscuit swarmed with red worms and spiders. He made a list of the negatives: stench, fumes, vomiting, fever, dysentery, heat, boils, scurvy, cancer, and mouth rot. Among the healthy, there were quarrels in the face of these frustrations. Friends reproached one another for having undertaken the journey. One day, during a heavy gale that tore the sail out of the sailors' hands, a pregnant woman was ejected from a porthole and fell into the sea. But that loss was made up for after they caught a big shark and opened him up: inside was an undigested man wearing silver-buckled shoes.

When the ship landed at Philadelphia, no one was allowed off unless he had paid his passage. The others stayed on board until they were purchased and released. The healthy, of course, were bought first, and the sick stayed on the ship, with the city so close, and often died. They might have recovered had they been allowed to get to shore. Every day, people came aboard to bargain, some from quite a distance, and parents could be seen trading away their children.

On the day after landing, Mittelberg was taken to the court-house to swear the oath of allegiance to the crown. What a hand-some city Philadelphia was, he thought, with its stone and brick houses with roofs of cedar shingles. People were friendly, greeting one another in the street with "How are you, good friend?" and replying, "So middling." There was a splendid town house with four entrances and tall plate-glass windows, as well as eight churches, one of the Quaker faith.

The religious diversity was unlike anything he had ever seen in Europe—there were Lutherans, Reformed, Catholics, Menno-nites, Moravians, Pietists, Baptists, Presbyterians, and Dunkers, who did not shave their beards and were not baptized until full grown, when they were immersed in deep water. Truly, he thought, what he had heard was true: in Pennsylvania everyone may not only believe what he will, but may say it freely and openly.

Mittelberg also noticed that there were no guilds. Anyone could work at whatever trade he wanted, and carry on ten trades if he so desired. There were no taxes on houses, property, or businesses. But one peculiarity was that unmarried men and women paid a tax according to their income, since they had no families to support. The tax was applied to the cost of the streetlights. By the look of it, few had to worry about this tax. All you saw in the street were women heavy with child, or women carrying children, or women leading children by the hand.

Although Mittelberg noticed great freedom, there was also severe punishment. If you stole so much as a handkerchief, you were tied to a post in the public market, stripped to the waist, and lashed with a switch until the skin hung in strips from your body. If you were caught stealing again, you were stood in a cart with a rope around your neck and driven beneath the gallows, and then the cart went off without you, leaving you to dangle. Mittelberg saw a hangman so unskilled that one of the spectators called out, "Why are you taking so long?," to which the hangman replied, "If you think you can do better, just come on."

The inquisitive German visited the courthouse, where a man, obviously poor, was being tried for swearing in public, after being turned in by an informer. According to the law, the informer was entitled to collect half the fine. In this case, the judge asked the informer whether he was willing to waive his half, since the offender was destitute. When the informer refused, the judge passed the sentence: fifty lashes to the posterior, twenty-five to the swearer and twenty-five to the informer.

In another case Mittelberg sat in on, a man accused of raping a woman and getting her pregnant looked at the judge without saying a word. He was found guilty and sentenced to a prison term. Not until the sentence was shouted in his ear did he recover his hearing, saying that when he had forced the woman she had screamed so terribly that he had been rendered temporarily deaf. "Oh you godless rogue," the woman exclaimed, "how can you say so? I did not speak a word at the time." The man then explained that he had only pretended to lose his hearing in order to get the woman to admit her silence. There had been other people in the house whom she could have alerted. "Had I known I was going to get pregnant, I would have," the woman replied, to general laughter. The man was acquitted.

For a broader view of the hinterland at mid-century, let us refer to Dr. Alexander Hamilton, a literate and inquiring Scotsman who arrived in Annapolis to practice medicine in 1739 at the age of twenty-seven. In 1744, he decided to travel through the different provinces for his health and recreation. He set out on horseback on May 30, armed with pistols, and accompanied by his slave Droma. There were few bridges, but plenty of ferries, and he crossed the Susquehanna near today's Havre de Grace and rode into Delaware. At New Castle, then a town of fifteen hundred, he baited the horses and stayed at a tavern, where he picked up from the conversation such expressions as "Damn my blood," "I am a plain honest fellow," "I'll box the saucy jacks," and "My little woman at home drinks tea twice a day."

The road to Wilmington was lined with neat farms and fine meadows, and farther on stood the villages of Chester and Darby, the latter boasting one of the first subscription libraries in America. At the inn, a Quaker and a boatswain, arguing about the lawfulness of using arms against an enemy, almost came to blows. There was a certain amount of rivalry between provinces, Hamilton observed. He heard Pennsylvanians running down Maryland and calling Marylanders cunning sharpers. The Pennsylvania boosters extolled their province as having better soil and better people. In these feelings of regional pride one can discern a nascent nationalism.

On June 6, Hamilton and Droma took the Schuylkill Ferry to Philadelphia. Here they found most of the streets unpaved and obstructed with rubbish, but noted the many fine buildings. When it was time for a shave, Hamilton's barber, giving voice to the perennial American hope of self-advancement, uttered this classic phrase: "I despair not of preferment before I die."

Hamilton was invited to a meeting of the Governor's Club at the Old Tun Tavern, where the writing of Cervantes was discussed. The Quakers, he thought, were an obstinate and stiff-necked lot. A perpetual plague to their governors, they opposed all methods of defense. They were, however, industrious, and he was astonished to see that the shops opened at 5:00 A.M. There was never music or dancing, and ladies seldom appeared in the street.

On June 13, he took the ferry over the Delaware to Trenton, where he stayed at the sign of The Wheat Sheaf and listened to New Jerseyans complain about their Assembly, which was, they said, made up of ignorant wretches. Grousing about the government was a common trait wherever he went. From Trenton, he headed toward New York, via the villages of Princeton and Perth Amboy, where he stayed at the sign of The King's Arms and had the best oysters he'd ever tasted. He took the ferry to Staten Island, which was peopled with Dutch. When Droma asked a black girl,

"Dis de way to York?" she replied "Yaws, mynheer." Annoyed by a term he did not comprehend, Droma said, "You a damn black bitch."

Hamilton found New York a livelier city than Philadelphia, with more shipping, and flutes and violins in the taverns, and the women more gaily dressed. He stayed at the sign of The Cart and Horse on William Street, where vendors sold water on the sidewalk from great casks. The people he met in the taverns were topers and punsters, bawdy talkers. One of them spoke to the discredit of Old England, preferring New York in every respect. They were generally civil and courteous, except for one man at dinner, who exceeded anything he had ever seen for impertinence by saying he suffered from piles and pulling out a linen handkerchief all stained with blood to show the company.

From New York he went up the Hudson to Poughkeepsie, noting that there were forty different ways to spell it and every year the post office adopted a new one. Albany was still mainly Dutch, with a population of four thousand. It was surrounded by a wooden palisade. All the Dutch thought about was money, Hamilton remarked, but they kept their houses tidy, with scrubbed floors, and Delft plates in the kitchen. They made their own wampum for trade with the Indians, who had lost the art of making it themselves. The women were the homeliest he had ever seen.

From Albany, Hamilton returned to New York and went up the Connecticut coast, glad not to hear Dutch spoken. He stopped at New Haven, a scattered town laid out in squares, with the cemetery facing the college, a three-story wooden building with a little cupola. Then on to New London, where he stayed at the sign of The Anchor, and heard of a town famous for onions as big as a child's head. As he left the province, he said to himself, "Farewell, Connecticut, I have had a surfeit of your ragged money, rough roads, and enthusiastic people." His next stop was Newport, Rhode Island, which was famous for privateering and pretty women.

From Newport, he headed north to Providence, where he went to the sign of The White Horse, asking an old fellow at the door if this was the place kept by one Angel. "No," the old fellow said, "Angel don't keep the house, the house keeps Angel." It was another fifty miles to Boston, then the largest city in North America, a city the size of Glasgow, with a population of about twenty thousand. The streets were narrow, and there were a hundred ships in the harbor. The recently built Long Wharf extended six-teen hundred feet into the water from the foot of King Street.

Hamilton liked Boston better than Philadelphia or New York, finding there more men of learning and greater hospitality. Also, the women were affable and pretty, and even a little flirtatious. "I saw not one prude while I was there," he observed. He dined at Wethered's, at the corner of Kilby and King streets, where he heard rumors of an intended expedition against the French fortress at Cape Breton. The conversation, he said, "had that subtlety and acuteness so peculiar to the New England genius." He was taken to a book auction on King Street, where a witty auctioneer plugged each book. "Here you have everything concerning popes, cardi-nals, anti-Christ, and the devil," he said. Or, "Here you have in Tacitus an account of that good and pious person, Nero, who loved his mother and kindred so well that he sucked their very blood." The best-sellers included Ovid's *Art of Love* and *The Marrow of Modern Divinity*, and Hamilton bought a copy of Clarke's *Homer*.

From Boston, he headed north to New Hampshire, encoun-tering a fellow traveler who peppered him with questions. "Pray sir, if I may be so bold, where are you going?" he asked. And then, "Pray sir, from where do you come?" When Hamilton told him, the fellow exclaimed, "Maryland! Where the devil is that place? I have never heard of it." "What an inquisitive rustic," thought Hamilton.

New Hampshire, which had a distinct government from Mas-sachusetts, was well peopled, and the town of Portsmouth had between four and five thousand. The chief trade was in fishing and masting for ships. But here Hamilton stopped, for New Hamp-shire was the frontier, and the governor of the fort at York, over the border in Maine, kept geese to give the alarm, as the ancient Romans had done.

Hamilton returned to Annapolis in September, having been gone more than three months and covered 1,624 miles. The most civilized place, he thought, was Boston, and the most peculiar, Dutch Albany. On the whole, however, his impression was that there was "but little difference in the manners and character of the people in the different provinces I passed through." And what was that character but hybrid . . . not completely English, and not completely anything else . . . yet.

Another aspect of the hinterland, observed by the Swedish botanist Peter Kalm in 1749, was the near absence of Indians.

Hamilton had seen some Mohawks parading up the street in Boston on their way to a conference with other tribes, but Kalm pointed out: "In most parts, you may travel 120 English miles from the coast before you reach the first habitations of the Indians. It is very possible for a person to have been at Philadelphia and other towns on the sea shore for half a year without so much as seeing an Indian."

In the colonies' brief history, there was already a "remember when" nostalgia. The old-timers reminisced: "I remember when the Indians boiled their meat in clay pots pierced at both sides near the rim with holes to pass a stick through. . . . I remember seeing them catch fish with hooks made from bird claws. . . . I remember them making fire by rubbing hard wood against soft." All that was gone, already a vanished way of life in the hinterland by mid-century.

There were now a number of distinct Americas, one English, one Spanish, one French, as well as one where the Indians were and one where they weren't, the frontier and the hinterland.

CHAPTER SIXTEEN

THE FRONTIER
IN 1750

By 1750, a handful of frontiersmen were trading in western
Pennsylvania and Ohio on land claimed by the French.
This led the French to build a chain of forts south of Lake
Erie on land claimed by Virginia. In May 1754, a skirmish
in the Pennsylvania woods became the first battle of the
French and Indian War.

New York Public Library

This plan of the Battle of Lake George in the French-Indian war in
1755, drawn by an eyewitness, shows "our men breaking their order
and hastily running," as well as the manner "in which a great number of the enemy (chiefly Indians) ran naked, for it is their manner
to fight without any other covering than a flap over those parts it is
decent should be concealed."

A volley fired by a young Virginian in the backwoods of America set the world on fire.

HORACE WALPOLE

In the 1750s, something extraordinary happened on the American frontier: a handful of little-known frontiersmen started a chain of events that led to history's first authentic world war, fought in America, Europe, Asia, and India. The British called it the Great War for Empire, while in America it is remembered as the French and Indian War. Involving the principal powers of Europe, it was the last great conflict to take place before the American Revolution.

The war began with friction in the unsettled trans-Appalachian west, claimed by the French, where American traders were making inroads upon the tribes in Pennsylvania and Ohio. The French in 1749 and 1750 undertook to fortify their water routes south of Lake Erie, between Erie and Pittsburgh, with a series of forts. But this Pennsylvania land was also claimed by Virginia, which set the stage for collision.

The opening of hostilities came in 1749, when a French military detachment marched into Ohio to oust the American traders. No one could imagine that these skirmishes in the wilderness would spread to Europe and the rest of the planet, but they did. For by 1755, the war had escalated in Pennsylvania, and both the British and the French were sending reinforcements across the Atlantic. That June, Admiral Edward Boscawen captured two French ships off Cape Breton Island, north of Nova Scotia. This naval action inflamed the French, who carried the war to Europe after spending eleven months maneuvering for allies.

In the choosing of sides, France, Austria, and Russia lined up against Britain and Prussia, opening a second front that was called the Seven Years' War (it lasted from 1756 to 1763). There was fighting in Minorca, in Calcutta, in the Philippines, fighting all over the globe, on land and on sea. On the North American front, the war lasted until 1760 and led to the expulsion of the French. Elsewhere, many places on the map changed hands, notably the subcontinent of India, which was won by the British from the French.

The French and Indian War was the final struggle between the French and the British-run American colonies for control of the

North American continent. In this struggle, a small number of frontiersmen played major roles, helping to disprove the assumption that history was made in the chancelleries of Europe. Men like Thomas Cresap, George Croghan, Conrad Weiser, and Christopher Gist were the instigators of these events, and it is with them that the story should begin.

Thomas Cresap arrived in Maryland in 1718, at the age of fifteen. First settling near today's Havre de Grace, he heard opportunity knock in the ongoing border dispute with Pennsylvania. Cresap obtained a dirt-cheap five-hundred-acre Maryland land grant in a contested zone where the Calverts were looking for settlers to help bolster their claims. It was on the western bank of the Susquehanna, at today's Wrightsville, across the river from present-day Columbia, Pennsylvania, west of Lancaster.

From the start, Cresap was at odds with the Pennsylvanians, particularly when he started operating a ferry across the Susquehanna and helping indentured servants run away from their Pennsylvania masters on the eastern bank. Hot-tempered and hard-muscled, Cresap liked tests of strength, and, in the words of a contemporary, "preferred the cudgel to the olive-branch." He made a number of enemies, and was in and out of court—for calling a man a thief and a rogue; for buying a stray horse and rebranding it; for assaulting the owner of the horse when he came to claim it; for beating and wounding an Indian woman who had taken an apple from his orchard.

On October 31, 1730, Cresap heard three rifle shots on the other side of the river, the signal that someone wanted to cross. He rowed over with his assistant, Samuel Chance, one of the servants he had helped escape. They picked up two men on the eastern shore, Edward Beddock and Rice Morgan. After they had rowed about seventy yards with their backs to the men, one said in an angry tone, "Damn you, Cresap, turn to shore or you are a dead man."

Morgan then threw Samuel Chance overboard and knocked Cresap down. Cresap grabbed an oar and poked Morgan with it, throwing him off balance, but the two men overpowered him and threw him overboard too. He hung on to the side of the boat as they banged on his hands to pry them loose. "Do you intend to murder me?" he asked, and they said they did. By then, the boat had been carried by the current to shallow water. Cresap felt rocks under his feet and, while his boat was carried downstream on the current, waded to an island, where a friendly Indian helped him get home. The incident seems to have been an attempt, by a competing ferry several miles up the Susquehanna or by the Pennsylvania authorities, to get rid of a troublesome borderer.

The Pennsylvanians were determined to oust Cresap, the northernmost of the Maryland claimants, from his land, and he was equally determined to resist them. In 1733, a group of vigilantes surrounded his house and ordered him to come out. When he refused, they forced his front door off its hinges. Cresap was waiting for them with a rifle. He killed Knoles Daunt, the first man to cross his threshold, which gave the sheriff of Lancaster, Samuel Smith, cause to arrest him, though he didn't set out to do it until 1736. By that time, Cresap had fortified his house and hired six men to help him defend it.

On November 24, 1736, Sheriff Smith and twenty-three men surrounded his house and told him to come out. Cresap called them "damned Scotch-Irish sons of bitches" and "damned quirking dogs and rogues." Smith offered immunity to any of Cresap's men who surrendered. One of the six made his way up the chimney. Cresap opened fire, and the sheriff set fire to his house.

Cresap was captured and brought in irons to Philadelphia. "Damn it," he cried, "this is one of the prettiest towns in Maryland!" He was kept in jail until May 1738, when there was an order from the king in council that each province should release the prisoners they had taken from the other. Now Cresap decided to put some distance between himself and lawmakers. He obtained a grant on the Potomac and moved to an ancient Indian crossroads and rendezvous, which he called Oldtown.

In 1747, fifteen-year-old George Washington visited Cresap on his surveying rounds, after taking what he called "the worst road that ever was trod on by man or beast." He stayed five days, during which he saw an Indian dance and observed, "The best dancer jumps up as though awakened out of a sleep and jumps about ye ring in a most comical manner."

There were always Indians at Oldtown, but they didn't trust Cresap, who was known as a person "of hot resentment and great acrimony." Whenever he felt wronged, his first reaction was to reach for his gun. In 1749, he complained to the governor of Maryland, Samuel Ogle, that some of the Indians were "very insolent and saucy." The more he gave them, the more they wanted. When he fed them, they demanded a cow. When he refused the cow, they killed some of his hogs.

Three years after Cresap's release from prison in 1738, a twenty-one-year-old Dubliner named George Croghan left Ireland during one of the potato famines and came to Pennsylvania. He settled across the Susquehanna from Harris' Ferry, near today's Carlisle. Croghan set up as an Indian trader, sending his pack trains along the rivers toward the Alleghenies. He had a tannery to process deer hides and a store that sold goods to the Indians, and by 1744 he was on Lake Erie, trading with the Senecas at the site of today's Cleveland. Croghan had his faults—he was slow to pay debts and vague about keeping promises—but if you needed someone to negotiate with the Indians or carry out any frontier assignment he was your man. He got along with the red man, and as a result he became an Indian agent for both Virginia and Pennsylvania.

At this time, the English and the French were competing for the allegiance of the tribes south of Lakes Erie and Ontario. In 1747, some Lake Erie Indians sent a belt of wampum and a French scalp to Philadelphia via Croghan as a sign that they would not be averse to an English alliance. Croghan became the architect of the diplomatic shift.

In 1748, the Pennsylvania Assembly voted to send a present of two hundred pounds' worth of goods to these Indians. Commissioned to deliver it to them, Croghan sent the Assembly a hefty bill covering wampum, tobacco, rum, transportation, and wages for his men. Around the same time, in June 1748, the Six Nations came to Lancaster and signed a treaty of friendship. The interpreter on that occasion was Conrad Weiser, another frontier diplomat.

Born in Württemberg, Germany, in 1696, Weiser had come to America with his father in 1710. They were part of a group of palatines who rented land on the vast Livingston estate on the Hudson. In 1714, they moved to Schoharie, forty miles west of Albany, in Mohawk country, where Conrad learned Indian ways. In 1729, he moved to Lancaster with his wife and five children, and established himself as an Indian expert.

So, in August 1748, Weiser was sent with Croghan to deliver the present to the large Indian village and trading center of Logstown, situated on the Ohio River, about eighteen miles above today's Pittsburgh.

They reached the Ohio on August 25, and came to the site of Pittsburgh, then an Indian village called Shanopin's Town, on the 26th. The next day, they arrived at Logstown, where there were reciprocal gun salutes. About twenty English traders were present, and the mood was festive. There was a lot of ceremonial firing and drinking. Weiser raised the Union Jack on a long pole, and they all drank to the king's health.

Familiar with Indian ways, Weiser met with each tribe separately. The Wyandots, settled around Detroit, said they had fallen away from the French because of hard usage: the French took their young men like slaves to make war. Weiser gave them some tobacco and whiskey.

Then he met with the friendly Senecas, who said that some of their warriors had been taken captive in Carolina. Weiser said he would see what he could do about getting the warriors released. Another Seneca complaint was that the traders were bringing too much rum into their towns. "It appears you love it so well that you cannot be without it," Weiser replied. He felt that rum was an Indian problem. On September 19, he left, having reached a better level of understanding with a number of tribes.

All this activity among the tribes was viewed with alarm by the French. The English traders had extended their routes across Pennsylvania and into western Ohio, as far as the trading post of Pickawillany, at today's Piqua, Ohio (the underwear capital of America), 120 miles south of Toledo. They had spread all over lands claimed by France. Complaints from the governor of New France to the governors of the various colonies were useless. The marquis de la Galissonière, who became governor in 1747, wrote home urging a bold advance into the Ohio Valley to consolidate French holdings and win over the Indians. The idea was to keep the English traders east of the Alleghenies. In June 1749, to implement this policy, a French military expedition of more than two hundred men started down the St. Lawrence under the command of Captain Pierre-Jacques de Céloron de Blainville. Their method was to find a series of linked waterways and portages from Lake Erie to the Ohio River. At today's Barcelona (on the southern shore of Lake Erie, about eighty miles west of Buffalo), they portaged to Lake Chautauqua. "This road is very difficult," Céloron wrote in his journal.

It took them three days to cover twelve miles, carrying canoes, supplies, weapons, and merchandise for gifts over rocky, hilly ground that had to be cleared before it could be walked. By July

29, they had reached the Allegheny, after burying a lead plate as a mark of possession. On the 30th, they reached the Indian village of Paille Coupée (Cut Straw). Céloron gave the locals a *coup de lait* (shot of milk—i.e., brandy) and read a message from the marquis de la Galissonière. "This land," he wrote, "belongs to me and the English cannot come here without being chased away." Céloron was shocked to see a cabin for the use of English traders. The Indians promised that the house would serve "only to amuse our youth."

The Indians asked Céloron for permission to keep the English gunsmith who came regularly to prepare their rifles for hunts. "If thou makest the English retire . . . ," they said, "we would be without help and exposed to die of hunger. . . . Have pity on us."

Continuing down the Allegheny, Céloron came to Venango, at its juncture with French Creek, at today's Franklin. Here, he had been told, were an English merchant and another gunsmith, but they had fled. He traveled on down the river like a circuit-riding evangelist, spreading the gospel of friendship with the French. On August 6, he came upon a village where six English traders had stopped with their fifty horses and nearly 150 packs of peltry. They said they were on their way to Philadelphia. Céloron told them that he would treat them with humanity this time. But if he ever saw them again, he warned, he would seize their goods.

On August 7, he came to Queen Alliquippa's village, the site of Pittsburgh. "She is entirely devoted to the English," he wrote of the queen. Six English traders were there, "who came before me trembling." They said they were only trying to make a living.

Céloron continued on to Logstown. Word of the French expedition had evidently preceded him, for the villagers, hedging their bets, flew one English and three French flags. "This mixture of flags is not seemly," Céloron told them. They said the English flag "was only placed for show, and to divert the young men." He told them to lower it or he would pull it down himself. The Indians assured him that "our heart is entirely French." Céloron had his doubts.

Céloron continued down the river, across southern Ohio and what today is Indiana, to a point west of Evansville, where the Wabash runs into the Ohio. He buried lead plates, gave speeches, and distributed presents. It was a good-will tour: the idea was to win over the Indians, not start fights. By September 19, he was back at Niagara, heading for Quebec to report. He had the distinct impression that the French could not hold on to the area on the forks of the Ohio without establishing a military presence there.

Besides the French and the Pennsylvanians, there was a third party interested in the forks of the Ohio. In 1747, a group of prominent Virginians, including the Fairfaxes, Lees, and Washingtons, had formed the Ohio Company and petitioned the crown for five hundred thousand acres in what is today western Pennsylvania. In 1749, Governor William Gooch was directed to make an initial grant of two hundred thousand acres, and the company built a storehouse at Will's Creek, Maryland (today's Cumberland). They asked Thomas Cresap, who lived nearby, to open a road to the Youghiogheny River, about thirty-five miles to the west.

In 1750, the Ohio Company asked the frontiersman Christopher Gist, who lived on a farm on the Yadkin River in North Carolina, to do a little exploring and reconnoitering on the lands they had been granted. So little was known about the area that his instructions were to "go out westward of the great mountains . . . and look for good level land." He set out on October 31 from his friend Cresap's place at Oldtown, but by the time he got to Shanopin's Town (Pittsburgh) in November, he had the fever. He sweated himself in the Indian manner until it abated.

On November 17, Gist reached Logstown and learned that he had just missed Croghan, who had been there trading the week before. The news was that the Ottawas were no longer safe to trade with. The Logstown Indians asked him what he was doing there, since he had no trading goods. When he gave evasive answers, they began to suspect him of coming to scout their land, and it was suggested that he might not get home safely. Gist said he was carrying a message from the king, which "obtained for me quiet and respect. . . . Otherwise I doubt not they would have contrived some evil against me."

By December 14, Gist had arrived at a Wyandot village of a hundred families at the juncture of the Muskingum and the Tuscarawas, where Coshocton, Ohio, now stands. He was told that the French had lately been there and had captured four English traders—making good on Céloron's earlier threat. The English colors were hoisted, in spite of the French attack, and Gist stayed for a while in the village, where Croghan arrived on January 14, 1751. After he gave the Wyandots four chains of wampum, he and Gist proceeded to the juncture of the Scioto and Ohio rivers, at today's Portsmouth, Ohio.

Croghan told the Indians in council that the French had placed a price on his head, if alive; on his scalp, if dead. In each village, Gist and Croghan did the same kind of missionary work Céloron had done, asking the tribes to be their allies against the French.

On March 3, 1751, Croghan went his own way to Logstown, to give the Indians a present. He was there on May 21, 1751, for the arrival of the French frontiersman Philippe Joncaire, who lived among the Senecas at Niagara and picked up money portaging goods around the falls.

When Joncaire told the Indians in council to turn away from the English, a chief of the Six Nations rose and said: "You are always threatening our brothers what you will do to them and in particular to that man," pointing to Croghan. "Now if you have anything to say to our brother tell it to him, if you be a man as you Frenchmen always say you are. . . . Our brothers are the people we will trade with and not you."

In spite of this rebuff, Joncaire stayed on good terms with Croghan, and asked him not to think too badly of his speeches, for he was under orders from the governor of New France. Even though he knew that the Indians of the Six Nations would not side with the French, he still had to try.

Joncaire was getting the worst of it. One of the Six Nations chiefs, stamping the ground with his foot and shaking his finger under Joncaire's nose, said: "Is this not our land?" Then the chief told Croghan that it was their custom to have their guns, kettles, and hatchets mended when they went to council, and Croghan promised to see to it. This meant that he had a treaty of alliance with the Logstown Indians.

A year later, in June 1752, Croghan and Gist took some Virginia commissioners to Logstown to negotiate with the Iroquois, Delaware, Shawnee, Wyandot, and Miami tribes. The Virginians were given permission to settle in the area south of the forks of the Ohio. They were allowed to build two trading houses on the river, one at the site of today's Pittsburgh and the other at Redstone Old Fort, about twenty miles south of Pittsburgh on the Monongahela, at today's Brownsville. By this time, Croghan's trading business had gone broke. He was always gambling, always in debt, always promising, "I won't owe a groat by Christmas." He vanished into Indian territory to avoid his creditors.

Around the time of the Treaty of Logstown, the French launched another military effort to contain the English. Pickawillany was a particular annoyance, because it was so far west. There were sometimes as many as fifty English traders there, guests of the Twightwees and their chief, who was so pro-English he was known as "Old Britain."

On June 21, 1750, a force of 240 Frenchmen and Indians marched from Detroit under the command of Charles de Langlade. They surprised the Pickawillany residents, killing one trader and taking five prisoners. The traders' storehouses were destroyed, and fifteen Indians were killed—including "Old Britain," who was boiled and eaten by the pro-French Indians.

The new governor of Canada, the Marquis Duquesne, reported to Versailles: "I trust that this blow, added to the complete pillage suffered by the English on this occasion, will discourage them from trading on our lands."

He was right. The French attack ended English influence in "Pick's Town," which had been known far and wide as "the village where George Croghan trades." Croghan returned to his plantation at Pine's Creek, four miles above the forks of the Ohio.

By this time, there was a new governor of Virginia: Robert Dinwiddie, who supported western expansion and was an investor in the Ohio Company. In December 1752, Dinwiddie heard that a large party of French had landed on the southern bank of Lake Erie and had begun to build a string of forts there. He wrote the Board of Trade that the forts "will, in time, much annoy our back country."

A thousand men, under the command of Captain Pierre-Paul Marin, had taken Céloron's route from Lake Ontario to the southern shore of Lake Erie. Marin continued down the lakeshore until he reached a peninsula with a good natural harbor, today's Erie, Pennsylvania—Presqu'Ile to the French. From Erie, there was a ten-mile portage to French Creek, which ran into the Allegheny, with its linkage to the Ohio and the Mississippi. Here, south of Lake Erie, the French started building a chain of forts that would serve as their boundary with the English. One fort was located on the lake at Presqu'Ile. Another, Fort LeBoeuf, lay twenty miles down, where the portage reached French Creek. A third, Fort Venango, was situated about forty miles farther down French Creek, where it ran into the Allegheny. Impressed by this show of force, the Twightwees shifted their allegiance to the French, and the English traders had to pull back.

An English response was in order, but the Pennsylvania Assembly would not vote funds for the construction of a fort, so it was left to the Virginians. Motivated by both his patriotic zeal and his shares in the Ohio Company, Governor Dinwiddie resolved to send an emissary to confer with the French. He first sent William Trent, Croghan's partner and brother-in-law, who turned tail the minute he saw a French flag.

Dinwiddie then decided to send a young but energetic adjutant who had some backcountry experience as a surveyor for Lord Fairfax. On October 31, 1753, twenty-one-year-old George Washington was promoted to major and given orders to go to the forks of the Ohio, present a letter to the French officer in charge, ask for a reply, and gather intelligence. He left Williamsburg that day for Fredericksburg, where he picked up a French-speaking Dutchman, Jacob Van Braam, as interpreter. They went north to Alexandria for supplies, and west to Winchester for baggages and horses. They then continued westward to Will's Creek (Cumberland, Maryland), where their guide, Christopher Gist, was waiting.

It was a bad time of the year to be traveling. The valleys were flooded, and the hills were already covered with snow. On November 14, the day Washington arrived at Will's Creek, the soldiers were restricted to quarters. Gist—a veteran frontiersman, survivor of many wilderness trips—thought the young man would require a lot of coddling.

Gist led the way across territory he knew well. They traveled due west to the forks of the Youghiogheny, then bore northwest toward the Monongahela. Because of the weather, it took them from the 15th to the 22nd to reach John Frazier's place at the mouth of Turtle Creek and the Monongahela. Having been ousted from his trading post at Venango, Frazier had relocated. Gist borrowed a canoe from him, for the rivers were impassable.

On November 23, they paddled across the Monongahela, swimming their horses over. Next they headed north to Logstown, where Gist found his old friend the Indian chief Half-King (so known because of his subordination to the Iroquois). When Gist told Half-King that they were headed for Venango, the Indian asked to come along; he wanted to return the wampum the French had given him. Gist knew that this represented the breaking of ties. The Half-King said he had already been to Venango and had told the French to get out, but that the French commander had rebuffed him, saying: "I am not afraid of flies or mosquitos, for Indians are

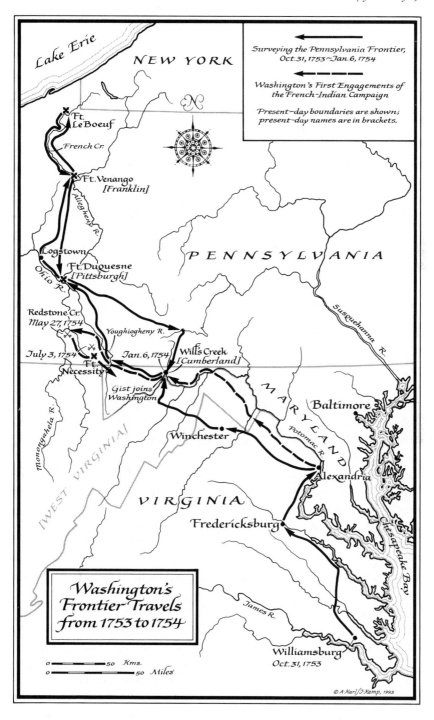

Lake Erie

NEW YORK

Surveying the Pennsylvania Frontier,
Oct. 31, 1753 ~ Jan. 6, 1754

Washington's First Engagements of
the French-Indian Campaign

Present-day boundaries are shown;
present-day names are in brackets.

✗ Ft.
LeBoeuf

French Cr.

N

Ft. Venango
[Franklin]

Allegheny R.

Logstown

Ft. Duquesne
[Pittsburgh]

Ohio R.

PENNSYLVANIA

Susquehanna R.

Redstone Cr.
May 27, 1754

Youghiogheny R.

July 3, 1754

Jan. 6, 1754

Wills Creek
[Cumberland]

Ft.
Necessity

Gist joins
Washington

MARYLAND

Baltimore

Monongahela R.

[WEST VIRGINIA]

Winchester

Potomac R.

Alexandria

VIRGINIA

Fredericksburg

Chesapeake Bay

James R.

Washington's
Frontier Travels
from 1753 to 1754

0 ____ 50 Kms.
0 ____ 50 Miles

Williamsburg
Oct. 31, 1753

© A. Karl/J. Kemp, 1993

such as those. . . . My force is as the sand upon the sea shore. . . . Child, you talk foolish; you say this land belongs to you, but there is not the back of my nail that is yours. . . . It is my land, and I will have it."

On November 30, 1753, Gist and Washington left Logstown with Half-King and three other chiefs. Venango was about sixty miles to the north. They reached it on December 4 and saw the French colors hoisted. Who should be in command of the small fort but Daniel Joncaire, brother of Philippe, who in 1751 had been at Logstown with Croghan to try to win over the Indians.

Daniel Joncaire was as welcoming to Gist and Washington as Philippe had been to Croghan. He invited them to dinner. "The wine," Washington recorded in his journal, "as they dosed themselves pretty plentifully with it, soon banished the restraint which at first appeared in their conversation and gave a license to their tongues to reveal their sentiment more freely." Joncaire said it was their plan to take possession of the Ohio and by God they would do it. They had a right to the river, because of the discoveries made by La Salle, and they already had a fort on Lake Erie and another on French Creek. They knew the English could raise twice as many men but felt confident that their rivals had lost the initiative.

The next day, December 5, Joncaire called in the Indians and asked them why they had not come to visit, since they were so close by. He offered presents, and plied them with brandy until the Indians were too drunk to leave. Washington and Gist had to stay an extra day, leaving on December 7 for Fort LeBoeuf. It was forty miles north from Venango to LeBoeuf, but the weather was so bad, and the creeks so difficult to cross, that it took them five days to get there. Washington presented his letter from Dinwiddie to the French commander, Legardeur de Saint-Pierre, whom he described as "an elderly gentleman, [who] had much the air of a soldier."

While the French drafted their reply to the letter, Washington took a look around, and saw that the rectangular fort on the western fork of French Creek had twelve-foot-high bastions, sharpened at the top, with eight six-pound pieces in each bastion. There were about a hundred men in the fort, and 120 canoes.

On the 14th, the reply was ready, and the French helped to load Washington's canoes with food and brandy. Washington realized, however, that they were trying to draw Half-King and the other Indians away, "to prevent their going after our departure.

. . . I cannot say that ever in my life I suffered so much anxiety as I did in this affair." Washington complained to the French commander, for the Indians were part of his company. Legardeur replied that he didn't know why they were staying, but Washington soon learned they had been promised guns. On the 16th, the guns were handed over, and the French also tried "the power of liquor," but Washington was insistent that Half-King keep his word, and they all left as planned.

The journey down French Creek was perilous. They just missed being dashed against the rocks, and had repeatedly to get out and wade in the freezing water to get over the shoals. At one place, the river was frozen and they had to portage a quarter-mile in the December cold. Their wet clothes turned to ice on their bodies. One of their canoes capsized, and they saw several brandy kegs go bobbing down the river. They didn't reach Venango until December 22; here they found their horses, which they had sent ahead.

The next day, Half-King said he could not go on: he had to attend Chief White Thunder, who was sick. Washington worried that Joncaire would keep the Indians in Venango and set them against the English, and warned Half-King to guard himself against French flattery. The Indian said not to worry—he knew the French too well.

Now their horses were so feeble that they couldn't be ridden. Eager to get his report to Dinwiddie, Washington left the horses and servants behind, and headed out on foot with Gist. Both men wore Indian dress—hip-length skin leggings and knee-length coats of matched skins, belted at the waist. They carried packs on their backs and guns in hand as they crossed trails covered with snow or ice. On December 26, some pro-French Indians lying in ambush fired at them from a distance of fifteen feet, and missed. That night, they slept in an Indian hut. Washington was near exhaustion. All the small runs were frozen, making it hard to collect drinking water.

On the 27th, the two got to Beaver Creek, a few miles above Logstown, and ran into an Indian who called Gist by his Indian name. Gist asked him to show them the shortest way. The Indian seemed willing and took Major Washington's pack. They walked for about eight miles, until Washington wanted to stop and camp for the night. Gist would have kept going, but he was held back by the greenhorn.

The Indian asked Gist if he could carry his gun, although he had a rifle of his own. When Gist refused, the Indian grew sullen. He said he would go his own way, warning that there were Ottawa Indians in the woods who would scalp them if they stopped.

"I thought very ill of the fellow," Gist wrote in his journal, "but did not care to let the Major know I mistrusted him."

As they walked on, Gist suspected that the Indian was taking them in the wrong direction. The Indian insisted, however, that he was within two whoops of his own cabin. Then Major Washington said they should stop at the next water. When they came to a snow-covered meadow, the Indian wheeled around and fired his rifle at them. "Are you shot?" the astonished Washington asked Gist. He replied that he wasn't. The Indian hid behind a big white oak, but they grabbed him before he could reload.

"I would have killed him," Gist wrote, "but the Major would not suffer me to kill him."

Pretending that he and Washington intended to sleep there, Gist asked the Indian to make a fire by a little stream. Washington didn't realize that the Indian, having been allowed to go free, would now hold them in contempt and try to kill them in their sleep. Gist explained: "As you will not have him killed, we must get him away, and then we must travel all night."

He then told the Indian, "I suppose you were lost, and fired your gun." The Indian said he was not far from his cabin. "Well," Gist said, "do you go home; and as we are much tired, we will follow your track in the morning; and here is a cake of bread for you, and you must give us meat in the morning." When the Indian started off, Gist followed him until he was out of earshot. Then he and Washington walked about a half-mile in the other direction, made a fire, set their compass, fixed their course, and traveled all night. The next morning, December 28, they landed a couple of miles above Shanopin's (Pittsburgh) and continued eastward until they reached the Allegheny.

There was no way to cross except on a raft, but making one with only a hatchet in the freezing cold was a full day's work, and they didn't get it launched until sunset on the 29th. Gist's fingers were frostbitten from lashing the logs together. They had poles to steer them across the swift-running river, but before they were halfway across, Washington wrote in his journal, "we were jammed in the ice, in such a manner that we expected at every moment our raft to sink and ourselves to perish."

Losing his balance, Washington fell into the ice-packed Allegheny, but saved himself by catching hold of the edge of the raft. They tried again to pole to the other shore, but could not, and were forced to abandon the raft and clamber to a small island (today called Herr's Island).

For the young officer, it was a rehearsal of hardships to come. They spent a sleepless, freezing night, wondering how they could cross with their raft gone. "But the cold did us some service," Gist wrote, "for in the morning it was frozen hard enough for us to pass over on the ice." The worst was over, and they were back at Will's Creek on January 6, 1754.

Washington was in Williamsburg with his report on January 16. It had been, he concluded, "a most fatiguing journey," with nothing but cold, wet weather, and only one day when it did not rain or snow incessantly. Without Gist to guide him and make the right decisions, the twenty-one-year-old major's life might well have been cut short. As it happened, it was Gist who did not have long to live: he died of smallpox in 1759, and was given a footnote in history, for twice having saved a great man's life.

In January 1754, Dinwiddie ordered William Trent to build a fort at the forks of the Monongahela and the Ohio, on the site of today's Pittsburgh, about sixty miles from the nearest French fort at Venango. Trent got there on February 17 with forty men and went to work, but early in April he went off again to fetch more men and supplies. He left the fort in command of Ensign Edward Ward, who happened to be George Croghan's half-brother.

Meanwhile, upon Major Washington's return, the Virginia Assembly voted ten thousand pounds to form a regiment, to be commanded by Colonel Joshua Fry, Dinwiddie's old friend and a professor at William and Mary. Washington, who had turned twenty-two in February, was commissioned a lieutenant-colonel on March 31 and made second in command. His orders were to proceed with a detachment to the forks of the Ohio and reinforce the unit that was building the fort. Fry would follow and build a second fort at Redstone Creek (today's Brownsville).

Washington set out on April 2, 1754, from Alexandria with 165 men and two wagons, reaching Thomas Cresap's Oldtown on April 20 and Will's Creek on April 23. Cresap, in the meantime, had blazed a sixty-mile trail with the Indian Nemacolin, from Will's Creek to Redstone Creek.

On the forks of the Ohio, Ensign Ward and his men were

building their humble but grandly named Fort Prince George when, on April 17, they saw a large French force in sixty bateaux and three hundred canoes full of painted Indians moving toward them on the three-hundred-yard-wide Allegheny. The two groups landed near the uncompleted fort, marching in step until they were a gunshot away. Captain de Contrecoeur, the French commander, sent an officer to the fort with an interpreter called Mingoes the Owl and two drums. The officer told Ensign Ward that he had an hour to surrender, and must come to the French camp with his answer in writing. Ward then spent a half-hour in council with Half-King, who had left Venango and sided with the English. Half-King advised him to tell the French that he was but a lowly ensign, unfit to make such an important decision, and they must wait until a higher-ranking officer arrived.

When Ward went to the French camp to try to buy time, Captain de Contrecoeur said that he must give his reply at once or the fort would be taken by force. Looking around, Ward estimated the number of French and Indians to be roughly one thousand. Since he had only thirty-three men, he surrendered. A few days later, Ward arrived at Will's Creek, where he gave Lieutenant Colonel Washington a belt of wampum from Half-King and reported that the fort he was to have reinforced had fallen and was now in the hands of a French force far superior to his own. They had renamed it Fort Duquesne.

What should Washington do, now that he was unable to carry out his orders? He decided to march into Pennsylvania on the trail blazed by Cresap and start building a fort at Redstone Creek, forty miles from the French. On May 24, he crossed the Youghiogheny and reached Great Meadows, about ten miles southeast of today's Uniontown. His were the first wheeled vehicles and artillery to cross the Alleghenies. That day, he received a message from Half-King that a detachment of French were on the march and "are resolved to strike the first English they see."

On May 23, Joseph Coulon de Villiers, sieur de Jumonville, had left Fort Duquesne with thirty men, carrying orders to seek out the English and give them a summons if they were found "on the lands of the [French] king." So here were a French and a British detachment heading for exactly the same spot. Jumonville followed the Monongahela, which the French called the "Mal-Engueulée," to the north of Redstone Creek, forty miles away. Washington too was heading for Redstone Creek.

Christopher Gist joined Washington on May 27. Another message arrived from Half-King: "they had seen along the road the tracks of two men which went down into a gloomy hollow, and . . . he imagined that the whole party was hidden there." Washington had several reasons to be suspicious: Had not the French themselves, their tongues loosened by wine, told him five months before at Venango that they intended to take the Ohio, whatever the cost? Then there was the message from Half-King that the French were "resolved to strike the first English they see." If their intentions were peaceful, why were they taking such precautions to camp in an out-of-the-way, hidden glen? Washington resolved to go after the French before they came after him, since his orders said that he should meet force with force.

That night, he took forty of his men along a narrow trail, in rain that fell in such sheets they had trouble keeping their powder dry. They "frequently tumbled one over the other," Washington wrote Dinwiddie, "and were so often lost that a 15 or 20-minute search would not find the path again." But the Indian guides picked up the French tracks, and on May 28, at sunrise, they reached the Indian camp where Half-King was waiting.

After holding council with Half-King, Washington decided to confront the French. Half-King led them to the French camp. Here is where accounts begin to differ. The French insisted that Jumonville, upon seeing the British, waved his arm to indicate that he had a letter to convey, and was stopped by a rifle shot in the head. The French officer Drouillon, who was taken prisoner, wrote Governor Dinwiddie that, when Washington and his men attacked, "neither we nor our own men took to arms. . . ." Washington, leading his men in single file toward the French, later wrote Dinwiddie: "I was the first man who approached them, and the first whom they saw, and immediately upon it [they] ran to their arms and fired briskly till they were defeated."

In the ensuing battle, Washington had one man killed and three wounded, while the French had ten killed and one wounded. The French powder was dry, protected by the bark huts they slept in, but the British powder was damp from the night's rain. It is possible, as Washington said, that the French opened fire, causing the English casualties, and then the British shot or bayoneted the French at close range. The English deserter Denis Kaninguen told the French that Half-King hovered over the fallen Jumonville and said, "You are not dead yet, my father," striking him in the head with his hatchet. Despite his dislike of the procedure, Washington had to stand by and watch his Indian allies scalp the French dead.

The French version was that a peaceful mission, with orders to treat the British courteously, had been bushwhacked. Captain de Contrecoeur wrote Governor Duquesne: "I think, sir, that you will be surprised at the shameful way the English are acting; this is something which has never been known, even among the most uncivilized nations, striking at ambassadors by assassination."

It was Washington's first taste of battle, and he wrote his brother that "I have heard the bullets whistle, and believe me, there is something charming in the sound." Upon which George II, who had been at Dettingen, is said to have observed: "He would not say so if he had been used to hear many."

Sir William Johnson, the highly respected superintendent for Indian affairs, felt that Washington had acted rashly. "I wish Washington had acted with the prudence and circumspection requisite in an officer of his rank," he wrote. "He should have avoided an engagement until our troops were all assembled. . . . I can without much of a prophetic spirit foresee the ruin of this country very shortly without the immediate interposition of His Majesty and Parliament."

Johnson was right in thinking that this would not be an isolated incident; in fact, it was the opening of the French and Indian War. Retribution was not long in coming. In June 1754, Washington started building the fort he called Necessity, in a waterlogged creek bottom with the woods on three sides and a bare hill on the fourth. Reconstructed on its exact site on the basis of digs, Fort Necessity stands today between Farmington and Chalkhill. This so-called fort was nothing but some logs carved to points and stuck in the ground side by side. Instead of placing his fort on the hill, Washington had chosen a clearing surrounded by woods, showing no understanding of position or strategy.

On June 6, Washington heard from Gist that Joshua Fry was dead in a fall from his horse, and that he was now in command. Reinforcements arrived, until he had a total of 293 officers and men, plus nine swivel guns, but on July 3, a French force twice the size attacked Fort Necessity, led by Louis Coulon de Villiers, who had arrived from Montreal to avenge his brother, Jumonville. After a nine-hour battle in the rain, the French, firing from forest cover, killed thirty of Washington's men, and he surrendered at midnight. His disarmed men were allowed to march back to Virginia with their flags flying, but he had to promise that Virginia would not build another fort on the Ohio for a year, and to turn over two officers as hostages in exchange for the twenty-one prisoners he had taken in the attack on Jumonville.

The worst humiliation for Washington, however, was having to sign a capitulation agreeing to the immediate return of the French prisoners taken "when he assassinated sieur de Jumonville." He later said he didn't understand what he was signing. Washington had not personally killed Jumonville: the French officer was killed by Half-King. Governor Duquesne, however, wrote: "Washington was stupid enough to admit it in his capitulation."

Whatever Washington's distress at being designated a war criminal, it was peripheral to what was now a full-fledged war between France and England in North America. This time, the frontier had dragged the hinterland into war, for the Fort Necessity defeat led the English crown to send General Edward Braddock with instructions to drive the French out of the Ohio.

With Washington's defeat, British power at the forks of the Ohio collapsed, and George Croghan pulled back to Aughwick Creek, forty miles west of Carlisle. Conrad Weiser came to visit in September 1754 and saw two hundred Indians there, still loyal to the British in spite of French successes. Croghan was keeping them happy at his own expense, and had planted twenty-five acres of corn for them. Around this time, Half-King, their old ally, died of alcoholism, convinced that the French had put a curse on him for scalping Jumonville.

Indians drifted in from the French zone, bringing news of Fort Duquesne, which Croghan passed on to Philadelphia. He complained to Weiser that Pennsylvania was doing nothing to defend its western lands, and that its "slow moshuns" would result in the desertion of the Indians. He did what he could to keep them happy, with a keg of rum once a month for a frolic, and believed that he had rallied the only bunch who were fit to fight the French. "If the French build more forts," he told Weiser, "I don't know what will become of the back parts of Cumberland county."

As if in answer to Croghan's prayers, the man the county was named for, the duke of Cumberland, son of George II, convinced his father to send troops to America. General Braddock, a short and stout sixty-year-old veteran of forty years in the army, was appointed commander of British forces in America, and arrived at Williamsburg with two regiments on February 23, 1755. He marched his men to Will's Creek, that old staging ground, where Fort Cumberland had been built for his operations; a seventeen-gun salute of four-pounders announced his arrival on May 10. There his thousand redcoats were joined by George Washington and eight hundred colonial militia, as well as by Croghan and about a hundred braves from Aughwick, who brought their wives and children.

Soon the fur-and-feather-clad warriors were dancing in the moonlight, while the squaws fraternized with the regulars, proudly turning over the proceeds of their amours to their husbands. Richard Peters, secretary to the Council in Pennsylvania, said, "Their squaws [were] bringing them money in plenty, which they got from the officers, who were scandalously fond of them." This was bad for discipline, and Braddock ordered the women and children sent home. When they left, the men left with them, except for eight who remained as scouts.

Braddock's objective was Fort Duquesne, the French fort on the Ohio, about 110 miles from Will's Creek. He was glad to see Washington, who had actually been to the forks of the Ohio, and who knew how to draw a map. Braddock also met Thomas Cresap and enlisted him as a supplier, until he decided that he had been "deceived and met with nothing but lies and villainy" from the man. Among Braddock's officers, Cresap was known as "the rattle-snake colonel."

The two-thousand-man army got going on June 7, 1755, along the path blazed by Cresap and Chief Nemacolin. Among the recruits, besides Washington and Croghan, was a twenty-one-year-old wagon driver in the North Carolina company named Daniel Boone.

By June 16, they had reached Little Meadows, at today's Grantsville, Maryland. In ten days, they had advanced about twenty-three miles. Braddock had three hundred axmen widening the trail so that it could accommodate artillery and supply wagons. His army on the march formed a line four miles long, hauling cannons and tons of supplies.

Washington, who recorded that Braddock "halted to level every mole-hill and to erect bridges over every brook, by which means we were four days in getting twelve miles," suggested they might push on more rapidly with a flying column of twelve hundred men and a minimum of artillery. Braddock agreed, despite his barely veiled contempt for colonials. These so-called

Americans, he thought, who had sold him lame horses and rotten meat, were worse than useless. On July 3, Christopher Gist went on a reconnaissance and said the way was clear. His scouts had approached to within a half-mile of Fort Duquesne and scalped a French officer.

On July 9, 1755, after cutting one hundred miles of road, this force of light infantry crossed the shallow Monongahela twice, on the outskirts of today's Pittsburgh, in the Turtle Creek Valley. Braddock ordered his men to march as if on dress parade, in colorful uniforms and with flags flying, drums beating, and music playing. They were ambushed a quarter-mile farther on, by a band of two hundred French and four hundred Indians led by Daniel Beaujeu, who was killed early in the battle and replaced by Lieutenant Dumas.

Croghan, who was at the front of the column, saw French officers signaling with their hats for their men to open fire. The French fired down on the British from a forested hill. Washington's Virginia troops took heavy losses as flanking scouts. Many were killed by friendly fire. Braddock insisted on massed men and orderly volleys, even though they could not see their assailants. He discovered that platoon firing was ineffective on a twelve-foot-wide trail in the middle of the woods. There was panic in the British ranks, which broke and fell back, creating an accordion effect, with the front lines pushing up against the advancing center. Dumas deployed his men "like ants around a caterpillar." Braddock was wounded and ordered a retreat. It became a rout.

Croghan saw the redcoats run, not one stopping to carry off their gravely wounded general, not even when Washington offered a fifty-guinea reward. He helped Washington lift Braddock into a wagon. The general tried to seize Croghan's pistols so that he could die in the field. He died on July 13, one of the 977 killed and wounded in his army, and was buried by the side of the road as Washington read the burial service. His dying words to Washington were: "We shall better know how to deal with them another time."

Croghan was appalled at the English tactics. "Many of our people fired 24 rounds and never saw the enemy," he said. He believed that, "had we had 50 Indians instead of eight, we might in a great measure have prevented the surprise." The Indian scout Scarouady said of Braddock: "He was a bad man. He looked upon us as dogs; and would never hear anything what was said to him.

. . . He never appeared pleased with us, and that was the reason that a great many of our warriors left him." William Johnson had warned Braddock that "a delicate conduct" was necessary with the Indians, but the warning had fallen on deaf ears.

CHAPTER SEVENTEEN

THE FRENCH DEPARTURE

After Braddock's defeat, the British brought in more regulars and in 1759 defeated the French decisively on the Plains of Abraham. France was evicted from North America. England won Canada, and Spain, as the result of a secret treaty with France, acquired the Louisiana Territory. But no sooner was the Seven Years' War over, in 1763, than Pontiac and his Indian warriors attacked British forts in Pennsylvania, Ohio, and Michigan and had to be turned back.

Heart of oak are our ships, heart of oak are our men:
We are always ready, steady! boys, steady!
We'll fight and we'll conquer again and again.

DAVID GARRICK

With Braddock's defeat came the dawn of skepticism concerning British military prowess. On the frontier, British prestige was completely eroded, and the settlers were tense. Some of them cut loopholes in the walls of their cabins, and some of them fled east. The western frontiers of Maryland and Pennsylvania became a no-man's-land where Indian marauders tied scalps to their wampum belts.

The atrocities began with Braddock's defeat, when pro-French Indians tied twelve redcoats to stakes and burned them alive, and continued until the French and Indian War ended in 1763. The smoke of burning plantations darkened the skies. German settlers were massacred at Penn's Creek, near the settled regions along the Susquehanna. Carlisle and Lancaster were in danger. "The roads are full of starved, indigent multitudes," Richard Peters wrote Thomas Penn on November 8, 1755. "Not one twentieth man has arms." Croghan remained at Aughwick in a stockade with forty men.

The maiming and eating of white prisoners was commonplace. A letter from Detroit dated July 9, 1763, was published in the Newport, Rhode Island, *Mercury*, reporting the boiling and eating of Sir Robert Davers. "And," the writer continued, "we are informed by Mr. Pauley, who escaped the other day, that he had seen an Indian with the skin of Captain Robertson's arm for a tobacco pouch." Captain Robertson's arm must have been distinctively tattooed to be so recognizable.

In August 1755, after Braddock's loss, which Samuel Eliot Morison termed "the Pearl Harbor of the Seven Years' War," the British brought in more regulars. But a plan by General William Shirley for an attack on Fort Niagara came to nothing. Instead, the French General Montcalm destroyed Fort Oswego, the British window on Lake Ontario, in August 1756. The following year, the English took another drubbing when Montcalm captured Fort William Henry, at the head of Lake George (Ticonderoga). The August 9 surrender led to a massacre by Montcalm's Indians, whom he could not restrain. Some said it was a stain on his blotter.

By 1756, the war had spread to the great European caldron, a stew of shifting alliances and conflicted monarchs—the Hapsburgs, the Hanovers, the Prussians, Louis XV of France, the Russians. There was much changing of sides, and many disputes within the coalition. England's fortunes improved when William Pitt the Elder became prime minister in 1757. His strategy was to let England's ally Prussia do the brunt of the fighting in Europe. This freed up men to fight the French in America. After Pitt doubled the number of regulars, the stage was set for a British victory. There was one more humiliating British defeat in 1758, when General James Abercromby attacked an entrenched French force at Ticonderoga over an open field. He lost two thousand men.

Then came a period of French reverses. Croghan and Weiser played roles here, serving as advisers to Pennsylvania Governor William Denny as he tried to regain the friendship of the Delaware tribes, who had sided with the French partly as a result of their outrage over the Walking Purchase. Between 1756 and 1758, there were four conferences with the Delawares. These led to the Treaty of Easton in October 1758, in which the Penn brothers gave up their claims to Pennsylvania lands west of the Alleghenies. The Delawares were led by Tedyuscung, one of the chiefs who had signed the Walking Purchase. He claimed to speak for all the tribes, which prompted Sir William Johnson to comment: "Indian manner of speaking is indeed somewhat figurative, but this is a rant beyond what I ever met with."

At first, Tedyuscung complained to the Pennsylvanians for taking lands without giving them so much as "broken pipes and such trifles." In July 1757, he insisted on having a clerk to record the minutes of the meeting. Governor Denny wondered if the Quakers had put him up to it. One day, the conference had to be put off because Tedyuscung was drunk.

At the July 6, 1758, conference in Easton, Tedyuscung agreed to bury the hatchet. Governor Denny displayed his negotiating skills, adopting Indian rhetoric. "Brothers, as you go through thick dark woods, where many bushes of prickly briars grow that may have hurt your legs, I will pull out the briars and anoint your legs with healing salve, Brothers, with this string [of wampum]."

Denny promised that a boundary would be fixed "in strong clear terms" indicating the return of lands to the Delawares. He also promised an inquiry into the Walking Purchase. Presents were handed out, and Tedyuscung said: "I will not sit as I have done with my pipe in my mouth and let the enemy Indians come and do mischief and strike on your frontiers."

The pacification of the Delawares and the Shawnees, a policy patiently pursued through the initiative of Croghan and Weiser, was the turning point in the wilderness war. In August 1758, Fort Frontenac, on the Canadian side of Lake Ontario, fell to Colonel John Bradstreet's expedition. Louisbourg, which had been re-turned to the French in 1748, fell to General Jeffrey Amherst, giving the British a strong position at the mouth of the St. Law-rence.

Now came the battle for the 987-mile-long Ohio River. The winner would hold the key to the American heartland. General John Forbes, who had learned the lesson of Braddock's defeat, wrote the Swiss-born officer Henri Bouquet: "I have been long of the opinion of equipping numbers of our men like savages. . . . In this country we must learn our art of war from the Indians." Want-ing to sidestep the ambush-prone road that Braddock had taken from Fort Cumberland, he suggested that the troops should start from Raystown (today's Bedford) and blaze a new road, 104 miles long, to the forks of the Ohio. They would build forts along the way to secure their advance.

Forbes had three times as many men as Braddock, nearly seven thousand, including one thousand wagoners and laborers. The provincials from Virginia, North Carolina, and Maryland were under the command of Washington. The Pennsylvanians at Bedford were under Bouquet. By September 17, when General Forbes finally got to Bedford, Bouquet was opening the road with twenty-five hundred workers; the road he cut is more or less today's Route 30. In the meantime, Colonel James Burd was sent to Loyalhanna Creek to build Fort Ligonier.

General Forbes reached Ligonier on November 2. He had the men practice Indian-style fighting, such as loading their muskets from behind a log, a daring departure from the British drill manuals. To withstand the increasing cold, they made overcoats from flannel blankets. Washington arrived on November 6, concerned that a winter attack was imprudent: if they took the French fort at Pittsburgh, they wouldn't have enough provisions to hold it. On November 11, all arguments against proceeding were mustered at a council of war. These included lack of clothing, scarce provisions, and the risk of defeat. Also, if they were beaten in the field, they would have to leave their artillery behind, because they couldn't haul it back across the mountains in the snow.

Nevertheless, they decided to go ahead. Croghan arrived with his Catawba Indians. On November 17, 1758, Washington arrived at Bushy Run—twelve miles away from Fort Duquesne, on a narrow neck of land at the confluence of the Allegheny and Monongahela rivers—"sadly puzzled for want of a guide." Bouquet was on the march with twenty-five hundred picked men and a light train of artillery. He made fifty miles in five days. On November 23, he too arrived at Bushy Run.

Bouquet halted and sent Indian scouts to survey the fort. When they reported that they had seen thick smoke billowing from its site, he sent a troop to put out the fire. It was too late. The outnumbered French had abandoned the fort and gone to Venango, leaving the forks of the Ohio to the British. The French chain between Canada and Louisiana was broken.

As the British marched to the fort on the morning of the 24th, it was still burning. The French had tried to destroy their Indian goods, but had left in such haste that piles of ammunition, gun barrels, and scalping knives remained. Some British prisoners held at the fort had been killed, and their bodies were strewn around the debris. "So many monuments to French humanity," wrote the

Pennsylvania Gazette on December 14. The British flag flew over the ruins of Fort Duquesne, now renamed Fort Pitt.

Bouquet gave credit to the Easton Treaty, which "kept such a number of Indians idle." His men, however, were in sorry shape, "reduced, deficient of every necessary, half naked, without shoes." A veteran soldier of fortune, Henri Bouquet played a large part in the opening of the Ohio frontier.

On December 17, Hugh Mercer, a physician and a colonel in the Pennsylvania Regiment, arrived to take command. He found the work on Fort Pitt already under way. The barracks were raised and roofed, and the five bastions—Music, Grenadier, Flag, Ohio, and Monongahela—almost enclosed. This was the mightiest fort built by the British in America, but there were still problems with the Indians and the French. The former were coming to the fort at the rate of 150 a day, asking for food. The French, Mercer heard from his Indian spies, were preparing for a counterattack, having brought up a number of bateaux.

Mercer sent Croghan, the man of many missions, to obtain the release of English prisoners held by the Indians. But when they asked for rewards, Mercer replied: "We are not come into your country to purchase our people of you, but to offer you peace, on condition the captives are brought home."

The Indians remained wary, for, as Mercer put it, after having been allies of the French, "they can scarcely reconcile their numerous barbarities with forgiveness on our part." In the winter, the fort was iced in, and scurvy and measles made their appearance. Five hundred Indians set up winter quarters near the fort, expecting to be fed. They were very troublesome, Colonel Mercer reported, having been indulged in too many of their extravagant demands. On the strength of their mere promise to bring venison, for instance, they demanded an advance of five cows.

In February 1759, most of the Indians left, having heard rumors of an attack from the north. Mercer heard that a French army of a thousand men was on the march from Niagara. They were ready to strike Fort Pitt from Venango as soon as the ice melted. In March, there was news of a dangerous French concentration at Presqu'Ile (Erie), and work was speeded up to complete the ditch around the fort and the glacis. Meanwhile, some sad news arrived: General Forbes, the strategist of the conquest of the Ohio, had died. Hugh Mercer wrote Bouquet: "His name for ages to come will be dear to Americans."

In April, escaped captives reported a buildup of enemy strength at Venango. Mercer was concerned that many Mingos (Ohio River Iroquois) and Delawares still did not support the English. The French buildup might send them back to their old allies.

So he asked Croghan, who now had a house four miles up the Allegheny and was back in the fur trade, to win over the Indians, with whom he had a reputation for generosity. They called him "the Buck," and told one another: "If the Buck is in your road, he will provide for you."

Fort Pitt was by now part of a larger, continental strategy against the French. On June 19, 1759, General Amherst approved a plan for a four-pronged attack: General James Wolfe was to take Quebec; General Amherst, with his army of fourteen thousand, was to join him there by way of Lake Champlain; General John Prideaux was to take Niagara as the staging area for the capture of Montreal; and General John Stanwix was to mop up the isolated forts on the Great Lakes.

But news traveled slowly from one battle area to another. During July, Mercer came to believe the French were about to attack Fort Pitt in force, and he asked Croghan to send his spies out. On July 8, Croghan sent two Indians to Venango, sixty miles away, to observe the French. They saw seven hundred French and four hundred Indians there, waiting to attack the fort. Lignery, the French commander, told them he was going to destroy the English in a few days. He was waiting for six hundred more Indians, who were, in fact, arriving at the rate of two hundred per day, and being supplied with guns and ammunition by the French.

But a packet of letters arrived for Lignery, informing him that the French fort at Niagara was under siege; the French were faltering and needed reinforcements. Lignery gathered the Indians and said: "My children, I have bad news to tell you, there is a great army of English coming against Niagara. . . . I have received orders to go directly to Niagara and take you with me. We must drive the English away from Niagara."

The strategy of multiple attacks was a success. The French were too thinly strung out to defend all their positions. They had to deplete one fort to reinforce another, where the threat was greater. Thus, the attack on Fort Niagara saved Fort Pitt. On July 31, Croghan reported to General Stanwix that only a hundred Indians were left at Venango. Very few had wanted to follow the French to what seemed like a losing battle at Niagara, which by the end of July had already fallen to the British. General Prideaux was dead, but the French water route was severed, and the back door to Montreal was open.

By mid-August 1759, the French had abandoned and burned their three remaining forts (Venango, LeBoeuf, and Presqu'Ile) between the Ohio and Lake Erie. They would not be back, for the pendulum of battle took a decisive swing that September: Major General James Wolfe, only thirty-one years old, took the great fortress city of Quebec with four thousand men. In a single concentrated volley on the Plains of Abraham above the city, the battle was won in barely ten minutes. Few battles were as short as this one was, and few battles changed the course of history as this one did. For in those ten minutes, the French hold on Canada was broken. The French commander, Louis-Joseph Montcalm, died on the battlefield, and so did Wolfe. It was lucky, some later said, that Wolfe did not live to command armies against the United States.

In the meantime, at Fort Pitt, Croghan had to reward his Indian allies with presents. On July 31, he gave General Stanwix this explanation: "I have been as frugal as the good of the company would permit, without running into an ill-timed parsimony." Now that the war was all but won, Amherst started restricting the presents. In retaliation, the Indians at Fort Pitt stole horses. Croghan sounded the alarm of Indian discontent, but Amherst dismissed the warnings, claiming that they were "of little consequence, as it is not in their power to hurt us."

Croghan, who always had one eye on profit, took charge of the pack trains supplying Fort Pitt. Responding to accusations of overcharging, he wrote Bouquet, "I never put a dirty six-pence in my pocket." He became the leading figure of Fort Pitt society, which in 1760 consisted of a garrison of three hundred men, with twenty-nine women and thirty-two children. Drunken Indians roamed the streets, and squaws peddled their eleven-year-old daughters.

There were still ten thousand French soldiers in Montreal in 1760, but that September they surrendered to Amherst's three columns. The French had lost North America, though the war would drag on for three more years, until the Treaty of Paris was signed on February 10, 1763. In Canada, sixty-five thousand French citizens became British subjects.

The Treaty of Paris was like that point in a card game where a new deck is brought in. The consequences were far-reaching. For one thing, the British, having got rid of the French for the benefit of the Americans, would soon outwear their welcome. Now they had to garrison the many western forts, which was expensive. To pay for the troops, they would tax the colonists, who would rise up against them.

More North American territory changed hands at the Treaty of Paris than through any other international agreement before or since. In the reshuffle, France was the big loser, ousted from the continent except for the islands of Saint-Pierre and Miquelon. The empire won by a succession of valiant explorers—Cartier, Champlain, La Salle, those fearless finders of lakes and rivers—was lost by bewigged and perfumed politicians in Paris with a stroke of the pen. Now the English presided in Canada over a bilingual society that saw itself not as French or English, but as distinctly North American. Meanwhile, in the English colonies, the idea that the British were not needed began to spread.

Without taking part in the fighting, Spain was both winner and loser. In a secret 1762 treaty, the French Minister Choiseul had brought Spain in on the side of France by dangling the Louisiana territory as bait. Spain's entry into the war gave the British the chance to take Havana. In the Treaty of Paris, Spain traded Florida for Cuba, and English Florida was divided into two provinces, east and west, the former being more or less the present state of Florida and the latter the southern halves of Alabama and Mississippi. In addition, all the land claimed by France west of the Mississippi now went to Spain, from the Illinois country to Louisiana. The Father of Rivers was now the boundary between England and Spain in North America.

In Florida, the Union Jack flew over the *castillo* at St. Augustine, ending two centuries of Spanish rule. Three thousand Spaniards were shipped from St. Augustine to Havana. They were instructed to take "all the royal property," from cannons to saddles, from baptismal fonts to the bunches of dried flowers used to decorate church altars.

In Sainte Genevieve, the French town on the western bank of the Mississippi, the inhabitants woke up one morning to find themselves subjects of the king of Spain. His governor, De Leyba, privately referred to the town as *misería*. He was upset to see the blurring of social distinctions and observed that "the classes of people are so mixed up that one cannot tell who is a farmer and who is a merchant." Because of the shortage of women, the French settlers had married Indian women, and the streets were full of mestizos, children who spoke Indian dialects and played with bows and arrows. With the arrival of slaves to work the lead mines, mulatto children grew up alongside the mestizos. Charles Valle, a member of the town's most prominent family, was charged with "continual debauchery" for keeping a mulatto mistress.

In terms of English settlement, the victory over the French had cleared large areas and pushed the frontier forward. There was a "swarming" out of crowded New England toward less settled areas of New York and New Hampshire. Connecticut residents moved into Pennsylvania. Pennsylvanians moved south through the Roanoke Gap into North Carolina's cheap land. But with the euphoria of new lands came the bad news of the Pontiac uprising, a reaction, at least in part, to English expansion in the Great Lakes area vacated by the French.

The Ottawa Chief Pontiac was a seasoned enemy of the English, having fought alongside the French against Braddock. Indian animosity increased when General Amherst cut down on the practice of gifts to the Indians and said they must learn to hunt again and trade at Fort Pitt, where a price schedule was posted. The Indians had it best when rivals were competing for their friendship. The French had long realized that it was cheaper to be generous than to keep a standing army, and the English had to match them; but now the French were gone. Croghan warned in May 1762 that Indians were asking him "ye reason why we always was calling them to council during ye war and giving them presents and now take no notice of them. They say ye French was but a poor people but they always clothed any Indians that was poor or naked when they came to see them."

Croghan predicted that the Amherst policy of "distressing" the Indians would have grave consequences. He wanted to follow Sir William Johnson's lead and give the Indians blankets to cover their dead so they would not have to proceed "with blood on their garments." Amherst did not listen to the advice of either Johnson or Croghan. He believed the Indians to be "an execrable race," and was determined to "extirpate them root and branch" if they made trouble.

By the start of 1763, Croghan was constantly asking for powder and lead for the Indians at Fort Pitt. The requests were rarely honored, but there was as yet no sign of disturbance. Garrison life had its pleasures and small sorrows. On April 20, Captain Donald

Campbell at Detroit asked for leave for one of his officers: "Poor Lt. MacDonald has been troubled with a melancholy disorder for some time past, it proceeded from a love affair with one of our young ladies."

In May 1763, however, only three months after the signing of the Treaty of Paris, Pontiac's Indian coalition began to attack British forts. Pontiac used trickery to gain admittance. At Detroit on May 6, Indians began straggling into the fort, which was open for trade. They stood at the street corners, with guns cut short and hidden under their blankets, until there were three hundred of them inside the palisade, three times the number of soldiers in the garrison. Seeing the men under arms, they didn't try anything, but instead protested undying friendship to Major Henry Gladwyn, the fort commander, who suspected that they were planning some mischief. They left in a surly mood and encamped across the river.

On the 8th, Pontiac and some of the chiefs came into the fort wanting to smoke the peace pipe, but Major Gladwyn snubbed them, so they informed Captain Campbell that the whole nation would come to council the next day. Everything would be settled, after which they would disperse. On May 9, the British officers counted fifty-six canoes crossing the river, with seven or eight men in each canoe. An interpreter was sent to tell them that no more than fifty or sixty would be admitted.

Pontiac replied "in a peremptory manner" that if they were not given free access to the fort none would enter, but that the countryside was his. His men went to an island where the English kept their cattle and killed twenty-four steers and three soldier-herdsmen, as well as two families of settlers. They ordered a Frenchman who had seen the settlers scalped to go to the fort and inform the soldiers of it.

On May 11, Pontiac attacked, advancing boldly over the open plain and coming to within sixty yards of the fort. After three Indians were killed and a dozen wounded, the rest retired as fast as they had advanced. Inside the fort, there were only 120 white men, including the traders, and Pontiac asked them to surrender with all their goods. Major Gladwyn replied in the negative. "I only regret," General Amherst commented when the incident was reported, "that when the chiefs of the Ottawa returned with the pipe of peace, they were not instantly put to death."

Elsewhere, things did not go as well. On May 16, at Fort Sandusky, on the shore of Lake Erie between Toledo and Cleveland, Ensign Pauli foolishly allowed seven Indians to come into the post. He gave them tobacco, but they tied him up and massacred everyone. A few days later, at Fort Miami, at today's Fort Wayne, Indiana, Ensign Holmes was told by his Indian concubine that there was a sick squaw in a cabin three hundred yards away who needed to be bled. She begged him to help. When he left the fort, he was ambushed and murdered.

On May 29, Captain Simon Ecuyer, a Swiss-born officer who had replaced Colonel Mercer as commandant of Fort Pitt, reported that the Mingos and the Delawares had come to the fort to sell three hundred pounds' worth of peltry, which they used to buy powder and lead. They then stole three horses and a keg of rum at nearby Bushy Run, as well as fifty pounds from a man named Coleman on the Bedford road, and killed a settler named Clapham and two men at the sawmill, taking scalps and leaving a tomahawk —a declaration of war. Ecuyer heard that Sandusky was cut off and, realizing that the uprising was general, prepared for the worst. By June 2, the Indians were a mile away, but not showing themselves. The people from the towns had been brought into the fort. Wood had been cut, and water prepared in case of fire. Platforms and embrasures for the cannons had been built, and beaver traps had been set along the rampart.

On June 3, at Michilimackinac, on the straits that divided Lakes Huron and Michigan, some Indians playing lacrosse outside the fort threw the ball inside. Captain Etherington and Lieutenant Lessley brought the ball out to them—and were seized and carried into the woods. Other Indians ran into the fort, where their squaws were waiting with hatchets hidden under their blankets. They killed seventeen men and took fifteen prisoners.

On June 4, at Fort Ligonier, Lieutenant Archibald Blane reported that his garrison had been attacked at 5:00 A.M. by a band of Indians firing from the skirts of the wood. All the inhabitants from Bushy Run and Stony Creek were safe inside. A few days later, the Indians made off with some of their horses. On June 17, communications with Fort Pitt were cut off. Then, on the 21st, some of the soldiers, seeing four Indians show themselves, insisted on being let out to pursue them. It was a ruse: a hundred more lay in ambush by the side of the creek, four hundred yards from the fort, and fired volley after volley at the exposed soldiers. Miraculously, no one was hit. Ligonier was the only small fort that did not fall. Even though there were so many desertions that only a handful of men were left to defend it, and the outer perimeter was open on three sides, Blane raised a parapet all around and made the fort impregnable.

At Fort Bedford, the principal depot for supplies and troops between Carlisle and Fort Pitt, Captain Louis Ourry reported on June 7 that his greatest problem was keeping his undisciplined militia from wandering off by twos and threes to their dear plantations. He worried about their needlessly exposing themselves to the Indians. Ninety-three families had taken refuge in the fort, and more were arriving hourly. He had built pens nearby for the cattle, and the residents were living on fresh beef to save their salt pork. He ordered biscuits to be baked for his parties of Indian scouts, who wore a piece of the regimental white lace to distinguish them from enemy Indians. Even though he only slept between midnight and three in the morning, he was in good spirits; he didn't know what the bad news was elsewhere.

On June 18, 1763, George Croghan reached Fort Bedford with a supply train and reported to Colonel Bouquet in Philadelphia, "We have madeira, claret, and good spirits in plenty."

General Amherst, who badly underestimated the Indians, was vexed to learn that at Bedford and Ligonier, "on the appearance of a few Indians," all the outbuildings had been burned and destroyed, "for I can see no sort of necessity for that on the approach of so despicable an enemy as the Indians are, without any kind of warlike implements, but those of ill-provided small arms."

Next came the turn of the three forts to the north of Fort Pitt—Venango, LeBoeuf, and Presqu'Ile. On the night of June 18, at Fort LeBoeuf, Ensign George Price was attacked by Indians who fired flaming arrows at the fort and set it on fire. He retreated in the night unseen, accompanied by seven men. They made their way to Venango and arrived on the 20th, to find it deserted and burned to the ground. The captured officer at Venango had been made to write down the Indians' grievances: First was the scarcity and high cost of powder during the last two years, for a gill's worth of which they were obliged to pay two deerskins; when they complained, they were ill-treated. Second, the large number of posts the English took possession of made them believe the English intended to take over all their country and were determined to destroy them. After taking down this dictation, the officer was put to death.

On June 20, at the Presqu'Ile fort on Lake Erie, Ensign John

Christie was surrounded by two hundred Indians who fired at the blockhouse all day. The next day, they invested the fort and approached as far as the commanding officer's room on the parade, to which they set fire. At midnight, an Indian who spoke French told the English it was no use trying to hold out, since they could set fire to the rest of the fort whenever they liked.

Christie's men were exhausted and unable to extinguish the fires. He asked if anyone among the Indians spoke English. One replied that they were Hurons, compelled to take up arms against the English by the Ottawas, and that they wanted only to occupy the fort. Now that they had it, they would allow the soldiers to leave when they pleased, with six days' provisions. Christie told them to cease firing and said he would give them his answer in the morning. But when he came out with his men, most were massacred. Christie and two others fled into the woods.

How could Christie have put faith in Indian promises? Amherst wondered. They should have defended themselves to the last. It was to some extent his own fault, for leaving weak garrisons in the western forts and for paying no attention to his own intelligence that an uprising was in the works. Now Pontiac and his men were accomplishing what the French had failed to do—ousting the English from the entire area.

Amherst ordered Bouquet to mount an expedition of five hundred men against Pontiac, from Carlisle. The British army had taken losses from and been humbled by "barbarians" who must be taught a lesson. Amherst was out for blood. "I wish to hear of no prisoners," he wrote Bouquet on June 29, "should any of the villains be met with in arms."

In Carlisle, on June 29, 1763, Bouquet saw that a general panic had seized the country and the residents had abandoned their farms and mills. "There appear to be few savages yet on these frontiers," he wrote, "but every tree is become an Indian for the terrified inhabitants." It was a bad time to raise troops, because of the harvest, but Amherst was urging him to leave for Fort Pitt at once. On July 13, however, Bouquet was still in Carlisle getting ready. He reported, "The savages have begun to kill on the upper part of Patowmack and within 16 miles of this town, which is suddenly become the frontier." Refugees were streaming into Carlisle and complaining that the government of Pennsylvania was worse than useless.

The scene was "painful to describe," said Bouquet. Two thousand families had left their homes and were crowded into barns, stables, cellars, and leaky sheds, desolate families reduced to despair. The streets were filled with distracted women looking for their children, and weeping children who had lost their parents.

In the meantime, at Fort Pitt, the Indians were closing in. On June 15, a party had been sent out to cut grass, and a militiaman was killed. That night, the Indians fired on the fort. Captain Ecuyer remained his usual optimistic self, writing Bouquet on June 16: "I have collected all the beaver traps which our merchants had and they were set in the evening outside the palisades. I would be happy to send you one, with a savage's leg in it, but they haven't given me that satisfaction."

Ecuyer didn't know whether to be more worried about the Indians or the smallpox that had broken out in the fort, which was crowded with refugees. There were a total of 540 mouths to feed. He had a hospital built, fearing the spread of the disease.

On June 23, Bouquet relayed this information to Amherst. On the following day, two Delaware Indians came to Fort Pitt, perhaps to trade. One of the traders there at the time was William Trent, George Croghan's brother-in-law, who had been sent with Ensign Ford roughly ten years earlier to build the original fort, which had been seized by the French. Trent was now a partner in the firm of Simon, Trent, Levy, and Frank. In his journal, the entry for the date of June 24 mentioned the visit of the two Indians and added: "Out of regard to them, we gave them two blankets and a handkerchief out of the smallpox hospital, I hope it will have the desired effect."

It was germ warfare in the eighteenth century: traders and officers at the fort seemed to think it was a splendid idea to spread smallpox among the tribes. And, indeed, smallpox would rage among the Delawares, Shawnees, and Mingos that summer and into the following year.

General Amherst, responding to Bouquet's news of smallpox at the fort, appears to have had the same idea independently. In an undated paper signed "J.A.," which seems to have been a postscript to a July 7 letter in the same handwriting, he commented: "Could it not be contrived to send the smallpox against the disaffected tribes of Indians? We must on this occasion use every stratagem in our power to reduce them."

In the July 13 letter in which Bouquet described conditions in Carlisle, he added a postscript of his own: "P.S. I will try to inoculate the bastards with some blankets that may fall into their hands, and take care not to get the disease myself. As it is a pity to expose good men against them, I wish we would make use of the Spanish method to hunt them with English dogs supported by rangers and some light horse, who would I think effectively extirpate or remove that vermin."

Amherst replied: "You will do well to try to inoculate the Indians by means of blankets, as well as to try every other method that can serve to extirpate this execrable race. I should be very glad if your scheme for hunting them down by dogs could take effect; but England is at too great a distance to think of that at present."

Another aspect of this episode came out in 1764, when Gershon Hicks, the servant of an Indian trader, who had been captured in May 1763 by some Shawnees, found his way back to Fort Pitt and made a statement to Captain William Grant (Captain Ecuyer's successor), in which he said that "the smallpox has been raging among the Indians since last spring (of 1763). Thirty or 40 Mingos, as many Delawares, and some Shawnees died, all of them of the smallpox. Since that time, it still continues among them."

According to Hicks, the smallpox had already started among the tribes by May of 1763. The gift of infected blankets, however, took place in late June, and could have had nothing to do with the outbreak of the disease. It may have been the other way around, with infected Indians bringing smallpox into the fort. But, in any case, the intent was odious, and showed the callousness of the British military when dealing with "natives."

Further evidence that smallpox still raged in 1764 came in a letter to Bouquet from Colonel Andrew Lewis, on the Virginia frontier: "The poor rascals are dying very fast with the smallpox; they can make but little resistance and when routed from their settlements must perish in great numbers by the disorders."

In the meantime, as Bouquet was putting his force together in Carlisle in July 1763, the situation in the backcountry was deteriorating. On July 16, Thomas Cresap reported that the Indians were killing settlers a hundred yards from his house at Oldtown. They had fired on six men cutting wheat in his field, killing one, and on some men who were lying under a large tree at the end of the lane leading to his front door. They had also attacked his neighbor Mr. Welder, who lived three hundred yards away; one bold Indian had cut Welder in the back, dividing his ribs from his backbone.

On July 28, Fort Pitt was attacked again, but Captain Ecuyer reported, "As soon as they showed their noses they were picked off like flies, for I have good marksmen." General Amherst chided him for firing his cannon, but he wrote Bouquet: "By the way, why should I not have fired the cannon when they attacked my men in the garden. . . . They stole all our horses and 40 cows. . . . They pushed me to an extreme and provoked me. . . . They shot burning arrows to set fire to our works. . . . Only two arrows came into the fort, one of which had the insolence to caress my left leg."

By this time, Bouquet was on the march and had reached Fort Bedford. The locally recruited militiamen had a tendency to "lose themselves in the woods" as soon as they were on the road, and could not be employed as flankers, so he had to hire thirty woodsmen to do the job. In addition, the temporary bridges had been swept away during the winter, and the roads were in poor condition, so he was advancing at a crawl. On one occasion, it took him thirty-six hours to go three miles.

From Fort Bedford to Pittsburgh was ninety-seven miles, and by August 5 Bouquet had reached Bushy Run, twelve miles east of Fort Pitt. That afternoon, at one o'clock, his advance guard was attacked by a force of Delawares, Mingos, Shawnees, and Hurons, and Bouquet ordered a general charge to dislodge the Indians from the height. The fighting lasted until nightfall, with heavy losses on both sides: Bouquet had sixty killed and wounded.

The next morning, the Indians surrounded his camp at a distance of about five hundred yards. They were shouting and leaping "to terrify us with their numbers," as Bouquet put it. They attacked in waves, trying to get inside the camp. Bouquet had run out of water, and his surrounded men were thirsty, and tired from the long march. "The savages growing every moment more audacious," he wrote, "it was thought proper . . . to entice them to come close upon us." So he pretended to retreat, and "the barbarians . . . hurried headlong on, advancing upon us with the most daring intrepidity." But, at the very moment when they thought they were masters of the camp, Major Campbell appeared at the head of two companies, from behind a hill, and fell upon their right flank.

"They could not stand the irresistible shock of our men, who rushing in among them killed many of them, and put the rest to flight." And so the battle of Bushy Run ended in triumph for Bouquet, even though he had lost a hundred men. On August 11, 1763, he arrived at Fort Pitt, and the siege was lifted. Bouquet was pleased with himself, feeling that the Indians could no longer claim to be invincible in the forest.

Now only Detroit remained under siege. During the summer, it was relieved with reinforcements and supplies by the lake route from Niagara, but in October 1763 Major Gladwyn was so short of flour and firewood that he was on the point of abandoning the fort. The Indians, tired of waiting, abruptly dispersed to their hunting grounds. Abandoned by his Indian allies, and realizing that it was chimeric to expect help from the French, Pontiac sent a message to Gladwyn on October 12 asking for a truce. He hoped, he said, that His Excellency the British commander would forget what had passed. Pontiac wanted to come to the fort and plead his case in person, but Major Gladwyn could not allow it, for he was under orders to kill the chief on sight.

Pontiac retreated to the Maumee River, and in August of the following year, 1764, Colonel John Bradstreet entered Detroit with his troops to prevent a renewal of the siege. The formal peace didn't come until July 1766. In 1769, Pontiac was killed by another Indian.

The frontier settlers who took the brunt of the Pontiac rebellion learned the hard way that the hinterland was unwilling to come to their aid. The Pennsylvania government in particular did nothing for their defense. Nowhere did the raw hatred of the frontier for both the Indians and the hinterland come out as clearly as in the incident at Conestoga in December 1763, when a mob from the town of Paxton, a few miles north of Harris' Ferry, massacred twenty peaceable and unarmed Conestoga Indians.

The principal result of the Pontiac rebellion was to awaken the British government to the need for a western policy. It had all been rather haphazard, with the king handing out large land tracts to friends and favorites, and with traders operating in the wilderness in an almost total vacuum of authority. To impose some order upon the situation, and to conciliate the Indians in the wake of the Pontiac revolt, the Board of Trade passed the Royal Proclamation of 1763, which drew a boundary line from Canada to Florida beyond which no settlement was permitted. The king restricted his "loving subjects" from the land west of the mountains, protecting the Indians from "whiskey purchases." The line could be moved westward as the population pressure dictated, but only by government purchase. Thus, nearly all the land that England had won from the French would be reserved for the Indians.

The two Indian superintendents, Sir William Johnson in the

North, and Colonel John Stuart in the South, called conferences with the tribes to mark out the line in two sections, north and south. In 1768, at Fort Stanwix, on the upper Mohawk River, more than three thousand Indians attended, receiving two hundred canoe-loads of presents. The line agreed upon ran from Oneida Lake, above today's Syracuse, New York, to the headwaters of the Delaware, across Pennsylvania to the forks of the Ohio, and down the Ohio to the Great Kanawha, at today's Point Pleasant, West Virginia. This line opened up western Virginia and southwestern Pennsylvania to settlement.

In the South, Colonel Stuart held two conferences, one at the South Carolina village of Hard Labor and the other at Savannah, running the line across Georgia to Mobile. The result was a north-south dividing line creating a white America to the east and a red America to the west. Confining western settlement was seen as a way of subordinating the colonies.

"I can never look upon that proclamation as anything but a temporary expedient to quiet the minds of the Indians," George Washington observed. How right he was. In 1763, the pioneers were already poised on the crest of the Appalachians, ready to move into the interior. For more than a century, they had been competing for overcrowded coastal strips, and now their moment had come, with the departure of the French and the piercing of the mountains by military roads. And so they followed Braddock's road to the forks of the Ohio, and the extension to Redstone Creek, where by 1760 there were already a dozen cabins.

At Fort Pitt, meanwhile, a town grew around the fort. In 1769, when a land office opened, three thousand buyers stormed the office on its first day of business. Within four months, a million acres had been sold. At the same time, the men who specialized in the mastery of frontier techniques moved into the bluegrass region of Kentucky and the winding valleys of the upper Tennessee. And the Indian traders softened up the Indians for the kill, and the professional squatters, who lived on a stream so they wouldn't have to dig a well, sold their "improvements" and moved on. And the point men of Manifest Destiny, for whom boundaries were hurdles, moved on to the aptly named Cheat River.

A British official wrote that the people "will remove as their avidity and restlessness incite them. They acquire no attachment to place but wandering about seems engrafted in their nature; and it is a weakness incident to it that they should forever imagine the lands further off are still better than those upon which they are already settled."

In the meantime, a smaller but long-festering boundary dispute was about to be settled. According to the conflicting claims of the vaguely drafted proprietary charters of Maryland and Pennsylvania, Philadelphia was in Maryland, and Baltimore was in Pennsylvania. The two colonies could have exchanged cities, but instead petitioned the royal astronomer in Greenwich to recommend two of his colleagues to assist local surveyors. A contract was signed with two respected astronomers, Charles Mason and Jeremiah Dixon, who arrived in November 1763. It took them nearly five years to establish the boundaries of Pennsylvania, Maryland, Virginia, and Delaware, ending the long struggle between the Penns and the Calverts, and tracing what would one day be the dividing line between slavery and abolition.

They started from the forks of the Brandywine River, thirty-one miles from Philadelphia, at the house of John Harland. The Philadelphia Observatory, on Cedar Street, was disassembled and rebuilt in Mr. Harland's yard. These Greenwich astronomers wanted no halfway measures. The fragile instruments were placed in a wagon on down mattresses, and were carried with the utmost prudence over the thirty-one miles, which took two days.

In June 1764, after finishing their preliminary calculations, they went to New Castle, Delaware, with their axmen, chain men, stewards, and cooks—the party totaling thirty-nine. At the ninety-five-mile mark, they reached Antietam Creek, near today's Waynesboro, Pennsylvania. Their progress was stalled as they waited for more boundary stones from England, with the arms of the Penns on one side and those of the Calverts on the other, which they placed every five miles. When it got cold, they took their winter break. Although working with deliberate lack of speed, they got the job done; in 1768, they turned over the boundary maps of the Mason-Dixon Line to Richard Peters, secretary to the Council in Pennsylvania.

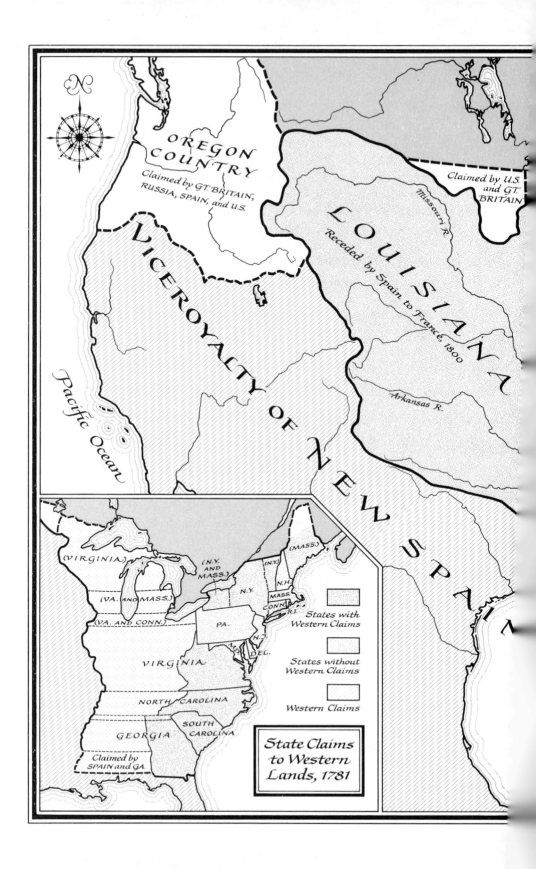

N

OREGON
COUNTRY
Claimed by GT. BRITAIN,
RUSSIA, SPAIN, and U.S.

Claimed by U.S.
and GT.
BRITAIN

L O U I S I A N A
Receded by Spain to France, 1800

Missouri R.

Arkansas R.

V I C E R O Y A L T Y   O F   N E W   S P A I N

Pacific Ocean

(VIRGINIA)

(N.Y.
AND
MASS.)

(N.Y.)

(MASS.)

(VA. AND MASS.)

N.Y.

N.H.

(VA. AND CONN.)

PA.

MASS.
CONN.
R.I.

States with
Western Claims

N.J.
DEL.

MD.

States without
Western Claims

VIRGINIA

NORTH CAROLINA

SOUTH
CAROLINA

Western Claims

GEORGIA

Claimed by
SPAIN and GA.

State Claims
to Western
Lands, 1781

BRITISH NORTH AMERICA

CANADA

Claimed by U.S. and GT. BRITAIN

(MASS.)

VT.

N.H. (Independent republic, 1777; state, 1791)

NEW YORK

MASS.

CONN.

R.I.

Hudson R.

British

French

Spanish

13 Original States

The United States as of 1800

INDIANA TERRITORY

TERRITORY NORTHWEST OF OHIO RIVER

PENNSYLVANIA

MD.

N.J.

DEL.

Ohio R.

Mississippi R.

VIRGINIA

KENTUCKY (1792)

TENNESSEE (1796)

NORTH CAROLINA

TERRITORY SOUTH OF OHIO RIVER

SOUTH CAROLINA

GEORGIA

MISSISSIPPI TERRITORY

WEST FLORIDA

EAST FLORIDA

Gulf of Mexico

Atlantic Ocean

Miles
0 ————— 300

Kms.
0 ————— 300

PART IV

AMERICA for the AMERICANS

© A. Karl/J. Kemp. 1993

CHAPTER EIGHTEEN

STARS
TO THE FLAG

In 1765, the colonies exploded in rage over taxes levied to finance the crown's military expenses. Ten years later, the Continental Congress commissioned George Washington to lead an army of citizen-soldiers in a war against England. In 1777, in upstate New York, an American-held fort fought off the British and flew, for the first time, an American flag in combat.

A patriot is not a weapon. A patriot is one who wrestles for the soul of his country.

ADRIENNE RICH

I n 1760, Americans joined in the celebration of the accession of George III to the throne. In the colonies, from Maine to Georgia, there was a mood of astonishingly uncritical pro-Britishness. England was "the wise and good mother." The Union Jack flew proudly everywhere. General Braddock's death was seen as a heroic sacrifice.

The passage of the Stamp Act in 1765 changed all that, as opinions altered and old attachments were surrendered. Loyalty was weighed against the *cost* of loyalty. The character of the nation was formed by what Jefferson called the need to break out of "the dull monotony of colonial subservience."

In Charleston, South Carolina, Charles Woodmason saw the Stamp Act as a splendid opportunity. Arriving in the colony in 1752, he had succeeded in buying a plantation, but he was a poor manager, and before long his lands were sold to pay his debts. In 1765, he obtained a job as distributor of stamps, which made him so disliked that he decided to change his life, both professionally and geographically. There was a need for Anglican ministers in the backcountry, and so Woodmason returned to England to be instructed and take holy orders. In 1766, he was back in South Carolina as "Reverend" Woodmason, ready to move to the backcountry.

The sand hills a hundred miles from the Atlantic shore marked the line where the Piedmont began. Settlers there were regarded as useful clods, absorbing the shock of Indian raids and Spanish or French attacks, and freeing coastal planters to focus on the enemy within—the slaves. As Lieutenant Governor William Bull described the situation in 1768: "The few inhabitants of the maritime settlements have a numerous domestic enemy, thick sown in our plantations, and they require our utmost attention to keep them in order."

Frontier settlement was encouraged with hundred-acre land grants and ten years' worth of free quitrents. The Piedmont was opened up to an ethnic and religious potpourri of settlers. First came the Germans and the Welsh, then the French Huguenots, the Ulster Irish, the Dunkers, the Seventh-Day Baptists, and a hundred other sects. By the 1730s, they had settled towns like Orangeburg, on the north fork of the Edisto. By 1759, the backcountry population of the two Carolinas had reached about twenty thousand.

The rough frontier life wore down the habits of polite society. Visiting the backcountry in 1753, South Carolina Governor James Glen observed that the people "take so much care in raising a litter of pigs that their children are equally naked and full as nasty. . . . It is not to be wondered at that the offspring of such loose embraces would be little looked after."

In 1760, the Cherokees began raids all along the frontier settlements, some of which had to be evacuated. The brutality of their lives, as when a wagon train on the way to Augusta was attacked and the bodies of the adults were butchered and the children were scalped, took its toll on the white settlers, turning them into hardened cases.

James Francis, a defender of the village of Ninety-Six in western Carolina, wrote South Carolina Governor Lyttleton: "We now have the pleasure, sir, to fatten our dogs with Indian carcasses and to display their scalps, neatly ornamented on the top of our bastions." Rooting them on from the cheap seats, the Assembly in Charleston raised the bounty on Indian scalps from twenty-five to thirty-five pounds.

Finally, the Cherokees were defeated in the summer of 1761,

and a peace treaty was signed. The backcountry, however, was left a disaster area. Settlements had been destroyed, and farming long interrupted. Still, the Indians were gone. One old woman said the most beautiful thing she had ever seen was a young man dying a natural death in bed—without a hatchet in his head.

In the absence of authority, bands of outlaws replaced the Indians. There were no courts and no sheriffs, and hardly any roads. The Piedmont was isolated and self-regulating. Settlers on the Carolina frontier couldn't get worked up about the tax on tea, which they didn't drink. They had their own perspective on taxation without representation, since they were themselves under-represented in the colonial legislature at Charleston. The one link between frontier and hinterland was the wagoner, who came from Charleston to collect produce, and who also served as postman, and as stringer for the Charleston gazettes.

It was into this ungoverned country that the Reverend Charles Woodmason arrived in September 1766. His parish headquarters was Camden, on the Wateree River, 120 miles northwest of Charleston. His territory as a circuit-riding minister included thirty scattered congregations in the huge, practically roadless parish of St. Marks, between the Congaree and Lynches rivers, extending from South into North Carolina.

Crossing the Wateree on the way to Camden, Woodmason's clothes were torn to pieces as he cut his way through canebrake and swamp. When he arrived, hungry and exhausted, "their provisions I could not touch—all the cookery of these people being exceeding filthy, and most execrable." His parishioners were poor and ignorant folk who lived in one-room log cabins. He had to take up quarters in a tavern, where he had to put up with the drunken clientele.

As an educated man who contributed an occasional poem to *The Gentleman's Magazine* in London, Woodmason was horrified by the lax morality of his flock. During the first wedding ceremony he performed, he noticed that the woman was "very big." Nine out of ten men had venereal diseases. He would have to rewrite his sermons for "a vile, disorderly crew."

In January 1767, he set out on his first tour, heading north about forty miles to preach at Lynch's Creek, on the border of North and South Carolina, west of today's Pageland. He did not think much of his parishioners there. These Scotch-Irish Presbyterians from the North of Ireland were "a set of the most lowest vilest crew breathing."

"Many hundreds live in concubinage," he noted, "swapping their wives as cattle." To counteract the immorality, he read them the 1760 Royal Proclamation for the encouragement of piety and virtue, and offered to marry and baptize anyone gratis. From then on, he was kept busy "marrying rogues and whores and baptizing their brats."

On January 25, Woodmason preached to a great multitude at Lynch's Creek, drawn there by the curiosity of seeing their first Anglican minister. "They complained of being eaten up by itinerant teachers, preachers, and imposters from New England and Pennsylvania, Baptists, New Lights, Presbyterians, Independents, and 100 other sects, so that one day you might hear this system of doctrine, the next day another, and the next day another retrograde to both. . . . They seemed so pleased with their native ignorance as to be offended at any attempts to rouse them out of it."

At his next stop, Hanging Rock Creek, the reverend was insulted and menaced by the tavern regulars, who saw the presence of a minister as inhibiting their frontier freedom. "These lawless ruffians telling me they wanted no damned black-gowned sons of bitches among them," he noted in his journal, "and threatening to lay me behind the fire." But others took him under their wing and guarded him all night.

He knew that the Presbyterians had put his detractors up to it, obviously wanting to get rid of the competition. Religious rivalries on the frontier had a gloves-off, bare-knuckled rawness. The idea was to win, no matter how. As part of their campaign against Woodmason, the Presbyterians hired a gang of hecklers "who kept hallooing and whooping like Indians." Thousands of immigrants had come to America to escape the religious wars of Europe, only to find them repeated on the frontier.

When Woodmason got back to Camden in February, he found that his lodgings at the tavern had been burglarized. Thirty valuable books were gone, as well as his linen, letter folder, and portfolio. The Presbyterians, he surmised, thinking them capable of every dirty trick.

Refusing to become discouraged, Woodmason set out again, this time to High Hills and Rafting Creek and Thompson's Creek, swimming himself and his horse across bridgeless creeks and spending the night in dirty, smoky cabins where he was offered inedible food.

At Thompson's Creek, the water was too deep and the current too swift to cross. One man made a raft so that he could go and tell the people on the other side that the minister could not get to them. The raft was soon engulfed by the torrent as Woodmason watched from the bank, feeling remorse: if the man drowned, it would be his fault. He was relieved to see him bob up in the water and take hold of a floating tree. The others threw him ropes and pulled him back to shore—where he was as merry as though nothing had happened. Then a man came by with a strong high horse, and bravely offered to take Woodmason behind him. Once he was over, it was twelve more miles to the Pee Dee River. And so it went, through the spring and summer of 1767.

Another problem Woodmason had to contend with was the absence of roads. Often so-called roads were barely visible paths, overgrown with grass and covered with leaves. And wherever he went, it seemed, the Presbyterians were already there, hiring hecklers to disrupt his meetings. He also had to compete with a few Baptist and Methodist ministers, low and ignorant persons, he thought, "yet the lowest class choose to resort to them rather than hear a well-connected discourse." He knew that his own meetings were well attended because of the oddness of his being there.

And yet there must have been more to it than that. These impoverished and ignorant borderers, who could not afford a Bible and lived like aborigines, seemed to have a hankering for religion, perhaps because it helped anchor their incoherent, wilderness-tossed existence.

The quaint names of many a frontier settlement were checked off Woodmason's list—Granny's Quarter, Dutchman's Creek, and Rocky Mount (on the Tar River in North Carolina). On September 25, at Beaver Creek, Woodmason fell into an ambush of horse thieves. But it turned out that they wanted a sermon, which he agreed to on the condition that they return their stolen horses. On October 3, he was preaching at Camden when the same rogues came into town and made off with several more horses. The congregation rode off after them, caught up with them at Twenty-Five-Mile Creek, and recovered the horses.

In December, at a congregation where there had never been an Anglican service, the Presbyterians sank to a new low. Not only did they provide two barrels of whiskey to get the congregation drunk, but the Presbyterian militia captain suddenly appeared in the middle of Woodmason's sermon and ordered all the able-bodied men to muster. When they refused, he threatened to fine them. But when they told him to get lost, he backed off.

The Presbyterians were a real threat, for by this time they had twenty churches scattered through the Carolina backcountry. Only two had ministers, but even so Woodmason was outnumbered: he was the only Anglican in the area. In his view, the Presbyterian method of worship, which was to meet in private homes without a minister for an evening of singing and sociability, was bound to lead to debauchery, assignations, and the singing of blasphemous songs. Religion was seen as a form of entertainment among these heathens, so Woodmason believed.

Tallying up the results of his first year in service, Woodmason figured that he had married forty couples and baptized 760 children. On his one horse, he had covered four thousand miles. "Thus you have," he wrote, "the travels of a minister in the wild woods of America. Destitute often of the very necessaries of life—sometimes starved, often famished, obliged to fight his way through banditti, profligates, reprobates, and the lowest vilest scum of mankind."

Although disgusted with his parishioners, Woodmason had a sense of what they were up against. They had been deliberately sent into the wilderness as a barrier between the Indians and the rich planters in Charleston, without laws or government, schools, churches, or police.

Coexisting in the lawless Piedmont with the planters and family men who made up Woodmason's congregations was a backcountry underworld that took advantage of the absence of government. This included squatters, runaway debtors, idlers, gamblers, mulattos, crackers, and others too lazy to be outright criminals: malingerers, poachers, chicken rather than horse thieves, marginal men.

There was also a class of outlaws, veterans of the Cherokee wars, who simply turned their depredations on the settlers, men who started out stealing deerskins and graduated to more serious crimes. They formed interracial gangs who were in cahoots with gangs in other colonies to move stolen horses, fence goods, and sell slaves.

In 1767, the year Woodmason hit his stride, Charleston newspapers reported "gangs of villains" on the "western frontiers." These groups of 200 to 300 men had "for some years past infested those parts," and possessed "regular communications with each other from the back settlements of Georgia to those of Virginia."

They bribed local constables to give them advance warning of warrants, so that they could clear out in time. When William

Silkes, a Camden horse thief, was caught, he boasted that he had escaped from twenty-eight jails. It was the start of the no-jail-can-hold-me outlaw bravado.

In Woodmason's parish, gangs openly rampaged the land, taking over planters' houses, raping wives, and kidnaping young women. Sometimes they were painted and dressed like Indians. A movement started among the people, who were fed up with the absence of law and order.

In October 1767, as Woodmason finished his first year of preaching, a thousand backcountry settlers formed a group they called "Regulators," becoming the granddaddies of all vigilante movements. The *South Carolina Gazette* reported on October 19: "Peaceable inhabitants . . . in a kind of desperation . . . have formed associations to expel villains from wherever they can get at them, and to do themselves justice in a summary way."

Regulator branches sprang up in the beleaguered settlements of Ninety-Six and Pee Dee. As a witness to the degree of lawlessness in his parish, Woodmason became sympathetic to the Regulator cause. Even though he professed to despise the backcountry people, finding their manners deplorable and their food indigestible, he believed in the justice of their cause. The people in the Piedmont were treated as second-class citizens and had no recourse against the outlaws. There was only one criminal court—in Charleston. It was a hardship to take prisoners over long distances, and the case would be decided by a jury unfamiliar with frontier problems.

Woodmason not only sympathized with the Regulators, he became their scribe, drafting a petition that was eventually signed by four thousand backcountry residents. Among their complaints were the following:

• The outlaws stole their cattle and horses and "wantonly tortured them in the Indian manner for to be made to confess where they secreted their effects from plunder."

• They had to travel three hundred miles round-trip to sue for a twenty-pound debt, and spent ten times that sum in legal costs and travel expenses.

• They could be arrested in their homes and taken to Charleston without knowing why, and be clapped in jail, unable to raise bail while they waited in a filthy dungeon for their cases to be tried. Or else they were subpoenaed to appear at court in Charleston and not called upon when they got there.

- They had no judges, no police, and no laws.
- Rowdy, uninvited guests came to their homes during weddings and christenings, mixed with the company, and started riots.
- Insolent tavern-keepers charged whatever they pleased.
- There were so few roads and bridges that they had to ride a hundred miles to advance ten miles as the crow flies, and the ferries were fifty miles apart and often unattended.

Woodmason transcribed these and other grievances in the petition, ending with a plea for circuit courts. On November 7, 1767, four Regulator leaders who were also members of the Charleston Assembly submitted the petition and threatened a march on Charleston if their demands were not met. The backcountry, created as a buffer against an external enemy, had itself become the enemy.

Woodmason, who thought of himself as a man of letters, insulted the members of the Assembly, many of whom were lawyers, by stating that Charleston was as infested with lawyers as Spain and Italy were with priests. He chided the Assembly for appropriating a thousand pounds in May 1766 for the erection of a statue of William Pitt: "It would be more useful to the province to spend money among the poor and for the distribution of bibles."

Taking offense, the Assembly tabled Woodmason's petition. It did, however, begin work on a circuit-court act, which was signed by the governor, Charles Montagu, in April 1768. The proposal then had to be sent to England for ratification. In the meantime, Montagu took action to restore law and order on the frontier, offering rewards for outlaws brought to the Charleston jail. He also assembled two companies of rangers, who tracked the outlaws into their lairs. They had some success, hanging sixteen fugitives, recovering ten stolen horses, and rescuing thirty-five young girls and returning them to their families.

At the same time, Montagu had to act against the Regulators, now numbering three thousand, who were planning a big demonstration in Camden. On October 5, 1767, he informed the South Carolina Council that some settlers between the Santee and Wateree rivers had "in a rioting manner" traveled the country inciting riots and disturbances and burning the houses of those rumored to be harborers of horse thieves.

Montagu asked for legislation to suppress the Regulators. But constables who tried to arrest them were beaten and shot at. This was a new phase of the uprising, as the rebels battled the lawmakers as ardently as they had fought the criminals.

To calm the Regulators, Lieutenant Governor Bull announced new Assembly elections in 1768. Settlers surveyed parish lines to establish backcountry voting districts, even though few of them could meet the property qualifications: five hundred acres and ten slaves. In October, the voters of South Carolina went to the polls, sometimes riding 150 miles or more to vote at parish churches. The backcountry voters elected some of their candidates, but it was a Pyrrhic victory, for news arrived that the crown had disallowed the circuit-court act: there was opposition in the Board of Trade and the Privy Council, based on considerations of expense. All in all, it seemed that England had little understanding of local problems in the colonies.

Thanks to the combined action of the rangers and the Regulators, however, the outlaw situation improved. Many fled to other states. Now unemployed, but not wishing to disband, the Regulators shifted their attention to the "poor white trash"—the "roving wretches" of the backcountry, the vagrants who lived by pilfering orchards and vegetable gardens. Soon they were not only chasing vagrants but involving themselves in debt collection and domestic disputes. Bennet Dozier was a wastrel whose wife complained to the Regulators that she and her children were indigent because of her husband's laziness. The Regulators went to Dozier's house, stripped him, tied him to an oak tree, and gave him thirty-nine lashes.

Sometimes the Regulators went too far, setting themselves up as supervisors of public morals. The pendulum swung from grievances about lawlessness to grievances about the Regulators. In 1768, some of their victims filed suits in Charleston, and some Regulators were convicted and fined for flogging people. Witnesses described flogging sessions that turned into festive occasions, with plenty to drink and fiddlers playing.

At the same time, there was finally some recognition in Charleston of the backcountry predicament; on September 10, 1768, Lieutenant Governor Bull wrote Lord Hillsborough, the colonial secretary, that the Regulators were not "the mere dregs of mankind" but rather "land-holders. . . . Though poor, they are in general an industrious and hardy race of men." The best way of dealing with them, he said, was to "treat them with moderation and their complaints with attention and their grievances with reasonable redress."

Governor Montagu urged the new Assembly to pass another circuit-court act, and it was approved by the crown in December 1769. This appeased the Piedmont population and calmed the Regulators. Those under indictment were pardoned. Little jails and courthouses sprang up, and the circuit courts started operating in 1772. By that time, ill and discouraged by his battle with the Presbyterians, Charles Woodmason had quit his parish and gone back to England.

In December 1773, Philip Vickers Fithian, a young man from New Jersey, arrived at the Virginia plantation of Robert Carter III, to serve as tutor to his children. Fithian was a Princeton-educated theological student, Presbyterian by denomination, and somewhat solemn and judgmental by temperament. The distance from Princeton to the plantation near Williamsburg was only 260 miles, yet Fithian found himself in a very different society, and experienced a kind of culture shock.

His friends had warned him. Virginia was malarial, they said, and the people there were profane and wicked, and wasted their time. They had no Calvinist books, and heard no Presbyterian sermons. He would spend more than his salary trying to keep up with their profligate way of life. Virginians preferred entertainment to religious devotion, and he would see daily examples of intemperance and impiety. Fithian listened to all their warnings and was gone.

On a crisp December day, he arrived at the plantation after a seven-day journey, on the Nomini River, five miles from the Potomac. He was greeted by a long entrance road lined with rows of poplars and paved with bricks dusted with burned oyster shells. The house was an imposing white-mortared brick structure with twenty-four-pane windows and five stacks of chimneys.

The terms of his one-year engagement were sixty-five pounds a year, a room with a study, the use of the library, a horse to ride, and a servant to light his fire, shine his shoes, and run errands. Mr. Carter would have preferred a tutor educated on the continent, on account of the English pronunciation, but had settled for Fithian. There were seven children under his care, five girls and two boys, aged from five to seventeen.

Fithian was struck by the division of land and labor. In New Jersey, land was divided into small properties, all more or less the same. This created an equality of wealth among people. Landowners worked alongside their laborers, holding one another in mutual esteem.

In Virginia, history had created a different sort of tradition. Carter's grandfather had arrived there in 1649, acquiring 13,500 acres on the Rappahannock. It was the duty of each generation to increase the family's landholdings, and Robert Carter's father did so well that he became known as "King Carter," the richest and most powerful man in Virginia. He amassed 333,000 acres, the bulk of which went to his eldest son, John, though the other sons were amply provided for. Robert III had sixty thousand acres and six hundred slaves, but not in one place—his lands were scattered among all the counties in the colony. He also had a big house in Williamsburg, and owned part of an ironworks near Baltimore.

It was Fithian's conviction that possessing these great estates often inflated their owners into "powdered coxcombs" whose aims in life, instead of working and praying, were dancing, scratching the fiddle, playing cards, fencing, and discussing the lineage of horses. If you did not attend to these activities, you did not fit into the plantation society.

Mr. Carter, however, was an exception in some ways, a thoughtful, scholarly man who spent a great deal of time in his library with the works of Addison, Pope, Swift, and Dryden. Carter, who played the pianoforte, had married a southern beauty, Frances Anne Tasker, who was lighthearted and cheerful and provided a welcome contrast to her husband's glumness and gallows humor. He told Fithian that he wanted to make his own coffin and keep it for a chest until its proper use was required. He also wanted a plain tombstone, with not even a *hic jacet* on it.

At dinner on December 23, shortly after Fithian's arrival, conversation turned to what makes a pleasing person. Mrs. Carter said she loved a sociable, open, chatty person, and could not bear sullenness and stupidity. Mr. Carter, however, observed, "There is a time for all things under the sun," as Solomon had put it. It was fine to laugh in season, and just as fine to be taciturn.

On Christmas Day, guns were fired all around the house, and the topic at dinner was marriage. Mrs. Carter said that if she were a widow, she would hesitate to remarry, for how could a man love her grown old, when the world was thronged with blooming, ripening virgins? Perhaps she was fishing for a compliment: Fithian thought she looked better than some unmarried ladies he knew.

Fithian got on fairly well with the children. The girls all studied musical instruments, and each day the music master arrived with his violin. Fithian sometimes had to arbitrate quarrels, as when Nancy said that Bob had stolen some rum and got drunk, and Bob called her a liar and hit her. Another time, Bob accused his brother, Ben, of taking his mother's Negro maid, Sukey, into the stable and locking himself in with her for a considerable time. Bob was the troublemaker, quarrelsome and abusive, and Fithian feared he would come to an unhappy end. Whenever he had trouble with him, Fithian said, "If you don't behave, I'm sending you to your father." Bob was in the habit of taking his dog into his bed at night for companionship, so Fithian read the boy chapter 27 of Deuteronomy: "Cursed be he that lieth with any manner of beast."

Plantation days were filled with parties, balls, fox hunts, country dances, and innumerable games, such as "break the pope's neck." On one occasion, Fithian escorted Mrs. Carter to a ball, though he declined to dance. There were minuets, gigues, and reels, to music from a French horn and two violins, and the ladies' silks and brocades rustled as they spun and swirled. While the dancers danced, others played cards and drank, toasting the Sons of Liberty, and singing anti-English songs, for the most part unharmonious. One of the planter-society coxcombs, George Lee, half drunk, asked Fithian why he came to the ball, since he neither danced nor played cards. "My invitation justifies my presence," Fithian replied with hauteur, adding that Lee was ill-qualified to judge his conduct.

The young Virginia gentlemen were pranksters. In January 1774, at a gathering in mixed company in Dr. Thompson's rooms, there was a skeleton hanging against the wall. When James Balenine, a young merchant, turned the bones into many improper and indecent positions, Fithian was offended. They might think he was dull and unsociable, but he thought they were vulgar.

These were people who not only spent most of their time on their own amusement, but did not take the Sunday service seriously. Fithian went to church every Sunday, and usually ran into John Lowe, a fellow tutor and a Scotsman. One day, Lowe observed some hogs in the graveyard next to the church. "If I was buried here," he said, "it would grieve me to look up and see swine feeding over me."

To Fithian, the hogs in the graveyard were not unlike the Virginians in church. Sunday service here seemed to him to be no more than a pretext to socialize. Before the service, letters were exchanged, advertisements were read, and knots of young bloods formed to discuss the price of tobacco and grain, or the qualities of favorite horses. There were endless conversations about the horses' family background, about their brothers, sisters, uncles, aunts, nephews, nieces, and cousins. After the service, crowds once again collected, and there were invitations to balls, fish feasts, christenings, cockfights, and horse races.

As he discovered the diversions of plantation life, Fithian also learned about its underside. Morgan the overseer told him that he had, through trial and error, perfected two forms of punishment for the slaves. The first was for sullenness, obstinacy, and idleness. "You take a negro," Morgan said, "and you strip him, and you tie him fast to a post. You take then a sharp curry-comb and curry him severely till he is well scraped. You call a boy in with some dry hay and you make the boy rub him down for several minutes. Then you salt him. After that he will attend to his business."

"Savage cruelty," thought Fithian, but he kept his own counsel.

"To get a secret from a negro," Morgan went on, "lay upon your floor a large thick plank, with a peg 18 inches long of hard wood and very sharp on the upper end, fixed fast to the plank—then strip the negro, tie a cord to a staple in the ceiling, hang him so that his foot just rests on the sharpened peg, then turn him briskly round. You would laugh at the dexterity of the negro, while he relieves his feet on the sharpened peg."

"There is a righteous God," Fithian thought, "who will take vengeance on such inventions."

It seemed unbelievable to Fithian that Carter was somehow able to reconcile the ownership of slaves with humane principles. Such was Virginia, he thought, that these people could live a contradiction, professing enlightened principles while keeping slaves.

At dinner on March 24, 1774, Mr. Carter said he had been troubled by some cruelty he had seen at dinner at Squire Lee's with George Turberville and his wife. As he had ridden up, he had seen Turberville's coachman on the chariot box, although there were no horses harnessed to the coach. Then he saw that the coachman was chained to the coach—because, it turned out, on one occasion he had tried to run away. When he got home, he would be turned over to the overseer and chained again.

Perhaps there was a connection between Turberville's treatment of his coachman and an incident that took place later that year. His barn burned down, a loss worth three hundred pounds. Quite a lot, observed Mr. Carter, for a man who was eager to turn every ear of corn into cash.

Fithian found the Virginians' strange blend of cruelty and kindness baffling. "The Virginians are so kind," he wrote, "that one can scarce know how to dispense with, or indeed accept their kindness shown in such a variety of instances." They were even, on occasion, kind to their slaves. At Easter, there was a general holiday, and they were disbanded from Sunday to Wednesday. On every plantation, there were dances and cockfights at which large sums were bet. Fithian stayed in his room reading Plato.

His final argument was that slavery was not economically sound. "How much greater," he wrote, ". . . would be the value of an estate if these poor enslaved Africans were all in their native desired country and in their place industrious tenants, who being born in freedom . . . would not only enrich their landlords but would raise a hardy offspring to be the strength and honor of the colony."

Fithian went home on leave in April 1774, glad to be restored to his old habits of pious worship. How unlike Virginia his church in Princeton was, with no rings of beaux chatting about gallantry before and after the sermon, and no idle chitchat after the service. Here the minister and his flock seemed to commune in reverence, quite unlike the spiritless harangues in the Virginia church. Soon, however, Fithian's attention was turned away from spiritual matters.

Everyone in New Jersey was in an uproar over the events in Boston. "The lower class of people here are in a tumult," Fithian wrote in his journal for May 31, "on account of reports from Boston. Many of them expect to be pressed and compelled to go and fight the Britains. [sic]" The Tea Act of 1773, which allowed the East India Company to sell its tea surplus directly to America, had undercut the local importers and merchants. When the tea ships arrived in December 1773, a number of "tea parties" were held to protest the unfair competition. One of the first, that December, was at Boston; at Portsmouth, New Hampshire, and in Philadelphia, the ships were turned away. In New York, the mob burned down the house of Governor Tryon for saying that if the orders for landing the tea had been transmitted to him he would have landed it even under the mouths of cannons.

Early in June 1774, the governor of New Jersey dissolved the

Assembly after it voted for a sympathy fast to protest the enforcement of the Acts of Parliament. The "Intolerable Acts" included
the closing of the port of Boston and the suspension of the province's charter. The people of New Jersey agreed to unite with the
people of Boston and the other northern trading cities. They would
not fight the British but they would remain independent. The
captain of a British ship who wanted to land on the New Jersey
coast on June 2 to load tobacco was kept from landing until they
had further news from the north. The tea business was uniting the
colonies.

When Fithian returned to Virginia, in the June heat, with a
flaming, sultry sun and the ground scorched and dusty, he found
that people there were also in an uproar. "The Virginians," he
wrote, "are warm and active in supporting the liberties of America.
. . . The warehouses are already hindering the shipping of tobacco. . . . The people here wish for the union of all the colonies.
. . . Notwithstanding, this colony and Maryland will suffer vastly,
because tobacco is a commodity less saleable among ourselves than
most of the produce of the northern colonies."

On June 18, Mr. Carter showed Fithian a London newspaper
in which it was reported that the Acts of Parliament had taken
from the people of Boston the power to try any soldier or person
for committing a crime: all such offenders had to be sent home for
legal trial. In Richmond, Prime Minister Lord North, who had
responded with harsh measures to the dumping of the tea, was
burned in effigy.

That September and October, the First Continental Congress
sat in Philadelphia with fifty-six delegates from twelve colonies,
including Virginia. A Declaration of Rights was adopted. Fithian
was astonished to find that the flighty Mrs. Carter, who paid scant
attention to serious subjects, had "a perfect acquaintance" with the
developments in Philadelphia.

Not everyone took the anti-British position. On September
18, an old friend of Mr. Carter's, Captain Walker, came to dinner
and "threw out exceeding unpopular sentiments with regard to the
present amazing disturbances through the colonies. . . . He asserted that no officers at Boston or elsewhere could question or
refuse any orders received from their sovereign or commanding
officers." Such was the Loyalist platform, which a minority would
adopt.

The general agitation was contagious. A slave uprising was

uncovered that September, leading Fithian to remark: "The ill treatment which this unhappy part of mankind receives here, would almost justify them in any desperate attempt for gaining that civility and plenty which tho denied them, is here commonly bestowed on horses."

The uprising, as it turned out, was limited to the slaves belonging to a Mr. Sorrel, who were charged with entering their master's house to murder him. It came out during the trial that Sorrel's own brother had put them up to it, bribing them to poison him. When that hadn't worked, he had paid them to assault him. The evidence was weak, since under Virginia law the testimony of a Negro could not be used against a white man. Fithian heard one of Sorrel's slaves say under oath at the trial that Sorrel's brother had guided their hands, and this sounded pretty convincing to him. However, the judge dismissed the case and ordered the slaves whipped.

When Fithian's contract came up for renewal later that year, Mr. Carter asked him to stay, but he had had enough of Virginia and told his employer that he was returning to his studies. On the eve of the War of Independence, Fithian found an America made up of two distinct and incompatible societies, north and south of the Mason-Dixon Line. Though there were slaves in the north, 90 percent of them were in the south.

On his tour of the north in 1744, Dr. Hamilton had found all the colonies pretty much alike, but thirty years later Fithian had reason to differ. Virginia society, he felt, was pleasure-loving and empty. Even Mr. Carter had little faith in some of its institutions. He said that he would never send his children to William and Mary, because the professors spent their nights in taverns playing cards. He had often seen them weaving through the streets drunk. Virginians were mercurial, quick to befriend you but also quick to quarrel. It didn't take much to start a fight: it was enough to call someone a lubber or a thick-skull, or to mislay his hat, or to knock a peach out of his hand, or to offer a dram without wiping the mouth of the bottle.

Coming from New Jersey, Fithian found Virginia so foreign that there was even a language problem. A person arriving at someone's house didn't ask, "Is anyone in?," but "Who keeps home?" What they called a "vendue" in New Jersey was called a "sale" in Virginia, and taverns were called "ordinaries." A mischievous horse was "vicious," and a brisk horse was said to go "gaily." In any case, Fithian was happy to be going home to New Jersey, where there was entirely less talk of horses.

In February 1775, the year after Philip Fithian left Virginia, Nicholas Cresswell, a twenty-three-year-old English traveler who had come to America for "a change of air," reported from Maryland that "the people are arming and training in every place. They are all liberty mad." Cresswell soon found himself an observer of America at war, for hostilities broke out that April in Lexington and Concord. Still, he managed to continue his travels and crossed the Alleghenies, which he found to be "not one entire mountain, but a number piled one on top of the other, with narrow valleys between them."

Cresswell made friends easily. When he got to Fort Pitt, which was now surrounded by thirty houses, mostly belonging to traders, he visited some Indian villages, where he took part in dances and whooped around the fire striped with Indian paint. He got "most feloniously drunk," and cavorted with so many squaws that he was "alarmed with symptoms of the itch."

By September 1776, he had returned to the Atlantic Seaboard. In Newark, he found himself under some pressure to enlist in the American ranks, but "I am determined to rot in jail rather than take up arms against my native country." It was no easy job: Newark was crawling with George Washington's troops. "Yankee men," Cresswell observed, were "the nastiest devils in creation. . . . The army here is numerous, but ragged, dirty, sickly and ill-disciplined. If my countrymen are beaten by these ragamuffins I shall be much surprised."

Cresswell left Newark to avoid conscription and headed south to Virginia. In Alexandria, he was arrested under suspicion of being a spy but was released when he promised to move on. Cresswell followed Washington's campaign against General William Howe closely. He was horrified in December and January, when Washington picked the British off at Trenton and Princeton. "That a negro-driver," he wrote, "should, with a ragged banditti of un-disciplined people, the scum and refuse of all nations on earth, so long keep a British general at bay, even oblige him to retreat—it is astonishing. It is too much . . . for General Howe to be puzzled and plagued by a Virginia tobacco planter."

By July 1777, Cresswell had taken passage home in a brig anchored in Long Island Sound. He was glad to be leaving "this unhappy country, this country turned topsy-turvy, changed from an earthly paradise to a hell upon terra firma. . . . The whims, cruelty, and caprice of a vile Congress give them laws, and a set of puritanical rascals retails the scriptures and gives them the little religion they have. . . ."

Cresswell did not understand the national feeling that had grown out of the Seven Years' War. Americans had made the land their own by fighting for it. England had won Canada with American help, but Americans had won their own country as well, and now they had to win it again.

Nor did Cresswell grasp the paradox that America, although never a classless society, had an army of citizen-soldiers. At the time of Cresswell's tour, America was a land of social stratification. John Quincy Adams wrote that, when his father was at Harvard, "the distinction of rank was observed with such punctilious nicety that . . . precedence was assigned to every individual according to the dignity of his birth, or the rank of his parents." John Adams was thus placed fourteenth in a class of twenty-four.

All that was an imitation of England. But the urge to re-create the social organization of the mother country was being replaced by a sense of American nationhood. Benjamin Franklin's "Join or Die" cartoon, with its drawing of a sectioned snake, had been published in the *Pennsylvania Gazette* in May 1754, during the French and Indian War. Now its message of strength through unity had a new relevance. Americans had found a voice in Patrick Henry: "The distinctions between Virginians, Pennsylvanians, New Yorkers, are no more. I am not a Virginian but an American."

This was not a statement of fact but a rallying cry, for there were plenty of distinctions. But there was also a common purpose. The right that allowed New England congregations to depose their ministers allowed Americans to oust the British.

And always in the background was the double-edged frontier, a line of defense for the Indians, a line of penetration for the settler. Now, with America at war, the frontier was threatened by Indians who were loyal to the crown because they saw in an American defeat the last chance to keep their lands.

Samuel Kirkland, a Princeton graduate like Philip Fithian, was ordained in 1766, at the age of twenty-five. A Connecticut Puritan, and a Presbyterian, he had the call, and was sent out by the Scotch Missionary Society to spread God's word—first among the Senecas and then among the Tuscaroras, near Oneida, New York. The spiritual muscle of Puritanism was getting flabby in New England, but there was still the prospect of its vigorous exercise in the wilderness.

The Tuscaroras were Iroquois who had strayed south and been pushed out of their lands in North Carolina in 1713 by settlers. They moved back north to upstate New York and were taken into the Great League of Five Nations—Senecas, Cayugas, Oneidas, Onondagas, and Mohawks—as a "Younger Brother." These self-governing Indian nations banded together for political and military reasons. They pledged never to fight on opposite sides in a war and, when united, were able to produce armies of several thousand men. The apex of their power was the French and Indian War, when they were courted by Sir William Johnson to side with the English. Once the war was over, however, they were no longer of use.

Having been "civilized," the Tuscaroras were dependent on the white man by the time Kirkland arrived. They concentrated on the business of surviving in their log houses and wigwam villages and cultivated the "three sisters"—corn, beans, and squash.

Kirkland learned their language, married Jerusha Bingham, an idealistic young woman who wanted to share his life in the wilderness, and in 1770 they settled in the wigwam town of Kanowalohale, near Oneida. He now worked under the auspices of the Boston-based London Company for the Propagation of the Gospel.

Kirkland found that his job wasn't simply a matter of preaching the gospel to the Indians. He ran what amounted to a social-services and welfare bureau, and also acted as the tribe therapist. "I sat with the headmen till midnight," he wrote in November 1770, "to consider the case of a Tuscarora whose wife left him for ten years and took another husband. . . . Every little difference in families or between relations must be brought to me to [achieve] reconciliation." He also gave them medical care, bleeding them when he thought they needed it.

Kirkland distributed food to the Indians in five villages when they lost their crops to worms. Families came to him, saying, "The last mess of corn we have in the world is already in the kettle over the fire. We know not where to go for subsistence, unless you can relieve us. The fishing season is not yet come, and good hunting is no more known among us since the encroachment of the white people." It wrenched him to see them arrive in winter wearing only "an old wornout blanket without any shirt, or even shoes to cover their feet."

Kirkland knew that donations of food and clothing were not the answer: he had to make them self-sufficient. He gave them farming utensils such as scythes, chopping axes, hoes, whipsaws, and augurs. He hired a man to teach them plowing and mowing. He gained their trust. His meetings were so crowded that some of his flock had to stand outside. When he preached, the Divine Power seemed to attend his words, many wept abundantly, and some made public confessions of their sins. This kind of zeal was rarely found among his own people, but Kirkland prayed that God would take away the Indians' "ugly wicked hearts." In December, he preached: "Thou Blind Pharisee—cleanse first the inside of thy cup."

On one occasion, an Indian couple had come from some distance to ask for baptism. But Kirkland did not dispense baptism easily, the way Catholic missionaries did. He insisted on spiritual progress, which caused resentment, for the Indians complained that thirty of their babies had died unbaptized. He also appointed a committee to enforce temperance in his village and gave the Indians an ultimatum: he would leave if there was any backsliding.

Kirkland served under the jurisdiction of Sir William Johnson, the superintendent of Indian affairs, who suspected him of preaching the views of the American revolutionaries to his Tuscaroras and Oneidas, and was thinking of having him banned from the area. On July 11, 1774, however, Johnson died.

In 1775, when the troubles between Great Britain and the colonies heated up, Guy Johnson, who had taken his uncle's place, reported to his superiors that Kirkland had explained the political situation to his Indians in the following terms: "My brothers, the King required a payment for the great expenses of the late war and laid duties for that purpose which the Americans would not pay, whereupon troops were sent to compel them." The Indian reaction was, What are these crazy white men up to now, quarreling among themselves?

In January 1775, a delegation of Oneidas brought a list of complaints about Kirkland to Guy Johnson. Besides his stinginess over baptism, and his meddling in Indian affairs, he tended to explain the grievances between the British and the colonies in terms favorable to the latter.

Johnson gave the Oneidas his own version of events, which

was that the dispute between the English and the Americans had to do with some people who, instead of letting a shipload of tea be unloaded, had destroyed it, which had made the king very angry, so that he sent some troops. Johnson would have to put a stop to Kirkland and other missionaries who were spreading the patriot gospel.

An Oneida chief told Kirkland: "We have heard of the unhappy differences and great contention betwixt you and Old England. We cannot meddle in this dispute between two brothers. You are two brothers of the blood, and we bear an equal affection to both of you. Should the great king of England apply to us for aid, we shall decline him; if the colonies apply to us, we shall refuse. We Indians cannot recollect in the tradition of our ancestors a like case. . . ."

The Six Nations wanted to stay neutral, but neither side would let them. Working for the patriot cause, Kirkland urged the Continental Congress to send a formal speech of friendship to the Six Nations. He also offered the Mohawks a speech from the Massachusetts patriots. General Thomas Gage, governor of Massachusetts and commander-in-chief of British forces in North America, alerted by Guy Johnson to Kirkland's activities, wrote Johnson on February 5, 1775: "Missionaries have it often in their power to lead the minds of people wrong. Therefore by all means do what you can to get the Indians to drive such incendiaries from among them."

Johnson reported to Gage that Kirkland had left for Boston to see his superiors "with many grievances (as some say) and accounts of obstructions to his pious endeavors." Gage replied on April 13 that Johnson must "rout . . . the troublesome missionaries." As for Kirkland, "before he attempts to return from his excursion here [in Boston], great pains should be taken to prejudice the Indians against him."

Six days later, hostilities broke out at Lexington and Concord. When Kirkland came through Johnson Hall in upstate New York that May, on his way back from Boston, Guy Johnson put him under house arrest. But Kirkland slipped away and managed to get to Philadelphia to appear before the Second Continental Congress that July of 1775, to testify on Indian affairs. He spent a week instructing Congress on Indian diplomacy, which led to the naming of Indian commissioners. It was largely thanks to Kirkland that the Continental Congress developed an Indian policy. When he left

Philadelphia on July 18, a grateful Congress gave him three hundred dollars for expenses, making him a paid agent.

While the Continental Congress met in Philadelphia, Guy Johnson convened the Six Nations in Montreal. On hearing rumors that Kirkland had been to Philadelphia, Johnson said that, if he could find proof that he had advised the Congress, "I would cut off Mr. Kirkland's head as soon as I would a snake's."

In July 1776, the Continental Congress passed the point of no return, adopting a resolution "that these United Colonies are, and of Right ought to be Free and Independent States." In August, with Kirkland interpreting, representatives of the Six Nations met in Albany with some of the Indian commissioners appointed by the Continental Congress. "The king has broken the covenant chain with his American children," the commissioners told the Indians, who appeared to agree. But they also agreed to what Johnson told them. Agreeing was part of their strategy of staying neutral.

Kirkland returned to the Oneidas and Tuscaroras, who told him that they were resolved to die with the Americans in this contest. At the same time, Joseph Brant, the Mohawk whom Sir William Johnson had educated and made his assistant, and who had visited England in 1775 and been made much of (his portrait was painted by Romney), was strongly pro-British. He took the Seneca, Cayuga, and Onondaga nations over to the British, while the Oneidas and Tuscaroras stayed on the American side, creating a split in the Iroquois League that would never heal.

Kirkland urged General Philip Schuyler to garrison Fort Stanwix, at today's Rome, New York, which the British had abandoned in July 1776. Kirkland became the fort chaplain, commuting from his Indian villages. Ebenezer Elmer, a lieutenant in the Fort Stanwix garrison, wrote in his diary for September 14, 1776, that Kirkland had given the following sermon: "He that is not for me is against me, and he that gathereth not with me, scattereth abroad."

Because of the trading post at the fort, Kirkland wrote, the Indians "pour in by shoals." In the winter, he went to the Oneida village to report George Washington's victories at Trenton and Princeton. They shot off their two cannons in celebration. On this happy occasion, he gave them six barrels of rum, one for each nation. In the interest of the Indian alliance, he had given up his pro-temperance principles.

• •

In 1765, the people of Charleston celebrated the resignation of its stamp officers. One was Charles Woodmason, the stamp distributor turned backcountry preacher. Citizens banded together to prevent the stamps from being unloaded, and the Sons of Liberty burned effigies and unfurled a Union Jack in the street with the word "Liberty" painted across it. The numerous slaves in Charleston couldn't read, but you can bet they got the message. Henry Laurens, a prominent Charleston merchant and importer of slaves, noted, "Some negroes . . . apparently in mere thoughtless imitation, began to cry 'Liberty.' "

The slaves believed that freedom was in the air and there might be some left over for them. It was natural that white activism would beget black activism, that the colonists' effort to shrug off England would lead to a corresponding effort among the slaves to be rid of their masters. At the same time that the Navigation Laws were broken by whites, the slavery laws were broken by blacks. As the southern colonies rebelled along with their northern neighbors, they worried that the British would encourage their slaves to rise against their rebellious masters.

In December 1765, Lieutenant Governor Bull heard shocking news: Mrs. Isaac Huger, the wife of a white merchant, had overheard, from the balcony of her home, two slaves discussing an insurrection on Christmas Eve. Bull was concerned. Christmas was the perfect time to start a revolt, for blacks were allowed to assemble then. There was also the "pernicious custom" of rejoicing by the firing of guns. Bull distributed a hundred rifles to the sailors on the ships in harbor. Their job was to guard the wharves at night. He also enlisted the friendly Catawbas to go after the runaways in their camps, "as Indians strike terror into the negroes."

The rumored revolution among the slaves turned out to be a bust: there were only seven runaways. Bull wrote London in January 1766: "The apprehension of a negro insurrection last December happily proved abortive. The vigorous execution of our militia and patrol laws for 14 days before and after Christmas Day prevented the festivity and the assembling of negroes usual at that time, and disconcerted their schemes."

Despite the absence of a slave revolt, the South Carolina Committee of Safety established a subcommittee "to secure the province against an insurrection of slaves or counter-revolutionary moves." Their anxieties were not unreasonable. In South Carolina at that time, the eighty thousand slaves made up more than half the population. They did the bulk of the physical labor, clearing land, digging canals, harvesting rice and indigo, tending cattle, and catching shrimp.

Not all slaves were field hands. In Charleston, many were trained in crafts and trades. They took over certain kinds of jobs and businesses. The rise of a distinct class of urban slave workers is reflected in the labor legislation of the period. One of the earliest antitrust actions in North America took place in 1736, when the Charleston Grand Jury protested that Negro apprentice chimney sweeps had combined to fix prices.

Charleston was a busy import-export hub, with ships bringing in slaves and other goods and taking out rice and indigo. The question for slave-owners in the city was: How do you make urban slaves profitable? And the answer was: Hire them out on a short-term basis to perform skilled tasks. But in making slavery profitable, they weakened the institution, by placing between the slave and his master an employer who paid him directly. Some masters placed want ads in the gazettes: "For hire, a very orderly negro man that understands how to wait on a gentleman and take care of horses as well as any servant in this province." Some slaves found their own jobs, made their own hours, kept part of their pay, and otherwise ran rings around their masters. Or else they free-lanced without telling them, as noted by Henry Laurens: "Ishmael— brought in 30 shillings. Said he had earned as a porter. I gave him the money together with a reprimand, which he thought a good couplet." Thanks to their outside work, plenty of city slaves had spending money.

Having joined the urban work force, slaves looked for ways to improve their condition, by stretching rather than breaking their bonds. New labor legislation followed. Efforts were made to set the going wage rate, so that the masters would know what their slaves were paid. In 1764, the Board of Commissioners fixed the payment for licensed slave porters who were rented out by the day at ten shillings for "labor in ships at the wharves" and "cleaning of wells," and six shillings for "common porterage" and "rolling of rice" (barrels). A hiring hall was designated where the slaves could be kept track of and accounted for.

A lot of slaves came from coastal areas in West Africa, where they had learned fishing and boating skills. Over the years, they took over the rivers, creeks, and other waterways around Charleston. A law required the owners of coastal vessels to have at least one white person aboard, but being impractical, it was ignored. The boatmen came to know the coast and the inland waterways better than their masters, acquiring a fund of useful knowledge that could be turned to profit. Slaves with boats could burglarize riverfront plantations and fence stolen goods, and the "fishing ne-groes" could sell their catch at the going rate, with their masters none the wiser.

The ancient West African tradition of market vendors and street callers was easily adaptable to the New World. In Charles-ton's Lower Market, Negro women who sold produce formed a kind of guild and were able to obtain a monopoly on certain goods, which they sold at high prices. For instance, the price of drumfish rose tenfold, and they also sold cooked rice with sauce and other tasty dishes. It was reported in the gazettes that the profits from this commerce were used to maintain runaway slaves who were hiding in the bustling city. The urban slaves of Charleston now formed a community resourceful enough to absorb and assist run-aways.

"The negroes receive too much countenance"—that was the refrain. The hiring-out system and the market-vendor guild brought them a measure of autonomy. Slaves with money in their pockets could bribe town watchmen with a few shillings and stay out after curfew. They gathered on Sundays to gamble while the white folk were at church. In 1773, a complaint arose that the law preventing extravagant dress among slaves was not being enforced. In response, one slave was detained for wearing silver buckles on his shoes. Tavern-owners weren't supposed to sell intoxicating drink to slaves, but this too was ignored. They came in through the back door, and staggered out the same way. Some of the dram-keepers were watchmen, but they were glad of the business.

There was quite a bit of slippage in the enforcement of slave legislation, not only because of the money to be made but also because the white leadership was absorbed in the political debate that would lead to the revolution.

In the late spring of 1775, news of Lexington and Concord reached South Carolina, which was already on the brink of rebel-lion. Rumors of British-engineered slave revolts mounted again. The Committee of Safety heard reports that two Tory merchants were rejoicing at the news that the British were about to arm the slaves. They were tarred, feathered, carted through the town, pa-raded in front of every Tory house, and made to proclaim, "Damn John Bull." At one house, the mob threw a bag of feathers on the porch and said, "Take care of it till your turn comes." Then they called for grog and said, "Charge it to the account of Lord North." The mob was in such a humor that shopkeepers dropped their shutters in fear.

When Lord William Campbell, the new royal governor, arrived in June 1775 on the sloop-of-war *Scorpion*, rumors flew that he had brought fourteen thousand rifles for the redcoats. Notorious falsehoods were spread to work people up into "a pitch of madness and fury," Campbell reported. He saw perfectly well that the best way to rally support for the revolutionary cause was to accuse the British of inciting a slave rebellion.

One of the victims of this campaign was a freed slave, Thomas Jeremiah. His was a rags-to-riches-to-rope story. Jeremiah, or "Jerry," was a licensed harbor pilot who had often brought in men-of-war through the shoals around Charleston Harbor. He built up his business until he had several slaves of his own and a thousand pounds of capital. Governor Campbell called him "one of the most valuable and useful men in his way in this province."

In June 1775, Thomas Jeremiah was brought to trial before two judges and five freeholders for plotting an insurrection. The evidence was weak, so he was jailed for two months until new information could be collected. On August 11, the trial resumed, and this time the testimony against him came from two slaves. One of them, Sambo, who worked on a schooner in Charleston Harbor, said under oath: "About two or three months ago, being at Simmons Wharf, Jeremiah says to me, do you hear anything of the war that is coming?" Sambo answered no, at which Jeremiah said, "Yes, there is a great war coming soon." Sambo said, "What shall we poor negroes do in a schooner?" Jeremiah said, "Set the schooner on fire, jump on shore, and join the soldiers—the war is come to help the poor negroes."

Another slave, Jemmy, had been deposed on June 16 before Justice of the Peace John Coram. Jemmy, who was owned by Peter Croft, said that ten weeks before, at Peolia's Wharf, he had been approached by Jeremiah, "who declared he had something to give Dewar, a runaway slave belonging to Mr. Tweed. He asked Jemmy to take a few guns to the said Dewar, to be placed in negro hands to fight the inhabitants of this province." Jeremiah further said, according to Jemmy: "I am to have the chief command of the negroes. I believe I have powder enough already, but I want more arms, and will try to get as many as I can."

It came out in the course of the trial that Jeremiah had been convicted for assaulting a white ship's captain four years before. At that time, he was sentenced to lie in stocks for an hour and receive ten lashes, but Lieutenant Governor Bull pardoned him, presumably because of extenuating circumstances. Now he appeared as a recidivist, a confirmed violent and seditious Negro. In addition, Jeremiah denied knowing Jemmy, who was in fact his brother-in-law. At a time when rumors were rife that the British were planning to free the slaves, Thomas Jeremiah didn't have a hope. He was sentenced to be hanged and burned.

Governor Campbell had the power to pardon him, and wanted to use it. "My blood ran cold," he wrote, "when I read on what grounds they had doomed a fellow creature to death." But his attempt at intervention "raised such a clamor among the people, as is incredible, and they openly and loudly declared, if I granted him a pardon they would hang him at my door." A leading citizen of Charleston wrote Campbell that a pardon "would raise a flame all the water in the Cooper river could not extinguish."

A local minister, the Reverend Mr. Smith, visited the condemned man shortly before his execution on August 18. Smith tried in vain to get a confession out of Jerry. The reverend told Governor Campbell afterward that Jeremiah was "perfectly resigned to his unhappy, his undeserved fate. He declared he wished not for life, he was in a happy frame of mind, and prepared for death." According to Campbell, Jeremiah to the end "asserted his innocence, behaved with the greatest intrepidity as well as decency, and told his implacable and ungrateful persecutors, God's judgment would one day overtake them for shedding his innocent blood."

Was Thomas Jeremiah railroaded? Clearly, in the climate of the times, he could not get a fair trial, and his right to a pardon was denied. According to one astute observer, it was a tough call. The merchant Henry Laurens noted that the evidence was weak, that his brother-in-law, Jemmy, later recanted, that the sentence was harsh, and that the noble bearing of the victim was perhaps a sign of his innocence. But . . . Sambo and another witness did not recant, and Laurens ended up believing that "Jerry was guilty of a design and attempt to encourage our negroes to rebellion and joining the king's troops if any had been sent there."

Jeremiah's death sentence gnawed at Governor Campbell for the rest of his days. He thought the witnesses, "terrified at the recollection of former cruelties," had perjured themselves to escape punishment. Why would a free Negro want to foster resistance, particularly since, being "remarkably sensible and sagacious," he was more successful than many whites? His public services to the city in putting out fires were widely acknowledged. It was a genuinely anguished Governor Campbell who wrote: "I could not save him, my lord! The very reflection harrows my soul."

My sense is that Thomas Jeremiah was guilty. A free Negro might have a strong feeling of obligation to those who were still slaves, and might use his advantages to organize a rebellion. As a skilled navigator with some capital, he was in a position to buy and distribute weapons. He seems also to have been a natural leader who could unite the Charleston slaves as allies of the British against the Americans. It was a question of "Call me a dog and I'll bark," of the rumors encouraging the slaves to act accordingly.

The rumors about the British co-opting the slaves did not take long to become fact. On November 7, 1775, the Virginia governor, Lord Dunmore, announced that Negroes willing to bear arms in His Majesty's army would be set free. In less than a month, three hundred slaves were wearing British uniforms with a patch on the jacket that said "Liberty to Slaves," in a unit known as the "Ethiopian Regiment."

As 1776 ended, the British began to revise their military strategy. Reconquest, rather than policing the colonies, became the priority. The theater of battle was a long narrow north-south corridor bisected by the Hudson River. This route, which connected Montreal to New York City, was considered the key to the capture of all the colonies.

The campaign of 1777 was a three-pronged attack: General John Burgoyne marched south from Montreal to take Fort Ticonderoga, at the northern end of Lake George, intending to continue on to Albany. General William Howe moved up the Hudson Valley from New York City, planning to meet Burgoyne in Albany. The third prong was a sideshow, in which Colonel Barry St. Leger advanced from Oswego on Lake Ontario to Oneida Lake and Wood Creek to take Fort Stanwix, at the portage point between Wood Creek and the Mohawk River. If this three-pronged approach succeeded, the British would have control of all the territory from Canada to New York City, completely cutting off New England. It was a colonial version of the domino theory: if New York fell, New England would fall next, and so on.

Fort Stanwix, renamed Fort Schuyler by the Americans, had been built by the British in 1758 at the portage known as the Oneida Carrying Place, near today's Rome, New York. This portage, which varied in length from one to five miles depending on the water level, consisted of a narrow trail across a low ridge. The ridge divided two major watersheds, the Mohawk flowing east into the Hudson, and Wood Creek flowing west into Oneida Lake. The location was strategic, because there were no roads, and because it was the second-shortest route from the Atlantic to the Great Lakes, via the Hudson, the Mohawk, Wood Creek, Oneida Lake, the Oswego River, and Lake Ontario. (The shortest was down the St. Lawrence from the north.)

Samuel Kirkland saw the importance of having the fort, abandoned by the British, rebuilt and garrisoned by Americans. General Philip Schuyler agreed, and in July 1776 he sent a detachment of ninety men from the Third New Jersey Regiment, under the command of Colonel Samuel Elmore. There was nothing left of the English fort except the visible outline of where it had been. The site was in the heart of the wilderness, surrounded by Indian villages, with only five families of settlers clustered round the ruins.

John Roof had been there since 1760, and his log cabin on a piece of cleared land was a stopping place for portaging travelers. When another settler, Thomas Mair, grumbled about the presence of the soldiers, he was suspected of Loyalist leanings. Since his house was right in front of the fort and obstructed the field of fire, it was torn down, and he was ordered to leave.

The men from New Jersey had a crucial assignment. If the British were to invade the Mohawk Valley, they would have to use the water route from Lake Ontario. Fort Stanwix was the plug. That fall, as they built barracks, the Americans lived in tents, complaining bitterly about the weather in upstate New York. On September 19, Lieutenant Ebenezer Elmer griped that it was a "cold stormy day and I obliged to live in a cold wet marquee [a large tent with open sides] which leaks considerable, whilst the captain, with two field officers and other great men, have good rooms in barracks." "The way of the world," Elmer concluded.

October was worse than September. On October 1, Lieutenant Elmer wrote: "Being on guard all night, we came near perishing, having our bodies exposed to a severe white frost, which froze the ground hard, and some of the men barefoot." One reason they

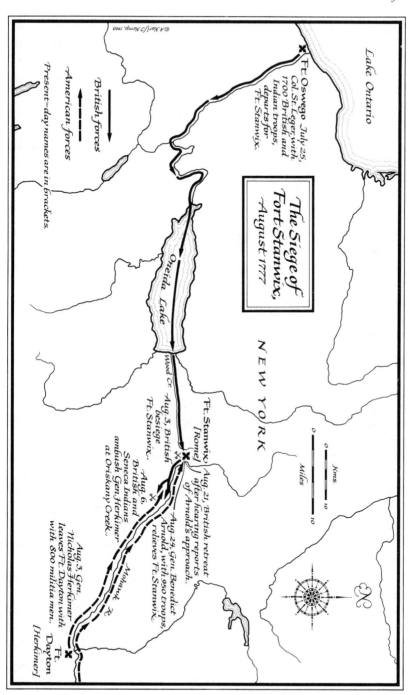

The Siege of
Fort Stanwix,
August 1777

Lake Ontario

NEW YORK

© A.Karl/J.Kemp, 1993

Ft. Oswego July 25,
Col. St. Leger, with
1700 British and
Indian troops,
departs for
Ft. Stanwix.

British forces

American forces

Present-day names are in brackets.

Oneida Lake

Wood Cr.

Ft. Stanwix
[Rome] Aug. 21, British retreat
after hearing reports
of Arnold's approach.

Aug. 3, British
besiege
Ft. Stanwix.

Aug. 24, Gen. Benedict
Arnold, with 950 troops,
relieves Ft. Stanwix.

Aug. 6,
British and
Seneca Indians
ambush Gen. Herkimer
at Oriskany Creek.

Mohawk R.

Aug. 3, Gen.
Nicholas Herkimer
leaves Ft. Dayton with
with 800 militia men.

Ft.
Dayton
[Herkimer]

Kms.
0   10

Miles
0   10

might have been barefoot was that they sometimes bartered their army-issue clothing and shoes to traders who came to the fort to sell rum. This was a punishable offense, as were being drunk on parade, insulting an officer, and cheating an Indian. There were so many offenders that in the middle of the parade ground stood a white cedar whipping post big enough to accommodate four men at a time—its remains were dug up by archaeologists in 1970. The youngest soldiers at the fort were an eleven-year-old fifer and a twelve-year-old drummer. Oddly enough, the whippings, usually fifty to 150 lashes, were administered by the drummer, whose blows must have been fairly light.

In the early months at Fort Stanwix, there were one or two desertions a day, a reflection on the living conditions. Three deserters were shot, and others were whipped or court-martialed. The officers found themselves attending trials almost daily, and Lieutenant Elmer observed on October 2 that after a court-martial they repaired to John Roof's to drink and play cards. They drank so much wine that "many of them got very happy . . . and knocked up an Indian dance, at which they yelled much. . . . All this was done within the fort."

Aside from the biting cold, disciplinary problems, and seasonal illnesses, the winter of 1776–77 was quiet, and the men were able to devote themselves to rebuilding the fort. Some of the noncoms and officers had their wives and children with them. This was allowed as long as the wives agreed to wash the soldiers' laundry. Not everyone, however, had a wife—or a need for clean clothes. Lieutenant Elmer, who was interested in medicine and later became a military surgeon, visited the sick "in their lousy old hospital . . . such a case of wretchedness that one could hardly bear to behold the abject souls therein confined." Samuel Kirkland served as chaplain, leading the prayers and visiting the sick, when he was not among the Oneidas to preach the patriot cause.

In the spring of 1777, there were three new arrivals. The first, on April 20, was Captain de la Marquisie, a French military engineer whose plan for building a new fort had been approved by General Schuyler. He was followed in May by Lieutenant Colonel Marinus Willett, who commanded the five hundred men of the much-welcome Third New York Regiment, and by the new fort commander, Colonel Peter J. Gansevoort, Jr., a Princeton-educated twenty-eight-year-old six-footer. Courteous and methodical, Gansevoort joked about the fact that he had no teeth in his mouth.

De la Marquisie resembled a comic character out of a Molière play, a bumbler whose motto seemed to be "The lower the chair, the higher the table." His plan was to build an expanded new fort rather than restore the ruins of the old one. But upon his arrival, he complained that he didn't have enough men to carry out his grand design.

Colonel Willett, a thirty-seven-year-old veteran of the 1776 campaign, began to wonder about the French engineer. His doubts multiplied when the man sent large parties into the swamp to look for logs and they brought back the wrong size. Willett urged Gansevoort to get rid of him, but Gansevoort hesitated, since the Frenchman had General Schuyler's backing.

Colonel Willett became convinced of "the incompetency of the engineer," since he built a barracks outside the fort, which would have to be burned down when the British attacked. De la Marquisie got so muddled in his calculations that he couldn't line up the pickets in the palisade with a salient angle he had built. Willett saw the mistake coming, but he let de la Marquisie self-destruct and then asked Gansevoort to arrest him. He was sent back to headquarters in disgrace, and after his departure, it was discovered that he hadn't even built a gunpowder magazine.

That summer saw the first incident of Indian harassment. On June 25, 1777, after breakfast, Captain Gregg and Corporal Madison saw great flocks of pigeons flying over the trees, quite close to the fort. Although they were disobeying orders, the temptation was too great. They went out to bag a few, and were ambushed by Indians. Both were shot, and Captain Gregg played dead while an Indian removed his scalp, leaving a bad cut on his forehead. Scalpless and bleeding, his corporal dead beside him, he took out his pocket watch and noted that the time was 10:00 A.M.

The boldness of the Indians may have been linked to the June 23 departure from Montreal of Lieutenant Colonel St. Leger, of the Thirty-fourth Regiment of Foot. Aside from his regulars, he had some Canadian militia, a total of eight hundred white men and about seven hundred Indians under the command of Colonel Daniel Claus, an experienced frontiersman. This small army sailed down the St. Lawrence to Oswego, which they reached in late June. There, three hundred Mohawks under Joseph Brant joined them.

Colonel Claus sent out a reconnaissance party to Fort Stanwix, about fifty miles away. On July 3, this group attacked a party of sixteen Americans who were digging turf under the command of Ensign John Spoor. Colonel Claus reported that the party "returned with five prisoners (one a Lt.), and four scalps, having defeated a working party of the rebels as they were cutting sod." He learned from the prisoners that there were about six hundred men in the fort. Colonel Gansevoort wrote that one of the dead was brought back "inhumanely mangled." He knew what to expect from St. Leger's Indian auxiliaries if the fort was taken.

Realizing that the attacking army was on its way, Colonel Gansevoort asked General Nicholas Herkimer, commander of the Tryon County militia, for assistance. Herkimer, a palatine settler who lived down the Mohawk River, in German Flats—about thirty miles east of the fort, near today's Little Falls—promised to bring some of his men.

Then, on July 27, three little girls left the fort to pick berries at the edge of the cedar swamp five hundred yards to the southwest. They were attacked by Indians. Two were killed, but the third one, though wounded, made it back to the fort. Gansevoort decided to send the women and children to Fort Dayton, at German Flats—except for one pregnant woman who was past due, the wife of an artilleryman. Because of de la Marquisie's bungling, the work on the fort wasn't finished. Gansevoort still had men working on the parapets, and could only hope that they would finish by the time the British arrived.

When the Continental Army came into existence on January 1, 1776, there was a ceremony on Prospect Hill in Charlestown, outside Boston, at which a Grand Union flag was raised on a seventy-six-foot flagpole. This hybrid flag had seven red and six white stripes, representing the thirteen colonies. In the upper left-hand corner, or canton, were the crosses of St. Andrew and St. George—otherwise known as the Union Jack. The retention of the British emblem signified the possibility of continued loyalty. But July's Declaration of Independence made that irrelevant, and the Grand Union flag fell into disfavor.

Then, on June 14, 1777, the Continental Congress passed a resolution in Philadelphia: "Resolved, that the flag of the thirteen United States be thirteen stripes alternate red and white; that the union be thirteen stars, white on a blue field, representing a new constellation." It's been said that this resolution was proposed by the Marine Committee, and that the flag described was intended as a naval ensign to identify American ships, not as a military standard. But the resolution says quite clearly that the flag described was to be "the flag of the United States." It does not say "the maritime flag."

This brief resolution went unnoticed among more pressing matters. None of the new flags were supplied to the army until six years later, in 1783, although the new design was flown on ships. The first mention of the new flag in a newspaper appears to have been an item in the *Pennsylvania Evening Post* on August 30, 1777. But perhaps it was mentioned before, in newspapers that have not been traced. There is such an implication in a journal entry made on August 3, 1777, by Dr. James Thacher, a military surgeon at the Albany General Hospital: "It appears by the papers that . . . the flag of the thirteen United States be 13 stripes, alternate red and white, that the union be 13 stars, white in a blue field." News of the flag had apparently reached Albany by then.

Dr. Thacher had been anxiously following General Burgoyne's advance down the Hudson with his army of nine thousand. He was disheartened when Burgoyne announced that he could recruit as many Indian auxiliaries as he needed. Why, Dr. Thacher wondered, were the Indians joining the cause of tyranny?

On July 5, Dr. Thacher heard that Burgoyne had dragged his cannon up steep Sugar Hill (Mount Defiance), overlooking Fort Ticonderoga. Shortly after midnight on July 6, General Arthur St. Clair abandoned the fort to the British. King George III exclaimed: "I have beat them! I have beat all the Americans!" The surrender of Ticonderoga caused great alarm in the patriot ranks, Dr. Thacher reported in his journal, saying: "No event could be more unexpected nor more severely felt throughout our army and country."

On July 6, Dr. Thacher joined a force leaving Albany, heading north to evacuate the wounded. They were attacked south of Ticonderoga and retreated to Fort Edward, only fifty miles north of Albany. On July 7, 1777, there was a severe engagement, with General Schuyler, at Fort Edward, trying to stop Burgoyne's advance.

On July 25, Dr. Thacher started downriver from Fort Edward with the wounded, heading back to Albany. In his absence, a detachment of the Ninth Massachusetts Regiment came through Albany on July 20, on the way to reinforce Fort Stanwix. The Massachusetts men may also have heard in Albany about the new flag, since Dr. Thacher heard about it upon his return with the wounded: his August 3 journal entry was written two weeks after their passage.

On July 30, the men of the Ninth Massachusetts reached Fort Dayton. It had taken them ten days to cover about 108 miles. A hundred men under Colonel James Mellen were assigned to escort several boatloads of supplies on their way to Fort Stanwix. They arrived on August 2, just in time for the siege: this was the day when Colonel St. Leger reached the fort with his eight hundred British troops and one thousand Indians. The Massachusetts men may have brought news about the new flag to Fort Stanwix.

August 3 was a Sunday, and on that day the besieged Fort Stanwix garrison raised a homemade flag. According to the diary of an eyewitness, Lieutenant William Colbrath of the New York Regiment, "Early this morning a Continental Flagg made by the officers of Col. Gansevoort's regiment was hoisted and a cannon pointed at the enemy's camp was fired on this occasion."

It's too bad Colbrath didn't describe the flag. Was it the Grand Union flag with the Union Jack in the corner, or was it the new flag described by Dr. Thacher, thirteen stripes and thirteen stars? A second eyewitness, Lieutenant Colonel Marinus Willett, who was Lieutenant Colbrath's commanding officer, gave a more detailed description in the narrative of his wartime experiences: "The fort had never been supplied with a flag. The necessity of having one, upon the arrival of the enemy, taxed the invention of the garrison, and a decent one was soon contrived. The white stripes were cut out of ammunition shirts furnished by the soldiers; the blue strips of a camlet cloak taken from the enemy at Peekskill; while the red stripes were made out of different pieces of stuff procured from one and another of the garrison."

We know that the flag had red and white stripes, but there is no mention of stars. The blue "strips" could have been either for the eight blue triangles in the Union Jack (the canton of the Grand Union flag), or strips sewn together to make the blue field of the stars. "Strips," however, seemed more suited to the Union Jack, since the blue field for the stars could have been cut as a single piece.

We also know that the blue cloth was cut from a voluminous camlet (camel's hair and silk) cloak taken from a British officer at the battle of Peekskill in 1776, and belonging to Captain Abraham Swartwout of the Third New York Regiment. Captain Swartwout parted with it on condition that he be given in exchange eight yards of broadcloth to make another.

The only other evidence consists of two powder horns engraved by soldiers who were supposedly at the siege. It seems to have been a popular pastime among colonial soldiers to personalize powder horns with illustrations. Unfortunately, these two contradict each other.

The first one, dated Fort Schuyler, December 25, 1977, four months after the siege, shows a diagram of Fort Stanwix with a flagpole and a flag. The flag distinctly shows a canton with an "X" in it, which is closer to the Union Jack than to the Stars and Stripes. The owner of this powder horn was John McGraw, a private in the New York Regiment commanded by Colonel Visscher. But this regiment was not at the fort during the siege, or in December, when the powder horn is dated.

The other powder horn, now owned by the Montgomery County Historical Society at Fort Johnson, New York, was engraved by Lieutenant Christopher Hutton, whose name is on the original siege muster as well as on the official New York State regimental list. Hutton was at Fort Stanwix from March 1777 to November 1780. His powder horn is marked "Chris Hutton 1777." It shows a drawing of an Indian with a musket and a tomahawk, and a mounted figure with the caption "Peter," who is evidently Colonel Gansevoort. And then, curled and blowing in the wind, there is a very evident Stars and Stripes, with six stars clearly visible.

So it's a toss-up. There's only circumstantial evidence that the Stanwix garrison knew about the flag resolution. There's no mention of stars in either eyewitness account. And yet Christopher Hutton, who was there, engraved his powder horn with the Stars and Stripes, and no one has questioned the powder horn's authenticity. Whereas John McGraw was not at Fort Stanwix in 1777, and his powder horn seems to have been engraved after the fact. When I spoke to Anthony Tommell, the Fort Stanwix military historian, who is convinced that the flag flown during the siege was not the Stars and Stripes, he said: "I've been studying the 1777 campaign for all my adult life, and the wishful-thinking issue always comes into play."

If it *was* the Stars and Stripes, it was raised for the first time in presence of an enemy at Fort Stanwix. (The so-called Bennington flag, which supposedly flew at the battle of Bennington on

August 16, 1777, was examined by fabric analysts from the Smith-sonian Institution, who dated it circa 1876.) Even if it wasn't the Stars and Stripes, it was a "people's flag," improvised from articles of clothing donated by occupants of the fort. This makeshift ban-ner, stitched together from strips of red, white, and blue fabric, became the emblem of what the men in the fort were fighting for: freedom from foreign sovereignty, and the chance to make their own nation.

On August 3, Colonel St. Leger asked for the surrender of Fort Stanwix. His offer, according to William Colbrath, was "re-jected with disdain." Colonel Gansevoort sent out parties to bring in hay for the cattle penned in the fort ditch, and then set fire to a house and barn in their field of fire. Indians fired at the fort from behind tree stumps, and an Indian sniper in a tree was blasted out of it with a load of grapeshot. The Indians encircled the fort and yelled through the night.

Gansevoort was waiting for Herkimer's militia column to ar-rive. Herkimer had called up every able-bodied man from sixteen to sixty, and by August 3 he had collected eight hundred men at Fort Dayton. One can imagine these citizen-soldiers taking their muskets off the cabin walls, kissing their wives and children good-bye, and leaving their unharvested wheat. It was only thirty miles to Fort Stanwix, though the going was slow because Herkimer had ox-drawn baggage wagons, and you couldn't hurry the oxen. He also had about sixty Oneida Indians, who had remained loyal to the Americans thanks to the efforts of Samuel Kirkland.

Herkimer sent three men to Fort Stanwix to say he was on his way, and that they should fire three cannon shots as the signal for him to attack. But it took the men longer than expected to get through the British lines. They reached the fort only on the morn-ing of August 6, after wading through the swamp. In the mean-time, Herkimer stopped on the evening of August 5 near Oriskany Creek, presumably within earshot of the fort, waiting for the sig-nal. Some of his officers, impatient for battle, accused him of mark-ing time. It was suggested that he was reluctant to fight because he had a brother, Joost Herkimer, fighting with the British. This underlines the agonizing divisions that took place during the Rev-olutionary War, when close relatives fought on opposite sides. The palatines, for instance, had no feelings of loyalty toward England. On the other hand, they disliked the patroons, whose tenants they had been in the Hudson Valley, and who had taken up the patriot cause. It could go either way, and in the Herkimer family it did.

The forty-nine-year-old soldier-farmer yielded and set out on the morning of August 6, moving in a double column with no flankers. They marched into a fifty-foot-deep ravine with steep sides, where they were ambushed by an English force of about 250 men, including the Seneca Indians commanded by Daniel Claus. Herkimer was shot in the leg but continued to lead his troops, sitting on a saddle with his back against a tree. He told his men to shoot from behind trees, two to a tree, so that one could load while the other fired.

His rear guard, which had not yet entered the ravine, ran off, and his detachment of farmers with no combat experience were trapped in the ravine and badly mauled. The Senecas came at them with hatchets. One of them, Blacksnake, whose recollections were later recorded, said, "We thought no more of killing a man than of killing a beast." The Americans took such heavy losses that there was no question of going on to Fort Stanwix, and Herkimer ordered them to pull back to Fort Dayton. Of his eight hundred men, about 550 were killed or wounded.

"Many of the latter," reported the British Colonel John Butler to General Guy Carleton, "were conformable to the Indian custom afterwards killed." The German Flats Committee of Safety said: "The Flower of our Militia are either killed or wounded except 150 who stood the field and forced the enemy to retreat." As for Herkimer, shot below the knee, his leg was amputated at Fort Dayton, an operation that he survived by only a few hours, owing to loss of blood. The slightest wound could be fatal. Nelson Greene, in his *History of the Mohawk Valley*, wrote: "In the valley homes was great mourning. For such a small population, the losses were almost overwhelming. In some families the male members were wiped out."

Of great significance in the battle of Oriskany was that Indians of the Six Nations Confederation fought one another for the first time. On the British side, the Senecas seem to have done the brunt of the fighting. Thirty-three of them were killed, including five chiefs. The British used them as kamikazes, sending them in with hatchets against muskets. Oriskany was the opening battle of a civil war among the Six Nations. They had broken their pledge of never fighting one another, and followed the white man's example, pitting brother against brother, with ruinous results.

One final remark concerning Oriskany. The history of the United States is so recent that there are amazing examples of oral history being handed down to the present through a tiny number of people. George Walter, a German militiaman at Oriskany in 1777, told the following story to Job Babcock around 1800, when Babcock was a boy. In May 1853, Babcock repeated it to John Albert Scott, the historian of Rome, New York, who published it in his book *Fort Stanwix and Oriskany*. Walter told of his being wounded and then scalped: "Dat Indian tot I vash det, but I knows petter, but I tot I would say noddings so as he would go off."

While Herkimer was trapped on August 6 in the ravine at Oriskany, his messengers arrived at Fort Stanwix, and three cannon shots were accordingly fired—too late. Colonel Willett was sent out with 250 men and a cannon on a traveling carriage, but, with one thing and another, including an August shower that would have dampened his powder, he didn't get going until mid-afternoon. On the way to his planned meeting with Herkimer, he got sidetracked, deciding to loot some half-deserted Indian camps he came to. There was so much loot, such as blankets, kettles, and muskets, that it took the fort's three horse-drawn wagons to collect it, each wagon making three round trips. Willett also collected five regimental flags, a first for the Continental Army. These were hoisted on the flagstaff below the American banner, "when all the troops in the garrison, having mounted the parapets," Willett wrote, "gave three as hearty cheers as perhaps were ever given by the same number of men."

When the Indians who had taken part in the battle of Oriskany returned to their camp, they found all their personal belongings gone, even their medicine bundles, which they took as a bad omen. This, on top of their losses in battle, caused the Indians to wonder why they had come on the expedition.

On August 7, Colonel St. Leger brought up his artillery and fired at the fort, but his popgun cannons did little damage. The following day, at 5:00 P.M., the men inside the fort heard the beating of the chamade (the signal for a truce) and saw a white flag wave. Three British officers stood before the fort; they were allowed inside blindfolded and led into a closed candlelit room, where they were offered cheese and crackers and wine. Once again they asked for the fort's surrender, saying they were having trouble holding back their Indian allies. Colonel Willett replied that the offer was insulting and that, before delivering the garrison "to such a murdering set as your army, I would suffer my body to be filled with splinters and set on fire, as you know has at times been practiced by such hordes as belong to your army on women and children." Colonel Gansevoort rejected the British demand out of hand. That night, Willett slipped out to get reinforcements.

There followed twelve days of inconclusive firing, during which it became clear that the British could not damage the fort, although on August 15 the pregnant woman was wounded. Colonel St. Leger dug a siege trench 150 yards from the fort, so that he could bring his cannon closer and perhaps dig a tunnel under the bastion. In the meantime, the relief column that Colonel Willett had gone to fetch was in Fort Dayton—eight hundred men under the command of General Benedict Arnold.

The story goes that General Arnold sent a half-wit, Yost Schuyler, to the British camp on August 21, to tell them that two thousand Continentals were marching in their direction. Apparently the Indians believed that Yost communed with the spirits. When he waved at the trees, saying there were as many men on the march as there were leaves in the branches, they were impressed.

More likely, the Indians were generally fed up with the way things were going. According to Dr. Thacher's journal, the Indians told Colonel St. Leger: "When we marched down, you told us there would be no fighting for us Indians, we might go down and smoke our pipes; but now a number of our warriors have been killed, and you mean to sacrifice us." According to Daniel Claus, "The Indians finding that our besieging the fort was of no effect, our troops but few . . . began to be dispirited and file off by degrees; the chiefs advised the Brigadier to retreat [to] Oswego and get better artillery from Niagara and more men, and return and renew the siege."

Colonel St. Leger took their advice, and retreated on August 22. That morning, the British bombarded "very smartly," according to Colbrath, wounding the sergeant major and two privates. At noon, a British deserter came into the fort and said that St. Leger had ordered his troops "to strike their tents and pack up." The lifting of the siege coincided with the birth of a daughter to the wounded woman, and "she and the child are like to do well." The garrison was free to walk about and take the free air that they had been denied for twenty days.

On September 3, James Rix, a Haverhill man who was in the

Ninth Massachusetts, wrote his wife: "We got here just as the enemy did. . . . None of the Haverhill people have been hurt. . . . They are all well men to a man. . . . I want to hear from you very much. . . . I am almost beat out with hardship for I never had so hard a campaign before. . . . I desire to be remembered to all enquiring friends and pray God to protect you under his wing." A citizen-soldier, glad to be alive, longing for his wife. High above his head flew his flag, with, instead of heraldic devices, white strips cut from soldiers' shirts, the red of a petticoat, and the blue of a British cloak taken in battle.

CHAPTER NINETEEN

THE
LAND HUNGER

While the war was fought in the east, settlers crossed the Appalachians westward into Kentucky and Tennessee. In 1781, Cornwallis was defeated at Yorktown, and two years later a treaty was signed that severed the American colonies from the British Empire. The Continental Congress, which continued to govern until 1789, took measures to regulate the enormous domain of public lands it had inherited thanks to the war and concessions from the states.

Musuem of Fine Arts, Boston

In George Caleb Bingham's *The Squatters*, two generations of settlers are shown. The men, looking outward, seem ruminative, while the lone woman, bent over a washtub, shows the female role on the frontier as laborious. To the right is a vast distance of unsettled land that beckons the squatters onward.

393

In front the sun climbs slow, how slowly,
But westward, look, the land is bright.

ARTHUR HUGH CLOUGH

This is the story of America. Everybody's doing what
they think they're supposed to do.

JACK KEROUAC

L ong before the colonies rebelled, settlers were pressing westward. Their desire to own land was stronger than the Indian
danger or the absence of government. By 1748, Scottish and
Irish emigrants from Pennsylvania had crossed the Blue Ridge
Mountains in western Virginia and found a green spread at the site
of today's Blacksburg.

The first settler to arrive cut his name into the bark of a dead
tree, which was known as a "tomahawk claim," and the place was
called Draper's Meadow. The squatters didn't know what tribe the
land belonged to, and they didn't care. They built cabins with
notched logs, because they had no nails, and they burned green-
timber fires, called "smudges," to protect their cattle from the insects that bred in the heavy dew.

In 1750, Mary Draper, an eighteen-year-old tomboy who
loved to ride horses and jump ditches, married twenty-one-year-
old William Ingles. Five years later, the Shawnees attacked
Draper's Meadow, killing or capturing nearly all its inhabitants.
The Shawnees cut off Philip Lybrook's head and put it in a bag.
They took the bag to his place on Sinking Creek and showed it to
his wife, saying: "Look in the bag and you will find an acquaintance."

Chased by Shawnee warriors through his cornfield, William
Ingles hid under a fallen tree, but his pregnant wife and her two
boys were captured. The Shawnees took them up New River,
where it runs into the Kanawha, in today's West Virginia. Mary
Ingles gave birth there and rode on with her baby in her arms.

When they reached a salt lick, the prisoners were told to boil
brine to make salt to take to the Shawnee village on the Ohio. Once
they got to the village, Mary was separated from her boys, aged
two and four, and taken to Chillicothe, on the Scioto. Some French

traders sold the Indians a stock of checked shirting, and Mary Ingles was put to work sewing shirts. She became known as a good squaw because of her proficiency with the needle.

When the Shawnees moved her farther along the Ohio to Big Bone Lick (in present-day Boone County, Kentucky), Mary found a Dutch woman there who had been captured in Pennsylvania. The two were sent out to pick walnuts and grapes, thus gaining a certain amount of freedom. Mary gave walnuts to a French trader, who placed them on a mastodon bone and cracked them with a tomahawk. Taking pity on her, he gave her a blanket and a tomahawk.

The women resolved to escape. Mary kissed her baby as he lay in his bark cradle, and slipped away with the Dutch woman. When the Shawnees realized the women were gone, they concluded the two had lost their way, and fired guns in the air. It did not occur to them that women might try to escape through the wilderness. Thinking they had been killed by wild animals, the Indians gave up the search.

The women followed the banks of the Ohio eastward, past today's Cincinnati. They saw a corn patch and an empty cabin, and the next day they found an old horse with a bell around its neck. Muffling the clapper with rags, they took turns riding the horse along the banks of the Ohio, past the present-day towns of Greenup and Ashland.

At today's Cattlesburg, Kentucky, the Big Sandy ran into the Ohio, and there seemed to be no way to cross either river. They managed to find a driftwood barrier that made a serviceable bridge across the Ohio, but the horse's legs got caught in the driftwood and it had to be left behind. The Dutch woman removed the bell from around the horse's neck and carried it as a charm. Unable to cross the Big Sandy, they had to walk up one bank as far as today's Louisa, Kentucky, where they found a sandbar, and then down the other bank back to the Ohio at today's Huntington, West Virginia.

The Dutch woman began to brood, and to blame Mary for inciting her to escape, but Mary calmed her, and they were to some extent reconciled. As they were slogging along together, it got cold, and their clothes were in shreds from the sharp branches and briars. They wore out their moccasins and tore strips from their dresses to wrap their feet. At night, they slept under rock shelves or in hollow logs, with moss for a blanket. One day, they ate a decomposing deer head discarded by an Indian hunting party.

Farther up the Ohio, they reached the mouth of the Kanawha, which Mary Ingles knew ran into the New River and toward home. Down the banks of the Kanawha they marched, crossing the Coal River at today's St. Albans, West Virginia, walking over paths beaten down by buffalo and elk. They came to the salt springs where they had stopped with the Shawnees, and went through the New River gorges, to the juncture with the Bluestone. Mary knew she was close to home.

By this time, they were starving. The Dutch woman said she could no longer stand it; she threatened to kill Mary Ingles and eat her. Mary Ingles proposed that they at least be fair about it and "draw cuts" to see who would be the victim. They did, and she lost. The Dutch woman grabbed her, but neither was strong enough to overpower the other. Mary escaped, leaving the other woman lying on the riverbank.

That night, a full moon lit up the river, and Mary Ingles noticed an old canoe tethered to the bank, half full of windblown leaves. There was no paddle, but she found a tree branch for rowing. There was not much current and she was able to cross the Bluestone. On the other side, she found an empty hunter's cabin, crept in, and spent the night. The next morning, after eating two raw turnips scratched out of the ground, she saw the Dutch woman on the other side of the river, waving her arms and shouting, pleading to be brought over. Mary decided it would make sense to keep the river between them.

She canoed through the New River narrows, past the mouth of Wolf Creek and soon she spied a settler's home and patch of corn. The settler was Adam Harmon, once her neighbor at Draper's Meadow. It was late November, and snow was falling. Harmon and his wife warmed some water in a skillet and bathed Mary's swollen feet and limbs, wrapped her in a blanket, and fed her venison. She had not seen a fire or tasted hot food for forty days.

Mary Ingles was reunited with her husband. Years later, they ransomed one of their sons. He was seventeen, and could not speak English. After his return to the family, he would wander off to spend days in the forest. Mary Ingles heard that the Dutch woman had somehow got back to Pennsylvania.

Mary Ingles' story is a New World fable of self-reliance. She overcame great obstacles, hostile Indians, hunger, unpassable rivers, and the treachery of her only ally. She had to abandon her baby. And yet she survived.

There were thousands of couples like the Ingleses, willing to risk their lives in ungoverned territories because of land hunger. From Draper's Meadow, it was just a hop through the Cumberland Gap into Kentucky, which was then a trans-Appalachian territory belonging to Virginia.

Kentucky was the great Middle Ground where the Indians hunted, fought over by many tribes but never lived on. When white men came in, the Cherokees sold them land that belonged to the Shawnees, and vice versa, so that they were always buying land from the wrong tribe.

Just to the south, Tennessee belonged to North Carolina. In the 1760s, people started settling on the Watauga, a stream that emptied into the Holston, in the northeastern corner of Tennessee. It didn't matter that a bunch of quill-pushing English lords had, in 1763, barred settlement west of the Appalachians. No one paid any attention to that imaginary and unenforceable barrier, except perhaps as a starting line. People streamed across it—people who would make any sacrifice for a piece of their own land.

Their main concern was not whom the land belonged to but how to get to it across the Appalachians, a series of mountain chains. The passes didn't line up from chain to chain, and the settlers had to figure out how they connected. For instance, the Saluda Gap, through the Blue Ridge Mountains, tied in with a valley through the Great Smokies. Some of the passes were held by Indians. The riddle of the mountains and Indian hostility had more effect on the way the population moved west than did the Proclamation of 1763.

The route through the Appalachians, with its likelihood of disasters, from rockslides to ambushes, was about 225 miles. It was said, when a man left the colonies, "He is gone to hell or Kentucky." The settlers not only moved into the wilderness but often regressed to a wild state, in many ways resembling the Indians they feared and detested. They even adopted the practice of scalping.

The saving grace was that if you didn't like it where you were, you could move on. With a continent for a backyard, men were bound to be restless. Timothy Flint, a Presbyterian minister traveling through Kentucky, noticed two families crossing on the road. One was leaving Kentucky and heading farther west, the other returning to Kentucky after having been west. "Why are you leaving old Kentucky?" the latter asked. "The range is all eaten up," said the other. "Why are you coming back?" "Oh," said the first, "the people are dying like rotten sheep. They have filled one grave-yard already and have begun on another. Turn about and go back; after all there is nothing like old Kentucky."

When the war with England came, that didn't stop settlement either; in fact, it probably accelerated settlement, in spite of the English policy of inciting the Indians against the Americans. "We need not be tender of calling on the savages," wrote General Gage to Lord Dartmouth from Boston on June 12, 1775.

That same year, a group of nine North Carolina citizens, who had organized the Transylvania Company to buy wilderness land from the Indians, took advantage of the relaxation of constituted authority. On March 14, one of the nine, Judge Richard Henderson, signed the famous Treaty of Sycamore Shoals, at today's Elizabethton, Tennessee. For a cabin-full of trade goods, he bought seventeen million acres of land from the Cherokees—most of Kentucky and middle Tennessee.

The purchase was denounced by the British governor of North Carolina and later invalidated, but that didn't stop the Transylvania Company from sending settlers in. To the east, the war was raging, with George Washington's victory at Monmouth in 1778, and the British capture of Savannah. No one was paying attention to what a private land company was doing in Tennessee.

In 1779, the year the British took Augusta but surrendered at Vincennes to George Rogers Clark, the Transylvania Company hired a Watauga settler named James Robertson to reconnoiter the area of French Lick on the twisting Cumberland River (today's Nashville). Robertson built some cabins, planted some corn, and posted men to keep the buffalo out.

Finding the site promising, he hired the surveyor and militia captain John Donelson to take a flotilla of boats filled with settlers over the water route to French Lick. An educated man who counted Thomas Jefferson among his friends, Donelson kept a journal of the trip, entitled "Journal of a Voyage intended, by God's permission, in the good boat *Adventure*, from Fort Patrick Henry on Holston river, to the French Salt Springs on Cumberland river."

Overland to Nashville, this was a three-hundred-mile trip, but by river it was 750 miles. Instead of going due west, as one would today, from Knoxville to Nashville, Donelson had to float down the Holston and into the Tennessee, which meandered across eastern Tennessee and down into Alabama for a couple of hundred miles. Then it turned north, moving across western Tennessee and into Kentucky, where it led to the Ohio and the Cumberland, which took him eastward to French Lick.

The entire party of about 160 settlers, including women and children, started down the Holston on December 22, 1779. Two months earlier, a Franco-American force had lifted the siege of Savannah after thirty-four days.

The dozen or so flatboats, finding "excessive hard frost and low water," were stuck on the Holston for two months. When they finally got going, on February 27, 1780, three boats were grounded on the shoals "in much distress." On March 2, one of the boats sank, and "Reuben Harrison went out a hunting and did not return that night, though many guns were fired to fetch him." He could not be found, "to the great grief of his parents and fellow travelers."

On March 6, "Captain Hutchin's negro man died, being much frosted in his feet and legs, of which he died."

By then, they were on the roiling Tennessee River, and Indians along the banks were keeping pace with the boats. The Indians invited them to come ashore, saying, "This side of the river is better for boats to pass," but, as Captain Donelson learned, it was a ruse. "Young Mr. Payne, on board Captain Blakemore's boat, was mortally wounded by reason of the boat running too near the northern shore . . . where some of the enemy lay concealed."

Payne's death was a minor incident compared with "the more tragic misfortune of poor Stuart, his family and friends, to the number of 28 persons." Captain Donelson had allowed the party to join his company with some reluctance, since the family was diseased with the smallpox. It was agreed "between Stuart and the company that he should keep at some distance in the rear, for fear of the infection spreading, and he was warned each night when the encampment should take place by the sound of a horn." The Indians, "observing his helpless situation singled him off from the rest of the fleet, intercepted him and killed and took prisoner the whole crew. . . . Their cries were distinctly heard."

The demise of the Stuart party, soon to be avenged when their captors came down with smallpox, was followed by a running battle with Indians stationed on the bluffs of both shores at a point where the river narrowed and boiled through a canyon. The entry for March 8 ended with "Jonathan Jennings' boat is missing."

At four o'clock on the morning of March 10, Captain Donelson was awakened by cries of "Help poor Jennings" coming from some distance behind him. His boat had run aground, with the Indians "keeping up a most galling fire." In the boat were Mrs. Jennings, their nearly grown son, a young man, a Negro couple, and the wife of Ephraim Peyton, who had the previous day given birth.

"A good soldier and an excellent marksman," Jennings returned the fire as he commanded the others to throw their goods in the river to lighten the boat. "But before they had accomplished their object, his son, the young man, and the negro jumped out of the boat and left."

Deserted by his own son, who fled with the two others, Jennings was left with the women. "Mrs. Jennings, and the negro woman, succeeded in unloading the boat. . . . Mrs. Peyton . . . assisted them, being frequently exposed to wet and cold. . . . Their clothes were very much cut with bullets." As for Mrs. Peyton's one-day-old baby, it was "unfortunately killed upon the hurry and confusion consequent upon such a disaster."

Even after they had jettisoned their goods, the boat remained stuck on a rock, so the brave Mrs. Jennings "got out of the boat and shoved her off, but was near falling a victim to her own intrepidity on account of the boat starting up so suddenly as soon as loosened from rock." "Upon examination," Captain Donelson concluded, Jennings "appears to have made a wonderful escape, for his boat is pierced in numberless places with bullets." As for the three who fled, the Negro was drowned, and the young man and Jennings' son were captured by the Chickamaugas. The young man was burned at the stake, but the son was ransomed with a large payment of goods.

On March 12, Donelson's flotilla reached Muscle Shoals, in northwestern Alabama, and "the water made a terrible roaring . . . with the current running in every possible direction. . . . We did not know how soon we should be dashed to pieces. . . . Our boats frequently dragged on the bottom. . . . They warped as much as in a rough sea." On March 14, two boats were fired at, and five crewmen were wounded. At night, the barking of dogs told them the Indians were near.

It took another eight days to navigate the river northward across Tennessee and into western Kentucky, where it merged with the Ohio. On March 20, they landed on the banks of the Ohio, which they would have to follow eastward against the current to reach the Cumberland.

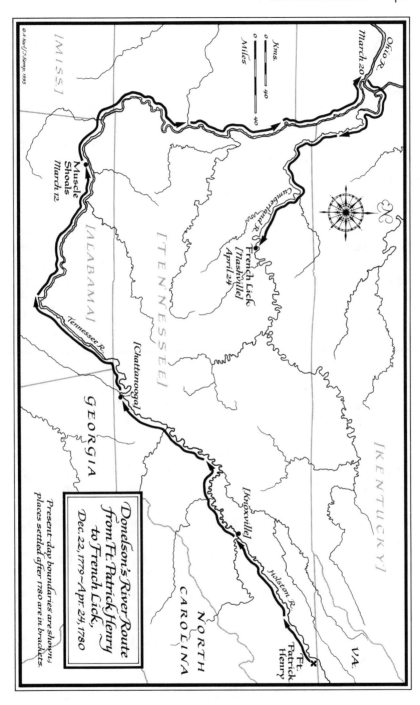

Donelson's River Route
from Ft. Patrick Henry
to French Lick,
Dec. 22, 1779–Apr. 24, 1780

Present-day boundaries are shown;
places settled after 1780 are in brackets.

"Our situation here is truly disagreeable," Captain Donelson wrote. "Our provisions exhausted, the crews almost worn down with hunger and fatigue . . . The scene is rendered still more melancholy as several boats will not attempt to ascend the rapid current."

Some of the members of the party mutinied and refused to follow Donelson. They planned to take the Ohio west with the current instead of east against it, easily reaching the Mississippi, which would take them down to Natchez, where the Spanish were offering land to settlers.

"We now part," Donelson wrote of the seceding boats, "perhaps to meet no more, for I am determined to pursue my course." That meant rowing up the Ohio and finding the Cumberland, without a map. Everyone was already suffering from hunger and fatigue. On March 24, they came to the mouth of a river, which Donelson said was the Cumberland. The others said it couldn't be, it was too small. "We determined however to make the trial," Donelson wrote, "and encamped for the night." The next day, his intuition was rewarded, for the river widened and "we are now convinced it is the Cumberland."

Food became the priority, and on March 26 they killed a buffalo. The meat was "poor, but palatable." The next day, they killed a swan, "which was very delicious," and two days later they "gathered some herbs . . . which some of the company called Shawnee salad."

A month later, they reached their destination, the bluffs at French Lick. Navigating the river route had been like running a perilous 750-mile gauntlet. "Though our prospects at present are dreary," Donelson wrote on April 24, 1780, "we have found a few log cabins which have been built on a cedar bluff above the Lick, by Captain Robertson and his company."

Donelson found a clearing twelve miles from the bluffs, named it Clover Bottom, and planted corn and cotton. Near the cabins on the bluff, vast burial mounds and the ruins of a walled town were reminders of a vanished civilization. Its dream of permanence had evaporated like the dawn mist on the river. Now another group of settlers had arrived with the same dreams. In 1785, Donelson was killed by Indians.

While settlers crossed the Appalachians, in the East a war was being fought, and a government was taking shape. Americans now saw themselves as a separate people.

In September 1774, a Continental Congress was assembled in Philadelphia, with fifty-six delegates from twelve colonies (Georgia did not attend). It served as an advisory council to the colonies in their disputes with England. When the Continental Congress met again on May 10, 1775, it was overtaken by events. Blood had been shed in Lexington and Concord on April 19, and militia units were forming in the colonies.

The Congress took over the direction of the war and named George Washington commander-in-chief on June 15. Then, in recognition that this was a revolution and not merely a list of grievances, the Congress drafted the Declaration of Independence on July 4, 1776, which declared the colonies to be "Free and Independent States." That being the case, some instrument of union had to be framed.

While the Congress was engulfed in military affairs, a committee reported a set of articles on July 2, 1776, dealing with questions of government. Should large and small states have the same number of votes? Should Congress regulate Indian affairs and fix the western boundaries of states that claimed to extend as far as the Mississippi?

On November 15, 1777, the Continental Congress approved the committee's draft and sent it to the states for ratification. This took more than three years, since the states were like independent nations, suspicious of any central government. Once ratified on March 1, 1781, the Articles of Confederation created "a firm league of friendship" and became the law of the land.

The articles established a unicameral Congress of Confederation as the only agency of government. There was no executive or judiciary branch. Congress ran the show, managing the war as well as foreign and financial affairs, although it did not have the power to tax or to regulate commerce. It operated according to what one historian has called "government by supplication."

Each state appointed from two to seven delegates but had only one vote. Rhode Island, for example, had parity with New York. The states were supposed to supply money to the treasury and troops to the army, but they often ignored their obligations. Lacking any power of enforcement, the Congress of Confederation was a toothless tiger. It remained, however, a provisional government from 1781 until 1789, when the Constitution and its three-branch government would be adopted.

While Congress sat in Philadelphia, the war was fought, with its ups and downs. On October 17, 1777, Burgoyne and his entire army surrendered at Saratoga, which brought in the French, who saw a chance to dismember the British Empire. The Spanish also came in, hoping to increase their holdings in the New World.

Four years later, the end came for the British on a Virginia beach. It is curious to see how the opposing armies seemed to conspire to stage a decisive battle that would determine the outcome of the war.

First General Charles Cornwallis, the commander of British forces, chose an obscure hamlet on the high western shore near the mouth of the York River, at the southeastern tip of Virginia, as the site for a naval base. The British wanted to send out gunboats to intercept American ships.

With the war in its seventh year and no end in sight, Cornwallis dug in at Yorktown with about eight thousand men. This concentration of British forces in an isolated spot was too tempting to resist. While the French fleet under de Grasse blockaded Yorktown and kept the British fleet at bay, Lafayette and Washington, with seventeen thousand men (half of them French), opened a formal siege in September 1781. The allies patiently dug their way to within three hundred yards of the British earthworks.

On October 14, a night attack led by Colonel Alexander Hamilton pushed in the British left. Three days later, and four years to the day after Burgoyne's defeat, Cornwallis opened surrender negotiations. There had been little fighting, but his troops were demoralized, and he believed he was surrounded.

Saratoga had been the first occasion in the long history of the empire on which an entire British field army had ever capitulated. Yorktown was Saratoga redux, giving the king's loyal opposition in Parliament sufficient grounds to stop the war. Victory at Yorktown ended all major combat.

It was two years before a treaty was signed, in Paris on September 3, 1783. The thirteen colonies were severed from the British Empire and recognized as the United States of America. The young nation's new western border was the Mississippi, on a line that started at the western tip of Lake Superior and continued south until it touched the Spanish possessions in present-day Mississippi.

Out of this land won by conquest, beyond the thirteen original states, would be carved the following eight states: West Virginia, Ohio, Kentucky, Tennessee, Indiana, Illinois, Michigan, and Wisconsin.

The Spanish remained a formidable presence, since they had obtained the Louisiana Territory from the French. This gave them New Orleans and control of navigation on the Mississippi. They also took back East and West Florida, which included the lower third of the present states of Alabama and Mississippi. The Spanish owned America's southern coast on the Gulf of Mexico.

The acquisition of a great mass occupied only by Native Americans opened up the issue of land policy. This was a complicated matter, given the tangle of triple ownership. First the land had to be obtained from a foreign power by treaty. Then it had to be ceded by the states to the central government. And, finally, it had to be bought from the Indians.

As soon as the ink was dry on the Treaty of Paris in September 1783, the Continental Congress began to grapple with the claims of the states on western lands. Seven of the thirteen states had western claims based on colonial charters. The other six, who wanted a share in the potential of the West, lobbied for cession. They felt that the land had been won from the British by the combined efforts of all thirteen. New York was the first to yield its claim, in 1781, followed by Virginia in 1784. The other states came around, with Georgia the last to cede in 1802.

Like an heir to a great fortune, the Congress acquired a public domain requiring management. This vast and growing capital of government-owned land was the key difference between the United States and other countries. The means of disposal, perhaps more than anything else, would determine the nation's character. In America, the history of land distribution is more instructive than the history of the battles. Behind most events, there is a little voice whispering, "Cheap land, cheap land, cheap land," and in the modulations of that voice much can be learned.

When Virginia ceded some of its trans-Ohio lands in March 1784, Congress was jogged into action, and a committee was named, headed by Thomas Jefferson, to study the formation of new states. Under the Articles of Confederation, it was one of the duties of Congress to create new states in the West that would be the equals of the first thirteen, a reaction to the previous subordination of the colonies to England.

Influenced by Montesquieu, Jefferson believed that small states like Switzerland made the best republics. He also wanted free public lands to be made available to settlers, with a large degree of self-government in any interim period.

While the cessions were coming in, the much-maligned Congress of Confederation prepared to deal with the fundamental question of who owned the West. Was it the government, which by selling land could raise urgently needed revenue? Was it the veterans, who had been promised bounty lands to reward their term of service? Or was it the squatters, those risk-taking entrepreneurs who had cleared the wilderness and fought off Indians?

The work of the Jefferson committee led to the Land Ordinance of May 20, 1785. This document was as important as any that Congress ever passed, because it regulated the distribution of land. (Active in the discussions was the onetime surveyor named George Washington.)

Under the ordinance, the basic unit of public land was a square, six miles to one side. This square was called a "township," and inside it were thirty-six square miles. Each square mile was called a "section." These 640-acre sections were the smallest pieces of land that a settler could buy, although later they were subdivided into half-sections and quarter-sections. Purchase would be at public auction, with the lowest bid a dollar an acre, and payment in cash.

The Congress (there being as yet no executive branch) became a friendly real-estate agent. With this one decision on the division of land into townships and sections, they determined what kind of country America would be. It would not be a country of great estates and tenant farmers. It would not be like Europe, where only kings, the nobility, and the church could own land. It would be a country where *anybody* could own land, a pie with millions of slices, a country where the buying and selling of acreage was as simple as a day's shopping. (It was so simple that it encouraged speculation and fraud, as we will see.)

After the 1785 Land Ordinance was passed, Congress began to tinker with the land laws, changing the purchase price, terms of credit, and minimum acreage. But the principle remained the same. Public land was thrown open for sale on a first-come, first-served basis.

The original plan was to fashion new states from the great slab of Old Northwest, which had been won in battle. No one was yet talking about a coast-to-coast America. It was simply that the new government owned the land and people were moving into it and they needed some kind of orderly system. As George Washington put it, "If you cannot stop the road, it is yet in your power to mark the way."

With the township and section system, every buyer knew exactly what he owned, and, as it turned out, most of the continent was carved up into squares, ignoring landscape features and giving the country the gridiron aspect so startling to see from a plane, the states themselves being rectangular, as if part of an enormous township.

If one believes that people are as much a product of their physical environment as of their principles and beliefs, the township system shaped the American character as definitively as the Declaration of Independence. This invisible grillwork stamped upon the nation became a part of the American consciousness, showing up in architecture and urban design, in main streets and front porches, in baseball diamonds and square dances.

For the townships to be sold, they had to be surveyed. The Land Ordinance provided for surveyors to lay out the land in rectangular blocks. The first survey would begin with an east-west baseline starting at the point where the Ohio River intersected with the western boundary of Pennsylvania (more or less at today's East Liverpool, Ohio). Along this baseline, seven rows of townships were to be measured off from north to south, and these rows were called "ranges."

Since each township had a six-mile side, and since there were seven rows, the baseline was forty-two miles long, stretching across Ohio to the vicinity of today's Magnolia. Each of the seven ranges would continue north-south until it reached the Ohio River, making each successive range a little longer than the last, since it was farther from the river. Overall, these first seven ranges formed a triangle, with one side being the forty-two-mile horizontal baseline, the second side, at a right angle, being the vertical line of the seventh range, about ninety miles long, and the third side being the ragged line of the Ohio, meandering south by southwest.

Each township was to be divided into thirty-six numbered sections, one of which would be reserved to provide the revenue for a church and a school. One might term this the ideological content of the Land Ordinance. It was not merely a division of land, but also a way to promote the social goals of an educated and churchgoing population. William Grayson, a member of the committee that drafted the ordinance, wrote Washington: "The idea of township, with the temptation of a support for religion and education, holds forth an inducement for neighborhoods of the same religious sentiments to confederate for the purpose of purchasing and settling together." It would be a furtherance of early settlement patterns by religious groups such as the Puritans.

Congress appointed a Geographer of the United States to conduct the survey of the seven ranges with a corps of deputy surveyors. They would be paid two dollars per mile, out of which would come all their expenses, such as chain carriers and equipment. As soon as the seven ranges were done, the Geographer of the United States would convey his plats (scaled diagrams) to the Board of Treasury, which would put the land up for sale.

The first and last man to hold this impressive title was fifty-year-old Thomas Hutchins, a career soldier in the British army. New Jersey–born, he had served for twenty-eight years in the colonies. In 1777, refusing to bear arms against his fellow Americans, he was arrested on a charge of high treason, and spent three years in a British jail. Upon his release, he was named geographer to the American army, and with the war over, he was assigned to the seven ranges.

On September 15, 1785, Hutchins and five deputies were in Pittsburgh, hiring chain carriers and buying horses and supplies. He planned to go into the wood and stay until December, when winter would force him back. Hutchins waited for his Indian guides until September 30, then started without them, pushing a line due west from the Pennsylvania border.

Hutchins began cutting out the first township in the first range, south of the baseline. On October 15, Indian messengers came to his camp and told him to cease. Intimidated, Hutchins returned to Pittsburgh. In 1785, about two weeks' worth of surveying was done.

In March 1786, Hutchins began to prepare for his second season, but was alarmed by reports that the British around Detroit were giving the Indians arms and whiskey. Young Indians were boasting: "The whites shall have as much land as they want, that is the breadth of their back, belly, or side, whichever way they fall."

The unarmed surveyors made a tempting target, and Hutchins returned to Pittsburgh with some apprehension on June 25, 1786, to wait for his deputies. Pittsburgh was then a log fort with about eighty two-story log houses strung along the Monongahela. Hutchins pleaded with Colonel Josiah Harmar for an escort, but the colonel said that if Indians saw soldiers flanking the surveyors it might "bring on a war, which, I conceive, the United States wish to avoid."

The colonel did have, however, 160 men under Captain John Francis Hamtramck, who was leaving on a squatter search-and-destroy mission (army policy then was to send squatters back from wherever they had come). They could assist the surveyors in the event of attack.

On July 14, 1786, Hamtramck with his men and Hutchins with his deputies moved out of Fort Pitt in bateaux and headed down the Ohio. Hutchins pitched camp at the juncture with Little Beaver Creek, while the troops continued downriver. Ranges two through seven were assigned to the deputies by the drawing of lots. Expressing a marked reluctance to start out without an escort, they told Hutchins on July 22: "We think it our duty to inform you . . . that a body of troops will be necessary to cover us in our operation."

Hutchins sent back to Fort Pitt for men, who arrived in his tiny camp in August. The eight deputies then laid out the first range of townships, and pushed the baseline farther west. By August 22, the baseline stretched twelve miles from the Ohio River—the first two ranges.

But on September 18, word spread that the Indians were assembling for an attack. Once again the deputies laid down their tripods, also complaining that they had not been paid. In October, they quit for the season. One by one, they drifted home.

CHAPTER TWENTY

THE OHIO COMPANY

In 1787, an association of veterans who wanted to move to
Ohio lobbied the Continental Congress and won the right
to buy 3.5 million acres with depreciated Continental
certificates. They settled Marietta, Ohio, which was briefly
the capital of Ohio Territory.

In this America, this wilderness
Where the axe echoes with a lonely sound,
The generations labor to possess
And grave by grave we civilize the ground.

LOUIS SIMPSON

W hen Thomas Hutchins was appointed geographer of the United States in 1785, he chose Brigadier General Rufus Putnam to be his deputy. Putnam was a war hero from Rutland, Massachusetts, a strong-willed six-footer with an odd squint, owing to a childhood eye injury, who carved this verse on his powder horn:

> *Amour of words and not of deeds*
> *Is like a garden full of weeds.*

In 1783, the year the Treaty of Paris was signed, Putnam had circulated a petition signed by 288 officers, asking for land south of Lake Erie. George Washington supported the petition, but it was premature: Congress had not yet passed the Land Ordinance, and the question of land cessions from the original states was unresolved.

When Putnam's appointment as deputy surveyor for the seven Ohio ranges came up, he was in the middle of a survey in Maine, and delegated young Ben Tupper, who was engaged to his daughter, Martha. After the short surveying season of 1785, Tupper went to Rutland to brief Putnam about what he had seen in Ohio.

In a conversation by the fireside that fall, they decided to form a company to buy Ohio land for veterans, using the depreciated continental certificates they had been paid. The company would issue a thousand shares worth a thousand dollars each, providing itself with a capital of a million dollars in certificates. Shareholders also had to pay ten dollars a share in coin.

William L. Clements Library, Ann Arbor, Mich.

This is a diagram of the basic unit in the division of public land, the township of 36 square miles. It was divided into 36 one-mile-square sections (640 acres). Some sections were broken up into smaller parts. Section 16 was set aside for a school, section 20 for a church, and sections 8, 11, and 26 were earmarked for future sale by Congress. The diagram is signed by Rufus Putnam, a founder of the Ohio Company and later surveyor general of the United States.

Putnam and Tupper organized veterans' meetings at taverns like the Bunch of Grapes in Boston. They also placed advertisements in Massachusetts newspapers asking for veterans "who wish to become adventurers in that delightful region," Ohio. The term "adventurer" was used in the English sense of a speculator in a land company.

Directors were appointed, including the irrepressible Manasseh Cutler, a Congregational minister and bon vivant, who was a veteran by virtue of having been chaplain to the troops. Cutler wrote his friend Jeremy Belknap: "What do you think, my friend of the Ohio country? Is it not preferable to these frozen regions?" Cutler thought so, confiding to his diary: "I had suffered exceedingly in ye war. . . . I thought ye people had not done me justice and I meditated on leaving them. Purchasing land in a new country appeared to be ye only thing I could do." Such was the situation of many veterans impoverished by the war.

Another Ohio Company director, Winthrop Sargent, took a surveying job in 1786 in order to scout locations in the area where the Muskingum River joined the Ohio. Sargent was not fully qualified, and his measurements were off; most of his work had to be done over. But while Hutchins waited for a military escort in the summer of 1786, he took a three-week trek into Muskingum country, in the company of a trader who sold liquor to the Indians. The land was inviting, but already infested with squatters. When the troops from Fort Harmar came round to evict them, they simply rafted across the river to Virginia. As soon as the troops left, they rafted back.

In 1787, the township system was under review in Congress, which was displeased with Hutchins' slow progress—twenty-six townships surveyed and platted in the first four ranges was the sum of the 1786 season. The total for two years was seven hundred thousand acres, whereas the veterans, who were clamoring for their bounty lands, had been promised three million. In addition, the government was going broke, and urgently needed the revenues from land sales.

To speed things up, it was proposed that large parcels of land be offered for sale. They would be surveyed by the buyers, according to the township system. This was exactly what the Ohio Company was hoping for, since unsurveyed land would be sold at a bargain.

In 1787, Hutchins and his deputies went out for their third

and final season, with their usual pattern of advance and retreat. This time, they completed the seven ranges, and then Hutchins resigned his post, fed up with congressional criticism and stinginess. He had to pay the surveyors' overtime out of his own pocket.

Seventeen eighty-seven was one of those years when a lot of important things were going on at the same time. The Ohio Company was gearing up for a big lobbying effort in New York with the Continental Congress, which was coming to grips with the form of government that should exist in the western lands. And the Constitutional Convention was busy in Philadelphia's Old State House from May 27 to September 17. Some of its delegates, such as James Madison of Virginia and Gouverneur Morris of New York, were also members of the Confederation (or Continental) Congress, and had to shuttle between the two cities.

The Continental Congress, which was, in effect, the government, was disorganized and peripatetic. In little more than a year, it sat in five different cities. It left Philadelphia for Princeton in 1783, but Princeton was so cramped that Madison had to share a bed. In Annapolis, the members disliked the muggy Chesapeake Bay summer, so they moved to Trenton, where they were chilled by the New Jersey winter. In December 1784, the Congress moved to New York, where it remained.

There was much absenteeism, since there was no way to compel attendance. Distance was obviously an issue; the state with the best attendance record was New York, and New Hampshire members were the worst slackers. The Continental Congress sat in continuous session, but there was no continuity. For months at a time, Congress was unable to reach the quorum of seven states out of thirteen required by the articles. The sixty or so members wandered in and out, going home to attend to state problems, family matters, or private business. Some were sick, some were worn out, and some blamed the weather.

The transaction of business was intermittent. In July 1787, there was a rare quorum of eight states. A five-man committee, consisting of Edward Carrington and Richard Henry Lee of Virginia, John Kean of South Carolina, Melancton Smith of New York, and Nathan Dane of Massachusetts, was formed to draft an ordinance concerning the government of western lands.

The notion that lands inhabited only by Indians should be opened up to settlement and divided into territories and eventually into states was hotly contested. Eastern skeptics said, We have enough land already, we can't afford this expansion, there will be a brain drain in the East. An elitist like Gouverneur Morris did not think that the western states should have rights equal to those of the original states. The interior, he said, "would not be able to furnish men equally enlightened to share in the administration of our common interests, because the busy haunts of men, not the remote wilderness, is the proper school of political talents."

This was on July 11, when the Continental Congress, in its debate on the revised ordinance, expressed compelling reasons for passage. You couldn't sell surveyed lands in a political vacuum. The people who bought those lands had to be under some type of government. Squatters were already on the land, and they too had to be governed. The British were still a threat, hanging on to forts on the Great Lakes which by treaty they were supposed to have vacated, egging on the tribes, putting pressure on the western fringes, and secretly hoping for the collapse of the young nation. The American government had to make its presence felt in the West.

All this helped to explain how, in four days, between July 9 and July 13, the Northwest Ordinance was drafted, introduced, read, amended, and unanimously passed by the eight voting states: Massachusetts, New York, New Jersey, Delaware, Virginia, North and South Carolina, and Georgia. The absent states were Pennsylvania, Connecticut, Maryland, New Hampshire, and Rhode Island. On July 13, 1787, William Grayson of Virginia, the acting president of Congress, pounded the gavel and said, "The ayes have it."

The Northwest Ordinance was the logical continuation of the 1785 Land Ordinance. The Land Ordinance determined the method of distribution, and the Northwest Ordinance the type of government. These newly settled areas would be called territories until they qualified for statehood, when they were sufficiently pop-ulated. As territories, they would go through three stages of growth, corresponding to childhood, adolescence, and adulthood. In the first stage, they would be ruled by a governor, appointed by the president with the consent of the Senate, a secretary, and three judges. The governor, with broad powers, could establish coun-ties, appoint officials, and adopt laws.

The second stage would come when the territory had an adult male population of five thousand. At this point, the inhabitants would be entitled to elect a House of Representatives for a two-year term. There would also be a five-man Council, a sort of upper house, appointed by Congress from a list of ten nominees submitted by the territorial House, and serving for five years. In addition, the House and the Council could elect a nonvoting delegate to Congress; the first of these was William Henry Harrison of Ohio in 1800.

In the third and final stage, when the population of the territory reached sixty thousand, it could petition Congress for admission to the Union. At this point, a constitutional convention would be held and a constitution drafted. The people would vote to ratify it, and the territory would become a state.

The Northwest Ordinance stipulated that the territory of the Old Northwest should be divided into no more than five or no fewer than three states. The men of the Continental Congress, representing the first thirteen, did not want to be outnumbered by western upstarts. As it turned out, the system was extended to the rest of the continental United States (with a few exceptions such as Kentucky, Vermont, and Texas), so that, between 1787 and 1912, twenty-eight tracts of land acquired by the United States were governed by Congress and the executive branch as territories, with an average wait of twenty years for statehood.

It has been charged that the territorial system was a form of colonialism, borrowed from the British. But the difference is that the colonies had no hope of change, whereas territories were states in the making. Territorial government was often despotic, but there seemed few other options. It was irresponsible to admit states with tiny populations, and the territorial system was a useful apprenticeship. In fact, the territories were more independent from federal regulations than they would be as states, which is why there was sometimes resistance to statehood. But, just as the character of the nation was formed by the distribution of land, it owed an equal debt to the interim years each state spent as a territory. During those years, the foundation was built.

In addition, the Northwest Ordinance, which was passed while constitutional deliberations were going on in Philadelphia, had its own bill of rights in six articles. These included freedom of worship, habeas corpus, and trial by jury.

But the most remarkable item was Article Six, which prohibited slavery. How was it possible that an ordinance drafted by a committee, three out of five of whose members were southerners (and passed unanimously by eight states, half of which were southern), could have included an article banning slavery? One hundred miles away, in Philadelphia, the framers of the Constitution, who were also deliberating in the summer of 1787, were unable to include such an article, and in fact recognized slavery in three different passages in veiled language.

First, in the Constitution, there was a provision by which a slave was to be counted as three-fifths of a person for purposes of congressional apportionment. The term used was "three fifths of all other persons," besides freemen and indentured servants. Second, it was agreed to maintain and prolong the slave trade, the language being: "The migration or importation of such persons as any of the states now existing shall think proper to admit, shall not be prohibited by the Congress prior to the year 1808." You would not know on the face of it that this item was about the slave trade. Third, there was a fugitive-slave clause, which said that "a person . . . who shall flee from justice, and be found in another state, shall on demand . . . be delivered up, to be removed to the state having the jurisdiction of the crime."

How did a ban on slavery pass in the Northwest Ordinance? On July 11, the ordinance was reported with no slavery article; on July 12, it went through a second reading, still with no mention of slavery. But on July 13, it was accepted without debate and passed by unanimous vote, with the slavery article attached.

The article was, apparently, the brainchild of Nathan Dane, an Ipswich-born, Harvard-educated lawyer, who took a large part in drafting the ordinance. Article Six was written on a separate sheet of paper, in his handwriting, and attached at the last minute to the ordinance. There were no objections when it was read. In fact, years later, Dane wrote in a letter dated May 12, 1831, that the article had been unanimously agreed to, "to the great honor of the slave-holding states."

The reasons for the southerners' agreement are threefold. The first was that the Constitution applied to all the states, including the South. A constitutional ban on slavery would have been a direct threat to the practice in existing states. The Northwest Ordinance applied only to new states and left slavery intact in the South.

There was also an economic explanation. Southern congressmen who voted for the ordinance sought to protect their plantation system, which produced cotton, tobacco, and indigo with slave labor: additional slave states with similar products would have been a threat. William Grayson of Virginia told James Monroe that Article Six "was agreed to by the southern members for the purpose of preventing tobacco and indigo from being made."

The third reason was that there was a good deal of antislavery sentiment among leading Virginians, among them Thomas Jefferson and Patrick Henry. This feeling permeated the Virginia delegation at the Continental Congress.

Yet, although they may have been opposed to slavery in theory, the Virginians also wanted to protect the property rights of slave-owners. In that sense, Article Six was a compromise, for, besides prohibiting slavery, it also contained a clause forbidding the harboring of fugitive slaves in the territories—the price of southern support. The southerners were able to thwart potential cotton and tobacco growers while maintaining their right to pursue runaway slaves.

One of the far-reaching implications of Article Six would be victory for the North in the next century's Civil War, when all the free states of the Old Northwest—Ohio, Illinois, Indiana, Michigan, and Wisconsin—joined the Union and sent a million men to fight for it.

Since the Northwest Ordinance applied to territories occupied by Indians, it also included the germ of an Indian policy. The Constitution did not mention Indians, who were not considered citizens and therefore did not fall under its jurisdiction. The Northwest Ordinance, however, contained a clause saying that the Indians "shall never be invaded or disturbed, unless in just and lawful wars authorized by Congress." This was double-speak, in which the second part contradicted the first. In effect, the Northwest Ordinance served as a potential declaration of war, warning the tribes that, if they did not cede their land by purchase, they would be forced off. The implications soon became apparent, when commitments were made to veterans for lands the Indians still owned, and when treaties signed with minor subchiefs became binding on entire tribes.

The link between the passage of the Northwest Ordinance and the goals of the Ohio Company was plain to see. Once a system of government was established in the West, Congress would be more receptive to sales of large tracts of unsurveyed land. But there was still a hostile minority to win over, so in July 1787, even as the ordinance was being drafted, Rufus Putnam dispatched to New York his number-one lobbyist and glad-hander, Manasseh Cutler.

A charming and vigorous forty-five, Cutler was a sort of Renaissance man, who had studied divinity, medicine, and botany, but wore his learning lightly. His job was to mix and mingle with the congressmen and push the company's case, for at that time only 250 of the Ohio Company's thousand shares had been subscribed. It was hoped that with congressional approval the subscription list would quadruple.

Cutler arrived in New York on July 5 and stayed at the Plow & Harrow, on the Bowery. He had forty-four letters of introduction, and wrote in his diary, "I hardly knew which to deliver first." On July 6, he went over to City Hall, at Wall and Broad streets, where the Continental Congress was sitting, and introduced himself to Edward Carrington of Virginia, the chairman of the Ordinance Committee. Carrington took him on the floor of Congress to meet some of the other members, thus giving him the opportunity to deliver some of his letters as well as the Ohio Company petition.

The wily lobbyist invited Nathan Dane to dinner and consulted with Thomas Hutchins, still geographer of the United States, on the best Ohio location. On July 7, he dined with the secretary of war, Henry Knox, and on July 8 with Arthur Lee, one of the three members of the Board of Treasury, who happened to be the brother of Richard Henry Lee, the Virginia congressman who was a member of the Ordinance Committee.

Cutler touched all the bases, being pleasant and pouring good wine on company expenses. He was invited to sit in on the deliberations of the committee studying his petition. Afterward, he was shown around the City Hall rooms.

On July 10, he met with the man who would turn out to be the key figure in the negotiations, William Duer, the secretary of the Board of Treasury, an old soldier in the British army who had espoused the American cause. Duer invited Cutler to dinner with the president of the Board of Treasury, Samuel Osgood, and told him he would push for the Ohio sale because it would bring funds into the public treasury.

By now, Cutler was on such friendly terms with members of Congress that he was given a copy of the Northwest Ordinance draft. He claims to have made suggestions that the committee adopted. On July 11, while waiting for Congress to act on his petition, he went to Philadelphia, where great events were also occurring.

The State House, where the fifty-five drafters of the Constitution were sitting, was directly across the street from a forbidding four-story stone prison. From the barred windows, inmates called to passersby and extended long reed poles with cloth caps on the end to receive alms. "If you refuse them," Cutler noted, "they load you with the most foul and horrid imprecations." The contrast struck him as having all the characteristics of a morality play, with the high-minded drafters of the Constitution working for the general good on one side of the street, and the foul-mouthed beggar-criminals on the other.

In Philadelphia, Cutler found a more cultivated society, a world a million miles removed from the "savage Ohio" that was his purpose. When he visited Benjamin Franklin, he felt as awed as if he were going to be introduced to a European monarch. To his surprise, there appeared "a short, fat, trunched old man, in a plain Quaker dress, bald pate and short white locks, sitting without his hat under a tree." Then eighty-one, Franklin was being cared for by his only daughter, "a very gross and rather homely lady," but "everything about him seems to diffuse an unrestrained freedom and happiness."

On July 17, Cutler learned that the Northwest Ordinance had passed, which bolstered his hopes, and he paid his respects to the president of Congress, General Arthur St. Clair, who was being touted as governor of the first territory. At the same time, he realized that his petition was in trouble, and that there were "a number in Congress decidedly opposed to my terms of negotiation, and some to any contract. . . . I must if possible bring the opponents over."

Cutler figured that the two Virginians, Carrington and Lee, were "certainly my warm advocates." Samuel Holton of Massachusetts also "may be trusted." Four or five of the others, however, were "troublesome fellows," who "must be attacked by my friends at their lodgings. . . . If they can be brought over, I shall succeed. If not, my business is at an end."

On July 20, Congress offered Cutler unacceptable terms. But on that same day, William Duer came to him with an offer he couldn't refuse, "proposals from a number of the principal characters in the city," which had to be kept "a profound secret." Although a public official, Duer was involved in land speculation. His group was interested in Ohio lands, but they could not buy in their own names, since some of them, including New York Congressman Melancton Smith, were government officials using inside knowledge for private gain. Manasseh Cutler, with his Ohio plan, would provide cover.

In essence, the deal was that Duer would pull strings for Cutler if Cutler would agree to buy land for the speculators in the name of the Ohio Company. Duer and his people would become the company's silent partners, and in exchange would use the Board of Treasury's influence with Congress to obtain the terms that Cutler sought. Cutler found Duer "a man of the most sprightly abilities."

After their meeting, Duer and Cutler took the ferry to Brooklyn and sealed their partnership at the Stone House Tavern with "oysters cooked in every possible form, but the fried were most delicious." After dinner, he was "closeted with Colonel Duer and agreed to purchase more land . . . for another company, which will probably forward the negotiations."

At the start, Cutler had been asking for 1.5 million acres at the mouth of the Muskingum. Duer wanted him to ask for a further tract of 3.5 million acres between the Muskingum and Scioto rivers. Duer and his associates would form the Scioto Company, with thirty shares, representing about 115,000 acres each. Some of these shares would be turned over to the Ohio Company, and in exchange Cutler would transfer the deed for roughly 3.5 million acres to Duer. Cutler would make the down payment on both tracts, and Duer and his group would acquire an option on a huge amount of land at little or no expense.

Cutler worried that some individual on the Board of Treasury, such as Arthur Lee, might get wind of the deal, but Duer reassured him: "You have got the length of his foot. He calls you an open, frank, honest New England man, what an uncommon animal."

On July 21, Cutler submitted an expanded proposal to Congress. He offered to buy two tracts totaling nearly five million acres at a dollar an acre, with a one-third discount on untillable lands such as swamps. Payment would be in depreciated Continental Certificates, worth about ten cents on the dollar in the open market, but redeemed by the government at face value. He offered to pay $250,000 down, 400,000 when the exterior lines of the survey were run, and the rest in six installments.

On July 23, there was a flurry of lobbying to win over his opponents. "We were obliged to engage three or four persons before we could get at them," he noted. "In some instances, we engaged one person, who engaged a second, and he a third, and so on to a fourth, before we could effect our purpose. In these maneuvers, I am much beholden to the assistance of Col. Duer and Major Sargent," the last being Winthrop Sargent, the secretary of the Ohio Company.

That evening, Cutler felt that favorable winds were blowing when he dined with members from southern states. To move things along, he agreed to support General St. Clair for governor of the territory, and St. Clair joined the lobbying effort.

On July 24, Cutler made a final push to convince three congressmen still adamantly opposed to the deal: William Few of Georgia, William Bingham of Pennsylvania, and Dyre Kearney of Delaware. "Every machine in the city that it was possible to work we now put into motion," Cutler wrote. ". . . Of Few and Bingham there is hope, but to bring over that stubborn mule of a Kearney, I think is beyond our power."

To force a vote, Cutler planned to bluff Congress into thinking that he was giving up the fight. On July 26, he buttonholed congressmen and told them he was discouraged and going home the next day. Besides, he could buy land on better terms from individual states: Massachusetts was offering land in Maine at fifty cents an acre; both New York and Connecticut also had land at that price. The congressmen advised him not to be hasty. This was a matter of great magnitude, far exceeding any private contract ever made in the United States. Never had an individual received such attention from Congress.

On July 27, Cutler packed his bags and went to pay his respects to various members, repeating his intention to find better terms elsewhere. That afternoon, at three-thirty, he was still at his inn when he was informed that his petition had passed. The final deal was a dollar an acre, with 33 percent off for bad lands, and five hundred thousand dollars down, with another five hundred thousand on completion of the exterior survey lines. At that point, he would be given a deed to the 1.5 million acres of the Ohio Company, which pledged to pay the balance in six installments— all in depreciated certificates, which amounted to a real purchase price of about seven cents per acre. The additional land, secretly reserved for the Scioto Company, would be doled out as more payments were made. There would be one deed for the Ohio Company land, and a second deed for the Scioto lands, made out in the names of Manasseh Cutler and Winthrop Sargent. This second deed was made out for options on land as yet not paid for.

It was easy to draw up contracts to the mutual advantage of Cutler and Duer, since they were drafted by the Board of Treasury, under Duer's guidance. The arrangement was that of the Scioto Company's thirty shares (which represented an option to buy nearly four million acres) thirteen shares went to Cutler and Sargent, another thirteen went to Duer's consortium, and the remaining four were called "shares at large." As it turned out, Duer's group did have to advance some cash, because the Ohio Company was still having trouble selling its shares and could not make the down payment. So Duer stepped in and advanced $143,000. Since the contracts were linked, the Scioto deal would fall through if Cutler defaulted on the down payment.

As Cutler noted in his diary, "By this ordinance, we obtained the grant of near five millions of acres of land, amounting to three million and a half of dollars, one and a half million acres for the Ohio Company, and the remainder for a private speculation in which many of the principal characters of America are concerned. Without connecting this speculation, similar terms and advantages could not have been obtained for the Ohio Company."

Two distinct contracts were signed at the Board of Treasury on October 27, the transfer of shares was made, and the fate of the Ohio and Scioto companies, one honest and above-board, the other clandestine and underhanded, became entwined. The leading figure in all this was of course William Duer, whose two principles seemed to be, never be honest when you can be crooked, and never pay your bills. As one of his disillusioned partners said, "When the business is done, the tone is changed and obligation no longer acknowledged." It was somehow fitting that, years later, Duer died in debtor's prison. As for the Scioto Company, its promise of huge profits came to nothing.

After his victory in New York in the summer of 1787, Manasseh Cutler returned to Boston and applied his promotional skills to producing a pamphlet on the bountiful blessings of the Muskingum. It would soon be the center of population and the seat of the national government. How could it be otherwise, when it had "cotton . . . in great perfection, sugar . . . equal in flavor and whiteness to the best Muscovado, and tobacco . . . superior to that of Virginia"?

Although newspaper articles ridiculed the purchase as "Cutler's Indian Folly," the response was encouraging, and enough subscribers signed up to finance the first stage of the operation.

On December 3, 1787, only four months after the purchase, forty-seven men set out from Ipswich, Massachusetts, in covered wagons labeled in large letters FOR THE OHIO. Rufus Putnam joined the party in Hartford on January 1, 1788. It took them several weeks to reach Sumrill's Ferry on the Youghiogheny, about twenty miles south of Pittsburgh. There they remained, building boats, until April 1, 1788, when they embarked down the Youghiogheny, into the Monongahela, and down the broad Ohio. They called one of their boats the *Mayflower*, connecting themselves to the Pilgrims and their ideals.

On April 7, they arrived at the mouth of the Muskingum, which was concealed by sycamores. They went right by it and had to be towed back upstream with help from Fort Harmar, which stood near where the Muskingum and the Ohio joined. Losing no time, the New Englanders unloaded their goods and pitched a tent for General Putnam. The next day, they "commenced with great spirit" to clear the land, and sent out surveying parties. By April 12, they had cleared five acres in the triangle between the Ohio and the Muskingum.

By April 19, surveyors were laying out eight-acre lots, which were numbered and drawn in a lottery. It was done with such scrupulousness that none of the directors drew a lot in the center of town.

Putnam's people were in a hurry, since land could not be sold until it was surveyed. Every day, boats were coming down the river on the way to Kentucky, filled with potential settlers who were bypassing Ohio. Putnam watched in frustration as a hundred boats passed by in a single day. He was cheered only by the fact that the site matched his expectations. They wondered at the scale of nature, a black-walnut tree twenty-two feet around, clams the size of dinner plates, catfish as big as baby whales. Here was the earthly paradise in all its splendid abundance. After planting corn, they were amazed to find that it had grown nine inches in twenty-four hours. You could almost watch it grow.

At first, it was an all-male society, run along quasi-military lines, like early Jamestown. Settlers carried their weapons into the field, and men stood watch at night. Even though Fort Harmar was directly across the Muskingum, they built their own stockade, which they called Campus Martius. Inside the enclosure were rows of houses for shareholders, connecting the four corner blockhouses.

In spirit, the settlement was reminiscent of a New England

village, with its vestigial Puritanism, its busybody concern with everyone's personal conduct, its need for conformity, and its guardianship of moral values. The town was called Marietta, after the soon-to-be-beheaded queen of France, Marie Antoinette, in gratitude for her warm reception of Benjamin Franklin, and to thank the French monarchs for helping in the War of Independence.

Manasseh Cutler arrived on August 19 in a driving rain and stayed three weeks. General Putnam was still living in a tent. The cornfield was so vast that "I should be as soon lost in it as in a cedar swamp," Cutler wrote. He took the garrison's twelve-oared barge across the Muskingum to Fort Harmar. On the blade of each oar was painted the word CONGRESS. On September 2, he attended the Court of Common Pleas, and on September 6 the directors ordered that some of the biggest trees be cut down so that the rings could be counted. The rings on a tulip tree, counted with a magnifying glass, came to 441, which dated it back to 1346.

A month earlier, on July 9, 1788, Governor Arthur St. Clair had come to Marietta to make it his territorial headquarters. He had a vast area to cover, from the Ohio to the Mississippi, and spent much of his time traveling. From June 1790 to February 1791, he traveled five thousand miles on horseback or in an open boat. Aside from governing the settlers, he was in charge of Indian affairs. The policy was to keep the peace by paying them for their lands. To this purpose, Congress had voted seventeen thousand dollars for St. Clair in 1787 and twenty thousand in 1788, for the settlement of Indian claims.

But St. Clair soon learned that negotiation would be no simple matter. The tribes remained under the influence of the British, who maintained a presence on the American shores of the Great Lakes. He made ineffectual overtures to various chiefs.

The problem was that the land was filling with squatters who considered themselves beyond the reach of government. Why, St. Clair asked himself, should the Indians negotiate with a government that they believed was assisting the squatters? "Though we hear much of the injuries and depredations that are committed by the Indians upon the whites," St. Clair wrote Secretary of War Henry Knox, "there is too much reason to believe that at least equal if not greater injuries are done to the Indians by the frontier settlers, of which we hear very little." If the squatters were not restrained, an Indian war was inevitable, said St. Clair, who found himself reluctantly acting as mediator between the tribes and the squatters.

In Marietta, St. Clair's arrival marked the beginning of civilian government in the Northwest Territory. Laws were passed, counties formed, and courts established. The first law called for a militia. As more settlers arrived, with single women and young people, a marriage act specified the minimum age—fourteen for women and seventeen for men. St. Clair explained in October 1788 that fourteen was more suitable than twelve: "It very rarely happens in this climate that girls of twelve years are even as animals fit for the reception of the male. . . ."

In September, three judges were named, and Ebenezer Sproat was appointed sheriff. He had been a colonel in the war, after which he had sold pins and needles in Rhode Island. Not long after his appointment, a court was opened "for the administration of even-handed justice to the poor and the rich." In a holdover from New England, stocks and a pillory were built. Some of the Puritan laws were also brought to Ohio. There were prohibitions against "idle, vain, and obscene conversation" and "irreverence to the Supreme Being." The fine for public drunkenness as a first offense was "five dimes," or an hour in the stocks. "House-burning" was punishable by death.

As 1788 ended, however, the British were still trying to incite the Indians, and Spain was also a problem, enticing settlers with offers of land in the Natchez area. By the end of the year, Marietta had a population of two hundred, of whom 133 were men. James Backus wrote his father in December that it was cruelly cold, and the saucer of tea standing not five feet from a good fire was frozen. There were as yet no Indian hostilities, apart from occasional theft. A party of Chippewas had stolen a soldier's cartridge box, and when they were caught one of their women claimed to have found it in the woods.

In January 1789, St. Clair managed to bring some of the tribes to Fort Harmar to sign treaties and negotiate land purchases. In attendance were the Wyandots, Delawares, Ottawas, Chippewas, Pottawatimas, and Sacs. It was a complicated business, since they were not one people but tribes with overlapping claims. Still, the treaty was important, because it introduced the principle of paying for Indian lands rather than simply seizing them.

Three months later, on April 30, George Washington took the oath of office as president of the United States in New York. His first administration did not change any of the policies concerning the Northwest Territory. St. Clair remained governor, and Winthrop Sargent was secretary. Henry Knox remained secretary of war, in charge of Indian affairs. Knox was a soldier, who saw no benefit in Indian wars. He wanted an orderly western advance through land sales and a humane Indian policy.

But policy had little to do with reality, for the frontier never stood still. The westward movement had a will of its own. "The spirit [of settlement] has gone forth, and cannot now be restrained," St. Clair wrote President Washington in August 1789. He had grave doubts about the settlers. Would they be national in spirit, or vulnerable to British and Spanish intrigues? In case of war, would they fight, or throw off all connection with the parent states? And how would treason in a territory be punished, when the inhabitants were not full-fledged citizens? In his view, it was all happening too fast, and going in too many directions.

When George Washington was inaugurated, he may have wondered what he was getting into. Here was a baker's dozen of debt-ridden and war-exhausted states, with a great expanse of unexplored continent promising more conflict and strife. Beyond that, England and Spain were waiting for the young nation to trip and fall so they could pick up the pieces.

Besides foreign and domestic policies, Washington had to formulate an Indian policy, with only the British precedent to guide him. The Indians were a contradiction in terms: resident aliens with priority of occupation. The continent's first inhabitants, they were now being displaced by an expansionist white society, often beyond the control of government.

No one suggested that the Indians should become American citizens; the two societies were considered incompatible. One was pagan, preliterate, and nomadic. The other was Christian, literate, and agricultural. The tribes had lost their self-reliance and become dependent on the white man for trade goods; they were unable to make their own guns and ammunition. As the dispenser of trade goods, the white man had the means of obtaining land. There was no need to go to war to take Indian land when it could be bought for a pittance. But the question remained of what to do with the Indians once their land had been acquired. Policies were patched together, in keeping with the experimental nature of the United States themselves, a nation not stable and unified, but complex and improvised—"an expedient developed under duress," in the words of the historian D. W. Meinig.

The anomalies of Indian policy were evident before the ink was dry on the Treaty of Paris in 1783. No Indians were invited to the signing of the treaty, even though they had fought in the war, for their views were irrelevant; the peace was negotiated without them. Why, then, should they recognize the rights of diplomats in Paris to give away their land? Because, having sided with the British, they were in a poor negotiating position.

Washington realized this as early as September 1783, when he was trying to articulate a coherent Indian policy in a letter to James Duane, a congressman on the Committee on Indian Affairs. The Indians, he wrote, "were determined to join their arms to those of Great Britain and share their fortunes." They could now be listed among the defeated.

They could have been "compelled to retire along with them [the British] beyond the lakes," or evacuated to Canada. "But," he went on, "as we consider them a deluded people . . . and as the country is large enough to contain us all . . . and as we are disposed to be kind to them . . . we will draw a veil over what is past and establish a boundary line."

A boundary separating Indian territory from lands owned by the whites would ensure orderly settlement and keep squatters at bay. Without it, Washington warned, the western country would be settled "by a parcel of banditti, who will bid defiance to all authority while they are skimming and disposing of the cream of the country at the expense of many suffering officers and soldiers."

Once the line was drawn, Indian lands could be purchased in an orderly manner, which was preferable "to attempting to drive them by force of arms out of the country." On September 22, 1783, in the spirit of Washington's letter, the Continental Congress issued a proclamation banning squatters, and troops were sent west to enforce the ban.

A year later, on October 22, 1784, in the Treaty of Fort Stanwix, the Iroquois, greatly weakened by the war, yielded one-fourth of the state of Pennsylvania in exchange for "goods . . . for their use and comfort." There was some discrepancy between Washington's policy and its application. At Fort Stanwix and elsewhere, the Indians were simply ordered off the lands that the British had lost by conquest. Barely understanding what was going on, they were told what to give up and what to keep. It wasn't surprising that the treaties were later repudiated. At Fort Stanwix, for instance, the Iroquois relinquished their claims to lands west of the Ohio, which belonged to other tribes.

Henry Knox, the enlightened secretary of war, genuinely believed that "the Indians, being prior occupants, possess the right of the soil." But, whereas in Philadelphia there were assertions of justice, in the West there was encroachment on Indian land.

Although the Constitution made no mention of who would govern the Indians, it gave the president the power to make treaties. Washington took this to mean treaties with the tribes as well as with foreign nations, although equating the tribes with foreign nations was a fiction, since they had no sovereignty; they could not dispose of their land as they wished. The tribes were "nations" allowed to negotiate with only one other nation—the United States. Thomas Jefferson explained the situation to a British minister in 1792: the United States insisted on "a right of pre-emption of [Indian] lands; that is to say, the sole and exclusive right of purchasing from them whenever they should be ready to sell."

In his third annual message to Congress, on October 25, 1791, Washington called for the regulation of land purchases and for dealing honorably with "an unenlightened race of men." The policy was "expansion with honor." But in fact the tribes were still being driven off their lands.

John May, a subscriber and a veteran, arrived in Marietta in May 1789. Subscribers were divided into groups of owners of twenty shares, which were called "divisions," and each division appointed an agent. Each share was worth a thousand dollars in certificates, plus ten dollars in cash, and entitled the owner to sixty-four acres in the country and one city house lot. Veterans had been given certificates as severance pay, and by buying land with these certificates, they retired the government's debt.

May had come to build a house and check things out as division agent. He had brought a wagonload of goods to sell, but at first found no buyers, since no one had any discretionary income. Even though May noted that sixty houses had been built and four hundred acres of corn planted, his overall impression was that "little appears to be done, and a great deal of time and money misspent." He drew for his lot, and hired six men to clear his land and hew timber for his house. They all caught poison ivy.

While waiting for the house to be finished, May slept on his boat, but the catfish and perch in the Muskingum made so much noise they kept him awake half the night. Although noisy, the animal world was amazingly friendly. When he went swimming, a flock of yellow-legged snipe lit on the water by his side. On his land, four fawns "as tame as cats" became his pets, climbing all over him and sucking on his ear.

Equally amazing was the abundance of food, the best of venison and turkey, as many gray and black squirrels as you pleased, and as much fish as in any market. "In a word," he summed it up, "we live superbly."

On the Fourth of July, 1789, a banquet that started at one in the afternoon went on past midnight. A table sixty feet long was set by the river, and the feasters were joined by officers not on duty at Fort Harmar. A great many toasts were offered; when they ran out of the obvious ones, such as "the United States" and "the Constitution," they drank to "the memory of heros," "the amiable partners of our delicate pleasures," and, last but not least, "all mankind."

Despite the good cheer and optimism of frontier life in Marietta, there were casualties. "A number of poor devils," May noted, "five in all, took their departure homeward this morning. They came moneyless and brainless, and have returned as they came." Then there was "poor Dr. M," who was broke and out of provisions. May took pity on him, gave him a gun with powder horn and shot bag, and hired him to stand in his cornfield and keep away the crows.

On July 14, May ate green peas, planted five weeks before, from his own garden. At the end of the month, his house was ready for the installation of windows. He had packed eighty panes of glass in Boston, and all had survived the trip intact. On August 1, he dismantled his boat to obtain the flooring for his house. No sooner had he finished it, however, than he decided to return to Boston for another wagonload of goods, and to see his wife, whom he missed.

In spite of the abundance of fish and game, there were still food shortages at Marietta. The great cornfield had been fenced, grubbed, girdled, and planted, but for some mysterious reason the first crop was inedible; it even made the hogs sick. A group of settlers went up the Ohio to Isaac Williams' place, on the Virginia side, and said they needed corn for their families, offering a half-guinea in gold in exchange. Williams, an old soldier who had fought with Braddock, owned four hundred acres, which were cultivated by thirteen families of tenant farmers.

"How many is there of you?" he asked. "Rising of twenty," he was told. "Dang it, there is a heap of you, but you must have half a bushel apiece." And he gave them ten bushels.

In 1790, the Indians' harassment took the form of overhunting game. They hoped by this stratagem to force out the whites and repossess their lands. So thoroughly did they destroy the game within ten miles of Marietta that a deer was seen only rarely, whereas before a hunter could kill from ten to fifteen a day. One old Indian, when he came to Fort Harmar to draw his treaty blanket, threw it over his shoulder, saying he had his cornfield on his back but he would have it to walk on next year.

As a result of the overhunting, 1790 was a year of scarcity. It was no time, the settlers said, "to catch penny and chuck farthing." Potato tops were used for greens, and nettles, pigweed, and pokeweed sprouts for soup. Coffee, tea, and sugar were out of the question. Spicebush and sassafras were the beverages of choice.

Indian relations grew worse rather than better; in September, Secretary Knox authorized a military expedition "to punish the Wabash Indians for their hostile depredations." In October, General Josiah Harmar marched out of Fort Washington (today's Cincinnati) with 1,133 militiamen and 320 federal troops, to destroy the Indian towns about 120 miles to the north, near today's Fort Wayne, Indiana. He was soundly defeated on October 21 by the Miami Chief Little Turtle.

His debacle produced this angry letter from President Washington to Knox on November 19, 1790: "I expected *little* from the moment I heard he was a *drunkard*. I expected *less* as soon as I heard that on this account no *confidence* was reposed in him by the people of the western country. And I gave up all hope of success as soon as I heard that there were *disputes* with him about his command."

One of the eighty-nine casualties of that battle was Captain John McMurtry, who was wounded in the retreat. A friend named Woods rode beside him and managed to keep him on his horse, but the Indians were gaining. He told Woods to help him dismount and to hide him by the side of the road so he wouldn't be scalped.

McMurtry was never heard from again. His wife, Mary, the mother of eight children, maintained for several years that he would return. Eventually she remarried. Had he lived, McMurtry would have been eligible for bounty lands, and could have settled his family somewhere in Ohio.

The Indians who died in that battle also had families, friends, a future. For the dead on both sides, the tragedy was that they could not work out their differences when there was such an abundance of land. The opportunity was denied them by important men in remote places who gave orders for military actions.

The Indians were now emboldened to attack Marietta and its satellite settlements of Belpre, Waterford, Wolf Creek, and Big Bottom. When Joseph Barker arrived in Marietta in the summer of 1790, daily life was hazardous. There were mysterious fires, and some of his hogs were killed, and one of his cows came in from pasture with an arrow stuck in her side. Barker said he would have to hold on to his scalp with one hand while he dug holes to plant fruit trees with the other.

At the age of twenty-six, Joseph Barker had come to Ohio from Newmarket, New Hampshire, by ox cart and flatboat. He had seen only a few cheerless log huts along the way. By now, there were about 250 settlers, who thought of themselves as possessing the real Yankee character. The story was told of a Marietta settler showing his cornfield to a visiting Virginian and telling how long it had taken to clear it. The Virginian said, "Well I know one thing—you must have been goddamned poor or you would not have worked so hard."

Now, in the winter of 1790, every settlement was an armed camp, and every settler did guard duty. It was clear that the Indians were strongly opposed to new settlements, but a group of impatient young men was determined to go and cultivate the lots they had drawn at Big Bottom, on the Muskingum, thirty-three miles northwest of Marietta.

They left in December, even though Rufus Putnam and the other directors were strongly opposed and told them it was imprudent. Ignoring the warnings, the men built a blockhouse of beech-logs, large enough to accommodate them all, but left the filling in of the chinks between the logs for a rainy day. That was their first mistake; their second was not posting sentries.

On January 2, 1791, Indian warriors observed the Big Bottom settlement from across the frozen, snow-covered Muskingum. As it got dark, they slipped across the river and surrounded the unguarded blockhouse. By the light of the settlers' fire, some of the Indians took aim through the chinks in the logs, while others broke through the blockhouse gate. Everyone inside was killed or captured. Only the Bullard brothers, Asa and Eleazer, who lived in a cabin about a hundred yards from the stockade, escaped to Waterford, farther down the Muskingum.

The Indians broke up the floor so they could make a bonfire to incinerate the blockhouse and the bodies of the twelve dead. But the wood was green, and the fire subsided, so that some were only partly burned. The arm of William James, who at six feet four was reputed to be the biggest and strongest man in the county, was found clenching a piece of Indian bread.

When news of the massacre reached Marietta via Eleazer Bullard, a small crowd huddled around him to hear the details. In the midst of his report, a settler wandered by, asking, "Did anyone see my big pot?" "Damn your big pot," General Putnam exclaimed, in a town where swearing was a criminal offense. The other small settlements now feared that they would be next. At Belpre, about fifteen miles south of Marietta—on the Ohio, across from its juncture with the Little Kanawha—Israel Stone's wife would not let her two sons undress at night: "If anyone escapes, he will not be naked."

Several settlements were abandoned, among them Wolf Creek, about sixteen miles up the Muskingum from Marietta, where two Pennsylvania millwrights had built the only mill in the area. All the settlements used the Wolf Creek mill for their flour, but no amount of money would induce the people there to stay. Trips had to be made with an armed escort to get the corn ground. Everyone went with his grist and his gun. Never had the grinding gone so quickly: Joseph Barker timed with his watch the grinding of one bushel of corn in two minutes.

In the fall of 1791, St. Clair was appointed commander-in-chief of the tiny United States army and retraced the steps of Harmar's expedition from the year before. Although St. Clair was so gouty that he could not get on and off his horse unassisted, he set out on September 17 from Fort Washington with 920 men, most of them raw recruits.

On November 4, he was attacked on the banks of the Maumee, where he had carelessly pitched his camp. In the three-hour engagement, an estimated 632 men were killed. St. Clair's report to Secretary Knox said: "The most disgraceful part of the business is that the great part of the men threw away their arms." Like Harmar, St. Clair did not know the terrain; in fact, he hardly knew what river he was on. For the second year in a row, the Indians showed that they could inflict a decisive defeat on a well-armed troop of American soldiers.

Washington was angered when he heard the news, which took thirty days to reach Philadelphia, where he was dining with friends. The president waited until his guests were gone, and then burst out to his secretary, Colonel Lear: "St. Clair's defeated—routed. The officers nearly all killed, the men by wholesale, the rout complete! Too shocking to think of . . . And yet, to suffer that army to be cut to pieces—hacked by a surprise, the very thing I guarded him against. O God!, then he's worse than a murderer." St. Clair was stripped of his rank, but remained as governor in Ohio.

Some members of Congress felt that administration policy was to blame. Senator Benjamin Hawkins of North Carolina, later a famous Indian agent, wrote President Washington on January 26, 1792: "We seem to have forgotten entirely the rights of the Indians. They were treated as tenants at will, we seized on their lands and made a division of the same, allotted them certain portions for hunting grounds and did not even think of offering them compensation. . . . I shall make no remark on the defeat of the 4th of November."

The British were suspected. From Fort Knox in Vincennes, Indiana, Major Hamtramck reported to the secretary of war on March 31, 1792, that he had asked two Eel River chiefs if the British had given the Indians presents in the summer of 1791, and they had said, "Yes, my father, the goods were in large heaps like stacks of hay." "Did you get arms and ammunition also?" the major asked. "We got everything but big guns," they replied. "If you had done so, and if your people had not told the Indians that their lands belonged to you, you would have had no war."

As a result of this and other information, Knox reported to the president that Indian unrest was "a concerted plan between certain powers to check the growth of this rising country . . . diabolical as it may seem."

Not until August 1794 would General Anthony Wayne defeat the Indians who had beaten back Harmar and St. Clair. During that three-year interim, the Muskingum settlers were in a state of siege.

The Ohio Company spent so much money on defense that it couldn't pay the second installment of five hundred thousand dollars, which came due in 1792. Many subscribers were delinquent, but the primary problem was the company's involvement in the Scioto outfit's greedy schemes of wealth. When the Scioto Company unraveled, and it did so with spectacular speed, it took the Ohio Company with it. In addition, the Ohio Company treasurer, Richard Platt, was Duer's partner in other crooked ventures. He embezzled eighty thousand dollars of the Ohio Company's money, and soon joined Duer in debtor's prison. Rufus Putnam, Manasseh Cutler, and other Ohio Company directors who held Scioto shares all suffered big losses. Putnam wondered what the reaction of Congress would be, writing Cutler: "It is dangerous to quarrel with that power who may determine a fox's ears to be horns."

The Ohio Company asked Congress for relief, and a bill was introduced in early March 1792, releasing the company from its 1.5-million-acre purchase. On March 5, when there was no quorum, an irate Manasseh Cutler, who was in Philadelphia to press the matter, wrote his wife: "It is intolerable provoking that these idle, lazy, six dollar per day men, cannot rise in the morning, sip their coffee, and dismiss their barbers, early enough to attend Congress at 11 o'clock." Thanks to proddings from Cutler and Putnam, the bill passed on April 12, allowing the company to keep a little over a million acres of its original purchase without additional payment.

In the fall of 1792, General "Mad" Anthony Wayne succeeded Arthur St. Clair as commander-in-chief of the army. He was a hero of the Revolutionary War, present at Brandywine and Valley Forge, and had stormed the British fort at Stony Point, New York, in 1779. His nickname should have been "Ready" rather than "Mad," for he spent a year to train his troops in Cincinnati so that they would not repeat the blunders of Harmar and St. Clair.

On October 7, 1793, Wayne left Cincinnati with a disciplined force of several thousand men and advanced cautiously, building a chain of four forts between Cincinnati and Lake Erie. The first was Fort St. Clair, at today's Eaton, Ohio, halfway between Cincinnati and Greenville, which wasn't much more than a stockade for storage. Then came Fort Greenville (at today's Greenville), a more substantial affair, and then Fort Recovery, on the Maumee, at the site of St. Clair's 1791 defeat. At Fort Recovery, the soldiers' first task was to bury the bones of the men slain two years before. Finally, there was Fort Defiance, at today's Defiance, Ohio, at the juncture of the Maumee and Auglaize rivers, in the northwestern corner of Ohio. It was from Fort Defiance that Wayne marched down the Maumee in August 1794 to engage a force of eight hundred Indians on August 20 at Fallen Timbers, at the rapids near today's Toledo. The Indians, whom Wayne suspected were led by the British, still holding on to their Great Lakes posts, were routed in a two-hour battle.

It took another year to convene the twelve warring tribes at Fort Greenville for talks which culminated in the treaty of the same name on August 3, 1795. According to the terms, two-thirds of Ohio was turned over to the Americans, in exchange for gifts of $1,666 per tribe and annuities of between five hundred and one thousand dollars. The subjugation of the Indians was expressed by one of their chiefs: "We do now acknowledge the fifteen United States of America to be our father. . . . We must call them brothers no more." To which General Wayne responded: "I now adopt you all, in the name of the President of the Fifteen Great Fires of America, as their children. . . ." This patronizing model became a staple of many treaties that followed, even though the children were of a different race and had no interest in being adopted. What they had was land, which their "father" wanted.

At Greenville, the pattern was set. Treaties were followed by disputes, which led to military action and Indian defeats, followed by more treaties. As Henry Knox wrote Anthony Wayne, "If our modes of population and war destroy the tribes, the disinterested part of mankind and posterity will be apt to class the effect of our conduct and that of the Spaniards in Mexico and Peru together."

The Treaty of Greenville gave the westward movement its second wind, for it unlocked the river route to the west, via the Ohio, from Pittsburgh to Cincinnati and Louisville, and onward to the Mississippi. Now there were only the usual perils of river travel to contend with, such as currents and sunken logs. With the war over, settlers streamed in.

Two major developments on the international front showed the ripple effect of world events on the American frontier. One was the treaty signed by John Jay in London on November 19, 1794. Britain, expecting a collapse of the American federation, had delayed evacuating its northwestern forts. Now, with a constitutional government in place, the mother country finally gave in. The English promised to evacuate Detroit, Niagara, Oswego, and Michilimackinac, which had become propaganda centers to incite the Indians against the United States. In 1795, Spain signed a treaty with Thomas Pinckney (son of Eliza Lucas Pinckney of

South Carolina), which accepted America's boundary claims with Spanish Florida and restored free navigation on the Mississippi. These three treaties pacified the Indians, removed the British, and barred the Spanish from the Northwest.

While treaties were being signed in foreign capitals, fifteen-year-old Ben Stone could again pasture the family cows on Blennerhassett Island, in the Ohio, for hostilities had come to an end. He saw the last man to be killed by Indians on the Muskingum, just before the conclusion of the Treaty of Greenville.

Jonas Davis had come upon a skiff stuck fast in the ice at the mouth of Crooked Creek, three miles above Fort Harmar. He got some pincers and took the skiff apart to pull out the nails, which were a scarce commodity. As he was working on the water's edge, two Indians shot him from the top of the bank, scalped him, and took his clothes and tools. Ben Stone saw the body brought back on a bark-and-pole stretcher. The ravens had picked out his eyes.

One of the clauses of the Treaty of Greenville stipulated that white captives of the Indians must be returned. This created an odd test of loyalty among some of the captives, who had become, over the years, assimilated with the tribes. One of them was John Bricknell, who, during four years with the Delawares, had been adopted by and taken into the family of a chief, Big Cat, who doted on him.

Although Bricknell had Indian wives and children, Big Cat had to abide by the treaty. In the spring of 1796, he took Bricknell to Fort Defiance and told him: "My son, these are men the same color as yourself. . . . But have I not used you as a father would use a son? . . . Our treaty says you must be free. If you choose to go with the people of your own color, I have no right to say a word. But if you choose to stay with me, your people have no right to speak. Now, reflect on it, and take your choice."

Bricknell was torn between his Indian family and his allegiance to his own people. Finally, he said: "I will go with my kin." Big Cat felt the pain of loss. "I am getting old and I can no longer hunt," he said. "I thought you would be a support to my old age, and I leaned on you as on a staff, but now the staff is broken."

Another, far more ominous result of the treaty was that the annuities converted the tribes from hunters and warriors to welfare recipients. Acting Governor Winthrop Sargent wrote Secretary of State Timothy Pickering on August 9, 1796: "The Indians who are settled in the vicinity of our garrisons appear to enjoy much contentment. . . . Their cornfields look new and as whilst they are maturing they draw rations from the public stores, they give not themselves the trouble of hunting and they have now all the happiness of supreme indolence."

As for the Ohio Company, it was in liquidation. As a result of the Scioto losses, it was so deep in the red that it was forced to sell all its property at auction, including Campus Martius and its other fortifications. By 1796, the company was no more. Freed from his responsibilities as company director, Rufus Putnam was able to accept an appointment as surveyor general.

The town of Marietta continued to thrive, although it was soon outstripped in importance by other towns on major water routes, such as Cincinnati and Toledo. But in 1807 a New York visitor noted that "Marietta may be considered as New England in miniature. Her inhabitants are sober, honest, religious, and industrious, while dissipation and irrational amusements are not known in friendly circles."

CHAPTER TWENTY-ONE

THE CREEKS FIGHT BACK

In a unique example of successful resistance to the invading Americans, the half-breed Creek chief Alexander McGillivray negotiated with the Spanish to the south and the Americans to the north to maintain his Creek kingdom.

These Americans are a set of crafty, cunning republicans.

ALEXANDER McGILLIVRAY

From the Indians' point of view, American independence was a catastrophe. When France, Spain, and England vied for the North American continent, the tribes could play the Europeans off against one another. After the Treaty of Paris, America was dominant and the tribes were the losers. The game of alliances was petering out; the French and the British were gone.

With the restraining British hand removed, the Americans were heading in every direction, moving down every river and into every valley. Squatters invaded tribal lands like conquering armies. Some of the bounties given to soldiers to spur enlistment included land inside Indian hunting grounds. For the tribes, the options were not promising: they could move west, or permit the white man to pauperize them with trade goods, or they could resist.

Among the European powers, only Spain remained, trying desperately to maintain its hold on a long line of settlements from the Atlantic to New Mexico. In Paris, during the 1783 negotiations, Vergennes, the French foreign minister, told Floridablanca, the Spanish secretary of state, that the bucolic Americans would never be dangerous neighbors. But Floridablanca was not so sure. The Americans were moving south toward Spanish settlements in

438

Alabama and Georgia with a tremendous driving force. Florida-blanca had heard about the aggressive tactics of the American land speculators. They would get not one Indian drunk, but an entire tribe. They bribed not one state legislator, but the entire legislature. They operated on a grand scale, all the while stirring up resentment against Spain. At Muscle Shoals on the Tennessee River, and Chickasaw Bluffs on the Mississippi, the land jobbers were ready to show the Spaniards a thing or two about boundary fixing.

The Spaniards could invest in fortifications, or they could send surveyors out to blaze trees at boundary lines. But a general lethargy numbed them. Their conquering days were over. In Georgia and Alabama, between the Spanish and the Americans, there was a buffer zone of four formidable tribes—the Creeks, the Cherokees, the Chickasaws, and the Choctaws. Whoever controlled the tribes held the balance of power.

This was apparent to a man who would become one of the most remarkable tribal leaders in the annals of Indian-American relations, a leader who through clever diplomacy maintained the lands and independence of the Creek nation for ten years. He was perhaps the only authentic Indian statesman, using force the way the white man did—to implement policy. Frail and in poor health, he was usually too weak to ride a horse or fire a gun. But he was an educated man, who could hold a quill and carry on a diplomatic correspondence.

Alexander McGillivray was born of mixed racial heritage. His father was a Scottish highlander who arrived in Charleston in 1735 at the age of sixteen with one shilling in his pocket. Lachlan McGillivray became a trader, lived among the Creeks, and married Sehoy, sister of Chief Red Shoes. As part of the courtship ritual, he planted beans and set a pole for two vines to climb. When they were entwined, the ceremony took place. A son was born in 1759.

Alexander McGillivray is an example of that stereotypical American, the half-breed, seen as the recipient of the worst of both races. On the frontier, the half-breed was suspected of dual allegiance, of being quite literally two-faced. Since the whites didn't want him, he often ended up living with the tribe. When Francis Parkman traveled west in the 1840s, he would be told that half-breeds were, "according to the common saying, half Indian, half white man, and half devil."

Alexander McGillivray devoted his life to the cause of his

tribe. His father, who had increased his single shilling into a fortune worth a hundred thousand dollars, was a fervent Loyalist in the War of Independence. When the Americans won, he was expelled from Georgia and went back to Scotland. His son held a grudge against the Americans for confiscating his father's land, and vowed to keep them off Creek lands.

At fourteen, Alexander McGillivray was sent to Charleston, where his father's cousin, a Presbyterian minister, agreed to be his tutor. By the time his father left Georgia in 1783, Alexander was twenty-four and lived on a plantation called Coweta, at the juncture of the Coosa and Tallapoosa rivers, on Creek land. He had managed to weave together a life that drew on both white and Indian influences. Like a southern white plantation owner, he kept slaves. A French traveler who visited Coweta counted sixty, each with his own cabin. But Alexander practiced polygamy like an Indian chief.

The Creeks were surrounded. Their lands extended across the middle of Alabama and Georgia, with Americans to the north and east, and Spaniards to the south. McGillivray feared that the Americans who had taken his father's property were now after his mother's land. He turned to the Spanish for help, using the British trader William Panton, based in St. Augustine, as his intermediary.

The Spanish allowed the British firm of Panton & Leslie to operate in their dominion because it served their purposes. The way to control the tribes was to buy their skins and furs, but there was no market for either in sunny Spain. Panton bought their entire supply, sold it on the English market, and helped keep the Indians pro-Spanish. One of the reasons the Spanish trusted him was that he hated the Americans. He swore to his friend Esteban Miró, the governor of New Orleans, that he would never have anything to do with them, not even "Washington himself, had he the thirteen United States in his belly!"

Panton put McGillivray in touch with Miró. This all happened at a time when the other tribes in the area were being lured away from Spain with American gifts and rations. The Indians assumed that they could accept presents from anyone who offered, even if it meant signing conflicting treaties. As one chief expressed it: "I extend my arms to the south and to the north, waiting to see who will be the first to speak the truth."

In 1784, McGillivray decided to ignore the Americans, whom

he thought of as "a set of cunning, crafty republicans," and conclude a treaty with Spain. The Spaniards were eager to cement
relations with a bona-fide Indian leader who occupied the buffer
zone between their possessions and the American settlements.
McGillivray was invited to Pensacola in June to sign a treaty of
trade and friendship with Arturo O'Neill, the Spanish governor.
He was now on the Spanish payroll and in close touch with Miró
in New Orleans, O'Neill in Pensacola, and Vizente de Zespedes,
the governor of Florida, in St. Augustine. Hearing that Mc-
Gillivray's poor health had been traced to syphilis, Miró sent him
a package of Olivenza's famous powder remedy.

In 1785, the Continental Congress appointed five commissioners to negotiate a peace treaty with the Creeks, the one tribe not
falling into line. The commissioners wrote to McGillivray, but he
was displeased by the tone of their letters, which were patronizing,
addressed to the "warriors of the thirteen great fires" and including
crude threats, such as: "The hatchet once lifted is not easily buried."

When the commissioners arrived on October 24 on the Ogee-
chee River above Savannah, McGillivray refused to attend. One of
the commissioners, ex-senator Benjamin Hawkins, complained
that the Creeks were represented by only two chiefs and a handful
of warriors. "The Creeks alone," he wrote in his report, "seem
blind to their own interest and still desirous of provoking new
troubles."

In the meantime, Georgia settlers were encroaching on Creek
hunting grounds. McGillivray complained that the Americans "get
every straggling Indian hunter to sign an instrument of writing,
which they falsely call a grant." In March 1786, he decided to go
on the offensive to rid his land of squatters, but he needed Spanish
backing and military aid. This led to consultations among the
Spanish governors. O'Neill in Pensacola and Zespedes in Saint
Augustine were in favor of giving McGillivray what he asked for,
but Miró in New Orleans hesitated. He didn't want Spain dragged
into hostilities with the United States over the Creeks.

Zespedes proposed that the Creeks be given "the customary
amounts of powder and ball for the purpose of hunting." Under
this transparent pretext, McGillivray was issued a few thousand
rifles, eight thousand flints, five thousand pounds of powder, and
ten thousand pounds of ball, all to be brought to his headquarters
in Alabama by Panton's trading firm. Miró advised that these sup-

plies be delivered "with the greatest circumspection. . . . The Indians should come to get them with only two horses each time, in order that they would appear to have been purchased by different tribes."

McGillivray summoned the Creek chiefs on April 23, and all agreed to rid their lands of squatters. His power over the chiefs came from his ability to obtain Spanish aid. Surrounded on all sides, the Creeks had no wilderness to retreat to. "Our lands are our life and breath," McGillivray wrote. "If we part with them we part with our blood." He knew that the Spaniards were not expansionist: it was to their advantage to maintain the Creeks where they were. It was the Americans he had to worry about, and by acting forcefully now, he might give them pause.

Hearing that the Creeks were arming, the Georgians sent out a hit man, Daniel McMurphy, to arrange for McGillivray's assassination. He rode into Creek territory, offering four horseloads of goods to any Indian who would kill the Creek leader. McGillivray heard about McMurphy's mission. "I had the satisfaction to make that scoundrel McMurphy run off as hard as he could for his life," he said.

In May 1786, McGillivray sent his warriors into Georgia on the Oconee River and into Tennessee on the Cumberland to ravage squatter settlements. He reported to his Spanish allies that he had "much interrupted their cultivation for this year," and that on the Cumberland a few settlers had been killed. This was "unavoidable, as those people bear extreme hatred and rancor to Indians." "My warriors are victorious over the Americans," he wrote Governor Zespedes. "The people of Cumberland are drove over the Ohio river and the state of Georgia now lays at our mercy."

McGillivray was gravely ill that summer. On August 12, he wrote O'Neill: "The fever has reduced me very low and it has been succeeded by a breaking-out all over my body. I'm apprehensive that I shall lose all my fingernails and with difficulty can I take the pen in my hand to write." The rash on his body sounded like the second stage of syphilis, which in the third stage attacks the brain.

By the beginning of 1787, McGillivray's health had improved enough for him to launch another campaign against the settlers, who had come back in greater numbers. McGillivray was enraged: he had thought he was rid of them for good. He wrote O'Neill on March 4: "In the spring . . . I will go to the lower towns and every American I find shall either be drove away or put to death for the cowardly murdering villains they are."

From New Orleans, the prudent Miró warned against more attacks: "If you exasperate the Georgians with new hostilities all the states will make common cause." Miró did not want the Creeks to receive any more guns. On October 6, McGillivray wrote Zespedes to complain. "Miró may be under the influence of an impolitic delicacy. . . . It cannot be your intention after having encouraged me to resist the encroaching disposition of the Americans, to withdraw your support."

The Creeks had plenty of guns from the year before, and continued their skirmishes. Governor George Mathews of Georgia declared on November 15, 1787: "Our frontiers have been the scene of blood and ravages; they have killed 31 of our citizens, wounded 20, and taken four prisoners; they have burned a number of houses and towns." McGillivray was pushing the Georgia squatters hard, and by January 1788 there was not a single building left standing on the contested lands.

But the military campaigns had economic consequences. The Creek warriors were now out of ammunition and had little time to collect pelts and skins. McGillivray once again needed Spanish aid and reminded his silent allies that the war was "not entirely our own." The Spaniards were losing patience with the Creek leader. O'Neill wrote Miró on June 4, 1788: "McGillivray considers himself independent of our government, though employed by it at $450 a month, and proceeds with almost complete arbitrariness." The Spaniards had doubts also about the trader Panton, of whom it was now said that he had a "corazón británico" (British heart).

Just as he was on the brink of defeating the Georgians, McGillivray's supply of arms and ammunition dried up. Disgusted with his fickle allies, he began to suspect that the Spanish were deserting him. When he was told in September 1788 to "make instant peace with America but reserve your trade with Spain," he wondered whether Spain and America had made a secret deal. It seemed to be confirmed by an item in an American newspaper: "If the Creeks do not agree to terms of peace, the whole Union will take the matter up. They are no longer supported by a certain power."

In Philadelphia, work on Indian affairs was delayed until the Constitution could be ratified and a president elected. In the spring of 1789, McGillivray was notified by the Indian Affairs Office: "We are now governed by a president who is like the Old King over the Great Water. He commands all the warriors of the thirteen great fires." In September, three distinguished ambassadors were sent to the Creek country to try and reach an agreement with McGillivray. They were Benjamin Lincoln, the general who had taken Cornwallis' sword; Cyrus Griffin, the last president of the Continental Congress; and David Humphreys, a veteran of Paris negotiations at the side of Benjamin Franklin. These eminent Americans arrived at Rock Landing, on the Oconee River in central Georgia, in the fall of 1789.

McGillivray had not deigned to attend the last commission in 1785, but this time he came with nine hundred men, and drank the Black Drink with the commissioners. He was not impressed with David Humphreys, who he felt was "a great boaster of his political knowledge." After reading the proposed treaty, "I told him [Humphreys] by God I would not have such a treaty crammed down my throat."

The real reason for McGillivray's intransigence was that the Spanish, alarmed by his negotiations with the Americans, had promised to renew their aid. The Spanish promises, McGillivray wrote, "made me (to use the Indian expression), stout in my heart and strong in my mouth." He made conditions that he knew the Americans would find unacceptable.

Determined to make peace with the Creeks, President Washington searched for a man who could win over McGillivray. He chose Colonel Marinus Willett, a much-decorated war hero, the officer who had been in command of the Third New York Regiment at Fort Stanwix in 1777.

Washington briefed Willett on the Creek situation in March 1790. The Creeks had six thousand fighting men, and they were at war with Georgia. Their leader was irritated by the confiscation of his father's lands. But the immediate point of friction was a tract of land on the Oconee, which Georgia claimed, though the validity of the claim was denied by the Creeks. The people of Georgia wanted Congress to send them an army to crush the Creeks, which would cost fifteen million dollars. But, Washington said, if someone could settle with McGillivray without the Georgians' hearing about it, a war might be prevented.

Willett left New York on March 15 with a servant and two horses. His Charleston-bound sloop took fourteen days. On April 2, he continued alone on horseback and headed west into Georgia through Cherokee country, swimming his horse across rivers. On April 30, he reached the first Creek settlement, where he learned that McGillivray was in a village called Ofkuskee (southwest of Atlanta).

McGillivray sent for the chiefs of the lower towns. They gathered on May 17 at his Alabama plantation, Coweta. Willett asked the chiefs "to repair with me to the council fire that is kindled in our beloved town [New York], that we may form a treaty which shall be strong as the hills and as lasting as the rivers." He withdrew then to let the chiefs discuss his proposal.

McGillivray was flattered that President Washington had sent his special emissary to negotiate with him as an equal, one head of state to another. He also knew that if he did not make a deal this time he might face the entire American nation. Whereas, if he did make a deal, he would be able to remain on good terms with both the Spanish and the Americans; it would be the triumph of Creek diplomacy.

Willett returned an hour later to hear the Creek reply: "You say you come from your beloved chief, George Washington, to invite our beloved chief to a council fire in your beloved town. The road is very long, and the weather is very hot; but our beloved chief will go with you."

On June 1, 1790, Willett started back to Charleston with McGillivray and his entourage. They reached New York in mid-July, where the Creek delegation was welcomed by the newly created Society of Tammany, a patriotic and fraternal organization founded in 1789, whose members adopted Indian rituals and dressed up in Indian costumes. The society escorted them up Wall Street to Federal Hall, where Congress was sitting. Henry Knox took McGillivray to meet President Washington. The president told the chief that the federal government was willing to concede favorable terms to the Creeks in order to put an end to hostilities.

The treaty that was concluded on August 13 was a compromise. The Creeks were to cede the Oconee lands claimed by Georgia and already occupied by settlers. In exchange, they were given a large and valuable hunting ground on the Altamaha, extending to Georgia's Atlantic coastline. As payment for the cession on the Oconee, McGillivray was given a lump sum of ten thousand dollars, plus two thousand a year. In addition, the treaty had a secret clause in which McGillivray was made an American agent with the rank of brigadier general and a stipend of twelve hundred dollars a year.

McGillivray had established the borders of Creek lands, been given the honors of a foreign chief of state, and was now a rich man, his promised payments soon to arrive from New York in gold. Though he still professed to despise the Americans, he accepted the rank of brigadier general in their army, explaining that, "tired of being repeatedly pressed to do so, I agreed to add this plumage to my cap." He had to swear an oath of allegiance to the United States, which he had previously refused. He also had to accept that the Creeks were now "under the protection of the United States of America." The nationhood of the Creeks was denied by those words.

McGillivray seemed content, but the Spaniards were concerned that he had switched sides, and the Georgians felt betrayed by their own government. Representative James Jackson of Georgia said that the federal government had "ceded three million acres of land guaranteed to Georgia by the Constitution." President Washington had "invited a savage of the Creek nation to the seat of government, caressed him in a most extraordinary way, and sent him home loaded with favors."

The exertion of the midsummer return trip, during which several horses were drowned while fording rivers, was too much for McGillivray, who upon his return was laid up with bouts of fever and gout. "It mounts from my feet to my knees," he said of the gout, "and I am still confined to the fireside." A visitor, John Pope, who saw him in June 1791, said he looked forty-five instead of his actual thirty-two.

McGillivray could congratulate himself on having saved his tribe and its lands. He was serving two masters, since he was being paid by both the Americans and the Spanish, who still gave him six hundred dollars a year. On July 6, 1792, he signed another treaty with Spain, in New Orleans. Now that there was a border between Georgia and the Creek lands, he had to make sure it was respected. His policy was to attack settlers who ran the line and seize their cattle. On November 28, 1792, he wrote Panton: "I gave out general orders that as the Georgians had put over a great number of cattle and horses into the south fork of the Oconee and erected huts, that these cattle should all be seized and the huts burned."

At the start of 1793, a gravely ill McGillivray went south to stay at his farm in Pensacola with one of his wives. William Panton came to visit, and stayed by McGillivray's side as he lay dying. On February 17, he died, at the age of thirty-four. "He breathed his last in my arms," Panton wrote McGillivray's father in Scotland. "I found him deserted by the British, without pay, without mercy, without friends, and without property, saving a few negroes, and he and his nation threatened with destruction by the Georgians, unless they agreed to cede them the better part of their country. I had the good fortune to point out a mode by which he could save them all, and it succeeded beyond expectation."

One historian, Albert J. Pickett, called McGillivray "the Talleyrand of Alabama." He was a nationalist, who maintained the illusion of a Creek nation for a time, but it was a doomed cause. The Creeks would be beaten down a generation later in the campaigns of Andrew Jackson. Forced off their native ground, they would move west of the Mississippi. The boundary line that McGillivray and George Washington traced was a line in the sand. While he lived, the Creek leader held on to the territorial integrity of his people. He maintained the balance of power with his more powerful neighbors when the adjacent tribes were already in defeat.

CHAPTER TWENTY-TWO

THE STRUGGLE
FOR STATEHOOD

The first three states to be made after the first thirteen had to struggle for their independence from the states they had once been part of. Only one of the three went through the territorial interlude prescribed in the Northwest Ordinance of 1787.

Such as we were we gave ourselves outright
(The deed of gift was many deeds of war)
To the land vaguely realizing westward,
But still unstoried, artless, unenhanced,
Such as she was, such as she would become.

ROBERT FROST

As Winston Churchill put it in his *History of the English-Speaking Peoples*, in the early years of the republic, the government of the Continental Congress "had neither the power nor the opportunity in so vast a land of creating an ordered society out of the wreckage of revolution and war."

At the 1787 Constitutional Convention in Philadelphia, the delegates had to decide whether to extend the provisions of the Northwest Ordinance beyond the Old Northwest, at a time when other areas were asking for statehood. The debate on the equality of states that had just taken place in New York was repeated, ending in a compromise that said only: "New states may be admitted by Congress into this Union."

But it was only after the Constitution had been adopted and ratified that the process of nation-building could begin. The original thirteen had entered the Union as proud little fiefdoms jealous of their prerogatives. During George Washington's two terms, however (1789–97), three new states were added—Vermont, Kentucky, and Tennessee—none of them in the Old Northwest, all of them territories belonging to one of the original thirteen. New York had claims on Vermont, Kentucky was part of Virginia, and Tennessee was an extension of North Carolina. After the first thirteen had won independence from England, these three captive areas of their parent states had to struggle for their independence.

Vermont was a wedge of woods and mountains bounded on the north by Quebec, on the east by the Connecticut River, and on the west by the Lake Champlain–Hudson River waterway. Theoretically, Vermont belonged to New York by a royal grant of 1664. But as long as the French were in Canada, they kept settlers south of the Massachusetts line by holding the Lake George–Lake Champlain water route with forts at Ticonderoga and Crown Point.

It was only when the English swept the French away in 1759 that settlers advanced into western Vermont, a land of brooks and rivers running down in all directions from the backbones of mountains—a land of what the locals called "intervales," flats of rich alluvial deposits mixed with groves of white pine that were easily converted into greenbacks, with the one condition that the tallest and finest and straightest were by law reserved for the Royal Navy.

These first Vermont settlers were men used to the woods, men who felt cramped by village life, as well as the can't-hold-a-job types, tenured vagabonds. They roofed their cabins with bark and hung blankets over the windows, because they had no glass. The floors were beaten earth or split logs laid with the flat side up. Light came from tallow dips, heat from the open fire, and time was reckoned from a "noon-mark" cut into a windowsill.

Captain Whitmore, who settled in a beaver meadow (which would one day be Marlboro) to protect his oxen from the wolves, carried his grain on his back from Deerfield, Massachusetts, twenty miles away. In winter, he dragged the load on his sled in four feet of snow. There were no doctors, so they set their own broken bones and delivered their own babies. When the area grew more populated, Mrs. Whitmore became a midwife and had delivered two thousand babies before she died at the age of eighty-seven.

Wild animals were a danger to livestock and humans. It didn't take long for a four-hundred-pound bear to empty a pigpen. But with every blow of the ax they saw their fortunes improve. The farm turned into a settlement, with a gristmill and a sawmill. The settlement turned into a village, with a store, a tavern, a school, a church, and rising property values. Soon they were talking about the good old days of barn raisings and neighborhood wolf hunts.

In 1749, a period of confusion over land ownership arose in eastern Vermont when Governor Benning Wentworth of New Hampshire began to grant patents in parts of Vermont west of the Connecticut River. In 1764, King George III confirmed the original 1664 royal grant of Vermont to New York. In 1770, the New York Supreme Court ruled that all Hampshire grants were invalid, which meant that settlers who held those patents had to buy back their land or lose it.

Resolving to do neither, the owners of those grants formed military companies called the Green Mountain Boys, under the command of Ethan Allen. He and his brothers, Ira and Levi, owned a land company with title to over three hundred thousand acres in central Vermont. Their armed bands drove off the New York sheriffs, tore down fences, burned cabins, stole cattle, and branded the naked backs of New York settlers with the "birch seal."

When the revolution broke out, the Green Mountain Boys already had five years of fighting New York under their belts, and they espoused the patriot cause with some success. Ethan Allen took Fort Ticonderoga on May 10, 1775, and Vermont regiments fought at Hubbardton and Bennington.

Under the leadership of the Allen brothers, Vermont declared itself an independent republic in 1777, taking advantage of the confusion of war to slip the yoke of its acquisitive neighbors. Vermont hoped for recognition from the Continental Congress, but this body showed no inclination to carve a new state out of a territory claimed by New York. The Declaration of Independence was not an invitation for dissident factions within the original colonies to abscond.

Repeatedly rebuffed, Ethan Allen looked in another direction, and tried to negotiate a secret treaty with the British. After all, Vermont had a border with Canada. Because it was landlocked, its commerce depended on access to the sea, and the shortest route was northward to the St. Lawrence.

But by this time, peace was at hand. In the Treaty of Paris in 1783, Canada stayed British but it was agreed that Vermont was

American. When Britain recognized the independence of the American states, it lost all interest in Vermont. Unwanted by either side in the conflict, Vermont was left with the Swiss option of a small alpine state trying to maintain its independence and avoid partition between its greedy neighbors, New Hampshire and New York.

At the time of the 1787 Constitutional Convention, Ethan Allen was still making overtures to the British. In a recently discovered letter dated January 12, 1787, he wrote the governor of Quebec, Lord Dorchester: "Vermont is not in confederation with the United States." He proposed an alliance with Quebec, arguing: "Nature has situated the inhabitants of these territories to be friends and neighbors."

Some scholars see the letter as proof of Ethan Allen's treason. It might be argued that he was simply a businessman looking for the best deal. But, with Allen conspiring to make Vermont Canadian, there was little chance of its becoming a state. In 1789, Levi Allen went to England and offered to raise a regiment of Green Mountain Boys for George III, which would surely have been treason.

It was not until Ethan Allen died in 1789 that Vermont statehood moved ahead. Alexander Hamilton, the secretary of the treasury, prevailed upon New York to accept Vermont's independence against compensation to the titleholders of Vermont lands. Thomas Jefferson, once the advocate of small states, objected that Vermont was *too* small. "If Congress are not firm on that head," he said, "our several states will crumble into atoms by the spirit of establishing every little canton into a separate state."

The prevailing opinion, however, was that Vermont, although tiny in size, was Yankee in character. There were no objections to adding two senators and two representatives to the New England alignment. In October 1790, the Vermont Assembly called a convention which ratified the Constitution, and on March 6, 1791, Vermont became the fourteenth state.

Vermont did not have to go through the territorial process, since it was already populated, and for the same reason, neither did Kentucky. Land companies had begun exploring Kentucky in the 1740s and 1750s, and squatters had started staking their claims in the 1760s.

On March 14, 1775, the Transylvania Company bought sev-

enteen million acres between the Kentucky and Cumberland rivers
from the Cherokees at the Treaty of Sycamore Shoals. How could
a private company buy vast tracts that in principle belonged to
Virginia and spilled over into Tennessee, which belonged to North
Carolina? Such was the deranged condition of the country on the
eve of the revolution, when constituted authority was unraveling.

The Transylvania Company petitioned the Continental Congress for admission of their land claim as the fourteenth state, even
as the governors of Virginia and North Carolina were having the
purchase invalidated. Settlers complaining that the company was
charging exorbitant prices for land sent a petition of grievances to
the Virginia Assembly, where the legality of what one legislator
called "a snug little purchase" was debated. The final decision of
the Assembly in Williamsburg, on November 4, 1778, was that the
Transylvania title was void. As a consolation prize, the company
was awarded two hundred thousand acres in western Kentucky,
on the Green River.

To certify its claim over the area of the Transylvania purchase, Virginia made Kentucky a county, with its seat at Harrods-
burg, a few miles south of the Kentucky River. The Cherokee
Chief Dragging Canoe issued the prophecy that "a dark cloud hung
over the land," which was apparently the origin of the phrase "dark
and bloody ground."

The war years saw Indian harassment in the bluegrass. The
British were "hair buyers," paying the Indians for American
scalps. Yet, in spite of the dangers, settlers kept coming. As always, land hunger overrode all other considerations. A number of
Loyalists also moved to Kentucky, having been thrown off their
lands in Virginia and North Carolina.

During those years, Kentucky aspired to statehood but remained under Virginia rule. To its appeals, Virginia responded in
1780 by dividing the one county into three—Fayette, Jefferson,
and Lincoln.

Kentuckians strongly felt the logic of separation. Distances
were great and communications uncertain, and whereas the rivers
of Virginia flowed toward the Atlantic, Kentucky's rivers flowed
toward the Mississippi, giving it a border-state vocation. In 1783,
a petition to Congress again asked for statehood, in these terms:
"Much wisdom is not required to supply our wants. A fool can put
on his clothes better than a wise man can do it for him."

When the Land Ordinance was established in 1785, its provisions for the equitable distribution of land in 640-acre sections did not apply to Kentucky, which remained under Virginia land laws. These laws were confusing, since there were so many different kinds of titles. Squatters had claims, and soldiers had warrants for land, which were sold and exchanged like currency.

There was an epidemic of litigation, which made Kentucky a promised land for lawyers. Rich men who could afford sharp lawyers got the best land. Poor people were forced off their lands and reduced to tenantry. Kentucky became a place of landlords and tenants, rich estates and dirt farms, of slaves, plantations, and first families, all hand-me-downs from the Virginia model. In the first federal census, in 1790, there were 12,430 slaves out of a total population of seventy-three thousand, or roughly 16 percent. It was in Kentucky that the myth of the happy darky and the kindly massa first traveled west of the Alleghenies.

The abuse of land titles, wrote Humphrey Marshall, the historian of Kentucky, "more than the Indian wars, or anything else, has retarded the population, obstructed the improvement, distracted the people, and depreciated the value of the soil." Thousands of Kentuckians who felt cheated by the land laws wanted to be rid of the Virginia connection.

Once the federal government was in place in 1789, Kentucky applied for statehood. On April 3, 1792, in Danville, forty-five delegates met to draft a constitution. All but three were landowners, and all but twelve owned slaves, so it came as no surprise that there was an article in the constitution protecting slavery.

In several other provisions, however, the constitution showed hints of a frontier radicalism. Imprisonment for debt was abolished, and, for the first time in any state constitution, all religious and property qualifications for voting were voided. Any free white male over twenty-one who was a Kentucky resident could vote.

Kentucky became the fifteenth state, and the first frontier state, on June 1, 1792. Its first governor was the frontiersman Isaac Shelby, who had lived most of his life on his original pre-emption claim. This squatter-governor's claim had been validated in 1779, when Virginia sent out four commissioners to adjudicate the land laws. They held court at Logan's Fort, on the Holston River, in October, and the first certificate they issued was to Shelby, for making a crop of corn in 1776 on land "on a branch that heads at the Knob Lick and about a mile and a half or two miles from the said Lick on a southeastwardly course."

•   •

In the case of Tennessee, the struggle for statehood took a dozen years, because North Carolina would not give up its western extension. The Continental Congress kept urging the states to cede their western lands, which was like asking someone to leave his estate to a charitable foundation. Obviously, *they* preferred to sell those lands to settlers, rather than give them to Congress to sell.

In early 1784, Congress once again urged the states to make their cessions for the good of the Union, since a large national debt was "a chain of slavery." Virginia was the first to act, ceding some of its trans-Ohio lands, and putting pressure on North Carolina to do the right thing.

Following Virginia's example, the North Carolina General Assembly met in April 1784 and voted for cession. The bill stated that the ceded western lands would be laid out in a state or states that would eventually be admitted to the Union.

The people who lived on the ceded lands—primarily the Watauga settlers in northeastern Tennessee—were not consulted in any of this. For two years, they had been building up grievances against North Carolina, which taxed them but provided no services: not a single soldier for their defense, not a single road on which to carry their goods to market. Meanwhile, their property in the remote interior was taxed at the same rate as property on the North Carolina seashore.

Adding insult to injury, one of the North Carolina speakers in the debate over cession called the Watauga settlers "off-scourings of the earth, fugitives from justice, and we will be rid of them at any rate." This was one of the arguments in favor of cession—the idea of casting off these undesirable frontier ruffians.

The Watauga settlers felt grievously wronged. They had won the battle of Kings Mountain, one of the turning points of the revolution in the South. And now they were being dumped into a reserve of ceded western lands. They had no idea who would govern them, or what would happen to their land titles.

The Watauga settlers decided to take matters into their own hands. In August 1784, the settlers in the three North Carolina counties of Washington, Sullivan, and Greene elected delegates to a convention in Jonesboro, between the Nolichuckey and Holston rivers.

On August 23, the Indian fighter and frontiersman John Sevier was named president of the convention, which voted to form a new state and petition Congress for admittance to the Union. The delegates declared their independence from their parent state, as Vermont had done in 1777.

That August, while the willful Wataugans were proclaiming their statehood, Assembly elections were held in North Carolina. When the newly elected members met in the fall, they began having second thoughts about cession. In its rush to copy Virginia, the previous Assembly had neglected to claim credit for the cost of Indian expeditions, thus waiving one of the principal advantages of cession. On November 20, the Assembly repealed the act of cession that had been passed in April—not because of events on the Watauga, but to obtain better terms from Congress.

On the Watauga, plans still went ahead for statehood. Independence was a heady brew, and the Wataugans now had a new grievance against their mother state: North Carolina was paying annuities to the tribes for land purchases, but since the April cession had stopped payment. The unpaid tribes were taking their revenge on the Wataugans, raiding and harassing them.

Another convention was held in Jonesboro in December 1784, and a constitution was passed. A declaration of independence said, "It is our inalienable right to form ourselves into a new and independent state." The state was named Franklin, after Benjamin Franklin. An Assembly was elected, met in Jonesboro in March 1785, and named John Sevier governor.

This state, consisting of three breakaway North Carolina counties, was basically a valley in eastern Tennessee, bounded by three rivers, the Holston, the Watauga, and the Nolichuckey. There were other settlements farther west, around Nashville, but these did not join the secession. Many of the settlers there had military bounty grants awarded by North Carolina, which it would have been injudicious to disavow. Besides, more than one state might be formed from the North Carolina backcountry, and they were waiting to see what would happen.

The state of Franklin was short-lived, surviving a scant four years. It was never recognized by anybody—not North Carolina, not the Continental Congress, and not the constitutional government. It sputtered along, experimenting with various strategies to stay afloat.

Having repealed its act of cession, North Carolina now claimed ownership of the lands in eastern Tennessee of which Franklin was made up. North Carolina's governor, Alexander Martin, sent an emissary to Jonesboro in March 1785 to test the water. The emissary, Major Samuel Henderson, was handed a letter from the Franklin Assembly, listing its grievances.

"The western country," the letter said, "found themselves taxed to support government, while they were deprived of all the blessings of it." Because North Carolina had stopped paying annuities, there were "frequent murders on our frontiers." As a result, "we have declared ourselves a free and independent state."

In response, Governor Martin issued a manifesto in April 1785, threatening force if the Franklinites did not return to the fold. "I know with reluctance," he said, "that the state will be driven to arms." Had it come to that, and had the antiwestern Alexander Martin remained in office, there might have been a civil war in the United States before there was a constitution. But Martin was succeeded by Richard Caswell, who, being a friend of Sevier's, was more tolerant of the Franklinites. Once more, an emissary was sent to Franklin. He reported, "They seem to have a tendency to dissolve even the federal bands."

Franklin was ambivalent about its identity, not quite sure whether it wanted to be the fourteenth state or a free and independent nation. At first, the Franklinites wanted to join the Union; in May 1785, they sent one of their leaders, William Cocke, to New York to present the Continental Congress with a petition for admittance into the sisterhood of states.

According to the Articles of Confederation, "No other colony shall be admitted into the same unless such admission be agreed to by nine states." A committee was appointed to study Franklin's bid, but when the vote came, on June 1, Cocke could muster only seven states. Congress did not wish to offend North Carolina, just as it was beginning to comply with federal measures, and with the matter of cession still unresolved.

Seeing their chance to join the Union blasted, the Franklinites had a fit of freedom fever. Sevier began dating his letters "in the first year of our independence." The Franklinites decided to build a mint and coin thirty thousand dollars' worth of their own money, although whether they ever did so is open to question, since not a single Franklin coin has survived.

Currency was so rare that taxes and state salaries were paid in goods, according to a table of evaluation. Rye whiskey, for instance, was evaluated at two shillings and sixpence per gallon. The Franklinites did not like paying taxes any better than before, and devised a barter-based method of tax evasion. Since they could pay their taxes in furs, and since raccoon pelts were worth much more than opossum, they cut the tails off the raccoons and sewed them onto worthless opossum. This debased peltry was baled up with the coon tails hanging out for the gullible treasurer to count. The tailless coonskins were sold to hatters.

The ingenious Franklinites experimented in a number of ways. One was the formation of an integrated white-Indian state. This may have been no more than a trick to facilitate the acquisition of Indian lands, but there were rumors that they wanted to give the Cherokees a representative in their bicameral legislature. A letter from a Franklinite was published in the *Maryland Gazette* on October 11, 1785: "A negotiation is on foot with the Cherokees, and the aim is to incorporate them and make them useful citizens. I dare say that the project will startle your rigid sectaries. . . ." Regrettably, nothing ever came of this intriguing scheme, which might have provided a national model for authentic Indian assimilation with political representation. America had to wait until 1992 for the first Indian to be elected to the United States Senate.

In the spring of 1786, the Cherokees attacked settlers on the Holston. Sevier raised a company of mounted riflemen and went off in hot pursuit. In the summer, he concluded a treaty with them in which it was peremptorily stated, "We have the rights to all the ground we have marched over."

The state of Franklin was not prospering, and no coinage had yet been minted. In October, the rate of payment for state officials was set at one thousand deerskins per annum for the governor, down to one muskrat skin per warrant served by the justice of the peace. One sign that Franklin was in difficulty came in this letter from Sevier to Governor Caswell, on October 28, 1786: "Please let us finish what we have begun," it read. "We are getting into confusion and you know any government is better than anarchy."

In 1787, the state of Franklin continued to limp along, but events in the East that year permanently shut the door to statehood. First, the passage of the Northwest Ordinance in July spelled out the procedure for becoming a state, which Franklin had not followed. Help might come from the Constitutional Convention, but there was no one in Philadelphia to plead Franklin's case. When the delegates discussed new states carved from old states, admission was made to depend on a vote of the original state's legislature. Franklin's goose was cooked.

During the following year, 1788, the state of Franklin unraveled. In March, John Sevier's term as governor expired, and no one was elected to replace him. At the same time, North Carolina planted a provocateur in Franklin: John Tipton, an enemy of Sevier's, agitated for the return of the breakaway state. Franklin politics slid into a Sevier-Tipton feud, with armed raids, two sets of courts, and other forms of factionalism. The state veered toward total collapse.

In North Carolina, Samuel Johnston, more of a law-and-order man, had replaced Richard Caswell as governor. When Johnston learned that Sevier had recruited a private army of a hundred mounted riflemen to go after the Cherokees, he wrote Indian Superintendent Richard Winn: "Sevier . . . appears to be incorrigible, and I fear we shall have no peace in your quarter till he is proceeded against to the last extremity. . . . They can be considered in no other light but that of freebooters and robbers."

Desperately looking for some way to keep Franklin afloat, Sevier played his last trump—the Spanish card. There were as yet no strong feelings of nationalism on the American borderlands. Just as Ethan Allen was ready to hitch Vermont to Canada, Sevier explored the possibility of an alliance with Spain.

In May 1788, Don Diego de Gardoqui, the Spanish ambassador to the United States, approached Sevier through one of his agents, James White, a superintendent of Indian affairs in the Cumberland region. White gave Sevier a letter from Gardoqui assuring him, "If they wished to put themselves under the protection of Spain and favor her interest, they should be protected in their civil and political government," on condition that they took the oath of allegiance to Spain and renounced loyalty to any other power.

Gardoqui was using the office of ambassador to exploit sectional quarrels such as the one between Franklin and North Carolina. He hoped to achieve the secession of the West from the United States. The idea was that these outlying territories, ignored by their own government, could get a better deal with Spain, one of the enticements being freedom of navigation on the Mississippi.

Having nowhere else to turn, rejected by both North Carolina and the Constitutional Convention, Sevier replied with a letter asking for Spanish help in restraining the Indians. Although this did not get him in too deep, it kept the correspondence going.

In July 1788, however, Governor Johnston ordered Sevier's arrest on a charge of high treason for levying troops to oppose the laws of the state. He was arrested on July 20 in Jonesboro, where he had so many supporters that he was quickly moved to Morgantown, North Carolina, near the Tennessee border. There he was rescued by friends, and he never came to trial. One deposition taken in a Jonesboro tavern shortly after Sevier's arrest stated: "A certain stripling said that everyone that was at the taking of Severe [sic] was Damnd Raskels and Scoundrels and was not worthy of cleaning his Shoes and Buckels."

Now, under the threat of imprisonment, Sevier turned once again to the Spanish. Writing Gardoqui on September 12, he asked "for a few thousand pounds," and held out "the future possibility of an alliance and concession of commerce." Was this treason? Like Ethan Allen, he felt that he was representing an independent state. But in both cases it was a desperate gambit.

Events soon overtook the Sevier-Gardoqui negotiations. In February 1789, North Carolina offered all Franklinites an amnesty and a pardon, which they accepted. Sevier took the oath of allegiance to North Carolina, and Franklin once again became three transmontane counties of that state.

By this time, the United States Constitution had been ratified, a federal government was in place, and George Washington had been elected president. North Carolina still held out, but there was a swing of sentiment away from local interests and toward federalism; further separation from the sister states seemed unwise. On November 21, 1789, North Carolina ratified the Constitution, the next-to-last state to do so (Rhode Island was the last, in May 1790), and agreed to cession, this time for good.

In spite of his secessionist activities, Sevier had maintained close ties with North Carolina, and was still enormously popular in the western counties. North Carolina recognized his political usefulness, and at the November 1789 Constitutional Convention, Sevier was a delegate from Greene County. He was then elected to the North Carolina Senate, and became a leader in the government he had tried to secede from. Who said there are no second acts in American lives?

The question now was what to do with the western lands North Carolina had ceded to the federal government. It was decided to extend to them the provisions of the Northwest Ordinance. In May 1790, the land that would become Tennessee was designated "Territory of the United States south of the river Ohio."

William Blount, a cultivated North Carolinian who had been a member of the Continental Congress and the Constitutional Convention, was named governor, and proceeded to put the area through the paces of territorial government, appointing many of the Franklin leaders to office, laying off counties, setting up courts, and starting the machinery of government turning.

Indian affairs were a large part of his duties, and in July 1791 he negotiated the Treaty of Holston with forty-one chiefs. At the site of the treaty, he founded the town of Knoxville, in honor of Secretary of War Henry Knox. Blount built a house there, within earshot of Indian villages. The whoops of their dances competed with the minuets and quadrilles in the governor's house.

In September 1791, the census showed 6,271 free white males over the age of twenty-one, more than the five thousand required to advance to the next stage of territorial government. A General Assembly was elected, and a legislative council of five was appointed. Sevier was named to the council in 1794.

Friction between Indians and whites continued to be Blount's biggest headache, and, to keep the settlers happy, he periodically unleashed Sevier and his eight hundred gunslingers. He wrote Knox on January 14, 1793, "General Sevier's name carried more terror to the Cherokees than an additional regiment could have done." In January 1794, Blount estimated that the Creeks and Cherokees had killed and taken prisoner more than two hundred settlers and stolen at least a thousand horses.

Yet, in spite of the Indian situation, settlers were pouring into the territory. The population grew so rapidly that in November 1795 Blount announced that they had reached the magic number of sixty thousand, allowing Tennessee to apply for statehood. Each county elected five delegates to a constitutional convention that met in Knoxville in January 1796.

The document was drafted and Tennessee asked for admission in June, having taken a mere five years to graduate from territory to state. It became the sixteenth state, and the first to be admitted to the Union under the Northwest Ordinance, even though Tennessee was not exactly the Northwest.

The first governor of Tennessee was John Sevier, for whom the state of Franklin had been a dress rehearsal. Sevier served five two-year terms, from 1797 to 1801, and from 1803 to 1809. He was then elected to the Tennessee State Senate, and in 1811 to the U.S. House of Representatives, where he served until his death in 1815, at the age of seventy. His monument in Knoxville carries the legend: "Thirty-five battles, thirty-five victories."

CHAPTER TWENTY-THREE

THE
LAND OPERATION

The federal surveying of public lands for private purchase began in 1785, under the Continental Congress, and continued until 1946, when Harry S Truman was president. The surveyor is a crucial but neglected figure in the American epic.

Marietta College, Marietta, Ohio

General Rufus Putnam, founder of the Ohio Company and surveyor general of the United States.

461

The land operation would have been an immense one even with all the administrative resources of a later age. That it was accomplished literally by hand, with compass and chain, quill pen and ink, illuminated by candlelight in rough prairie offices, was in itself a herculean performance.

LEONARD WHITE

W hen the Continental Congress expired and the presidential system was enacted, in 1789, the responsibility for the management and sale of the public domain was left to the secretary of the treasury, Alexander Hamilton. Under Hamilton, the surveying of the Ohio ranges continued in spite of Indian wars and squatters.

It is with the surveyor's compass and chain that the western movement begins, told in plats and field notes. Before the soldier, before the settler, before the missionary, came the meticulous and peaceable surveyor, a neglected figure in the saga of the West.

Surveyors never became the stuff of legend, because their work was not dramatic. They did not get into gunfights, since they didn't carry guns. They were too busy making diagrams with their quill pens to tell tall tales. They did not stir the popular imagination or become the subjects of novels and movies.

A surveyor strode into the wilderness carrying a clock-sized compass with folding sights that were raised when it was mounted on a tripod or a Jacob's staff. The distances along the sight lines were measured with fifty- or hundred-link chains of brass or iron with triangular handles (one hundred-link chain measured sixty-six feet, and eighty chains made a mile). The surveyors carried paper and ink for their notes, which they transcribed to a clean copy by candlelight when the day's work was done.

The two-pole, fifty-link chain was for hilly country, and the four-pole chain was for flatlands. To measure the ground, the forward chainman carried eleven tally pins, each with a red cloth tied to a ring at the top. After stretching the chain, he struck a pin in the ground. At the eleventh pin, he cried "Tally!" The rear chainman then collected the pins and brought them up to the front and became the forward chainman for the next series of twelve stretches. Eight tallies with the thirty-three-foot chain made half a mile.

Nature was at best an obstacle to the surveyor, at worst a

deadly antagonist, and he seldom stopped to admire a sunset or a waterfall. He worked in all kinds of weather, and there weren't any inns along the way. The list of his hardships was all-inclusive, from drowning to freezing to scalping.

But, though it was extremely dangerous, the work had a plodding quality of boring sameness. There is no famous surveyor, as there are famous mountain men and cowboys. And yet it was the surveyor, with his link chains and Jacob's staff, who located, marked, and mapped most of the privately owned land in America.

In 1796, a new land law was passed, which provided for easier terms and a small down payment: 5 percent on signing, another 45 percent within thirty days, and the balance in a year. At the same time, the minimum price was doubled to two dollars an acre. A 640-acre section now cost $1,280, but the down payment was only sixty-four dollars. The 1796 law also called for land offices in Pittsburgh and Cincinnati and created the office of surveyor general.

The surveyor general's was such an important job, President Washington believed, that he spent three months searching for the right man. One candidate was "of too short standing in the community." Another was rejected because "I know too little of his real character." Finally, Rufus Putnam, who had twenty years of surveying experience, took the post.

After receiving his commission in October 1796, Putnam wondered where to begin. He asked for guidance concerning what to pay his crews, and whether to run boundary lines between federal and Indian lands. Oliver Wolcott, Hamilton's successor at the treasury, wrote him on March 14, 1797, that Congress had appropriated twenty-five thousand dollars to fund the surveys. Deputies would be paid no more than three dollars a mile. Putnam should get going at once, Wolcott urged, so that there might be "speedy sales on account of the United States."

From 1797 to 1803, Putnam surveyed the remaining lands in Ohio, turning them into tidy ranges ready for sale. Of course there were inaccuracies—if you bought 640 acres, you might end up with six hundred—but the allotment of public lands was under way. There were also problems with the military escort, since the soldiers refused to double as axmen to clear the way and mark corners.

The year 1800, while John Adams was president, saw an enormous change in the West. William Henry Harrison was elected to Congress as the first delegate from the Northwest Territory. Even though he couldn't vote, Harrison lobbied to have the huge territory divided into parts. He wanted a more liberal land law, with smaller units, easier credit, and land offices closer to where the land was sold. People didn't want to travel for days to Cincinnati or Pittsburgh to buy their sections.

In a single week, Harrison managed to accomplish his goals. On May 7, 1800, the Northwest was divided into Ohio and Indiana territories, with Chillicothe and Vincennes as the respective capitals. The new and improved land-sale law of May 10 called for selling 320-acre half-sections for $640, and initiated a four-year credit plan. In addition, there would be land-sale offices in four Ohio towns, Marietta, Steubenville, Chillicothe, and Cincinnati.

Succeeding Adams, Thomas Jefferson was inaugurated in March 1801 and moved the Cabinet to the new capital of Washington, with its still-unpaved streets. Albert Gallatin, a shrewd Swiss immigrant from Geneva, became his secretary of the treasury. He wanted to cut the minimum lots even further, to a quarter-section, or 160 acres. But every time Congress eased the land laws to help the settlers, they bought more land with easier credit and went into debt. Then they pressured Congress to cancel their debts.

Installment buying meant that speculators could come in and buy a lot of land for quick resale. The opportunities for fraud were tempting, and every regulation seemed to come with a loophole.

Take the case of Thomas Worthington, a deputy surveyor who was promoted to register of the land-sale office at Chillicothe in 1800. Every land office had a register to identify each tract as it came up for auction, and a receiver to handle the payment. The register kept two books, a tract book showing the land up for sale and recording the parcels sold. The second book was the plat book, with plats (or maps) of the land in each township. These land auctions were considerable social events in frontier areas where there was little recreation. People began to show up two weeks before the sale, as if for a fair. On the day of the sale, Worthington, flanked by his clerks, would come out of his office with a crier and move through the crowd to a raised platform. The crier would step forward and announce the location and number of the first tract, and bids were made in low voices.

This was high drama, ranking with birth, marriage, and death as one of the benchmark events in a man's life. In a few seconds, he could become a landowner, his life transformed. Land sales became something of a national ritual, an American ceremony of social advancement. The successful bidder went to the register and got a notation of his tract. Then he went to the receiver, handed over his down payment, and got his receipt in duplicate. He returned one copy to the register, who noted the location of the tract on his list and marked his diagram "AP" at the appropriate spot— Applied For. More than a commercial transaction, this was the culmination of a social policy promoting a nation of landowners. As Blackstone put it, "A set of words upon a parchment convey dominion over land."

In the summer of 1802, the settler Elias Langham went to the Chillicothe land sale with his eye on a thousand acres of high-bank prairie on Paint Creek, a few miles outside town. He arrived late because of rain, and the first thing he saw upon entering the crowded auction room was a roll of paper with a label that said: "Any person examining this map must pay 25 cents." Langham was shocked to find that Worthington was charging potential buyers a fee to look at the map of the parcels for sale, which should have been hung on the wall for everyone to see.

Langham told Worthington that he was interested in some Paint Creek acreage and wondered how high the bids would go. Worthington said there were bidders ready to go as high as sixteen dollars an acre. It was outstanding land, he said—low, rich, and level, already fenced and under cultivation.

Langham said he was willing to go as high as eight dollars. "You'll never get it for that," Worthington responded. "We'll see," Langham said. He asked Worthington to let him know when the tract came up, since he hadn't seen the map and didn't know the number.

When it was called, no one said a word, and there was only one bid, for $2.50 an acre. A murmur went around the room: "The high banks are gone off at two and a half dollars." Furious, Langham demanded of Worthington: "How did this happen? Why weren't the people informed the high banks were offered? Don't you remember I told you I'd go to eight?"

Looking perplexed, Worthington said he'd mentioned it to the crier. The next day, Langham learned that Worthington had received sixteen hundred dollars from the lucky buyer of the high banks. He made a formal complaint: "How could I suspect that the register would enter into a combination to prevent competition and keep down the sale of public lands?"

Worthington was suspected of being a secret partner in a number of highly lucrative deals. After a formal inquiry, however, he was cleared. His mentor was Albert Gallatin, himself a speculator in Ohio lands. Worthington sometimes acted as his land agent, recommending choice parcels. The concept of conflict of interest was not yet clearly defined. Worthington went on to become governor of Ohio and a United States senator.

Land registers were often willing to do a little business on the side. Although not allowed to buy land themselves, they had no trouble finding proxies. Thomas Flood, the register at Zanesville, Ohio, was known to use third parties to increase his holdings. Another method was to take a cash fee to reserve a half-section for a buyer. Registers also became loan sharks, advancing money to buyers at 20-percent interest. There were so many forms of chicanery that J. W. Brown, the register in Ionia, Michigan, in 1836, would write: "My present assistants are new in the business, and we may make mistakes, but they have not been long enough in a land office to become dishonest."

In 1803, President Jefferson replaced Surveyor General Rufus Putnam with Jared Mansfield, a Yale graduate, mathematician, and a captain in the army engineers. The disappointed Putnam suspected that his office had fallen to political patronage: he had been fired because he was not a Jeffersonian. "I am happy in having my name enrolled with many others who have suffered a like political death," he wrote in his memoirs.

Gallatin told Jared Mansfield on September 19, 1803: "As almost the whole of the public lands have already been surveyed, it is presumed that one clerk will be sufficient for your office." In other words, they had surveyed most of Ohio, and to the west was Indian land. Presumably, there wouldn't be much for Mansfield to do. When he moved to Marietta in November, he looked forward to having plenty of time for making astronomical observations.

Mansfield did not know that William Henry Harrison, now governor of Indiana Territory, was busily acquiring Indian lands, in accordance with administration policy. Jefferson instructed Harrison that, once the Indians were taught to farm, "they will perceive how useless to them are their extensive forests, and will be willing to pare them off from time to time in exchange for necessaries for their farms and families. To promote this disposition to exchange lands, which they have to spare and we want, we shall push our trading houses, *and be glad to see the good and influential individuals among them run into debt* [emphasis added], because we observe that when these debts get beyond what the individuals can pay, they become willing to lop them off by a cession of lands. . . ." This enticement of the Indians into debt in order to foreclose on their lands turned out to be an enormously successful tactic.

In 1802, Harrison bought 1.8 million acres from the tribes around Vincennes, in western Indiana, on the Wabash River. Then, in August 1803, he bought a big slice of the state of Illinois from the Kaskaskia tribe. He kept making purchases, until by 1810 another 110 million acres had been bought from the Indians in the Old Northwest Territory, providing steady employment for surveyors.

Gallatin created the office of the district surveyors, who were permanently assigned to one area. This gave the surveyor general a certain amount of patronage, since he appointed the district men. Applications and recommendations flowed into Jared Mansfield's office, such as the one for a gentleman who was "master of the art, of irreproachable character, and a good republican."

In 1804, a new land law further reduced the minimum parcel for sale to a quarter-section, or 160 acres. Mansfield, who had been busy with twelve deputies subdividing Ohio townships into half-sections, to comply with the land law of 1800, now had to go west to Indiana to survey the nearly two million acres of the Vincennes tract.

He hired surveyors at $2.50 a mile to place additional markers to indicate the quarter-section lines. One of these raw recruits, found through a Yale connection, was Zilba Foote, a twenty-year-old Connecticut-born graduate, who was sent out on the Wabash in March 1806. On May 16, he came to a pond thirty chains wide (a chain was sixty-six feet). He thought he could wade across, even though Mansfield had warned him to work around the ponds by offset. After fastening his compass and Jacob's staff to his belt, he plunged in, but the pond was deeper than expected, and he was soon over his head. He could not swim, and called out to his chain men. By the time they swam out to save him, he had sunk like a stone. By the time they pulled him out he was dead. They put him in a bark coffin and dug his grave on the bank. The chain men reported that the young man had been teased by friends, who said he would not be able to stand the rough outdoor life, and that he was determined to show he had what it took.

Mansfield himself went to Vincennes to supervise the work,

and found "insuperable" difficulties, owing to "swamps, ponds, briars, cane brakes and different kinds of bushes." Much of Indiana and Illinois were prairie, which the Connecticut mathematics professor thought of as a weird and unnatural landscape. Who would want these treeless lands? he wondered; "it would be impossible for cultivators to subsist without wood or water." And what was the point of surveying land that no one would want?

Despite his misgivings, Mansfield stuck to the system of baseline and ranges, and he and his men surveyed most of the southern half of Indiana.

In the meantime, Thomas Worthington, now a senator from Ohio, cast greedy eyes on the southern tip of Illinois, then known as the Kaskaskia district. In March 1804, he asked Mansfield for the contract to survey four million acres between the Wabash and the Mississippi. He saw this as such a golden opportunity that he was willing to resign his Senate seat. But Mansfield wasn't ready for Kaskaskia; he was looking for someone to survey the southernmost strip of Indiana.

The man he chose for the task was William Rector, one of the more intriguing figures in the annals of surveying. Rector applied for the contract "not with a view of making much money (as the nature of the business will not admit of fast running), but in order to gratify a desire I have of seeing the country." This laudable ambition aside, he neglected to mention that he had six brothers— Nelson, Elias, Thomas, Stephen, Wharton, and John—all seeking employment.

William Rector got going in July 1805, hiring his crew (including three of his brothers, Elias, Nelson, and John), and shipping provisions to the mouth of the Wabash. He asked Governor Harrison for a pass requesting the Indians to treat him well. In the tall Indiana prairie, he had his four pack horses lead the chain men in order to stamp down the grass. But he was nonplused when it came to marking corners. It was hard work in the rain and heat, he reported to Mansfield, and two of his men were sick. Strong men were needed, men used to the woods.

By January 1807, Rector was in the southernmost corner of Illinois. He wrote Mansfield of snow and rain and said he was suffering from exposure. In addition, he had lost some of his horses. "In truth," he wrote, "my tour so far has been almost a continual scene of disappointments and difficulties." Mansfield was disappointed too, because Rector was doing everything wrong. He was behind schedule and running lines contrary to instructions; he had hired three of his brothers without authorization. Mansfield wanted to fire him, but experienced surveyors were hard to find, so he kept Rector on, even though he did nothing but complain—about low wages, rugged terrain, and sick crews.

By the fall of 1807, the territory covered by the surveyors stretched from the western border of Pennsylvania to the Mississippi River, on the western border of Illinois. Three future states —Ohio, Indiana, and Illinois—had been surveyed, and settlers were flocking to the land sales. In the East, fall surveying had been the rule. Trees were bare, streams were low or frozen, and insects were scarce. In the treeless prairies, however, spring surveying was not only possible but relatively pleasant. Still, there was one recurring problem: the Indians were destroying the corner posts.

In 1810, a fresh impediment arose, with the crusade of Tecumseh and his brother the Prophet. Tecumseh tried to organize a tribal confederacy, advancing the position that land was the common property of all the tribes. "Sell our land," he asked, "why not sell the air, the clouds, and the great sea?"

On August 22, 1810, William Henry Harrison wrote Mansfield: "The Prophet's brother has sworn his determination not to suffer the new Purchase to be surveyed." This was the 1809 purchase of three million acres in Indiana and Illinois. When Tecumseh declared the sale invalid, raids began on outlying settlements. This of course led to Harrison's first-strike strategy in the Tippecanoe campaign of 1811, and a year later the Indian war merged into the War of 1812. It was not an auspicious time for surveying. Jared Mansfield, who had been offered a teaching job at West Point, took it.

In 1812, under the presidency of James Madison, the surveying and sale of public lands was transferred to the newly created General Land Office, which was run by a commission of public lands. It was up to the first commissioner, Edward Tiffin, who had been governor of Ohio and a United States senator, to appoint a new surveyor general. He chose the frontier schoolmaster Josiah Meigs, who had taught "under the forest oak" at the so-called University of Georgia at Athens. He was the "acting president" of that institution, which had no classrooms. Indeed, he was its entire faculty. When he was turned down for a salary raise, he called the board of trustees "a damned pack of Tories and speculators." Dismissed from the university in 1811, he was appointed surveyor general in August 1812.

Meigs was sent to Cincinnati, but the war was on, barring any serious surveying efforts. As Jared Mansfield pointed out to his successor in June 1813, "The distracted state of the country has suspended the surveys generally, whether in hand or in contemplation." In addition, some of the surveyors had gone soldiering. William Rector became a brigadier general in the Illinois militia, while his brother Elias was made adjutant general for Illinois Territory, and was wounded in battle.

When the British burned Washington in 1814, Edward Tiffin's records were moved to a safe place, but the activities of the General Land Office came to a standstill. "I can do nothing," he wrote Meigs on August 31, "while the enemy is still in sight." Tiffin then decided he wanted to go home to Ohio, and prevailed upon President Madison to let him change places with Meigs: he went to Cincinnati in 1815 and became surveyor general, while Meigs took over as commissioner of public lands in Washington.

In Cincinnati, Tiffin had before him a big and urgent job. He was to survey the six million acres that Congress had set aside for War of 1812 veterans in western Illinois, Michigan, and Missouri (which was part of the Louisiana Purchase). Congress had promised the soldiers good land, and it was up to the surveyors to find it.

Even though the war was over, Indians were still attacking isolated groups. Still, despite the danger, Tiffin wrote Meigs in March 1815, "I am much pestered with applications for surveying the military bounty lands." One of the lucky applicants, William Harris of Vincennes, wrote Tiffin to ask how, if he met "traveling bands of savages," he would know whether they were friendly or hostile. Tiffin might have replied that he was sure to know if they shot him full of arrows, but conceded that there was a genuine problem, for the surveyors "would not know whether to defend themselves, or run, or stand still, until the Indians first made the attack."

In Michigan, an area of strong British influence over the Indians, the threat was so great that the commander of American forces at Detroit refused to detail thirty men to guard the surveyors. Finally, some intrepid surveyors started out, but found the land so marshy that they could not advance until it had frozen over solid in order to support men and horses. One of them, Joseph Wampler, uttered a cry from the heart in a letter to Tiffin dated "Michigan wilds, Nov. 22, 1817: I have come to this miserable country to finish my surveys. . . . I have been unfortunate through sickness . . . but I will go wherever you please to send me. . . ."

A year and a half later, on June 3, 1819, Wampler reported Indian trouble: "A week ago the Indians began to plunder my camp . . . taking our provisions by force. . . . When we resisted, they chewed their bullets, loaded their rifles, and took aim as though they would fire on us; this so terrified my men that I could not prevail on them to stay."

In November 1820, there was another episode of Wampler's woes from "the Saganaw Wilderness": "I now take up my pen to relate a lamentable tale. . . . My best horse died. I got another and in ten days he also died, so that I lost about 110 dollars in horses. . . . I have just been detained by the Saganaw Indians, who will not suffer me to survey. . . . Though I have written a lamentable tale, I do not wish it to be considered a complaint or murmur. . . ."

Wampler was still in the "Michigan Wilderness" in February 1823, and wrote Tiffin that he had abandoned his lines because the snow was waist-deep. Over two years later, in November 1825, he reported another mishap: "Being scarce of paper (for I had the misfortune to get my ink bottle broken, and the ink spilled so over my paper that nearly all was spoiled), I crowded the meander of the lakes into the middle of the book."

But Tiffin kept Wampler on the payroll, for he knew that surveying in Michigan was difficult. Tiffin had seven deputies, one of whom, William Brookfield, was laid low with a fit of "Bilious Remittent Fever," and wrote Tiffin on February 8, 1827, "Patience is the lard of the lean meat of adversity."

His principal deputy, based in Detroit, was John Mullett, who was accurate but slow. While surveying near today's Kalamazoo in March 1825, Mullett came upon a village where the Indians were making maple sugar. They followed him, pulled up his posts, and took his compass. "The land is ours," they said, "you have no right to hack the trees, your chiefs are bad men." They told him that if he went any farther they would kill him.

On March 14, Mullett was out in the field, running a range line north from the St. Joseph River with his chain men and axmen, when two armed Indians came to his camp and told the guards there, Taylor and Baldwin, to vamoose. But first they wanted food and tobacco. After they'd smoked their pipes, they seemed to be in a better mood, and walked into the tents to examine the stores, noting the loaded rifles. They hung about in seeming doubt as to whether they should be friends or enemies. Then one of them drew his hatchet and demanded provisions.

Taylor said that if he parted with provisions the men would be hungry and offended when they returned. At this the other Indian went up to Taylor with a cocked rifle and told him to be quick about it. But Baldwin sneaked behind the armed Indian and knocked his rifle aside. As they scuffled over the rifle, it broke in two, and Baldwin was left holding the naked barrel, with which he brained his assailant. He then went to rescue Taylor, who was on the ground, wrestling with the Indian with the hatchet. One blow of the barrel, Mullett reported to Tiffin, saved Taylor "from his disagreeable situation." Taylor and Baldwin tied the Indians up, and waited for the others to return. Mullett decided to let them go, since they were seventy miles from the nearest white settlement and not equipped to take prisoners. After this, the surveyors went back to Detroit.

Such was surveying in Michigan. If the climate didn't get you, the Indians did. Another deputy, Calvin Brittain, wrote in July 1831 to the new surveyor general, Micajah Williams, that there were three main evils. First, "local attraction, which follows us through the district." ("Local attraction" was the surveyors' euphemism for Indians, as in "This is the most difficult country I have ever heard of, in consequence of the strength of local attraction.") "The second," Brittain went on, "more to be dreaded by surveyors than all others, is electricity caused by the friction of clothes upon the compass glass in dry weather." This sent the compass needle wandering and led to serious mistakes. Three, "an obvious difference in the length of my chain and that with which the exterior lines of the townships were measured." His chain, Brittain pointed out, had been made in Chillicothe and had never had a crooked link.

The most common complaint was that the work was destroying their health. From Illinois Territory in November 1832, Lucius Lyons reported that the snow was nine inches deep and they couldn't run lines. "I don't mean to write another lachrymose letter on the difficulties of surveying," he said, "for you will think by and by that we are spoiled children, badly brought up, to be always whining." And yet . . . the weather was uncommonly cold, three of his men had frostbite, one of whom would probably lose part of his foot, and there were mysterious variations in the compass, perhaps because of the proximity of the lead mines; everything had to be done twice.

It was becoming impossible to fine assistants, Lyons added. "Men cannot be hired at any price short of the pay of a member of Congress," he said, for "there is now a great rush to get over the river to Dubuque's mines, where every man expects to make his fortune."

Writing from Milwaukee in 1835, Hiram Burnham reported a considerable rush of squatters, who arrived hard behind the surveyor. It took the squatter about five minutes to become a real-estate agent. "They were making their pitches in many places," he said. "The general mode was to lay up a square pen of poles about four feet high, throw together a few brush, and put their name on a tree or two with red chalk. . . . They do not all stop at one claim—I learn from one that he has made six pitches. . . . Will hold on to one and sell out the others to other emigrants—his usual price $250 a claim."

As the nation's first emissaries to the wilderness, the surveyors were able to gather much firsthand information—which was buried in the files of the General Land Office.

We last saw William Rector in southern Illinois in 1807. Having served briefly in the War of 1812, Rector left Illinois in 1813 to become the principal deputy surveyor for Missouri Territory, based in St. Louis. He continued to find work for his brothers. One of them, Nelson, remained in southern Illinois.

On March 1, 1814, Nelson Rector was returning from a tour of surveying on the north fork of the Saline River when he was shot at by five Indians who lay concealed under a high bank twenty feet away. Three balls struck him, one through the left shoulder near the chest, another in the left arm, fracturing the bone, and the third grazing his temple, taking with it a lock of hair and a small piece of skin, and knocking off his hat.

This was in the middle of the War of 1812, when the British were arming and encouraging the Indians. Another ball struck his horse, which bolted ahead and then sank to its knees. The Indians moved closer, barring the road, and Nelson put spurs to his wounded horse, which rose up and made a desperate attempt to rush through. "In this miserable plight," his brother William reported to Surveyor General Josiah Meigs, Nelson rode on, with his broken arm dangling at his side, while with the other he gripped the saddle, thinking that if it had not been a Spanish saddle he would have fallen off and lost his life. Faint from loss of blood, he took the bridle in his teeth and rode twelve miles to a fort, where he arrived "so much exhausted that he could scarcely stick on his horse."

His surgeons said the outlook was favorable, William Rector reported. It was a narrow escape from the allies of His Britannic Majesty. Other surveyors in the area had deemed it prudent to leave the woods, but Nelson was determined to complete his range, and hoped to finish within the time limit mentioned in the contract.

That August, Nelson was fit enough to raise a company of volunteers to go after Indian marauders. His brother Elias wrote Meigs: "I hope and believe Nelson will have an opportunity of revenging himself on the savages who so unfairly wounded him." In 1815, the war ended, though Indian raids in Illinois Territory continued. Nelson Rector went back on the job in March, with a guard of rangers to protect his men.

But Nelson Rector was not himself, so traumatized by the incident with the Indians that he began to show signs of instability. On June 25, 1815, Nelson wrote a bizarre letter to Surveyor General Edward Tiffin (who had just changed places with Meigs), claiming that he had been slandered by his colleague John Messenger.

"What that insidious puppy has told you relative to the qualifications of my assistants are downright arrant lies," he wrote. If there was anything wrong with his work, "I will forfeit my standing in society as a surveyor and will forfeit my head if necessary."

Quarrels between surveyors over the accuracy of their work were not uncommon, but Nelson Rector's inflamed tone betrayed his distress. "Did I not finish my contract last winter under the most trying circumstances?" he asked. "I surveyed, sir, without a guard under the very muzzles of the most ferocious and inhumane enemies to the human family—I mean savages. I have been shot to pieces (comparatively speaking) by the Indians. . . ."

Perhaps as a result of his quarrel with Messenger, Nelson Rector left Illinois and took a contract on the Arkansas River. Six months later, on January 8, 1816, Josiah Meigs got a letter from a land commissioner in southern Illinois by the name of Thomas Sloo: "We have just received news of the death of Nelson Rector. Report says he went on to Arcansaw to survey and there blew out his brains." There were no further details. It seems that Nelson was driven to despair by the strains and dangers of his profession.

As for brother William, Meigs referred to him as "the most skillful and practical surveyor in the United States." In 1816, he was named to head a new surveying district that covered Illinois, Missouri, and Arkansas. From his headquarters in St. Louis, he continued to parcel out contracts to his friends and relatives. If you wanted a surveying job in Indiana Territory and you didn't know the Rectors, you were out of luck, as Gershon Flagg found out. Flagg was a young man who left Richmond, Vermont, in 1816 with a bad case of Ohio fever. In Vermont, times were hard and bread was scarce, whereas the word was out that in Ohio the corn grew fourteen feet high.

In August 1817, Flagg arrived in Cincinnati, which had a brick courthouse and a branch of the United States Bank. Most of the land on the Wabash was already taken, and Indiana was mostly Indian, so Flagg decided to go to Missouri, where the office of the district surveyor was located. Eighty companies of surveyors, Flagg heard, all contracted by Rector, were out measuring Indian purchases. There must be plenty of jobs, for there were more surveyors in Indiana and Illinois than in all the rest of the United States.

It was seven hundred miles from Cincinnati to St. Louis, down the Ohio on a flatboat. When he got there, Flagg went immediately to see Rector, but soon realized he did not have the right credentials. As he wrote home: "Some who are not surveyors (but favorites) make contracts for surveying and hire it done. I was offered $25 a month to go with another surveyor but did not choose to go under a man who did not know as much as I did myself."

Rector had a nice thing going, letting out contracts to his brothers, who subcontracted the work at a lower price and pocketed the difference. He soon extended his zone of influence to Arkansas, sending down his brother Thomas in April 1819. Thomas wrote Josiah Meigs that there was already a problem with squatters, "for there are many men of rambling dispositions who are able to pay for lands to live on, but will not purchase as long as they are permitted to occupy the best of public lands without paying anything for its use."

Rather quickly, the Arkansas surveyors got themselves into the real-estate business. They knew where the good land was, because they had walked it. They could translate field notes into real bottom lands. Chilo Moultier, an Arkansas settler and early-nineteenth-century whistle-blower, wrote Meigs on April 14, 1819, "It is easy for a crafty surveyor to become a crafty land speculator." The way it worked was this: Arkansas had been part of the Spanish domain. Numerous settlers held fraudulent Spanish land grants. The surveyors conspired with these holders to confirm their grants. A Spanish grant for 250 arpents was miraculously converted into a settlement right for 640 acres. Near Little Rock, there lived a former Spanish commandant who was willing, for a fee, to draw up a predated Spanish grant. Then the claimants found witnesses to perjure themselves for a fee, and surveyors willing to run the lines.

How curious that so many of those who had been given Spanish land grants before 1790 were still around to appear before the court in Little Rock in 1819. They must have received those grants as infants. How odd that these claims, originating in different places, should all have the same spelling mistakes, such as *tiera* for *tierra*. Genuine Spanish claims never contained a single misspelled word.

The name of the original Spanish surveyor, "Laveau Trudeau," was invariably misspelled "Lavieau Trudieau," and you would think he'd know how to spell his own name. Some of the paper used to draw up the claims had evidently been dipped in the Arkansas River to make it look old. Anyone who had ever seen a real Spanish claim would know at once that these were fake. And yet the court in Little Rock confirmed 117 claims, totaling sixty thousand acres.

Some of the claims were staked out on land that had already been earmarked for veterans of the War of 1812, so that the government had to buy it back. The worst offender, Chilo Moultier charged, was Thomas Rector's deputy, William Russell, who spent most of his time surveying phony claims. His conduct was so flagrant that William Rector reprimanded him. Russell complained that he was being singled out "to be tortured, vexed, and perplexed."

Another interesting swindle involved the New Madrid land warrants. New Madrid, on a bend in the Mississippi near the Tennessee-Missouri border, had been settled in 1789 in what was then Spanish Louisiana. Violent earthquakes in 1811 and 1812 pretty much flattened the place. The government issued earthquake victims warrants for land in other areas. Soon the number of these warrants multiplied like the proverbial loaves and fishes, and they were hawked on every street corner.

In 1821, when William Rector proposed to survey 559 townships for a total cost of $120,000, his surveying conglomerate came to the attention of Congress. By this time, Missouri had become a state, and one of its senators was David Barton, who was also chairman of the Senate Land Committee.

On August 21, 1823, Senator Barton wrote President James Monroe to urge that William Rector be indicted for misconduct. Barton described his nepotism and subcontracting methods. He and his brothers had turned surveying into a lucrative racket. There were complaints that the surveying by the subcontractors was botched because they were cutting corners and using unlicensed people.

The Senate then asked to see copies of Rector's contracts. It turned out that, of ninety-eight contracts, seventeen had been given to his brothers, and others to two nephews in Arkansas, Henry and James Conway. Rector left for Washington to defend himself. While he was absent from St. Louis, David Barton's brother Joshua asserted in the *Missouri Republican* that "the surveyor-general indulged in the practice of giving out the largest and best contracts to his family connections and personal friends . . . who sub-let them, and without incurring any particular labor, responsibility or risk, were enabled to pocket considerable emoluments." Since William Rector was not in St. Louis to defend his good name, his brother Thomas challenged Joshua Barton to a duel, which was fought on an island in the Mississippi called Bloody Island because it was a favorite site for duelers. According to a contemporary account, Thomas Rector killed Barton "as cool as if he was shooting deer from a prairie." He was himself killed in a tavern brawl a few years later.

William Rector, rather than deny that he'd employed his brothers, insisted that they were competent and that his surveys were accurate. But there were too many instances in which the work that was supposed to be done by a deputy surveyor had been done by an assistant. Senator Barton said that even if Rector's brothers were first-class surveyors they couldn't sit in St. Louis and run lines three hundred miles away, in Michigan and Arkansas, and then certify the execution of the work upon their official oaths. If that was the case, "the more appropriate certificate would have been that they were men of extraordinary optic powers, and regularly descended from Argus," the many-eyed monster.

President James Monroe removed William Rector from office in late 1824. Edward Tiffin wrote from Chillicothe: "If I have been correctly informed of his general conduct and that of his numerous needy relatives, he has been mercifully borne with too long." Rector was replaced by William McRee, whose mandate it was to clean up surveying practices. McRee wrote a classic description of the loophole mentality on November 29, 1826, in a letter to George Graham, a commissioner of the Land Office: "It would almost appear that apprehensions were entertained lest knavery should become extinct in the community, when the laws offer premiums for its exhibition or practice."

The surveying game having lost its allure, the Rector brothers fanned out in different directions. In 1831, Elias Rector became United States marshal for the territory of Arkansas, and in 1836 his brother Wharton was appointed agent to the Creek Indians.

William Rector was by no means unique. Also caught with his hand in the till was Valentine Y. Conway, surveyor general of Florida. In June 1843, Conway informed the commissioner of the General Land Office that his son, who had worked for him as a clerk, had died.

Conway had three clerks in all, the other two being A. A. Nunes and L. W. Prevost. There were special difficulties with Florida surveys. Most of the marks of the old Spanish surveys had been made by blazing pine trees, which meant cutting into the trees so that the turpentine flowed down into the ground. When the grass was fired up in the fall, the turpentine ignited and trailed up the trunk, destroying the tree and the survey marks. Aside from the pitch-pine trees, cypress swamps, muddy ponds emitting noxious effluvia, and rivers that became torrents when swollen with heavy rains were other obstacles that made surveying in Florida sheer hell.

In any case, Conway's three clerks were getting a thousand dollars a year each. Now that one was dead, he asked for permission to divide their total salaries of three thousand dollars a year between the remaining two, since they were willing to do the additional work. This would save them the trouble of hiring another clerk. Permission was granted.

Conway, however, continued to pay his two clerks a thousand a year, pocketing the extra thousand as a sort of private annuity, which increased his salary from two to three thousand dollars a year. Since he did not kick anything back to his clerks, they complained of extra work.

George M. Bibb, the secretary of the treasury, recommended to President John Tyler that Conway be removed from office, since, in addition to being an embezzler, he passed off "chimney corner" surveys, meaning that his plats and notes were sent in without his ever having covered the ground. In 1844, Conway was charged with malfeasance in office and peculation (embezzlement).

Most surveyors, however, were as straight as their sight lines, and did their patient, methodical work in the service of their country. Few were those whose health did not suffer because of it. Day in, day out, surveying was about the ugliest assignment of western expansion. Surveyors weren't cited for gallantry or awarded medals, but there was a drab heroism to their work.

In the summer of 1877, members of a surveying party on the James River in eastern South Dakota, with their tripods and chains, trespassed onto the summer hunting camp of Drifting Goose's band of Sioux. One day, they found themselves surrounded by seventy-five armed and mounted warriors, who ordered them to leave, firing into their wagon boxes for emphasis. The surveyors started back on the two-hundred-mile journey south to Yankton.

The following year, the surveyor John Marshall contracted to take another party out—six field men and a cook, who turned out to be as cranky as a sitting hen, and drank all the Perry Davis painkiller. For two weeks, they ran lines, measured miles, and built mounds. Then an Indian appeared and said that if they didn't leave they'd be driven out. "We'll keep working," Marshall told his crew.

A few days later, Sutley the flagman was riding three miles from camp when armed Indians jumped out of the tall grass. Sutley's horse bolted, and he was thrown. The Indians sliced his clothes off his body with their hunting knives, boots and all, and then let him go. It was a shot across the bow. The next night, Marshall's horses were stolen.

Marshall asked for a powwow with Drifting Goose, and told the chief that if the hostile acts continued they would leave, but they would come back with soldiers. Things calmed down. After they were finished and had gone, however, the Indians destroyed their work. They took the dirt from the mounds and put it back in the pits, down to the last handful. Many a homesteader who couldn't find his corners must have cursed the surveyors.

·   ·

In the summer of 1905, Charles B. Clark was surveying on the Cheyenne River in South Dakota. The line party was out. The flagman rode ahead on horseback, followed by Clark and the chain men, who measured off the miles. At every chain length, the chain men paused to push an iron pin into the ground and call out, "Stick stuck." The mound man followed with his spade, marking the corners.

They crossed a rolling tableland carpeted with short buffalo grass as smooth as a lawn. The flagman rode from point to point at a gallop. The men wouldn't have admitted it, thought Clark, but they were superstitious. They believed in luck, which came in streaks. If a flagman was kicked by a horse one day, a chain man was sure to be bitten by a rattlesnake the next. If the cook burned a mess of beans, the mess wagon would get mired in mud, which they called "gumbo."

When they reached the end of the tableland, their luck changed. A storm approached, peals of lightning seared the sky around them, and thunder shook the ground. The chain men staggered under a shock that numbed their arms to the elbows. "Drop your tools," Clark called out. "Get away from that horse and lie down. This table is the highest land for ten miles around and all the lightning in the country will strike here."

Five men lay down as the heavy artillery came at them from the heavens. "We'll all be skeletons by the time they find us," the flagman said. Cold rain poured down and beat through their shirts, setting their teeth chattering. But eventually the rain let up. They found a ranch and were received with the hospitality of cow country.

Federal surveying began in 1785 with the Ohio ranges, and in 1905, more than a century later, they were still at it, dividing those millions of acres into sections that people could live on, creating, for the first time in history, a nation of landowners. The work continued until 1946, until there was no more public land to survey, and the General Land Office was closed.

CHAPTER TWENTY-FOUR

THE
YOUNG NATION

Poised for western expansion, the United States at the end of the eighteenth century was shedding the Englishness of its former colonizers and acquiring a distinct and recognizable character.

Caesar, a slave on a Hudson River estate, was born in 1737. When he died in 1852, at the improbable age of 115, he was still a slave.

*Often there were people on the land, who lived in
continual danger, and yet were fond of this savage
freedom.*

WILLIAM STRICKLAND

A prehistoric people of Asian origin found itself stranded on the Bering Land Bridge during an interglacial. Their route back to Asia was cut off by the rising sea. In a migration forced by climatic change, they stumbled onto the North American continent.

These Stone Age hunters moved down the narrow neck of Alaska to the broad expanse of an uninhabited continent. Shaped like an inverted triangle, North America was the third largest of the world's continents, more than nine million square miles. But it was unknown and undiscovered, being washed on both sides by great breadths of ocean. Only one point on its surface was in proximity to an inhabited continent, and that was the Seward Peninsula, forty miles or so distant, over the Bering Strait, from the Chuckchi Peninsula of Siberia.

For thousands of years, these Asian people lived in North America undisturbed, honing their Stone Age skills, hunting and fishing in relatively isolated tribal groups. Theirs was an immeasurable land mass of great natural wealth, with vast forests, ample water resources, a wide range of climates and soils, and seemingly inexhaustible deposits of minerals and fuels. But they never learned to smelt metal or burn coal. They hardly tapped the timber reserves and did not harness the abundant waterpower. They sustained themselves without disturbing nature.

In the fifteenth century came the European navigators, who came upon the unknown continent while looking for a shortcut to China and its spices. They saw this "New World" as a place to settle and colonize. The natives were seen as savages to be converted and forced into peonage, or to be pushed off their lands. The Europeans had a long tradition of smelting and coal mining, of harnessing water and wind, of building mills below waterfalls. Equipped with firearms and religious convictions, they saw no reason why they should not claim this bountiful land.

Three European powers settled in different parts of the continent and pieced together a sense of its geography, a little like the blind men describing an elephant. The Spanish saw that there was a low coastal plain around the Gulf of Mexico and that a mighty river emptied into the gulf. They saw that Florida was not an island and that the Mexican sierras continued north into the Rockies. The French moved into the heart of the continent from Canada by discovering the water route that linked the St. Lawrence to the Great Lakes and the Mississippi. The British groped their way along the Atlantic coastline from Maine to Georgia and advanced westward as far as the barrier of the Appalachian highlands.

Mix well these ingredients: three expansionist European powers, a native people refusing subjugation, and a population of slaves brought against their will from West Africa. The result? A recipe for strife.

In the eighteenth century, the power of France gave way to British North America, and Canada became a part of the British Empire. The Spanish still held large areas, from Florida to California, but had lost their momentum and would eventually depart.

The removal of the French disrupted the community of interests between England and America. After 1760, Americans and Englishmen were no longer of one mind, with one common enemy. Assorted disputes arose, and Americans began to think they would be better off on their own, without the mother country.

These years saw the rise of an American personality. In Crèvecoeur's famous phrase: "Here individuals of all nations are melted into a new race of men." This new race rejected Europe, and turned west instead of east. When they looked west, they saw a seemingly infinite abundance of land, where they could settle and become Americans, liberated from the restraints and conventions of Europe. Here would be none of the privileges and inequalities of the old order, which were all founded on land scarcity. Like corn or wheat, democracy was a crop that sprouted from the ground.

The availability of land inspired the ideology. Only when there was enough land for everyone could the conviction be expressed that all men—with the exception of slaves and Indians—were born free and equal. The idea of America as a promised land was expressed by Thomas Paine with sledgehammer logic couched in the cadences of the King James Bible: "Every spot of the old world is over-run with oppression. Freedom hath been hunted round the Globe! . . . O! Receive the fugitive and prepare an asylum for mankind." And why was America rather than France or

Switzerland the asylum for mankind? Because there was enough
elbow room for mankind.

In 1776, resistance hardened into war. The colonies became
independent states, and the thirteen states formed a union. The
war was fought and won. Republicanism replaced monarchy.
Founded in 1789, the new Union was based on the principle of
divided sovereignty, or federalism.

And how did the young nation fare in its early years, on the
eve of the westward movement? How did it display its "Americanness"? An English traveler who visited a ten-year-old post-Consti-
tution America provided a description in his diary.

On August 19, 1794, a forty-one-year-old Yorkshireman
named William Strickland sailed from Hull Roads aboard the New
York–bound *Fair American*. A gentleman farmer and a baronet,
son of the fifth baronet of Boynton, he was not going to America
as an emigrant but as a tourist with a professional interest in agriculture. Mainly, however, he was motivated by a natural curiosity
to see how the infant nation was faring in the last decade of the
eighteenth century.

For five years now, this amalgam of former British colonies
had been under something called democratic rule, with an elected
president and two houses of elected congressmen. Brought up
under the traditional system of monarchy and peers, Strickland
wondered how this empowerment of the common folk would
work. God knows it had been a miserable failure in France!

How could these so-called United States, he also wondered,
remain united, when they had such varying interests? In the
North, small landholders of a Puritan bent labored. In the South,
large plantations with slave labor prospered. In the West, a squatter rabble was constantly at war with Indians whose lands they
were grabbing. It did not sound like a very successful formula for
nationhood, but it was nonetheless a fascinating experiment.

Suspicious of the ship's cloudy water, the fastidious Strickland
had bought some hampers of Bristol water in Hull. He also carried
letters of introduction to some of the Eastern Seaboard's finest
families.

What were Americans, thought Strickland, but the overflow
from other countries, mixed with Negroes and savages? Well, at
least they knew how to build boats. The *Fair American*, out of New
London, Connecticut, had timbers of white oak grown on the Hud-

son River, with a beam of Connecticut chestnut and planks of yellow pine. The cargo was woolen cloth from West Riding, and anvils and ironware for ballast. Among the passengers were a Quaker family of linen weavers on their way to the New World.

The captain was a bee of the New England hive, always first and last at work, never permitting an hour of idleness. When the crew was not spinning oakum, it was splicing rope, or rigging new sails, or weaving defenders for the shrouds, or making quarterdeck netting. Whatever one might think about these coarse Yankees, they were industrious.

Several hundred miles from shore, they saw their first American bird, a crested nuthatch with a yellow-tipped tail. The sea was alive with rising and plunging porpoises. As the 226-ton ship approached land on September 19, through heavy swells, the captain pointed out the peculiar color of the American sky, which was tinged with a purplish glow.

When they approached the coast of Long Island, Strickland saw the homes of Dutch rustics among green fields and orchards. He felt sure that they did not fully appreciate the lush beauty that surrounded them.

In New York Harbor, they joined a forest of masts, more ships than Strickland had ever seen except on the Thames below London Bridge. The captain delivered his letter bag to the post office and showed his receipt at customs. At this point, he was allowed to clear the cargo and the passengers, whose names would be listed in the next day's newspaper.

Strickland paid a visit to a prominent merchant, William Seton, who told him there were many opportunities for those with a mind turned to business. The circumstances of the country were completely different from any that had ever existed. America was wide open, with no privileged class to keep the little man down. Public lands were being sold by the millions of acres for ridiculously low sums. A man with a little money to invest could make a fortune in land or in any business from lumber to lucerne. The people here were not like those in the old settled countries of Europe; they were optimistic and enterprising and restless.

Strickland took this all with a grain of salt, for he had found everything he had so far seen just like England, except that there were a greater number of blacks, "who may be seen of all shades, until the stain is entirely worn out."

He called next on the British minister, George Hammond,

who told him that American debts to British merchants amounted to four million pounds. Hamilton, Jefferson, and other leading members of the administration were among the chief debtors, said Hammond, and had a personal interest in avoiding settlement.

The federal government was so weak, said Hammond, that it could not enforce its orders, which were disobeyed by the different states. In the five southern states, hardly any laws existed, and the people were lax, profligate, and debauched. South Carolina had fitted out privateers to cruise against the British. Hammond believed that the whole system was far too democratic, which could only lead to anarchy. As a good Tory, he gave Strickland his set propaganda lecture, which the visitor just off the boat absorbed without a murmur.

At dinner with the Setons on September 24, Strickland heard more about the weakness of the government and its inability to control its western part, by which, he gathered, was meant Pennsylvania. Vast fortunes were being made by land speculators, he was told. Immense tracts were bought for a shilling an acre and sold for a tenfold profit.

As an example, William Seton cited an estate in upstate New York belonging to the De Lanceys, and bought for seventeen hundred pounds. The estate had been confiscated, because they were Loyalists, and was now for sale for two hundred thousand pounds. Often there were people on the land, whom the land jobbers called "squatters" and who had to be ousted by force. They lived in a semibarbarous state and were constantly at war with their Indian neighbors. They cultivated their fields with rifles on their backs or fixed to their plows. Although always in danger, they seemed to be fond of their savage freedom.

Strickland persisted in his idea that America was like England, the only difference being the method of numbering the houses. In New York, one side of the street had odd numbers and the other side had even, whereas in London you had to go up one side of the street and down the other to find the number you wanted.

"Surely, this cannot be a new town in a new world," he wrote in his diary, "for I can find nothing different from what I have quitted in Hull, in Liverpool, in Bristol. The children are playing at Knacks and Taws [marbles] or running the hoop. No language is to be heard but English, more uniform because free of any provincial dialect. . . . Except for some street names that are not English, everything is the same. . . . The dress and appearance of people is the same, the houses are in the style we know, and within doors the furniture is English. The mode of living is English, and dishes and liquors are English. So where to find differences?"

Certainly not in New Jersey, which he visited on September 30, in a coach-and-four driven onto a scow, over to Hackensack, then two miles through a swamp to Passaic, only to find that "the people I passed on the road either nodded their heads or pulled off their hats, a proof of their perfect conviction of the inequality of rank which still exists in this republic."

On October 6, Strickland started on a trip up the Hudson, with a servant and two horses. He wondered whether it would be wise to carry pistols, but was told that, whereas pistols were a good idea when traveling south, they were entirely unnecessary when going north. After crossing Kings Bridge, which connected the island of Manhattan to the continent, he lost his way "for want of guide-posts, a convenience unknown in this country."

All along the road, he saw what he called "attempts at cultivation," which he found perfectly appalling. He frowned on "these forlorn cultivators, debarred from society, ragged, ignorant and loutish," who girdled the trees to kill them, turned over loose stones, tore up the ground a little among the stumps, and scattered their seed.

In Poughkeepsie, Strickland learned that the Dutch no longer kept to themselves, but were melting into the pot and getting rid of old prejudices and customs. The Dutch language was no longer taught; at church, the sermon was in Dutch every four or five weeks, for old times' sake.

Continuing up the Hudson, Strickland reached Albany, where a man he had met in New York, a Mr. Henry, had invited him to stay. Looking for directions, Strickland knocked on the door of an inn and asked the Irish innkeeper, a Mr. McQuirk, to hold his horse.

"Damn you for an English aristocrat," exclaimed McQuirk. "I would not hold a horse for the king of England."

Strickland said he had meant no offense, but this only made McQuirk angrier, and he said he was a much better man than Strickland, being a freeman and a republican, whereas Strickland was but an English slave.

Annoyed but also a little intimidated, Strickland said that all he wanted was to find Mr. Henry, and McQuirk finally agreed to help. Mr. Henry later assured the innkeeper that it was not unusual in England for one gentleman to hold the horse of another; it indicated no difference in rank.

"This is the first instance I have met with," Strickland commented in his diary, "of the folly and insolence of the low democrats of this country."

Strickland proceeded north of Albany. In a clearing in the woods he saw a log cabin, and inside the cabin a woman playing the pianoforte. This example of cultural refinement in the middle of the wilderness struck home, and for the first time Strickland thought: "Only in America."

He also came upon some young men "making a pitch," as they called it. "They proceeded in western country," he wrote, "found a place to their mind, and pitched upon it for their future residence, without any permission or inquiry whether anyone owned the land or not. This sort of acquisition the law somehow countenanced, in favor of these people called Squatters . . . who are the overflowing of the New England hive, and thousands emigrate each year, demonstrating that want of attachment for person or place which is so perceptible in the American character."

Once again, Strickland was judging America by English standards, failing to see that it was not want of attachment that beckoned the settlers onward, but available land. Conversely, in England, people stayed put because there was nowhere to go— unless they came to America.

In the pine forests near Albany, Strickland saw several families of freed Negroes, who lived the lives of Indians, cultivating a little maize but subsisting chiefly on the produce of the woods. To Strickland they seemed to have lapsed into a state of barbarism. They spent what they earned in the summer, and in the winter their children were naked and neglected.

Back in Albany on his return trip down the Hudson, Strickland's poor opinion of democracy was confirmed when he visited two of the biggest landowners, Schuyler and Van Rensselaer. These men had political influence to match their wealth, by the simple expedient of controlling the votes of their numerous tenants. "Thus has property an equal influence under every form of government," he concluded.

Strickland arranged to visit the State Supreme Court, where he saw the mix of nations so typical of America, "the clumsy chill Dutchman, the ignorant staring German too recently released from bondage in his own country to understand the freedom of this, the wild Irishman, and the savage backwoodsman." He could not help noticing the general stature of the people, who were most of them a little under six feet, lean and well limbed. Was it the air or the water?

The high point of his tour came when he visited Chancellor Livingston, "one of the first and richest persons of the country," in Clermont, New York. Then forty-eight, Robert R. Livingston was an interesting American type, the farmer-diplomat. He was also the grandson of the Dutch landholder Henry Beekman, Jr. (who previously appeared in Chapter Seven).

Livingston was a working farmer, who applied himself with great diligence to the management of his lands, as he would later, in Paris, apply himself to the negotiations for the Louisiana Purchase, and, even later, to financing the construction of Fulton's steamboat. He encouraged his tenants to use gypsum as manure, showing them some buckwheat he had grown that was five feet high.

His property was vast, more than two hundred thousand acres extending southwest to the Delaware River on the Pennsylvania border, and northeast twelve miles from the Hudson to Massachusetts. Many of his farms were leased to palatine Germans, "the merest drones, who had never stepped out of the paths of their ancestors or given any education to their children," Strickland observed. For every hundred acres they rented, they agreed to work one day a year for Livingston, to grind his meal, and to give him four fowls a year.

These terms struck Strickland as being closer to "the spirit of feudal aristocracy than might be supposed to be harbored in the breast of the staunchest republicans in the United States." Once again, Strickland had missed the point. Livingston was not a medieval baron, but an American entrepreneur, whose family had amassed great tracts of land in the days of the patroons, but whose mind was marinated in the juices of the Enlightenment. He believed in progress, the useful sciences, and just enough democracy to fuel the Protestant work ethic and the profit motive.

One highly un-English aspect of life at Livingston Manor was that the chancellor had to contend with Indian tribes. Some Stockbridge Indians were living on his land in a swamp near Clermont, though for the moment they were off hunting with the Cayugas.

"They are good workers," observed the chancellor. "Why they can do the work of three whites." But they were unreliable, quitting work suddenly and without notice. Civilization had entirely ruined them, the chancellor said. They pined away for want of their accustomed freedom, and used spirituous liquor immoderately.

Strickland did not dwell on the chancellor's remarks, for, on the paltry scale of Europe, with its patchwork, hemmed-in little countries and its frontiers every few hundred miles, this Indian attachment to an unlimited expanse was hard to grasp.

He did, however, experience a small epiphany during breakfast at the chancellor's house. The brick house covered with white stucco was built in the form of an H and situated on a natural terrace above the Hudson, a hundred yards from the edge. In the dining room, which was hung with French wallpaper, Mrs. Livingston, a somewhat formal though friendly woman, presided over breakfast.

"Four negro boys," Strickland wrote, "the eldest about 11 or 12, the youngest about five or six, clean and well-dressed but barefoot, waited on us at the table. After breakfast, Mrs. Livingston, a woman of one of the best families in the state . . . while we were sitting round the table, insensibly and almost imperceptibly washed and wiped the tea-things, which those boys carried away piece by piece."

At this point, all of Strickland's preconceptions about America being just like England flew out the window. In England, there would have been no slaves, and the mistress of a stately home would never have demeaned herself by doing the dishes in front of a guest. America was England turned inside out. Slavery and democracy were a contradiction in terms, but in America they coexisted, as he had just seen.

Chancellor Livingston had house slaves who served at table, but his wife, with egalitarian self-reliance, did the breakfast dishes herself, perhaps not trusting the young slaves to handle her imported china.

Slavery in New York State, of course, was not exactly like slavery in the plantation South. Slaves on the Hudson River estates were house servants rather than field hands. They grew up with their masters' children, who became their playmates, and were given the same religious instruction. As adults, they went to the same church as their masters, a gallery being set aside for them, and they believed in Predestination or Apostolic Succession, according to whether their masters attended the Dutch Church or the Church of England. When the young Negro boys and girls got married, the ceremony was conducted by an ordained clergyman, and the masters never separated husband and wife. Whippings were unheard of, and an adult slave was seldom sold. If he became incorrigible, he was shipped to the West Indies to be sold there.

When Strickland visited New York State, slavery was on its way out. In 1799, the legislature passed a law granting freedom to the children of slaves born after the Fourth of July in that year. Of course, those born before that date were out of luck until further laws were passed. A Negro named Caesar was the last person to die a slave north of the Mason-Dixon Line, in 1852, at the age of 115.

In 1736, in one of those matches based on acreage, Rensselaer Nicoll, who had thirteen hundred acres eight miles below Albany, married Elizabeth Salisbury, who had a few thousand acres on the western bank of the Hudson. Among their wedding gifts were some Negro slaves from the father of the bride. A year later, a boy was born to two of these wedding gifts, and named Caesar. He became a playmate of his master's eldest son, Francis, accompanying him on hunting and fishing trips in the Hudson River Valley.

Rensselaer and Elizabeth Nicoll settled on his estate, called Bethlehem. He had plenty of money and plenty of slaves to look after his needs, but he was beset by an implacable apathy. Nothing interested him. He was not a sportsman, he did not read books, he did not improve his estate, which his son Francis took over, and he had no hobbies. He stagnated, and in his sixties became senile.

Rensselaer Nicoll had built a heavy oak cradle more than six feet long, in which he spent much of the day. It became Caesar's principal duty to rock the cradle. Caesar must have sometimes wished that he could work in the fields rather than sit there day after day, rocking the cradle. Perhaps from time to time he dozed off. On August 5, 1776, old man Nicoll slipped out of the cradle, wandered off, and fell into a creek. It was only a foot and a half deep, but, being too feeble to raise himself, he drowned in those eighteen inches of water. The cradle was put to rest in the garret of the old house.

Caesar became the family coachman, driving the horses for Francis Nicoll and his wife when they made their annual winter trip to New York in the large sleigh, riding down the western side of the Hudson on the turnpike, and stopping for a few days at the homes of relatives and friends. After two weeks in the city, they drove back up the eastern bank, where hospitable mansions afforded a cordial welcome, and on to Albany.

In 1808, all slaves under the age of sixty-five in New York State were freed. Caesar, by then seventy-one, remained a slave. When Francis Nicoll died in 1817, eighty-year-old Caesar was still part of his master's property, which was inherited by a grandson, William Nicoll Sill. Caesar, who had trouble climbing stairs, was given a room on the ground floor of the kitchen extension of the old house, with an outdoor entrance, a stoop, and a large open fireplace. Here he lived for another thirty-five years, playing his fiddle and throwing chips of wood at his great-grandchildren. He had a testy temper and did not like being "bothered with young niggers."

By this time, Caesar was a picturesque fixture in the household, whom all the far-flung members of the Nicoll and Sill families came to meet. But he refused to be introduced to one of the young Nicolls who was crippled, perhaps from superstition, or resenting this example of physical deformity in the master's family. When he died in 1852, he was buried in the family graveyard, and a marble stone was placed at the head of his grave. He had been a slave under six generations of masters, and he lived all his life in the place where he was born.

William Strickland returned to England with several amendments to his original thesis that America was the duplicate of England. America was no one's clone, America was self-invented, *sui generis*, underivative and wholly original. America was a girdled tree and a clearing in the wilderness; it was an Irish innkeeper who mocked class differences and a Hudson River patroon who believed in the rights of man. America was a bundle of contradictions, but it was large enough and untested enough to live at the heart of a contradiction, as the Livingstons did, professing democracy while owning slaves.

Strickland had come to accept the immense diversity of the people, the sectional prejudices, the particular nature of life in a New England village, or on a southern plantation, or on the prairie. But where in all this was the national character?

One unifying link seemed to be a spirit of enterprise. In such a huge country, without title or rank, all hierarchies were based on enterprise, which became an accepted model, a tradition. The spirit of enterprise was usually expressed in the future tense, as in the oft-heard question "Does it pay?"

Americans were hyperactive. A bell sounded, a meal was eaten in minutes, and people scattered back to their various occupations. There was no high tea, and no looking back. The story was told of a traveler who asked whether the toll for a bridge covered the return trip. He was advised, "Everything is go ahead here."

In tandem with that forward motion of enterprise came egalitarianism. There was no primogeniture, so everyone had an equal stake in the country. Anyone could own land for a pittance, and men of all ranks could aspire to leadership, wealth, and political office. This egalitarianism had its offensive side, when it was expressed in defiant, free-of-the past attitudes.

The highest expression of egalitarianism was frontier life, which had a crude energy that Strickland disliked. The story was told of a squatter who brought a birdhouse to a quarter-section and swore to the land register that his house was eighteen by twenty— without specifying whether it was feet or inches.

These unscrupulous frontiersmen were constantly knocking heads with the original occupants, who were robbed of their lands and pushed back, farther and farther west. It seemed to Strickland that the young nation had two festering infirmities—the slaves and the Indians—for which there was no cure.

At the same time, there was in America a ferment and a will to action the likes of which Strickland had never seen. England was fixed in its boundaries and in its ways. England was a portly squire comfortably sipping tea by the fireside, quite satisfied with the status quo. America was a smoking test tube, a braying infant, a blank page; it was change made palpable, change glorified, change as a stated goal, fluid, undetermined, unfixed, defying the logic of the centuries, observing its distant horizon lines, a ship that had strayed from the fleet and was off on its own uncharted course.

Acknowledgments

I would like to thank the following for their help: the New York Historical Society Library, one of the half-dozen finest libraries in the country, with its splendid manuscript collection; its former librarian James Mooney, its present librarian, Janet Ashton, and its unfailingly helpful staff; the archaeologists David Hurst Thomas of the Museum of Natural History, Robert D. Shaw of Anchorage, Alaska, and Jean Aigner of Fairbanks, Alaska; Florida State Museum, Gainesville, Florida; Plymouth Plantation, Plymouth, Massachusetts; Nancy D. Egloff, Staff Historian, Jamestown Settlement, Jamestown, Virginia; Robert Silliman, Windsor Historical Society, Windsor, Connecticut; Historic St. Mary's, Maryland; Irvin G. Allen, Oldtown, Maryland; Pennsbury Manor, Morrisville, Pennsylvania; Fort Ligonier, Ligonier, Pennsylvania; Carl Gravelin, Salzburger Museum, Ebenezer, Georgia; Jamie and Marcia Constance, Chicora Wood Plantation, Georgetown, South Carolina; Anthony Tommell, Fort Stanwix National Monument, Rome, New York; Clement Biddle Wood, John Marquand, Moorehead Kennedy, Gerald T. Dunne, David J. Weber, Sally McMillen, Joseph A. Jiminez, John B. Briley, John Cooper, and Don Cook, for chapter readings.

Having visited all the places described in this book, I would like to thank my traveling companions for their patience: Eileen Bresnahan, Amber Morgan (who learned how to portage a canoe), and Gabriel Morgan.

Finally, for the many hours they spent improving this book, credit for a first-rate job goes to my editors, Alice Mayhew and George Hodgman. Without them, I would still be hacking my way through the wilderness.

Notes

Abbreviated titles of sources frequently cited:

NYHS: New York Historical Society.
TP: The Territorial Papers of the United States, compiled and edited by C. E. Carter (Washington, D.C., 1934), 27 vols.

INTRODUCTION

Frederick Jackson Turner, "Western State-Making in the Revolutionary Era," *American Historical Review*, vol. 1; *The Historical World of Frederick Jackson Turner*, by Wilbur R. Jacobs (London, 1968); *The Frontier in American History*, by Frederick Jackson Turner (Tucson, Ariz., 1986).
Henry Hollingsworth: *Tennessee Historical Quarterly*, vol. 9.

CHAPTER ONE
THE FIRST FIFTEEN THOUSAND YEARS

On St. Lawrence Island: Riley D. Moore, "Social Life of the Eskimo on St. Lawrence Island," *American Anthropology*, vol. 3 (1923).
On the Ice Age: William F. Fitzhugh and Aron Crowell, *Crossroads of Continents* (Washington, D.C., 1988); Alan Lyle Bryan, ed., *New Evidence for the Pleistocene Peopling of Americas* (Orono, Maine, 1986); Charles Matsch, *North America and the Great Ice Age* (New York, 1976); R. F. Flint, *Glacial and Pleistocene Geology* (New York, 1957).
On Beringia: Robert Kirk, ed., *Out of Asia* (Canberra, 1985); F. H. West, *The Archaeology of Beringia* (New York, 1981); William G. Haag, "The Bering Strait Land Bridge," *Scientific American*, Jan. 1962; D. M. Hopkins, ed., *The Bering Land Bridge* (Stanford, Calif., 1967).
On Ice Age mammals: Antony J. Sutcliffe, *On the Track of Ice Age Mammals* (Cambridge, Mass., 1985).
On Early Man: Fitzhugh and Crowell, *Crossroads of Continents;* Kenneth Mac-Gowan, *Early Man in the New World* (New York, 1950); H. M. Wormington, *Ancient Man in North America* (New York, 1957); Cynthia Irwin-Williams, *Early Man in Western North America* (New York, 1968); Jesse D. Jennings, *Prehistory in North America* (New York, 1968); Bryan, ed., *New Evidence.*
On Early Man in Alaska: Robert D. Shaw, Roger K. Harritt, and Don E. Dumond, eds., "The Late Prehistoric Development of Alaska's Native People," *Alaska Anthropological Association Monograph Series*, no. 4, 1988.
On archaeology: David Hurst Thomas, *Archaeology* (Fort Worth, Tex., 1989); Mark P. Leone and Parker B. Potter, Jr., "The Recovery of Meaning," *Smithsonian*, 1988; Franklin Folsom and Mary Elting Folsom, *America's Ancient Treasures* (Albuquerque, N.M., 1983).
On tree-ring dating: B. Bannister and W. J. Robinson, "Tree-Ring Dating in Archaeology," *World Archaeology*, vol. 7 (1972).

On the Folsom point: J. D. Figgins, "The Antiquity of Man in America," *Natural History*, vol. 27, no. 3 (1927).

On carbon-dating: Willard F. Libby, *Radio-Carbon Dating* (Chicago, 1952); L. S. Cressman, "Western Pre-History in the Light of Carbon 14 Dating," *Southwest Journal of Anthropology*, no. 3, 1951.

On the Meadowcroft dig: J. M. Adovasio, "Meadowcroft," *American Antiquity*, vol. 43, 1987.

On Russell Cave: John W. Griffin, *Investigations in Russell Cave* (Washington, D.C., 1974).

On the spread of early man: Edwin N. Wilmsen, *American Antiquity*, no. 31; Wormington, *Ancient Man in North America;* Linda S. Cordell, *Prehistory in the Southwest* (Albuquerque, N.M., 1984); Waldo R. Wedel, *Prehistoric Man on the Great Plains* (Norman, Okla., 1961).

On the Chubbuck bison kill: Joe Ben Wheat, "A Paleo-Indian Bison Kill," *Scientific American*, Jan. 1967.

On the hunter-gatherer life-style: Robert L. Bettinger, "Archaeological Approach to Hunter-Gatherers," *Annual Review of Anthropology*, no. 16, 1987.

On corn: Paul Mangelsdorf, *Corn: Its Origins, Evolution and Improvement* (Cambridge, Mass., 1974); Richard S. MacNeish, *The Prehistory of the Tehuacan Valley* (Austin, Tex., 1967).

On grave goods and burial mounds: Don W. Dragoo, *Mounds for the Dead* (New York, 1963); Robert Silverberg, *The Mound Builders* (Athens, Ohio, 1986).

On farming: Barbara Stark, *Early Plant Domestication in the New World* (New York, 1986).

On the Ohio culture: John B. Carlson, "Hopewell," *Early Man*, Winter 1977; David S. Brose, ed., *Ancient Art of the American Woodland Indians* (New York, 1985); Susan L. Woodward and Jerry N. McDonald, *Indian Mounds of the Middle Ohio Valley* (Blacksburg, Va., 1986).

On the Georgia and Alabama sites: Max E. White, *Georgia's Indian Heritage* (Roswell, Ga., 1988); John A. Walthall, *An Introduction to the Archaeology of a Mississippian Chiefdom* (Moundville, Ala., 1977).

On Cahokia: Melvin L. Fowler, "A Pre-Columbian Urban Center on the Mississippi," *Scientific American*, Aug. 1975; John E. Pfeiffer, *Cahokia: Indian City on the Mississippi* (New York, 1974).

On Richard Wetherill: Frank McNitt, *Richard Wetherill* (Albuquerque, N.M., 1966).

On Chaco Canyon: J. J. Snyder, "Chaco Canyon," *Early Man*, vol. 2 (1978); David Grant Noble, ed., *New Light on Chaco Canyon* (Santa Fe, N.M., 1984).

On early trading systems: W. Raymond Wood, *Contrastive Features of North American Trade Systems* (Oregon, 1972).

CHAPTER TWO
The Exploration Fever

On Columbus: *Select Letters of Christopher Columbus* (Hakluyt Society, 1870); Samuel Eliot Morison, *Admiral of the Ocean Sea* (New York, 1942).

On La Isabela: *New York Times*, Nov. 27, 1990.

"They all made fun": *Select Letters.*

On Caboto: Samuel Eliot Morison, *The European Discovery of America* (New York, 1971).

On Vespucci: Ibid.

Vespucci letter: *The Letters of Amerigo Vespucci*, Clements R. Markham, trans. (New York, 1884).

On the Spanish in the Caribbean: Gonzalo de Oviedo, *Historia General y Natural de los Indias* (Albuquerque, N.M., 1936); Antonio de Herrera, *General History of the West Indies* (New York, 1932).

On Ponce: Oviedo, *Historia General;* Herrera, *General History;* Edward W. Lawson, *The Discovery of Florida* (St. Augustine, Fla., 1946); Eugene Lyon, *The Enterprise of Florida* (Gainesville, Fla., 1976).

On Requerimiento: Oviedo, *Historia General;* Herrera, *General History.*

On Magellan: Morison, *European Discovery.*

On Verrazano: Letter to Francis I, NYHS collections, 1809.

On Cabeza de Vaca: A. F. Bandolier, ed., *Journey of Álvar Núñez Cabeza de Vaca* (New York, 1902); Morris Bishop, *The Odyssey of Cabeza de Vaca* (New York, 1933).

On Cartier: H. P. Biggar, *The Voyages of Jacques Cartier* (Ottawa, 1924); Justin Winsor, *Cartier to Frontenac* (Cambridge, Mass., 1894); Marc Lescarbot, *History of New France* (Toronto, 1907).

CHAPTER THREE

THE SPANISH PRESENCE

On Calvin Jones: David Hurst Thomas, interview.

On De Soto: James Alexander Robertson, ed., *True Relation of the Hardships Suffered by Governor Fernando de Soto . . . by a Gentleman of Elvas,* (New York, 1932); Edward Gaylord Bourne, ed., *Narratives of the Career of Hernando de Soto in the Conquest of Florida* (New York, 1904); *Final Report of the United States De Soto Expedition Commission*, 76th Cong., 1st sess., House Document no. 71, 1939.

On the white man's spreading disease: Ann F. Ramenofsky, *Vectors of Death* (Albuquerque, N.M., 1987).

On Coronado: G. P. Winship, *Coronado* (New York, 1904).

On the French and the Spanish in Florida: Charles E. Bennett, ed., *Three Voyages: René Laudonnière* (Gainesville, Fla., 1975); Anthony Kerrigan, ed., *Barcia's Chronological History of the Continent of Florida* (Gainesville, Fla., 1951); Charles W. Amade, *Florida on Trial, 1593–1602* (Coral Gables, Fla., 1959); Eugene Lyon, *The Enterprise of Florida* (Gainesville, Fla., 1976); Paul E. Hoffman, *The Spanish Crown and the Defense of the Caribbean, 1535–1585* (Baton Rouge, La., 1980); Jean Parker Waterbury, *Oldest City, St. Augustine* (St. Augustine, Fla., 1983).

On Gilbert and Roanoke: Samuel Eliot Morison, *The European Discovery of America* (New York, 1971).

On Oñate: George P. Hammond, *Don Juan de Oñate* (Albuquerque, N.M., 1953).

CHAPTER FOUR

THE FRENCH FRONTIER

On the Champlain astrolabe: NYHS manuscript collections.

On France in the New World: Marc Lescarbot, *History of New France* (Toronto, 1907); George M. Wrong, *The Rise and Fall of New France* (New York, 1928); L. P. Kellogg, *The French Regime in Wisconsin* (Madison, Wisc., 1925).

On Champlain: H. P. Biggar, *The Works of Champlain* (Toronto, 1922). All Champlain quotes are from Biggar.

On Hudson: G. M. Asher, ed., *Henry Hudson, The Navigator* (New York, 1963).

"Our master and his mate": Robert Juet, *Journal New Jersey Historical Society*, 1959).
"The first step": J. C. W. Armstrong, *Champlain* (Toronto, 1987).
On Sagard: Father Gabriel Sagard, *Long Journey to the Country of the Hurons* (Toronto, 1939).
On French-Indian relations: Cornelius J. Jaenen, *Friend and Foe* (Ontario, 1976).
"I have seen the time": Ibid.
On Indian overhunting: Calvin Martin, *Keepers of the Game* (Berkeley, Cal., 1978).
On Indian drinking: Lescarbot, *History of New France;* Jaenen, *Friend and Foe;*
Abbé Belmont, *Treatise on the Brandy Trade* (Toronto, 1967).
"I am but a tiny animal": Biggar, *Works of Champlain.*

CHAPTER FIVE
THE JAMESTOWN FRONTIER

On the impetus for settlement: Jamestown settlement museum, Williamsburg, Virginia.
On the Virginia Company: Susan Myra Kingsbury, ed., *Records of the Virginia Company of London* (Washington, D.C., 1906).
"Which bendeth most": Kingsbury, *Records.*
Bonds and lotteries: Ibid.
On the colonists' arrival in Virginia: Carl Bridenbaugh, *Jamestown* (New York, 1980); Charles E. Hatch, *The First Seventeen Years: Virginia, 1607–1624* (Charlottesville, Va., n.d.)
"The densely inhabited land": Jamestown settlement museum.
On Percy: Lyon Gardiner Tyler, ed., *Narratives of Early Virginia* (New York, 1907).
On John Smith: Edward Arber, ed., *Captain John Smith* (London, 1897).
"Fellow, either thou art": Arber, *Captain John Smith.*
"In all your passages": Kingsbury, *Records.*
"Making it known to them": Ibid.
Chilling recital: George Percy, *Discovery of the Plantations of the Southern Colony in Virginia by the English* (New York, 1913).
Joyful News: Jamestown settlement museum.
Book of Homilies: Ibid.
"Lascivious sons": Kingsbury, *Records.*
"As fast killing them" and "by all lawful means": Ibid.
On Ralph Hamor: Ralph Hamor, *A True Discourse on the Present State of Virginia* (London, 1615).
On John Rolfe: Tyler, *Narratives of Early Virginia;* Richard L. Morton, *Colonial Virginia* (Chapel Hill, N.C., 1960).
On Pocahontas: Philip L. Barbour, *Pocahontas and Her World* (Boston, 1970).
On the tobacco economy: A. P. Middleton, *Tobacco Coast* (Newport News, Va., 1953).
"The byting tast": Gloria L. Main, *Tobacco Colony* (Princeton, 1982).
Spreading of the colony: Kingsbury, *Records.*
"Coat-wearing people": Jamestown settlement museum.
"Right worthy statesman": Kingsbury, *Records.*
"Now, sir, here's another devil": Tyler, *Narratives of Early Virginia.*
"But five or six houses": Kingsbury, *Records.*
"Against teaching Indians": Ibid.
"Mr. Lambert has found out": Ibid.

"The plantation can never flourish": Ibid.
"She shall for such offense": Ibid.
"A more damned crew never vomited": Ibid.
On head-rights: W. F. Craven, *White, Red, and Black* (Charlottesville, Va., 1971).
On convicts and servants: *Virginia Magazine of History and Biography*, vol. XXX (1901).
On Richard Frethorne: Kingsbury, *Records*.
On the first legislative assembly in 1619: NYHS collections, 1857.
On court records: H. R. McIlwaine, ed., *Minutes of the Council and General Court* (Richmond, Va., 1924).
"Their darling tobacco": Kingsbury, *Records*.
On the massacre of 1622: Ibid.
On the demise of the London Company: W. F. Craven, *Dissolution of the Virginia Company* (Gloucester, Mass., 1964).

CHAPTER SIX

THE PILGRIM FRONTIER

On Pilgrim origins: William Bradford, *Of Plymouth Plantation, 1620–1647* (New York, 1987).
On Pilgrims in Leiden: B. N. Leverland and J. D. Bangs, *The Pilgrims in Leiden* (Leiden, 1984).
"Hunted and persecuted": Bradford, *Of Plymouth*.
On their arrival in America: Eugene Aubrey Stratton, *Plymouth Colony* (Salt Lake City, 1986); D. B. Rutman, *A Militant New World* (New York, 1979); Alexander Young, *Chronicles of the Pilgrim Fathers* (Boston, 1841).
"We are all weaned": Bradford, *Of Plymouth*.
"What profits might arise": Young, *Chronicles*.
"Let every man repress": Bradford, *Of Plymouth*.
"Ill-conditioned people": Ibid.
"Wherein 100 sails of ship": Dwight B. Heath, ed., *Mourt's Relation: A Journal of the Pilgrims at Plymouth* (Cambridge, Mass., 1986).
"Caused to cast and scour": Heath, *Mourt's Relation*.
"The savages had died like rotten sheep": Edward Arber, *The Story of the Pilgrim Fathers* (London, 1897).
On relations with the Indians: Bradford, *Of Plymouth*.
On early days: *John Pory's Lost Description* (New York, 1918).
"Leveled and sown": Bradford, *Of Plymouth*.
"So I am quit of you": Ibid.
"I will so far inform you": Ibid.
"Much daunted and dismayed": Ibid.
"All criminal facts": Young, *Chronicles*.
On Lyford and Oldham: Bradford, *Of Plymouth*.
On Morton: Thomas Morton, *New England Canaan* (Amsterdam, 1637); Bradford, *Of Plymouth*.
On the Pilgrims' dispersal: Ibid.
On court cases: *Records of the Colony of New Plymouth* (Boston, 1855).
On Thomas Granger: Bradford, *Of Plymouth*.

CHAPTER SEVEN
The Dutch Frontier

On the Dutch East India Company: J. F. Jameson, ed., *Narratives of New Netherlands* (New York, 1909).
"An oblong bead": Ibid.
On de Rasieres in Plymouth: William Bradford, *Of Plymouth Plantation, 1620–1647* (New York, 1987).
"Are better behaved than ours": Jameson, *Narratives*.
On Michaelius: NYHS collections, 1841.
On Heckewelder and the Indians: Ibid.
On Melyn in Staten Island: Ibid., 1857.
On Megapolensis: Ibid.
On De Vries: Jameson. *Narratives*.
"The French are doing more": Allen W. Trelease, *Indian Affairs in Colonial New York* (Ithaca, N.Y., 1960).
On the first Jews: Jameson, *Narratives;* Megapolensis, NYHS collections.
Jews in North America: Jameson, *Narratives*.
"Causes a great deal": Megapolensis, NYHS collections.
"What can my lord do": Jameson, *Narratives*.
On Beekman: Beekman Mercantile Papers, 1746–1799, NYHS; Philip H. White, *The Beekmans of New York* (New York, 1956).
"There is now but few": Trelease, *Indian Affairs*.

CHAPTER EIGHT
The Puritan Frontier

Background on the Puritans: Alden T. Vaughan, ed., *The Puritan Tradition in America* (New York, 1972); Perry Miller, *The New England Mind* (Williamsburg, Va., 1981) and *The American Puritans* (New York, 1956).
"Notorious whores": Miller, *The American Puritans*.
On Higginson: Young, *Chronicles*.
On Winthrop: John Winthrop, *History of New England* (Boston, 1853); Winthrop Papers, Massachusetts Historical Society.
On arrival: Winthrop, *History;* Alexander Young, *Chronicles of the First Planters* (Boston, 1846).
"All things to do": Winthrop Papers.
"From a paradise of plenty": Winthrop, *History*.
On the New England frontier: Richard I. Melvoin, *New England Outpost* (New York, 1989).
On Dudley: Winthrop, *History*.
"To prove ill neighbors": Winthrop, *History*.
"Lest an enemy": Ibid.
"Wandering, benighted coasters": William Wood, *New England's Prospect* (New York, 1954).
On Indian relations: Alden T. Vaughan and Edward W. Clark, eds., *Puritans Among the Indians* (Cambridge, Mass., 1981).
On court cases: N. B. Shurtleff, ed., *Records of the Massachusetts Bay Colony* (Boston, 1853).
On the expansion into the Connecticut Valley: William Bradford, *Of Plymouth Plantation 1620–1647* (New York, 1987); Young, *Chronicles;* Winthrop, *History*.

"We thought fit": Winthrop, *History*.
Encounter with the Dutch: Bradford, *Of Plymouth*.
On the John Stone incident: Winthrop, *History*.
"The strong bent of their spirits": Ibid.
"Their skin cleaving": Bradford, *Of Plymouth*.
"Leave to remove": Winthrop, *History*.
On Dorchester people: Bradford, *Of Plymouth*.
On William Pynchon: Henry Morris, *Early History of Springfield* (Springfield, Mass., 1876); Ruth A. McIntyre, *William Pynchon* (Springfield, Mass., 1961).
"The many desirable places": Morris, *Early History*.
"House room": Ibid.
"Encumbered with Indians": Ibid.
"Fifty families rich and poor": Ibid.
"From the Narragansett to the Pacific": *Dictionary of American History*, vol. VI (New York, 1976).
On Lion Gardiner: *Papers of Lion Gardiner* (St. Louis, Mo., 1883).
John Oldham's death: Winthrop, *History*.
"To put to death the men": *Ibid*.
On John Underhill: Captain John Underhill, *News from America* (London, 1638).
"If the case be never so dangerous": Morris, *Early History*.
On John Mason: Louis B. Mason, *The Life and Times of Major John Mason* (New York, 1935); John Mason, *A Brief History of the Pequot War* (Boston, 1736).
March on Pequots: Mason, *Brief History*.
On the Pynchon profiteering case: Joseph H. Smith, *Colonial Justice in Western Massachusetts, 1639–1702* (Cambridge, Mass., 1961).
"I care not who knows it": Mason, *Life and Times*.
"I will neither make": Mason, *Brief History*.
"An Indian promise": Smith, *Colonial Justice*.
"Unfaithful dealing": Ibid.
"A plain turning me out": McIntyre, *William Pynchon*.
On frontier and hinterland: Melvoin, *New England Outpost*; Sylvester Judd, *History of Hadley* (Northampton, Mass., 1863); James Deetz, *In Small Things Forgotten* (New York, 1977); Shurtleff, *Records*.
"The offscourings of civilized society": Melvoin, *New England Outpost*.
"Was ordered to be torn": Ibid.
"Ornamented or wanton clothing": Shurtleff, *Records*.
Chamber pots: Deetz, *In Small Things*.
Case of Sarah Smith: Smith, *Colonial Justice*.
"Unchaste miscarriage": Shurtleff, *Records*.
On Colonel Cartwright: NYHS collections, 1869.
On John Gyles: Vaughan and Clark, *Puritans Among the Indians*.

CHAPTER NINE
FRONTIERS IN COLLISION

On Father Allouez: L. P. Kellogg, *Early Narratives of the Northwest, 1634–1699* (New York, 1917).
On New France: George M. Wrong, *The Rise and Fall of New France* (New York, 1928).
On Louis XIV's instructions: Louis XIV to Sieur Gaudais, NYHS manuscript collections.

504 NOTES FOR PAGES 197–224

On Louis de la Hontan: *La Hontan's Voyages to North America* (Chicago, 1935).
On Marquette: H. W. Beckwith, ed., *Collections of the Illinois State Historical Library* (Springfield, Ill., 1903).
On La Salle: Kellogg, *Early Narratives;* Léon Lemonnier, *Cavelier de la Salle et l'Exploration du Mississippi* (Paris, 1942).
"Introduce by moonlight": Kellogg, *Early Narratives.*
"You will pardon us": P. Leprohon, *Cavelier de La Salle*, Paris, 1984.
"I know of no friends": Ibid.
"There are very few people": Ibid.
"As dangerous to the mind": Ibid.
"So much the better": Ibid.
On La Salle in Texas: Robert S. Weddle, *Wilderness Manhunt: The Spanish Search for La Salle* (Austin, Tex., 1973).
"There you lie": Ibid.
"Escape their crimes": Wrong, *Rise and Fall.*
On Alonso De León: Weddle, *Wilderness Manhunt.*
On the "Spanish tier": Howard Peckham and Charles Gibson, eds., *Attitudes of Colonial Powers Toward the American Indians* (Salt Lake City, 1969).
On St. Augustine: Kathleen Deegan, "St. Augustine, First Urban Enclave in the United States," *North American Archaeologist* 3 (1982); Jean Parker Waterbury, ed., *The Oldest City* (St. Augustine, Fla., 1983).
"No one comes to America to plant": George P. Hammond, *New Mexico in 1602* (Albuquerque, N.M., 1938).
Spanish missions in New Mexico: Ramon A. Gutierrez, *When Jesus Came, the Corn Mothers Went Away* (Stanford, Cal., 1991).
Don't let the Indian women: Hammond, *New Mexico.*
On Benavides: R. E. Twitchell, *The Leading Facts of New Mexico History* (Cedar Rapids, Iowa, 1911).
"Indian foolishness": Hammond, *New Mexico.*
Popé and Indian revolt: George Hammond, ed., *The Revolt of the Pueblo Indians* (Albuquerque, N.M., 1942); Charles Wilson Hackett, "The Revolt of the Pueblo Indians in 1680," *Quarterly of the Texas State Historical Association*, October 1911; Gutierrez, *When Jesus Came.*
On Otermín: Hammond, *Revolt.*
"What grieved us the most": Hammond, *Revolt.*
"We are quit with the Spaniards": Hammond, *Revolt.*
On the sequel to the Pueblo revolt: John F. Bannon, *The Spanish Borderlands Frontier, 1513–1821* (Albuquerque, N.M., 1974).

CHAPTER TEN
THE MANORIAL FRONTIER

On William Fitzhugh: Richard Beale Davis, ed., *William Fitzhugh and His Chesapeake World* (Chapel Hill, N.C., 1963).
"As durable as a brick wall": Ibid.
"Never courted": Ibid.
"Pledges of": Ibid.
"I understand there are": Ibid.
"You make some abatement": Ibid.
"I thank God": Robert Beverley, *The History of Virginia* (London, 1722).
"The pluckers and the cutters": Davis, *William Fitzhugh.*
"The lowness of tobacco": Ibid.

The tobacco economy: Gloria L. Main, *Tobacco Colony* (Princeton, N.J., 1982).
"In funky, foggy weather": Ibid.
On slavery legislation: NYHS manuscript collections; parish transcripts, Public Records Office, London.
On William Byrd: Kenneth A. Lockridge, *The Diary and Life of William Byrd of Virginia* (London, 1987); *The Secret Diary of William Byrd* (New York, 1963); *The London Diary of William Byrd* (New York, 1958); William Byrd, *History of the Dividing Line* (New York, 1973).
"She was in the wrong": *Secret Diary*.
"She lifted up her hands": Ibid.
"Eugene pissed abed": Ibid.
"The flourish was performed": Ibid.
"I rogered her" and "I gave my wife": Ibid.
"Because there seemed to be": Lockridge, *Diary and Life*.
"To stoop to a dirty": Ibid.
"I have no bills to pay": Ibid.
"We should hang bundles": Ibid.
Byrd and Spotswood: Pierre Marambaud, *William Byrd of Westover* (Charlottesville, Va., 1971).
Byrd in London: *London Diary*.
Running the boundary: Byrd, *Dividing Line*.
All quotes on running the boundary: Ibid.
Letter to the Earl of Egmont: *American Historical Review*, vol. 1.

CHAPTER ELEVEN
THE CHESAPEAKE FRONTIER

On George Calvert: David B. Quinn, ed., *Early Maryland in a Wider World* (Detroit, 1982).
"From the midst": Ibid.
Arrival of first Maryland settlers: Andrew White, *A Relation of Maryland* (London, 1635).
"Very careful": Quinn, *Early Maryland*.
On Quakers: *Dictionary of American History*, vol. V (New York, 1976).
On convicts and servants: E. I. McCormac, *White Servitude in Maryland* (Baltimore, 1904); Abbot E. Smith, *Colonists in Bondage* (Chapel Hill, N.C., 1947).
On Thomas Bradnox: Raphael Semmes, *Crime and Punishment in Early Maryland* (Baltimore, 1938).
On Lumbrozo: Ibid.
On other court cases: Ibid.
On slave legislation: Parish transcripts from the London Public Records Office, NYHS manuscript collections.
On Macnemara and Dulany: Aubrey C. Land, *The Dulanys of Maryland* (Baltimore, 1955).

CHAPTER TWELVE
THE BLACK FRONTIER

On the early settlements: R. M. Weir, *Colonial South Carolina* (New York, 1983); A. S. Salley, *Narratives of Early Carolina* (New York, 1911).
"Wine, oil, raisins": Weir, *Colonial*.

"We are here settled": Salley, *Narratives*.
"The dead were carried": Ibid.
"But I can make": Ibid.
On the rice culture: A. S. Salley, *Introduction of Rice Culture in South Carolina* (Columbia, S.C., 1919).
"I can see a goodeal": Peter H. Wood, *Black Majority* (New York, 1974).
On slave population: Ibid.
On Muhlenberg: NYHS manuscript collections, Muhlenberg.
"De buckruh habe scheme": Weir, *Colonial*.
"The greater [the] number": Wood, *Black Majority*.
On St. Augustine as a haven: NYHS collections, Montiano papers; *Letters of Montiano, Collections of the Georgia Historical Society*, vol. VII; Herbert E. Bolton, ed., *Arredondo's Historical Proof of Spain's Title to Georgia* (Berkeley, Cal., 1925).
"Four or five who were": Wood, *Black Majority*.
"To find their property": Ibid.
On the Stono Rebellion: Weir, *Colonial*.
On the siege of St. Augustine: Ricardo Torres-Reyes, *The British Siege of St. Augustine in 1740* (Denver, 1972).
"The English taste": *Letters and Journals of Eliza Lucas* (Wormsloe, Ga., 1850); H. H. Ravenel, *Eliza Lucas* (New York, 1896).
"I own I love": Ravenel, *Eliza Lucas*.
"I have greater hopes": Ibid.
On indigo: *Eliza Lucas Pinckney*, Historic Georgetown leaflet, Rice Museum, Georgetown, S.C., 1975.
"A mere bungler": Ravenel, *Eliza Lucas*.
"I have the business": Ibid.
"Not for all the riches": Ibid.
"Had been very much deluded": Ibid.
On Weberites: NYHS manuscript collections, Muhlenberg.

CHAPTER THIRTEEN
THE SALZBURGER FRONTIER

"Procure a quantity of acres": T. R. Reese, *Colonial Georgia* (Athens, Ga., 1963).
On the arrival of the first settlers: Ibid.
On the conflict over slavery: NYHS manuscript collections, parish transcripts, Georgia.
"Experience has shown": Parish transcripts.
Horton to Savannah: Ibid.
On Salzburgers: George Fenwick Jones, ed., *Detailed Reports on the Salzburger Emigrants Who Settled in America*, 8 vols. (Athens, Ga., 1968–1987); George Fenwick Jones, *The Salzburger Saga* (Athens, Ga., 1984).
All Salzburger quotes from Jones, *Detailed Reports*.
On William Stephens: *William Stephens, A Journal of the Proceedings in Georgia* (New York, 1966).
All Stephens quotes from *Journal of the Proceedings*.

CHAPTER FOURTEEN
The Quaker Frontier

On William Penn: Richard S. Dunn and Mary Maples Dunn, *The Papers of William Penn*, 5 vols. (Philadelphia, 1981–87).
On Quakers: F. B. Tolles, *Meeting-House and Counting-House* (Chapel Hill, N.C., 1948).
On Fenwick arbitration: A. C. Myers, ed., *Narratives of Early Pennsylvania* (New York, 1912).
On Philip Ford: Dunn, *Penn Papers*.
On Thomas Paschall: NYHS manuscript collections.
On Pastorius: M. D. Learned, *The Life of Daniel Pastorius* (Philadelphia, 1908).
"For upright people": Learned, *Life of Pastorius*.
"We cannot imagine why": Ibid.
"Obliged to play the role": Ibid.
"Brother love is not": Dunn, *Penn Papers*.
"Each prays for his neighbors": Tolles, *Meeting-House*.
Pennsbury: Pennsbury Manor, Morrisville, Pa.
Penn kept slaves: Dunn, *Penn Papers*.
"Ye Quakers do here": Ibid.
On James Logan: F. B. Tolles, *James Logan and the Culture of Provincial America* (New York, 1957).
"That muck worm": Dunn, *Penn Papers*.
"Unreasonable and voracious": Ibid.
William Penn, Jr.: Ibid.
"A troublesome swimming": Ibid.
"O Pennsylvania": Ibid.
"Their yea was yea": Tolles, *Meeting-House*.
"Under the pretense": Ibid.
On the Scotch-Irish: J. G. Leyburn, *The Scotch-Irish* (Chapel Hill, N.C., 1962); R. J. Dickson, *Ulster Migration to Colonial America, 1718–1775* (New York, 1970).
"There are at this time": Tolles, *James Logan*.
On Edward Marshall: Myers, *Narratives*.
On the Walking Purchase: "The Walking Purchase," *Pennsylvania History*, January 1970; William J. Buck, *History of the Indian Walk* (Philadelphia, 1886).

CHAPTER FIFTEEN
The Hinterland in 1750

"Our people must at least": Verner W. Crane, *Benjamin Franklin and a Rising People* (New York, 1954).
On Appolon de Rivoire: NYHS manuscript collections.
On Colden: NYHS, Colden papers.
On Mittelberg: *Gottlieb Mittelberg's Journey* (Philadelphia, 1898).
On Hamilton: *Journals of Alexander Hamilton* (New York, 1890).
On Peter Kalm: Peter Kalm, *Travels in North America* (New York, 1920).

CHAPTER SIXTEEN
The Frontier in 1750

On French and Indian Wars: Edward P. Hamilton, *The French and Indian Wars* (New York, 1962).

On Thomas Cresap: Kenneth P. Bailey, *Thomas Cresap* (Boston, 1944).

On Washington's meeting with Cresap: D. M. Larrabee, *Journals of George Washington* (New York, 1929).

On George Croghan: R. G. Thwaites, *Early Western Travels* (Cleveland, Ohio, 1904); Albert T. Votwiler, *George Croghan and the Westward Movement* (Cleveland, Ohio, 1926); N. B. Wainwright, *George Croghan* (Chapel Hill, N.C., 1959).

On Conrad Weiser: Thwaites, *Early Western Travels*.

On Céloron: Céloron de Blainville's Journal, *Ohio Archaeological and Historical Quarterly*, vol. 29, 1920.

On Christopher Gist: W. M. Darlington, ed., *Christopher Gist's Journal* (Pittsburgh, 1893).

Joncaire and the Indians: Thwaites, *Early Western Travels*.

"Is this not our land?": Ibid.

"I won't owe a groat": Votwiler, *George Croghan*.

On William Trent: *Journal of Captain William Trent* (Cincinnati, Ohio, 1871).

Gist and Washington: Darlington, *Gist's Journal*; Larrabee, *Journals of George Washington*.

On Washington and Jumonville: Marcel Trudel, "The Jumonville Affair," *Pennsylvania History*, vol. 26.

"I was the first man": Ibid.

"I think, sir": Ibid.

"I have heard the bullets whistle": Ibid.

"He would not say so": Ibid.

Washington's version: Donald H. Kent, ed., "Contrecoeur's Copy of George Washington's Journal for 1754," *Pennsylvania History* 19 (1952).

"I wish Washington": George P. Hunt, *Wars of the Iroquois*.

On Fort Necessity: Fort Necessity National Battlefield Museum, Great Meadows, Pa.

"If the French build more forts": Votwiler, *Croghan*.

"Their squaws [were] bringing them": Francis Jennings, *Empire of Fortune* (New York, 1988).

"Deceived and met with": Bailey, *Cresap*.

"Rattle-snake colonel": Ibid.

On Braddock's defeat: Stanley Pargellis, "Braddock's Defeat," *American Historical Review*, 1936.

"Many of our people": Votwiler, *Croghan*.

"He was a bad man": Ibid.

"A delicate conduct": Ibid.

CHAPTER SEVENTEEN
The French Departure

"The roads are full": Richard S. Dunn and Mary Maples Dunn, *The Papers of William Penn* (Philadelphia, 1987).

"We are informed": Francis Jennings, *Empire of Fortune* (New York, 1988).

"The Pearl Harbor": Samuel Eliot Morison, *Oxford History of the American People* (New York, 1965).

Governor Denny's negotiations: Gallatin papers, "Minutes of a Conference between Gov. Denny and Tedyuscung," NYHS manuscript collections.
"I have long been": Sylvester K. Stevens and Donald H. Kent, eds., *The Papers of Col. Henri Bouquet* (Harrisburg, Pa., 1942).
On capture of Fort Pitt: Ibid.
On Hugh Mercer: M.C. Darlington, ed., *Fort Pitt, Letters from the Frontier* (Philadelphia, 1960).
"We are not come": Ibid.
"If the Buck is in your road": Albert T. Votwiler, *George Croghan and the Westward Movement* (Cleveland, Ohio, 1926).
"My children, I have bad news": Darlington, *Fort Pitt*.
"I have been as frugal": Votwiler, *Croghan*.
"I never put a dirty six-pence": Stevens and Kent, *Bouquet Papers*.
Treaty of Paris: Kate Hotblack, "The Peace of Paris, 1763," *Transactions of the Royal Historical Society*, vol. 2, 3d series.
On Sainte Genevieve: Carl J. Ekberg, *Colonial Ste. Geneviève* (Gerald, Mo., 1985).
On the Pontiac rebellion: Howard H. Peckham, *Pontiac and the Indian Uprising* (Princeton, 1947); Cyrus Court, *Henri Bouquet and His Campaigns* (Lancaster, 1883); Francis Jennings, *Empire of Fortune* (New York, 1988); Stevens and Kent, *Bouquet Papers*.
"Poor Lt. MacDonald": Darlington, *Fort Pitt*.
"I only regret": Ibid.
"We have madeira": Stevens and Kent, *Bouquet Papers*.
"I wish to hear of no prisoners": Ibid.
"There appear to be few savages": Ibid.
"The savages have begun": Ibid.
"I have collected": Ibid.
"Out of regard": *Journal of Capt. William Trent* (Cincinnati, 1871).
On germ warfare: Bernhard Knollenberg, "General Amherst and Germ Warfare," *Mississippi Valley Historical Review*, Dec. 1954.
"I will try to inoculate": Stevens and Kent, *Bouquet Papers*.
Gershon Hicks: Knollenberg, "General Amherst."
"The poor rascals": Stevens and Kent, *Bouquet Papers*.
"As soon as they showed": Darlington, *Fort Pitt*.
"By the way": Stevens and Kent, *Bouquet Papers*.
Bouquet at Bushy Run: Court, *Henri Bouquet*.
Proclamation of 1763: *Dictionary of American History*, vol. 5 (New York, 1976).
"Will remove as their avidity": Jennings, *Empire of Fortune*.
On the Mason-Dixon line: *The Journal of Charles Mason and Jeremiah Dixon* (Philadelphia, 1969).

CHAPTER EIGHTEEN
STARS TO THE FLAG

"The wise and good mother": Max Savelle, *Seeds of Liberty* (New York, 1948).
"The dull monotony": Ibid.
On Charles Woodmason: Charles Woodmason, *The Carolina Backcountry on the Eve of Revolution* (Chapel Hill, N.C., 1953).
On the Carolina Regulators: R. M. Brown, *South Carolina Regulators* (Cambridge, Mass., 1963).
On Philip Fithian: *Journal and Letters of Philip Vickers Fithian* (Williamsburg, Va., 1957).

On Nicholas Cresswell: *The Journal of Nicholas Cresswell* (New York, 1925).

On Samuel Kirkland: Kirkland Papers, Hamilton College, Clinton, N.Y.

On Charleston: Leila Sellers, *Charleston Business on the Eve of the American Revolution* (Chapel Hill, N.C., 1934).

On Jeremiah: David Merrill Zornow, "A Troublesome Community: Blacks in Revolutionary Charles Town, 1765–1775," unpublished social studies essay, Harvard College, 1976.

Ethiopian Regiment: Geoffrey J. Rowe and Larry D. Tise, eds., *The Southern Experience in the American Revolution* (Chapel Hill, N.C., 1978).

On British strategy: Savelle, *Seeds*.

"Cold, stormy day": "Journal of Ebenezer Elmer," New Jersey Historical Society, vols. 2 and 3 (1848–49).

On Fort Stanwix: John F. Luzader, *Fort Stanwix: Construction and Military History* (Washington, D.C., 1976).

On de la Marquisie: William Willett, *A Narrative of the Military Action of Col. Marinus Willett* (New York, 1831).

On the first incidents of Indian harassment: John Albert Scott, *Fort Stanwix and Oriskany* (Rome, N.Y., 1927).

On the flag: Milo M. Quaife, Melvin W. Weig, and Roy E. Appleman, *The History of the United States Flag* (Philadelphia, 1966).

On Dr. James Thacher: *Military Journal* (Boston, 1823).

On the homemade flag: William Colbrath, "Journal of the Most Material Occurrences Preceding the Siege of Fort Schuyler (formerly Fort Stanwix), with an account of the siege etc." (microfilm, New York Public Library).

On Capt. Abraham Swartwout: James Weise, *Swartwout Chronicle* (New York, 1899).

On powder horns: William Rea Furlong and Byron McCandless, *So Proudly We Hail: The History of the United States Flag* (Washington, D.C., 1981).

On Oriskany: "Col. Claus' Account of the Battle of Oriskany and the Defeat of St. Leger's Expedition," Public Records Office, London; Scott, *Fort Stanwix and Oriskany*.

"I would suffer my body": Willett, *Narrative*.

James Rix letter: Fort Stanwix National Monument museum.

CHAPTER NINETEEN
THE LAND HUNGER

On Mary Draper: C. L. Skinner, *Pioneers of the Old Southwest* (New Haven, Conn., 1919).

"He is gone to hell": A. K. Moore, *The Frontier Mind* (Lexington, Ky., 1957).

"Why are you leaving": Ibid.

Sycamore Shoals Treaty: *Dictionary of American History*, vol. VI (New York, 1976).

On John Donelson: A. W. Putnam, *History of Middle Tennessee* (Nashville, Tenn., 1859); Skinner, *Pioneers*. All quotes on Donelson trip from Putnam.

On the Continental Congress: Edmund C. Burnett, *Letters of Members of the Continental Congress*, 8 vols. (Washington, D.C., 1848–49); F. N. Thorpe, *Constitutional History of the United States* (Boston, 1904).

Articles of Confederation: *Dictionary of American History*, vol. I (New York, 1976).

Surrender of Saratoga: *Dictionary of American History*, vol. VI (New York, 1976).

Treaty of Paris: *Dictionary of American History*, vol. IV (New York, 1976).

On the Land Ordinance of 1785: B. H. Hibbard, *History of the Public Land Policies* (Madison, Wisc., 1965); P. J. Treat, *The National Land System* (New York, 1910); B. A. Hinsdale, *The Old Northwest* (Boston, 1899).

On the township system: Thomas Donaldson, *The Public Domain* (Washington, D.C., 1880).

On Thomas Hutchins: Joseph W. Ernst, "With Compass and Chain: Federal Land Surveyors in the Old Northwest, 1785–1816," unpublished doctoral thesis, Columbia University, 1958.

CHAPTER TWENTY
THE OHIO COMPANY

On Rufus Putnam: *The Memoirs of Rufus Putnam* (Marietta, Ohio, 1963).

Powder horn verse: Campus Martius Museum exhibit, Marietta, Ohio.

On the formation of the Ohio Company: Putnam, *Memoirs;* S. P. Hildreth, *Pioneer History* (Cincinnati, Ohio, 1848); Thomas J. Summers, *History of Marietta* (Marietta, Ohio, 1903).

On Manasseh Cutler: *Life, Journals and Correspondence of Manasseh Cutler* (Athens, Ohio, 1987).

On Winthrop Sargent's surveying: Ernst, "With Compass and Chain."

On the 1787 Continental Congress: Roscoe R. Hill, ed., *Journals of the Continental Congress* (Washington, D.C., 1936).

On the Northwest Ordinance: Peter S. Onuf, *The Origins of the Federal Republic* (Philadelphia, 1983) and *Statehood and Union* (Bloomington, Ind., 1987); Jack N. Rakove, *The Beginnings of National Politics* (New York, 1979); F. D. Williams, ed., *Essays on the Northwest Ordinance* (East Lansing, Mich., 1989).

"Would not be able": Rakove, *Beginnings.*

"The ayes have it": Onuf, *Origins.*

On the Nathan Dane letter: *Indiana Historical Society Publications,* vol. 1.

"Shall never be invaded": Onuf, *Origins.*

On Manasseh Cutler in New York: Cutler, *Life.*

On the Scioto deal: Archer B. Hulbert, "The Scioto Company," *Mississippi Valley Historical Review,* March 1915; T. T. Belote, "The Scioto Speculation," *University of Cincinnati Studies,* ser. II, vol. 3, no. 3; Shaw Livermore, *Early American Land Companies* (New York, 1939).

"You have got the length of his foot": Cutler, *Life.*

"We were obliged": Ibid.

"When the business is done": Hulbert, "Scioto Company."

"Cotton . . . in great perfection": Cutler, *Life.*

"Commenced with great spirit": Putnam, *Memoirs.*

On early Marietta: R. C. Buley, *The Old Northwest* (Indianapolis, Ind., 1950); Archer Butler Hulbert, *The Ohio River* (New York, 1906).

"I should be as soon lost in it": Cutler, *Life.*

On Arthur St. Clair: William Henry Smith, *Arthur St. Clair* (Cincinnati, Ohio, 1882); *TP,* vol. 4.

On early government in Marietta: Summers, *History of Marietta.*

"Though we hear much": *TP,* vol. 4.

"It very rarely happens": Ibid.

"The spirit of settlement": Ibid.

On Washington's Indian policies: Francis P. Prucha, *American Indian Policy in the Formative Years* (Cambridge, Mass., 1962).

"Were determined to join": *TP*, vol. 4.

Treaty of Fort Stanwix: *Dictionary of American History*, vol. VI (New York, 1976).

"The Indians, being prior occupants": *TP*, vol. 4.

"A right of pre-emption": Francis P. Prucha, *American Indian Policy*.

On John May: Dwight L. Smith, ed., *Western Journals of John May* (Cincinnati, Ohio, 1961).

"How many is there of you": Joseph Barker, *Recollections* (Marietta, Ohio, 1958).

On Indian overhunting: Ibid.

"To punish the Wabash Indians": *TP*, vol. 4.

On Harmar's expedition: B. J. Griswold, *The Pictorial History of Fort Wayne, Indiana* (Fort Wayne, 1913).

"I expected *little*": *TP*, vol. 4.

On Captain John McMurtry: Richard K. McMurtry, *John McMurtry and the American Indian* (Berkeley, Cal., 1980).

On the Big Bottom massacre: Barker, *Recollections*.

On Israel Stone: Ibid.

On St. Clair defeat: Smith, *Arthur St. Clair*.

"The most disgraceful part": *TP*, vol. 4.

"St. Clair's defeated": Smith, *Arthur St. Clair*.

"We seem to have forgotten": *TP*, vol. 4.

Hamtramck letter: Ibid.

"A concerted plan": Ibid.

On the Ohio Company's request for relief: Cutler, *Life*.

"It is dangerous to quarrel": Putnam, *Memoirs*.

"It is intolerable provoking": Cutler, *Life*.

On Wayne campaign: E. O. Randall and D. J. Ryan, *History of Ohio* (New York, 1916).

On Treaty of Greenville: F. L. Paxson, *History of the American Frontier* (Boston, 1924).

"If our modes of population": *TP*, vol. 4.

On Ben Stone: Barker, *Recollections*.

On Bricknell: Francis P. Prucha, ed., *Documents of the U.S. Indian Policy* (Lincoln, Neb., 1990).

On the end of the Ohio Company: Cutler, *Life*.

"Marietta may be considered": Summers, *History of Marietta*.

CHAPTER TWENTY-ONE
THE CREEKS FIGHT BACK

On McGillivray: John Walton Caghey, *McGillivray of the Creeks* (Norman, Okla., 1938); Arthur Preston Whitaker, *Spanish-American Frontier, 1783–1795* (New York, 1927).

On half-breeds: William J. Scheick, *The Half-Blood: A Cultural Symbol in American 19th-Century Fiction* (New York, 1970).

"Washington himself": Caghey, *McGillivray*.

"A set of cunning": Ibid.

"The Creeks alone": *TP*, vol. 5.

"The customary amounts": Caghey, *McGillivray*.

"My warriors are victorious": Ibid.

"Our frontiers have been": *TP*, vol. 5.

"McGillivray considers himself": Whitaker, *Frontier*.

"We are now governed": Caghey, *McGillivray*.
On Willett Mission: William Willett, *A Narrative of the Military Action of Col. Marinus Willett* (New York, 1831).
"Tired of being repeatedly pressed": Caghey, *McGillivray*.
"It mounts from my feet": Ibid.
"I gave out general orders": Ibid.
"He breathed his last": Ibid.
"The Talleyrand of Alabama": Albert J. Pickett, *Alabama* (Birmingham, Ala., 1900).

CHAPTER TWENTY-TWO
The Struggle for Statehood

On Vermont: Chilton Williamson, *Vermont in Quandary* (Montpelier, Vt., 1949); Charles Miner Thompson, *Independent Vermont* (Boston, 1942).
"Vermont is not in confederation": *New York Times*, Dec. 2, 1990.
"If Congress are not firm": *TP*, vol. 2.
On Transylvania Company: *Dictionary of American History*, vol. VII (New York, 1976).
"A snug little purchase": Steven A. Channing, *Kentucky* (New York, 1977).
On land laws: Ibid.
"More than the Indian wars": Humphrey Marshall, *Kentucky* (Frankfort, Ky., 1824).
On Isaac Shelby: Channing, *Kentucky*.
"Off-scourings of the earth": S. C. Williams, *The Lost State of Franklin* (Johnson City, Tenn., 1924).
On John Sevier: Carl S. Driver, *John Sevier* (Chapel Hill, N.C., 1932).
"The western country": Williams, *Franklin*.
"I know with reluctance": Ibid.
"In the first year of our independence": Driver, *Sevier*.
"A negotiation is on foot": Williams, *Franklin*.
"We have the rights": Driver, *Sevier*.
"Sevier . . . appears to be incorrigible": Ibid.
Gardoqui letters: Williams, *Franklin*.
"A certain stripling": Eric R. Lacy, "Persistent State of Franklin," *Tennessee Historical Quarterly* (Dec. 1964).
On Tennessee's territorial period: Stanley J. Folmsbee, Robert E. Corlew, and Enoch L. Mitchell, *A Short History of Tennessee* (New York, 1960).

CHAPTER TWENTY-THREE
The Land Operation

On 1796 land law: Malcolm J. Rohrborough, *The Land Office Business* (New York, 1968).
"Of too short standing": Joseph W. Ernst, "With Compass and Chain: Federal Land Surveyors in the Old Northwest, 1785–1816," unpublished doctoral thesis, Columbia University, 1958.
Rufus Putnam as surveyor general: Ibid.
Thomas Worthington and Elias Langham: *TP*, vol. 3.
On Jared Mansfield: *TP*, vols. 3, 4, 5; Ernst, "With Compass and Chain."

"I am happy in having my name": *The Memoirs of Rufus Putnam* (Marietta, Ohio, 1963).
"As almost the whole": Ernst, "With Compass and Chain."
"They will perceive": *TP*, vol. 3.
On Zilba Foote: *TP*, vol. 4.
"It would be impossible": Ibid.
On the Rectors: *TP*, vols. 4, 5, 6, 7.
"The Prophet's brother": *TP*, vol. 7.
On Meigs and Tiffin: *TP*, vol. 10.
On surveying in Michigan: Ibid.
On surveying in Illinois: Ibid, vol. 11.
On Nelson Rector: Ibid., vol. 16.
On surveying in Indiana: Ibid., vols. 11, 12.
On Gershon Flagg: Gershon Flagg, *Pioneer Letters* (Springfield, Ill., 1912).
On William Rector's activities: Joseph Gillespie, *Recollections of Early Illinois* (Chicago, 1880).
On Thomas Rector in Arkansas: *TP*, vol. 19.
On Chilo Moultier: Ibid.
On New Madrid land warrants: *Arkansas Historical Quarterly*, Winter 1956.
On demise of William Rector: John Reynolds, *Pioneer History* (New York, 1852); *TP*, vol. 19.
"If I have been correctly informed": *TP*, vol. 19.
"It would almost appear": *TP*, vol. 20.
On Valentine Conway: *TP*, vol. 26.
On Marshall and Drifting Goose: *South Dakota Historical Collections*, vol. 8, 1910.
On Charles Clark in South Dakota: *South Dakota Historical Collections*, vol. 5, 1907.

CHAPTER TWENTY-FOUR
THE YOUNG NATION

On William Strickland: NYHS manuscript collections.

Index

About the Author

TED MORGAN is the author of the biographies *Maugham*; *Churchill: Young Man in a Hurry*; and *FDR*. His other books include *On Becoming American* and *Rowing Toward Eden*.

Mr. Morgan lives in New York City.